A Companion to the Hussites

Brill's Companions to the Christian Tradition

A SERIES OF HANDBOOKS AND REFERENCE WORKS ON THE
INTELLECTUAL AND RELIGIOUS LIFE OF EUROPE, 500–1800

Edited by

Christopher M. Bellitto (*Kean University*)

VOLUME 90

The titles published in this series are listed at *brill.com/bcct*

A Companion to the Hussites

Edited by

Michael Van Dussen
Pavel Soukup

BRILL

LEIDEN | BOSTON

Cover illustration: The Hussite heaven with commander Jan Žižka holding the Hussite banner. Jena Codex, fol. 5v (National Museum, Prague).

The Library of Congress Cataloging-in-Publication Data is available online at http://catalog.loc.gov
LC record available at http://lccn.loc.gov/2019920563

Typeface for the Latin, Greek, and Cyrillic scripts: "Brill". See and download: brill.com/brill-typeface.

ISSN 1871-6377
ISBN 978-90-04-39786-6 (hardback)
ISBN 978-90-04-41404-4 (e-book)

Copyright 2020 by Koninklijke Brill NV, Leiden, The Netherlands.
Koninklijke Brill NV incorporates the imprints Brill, Brill Hes & De Graaf, Brill Nijhoff, Brill Rodopi, Brill Sense, Hotei Publishing, mentis Verlag, Verlag Ferdinand Schöningh and Wilhelm Fink Verlag.
All rights reserved. No part of this publication may be reproduced, translated, stored in a retrieval system, or transmitted in any form or by any means, electronic, mechanical, photocopying, recording or otherwise, without prior written permission from the publisher.
Authorization to photocopy items for internal or personal use is granted by Koninklijke Brill NV provided that the appropriate fees are paid directly to The Copyright Clearance Center, 222 Rosewood Drive, Suite 910, Danvers, MA 01923, USA. Fees are subject to change.

This book is printed on acid-free paper and produced in a sustainable manner.

Printed by Printforce, the Netherlands

Contents

Acknowledgements　VII
Conventions on the Use of Proper Names　VIII
English Equivalents of Czech Names　IX
Notes on Contributors　X

Introduction: Hussite Histories　1
　　Michael Van Dussen and Pavel Soukup

PART 1
Influences

The Early Bohemian Reform　25
　　Olivier Marin

Wyclif in Bohemia　63
　　Stephen E. Lahey

PART 2
Major Figures

Major Hussite Theologians before the *Compactata*　101
　　Petra Mutlová

Major Figures of Later Hussitism (1437–1471)　141
　　Jindřich Marek

PART 3
Religious Politics

The Apocalyptic Background of Hussite Radicalism　187
　　Pavlína Cermanová

The Utraquist Church after the *Compactata*　219
　　Blanka Zilynská

PART 4
Theology and Religious Practice

Key Issues in Hussite Theology   261
    Dušan Coufal

Preaching, the Vernacular, and the Laity   297
    Pavlína Rychterová

Liturgy, Sacramental Theology, and Music   331
    David R. Holeton, Pavel Kolář and Eliška Baťová

PART 5
Later Developments

The Unity of Brethren (1458–1496)   371
    Ota Halama

The Bohemian Reformation and "The" Reformation: Hussites and Protestants in Early Modern Europe   403
    Phillip Haberkern

Index   439

Acknowledgements

The editors are grateful to Christopher Bellitto, the Editor-in-Chief for this series, for his unflagging kindness and patience. We thank Martin Pjecha for his work in translating the chapters by Jindřich Marek, Pavlína Cermanová, Dušan Coufal, and Ota Halama, and to Andrew Morris, who translated the chapter by Olivier Marin. Our thanks also go to Patrick Outhwaite, our assistant and indexer, Angela Jianu, for her help in copyediting, Ivo Romein and the production team at Brill, and to the readers whose comments at an earlier stage were remarkably supportive and helpful. The chapters by Pavlína Cermanová and Dušan Coufal, as well as the editorial involvement of Pavel Soukup, were sponsored by the Czech Science Foundation project "Cultural Codes and Their Transformations in the Hussite Period" (P405/12/G148).

Michael Van Dussen
Pavel Soukup
August 2019

Conventions on the Use of Proper Names

The orthography of names and places varies widely in international scholarship on the Hussites. The tendency in most recent scholarship in English is to use vernacular Czech forms, except when English forms have already gained widespread currency. The present volume usually renders a figure's name as it appears in the modern form of his or her vernacular language (e.g. Jakoubek of Stříbro). However, for persons whose names have long appeared in their Anglicized forms, we have followed suit. This is the case with names like Jerome of Prague, Nicholas of Dresden, Matthew of Cracow, and for well-known figures from the history of philosophy, such as Hugh of Saint-Victor, John Buridan, and John Stojković of Ragusa. Place names, too, usually take their regional forms, except when the Anglicized form is in widespread use (e.g. Prague). Names of rulers (Wenceslas IV, Ladislas Posthumous, George of Poděbrady, Louis of Bavaria) and saints (St. Wenceslas, St. Adalbert) also appear in English. Where the Latin name is often used in English scholarship, we retain the Latin (e.g. Iohannes Andreae, Nicolaus Magni); where helpful, we indicate both forms (Vojtěch Raňkův of Ježov/Adalbert Ranconis de Ericinio). Readers who may be unfamiliar with the non-Anglicized forms of certain names are referred to the following index.

English Equivalents of Czech Names

Arnošt = Ernest
Brikcí = Briccius
Eliáš = Elijah
Havel (diminutive: Havlík) = Gall
Jakub (diminutive: Jakoubek) = James
Jan = John
Jeroným = Jerome
Jindřich = Henry
Jiří = George
Kateřina = Catherine
Křišťan = Christian
Lukáš = Luke
Mařík = Maurice
Matěj = Matthias
Matouš = Matthew
Mikuláš = Nicholas
Oldřich = Ulrich
Ondřej = Andrew
Pavel = Paul
Petr = Peter
Řehoř = Gregory
Stanislav = Stanislas
Šimon = Simon
Štěpán = Stephen
Tomáš = Thomas
Václav = Wenceslas
Vavřinec = Lawrence
Vilém = William
Vladislav = Vladislas
Vojtěch = Adalbert

Notes on Contributors

Eliška Baťová
is a Researcher at the Association for Central European Cultural Studies, Prague.

Pavlína Cermanová
is a Researcher in the Centre for Medieval Studies, Institute of Philosophy, Czech Academy of Sciences, Prague.

Dušan Coufal
is a Researcher in the Centre for Medieval Studies, Institute of Philosophy, Czech Academy of Sciences, Prague.

Phillip Haberkern
is an Associate Professor in the Department of History at Boston University.

Ota Halama
is an Associate Professor at the Protestant Theological Faculty, Charles University, Prague.

David R. Holeton
is Professor Emeritus of the Hussite Theological Faculty, Charles University, Prague.

Pavel Kolář
is Lecturer in Liturgy at the Hussite Theological Faculty, Charles University, Prague.

Stephen E. Lahey
is a Professor in the Department of Classics and Religious Studies at the University of Nebraska-Lincoln.

Jindřich Marek
is a Faculty Member of the Institute of Information Studies and Librarianship, Charles University, Prague.

Olivier Marin
is a Lecturer in the Département d'histoire, Université Paris 13.

NOTES ON CONTRIBUTORS

Petra Mutlová
is an Associate Professor in the Department of Classical Studies at Masaryk University, Brno.

Pavlína Rychterová
is a Researcher in the Institut für Mittelalterforschung, Österreichische Akademie der Wissenschaften, Vienna.

Pavel Soukup
is a Researcher in the Centre for Medieval Studies, Institute of Philosophy, Czech Academy of Sciences, Prague.

Michael Van Dussen
is an Associate Professor in the Department of English Literature, McGill University, Montreal.

Blanka Zilynská
is a Faculty Member in the Institute for Czech History, Charles University, Prague.

Introduction: Hussite Histories

Michael Van Dussen and Pavel Soukup

The Hussites, as the Bohemian reformists have come to be called, became one of the most vocal and significant reform movements of the later Middle Ages, with roots in native reformist thought, influences from other European intellectual and devotional currents, and a continuing importance for the European reformations of the 16th century and later. One primary reason for their success – and for the alarm that they created among other groups in Latin Christendom – was that the Hussite movement represented an interchange between "town and gown," masters and laity, academic controversy and pastoral concern, that was largely unprecedented in Europe (the Wycliffites in England being one contemporary exception). This meant that debates that came to define the Bohemian Reform could not be confined to homogeneous social groupings whose exclusivity was reinforced by the Latin language and learning. In addition, the Hussite movement took shape within what was at that time the political center of the Holy Roman Empire, with Prague as its capital; the Hussites became entwined with contemporary outrage over the schismatic western church, and their reformist positions would come up for rigid scrutiny during the 15th-century general councils at Constance and Basel.

1   Who Were the Hussites and What Did They Represent?

"Hussites" is a term that was initially applied to the reformists who were perceived to be followers of the Bohemian preacher Jan Hus (ca. 1370–1415), though Hus himself began the process of appropriating the derogatory name (from Old Czech *hus* [mod. Czech *husa*], meaning "goose") as a rhetorical figure during his own lifetime. The association of the Bohemian reforms with the person of Hus (and with the term "Hussitism") tends to level the complicated history of reformist influence on Hus and his co-religionists. Jan Hus and his circle built on native reforms that stemmed from a previous generation in Bohemia, namely, the teachings of Milíč of Kroměříž, Konrad Waldhauser, and Matěj of Janov.[1] At the same time, they were influenced by (though no mere imitators of) the teachings of their near-contemporary English reformer John Wyclif and his followers, the Wycliffites. In fact, Wyclif's ideas often overlapped

---

1 See Olivier Marin's chapter in this volume.

with the concepts and feelings stemming from the Bohemian reform tradition, which made the creative adaptation of these Wycliffite ideas in Bohemia possible. Nevertheless, recent scholarship rightly points out that Milíč's generation did not merely prepare the way for subsequent developments. While Milíč and Janov did not escape accusations of heresy, the deliberate posture of opposition to the contemporary church was uniquely the choice of Hus and his followers. Hus certainly did introduce reforms and emphases of his own, and thus can be said to have initiated what would come to be called the Hussite movement.

One enduring emphasis throughout the reformist movement in Bohemia, though it underwent various changes, was an investment in the accessibility of the Eucharist. Devotion to the Eucharist surged throughout Europe in the later Middle Ages, alongside debates surrounding eucharistic theology, but this development manifested itself in unique ways in Bohemia. Reformists before Hus advocated the administering of frequent communion to the laity, going beyond the stipulation of the Fourth Lateran Council that stated that the faithful should receive the Eucharist at least once each year. During Hus's lifetime – though his own advocacy of the doctrine is fraught – reformists such as Jakoubek of Stříbro began to promote communion in both kinds (*sub utraque specie*), bread and wine.[2] After the Council of Constance (1414–1418), communion in both kinds, or Utraquism, would come to characterize the Hussite movement. The Hussites – including the radical offshoots of the movement – would even adopt the chalice as their symbol.[3]

The term "Hussites" itself originated with the enemies of Bohemian reformists. It was first coined as a term of abuse and was rejected by those to whom it was applied. The Hussites, however, did not adopt any common name for themselves other than "the faithful" and similar; neither was the term "Utraquists" used in the period. The official designation "Bohemians and Moravians who receive the Body and Blood of God under both kinds" (as we see in the *Compactata*, on which more below) is unwieldy in today's historiography.[4] In modern scholarship, the word "Hussites" is commonly used as a neutral, technical term. It is applied to the partisans of reform from Jan Hus's generation through the end of the 15th century. Most historians, however, tend to replace the term "Hussites" with "Utraquists" as the 15th century progresses.

---

2 For a discussion of liturgy and sacraments during the Bohemian Reformation, see the chapter by David R. Holeton, Pavel Kolář, and Eliška Baťová in this volume.
3 See Ota Halama and Pavel Soukup (eds.), *Kalich jako symbol v prvním století utrakvismu* (Prague: 2016).
4 Pavel Soukup, "The Waning of the 'Wycliffites.' Giving Names to Hussite Heresy," in *Europe after Wyclif*, eds. J. Patrick Hornbeck II and Michael Van Dussen (New York: 2017), 196–226.

Naturally, everyone who adhered to lay communion *sub utraque* can be called Utraquist from 1414 on. Yet the term gains a special meaning for the period after the *Compactata* (1436) and is commonly applied to the group that began to build an ecclesiastical administrative system of its own (the Utraquist Church).

The terms "Hussites" and (later) "Utraquists" – sometimes called by the synonym "Calixtines," especially in Czech (*kališníci*) – are thus employed in the historiography to describe the movement as a whole. And although no common nomenclature was used in the period itself, there were terms for the individual Hussite factions. Historians, relying in part on the terminology of the sources, distinguish the moderate Praguers and radical Taborites as the two major Hussite groups, joined by additional religio-military brotherhoods (the east Bohemian Orebites or Orphans); Hussite sects such as the Pikarts, who split from Tábor in the early 1420s;[5] and various groups of radical Utraquist enthusiasts in the mid-15th century. One of these latter groups, the Unity of Brethren, developed into a significant religious current and survived into the 17th century.[6] At this point, the term "Utraquists" takes on a more limited meaning as it comes to define the mainstream of Hussitism as opposed to both the Unity and the European, especially Lutheran, reformations that spread into the Czech lands.[7] The autochthonous non-Catholic groups are subsumed under the rubric "Bohemian Reformation" by some historians. This umbrella term covers the period reaching from the nonconformist reforming preachers of Milíč's generation to the Recatholicisation in the 1620s (and beyond, if we consider the exiled Brethren). While one must be careful not to construct continuity where it never existed or anachronistically assign Reformation intentions to the early generations, the term "Bohemian Reformation" admittedly reflects the sense of heritage that the early modern adherents of the Reformation in Bohemia and Moravia entertained.[8]

2   Realist Philosophy and Wycliffism

One of the most controversial developments in the early Hussite movement was its adoption of a brand of realist philosophy of universals (as opposed to the prevailing nominalism), derived from the writings of John Wyclif.[9] Many of

---

5   See Pavlína Cermanová's chapter in this volume.
6   See Ota Halama's chapter in this volume.
7   See Phillip Haberkern's chapter in this volume.
8   See Phillip Haberkern, "What's in a Name, or What's at Stake When We Talk about 'Hussites'?," *History Compass* 9 (2011): 791–801.
9   See Stephen E. Lahey's chapter in this volume.

the social and political implications of Hussite doctrine are rooted in or can be inferred from realist philosophy, the philosophy that claims that universals exist, and that they are to be distinguished from particulars. Eventually the association of Hus and Jerome of Prague with realism would contribute to the case for the execution of these men at the Council of Constance, used, for example, as evidence that the Bohemian reformers denied the doctrine of transubstantiation. Earlier, however, Wyclif's realist philosophy afforded the Czech-speaking Hussites a robust philosophical system that they used to gain leverage over the nominalist Germans who dominated the university at Prague. This dispute ultimately led to the exodus of the German masters, who left in 1409, after the Decree of Kutná Hora was issued, to found a new university at Leipzig. Not long after that time, when Wyclif's writings came under attack by the Archbishop of Prague in 1410 and following, several of the Hussite masters publicly defended Wyclif's realist teachings.

The advocacy of Wycliffite teachings, which the Hussites considered to be "evangelical truths," also played an important symbolic role. The decision not to surrender to the command of ecclesiastical authorities to abandon those teachings was a milestone on the Hussites' road to heresy and the Reformation. After communion in both kinds was condemned by the Council of Constance in 1415, the chalice became a symbol not only of Hussite liturgical practice, but also of Hussite resistance. The different degrees of consistency with which theoretical premises (including Wycliffite philosophy and theology) were applied to social and religious life gave rise to doctrinal stratification within the Hussite movement.[10] This can be seen in the case of teaching on the Eucharist, which was a point of dispute between Bohemian denominations from the early 1420s well into the 16th century.

3   Popular Support and Survival

The first generation of Hussites quickly recognized the importance of translating their reformist program into popular terms and through popular channels such as preaching, songs, images, manifestos, and processions.[11] This won the Hussite masters popular support as well as the political backing they needed to

---

10   For more on the principles of Hussite theology, see Dušan Coufal's chapter in this volume.

11   Thomas A. Fudge, *The Magnificent Ride. The First Reformation in Hussite Bohemia* (Aldershot: 1998), 178–266; Marcella K. Perett, *Preachers, Partisans, and Rebellious Religion. Vernacular Writing and the Hussite Movement* (Philadelphia: 2018); Petra Mutlová, "Communicating Texts through Images. Nicholas of Dresden's *Tabulae*," in *Public Communication*

institute their reforms in Bohemia. They succeeded on both fronts, giving rise to a movement that enjoyed the assistance not only of the Czech nobility and municipal leadership in Prague, but also of the commoners more generally. The methods the Hussites used to gain this support are also interesting for what they tell us about the history of media and communication, in both Latin and the vernacular.[12] Preaching was of course one of the primary means by which the Hussites conveyed and shaped the application of their reformist messages. The primary center of this activity in Prague was Bethlehem Chapel, founded by Prague burghers in 1391 as a space that was designated for preaching in the Czech vernacular. Jan Hus would take the pulpit there in 1402, as would other reformists after him, including Jakoubek of Stříbro.[13]

In contrast to other heretical movements of the Middle Ages, including the Wycliffites, the Hussites managed to establish themselves as a publicly active religious group that was practically distinct from the Roman Church. A crucial factor in Hussite survival was their successful military defense. From 1420 to 1431, a series of crusades was organized by the legates of Martin V and carried out primarily by King Sigismund and the Princes of the Empire. All expeditions in Bohemia failed. The Council of Basel introduced a new policy and started negotiations with the "heretics" in 1433. These negotiations resulted in a set of articles on fundamental positions – the *Compactata* (1436), supplemented by a series of agreements between the Hussites and Emperor Sigismund (1435–1436).[14] The Hussites thus secured their existence temporarily through the *Compactata* and on a long-term basis through political backing from the Utraquist Estates. The establishment of a Hussite Church was very close to a Protestant *Landeskirche*, but took shape a century earlier.[15]

---

in *European Reformation. Artistic and other Media in Central Europe 1380–1620*, eds. Milena Bartlová and Michal Šroněk (Prague: 2007), 29–37.

12   See Pavlína Rychterová's chapter in this volume.

13   The history of Hussite preaching after Hus is still to be written. For an overview of sources, see František Michálek Bartoš, *Dvě studie o husitských postilách* (Prague: 1955); for Jakoubek of Stříbro, see Jindřich Marek, *Jakoubek ze Stříbra a počátky utrakvistického kazatelství v českých zemích. Studie o Jakoubkově postile z let 1413–1414* (Prague: 2011); Pavel Soukup, *Reformní kazatelství a Jakoubek ze Stříbra* (Prague: 2011). On the founding generation of Hussite theologians and religious leaders, see Petra Mutlová's chapter in this volume.

14   František Šmahel, *Die Basler Kompaktaten mit den Hussiten (1436). Untersuchung und Edition* (Monumenta Germaniae Historica. Studien und Texte) 65 (Wiesbaden: 2019); Petr Čornej and Milena Bartlová, *Velké dějiny zemí Koruny české*, vol. 6 (Prague and Litomyšl: 2007), 11–19.

15   See Blanka Zilynská's chapter in this volume.

4   The Vicissitudes and Legacy of Later Hussitism

The ambiguous and precarious position of the Utraquists – theoretically a part of, yet practically independent from the Roman Church – influenced religious and political history after the *Compactata*. In the rest of the 15th century, and indeed onwards until 1627, we see waves of recatholicisation endeavors and Utraquist revivals. The late 1430s and 1440s witnessed a partial return to the pre-war situation and a renewal of more traditional religious practices, carried out by the Catholics and conservative Utraquists. In 1448, more radical Utraquists regained dominance by seizing Prague. Their leader, the Hussite nobleman George of Poděbrady, was elected Land Governor in 1452 and King of Bohemia in 1458. George was a *Compactata* legalist: he considered both the Catholics and the Utraquists to be legitimate members of the universal Church while he persecuted other religious groups such as the Brethren.[16] The legal basis of the status quo, however, was shaken in 1462 when Pope Pius II nullified the *Compactata*. The Second Hussite War followed Paul II's proclamation of a crusade in 1467, with the King of Hungary, Matthias Corvinus, waging war for the Bohemian Crown. The settlement stipulated that King Vladislav II the Jagellonian would keep rule over Bohemia while Matthias would rule in all the other crown lands.[17] The continuing tensions between Bohemian "confessions" were resolved in a satisfactory way by the Peace Treaty of Kutná Hora, concluded in 1485. This year is often considered the end of the Hussite period.

The Peace of Kutná Hora gave each adult individual freedom of choice between Utraquist and Catholic worship, thus going even further than the later Augsburg regulation of 1555. Yet the co-existence of religious groups in Bohemia was a consequence of a power stalemate, not the offspring of any conscious principle of religious freedom. Although few outstanding figures in the late 15th and 16th centuries might have professed some sort of supra-confessional Christianity, the situation in general can be termed "toleration out of necessity."[18] Neither of the religious parties was able to prevail over the

---

16   In English, see Frederick G. Heyman, *George of Bohemia. King of Heretics* (Princeton: 1965); Otakar Odložilík, *The Hussite King. Bohemia in European Affairs 1440–1471* (New Brunswick: 1965).

17   Antonín Kalous, *Matyáš Korvín (1443–1490). Uherský a český král* (České Budějovice: 2009).

18   Expression in František Šmahel, "*Pax externa et interna*. Vom Heiligen Krieg zur Erzwungenen Toleranz im hussitischen Böhmen (1419–1485)," in *Toleranz im Mittelalter*, eds. Alexander Patschovsky and Harald Zimmermann (Vorträge und Forschungen) 45 (Sigmaringen: 1998), 221–73. On supra-confessional convictions see Josef Válka, *Husitství na Moravě. Náboženská snášenlivost. Jan Amos Komenský* (Brno: 2005); Winfried Eberhard, "Das Problem der Toleranz und die Entwicklung der hussitisch-katholischen Koexistenz

other by force. The formation of alternative confessions in Bohemia was entangled with the development of the political system of Estates representation. This specific character of East-Central European confessionalization, developed in multi-confessional Estate-dominated societies (i.e. societies whose confessionalization was guaranteed by nobles, towns, and in some cases prelates), meant that Utraquism never became a state religion or a means of discipline, as we see in the early modern period in some Central and West European territories, where confessionalization was enforced by princes.[19] The nature and significance of later Utraquism has been the subject of some re-evaluation in the scholarship. Recent studies suggest that Utraquism did not suffer from the kind of intellectual impotence and theological necrosis that earlier historiography assumed, but rather developed original solutions to ecclesiological questions representing a middle way between Roman Catholicism and the Lutheran Reformation.[20]

5 Hussites in Late Medieval Europe

Convinced of the salutary nature of their teachings, the Hussites strove to proselytize outside of Bohemia. Hussite ideas spread among the local populaces in Poland, Flanders, some territories of the Empire, and in the Balkans.[21] This influence, however, must not be overestimated in terms of numbers of

---

im 15. Jahrhundert," in *Die Hussitische Revolution. Religiöse, politische und regionale Aspekte*, ed. Franz Machilek (Cologne, Weimar, and Vienna: 2012), 93–105.

19   Winfried Eberhard, *Konfessionsbildung und Stände in Böhmen 1478–1530* (Munich and Vienna: 1981).

20   Zdeněk V. David, *Finding the Middle Way. The Utraquists' Liberal Challenge to Rome and Luther* (Washington, Baltimore, and London: 2003). For a biographical and bibliographical overview of later generations of Hussite authors, see Jindřich Marek's chapter in this volume.

21   Research dedicated to this communication, especially that which is focused on "international cooperation" in the context of socialist countries in the second half of the 20th century, might make the Hussite influence appear to be more important than it was. Cf. Josef Macek (ed.), *Mezinárodní ohlas husitství* (Prague: 1958). New research includes Paweł Kras, *Husyci w piętnastowiecznej Polsce* (Lublin: 1998); Thomas A. Fudge, "Heresy and the Question of Hussites in the Southern Netherlands (1411–1431)," in *Campin in Context. Peinture et société dans la vallée de l'Escaut à l'époque de Robert Campin 1375–1445*, eds. Ludovic Nys and Dominique Vanwijnsberghe (Valenciennes, Bruxelles, and Tournai: 2007), 73–88; Franz Machilek, "Deutsche Hussiten," in *Jan Hus. Zwischen Zeiten, Völkern, Konfessionen*, ed. Ferdinand Seibt (Munich: 1997), 267–82; and Cristian Nicolae Daniel, "The Political and Confessional Landscape in Alexander the Good's Moldavia. The Hussites," *Annual of Medieval Studies at Central European University* 12 (2006): 125–41.

adherents (the same should be said for the fusion of certain German-speaking Waldensian groups with radical Hussites in the mid-15th century).[22] The reaction of Latin Christendom to Hussitism was largely hostile. The impact of Hussitism on contemporary Europe thus consisted mainly in provoking intellectual, political, and military responses. Recent research shows that the importance of the Hussite theme for learned discourse, politics, and everyday life was greater than what previous scholarship suggested. At the Council of Constance, for example, churchmen from across Europe became acquainted with the challenges of Hussite thought, and regional Hussite polemical debates now gained an international dimension. The sheer volume of anti-Hussite polemics has only recently begun to be appreciated by historians, emerging in the last decade as an extremely promising field of research. Indeed, approximately three hundred treatises written against the Hussites throughout the 15th century survive, and some of the most prominent intellectuals of the period – men like Jean Gerson and Nicholas of Cusa – played an active role in these controversies.[23]

The Council of Basel represented the peak of polemical and theological engagement with the Hussites. The unprecedented two-round theological debate involving four speakers from each side eventually led to the settlement between the council, representing the Roman Church, and the Hussites. The church, however, was simultaneously working through the question of who had the authority to speak on its behalf. From the point of view of the papacy, the *Compactata* period remained an interim that was both preceded and followed by military confrontation. The crusades against the Hussites spread the knowledge about Hussitism beyond ecclesiastical and political elites. The preaching of crusading indulgences in the hinterland and catechetical work in general reinforced the image of the Bohemian enemy among the illiterates. These specific crusading treatments of the Hussite wars still await full evaluation in the context of the flourishing research on the later crusades.[24] The

---

22 Amedeo Molnár, *Die Waldenser. Geschichte und europäisches Ausmaß einer Ketzerbewegung* (Berlin: 1973), 237–325; Albert de Lange and Kathrin Utz Tremp (eds.), *Friedrich Reiser und die "waldensisch-hussitische Internationale"* (Heidelberg, Ubstadt-Weiher, and Basel: 2006).

23 For an overview of the first phase of debates over Utraquism, see Dušan Coufal, *Polemika o kalich mezi teologií a politikou 1414–1431. Předpoklady basilejské disputace o prvním z pražských artikulů* (Prague: 2012). More research must be done before a synthetic evaluation of anti-Hussite polemics can be produced. For the time being, see the continually updated list of treatises in Pavel Soukup, *Repertorium operum antihussiticorum*, on-line database, www.antihus.eu.

24 In the context of crusading studies, only overviews within synthetic works are available: Frederick G. Heymann, "The Crusades against the Hussites," in *A History of the Crusades*,

difficult international position of the Utraquists led to attempts to gain support through diplomacy. King George of Bohemia sent out several embassies to other parts of Europe. In search of religious cognates or allies, the Utraquists dispatched their envoys as far as Constantinople in 1452; the Unity of Brethren sent several of their members to the Eastern churches to search for the remnants of the primitive church.[25]

Hussitism was by no means isolated from other developments in late medieval Christian Europe. In many respects, the Hussites profited from the "multiple options" that 15th-century Christianity offered to respond to diverse religious needs. The points of contact with other religious currents in Europe are numerous: the Hussites emphasised personal, self-conscious devotion as opposed to formalism and ritual; their religious concepts overlapped with late medieval christocentric tendencies, visible especially in eucharistic devotion and the emphasis on divine law derived from the imperative of *imitatio Christi*; they provide an extreme example of lay participation in religious matters that characterized the 15th century in general; they profited from the dramatic increase of religious writing in the vernacular – to name just few prominent examples.[26] The compromise with the Council of Basel may appear to be one of the many successful attempts at integration of innovative projects that the 15th-century church undertook. And yet, Hussitism eventually fell outside of what the Roman Church was able to accommodate. Despite the Basel intermezzo, the church never fully accepted the Hussites, and vice versa. This was primarily because the Hussites refused to blindly accept the doctrinal authority of the institutional church. They subjected the mandates of ecclesiastical authorities to discursive scrutiny and measured them against divine law. This approach constituted what can arguably be termed the Hussite Reformation – a phenomenon that continues to challenge traditional periodization boundaries and uniform religious landscapes.[27]

---

eds. Kenneth M. Setton and Harry W. Hazard, vol. 3 (Madison and London: 1975), 586–646. Most recently, see Pavel Soukup, "Crusading against Christians in the Fifteenth Century. Doubts and Debates," in *Reconfiguring the Fifteenth-Century Crusade*, ed. Norman Housley (London: 2017), 85–122. Soukup is preparing a comprehensive monograph on the subject of anti-Hussite crusades.

25   Milada Paulová, "L'Empire Byzantin et les Tchèques avant la chute de Constantinople," *Byzantinoslavica* 14 (1953): 158–22; Antonín Salač, *Constantinople et Prague en 1452* (Prague: 1958); for the Unity, see the chapter by Ota Halama in this volume.

26   John Van Engen, "Multiple Options. The World of the Fifteenth-Century Church," *Church History* 77 (2008): 257–84.

27   Winfried Eberhard, "Zur reformatorischen Qualität und Konfessionalisierung des nachrevolutionären Hussitismus," in *Häresie und vorzeitige Reformation im Spätmittelalter*, ed. František Šmahel (Munich: 1998), 213–38; Pavel Soukup, "Kauza reformace. Husitství

6 The Emphases of Modern Scholarship

Scholarship on the Hussites has a long and distinguished tradition, and indeed current studies must continually contend with a historiography that is not always easy to disentangle from nationalistic, confessional, and political projects of the 19th and 20th centuries. In recent decades, revisionist scholarship has added further nuance to our understanding of influences on the Hussites, as well as of the relationship that other reformist movements had to the group that was closely connected to the reformist preacher Jan Hus. Scholarship on the Hussites has always been – and continues to be – characterized by scrutiny of primary manuscript sources. Recent studies, however, have begun to devote renewed attention to the position of these sources, and of the movement that these sources mediate to us, in the context of wider European religious politics of the late Middle Ages.

In the wake of two influential synthetic surveys from 1993 (František Šmahel) and 2000–2007 (Petr Čornej),[28] modern scholarship has been looking for new areas of research, broadly inspired by cultural studies. One example of this is the recent study of Hussite theory of images and iconoclasm. Thanks to the continuing influence and activity of members of an older generation of scholars, research on legal history, the history of mentalities, and other key areas continues to develop. This is seen, for instance, in Čornej's pioneering study on the mental horizon of Hussite chroniclers; Šmahel's work on literacy, magic, and visual media; semantic studies by Josef Macek and Robert Novotný; and works on university history by Šmahel and Martin Nodl.[29] Areas of contemporary research include the study of polemics, commentaries, and

---

v konkurenci reformních projektů," in *Heresis seminaria. Pojmy a koncepty v bádání o husitství*, eds. Pavlína Rychterová and Pavel Soukup (Prague: 2013), 171–217; Berndt Hamm, "Abschied vom Epochendenken in der Reformationsforschung. Ein Plädoyer," *Zeitschrift für historische Forschung* 39 (2012): 373–411.

28 František Šmahel, *Husitská revoluce*, 4 vols. (Prague: 1993); German edition: *Die Hussitische Revolution*, trans. Thomas Krzenck (Monumenta Germaniae Historica. Schriften) 43, 3 vols. (Hanover: 2002); Petr Čornej, *Velké dějiny zemí Koruny české*, vol. 5 (Prague and Litomyšl: 2000); Čornej and Bartlová, *Velké dějiny*, vol. 6.

29 Petr Čornej, *Rozhled, názory a postoje husitské inteligence v zrcadle dějepisectví 15. století* (Prague: 1986); František Šmahel, "Literacy and Heresy in Hussite Bohemia," in *Heresy and Literacy, 1000–1530*, eds. Peter Biller and Anne Hudson (Cambridge: 1994), 237–54; idem, "Stärker als der Glaube. Magie, Aberglaube und Zauber in der Epoche des Hussitismus," *Bohemia* 32 (1991): 316–37; idem, "Die *Tabule veteris et novi coloris* als audiovisuelles Medium hussitischer Agitation," *Studie o rukopisech* 29 (1992): 95–105; Josef Macek, *Česká středověká šlechta* (Prague: 1997); Robert Novotný, "Staročeský výraz hejtman. Sémantická analýza," *Marginalia Historica* 4 (1999): 85–102; František Šmahel, *Die Prager Universität im Mittelalter. The Charles University in the Middle Ages* (Leiden and Boston: 2007); Martin

sermons with their textual traditions (Petra Mutlová, Dušan Coufal, Jindřich Marek, Pavel Soukup), as well as of the transformation of religious writings into the vernacular (Pavlína Rychterová, Marcela Perett);[30] work on Hus's momentous trial at Constance (Sebastián Provvidente, building on Jiří Kejř); studies of social history (Čornej, Novotný, Nodl, Robert Šimůnek); and the study of church administration (Jan Hrdina, Blanka Zilynská).[31]

Two major tendencies can be observed in contemporary research. One is the international character of Hussite research, which builds on the achievements of scholars such as Howard Kaminsky (USA), Ferdinand Seibt (Germany), Paul De Vooght (Belgium), and Stanisław Bylina (Poland) in the second half of the 20th century.[32] Most recently, Anglophone scholars have contributed to

---

Nodl, *Das Kuttenberger Dekret von 1409. Von der Eintracht zum Konflikt der Prager Universitätsnationen* (Cologne, Weimar, and Vienna: 2017).

30 See, for example, Petra Mutlová, "Mikuláše z Drážďan Sermo ad clerum 1416 (kritická edice)," *Studia historica Brunensia* 62 (2015): 295–312; Dušan Coufal, "Die katholischen Magister Peter von Mährisch Neustadt, Johann von Königgrätz, Nicolaus von Pavlíkov und die Formierung der utraquistischen Universität in Prag 1417," *Acta Universitatis Carolinae – Historia Universitatis Carolinae Pragensis* 49, 2 (2009): 127–41; idem, "Der Laienkelch im Hussitentum. Neue Quellen zu Johann Rokycanas Verteidigung des Laienkelchs auf dem Basler Konzil im Januar 1433," in *Die Hussitische Revolution. Religiöse, politische und regionale Aspekte*, ed. Franz Machilek (Cologne, Weimar, and Vienna: 2012), 39–56; Pavlína Rychterová, *Die Offenbarungen der heiligen Birgitta von Schweden. Eine Untersuchung zur alttschechischen Übersetzung des Thomas von Štítné* (Cologne, Weimar, and Vienna: 2004); Perett, *Preachers, Partisans, and Rebellious Religion*; and the works cited in note 13 above.

31 Sebastián Provvidente, "Inquisitorial process and plenitudo potestatis at the Council of Constance (1414–1418)," in *The Bohemian Reformation and Religious Practice*, eds. Zdeněk V. David and David R. Holeton, vol. 8 (Prague: 2011), 100–16; Jiří Kejř, *Die Causa Johannes Hus und das Prozessrecht der Kirche*, trans. Walter Annuß (Regensburg: 2005); Petr Čornej, "Kočička, Kurvička, Kokot a Múdrá Hlavička aneb Staroměstští řezníci v husitské revoluci," *Pražský sborník historický* 40 (2012): 7–129; Robert Novotný, "Die Konfessionalität des böhmischen und mährischen Adels in der Zeit der Regierung Sigismunds von Luxemburg," in *Kaiser Sigismund (1368–1437). Zur Herrschaftspraxis eines europäischen Monarchen*, eds. Karel Hruza and Alexandra Kaar (Cologne, Weimar, and Vienna: 2017), 57–74; idem, "Der niedere Adel um Wenzel IV. Ein Sonderfall?" in *Heilige, Helden, Wüteriche. Herrschaftsstile der Luxemburger (1308–1437)*, eds. Martin Bauch, Julia Burkhardt, Tomáš Gaudek, and Václav Žůrek (Cologne, Weimar, and Vienna: 2017), 193–208; Martin Nodl, "Sociální koncept pozdně středověkého městského přistěhovalectví," in *Sociální svět středověkého města*, ed. Martin Nodl (Colloquia mediaevalia Pragensia) 5 (Prague: 2006), 3–97; Robert Šimůnek, *Reprezentace české středověké šlechty* (Prague: 2013).

32 Howard Kaminsky, *A History of the Hussite Revolution* (Berkeley and Los Angeles: 1967); Ferdinand Seibt, *Hussitica. Zur Struktur einer Revolution*, 2nd ed. (Cologne: 1990); Paul De Vooght, *L'hérésie de Jean Huss* (Leuven: 1960); idem, *Jacobellus de Stříbro († 1429), premier théologien du hussitisme* (Leuven: 1972); Stanisław Bylina, *Rewolucja husycka*, 3 vols. (Warsaw: 2011–2016).

the study of major figures and events of 15th-century Hussite history (Thomas Fudge),[33] communication between England and Bohemia (Michael Van Dussen), political ideas of early Hussitism (Jeanne Grant), and Hus's posthumous reputation (Phillip Haberkern).[34] A comprehensive monograph of the reformist movement up to 1419 is available in French (Olivier Marin).[35] Polish scholars have dealt with the issues of Hussitism in Poland (Paweł Kras) and the diplomacy surrounding Hussite Bohemia (Jarosław Nikodem, Jacek Smołucha).[36] Germanophone and Anglophone historians of an emerging generation have contributed to the field of anti-Hussite polemics and warfare.[37] Since 1994, the bi-annual symposia on the "Bohemian Reformation and Religious Practice," organized by Zdeněk David and David R. Holeton, have facilitated academic contact between Czech and international scholars,[38] and further

---

33 See, for example, Thomas A. Fudge, *Jan Hus. Religious Reform and Social Revolution in Bohemia* (London: 2010); idem, *The Trial of Jan Hus. Medieval Heresy and Criminal Procedure* (Oxford: 2013); idem, *Jerome of Prague and the Foundations of the Hussite Movement* (New York: 2016).

34 Michael Van Dussen, *From England to Bohemia. Heresy and Communication in the Later Middle Ages* (Cambridge: 2012); Jeanne E. Grant, *For the Common Good. The Bohemian land law and the beginning of the Hussite Revolution* (Leiden: 2015); Phillip Haberkern, *Patron Saint and Prophet. Jan Hus in the Bohemian and German Reformations* (Oxford: 2016).

35 Olivier Marin, *L'archevêque, le maître et le dévot. Genèses du mouvement réformateur pragois. Années 1360–1419* (Paris: 2005).

36 Kras, *Husyci*; Jarosław Nikodem, *Polska i Litwa wobec husyckich Czech w latach 1420–1433. Studium o polityce dynastycznej Władysława Jagiełły i Witolda Kiejstutowicza* (Poznań: 2004); Janusz Smołucha, *Polityka Kurii Rzymskiej za pontyfikatu Piusa II (1458–1464) wobec Czech i krajów sąsiednich. Z dziejów dyplomacji papieskiej w XV wieku* (Cracow: 2008). Further Polish works on Hussite history include Krzysztof Moskal, *"Aby lud był jeden..." Eklezjologia Jana Husa w trakcie De ecclesia* (Lublin: 2003); Anna Paner, *Jan Žižka z Trocnova* (Gdańsk: 2002).

37 Christina Traxler, *Firmiter velitis resistere. Die Auseinandersetzung der Wiener Universität mit dem Hussitismus vom Konstanzer Konzil (1414–1418) bis zum Beginn des Basler Konzils (1431–1449)* (Göttingen: 2019); eadem, "Früher Antihussitismus. Der Traktat *Eloquenti viro* und sein Verfasser Andreas von Brod," *Archa Verbi* 12 (2015): 130–77; Hartmut Spengler, "Die Stärke der deutschen Aufgebote und Heere in den Hussitenkämpfen (ca. 1420–1438)," *Blätter für deutsche Landesgeschichte* 151 (2015): 311–416; Alexandra Kaar, "Neue Mittel der Kriegsführung? König/Kaiser Sigismund und das Handelsverbot gegen die Hussiten in Böhmen," in *Heilige, Helden, Wüteriche. Herrschaftsstile der Luxemburger (1308–1437)*, eds. Martin Bauch, Julia Burkhardt, Tomáš Gaudek, and Václav Žůrek (Cologne, Weimar, and Vienna: 2017), 223–42; Mark Whelan, "Between Papacy and Empire. Cardinal Henry Beaufort, the House of Lancaster, and the Hussite Crusades," *English Historical Review* 133 (2018): 1–31.

38 The proceedings (eleven volumes to date), edited by Zdeněk V. David and David R. Holeton, are accessible at www.brrp.org.

conferences and edited volumes enabled cooperation between historians working on the Hussites and related topics such as English Wycliffism and church reform in general.[39]

The second tendency is the renewed interest in unpublished sources. Scholars who entered the field after 2000 often base their work on manuscripts, thus enlarging the body of available evidence. The number of source editions, whether book-length or appended to articles, is reminiscent of editorial activities in the pioneering period of research in the late 19th end early 20th centuries. Over the past decade, several volumes of Hus's *Opera omnia* have appeared in print (Jana Zachová, Jana Nechutová, Helena Krmíčková et al.), as well as treatises by Štěpán of Páleč (Ivan Müller), Nicholas of Dresden (Petra Mutlová, Milada Homolková et al.) and Petr Chelčický (Jaroslav Boubín).[40] Further versions of the Old Czech Chronicles have been made accessible (Alena Černá, Markéta Klosová, and Petr Čornej), and several volumes of records from Sigismund of Luxembourg's chancery have been published (Petr Elbel et al.).[41] The body of visual sources from the Bohemian Reformation has

---

39 Michael Van Dussen and Pavel Soukup (eds.), *Religious Controversy in Europe, 1378–1536. Textual Transmission and Networks of Readership* (Turnhout: 2013); Hornbeck and Van Dussen (eds.), *Europe after Wyclif*; Elizabeth Solopova (ed.); *The Wycliffite Bible. Origin, History and Interpretation* (Leiden and Boston: 2017), and the forthcoming papers from the conferences "Before and After Wyclif: Sources and Textual Influences," held at the University of Milan in 2016, and "Wycliffism and Hussitism. Contexts, Methods, Perspectives," held at the University of Oxford in 2018.

40 *Dicta de tempore magistro Iohanni Hus attributa*, ed. Jana Zachová (Magistri Iohannis Hus Opera omnia) 26 (Corpus christianorum. Continuatio mediaevalis) 239, 2 vols. (Turnhout: 2011); *Magistri Iohannis Hus Enarratio Psalmorum (Ps. 109–118)*, eds. Jana Nechutová et al. (Magistri Iohannis Hus Opera omnia) 17 (Corpus christianorum. Continuatio mediaevalis) 253 (Turnhout: 2013); *Magistri Iohannis Hus Constantiensia*, eds. Helena Krmíčková et al. (Magistri Iohannis Hus Opera omnia) 24 (Corpus christianorum. Continuatio mediaevalis) 274 (Turnhout: 2016); Štěpán Páleč, *Commentarius in I–IX capitula tractatus De universalibus Iohannis Wyclif Stephano de Palecz ascriptus*, ed. Ivan Müller (Prague: 2009); Nicholas of Dresden, *Nicolai Dresdensis Apologia. De conclusionibus doctorum in Constantia de materia sanguinis*, ed. Petra Mutlová (Brno: 2015); Milada Homolková and Michal Dragoun (eds.), *Tabule staré a nové barvy Mikuláše z Drážďan ve staročeském překladu* (Prague: 2016); Petr Chelčický, *Spisy z Pařížského sborníku*, ed. Jaroslav Boubín (Sbírka pramenů k náboženským dějinám) 1 (Prague: 2008); idem, *Siet viery*, ed. Jaroslav Boubín (Sbírka pramenů k náboženským dějinám) 3 (Prague: 2012); idem, *Spisy z Olomouckého sborníku*, ed. Jaroslav Boubín (Sbírka pramenů k náboženským dějinám) 4 (Prague: 2016); idem, *Spisy z Kapitulního sborníku*, ed. Jaroslav Boubín (Sbírka pramenů k náboženským dějinám) 5 (Prague: 2018).

41 Alena M. Černá, Petr Čornej, and Markéta Klosová (eds.), *Staré letopisy české. Texty nejstarší vrstvy* (Fontes rerum Bohemicarum. Series nova) 2 (Prague: 2003); eidem (eds.), *Staré letopisy české. Východočeská větev a některé související texty* (Fontes rerum

been revisited (Kateřina Horníčková and Michal Šroněk), and we have seen a comprehensive monograph on Hussite art (Milena Bartlová).[42] Yet although current work, as in earlier scholarship, continues to profit from intensive work with original, unprinted resources, one point of departure from the historiography of the 19th and 20th centuries is that unabashedly ideological interpretations and heroic narratives have largely gone by the wayside, posing less of an obstacle to research than they once did.[43]

7   The Present Volume

A reassessment of the place of Hussitism in its contemporary European religious culture is already under way, though further comparative studies are needed. Our knowledge of Hussitism would benefit from further study of the parallels and differences not only with English Wycliffism, but also with Conciliarism and the Modern Devotion (to name just a few). The present state of research on Hussitism, especially that which is available in English, can be misleading to newcomers to the field. In general, work on the Hussites is largely ignored by scholars who are not Czech, or who do not themselves specialize in Hussite studies. At the same time, some of the most accessible scholarship on Czech history gives the impression that the Hussites were typical of contemporary developments in Europe (which they were not), or (to the contrary) were unique and out of touch with the pre-Reformation Catholic Church (which was also not the case). This Companion addresses a significant gap by providing reliable statements on the development of the Hussite movement in its European cultural context.

Each chapter in the present volume presents new scholarship on the Hussite movement, while at the same time providing students and scholars new to the Hussites a clear sense of the historiography and current trends in Hussite studies. Several chapters provide concise statements on major emphases in such areas as Hussite theology, ecclesiology, philosophy, and religious life or practice. As most scholarship on the Hussites has been written in Czech and

---

Bohemicarum. Series nova) 3 (Prague: 2018); Petr Elbel et al. (eds.), *Regesta Imperii*, vol. 11: *Regesten Kaiser Sigismunds*, Parts 1–3 (Vienna: 2012–2016).

42   Kateřina Horníčková and Michal Šroněk (eds.), *Umění české reformace (1380–1620)* (Prague: 2010); Milena Bartlová, *Pravda zvítězila. Výtvarné umění a husitství 1380–1490* (Prague: 2015).

43   An overview of older Hussite research can be found in Šmahel, *Die Hussitische Revolution*, vol. 1, 1–84.

German, this volume provides a valuable resource by presenting accounts in English on a variety of figures, texts, concepts, and topics that are central to the study of the movement, with particular attention to its religious aspects, and by taking stock of the state of scholarship at the beginning of the 21st century. The volume joins others in the Brill's Companions to the Christian Tradition series, including recent volumes on Jan Hus, John Wyclif, the Lollards, Jean Gerson, the Council of Basel, the Reformation in Central Europe, and Martin Luther (among others).

This Companion focuses primarily on religious aspects of the Hussite movement, whereas social and political contexts and intersections are dealt with only in passing. Given the recent publication of thematically related Companions, the figure of Jan Hus and the topic of the Christian art of the Bohemian Reformation are largely and intentionally left out.[44] The trajectory of the volume extends from the early inspirations of the Hussite movement (the native Bohemian reformist movement, Wyclif, and the early church); to the major figures and concerns of the movement as it developed throughout the 15th century; then to religious politics, theological emphases, and religious practice; and ending with the later history of the movement up to the Reformation. Each chapter concludes with a bibliographic survey that outlines the development of one aspect of the field since the 19th century, when modern academic study of the Hussites began in earnest. These surveys provide references to the most important or influential primary and secondary sources.

Bibliography

Editions of Sources

Černá, Alena M., Petr Čornej, and Markéta Klosová (eds.), *Staré letopisy české. Texty nejstarší vrstvy* [Old Czech annals. The earliest texts] (Fontes rerum Bohemicarum. Series nova) 2 (Prague: 2003).

Černá, Alena M., Petr Čornej, and Markéta Klosová (eds.), *Staré letopisy české. Východočeská větev a některé související texty* [Old Czech annals. The East-Bohemian branch and some related texts] (Fontes rerum Bohemicarum. Series nova) 3 (Prague: 2018).

---

44 František Šmahel and Ota Pavlíček (eds.), *A Companion to Jan Hus* (Brill's Companions to the Christian Tradition) 54 (Leiden and Boston: 2015); Kateřina Horníčková and Michal Šroněk (eds.), *From Hus to Luther. Visual Culture in the Bohemian Reformation (1380–1620)* (Turnhout: 2016).

Chelčický, Petr, *Spisy z Pařížského sborníku* [Writings from the Paris manuscript], ed. Jaroslav Boubín (Sbírka pramenů k náboženským dějinám) 1 (Prague: 2008).

Chelčický, Petr, *Siet viery* [The net of faith], ed. Jaroslav Boubín (Sbírka pramenů k náboženským dějinám) 3 (Prague: 2012).

Chelčický, Petr, *Spisy z Olomouckého sborníku* [Writings from the Olomouc manuscript], ed. Jaroslav Boubín (Sbírka pramenů k náboženským dějinám) 4 (Prague: 2016).

Chelčický, Petr, *Spisy z Kapitulního sborníku* [Writings from the Chapter manuscript], ed. Jaroslav Boubín (Sbírka pramenů k náboženským dějinám) 5 (Prague: 2018).

Elbel, Petr, Stanislav Bárta, Přemysl Bar, and Lukáš Reitinger (eds.), *Regesta Imperii*, vol. 11: *Regesten Kaiser Sigismunds*, Parts 1–3 (Vienna: 2012–2016).

Homolková, Milada, and Michal Dragoun (eds.), *Tabule staré a nové barvy Mikuláše z Drážďan ve staročeském překladu* [The Tables of the old and new color of Nicholas of Dresden. An old Czech translation] (Prague: 2016).

Hus, Jan, *Magistri Iohannis Hus Enarratio Psalmorum (Ps. 109–118)*, eds. Jana Nechutová, Helena Krmíčková, Dušan Coufal, Jana Fuksová, Petra Mutlová, Anna Pumprová, Dana Stehlíková, and Libor Švanda (Magistri Iohannis Hus Opera omnia) 17 (Corpus christianorum. Continuatio mediaevalis) 253 (Turnhout: 2013).

Hus, Jan, *Dicta de tempore magistro Iohanni Hus attributa*, ed. Jana Zachová (Magistri Iohannis Hus Opera omnia) 26 (Corpus christianorum. Continuatio mediaevalis) 239, 2 vols. (Turnhout: 2011).

Hus, Jan, *Magistri Iohannis Hus Constantiensia*, eds. Helena Krmíčková, Jana Nechutová, Dušan Coufal, Jana Fuksová, Lucie Mazalová, Petra Mutlová, Libor Švanda, Soňa Žákovská, and Amedeo Molnár (Magistri Iohannis Hus Opera omnia) 24 (Corpus christianorum. Continuatio mediaevalis) 274 (Turnhout: 2016).

Nicholas of Dresden, *Nicolai Dresdensis Apologia. De conclusionibus doctorum in Constantia de materia sanguinis*, ed. Petra Mutlová (Brno: 2015).

Páleč, Štěpán, *Commentarius in I–IX capitula tractatus De universalibus Iohannis Wyclif Stephano de Palecz ascriptus*, ed. Ivan Müller (Prague: 2009).

Secondary Sources

Bartlová, Milena, *Pravda zvítězila. Výtvarné umění a husitství 1380–1490* [The truth prevailed. Hussitism and the visual arts 1380–1490] (Prague: 2015).

Bartoš, František Michálek, *Dvě studie o husitských postilách* [Two studies on Hussite postils] (Prague: 1955).

Bylina, Stanisław, *Rewolucja husycka* [The Hussite revolution], 3 vols. (Warsaw: 2011–2016).

Čornej, Petr, *Rozhled, názory a postoje husitské inteligence v zrcadle dějepisectví 15. století* [Horizon, views and stances of the Hussite intelligentsia as mirrored in the 15th-century historiography] (Prague: 1986).

Čornej, Petr, *Velké dějiny zemí Koruny české* [A comprehensive history of the lands of the Bohemian Crown], vol. 5 (Prague and Litomyšl: 2000).

Čornej, Petr, "Kočička, Kurvička, Kokot a Múdrá Hlavička aneb Staroměstští řezníci v husitské revoluci" [Kočička, Kurvička, Kokot and Múdrá Hlavička, or The Old-Town butchers in the Hussite revolution], *Pražský sborník historický* 40 (2012): 7–129.

Čornej, Petr, and Milena Bartlová, *Velké dějiny zemí Koruny české* [A comprehensive history of the lands of the Bohemian Crown], vol. 6 (Prague and Litomyšl: 2007).

Coufal, Dušan, "Die katholischen Magister Peter von Mährisch Neustadt, Johann von Königgrätz, Nicolaus von Pavlíkov und die Formierung der utraquistischen Universität in Prag 1417," *Acta Universitatis Carolinae – Historia Universitatis Carolinae Pragensis* 49, 2 (2009): 127–41.

Coufal, Dušan, *Polemika o kalich mezi teologií a politikou 1414–1431. Předpoklady basilejské disputace o prvním z pražských artikulů* [Polemic about the chalice between theology and politics, 1414–1431. Preconditions of the Basel disputation about the first Prague article] (Prague: 2012).

Coufal, Dušan, "Der Laienkelch im Hussitentum. Neue Quellen zu Johann Rokycanas Verteidigung des Laienkelchs auf dem Basler Konzil im Januar 1433," in *Die Hussitische Revolution. Religiöse, politische und regionale Aspekte*, ed. Franz Machilek (Cologne, Weimar, and Vienna: 2012), 39–56.

Daniel, Cristian Nicolae, "The Political and Confessional Landscape in Alexander the Good's Moldavia: The Hussites," *Annual of Medieval Studies at Central European University* 12 (2006): 125–41.

David, Zdeněk V., *Finding the Middle Way. The Utraquists' Liberal Challenge to Rome and Luther* (Washington, Baltimore, and London: 2003).

de Lange, Albert, and Kathrin Utz Tremp (eds.), *Friedrich Reiser und die "waldensisch-hussitische Internationale"* (Heidelberg, Ubstadt-Weiher, and Basel: 2006).

De Vooght, Paul, *Jacobellus de Stříbro († 1429), premier théologien du hussitisme* (Leuven: 1972).

De Vooght, Paul, *L'hérésie de Jean Huss*, 2 vols, 2nd ed. (Leuven: 1975).

Eberhard, Winfried, *Konfessionsbildung und Stände in Böhmen 1478–1530* (Munich and Vienna: 1981).

Eberhard, Winfried, "Das Problem der Toleranz und die Entwicklung der hussitisch-katholischen Koexistenz im 15. Jahrhundert," in *Die Hussitische Revolution. Religiöse, politische und regionale Aspekte*, ed. Franz Machilek (Cologne, Weimar, and Vienna: 2012), 93–105.

Eberhard, Winfried, "Zur reformatorischen Qualität und Konfessionalisierung des nachrevolutionären Hussitismus," in *Häresie und vorzeitige Reformation im Spätmittelalter*, ed. František Šmahel (Munich: 1998), 213–38.

Fudge, Thomas A., *Magnificent Ride. The First Reformation in Hussite Bohemia* (Aldershot: 1998).

Fudge, Thomas A., "Heresy and the Question of Hussites in the Southern Netherlands (1411–1431)," in *Campin in Context. Peinture et société dans la vallée de l'Escaut à l'époque de Robert Campin 1375–1445*, eds. Ludovic Nys and Dominique Vanwijnsberghe (Valenciennes, Bruxelles, and Tournai: 2007), 73–88.

Fudge, Thomas A., *Jan Hus. Religious Reform and Social Revolution in Bohemia* (London and New York: 2010).

Fudge, Thomas A., *The Trial of Jan Hus. Medieval Heresy and Criminal Procedure* (Oxford: 2013).

Fudge, Thomas A., *Jerome of Prague and the Foundations of the Hussite Movement* (New York: 2016).

Grant, Jeanne E., *For the Common Good. The Bohemian Land Law and the Beginning of the Hussite Revolution* (Leiden: 2015).

Haberkern, Phillip, "What's in a Name, or What's at Stake When We Talk about 'Hussites'?," *History Compass* 9 (2011): 791–801.

Haberkern, Phillip, *Patron Saint and Prophet. Jan Hus in the Bohemian and German Reformations* (Oxford: 2016).

Halama, Ota, and Pavel Soukup (eds.), *Kalich jako symbol v prvním století utrakvismu* [The chalice as a symbol in the first century of Utraquism] (Prague: 2016).

Hamm, Berndt, "Abschied vom Epochendenken in der Reformationsforschung. Ein Plädoyer," *Zeitschrift für historische Forschung* 39 (2012): 373–411.

Heymann, Frederick G., *George of Bohemia. King of Heretics* (Princeton: 1965).

Heymann, Frederick G., "The Crusades against the Hussites," in *A History of the Crusades*, eds. Kenneth M. Setton and Harry W. Hazard, vol. 3 (Madison and London: 1975), 586–646.

Hornbeck II, J. Patrick, and Michael Van Dussen (eds.), *Europe after Wyclif* (New York: 2017).

Horníčková, Kateřina, and Michal Šroněk (eds.), *Umění české reformace (1380–1620)* [The art of the Bohemian Reformation, 1380–1620] (Prague: 2010).

Horníčková, Kateřina, and Michal Šroněk (eds.), *From Hus to Luther. Visual Culture in the Bohemian Reformation (1380–1620)* (Turnhout: 2016).

Kaar, Alexandra, "Neue Mittel der Kriegsführung? König/Kaiser Sigismund und das Handelsverbot gegen die Hussiten in Böhmen," in *Heilige, Helden, Wüteriche. Herrschaftsstile der Luxemburger (1308–1437)*, eds. Martin Bauch, Julia Burkhardt, Tomáš Gaudek, and Václav Žůrek (Cologne, Weimar, and Vienna: 2017), 223–42.

Kalous, Antonín, *Matyáš Korvín (1443–1490). Uherský a český král* [Matthias Corvinus (1443–1490). King of Hungary and Bohemia] (České Budějovice: 2009).

Kaminsky, Howard, *A History of the Hussite Revolution* (Berkeley and Los Angeles: 1967).

Kejř, Jiří, *Die Causa Johannes Hus und das Prozessrecht der Kirche*, trans. Walter Annuß (Regensburg: 2005).

Kras, Paweł, *Husyci w piętnastowiecznej Polsce* [The Hussites in 15th-century Poland] (Lublin: 1998).

Macek, Josef (ed.), *Mezinárodní ohlas husitství* [The international echo of Hussitism] (Prague: 1958).
Macek, Josef, *Česká středověká šlechta* [The medieval Czech nobility] (Prague: 1997).
Machilek, Franz, "Deutsche Hussiten," in *Jan Hus. Zwischen Zeiten, Völkern, Konfessionen*, ed. Ferdinand Seibt (Munich: 1997), 267–82.
Marek, Jindřich, *Jakoubek ze Stříbra a počátky utrakvistického kazatelství v českých zemích. Studie o Jakoubkově postile z let 1413–1414* [Jakoubek of Stříbro and the beginnings of Utraquist preaching in the Bohemian lands. A study of Jakoubek's postil from 1413–1414] (Prague: 2011).
Marin, Olivier, *L'archevêque, le maître et le dévot. Genèses du mouvement réformateur pragois. Années 1360–1419* (Paris: 2005).
Molnár, Amedeo, *Die Waldenser. Geschichte und europäisches Ausmaß einer Ketzerbewegung* (Berlin: 1973).
Moskal, Krzysztof, *"Aby lud był jeden..." Eklezjologia Jana Husa w trakcie De ecclesia* ["May the people be united..." The ecclesiology of Jan Hus in the tract *De ecclesia*] (Lublin: 2003).
Mutlová, Petra, "Communicating Texts through Images. Nicholas of Dresden's *Tabulae*," in *Public Communication in European Reformation. Artistic and other Media in Central Europe 1380–1620*, eds. Milena Bartlová and Michal Šroněk (Prague: 2007), 29–37.
Mutlová, Petra, "Mikuláše z Drážďan Sermo ad clerum 1416 (kritická edice)" [Nicholas of Dresden's *Sermo ad clerum* 1416 (a critical edition)], *Studia historica Brunensia* 62 (2015): 295–312.
Nikodem, Jarosław, *Polska i Litwa wobec husyckich Czech w latach 1420–1433. Studium o polityce dynastycznej Władysława Jagiełły i Witolda Kiejstutowicza* [Poland and Lithuania in relation to Hussite Bohemia in the years 1420–1433. A study of the dynastic policy of Władysław Jagiełło and Witold Kiejstutowicz] (Poznań: 2004).
Nodl, Martin, "Sociální koncept pozdně středověkého městského přistěhovalectví" [The social concept of late medieval urban immigration], in *Sociální svět středověkého města*, ed. Martin Nodl (Colloquia mediaevalia Pragensia) 5 (Prague: 2006), 3–97.
Nodl, Martin, *Das Kuttenberger Dekret von 1409. Von der Eintracht zum Konflikt der Prager Universitätsnationen* (Cologne, Weimar, and Vienna: 2017).
Novotný, Robert, "Staročeský výraz hejtman. Sémantická analýza" [The Old Czech term "hejtman" (captain). A semantic analysis], *Marginalia Historica* 4 (1999): 85–102.
Novotný, Robert, "Die Konfessionalität des böhmischen und mährischen Adels in der Zeit der Regierung Sigismunds von Luxemburg," in *Kaiser Sigismund (1368–1437)*.

Zur Herrschaftspraxis eines europäischen Monarchen, eds. Karel Hruza and Alexandra Kaar (Cologne, Weimar, and Vienna: 2017), 57–74.

Novotný, Robert, "Der niedere Adel um Wenzel IV. Ein Sonderfall?" in *Heilige, Helden, Wüteriche. Herrschaftsstile der Luxemburger (1308–1437)*, eds. Martin Bauch, Julia Burkhardt, Tomáš Gaudek, and Václav Žůrek (Cologne, Weimar, and Vienna: 2017), 193–208.

Odložilík, Otakar, *The Hussite King. Bohemia in European Affairs 1440–1471* (New Brunswick: 1965).

Paner, Anna, *Jan Žižka z Trocnova* (Gdańsk: 2002).

Paulová, Milada, "L'Empire Byzantin et les Tchèques avant la chute de Constantinople," *Byzantinoslavica* 14 (1953): 158–225.

Perett, Marcela K., *Preachers, Partisans, and Rebellious Religion. Vernacular Writing and the Hussite Movement* (Philadelphia: 2018).

Provvidente, Sebastián, "Inquisitorial process and plenitudo potestatis at the Council of Constance (1414–1418)," in *The Bohemian Reformation and Religious Practice*, eds. Zdeněk V. David and David R. Holeton, vol. 8 (Prague: 2011), 100–16.

Rychterová, Pavlína, *Die Offenbarungen der heiligen Birgitta von Schweden. Eine Untersuchung zur alttschechischen Übersetzung des Thomas von Štítné* (Cologne, Weimar, and Vienna: 2004).

Salač, Antonín, *Constantinople et Prague en 1452* (Prague: 1958).

Seibt, Ferdinand, *Hussitica. Zur Struktur einer Revolution* (Cologne and Graz: 1965).

Šimůnek, Robert, *Reprezentace české středověké šlechty* [The representation of medieval Czech nobility] (Prague: 2013).

Šmahel, František, "Stärker als der Glaube. Magie, Aberglaube und Zauber in der Epoche des Hussitismus," *Bohemia* 32 (1991): 316–37.

Šmahel, František, "Die *Tabule veteris et novi coloris* als audiovisuelles Medium hussitischer Agitation," *Studie o rukopisech* 29 (1992): 95–105.

Šmahel, František, *Husitská revoluce* [The Hussite revolution], 4 vols. (Prague: 1993).

Šmahel, František, "Literacy and Heresy in Hussite Bohemia," in *Heresy and Literacy, 1000–1530*, eds. Peter Biller and Anne Hudson (Cambridge: 1994), 237–54.

Šmahel, František, "*Pax externa et interna*. Vom Heiligen Krieg zur Erzwungenen Toleranz im hussitischen Böhmen (1419–1485)," in *Toleranz im Mittelalter*, eds. Alexander Patschovsky and Harald Zimmermann (Vorträge und Forschungen) 45 (Sigmaringen: 1998), 221–73.

Šmahel, František, *Die Hussitische Revolution*, trans. Thomas Krzenck (Monumenta Germaniae Historica. Schriften) 43, 3 vols. (Hannover: 2002).

Šmahel, František, *Die Prager Universität im Mittelalter. The Charles University in the Middle Ages* (Leiden and Boston: 2007).

Šmahel, František, *Die Basler Kompaktaten mit den Hussiten (1436). Untersuchung und Edition* (Monumenta Germaniae Historica. Studien und Texte) 65 (Wiesbaden: 2019).

Šmahel, František, and Ota Pavlíček (eds.), *A Companion to Jan Hus* (Brill's Companions to the Christian Tradition) 54 (Leiden and Boston: 2015).

Smołucha, Janusz, *Polityka Kurii Rzymskiej za pontyfikatu Piusa II (1458–1464) wobec Czech i krajów sąsiednich. Z dziejów dyplomacji papieskiej w XV wieku* [The Roman curia's policy on Bohemia and neighboring countries during the pontificate of Pius II (1458–1464). From the history of papal diplomacy in the 15th century] (Cracow: 2008).

Solopova, Elizabeth (ed.), *The Wycliffite Bible. Origin, History and Interpretation* (Leiden and Boston: 2017).

Soukup, Pavel, *Reformní kazatelství a Jakoubek ze Stříbra* [Reform preaching and Jakoubek of Stříbro] (Prague: 2011).

Soukup, Pavel, "Kauza reformace. Husitství v konkurenci reformních projektů [The case of the Reformation. Hussitism among competing reform projects]," in *Heresis seminaria. Pojmy a koncepty v bádání o husitství*, eds. Pavlína Rychterová and Pavel Soukup (Prague: 2013), 171–217.

Soukup, Pavel, "Crusading against Christians in the Fifteenth Century. Doubts and Debates," in *Reconfiguring the Fifteenth-Century Crusade*, ed. Norman Housley (London: 2017), 85–122.

Soukup, Pavel, "The Waning of the 'Wycliffites.' Giving Names to Hussite Heresy," in *Europe after Wyclif*, eds. J. Patrick Hornbeck II and Michael Van Dussen (New York: 2017), 196–226.

Soukup, Pavel, *Repertorium operum antihussiticorum*, on-line database, www.antihus.eu.

Spengler, Hartmut, "Die Stärke der deutschen Aufgebote und Heere in den Hussitenkämpfen (ca. 1420–1438)," *Blätter für deutsche Landesgeschichte* 151 (2015): 311–416.

Traxler, Christina, "Früher Antihussitismus. Der Traktat *Eloquenti viro* und sein Verfasser Andreas von Brod," *Archa Verbi* 12 (2015): 130–77.

Traxler, Christina, *Firmiter velitis resistere. Die Auseinandersetzung der Wiener Universität mit dem Hussitismus vom Konstanzer Konzil (1414–1418) bis zum Beginn des Basler Konzils (1431–1449)* (Göttingen: 2019).

Válka, Josef, *Husitství na Moravě. Náboženská snášenlivost. Jan Amos Komenský* [Hussitism in Moravia. Religious tolerance. Jan Amos Komenský] (Brno: 2005).

Van Dussen, Michael, *From England to Bohemia. Heresy and Communication in the Later Middle Ages* (Cambridge: 2012).

Van Dussen, Michael, and Pavel Soukup (eds.), *Religious Controversy in Europe, 1378–1536. Textual Transmission and Networks of Readership* (Turnhout: 2013).

Van Engen, John, "Multiple Options. The World of the Fifteenth-Century Church," *Church History* 77 (2008): 257–84.

Whelan, Mark, "Between Papacy and Empire. Cardinal Henry Beaufort, the House of Lancaster, and the Hussite Crusades," *English Historical Review* 133 (2018): 1–31.

PART 1

Influences

∴

The Early Bohemian Reform

Olivier Marin

1   Palacký's Paradigm and Its Limitations

The Early Bohemian Reform no longer means what it once did. For a long time, the expression remained associated with the search for a patriotic identity that motivated generations of Czechs in the name of "National Awakening." Here, as elsewhere, one needs to go back as far as František Palacký if the orientation of all of the subsequent historiography is to be understood. Swept along by his Protestant culture, this advocate for Austro-Slavism considered Hussitism to be a key to interpreting all that had gone before. In a lecture he gave to the Royal Czech Society in 1842, Palacký broached the idea that the way had been paved for Jan Hus's initiative in Bohemia by an uninterrupted chain of reforming precursors, in the persons of Konrad of Waldhausen, Milíč of Kroměříž, Matěj of Janov and Jan Štěkna. He was thus pouring new wine into old bottles, repeating a genealogy familiar to the Unity of the Brethren, while drawing on a considerably expanded documentary basis. The statement he made was not at all to the liking of the Austrian censors, who prevented its publication for four years.[1] Yet the Austrian regime was unable to stop the spread of the concept of continuity within the Bohemian reformist movement. Palacký soon had occasion to return to it. In the third volume of his monumental *History of Bohemia* (1845), he attempted to show that the roots of the Hussite movement were to be found against a background of Slavic values that were basically incompatible with both Latin Catholicism and German culture. He claimed that the evidence for this was to be found among the forerunners of Jan Hus, and he restated their succession with one modification: this time Tomáš Štítný was recruited instead of Jan Štěkna.[2]

The list of reformers would go on to become classic, along with the concept of a Bohemian religious movement that was inseparable from it. The only voices raised against this retrospective vision came from Bohemia's German-speaking historians, such as Konstantin Höfler, Johann Loserth and Adolf

---

[1]   Palacký's lecture was eventually published in German, under the pseudonym J.P. Jordan, as *Die Vorläufer des Hussitenthums in Böhmen* (Leipzig: 1846).
[2]   See Stanisław Bylina, "František Palacký a české reformní hnutí 14. století," in *František Palacký 1798/1998. Dějiny a dnešek*, eds. František Šmahel and Eva Doležalová (Prague: 1999), 123–37.

Bachmann. Their criticisms were not without foundation, but were too often expressed *cum ira et studio* for them to take hold, especially in the context of the birth of Czechoslovakia. It was then that their contradictor, Václav Novotný, laid down the authoritative interpretation under the title *The Czech Religious Movement* (1915). This work was a synthesis in the purest liberal and patriotic spirit of the time.[3] Nor did the Marxist historiography that soon took over bring any more substantial revision to the overall story. While changing the emphasis from doctrine to infrastructure, it popularised the expression "pre-Hussitism," which was able to encompass the whole of the 14th century without mentioning the Luxembourg dynasty as the rulers of Bohemia. The shadow cast by the Hussite revolution had become more invasive than ever. The explanatory design created by Palacký was thus maintained and even radicalised until the very end of the 20th century.[4]

This paradigm had indisputable merits, including the encouragement of the publication of large collections of source material that remain useful references even today. However, it raises some difficulties that have recently emerged, or rather re-emerged. Was the Bohemian Reform, as Clemenceau said of the French Revolution, a single entity? Nothing is less certain. Caution should be exercised in praising its unity since this could serve to minimise the external influences that have affected it. Waldensianism may have had some effect, but there was, above all, John Wyclif and the influence of the Wycliffites. Similarly, Palacký and most of his spiritual heirs decided to reduce German-speaking clerics to the role of mere extras. Only Waldhauser found grace in their eyes, on the grounds that he had been in some way "de-Germanised" through his contact with the people of Bohemia. In Prague, however, the Czechs did not have a monopoly on reform. The dispute that arose in 1371 when the scholar Vojtěch Raňkův of Ježov (Adalbertus Ranconis de Ericinio, d. 1388) opposed Heinrich Totting of Oyta (d. 1397) reversed the expected situation. In that particular case, it was the Czech who, as a devoted son of the church, called upon the curia to examine the six theses that his Saxon colleague had had the imprudence to advance on the subject of priests in a state of mortal sin. Things went badly for Vojtěch, however, since his case was dismissed and he had to leave Prague rather miserably for Paris.[5] Until the dawn of the 1390s, it was the German-speaking university dons who actually set the tone. By far

---

3 Václav Novotný, *Náboženské hnutí české ve 14. a 15. stol. Část 1. Do Husa* (Prague: 1915).
4 A historiographical clarification of the subject can be found in Pavel Soukup, *Reformní kazatelství a Jakoubek ze Stříbra* (Prague: 2011), 11–22.
5 Concerning this case, see Jaroslav Kadlec, *Leben und Schriften des Prager Magisters Adalbert Rankonis de Ericinio* (Münster: 1971), 14–6.

the most popular Prague text came from the pen of one of their number. This is the *Dialogus rationis et conscientiae de crebra communione* written by Matthew of Cracow, of which no fewer than 265 manuscripts, three translations into the vernacular (German, Czech and French) and seven 15th-century printings survive.[6] A rebalancing remains to be pursued if one is to better understand the milieu in which the German-speaking preachers and theologians lived.[7]

This remark also sheds light on another weak point in the historiographic model inherited from Palacký: the scant consideration applied to audience reception. For a long time, the four "precursors of Hus" were credited with having had a huge influence, but with no attempt to measure the extent of this influence. In the case of Tomáš Štítný, this hypothesis needs considerable revision, because his adaptations of Latin religious literature into Czech barely circulated outside his immediate family circle. Matěj of Janov did not fare much better. Only parts of the *Regulae Veteris et Novi Testamenti* that concern the Eucharist found relative favor (about twenty manuscripts have been preserved). As for the rest, they failed to find an audience, at least in the short term. If the criterion of manuscript circulation is adopted, a very different landscape emerges from that which is traditionally depicted. After the *Dialogus* of Matthew of Cracow, the next most widely circulated text in the region was the *Malogranatum*, of Cistercian origin. This influential work describing the way to spiritual perfection survives in more than 150 manuscripts and in three incunabula editions and was translated into German and Dutch. The third most popular text is Waldhauser's *Postilla studentium* (110 complete manuscripts, plus 15 or so published extracts and a translation into Czech), which very clearly surpasses the quantity of Milíč's homiletics collections. Finally, there were the provincial statutes promulgated in 1349 by Prague's new archbishop, Arnošt of Pardubice: apart from one early printing, more than 90 manuscripts have survived, out of the 2,000 or so that must have existed at the time. Even in this last case, a strikingly large number of manuscripts (at least 20 per cent) circulated outside the province of Prague.[8] This proves how the Bohemian Reform radiated outwards and found especially fertile ground in the

---

[6] These figures are based on Carmen Cardelle de Hartmann, *Lateinische Dialoge 1200–1400. Literaturhistorische Studie und Repertorium* (Leiden and Boston: 2007), 683–84.

[7] A recent monograph has begun this reassessment: Matthias Nuding, *Matthäus von Krakau. Theologe, Politiker, Kirchenreformer in Krakau, Prag und Heidelberg zur Zeit des Großen Abendländischen Schismas* (Tübingen: 2007).

[8] Ivan Hlaváček. "Kodikologisch-bibliotheksgeschichtliche Bemerkungen zu den Provinzialstatuten Ernsts von Pardubitz von 1349," in *Partikularsynoden im späten Mittelalter*, eds. Nathalie Kruppa and Leszek Zygner (Göttingen: 2006), 331–50.

neighboring regions of south Germany, Austria and Poland. Their longevity was no less remarkable. These four best-sellers were constantly copied and adapted into the vernacular throughout the 15th century, whether in Catholic or in Utraquist circles. In other words, contrary to what might have been thought, the Hussite revolution did not render them obsolete.

Consequently, the idea of linear and relentless progress that underlies the classic view of the Early Bohemian Reform also deserves to be criticized. Firstly, the process was polymorphic. The Reform was upheld by heterogeneous pressure groups. While all of them shared a vague common ideal of moral and spiritual regeneration, they did not necessarily agree on what methods to follow. Thus, the reforming movement was anything but a long, smoothly flowing river. It experienced alternate phases of crisis and resumption. The 1370s proved fatal for the disciples of Milíč before the influence of the new archbishop, Jan of Jenštejn and his university advisers gave them a second chance. Afterwards, not all reformers joined Hussitism. The path taken by Ondřej of Brod clearly shows that everything remained open. This Czech Master may well have been a preacher at the Bethlehem Chapel, as was Hus, and castigated ecclesiastical pomp in terms that Hus himself would not have rejected, but Ondřej refused to follow his colleague when he thought that sacramental orthodoxy was under threat.[9]

Current historiography, unsullied by a belief in progress, thus seeks to analyse the authors of the Early Bohemian Reform in terms of their own consistency and avoids reading them solely in the light of nascent Hussitism. The most recent biography of Milíč of Kroměříž is exemplary in this regard. Rather than depicting the Moravian preacher as the prophet of a new era, it shows him as the heir to the pastoral turning point initiated at the Fourth Lateran Council.[10] It also shows that Milíč conceived of the deepening of Christian life only in the strict context of the practice of the sacraments, listening to the Word of God and pious works. This perspective grants legitimacy to the proliferation of ideas that flourished in Bohemia during the second half of the 14th century while simultaneously rendering Hussitism a unique and unpredictable development.

It is in line with these historiographic reinterpretations that we here discuss the presence of reforming forces, their resources and their unfulfilled

---

9   Jaroslav Kadlec, "Reformní postila a synodální kázání mistra Ondřeje z Brodu," *Studie o rukopisech* 16 (1977): 13–26.

10   Peter C.A. Morée, *Preaching in Fourteenth-Century Bohemia. The Life and Ideas of Milicius de Chremsir († 1374) and his Significance in the Historiography of Bohemia* (Heršpice: 1999).

achievement.[11] The chronological bracket begins with the elevation of Prague to an archbishopric (1344), a real milestone in the history of Bohemian ecclesiastical reform, and does not go beyond the approximate date of 1400. The rapid spread of Wycliffism, the dethronement of Wenceslas IV as King of the Romans, and the concomitant death of Jan of Jenštejn opened up a new era that would eventually lead to other developments.

2 The Originality of the Bohemian Church in the Mid-14th Century

In the Christianity of the mid-14th century, reform was on everyone's lips. Everywhere could be found the same awareness of the intolerable gap between the Gospel ideal and current reality as well as an apparent will to remedy the situation, both by the conversion of hearts and the reform of institutions. This universal recognition took on a unique tone in Bohemia, owing to the special conditions of its development.

The first condition was that this was a new country, in the sense that Bohemia had long remained on the periphery of the Latin West. The church, however, had benefitted from mid-13th century conditions, when the national monarchy became stronger, foreign contacts intensified, and economic expansion allowed the local church to become a free power under its own administration, in accordance with the Gregorian Reform. This development was accelerated by the events that followed the Council of Vienne. The Bishop of Prague, Jan IV of Dražice (1301–1343), who attended it in person, assigned himself a chancellery upon his return, as well as other instruments of government that were indispensable to the extension of his authority throughout the diocese.[12] Pope Clement VI approved this *de facto* situation by creating an archbishopric in the Bohemian capital (1344), whose province covered the Moravian diocese of Olomouc and that of Litomyšl, as well as a university, the first situated east of the Rhine (founded 1347/48). At the same time, Charles of Luxembourg ousted Louis of Bavaria as King of the Romans (1346).

While the crisis weakened countries further to the west, Bohemian Christianity went on flourishing.[13] It was spared from plagues and wars, at least until

---

11 This chapter revisits and builds on ideas from Olivier Marin, *L'archevêque, le maître et le dévot. Genèses du mouvement réformateur pragois. Années 1360–1419* (Paris: 2005).

12 Zdeňka Hledíková, *Biskup Jan IV. z Dražic (1301–1343)* (Prague: 1992), 40–98.

13 A pessimistic panorama of Bohemia's ecclesiastical institutions is provided in František Šmahel, *Die Hussitische Revolution*, trans. Thomas Krzenck (Monumenta Germaniae Historica. Schriften) 43 (Hannover: 2002), vol. 1, 168–219. For a more balanced view, see Hledíková, "Úpadek nebo růst? K situaci církve v Čechách ve 14. století," in *Traditio et*

the 1380s, when it boasted two and a half million faithful: new churches were being built, but these were not always enough to welcome all who came. At the same time, religious holdings had become dense. Covering an average area of 28 km² each, the 2,084 parishes of the diocese of Prague could be compared in size to those of England. They were administered at the ratio of one priest for every 150 to 200 inhabitants, something that bore comparison with the countries in which Christianity was of ancient vintage. The clergy was numerous, even overabundant, and was becoming ever more tightly structured. The diocesan synods that had met regularly since 1310 were relayed by holding meetings at the level of the newly created deaneries and through the action of the archdeacons, thus ensuring a minimal form of hierarchical control over those who served the parishes. In short, in the space of less than a century, Bohemia had more than made up for lost time. It should be remembered that reform did not emerge from an atmosphere of decadence; on the contrary, it arose from a church that was expanding rapidly, both in terms of numbers of the faithful and of its institutions.

If we examine these developments more closely, it is striking to note that the movement was almost exclusively focused around Prague, which is consistent with the strong centralization of the Czech state and the church at the time. What was unique for Central Europe was that Prague, with its 40,000 inhabitants and 42 parishes, concentrated within its walls or at its gates everything that counted in Bohemia, namely, the three powers of *regnum*, *sacerdotium*, and *studium* – the imperial court, the seat of the archbishop, and the most prestigious ecclesiastical establishments (these were the Benedictine monasteries of St. George and of Břevnov, to which should be added the convents of the four mendicant orders, a charterhouse, and a Slavic rite monastery), as well as a university.[14] One can imagine what a cultural melting pot this small space represented, being both over-supplied and coveted, and where the level of teaching, the degree of political consciousness, and religious demands were of the highest order. The reformers themselves were well aware that in Prague, and particularly in the heart of the Old Town, they had found their Jerusalem.

The pace of change was also so swift that the historian has difficulty in separating it into phases of the creation of the local church and its reform. While the Latin countries had taken centuries to set up the elementary structures of religious life and subsequently to adjust to the new demands of canon law, the

---

cultus. Miscellanea historica Bohemica Miloslao Vlk archiepiscopo Pragensi ab eius collegis amicisque ad annum sexagesimum dedicata, ed. Zdeňka Hledíková (Prague: 1993), 51–62.

14   The best reference tool for the religious history of the Czech capital remains Václav Vladivoj Tomek, *Dějepis města Prahy*, vol. 3, 2nd ed. (Prague: 1893).

Czech lands telescoped these two phases. This speed of innovation and of the rifts witnessed over time demonstrates the proactivity of the Prague elites. In the long term, however, it reveals a factor of fragility, due to insufficient assimilation.[15]

Finally, there is another specifically Bohemian feature that deserves mention, that of its situation at the religious frontier. Since the late 13th century, German colonisation had embraced numerous clandestine Waldensian communities. After a phase of wait-and-see, the church began to react from 1310, when the Inquisition launched a pitiless campaign of repression in southern Bohemia, weakening the "heresy" forever, though never managing to eradicate it entirely.[16] The Bohemian Reform movement took on a militant character as a result. Even though its leaders did not become directly involved in persecution, they were aware of this danger from within and decided to take up the Waldensian challenge of a personal religious life without formalism. Through elevating the culture of the clergy, as well as the moralisation of Christian society as a whole, they sought to introduce an effective antidote to the Waldensians. In other words, the Early Bohemian Reform was, to an extent, a counter-reformation.

3 The Geopolitics of Reform: The Institutions

Faced with the threat of heresy, the reformers closed ranks. Yet they were divided among themselves, with tendencies that did not exactly overlap. Three main reforming centers can be distinguished: the governing diocesan circles, those connected with monastic or religious orders, and the University of Prague. They will each be examined in turn, in order to assess their synergies and the balance of power that was created by this situation.

It has now been proven that the Early Bohemian Reform was initiated from above, the initiator being Prague's first archbishop, Arnošt of Pardubice. This outstanding personality had been trained at the finest Italian universities and would soon emerge as a model of pastoral knowledge and zeal who was so

---

15 Zdeňka Hledíková, "Církev v českých zemích na přelomu 14. a 15. století," in *Jan Hus na přelomu tisíciletí*, eds. Miloš Drda, František J. Holeček, and Zdeněk Vybíral (Husitský Tábor. Supplementum) 1 (Tábor: 2001), 35–58.

16 Pavel Soukup, "Die Waldenser in Böhmen und Mähren im 14. Jahrhundert," in *Friedrich Reiser und die "waldensisch-hussitische Internationale,"* eds. Albert de Lange and Kathrin Utz Tremp (Heidelberg, Ubstadt-Weiher, and Basel: 2006), 131–60. See also the recent discussion in Reima Välimäki, *Heresy in Late Medieval Germany. The Inquisitor Petrus Zwicker and the Waldensians* (York, York Medieval Press: 2019).

universally respected that, during the conclave of 1362, his name was circulated as being among the potential successors to Innocent VI.[17] In Christianity at the time, very few prelates were moved by such a reforming ardor. The synodal activity he encouraged is just a barometer. Five years after the establishment of an archbishopric, Arnošt convened a provincial council and promulgated its statutes (1349). While borrowing much of their substance from the 1310 council of Mainz, these statutes were distinguished by both a more literal fidelity to canon law and the grafting on of pre-existing local by-laws. This founding deed gave rise to a continuous series of diocesan synods, no fewer than sixty having met before 1419, a record number since everywhere else synodal activity had run out of breath in the course of the 14th century. The impact of this annual (and sometimes biannual) legislation on diocesan life cannot be underestimated. Only the archdeacons, the representatives of chapters, the deans, and non-exempt orders could be convened to the cathedral, but the deans would then have to hand down the decisions to their colleagues who were affected, by providing them with the texts of the statutes and explaining them. All the rectors, in their turn, were required to own a copy in good condition, a provision that was considered significant since it was systematically checked by visitors.[18]

Not content with bringing together the flower of the clergy, Arnošt of Pardubice covered the length and breadth of the province to ensure that the rules laid down in the synod were being implemented in the field. For this purpose, he resorted to the instrument of the canonical visit as codified by Innocent IV.[19] He either made visits personally, as when he went to inspect the cathedral chapter of Olomouc, or through one of his archdeacons or other representatives appointed specially for the purpose. After the practice was ended by his successor, Jan Očko of Vlašim, the visits were resumed even more energetically at the start of Jan of Jenštejn's bishopric. The years 1379–1382 mark the date of the only official report of a pastoral visit preserved from the whole of central Europe, a visit performed by the archdeacon Pavel of Janovice to the nine deaneries surrounding Prague. The vices of Nicolaism, ignorance, simony and

---

17 Zdeňka Hledíková, *Arnošt z Pardubic. Arcibiskup, zakladatel, rádce* (Prague: 2008), 99–100.
18 Zdeňka Hledíková, "Synoden in der Diözese Prag 1280–1417," in *Partikularsynoden im späten Mittelalter*, eds. Nathalie Kruppa and Leszek Zygner (Göttingen: 2006), 307–29. In Moravia, synodal activity was much less regular; however: see Pavel Krafl, *Synody a statuta olomoucké diecéze období středověku* (Prague: 2003; 2nd ed. 2014).
19 Zdeňka Hledíková, "Die Visitationen des weltlichen Klerus im vorhussitischen Böhmen," *Mediaevalia Bohemica* 1 (1969): 249–74.

negligence by priests were severely stigmatised.[20] This document went far to nourish the dark legend of a Bohemian church plagued by excesses. Yet it can be interpreted less as a sign of deterioration in the state of the parish clergy than as an increase in the standards that the "good priest" had to meet.

Finally, as synods and visits were by nature intermittent, their effects were in danger of evaporating quickly if central authorities were not there to oversee them on a daily basis. New colleagues of the archbishop, people who were educated and had a stable position, would assist him in this area: these included an official, heading an episcopal or consistory court of law, vicars-general whose function was regularised from 1359, and "correctors of the clergy," a post unique to Prague, created *ex nihilo* to support the work of the archdeacons. Each of these prelates made a point of checking the suitability of clerics appointed to benefices. In an evocative image, Jan of Jenštejn compared their role to that of sheepdogs, helping to keep the flocks safe and warn them of imminent danger.[21]

This ambitious diocesan reform program was a long-term project that seems to have reached its apogee in the 1380s, when a whole system of bureaucracy operated, relying on the intensive use of written archives. The main features of this reform were the following: firstly, it was inspired by Rome. A few lawsuits were brought against Arnošt of Pardubice and the papacy concerning the appointment of archdeacons, but these did not deter the archbishops of Prague from seeking institutional models from the curia at Avignon and cultivating their networks of influence. To accuse them of having autonomist or nationalist tendencies would be anachronistic. This reform subsequently adopted an essentially disciplinary outlook, insofar as it standardised Christian behavior through the conduct of a reformed priesthood. Priests were required to remain celibate and suitably dressed, and the laity was expected to observe fast days, rest on Sundays, and pay tithes.[22] To deduce from this that the archbishops' initiatives favored conformance to completely external practices involves a significant step, albeit one that has often been taken by the historiography. This is

---

20   Pavel of Janovice, *Protocollum visitationis archidiaconatus Pragensis annis 1379–1382 per Paulum of Janowicz archidiaconum Pragensem factae*, eds. Ivan Hlaváček and Zdeňka Hledíková (Prague: 1973).

21   *De officio pastoris* sermon in Weltsch, *Archbishop John of Jenstein*, 196: "Sic episcopus deberet habere duos vel tres canes, id est officiales, qui simul cum eo gregem custodiant, et ubi ipse deficeret contra lupos, ut saltem illis canibus, videlicet officialibus seu vicariis, adiuvetur, ut sibi in testimonium adveniant et sue innocencie testes fiant."

22   An analysis of the various provisions can be found in Jaroslav V. Polc, "Kapitoly z církevního života Čech podle předhusitského zákonodárství," in *Pražské arcibiskupství 1344–1994*, eds. Zdeňka Hledíková and Jaroslav V. Polc (Prague: 1994), 30–57.

wrong, because diocesan reform did not neglect the internalization of Christian truths and values. It is significant, in this respect, that Arnošt of Pardubice, aware that he could not leave it to naive priests to direct souls, insisted on adding a manual of elementary theology to the provincial statutes of 1349, entitled *De tribus punctis essentialibus christiane religionis*, written by the Sorbonne University fellow Thomas of Ireland (1316). The lower clergy would find in it a succinct explanation of the articles of faith, the commandments and mortal sins, and from 1353 they were encouraged to use it to teach and guide their parishioners. This pioneering measure predated the first formal catechisms by almost two centuries, demonstrating the importance attached by the church of Prague to learning the principles of the faith.[23]

In this respect, the secular hierarchy of Prague concurred with some of the aspirations that had been at work for several decades in monastic circles in Bohemia. How to reform the inner man and open routes to salvation other than by the accumulation of good works: such was the lesson to be learned from the *Malogranatum*, an edifying Cistercian treatise that was finding increasing favor among prelates and pious faithful. This dialogue between a novice and his spiritual mentor had been composed before 1335 at the Zbraslav Monastery, by one of the abbots, perhaps Peter of Zittau (d. 1339). Its three volumes corresponded to the three stages of spiritual growth – novices invited to perform penitence, those still en route to perfection who need to fight against temptation by practicing virtue and frequenting the sacraments, and those who have achieved perfection and are promised the vision of God.[24] Through its christocentrism, its praise of solitude and renunciation, and its relative indifference to the social dimension of Christian values, the *Malogranatum* has often been quoted as the illustration of a hypothetical Bohemian *devotio moderna*. The Bohemian text contains neither methodical devotional exercises nor a particular insistence on the copying of books. At the same time, the frequent apology for the eucharistic communion to which the Master of Zbraslav devotes himself seems to have had no equivalent in the Dutch

---

23 Mary A. Rouse, and Richard H. Rouse, *Preachers, Florilegia and Sermons. Studies on the Manipulus Florum of Thomas of Ireland* (Toronto: 1979), 101–04. More generally, on the circulation of this type of handbook for priests in Central Europe, see Martin Nodl, "Mezi laickou a učeneckou zbožností. Katechetické příručky pro faráře v českém a slezském prostředí pozdního středověku," in *Náboženský život a církevní poměry v zemích Koruny české ve 14.–17. století*, eds. Lenka Bobková and Jana Konvičná (Prague: 2009), 176–91.

24 Manfred Gerwing, *Malogranatum oder der dreifache Weg zur Vollkommenheit. Ein Beitrag zur Spiritualität des Spätmittelalters* (Munich: 1986).

movement prior to the 15th century.[25] Let us not overestimate *Malogranatum*'s influence over the disciples of Geert Grote. Yet its contribution to the renewal of religious life in Central Europe is certain. The work's pedagogical structure and the simplicity of its contents which, though originally destined for monks, could easily be adapted to a wider readership, facilitated its circulation outside the cloister where there was a renewed attention to the inner life.

The fact remains that the direct participation by the Cistercians in the Reform was limited by the strict enclosure to which they were committed and by the exemption they enjoyed. Other orders or congregations that were more closely associated with the diocesan government would supplement their work, with the regular canons of St. Augustine at the forefront. In 1333, Jan of Dražice installed a canonical community in the episcopal city of Roudnice based on that of Pavia. His successors strongly favored founding similar institutions throughout the Czech lands; twelve other houses followed, some of whose members settled in Austria, Poland, and Upper Hungary. The priority given to the study of the church fathers in this Roudnice congregation can be clearly seen in the *Consuetudines Rudnicenses* and the catalogues of the extensive libraries it owned, contributing greatly to its success. The archbishops of Prague drew sustenance from it for their personal piety. It was to Roudnice that Jan of Jenštejn chose to withdraw and it was from here that he recruited his spiritual guide in the person of the abbot Petrus Clarificator.[26] Many vicars-general were chosen from among their ranks, including Štěpán of Uherčice. He was the confidant of Arnošt of Pardubice and may have studied with him in Italy, becoming his right-hand man, accompanying him on his most difficult inspections, and hearing his confessions. In this role, he was ordered to produce a manual for confessors, the *Questiunculae*. The work contains an encyclopaedic introduction designed to explain the key concepts of the ecclesiastical discipline, illustrated with concrete examples, followed by an examination

---

25   Eduard Winter even inferred a genuine descent through analogous emphases on the grounds that Florens Radewijns and other future canons of Windesheim had studied in Prague during the 1370s and might have been influenced by the spirituality of the *Malogranatum*. The comparison with *devotio moderna* is nevertheless far-fetched: Eduard Winter, *Frühhumanismus. Seine Entwicklung in Böhmen und deren europäische Bedeutung für die Kirchenreformbestrebungen im 14. Jahrhundert* (Berlin: 1964), 165–177. For an opposite view, see Stanisław Bylina, "Devotio moderna et dévotion des masses chrétiennes en Europe centrale aux XIVe–XVe siècles," in *Die "Neue Frömmigkeit" in Europa im Spätmittelalter*, eds. Marek Derwich and Martial Staub (Göttingen: 2004), 211–24; and Soukup, *Reformní kazatelství*, 25–43.

26   Jaroslav Kadlec, "Začátky kláštera augustiniánských kanovníků v Roudnici," *Studie o rukopisech* 20 (1981): 65–86; idem, "Petr Klarifikátor, duchovní vůdce a životopisec arcibiskupa Jana z Jenštejna," *Sborník Katolické teologické fakulty* 1 (1998): 101–50.

in dialogue form of the difficulties that the application of the provincial statutes posed in the field. The success of this combination of canonical literature and pastoral experience (more than 25 manuscripts of it are known) is a measure of the crucial role played by the canons of Roudnice in the organization of the new province of Prague.[27]

At a later date and more discreetly, the Benedictines also made their mark on the Early Bohemian Reform, to judge from the example of Břevnov. This ancient institution went through hard times in the mid-century but was able to recover under Abbot Denys II (1385–1409) and enabled the whole of the Bohemian church to benefit from its experience. One of the monks, Jan of Holešov (d. 1436), took up his pen in the service of pastoral reform, in which he participated through the *cura animarum* that the monastery exercised in its numerous incorporated parishes. Two of his treatises are designed to sanctify the Christian peoples as a whole. One of the treatises, written in 1397, determines the text and the correct interpretation of a popular Old Czech prayer, the *Hospodine pomiluj ny*, often attributed to St. Adalbert; the other, known as *Largum sero*, seeks to purify the Christmas festival from the superstitious or excessively profane customs attached to it (prior to 1405).[28] Jan of Holešov shows originality in the attention he pays to socio-linguistic realities and to folk culture, but shares with the other reforming elites a desire to draw the faithful away from obscurantism. It was considered in high places that it was no longer sufficient for the laity to accept the faith of the church; it was also necessary for the laity to understand it in order to live better.

At the time when Jan of Holešov was writing, Prague University was emerging from its initial lethargy and in turn became involved in the educational work that so brilliantly reinforced its social usefulness. It was not until the 1360s that the *studium* was given an institutional setting. The staffing levels then increased and were soon swelled by numerous masters and students escaping from Paris due to the Great Schism. Under the episcopacy of Jan of Jenštejn, the university emerged as a true cultural melting-pot, in which texts and doctrines originated from France (Hugh of Saint-Cher and other 13th-century masters, John Buridan, etc.), Italy (Johannes Andreae, Simon Fidati of Cascia), and England (Robert Grosseteste, Richard FitzRalph, Richard Rolle). This diversity resulted in a raft of disagreements among the various schools,

---

27 Rostislav Zelený, *The Questiunculae of Stephan of Roudnice* (Rome: 1966).
28 Kamil Harvánek, "Traktát Largum sero Jana z Holešova. Příspěvek k lidové zbožnosti ve středověku," *Studia historica Brunensia* 56 (2009): 105–20; Olivier Marin, "Aux origines médiévales de la slavistique. L'Expositio cantici Hospodine pomiluj ny (1397)," *Mélanges de l'Ecole française de Rome* 117 (2005): 615–39.

religious families, and rival nations, but these should not be exaggerated. Almost all those living in Prague, regardless of how they were labelled, experimented with a new way of viewing theology, which Berndt Hamm has rightly named *Frömmigkeitstheologie*.[29] This expression describes the eruption of morality and spirituality in university theology, i.e. a greater preoccupation with personal salvation and the affective participation in the life of faith. This movement, critical of speculative theology as cultivated by previous generations, resulted on the one hand in enabling the Bible to regain its place of honor, with biblical commentary recovering some of the prestige and the educational role it had lost in the course of the 14th century. It also opened up a space for practical issues concerning the conduct of daily life. The range of topics was extensive, from the ethics of economics to spiritual direction and the administration of the sacraments, via expressions of piety (superstition, indulgences, new liturgical festivals) or religious vows. The masters of Prague did not disdain to consult the regular circles mentioned above on these various matters. In their anti-intellectualism, they also did not hesitate to build on the certainties of intuition and enlightenment, as is proven by their ready acceptance of the *Revelations* of Bridget of Sweden.[30]

Yet while the University's theologians enthusiastically celebrated the "Sibyl of the North," going as far as to plead for her canonization at the curia, this was not merely because they sought to renew their discipline through contact with mysticism and visionary literature. It is also because they were sensitive to her vibrant appeals for the reform of the church. *Frömmigkeitstheologie* also made demands for collective action, something that is decisive for this discussion. It expressed the conviction that the mission of a scholar was not merely an intellectual one; he was also required to enlighten the faithful concerning their practices by allowing them to enjoy the fruits of his learning. This should be achieved either directly, through the pastoral responsibilities assumed by certain masters in their Prague parishes, or through a ricochet effect, by working with the archbishop to improve the training of priests and sometimes by patronizing the first attempts at translating religious literature into the vernacular.

A man such as Matthew of Cracow, who taught at Prague until ca. 1394, is characteristic of this reformist orientation. He had been a preacher at Our

---

29   Berndt Hamm, "Was ist Frömmigkeitstheologie? Überlegungen zum 14.–16. Jahrhundert," in *Praxis pietatis. Festschrift für Wolfgang Sommer*, eds. Hans-Jörg Nieden and Marcel Nieden (Stuttgart: 1999), 9–45.

30   This reception drew the attention of Pavlína Rychterová, *Die Offenbarungen der heiligen Birgitta von Schweden. Eine Untersuchung zur alttschechischen Übersetzung des Thomas von Štítné* (Cologne, Weimar, and Vienna: 2004).

Lady Before Týn and was invited four times by Jan of Jenštejn to address the diocesan clergy who had gathered in a synod. In his writings, the scholarly exercizes carry little weight in the face of the multitude of occasional sermons, manuals of confession, treatises of edification and prayer, including a confession formula written in German.[31] The same could be said, *mutatis mutandis*, of the Dominican theologian Heinrich of Bitterfeld (d. ca. 1405), who also aspired to be a moralist and person of influence with Jenštejn, and of the preacher of St. Gall, Nicolaus Magni of Jawór (d. 1435).[32] This confirms that the 1380s were indeed a golden age, thanks to the fruitful collaboration between the archbishopric and the *studium*. The subsequent development of *Frömmigkeitstheologie* at the universities of Vienna, Cracow and Heidelberg would certainly have been impossible if not for its initial incubation in Prague, in the course of which the masters learned together to enrich pastoral action with their knowledge and in return, open their minds to the shared sentiment of the faithful.

4   Practice: Preaching the Reform

Reform required a major initiative of communication and socio-cultural adaptation, the most important instrument for this being the pulpit. Prior to the 14th century, preaching had been limited in Bohemia to certain regular audiences. With the exception of a few unusual circumstances linked to the visit of a popular mendicant friar such as Berthold of Regensburg, the faithful usually found they were faced with clerics who were incapable of teaching them anything. With the multiplication of grammar schools and the subsequent improvement in the level of instruction of the laity, however, the situation became intolerable. Emperor Charles IV, who considered himself responsible for the salvation of his subjects, became anxious. He was not alone in this. As Pavel of Janovice discovered in the course of a pastoral visit, the parishioners openly

---

31   Dietrich Schmidtke, "Pastoraltheologische Texte des Matthäus von Krakau," in *Schriften im Umkreis mitteleuropäischer Universitäten um 1400. Lateinische und Volkssprachige Texte aus Prag, Wien und Heidleberg: Unterschiede, Gemeinsamkeiten, Wechselbeziehungen*, eds. Fritz Peter Knapp, Jürgen Miethke, and Manuela Niesner (Leiden and Boston: 2004), 178–96.

32   Koudelka, Vladimír J., "Heinrich von Bitterfeld († c. 1405), Professor an der Universität Prag," *Archivum Fratrum Praedicatorum* 23 (1953): 5–65; Manfred Gerwing, "Heinrich von Bitterfeld als Reformer," *Theologie und Glaube* 95 (2005): 409–22; Adolph Franz, *Der Magister Nikolaus Magni de Jawor. Ein Beitrag zur Literatur- und Gelehretengeschichte des 14. und 15. Jahrhunderts* (Freiburg im Breisgau: 1898).

complained about clerical ineptitude.[33] The ecclesiastical reformers were not deaf to this demand for teaching. The advice offered by Milíč of Kroměříž in 1367 to Pope Urban V included an exhortation above all things to send preachers to the four corners of Christianity, since for him they represented the last chance for Christian soldiers to defeat the Antichrist. The whole history of salvation depended upon them.[34] Subsequently, many people would repeat that preaching was one of the inalienable duties of a priest. As a sign of the price attached to it thereafter, in 1374, Archbishop Jan Očko decided to grant forty days of indulgence to those who attended sermons.

Under the joint influence of demands from the laity and the ongoing reconstruction of the church's diocesan structures, the Early Bohemian Reform – the difference from *devotio moderna* should once again be noted – placed the sermon at the heart of its initiative. But in what forms?

The first arena considered suitable for reformist preaching was that of the synod. Preaching in synods was a good way of reinforcing and modernizing the training of priests and consisted, in fact, of using the occasion to harangue them. The archbishops of Prague made intensive use of this method. Rather than preach themselves, they left it to personalities in the diocese whose thinking or pastoral initiatives they favored. The first synodal preacher of whom we are aware, in the late 1360s, was none other than Milíč. University masters took over from the end of the following decade. In addition to Matthew of Cracow, already mentioned, this prestigious function was performed successively by the Vicar-General Kuneš of Třebovle, the *scholasticus* Vojtěch Raňkův of Ježov, and the Masters Štěpán of Kolín and Stanislav of Znojmo. They were given this mission by the archbishop, explains Matthew, to "correct the clergy, and through the clergy the people of the whole province, of their past errors, to put them on guard against the errors to come, and show them what they had to do, applying a treatment that lasted for half a year."[35] In concrete terms, these synodal sermons served to reinforce the statutes. Of course, it was rare for a

---

33   Stanisław Bylina, "La catéchisation du peuple en Bohême aux XIVe et XVe siècles" in *The Bohemian Reformation and Religious Practice*, eds. Zdeněk V. David and David R. Holeton, vol. 3 (Prague: 2000), 25–33.

34   Peter C.A. Morée, "The Role of the Preacher According to Milicius de Chremsir," in *The Bohemian Reformation and Religious Practice*, eds. David and Holeton, vol. 3, 35–48.

35   *Sermo Digne ambuletis*, in Matthew of Cracow, "Sermones synodales," in *Mateusza z Krakowa De praxi romanae curiae*, ed. Władysław Seńko (Wrocław, Warsaw, and Cracow: 1969), 140: "Quid enim est predicare in sinodo, nisi quantum ad doctrinalem archiepiscopale officium exercere et debitum explere, totum clerum, immo per clerum totius provincie populum de preteritis malis corrigere, munire de futuris, ad ea que facienda sunt dirigere et quasi pro dimidio anno medicinam adhibere?"

preacher to comment upon them. Preachers would draw their inspiration from the Bible, the church fathers, and canon law, and sought to show the spirit in which the statutes should be understood. Moral discourse was naturally omnipresent and relied on a dual contrast between the perfection of the primitive church and contemporary decadence. It also highlighted the view that a priest had to be a man separated from the community that was in his care by his way of life, and yet altogether devoted to it.[36] This high ideal of the priesthood was in the spirit of a hierarchical ecclesiology of more or less Dionysian inspiration, which justified reform that began from above before reaching the Christian populace through successive mediations.

Some reforming clerics did not stop there and were brave enough to preach the good word themselves to the laity. In this, they faced formidable obstacles. They first noted the lack of specialized preachers' benefices in the city. In the mid-century, only St. Vitus Cathedral had one, thanks to an ancient provision updated to the tastes of the day by the Fourth Lateran Council. In an effort to reinforce the prestige of the diocesan clergy, Bishop Jan of Dražice appointed a secular preacher in place of the mendicant friars who had performed the function hitherto. Nevertheless, in 1363, when Emperor Charles IV called upon the regular Austrian canon Konrad Waldhauser to preach in Bohemia, he needed to find him an additional occupation. Through imperial intervention, Waldhauser became rector of Litoměřice, and subsequently that of the large parish of St. Gall, a strategic position from which he was able to attract all the high society in the capital. As for Milíč, he owed it to the support of the archbishop to be able to preach alternately at the Churches of St. Nicholas, St. Giles and in place of the rector at Our Lady Before Týn.

These expedients were too random to guarantee regular preaching in the secular churches of Prague, hence the feeling that the number of "preaching posts" needed to be increased so that priests could be specially assigned to preaching. Fifteen or so pulpits of this type were created in the capital before the end of the century. It was significant that the initiative for this could be traced, not to the king or the archbishop, but to wealthy citizens. Thus, the merchant Kříž, with the support of a member of the privy council, the Silesian knight Johann of Mühlheim, founded a chapel in 1391 on his land south-west of the Old Town of Prague, which he dedicated to the Holy Innocents of Bethlehem. This chapel was entirely dedicated to preaching. The letter of foundation is evidence of the care with which the preacher was chosen. He needed to be

---

36 Jana Nechutová, "Reform- und Bußprediger von Waldhauser bis Hus," in *Kirchliche Reformimpulse des 14./15. Jahrhunderts in Ostmitteleuropa*, eds. Winfried Eberhard and Franz Machilek (Cologne, Weimar, and Vienna: 2006), 239–54.

recruited from the ranks of the secular clergy, acknowledged to be able to preach in Czech, live locally, and obtain the approval of the Bohemian Nation of the University. It was even specified in this respect that the oldest three Czech masters of the Karolinum College should discuss the candidate with the head of the Old Town council. Under the auspices of this rapprochement between the *studium* and urban circles, preaching to the people thus took precedence over the traditional liturgical obligations and emerged as the supreme form of service to God.[37] From 1402, the Bethlehem Chapel became famous due to a certain John of Husinec, better known as Jan Hus. The new establishment had a difficult start and, in any case, was merely the result, among other things, of an unprecedented effort to teach religious education through preaching.

Once this institutional obstacle had been removed, the reformers needed to find a suitable communication strategy. The Prague sources sometimes make this hard to witness. In fact, very few *reportationes*, that is to say notes taken on the spot by listeners, are available.[38] The homiletical collections that have been preserved usually transmit model sermons that stand in a complicated relationship to oral preaching. They are generally the result of sermons, cleaned up after the event, that were originally preached by their authors, while at the same time conceived as working tools that could easily be used in turn by apprentice preachers. As a result, these anthologies of sermons stick to a rather dull literary formula. Histrionics and discussion of topical incidents, which might not serve as suitable examples, are almost systematically banished. If one wishes to reconstitute the *Sitz im Leben* of reform preaching, examples need to be compared with other sources of the narrative type, such as chronicles or documents from legal accusations.[39]

The first finding when examining sermon collections is that the times and places in which sermons were delivered began to diversify. Sermons tended to be given twice a day. In addition to the morning sermon, a university custom emerged of having an afternoon sermon or *collatio* as well. The most zealous of the preachers, like Milíč, might preach four of five times in a row on feast days. This proliferation in turn encouraged preaching to become detached from the religious context from which it had originally emerged. Some of the faithful would strive to attend as many sermons as possible, as if preaching were itself

---

37   Šmahel, *Die Hussitische Revolution*, vol. 2, 776–84.
38   A relative exception is that of the *Quadragesimale Admontense*, which resulted from the transcription of sermons by Johlín of Vodňany in the early 1390s. See Hana Florianová et al. (eds.), *Quadragesimale Admontense* (Fontes Latini Bohemorum) 6 (Prague: 2006).
39   Pavel Soukup, "'Ne verbum Dei in nobis suffocetur...' Kommunikationstechniken von Predigern des frühen Hussitismus," *Bohemia* 48 (2008): 54–82.

imbued with a sacramental function. Through a similar process, the orators did not long confine themselves to the interiors of churches and began to encroach upon urban space. Thus, the Church of St. Gall became so overcrowded that Waldhauser had to go out and speak in the open air, in the marketplace, where a mobile rostrum served instead of a pulpit. This resulted in lively competition between preachers who fought for the best access to public places. Every trick was permitted in this game. Witness the ridiculous squabble that occurred in Žatec, in May 1365, between Waldhauser and the local Franciscans: the latter forced him into silence by ringing the church bells as loudly and for as long as possible, then by marching in procession and destroying his pulpit.[40]

The result was that when addressing the people, preachers sacrificed the convoluted structure of the *sermo modernus*, preferring to revert to patristic homilies, commenting step-by-step on the entirety of the pericope. This choice was based on an evident didactic concern, namely that of giving access to the text of the Bible, mainly the New Testament, duly quoted or paraphrased. The Bohemian reformers subsequently distinguished themselves by their hostility to the *exempla*, those edifying anecdotes that had hitherto been widely used in the pulpit. Štěpán of Roudnice indicated the dangers of *exempla* on the grounds that they distorted Holy Writ. A number of preachers abandoned them out of theological scruples but made even greater use of the resources provided by proverbs and comparisons. These were borrowed from nature or social relationships and formed a sort of *koiné* that made it possible to play on cultural complicity with the public. Other additional resources for preaching were introduced, beginning with chanting. At the start of their sermons, preachers encouraged volunteers among their audience to recite a prayer in Latin or the vernacular. Visual aids were also used as reinforcements. Inscriptions were sometimes written on the walls of churches, presumably in support of preaching.[41] Expressive gestures had an even better chance of hitting the mark. If Milíč's adversaries are to be believed, in the course of one of his sermons, he grabbed jewels from a fashionable woman in the audience and smashed them to pieces. This translated into action, and in the sight of everyone, the hatred of luxury in the capital city inspired Prague's reformers.[42]

---

40   Ferdinand Menčík, *Konrád Waldhauser, mnich řádu svatého Augustina* (Prague: 1881), 23.
41   The text of the Ten Commandments was the main subject of these epigraphs. In the late 14th century, one could also read in St. Michael's Church in the Old Town authorities who favoured frequent communion, as has been shown by Pavel Spunar, "Neznámé pražské nápisy v kodexu ÖNB 4550," *Studie o rukopisech* 12 (1973): 175–90.
42   Jiří Kejř, "Žalobní články proti Milíčovi z Kroměříže," *Husitský Tábor* 10 (1991): 188.

These various techniques served a single objective: conversion. Occasionally, this might involve bringing the Catholic faith to non-Christians. Waldhauser, for example, did much to convert the few Jews who came to his assistance – apparently with little success. The main thrust of reformist preaching, however, was directed at Christians themselves and was designed to make them examine their consciences as a prelude to a change of lifestyle; sacramental confession was the immediate aim. The spiritual journey thus entailed, while it may not have reached the heights of mysticism, was no less demanding. It went not only through an imitation of the life and actions of Christ, but also through the purification of the heart. There are some indications as to the ardor with which some of women pursued this path. Kačka, for instance, was a lowly servant who in 1378 discussed with her friends the sermons she had heard and went so far as to write down a prayer of her own that she had devised.[43] A watertight barrier should not be erected between preaching and the spiritual literature of the time. Collective morality and introspection were not in opposition to each other; they were strictly coordinated for the greater effectiveness of the Word of God.

The plan applied to all walks of life. The preachers, conscious that they were addressing a mixed audience, nevertheless bore in mind that they needed to adjust their discourse depending on the various social classes and the vices that they were addressing. To city-dwellers, they stigmatized the ravages of usury; their wives were accused of sacrificing themselves to the vanities of fashion; the powerful were accused of burdening their subjects with taxes and unjust demands. Nor were the clerics spared. Prelates were castigated for their ambitions, monks and canons for their possessions, while those in holy orders were exposed to criticism for their simony. However, it was one thing to denounce ecclesiastical abuses behind the closed doors of the synod, but quite another to expose them to the light of day at the risk of scandalizing the laity. This strategy, consciously assumed, had serious consequences. It put to the test the Bohemian church's ability for self-regulation, as evidenced by the successive crises with which it had to deal.

---

[43] "Interrogata, utrum sermones faciat, respondit, quod non, sed quando de sermone venit, tunc habet collacionem cum aliqualibus dominabus et domicellabus de sermone audito. Interrogata, utrum fecerit aliquas orationes de proprio capite, respondit quod fecit unam orationem, cujus copiam dominis vicariis transmittere promisit." Ferdinand Tadra (ed.), *Soudní akta konsistoře pražské. Acta judiciaria consistorii Pragensis*, 7 vols. (Prague: 1893–1901), vol. 1, 398, 312.

5 Dynamics: Crises and Resistance

These crises deserve attention because they offer evidence of the resistance that the Early Bohemian Reform encountered. They thus make it possible to assess the room for manoeuvre that was available to its leaders when negotiating with the ecclesiastical hierarchy for the application of their ideas. Many historians have considered that an orthodox reform had no chance to succeed in late-medieval Bohemia. According to his biographer Ruben E. Weltsch, Jan of Jenštejn tried to square the circle.[44] In reality, depending on the moment and on what was at stake, the church of Bohemia proved to possess a varying mixture of introspection, adaptation, and creativity.

The first serious conflict emerged in 1363–1364, when the mendicant orders, led by the Dominicans and Hermits of St. Augustine, accused Waldhauser of heresy. The confrontation turned to Waldhauser's advantage, since he could count on the support of the emperor, the archbishop and the aldermen of Prague. The parish clergy also seem to have made common cause with him. For decades there had been an endemic rivalry between the rectors and the friars over funeral fees. They also applauded Waldhauser's indictment of the mendicant apostolate. By recycling a good share of the arguments proposed by William of Saint-Amour and other secular Parisian masters, the early reformist movement helped to crystallize a new self-awareness by the diocesan church. This allowed it to acquire a powerful capacity to mobilise the populace. Thus, on 28 December 1363, Waldhauser marched to the court of the archbishopric backed by a demonstration which turned into a riot in front of the Dominican convent of St. Clement.[45]

Ten years later, the demarcation lines had clearly changed. This time, it was Milíč who found himself on the front line. This former archdeacon had drawn penitent prostitutes to himself through his fiery preaching and the example of his personal conversion. At first, he tried to procure material assistance for them and rehabilitate them through work or marriage. In the autumn of 1372, however, he resolved to assemble them around him in a community. Thanks to certain legacies and a shrewd policy of acquisition, a former brothel south of the Old Town became the headquarters under the name of Jerusalem.[46] This endeavour did not lack precedents. It was nevertheless innovative in that it

---

44 Weltsch, *Archbishop John of Jenstein*, 178–79.
45 With respect to this conflict, see David C. Mengel, *Bones, Stones and Brothels. Religion and Topography in Prague under Emperor Charles IV (1346–1378)* (PhD dissertation, University of Notre Dame: 2003).
46 David C. Mengel, "From Venice to Jerusalem and Beyond: Milíč of Kroměříž and the Topography of Prostitution in Fourteenth-Century Prague," *Speculum* 79 (2004): 407–42.

ploughed a middle furrow between the lay and the religious estates. While, for example, the female penitents of St. Mary Magdalene favored the rule of St. Augustine, the Jerusalem community did not live by any specific rule, nor did its members wear a distinctive habit that would make them appear to be members of a religious order. This legally ambiguous position was similar to that of a Beguine house; just as singular was the coexistence between men and women that prevailed at Jerusalem. That is because Milíč had attracted priests and students, partly to assume spiritual responsibility for the penitent women, but also to train them at his school for preachers. They led a communal life here, again without following any particular religious rule. This could not but set tongues wagging. As a man who favored unanimity, the founder of Jerusalem, through the mixing of social conditions and the sexes, was ostensibly breaking down the barriers of Prague society.

The reaction was swift in coming. From 1373, the mendicant friars and the rectors of neighboring parishes banded together against Milíč, accusing him of being in breach of canon law. Archbishop Jan Očko and the emperor abandoned him. Milíč, who had not, however, lost all of his connections with the higher echelons of the clergy and the Czech-speaking patricians, meanwhile set out to defend himself at the curia at Avignon. Did he succeed *in extremis* of being found innocent, as his *Vita* claims? The point has never been clarified. After he died of the plague on the shores of the Rhône on 29 June 1374, the repression resumed with greater vigor. His supporters among the Prague clergy were routed, the Jerusalem community dissolved and the buildings handed over to the Cistercians.[47] Yet the aspiration to a spiritual life in the temporal world was not dead. Small Beguine houses continued to multiply, for example the house of Kateřina of Sulevice, which lodged six widows and eight virgins beside the Church of St. Benedict at Hradčany. Although these houses were more modest than Jerusalem had been and were closely tied to the vicar-general or the local rector, they did not escape suspicion. In 1388, they were subjected to a royal expulsion decree, causing Archbishop Jan of Jenštejn to attenuate their scope so as to protect orthodox communities. The Early Bohemian Reform thus gave birth at its margins to groups of devotees who could no longer be treated as mere passive recipients of clerical teaching.[48] But what form of life should be offered to them? What status should be given to what they said? The church had difficulty in finding satisfactory replies to these questions.

---

47   Šmahel, *Die Hussitische Revolution*, vol. 2, 747–52.
48   Rostislav Nový, "Ženské řeholní a laické komunity v předhusitské Praze," *Documenta Pragensia* 13 (1996): 41–6.

In the meantime, a new front opened up, that of ecclesiology. From this point of view, the Great Schism traces a clear dividing line between two generations. Until 1378, the reformers of Prague only paid a certain amount of attention to the constitution of the church. The very few pages on which they express themselves on the subject have a strong papalist flavor. Milíč exalted the primacy of the pope's jurisdiction and the spiritual role that was due the pope by right; consistent with these principles, in 1367 he handed over to Pope Urban V the reins of the universal Reform of which he had dreamed.[49] When Christian unity fractured, however, minds began to change. Officially, Bohemia had indeed rallied unconditionally behind the banner of the pope of Rome, Urban VI. There were nevertheless quite a few clerics who defended the rights of his rival, Clement VII. Jan of Jenštejn had to take a hard line with them.[50] Calls also emanated from the University of Paris for the convocation of a general council. The *Tetragonus Aristotelis*, a fictional epistolary collection written in Prague, probably in early 1382, contributed to a similar conciliar fervor. The aim was to persuade King Wenceslas IV, at the insistence of the *studia* of Oxford, Prague and Paris, to convene a council for the purpose of establishing the legitimacy of Pope Urban VI.[51] Interest waned, however. For lack of political support, the conciliation plan in Bohemia evaporated almost immediately.

Yet as time passed, Wenceslas realized that unconditional support for the pope of Rome might harm his imperial ambitions and that he had an interest in remaining equivocal. This was all that was needed for Vojtěch Raňkův of Ježov to present the archbishop with a counter-ecclesiology. The polemic between these two men broke out in the mid-1380s. According to Jenštejn, Vojtěch refused to believe that obedience to Urban VI was an article of faith since it was up to each Christian to decide in conscience which pope he ought to recognise. The failure of the *via facti* and the tolerance that had developed between the two obediences justifies this assessment. Yet this pragmatism also nourished an original concept of the church, one that was inspired by the *Epistola concordie* of Konrad of Gelnhausen, which saw the pontiff as occupying a subordinate position. Vojtěch deduced that only the universal church, as a

---

49   Milíč of Kroměříž, "Epistula ad papam Urbanum V," in Milíč of Kroměříž, *The Message for the Last Days. Three Essays from the Year 1367*, eds. Milan Opočenský and Jana Opočenská (Geneva: 1998), 18–31.
50   Rudolf Holinka, *Církevní politika arcibiskupa Jana z Jenštejna za pontifikátu Urbana VI.* (Bratislava: 1933).
51   See Michael Van Dussen, "Aristotle's Tetragon. Compilation and Consensus during the Great Schism," in *Religious Controversy in Europe, 1378–1536. Textual Transmission and Networks of Readership,* eds. Michael Van Dussen and Pavel Soukup (Turnhout: 2013), 187–210.

gathering of all the faithful in a state of grace, received from Christ the guarantee of infallibility. Without advocating predestination as Wyclif had, he thus marked a distinction between the mystical body and the militant church.[52] This clearly weakened the link between salvation and the institution.

As a sign of the times, more and more voices were raised in Prague to recommend frequent eucharistic communion. The idea had already been in the air for half a century.[53] The author of *Malogranatum* was the first to dispute the fact that access to the sacrament should be reserved for those who were perfect. He was not preaching in the desert. Around 1370, Milíč in turn exhorted his audience, which included lay people, to take communion frequently. Putting words into deeds, he permitted several women from the Jerusalem community to approach the altar up to three times a week, thus adding to the discredit of the young foundation. Wary of those who considered it to be a scandalous innovation, the ecclesiastical authorities rejected this practice as flirting with the boundaries of orthodoxy. Yet the debate was not over. It reemerged in the late 1370s, when it was taken up by the university masters. Numerous questions and treatises were devoted to the subject, showing how all protagonists had become aware of how much was at stake. This was a matter of the relationship between the church and its history. To what extent could it distance itself from patristic practice? Liberalizing access to the Eucharist also raised questions about the believer's responsibility. Were the faithful capable of judging their own frame of mind, or should they seek the opinion of their rector? Finally, the controversy came to involve the whole sacramental discipline, depending on whether one opted for a pastoral approach that emphasized the fear of damnation, or whether one preferred to exalt the power of divine grace. The Prague masters were far from presenting a common front on any of these issues. The Dominican friar Mikuláš Biceps was categorically opposed to frequent communion, while Vojtěch Raňkův of Ježov hesitated to make a clear pronouncement. It was Matthew of Cracow and especially the Dominican Heinrich of Bitterfeld who emerged as the most resolute advocates of frequent communion and who finally won the debate: in June 1391, repealing the former restrictions, Jan of Jenštejn ruled in a synod that the faithful

---

52 Kadlec, *Leben und Schriften*, 50–7.
53 There is a considerable bibliography on this subject. See the overview by Stanisław Bylina "La dévotion nouvelle et le problème de la communion fréquente en Europe centrale, XIVe–XVe siècles," in *The Bohemian Reformation,* eds. David and Holeton, vol. 4 (Prague: 2002), 31–42. For an assessment in greater depth, see Jaroslav V. Polc, *Česká církev v dějinách* (Prague: 1999), 169–239, as well as Stephen Mossman, *Marquard von Lindau and the Challenges of Religious Life in Late Medieval Germany* (Oxford: 2010), Ch. 2.

who had confessed and who were worthy could take communion as often as they wished.

The measure was unique in Christianity at the time. It enshrined a form of recognition of lay piety that would have been inconceivable without the contacts made locally between the Prague intelligentsia and the faithful, especially the women. Yet this was not an unequivocal victory. The debate about frequent communion firstly gave a platform to the controversial Matěj of Janov. This preacher and confessor at St. Vitus Cathedral had studied in Paris in the 1370s, where he had come under the influence of the school of Marsilius of Inghen.[54] Upon returning to Bohemia, he started work on the *Regulae Veteris et Novi Testamenti*, a voluminous and often repetitive work, in which he comingled the genres of biblical commentary, prophetic pamphlet, university *quaestio*, hagiography, and the collection of authorities. The theme that runs through it – and in which it is not hard to see a symptom of the disquiet caused by the Great Schism – is how to discern between true Christianity and its imitations.

Matěj of Janov harbored the conviction that the Christianity of his day constituted an enclosed battlefield in which the disciples of Christ were required to wage a decisive war against the forces of the Antichrist, the latter having invaded the higher spheres of the church. Nor did civil society and the State find grace in his eyes. He claimed that reform needed to begin from below, through a drastic reduction in devotions and current religious practice: observances, pilgrimages, indulgences, and canon law were all human inventions that should be reduced, or even eliminated, in order to bring mankind back to the essentials, to the twin sources of the Bible and the Eucharist. Matěj of Janov did not flinch from what he knew to be the destructive consequences of his theories. Without denying its legitimacy, he wrote vitriolically against the cult of images. He was also critical of the pontifical system of centralization and began to profess an ecclesiology of the presbyterian type, pleading for the complete abolition of the religious orders.[55] Such ideas could not but place its author at odds with the Prague hierarchy. In 1389, Matěj was suspended from preaching. Shortly thereafter, the Inquisition arrested some of his friends who

---

54 Martin Dekarli, "*Regula generalis, principalis, prima veritas*. The Philosophical and Theological Principle of *Regulae Veteris et Novi Testamenti* of Matěj of Janov," in *The Bohemian Reformation,* eds. David and Holeton, vol. 8 (Prague: 2011), 30–41.

55 With respect to its iconophobia, see Ota Halama, *Otázka svatých v české reformaci. Její proměny od doby Karla IV. do doby České konfese* (Brno: 2002), 111–16. His ecclesiology is dealt with in Emil Valasek, *Das Kirchenverständnis des Prager Magisters Matthias von Janow (1350/55–1393). Ein Beitrag zur Geistesgeschichte Böhmens im 14. Jahrhundert* (Rome: 1971), who tends to underestimate its subversive aspects.

were reading dissenting prophecies in secret.[56] Although he died in 1393 within the communion of the church, Matěj of Janov had shown the potential for radicalization within the Early Bohemian Reform, and he had done so independently of Wyclif.

Other, even more serious concerns awaited Jan of Jenštejn. Since the late 1380s, he had been in a merciless conflict with Wenceslas IV, of which the murder of the Vicar-General Jan of Pomuk (the future St. John Nepomuk of the Counter-Reformation) was one of the most dramatic episodes.[57] The archbishop was defeated. After having been forced to resign his post in 1396, Jan of Jenštejn left for exile in Rome, where he died four years later. The defeat had serious consequences for the future of the reformist movement. The Jenštejn episode did the archbishopric considerable damage. It lost its right to supervise the university and, more generally, the leading role that it had enjoyed hitherto. The clergy, far from being unanimous in supporting its head, proved increasingly aware of what royal intervention could accomplish: the court began to be seen as an institution better equipped to achieve reform, even against the ecclesiastical hierarchy if necessary.

Around 1400, at a time when a new generation of Czech masters was emerging at the University, the Early Bohemian Reform found itself at a crossroads. It had some magnificent achievements behind it and seemed to be animated by an irresistible impetus. Yet it found itself headless and exposed to internal tensions that were becoming harder and harder to manage.

6 From the Early Bohemian Reform to Hussitism: Split or Continuity?

The Hussites did not make a *tabula rasa* of their past. Their anchorage in the institutions and their communication strategies remained fundamentally the same, at least until 1412. They also collated the texts written by their predecessors, often copying them and mixing them haphazardly with their own, so as to form a codicological continuum. Hus and his disciples drew much of their inspiration from these texts. The young preacher from the Bethlehem Chapel possibly copied a large number of pages, although *suppresso nomine*, from Waldhauser's *Postilla studentium*.[58] Matěj of Janov exerted an even more

---

56 Ivan Hlaváček, "Zur böhmischen Inquisition und Häresiebekämpfung um das Jahr 1400," in *Häresie und vorzeitige Reformation im Spätmittelalter*, ed. František Šmahel (Munich: 1998), 116–17.
57 Jaroslav V. Polc, *Svatý Jan Nepomucký* (Rome: 1972), 155–239.
58 Jana Zachová, "Waldhauser a Hus," in *Husitství – reformace – renesance. Sborník k 60. narozeninám Františka Šmahela*, eds. Jaroslav Pánek, Miloslav Polívka, and Noemi

decisive influence over Jakoubek of Stříbro and Nicholas of Dresden, who made the *Regulae Veteris et Novi Testamenti* into their bedside book.

Can it thus be said, for instance, that from frequent communion to Utraquism, there was a direct line of descent? It is true that, in this development, the Hussites rearranged the themes for which the controversies of the 1380s had already set the tone – these being the exemplarity of the primitive church, the rehabilitation of the status of the laity, the superiority of sacramental communion over that of mere spiritual communion? Perhaps that would be an oversimplification. In claiming adherence to Matěj of Janov, for example, Jakoubek of Stříbro was nevertheless forced to introduce interpolations into the meaning of what the former had written. Matěj had never cast doubt on the scholastic doctrine of concomitance.[59] Nor was this theological content the only point of difference. Sociologically, the two practices, frequent communion and Utraquism, had little in common. While frequent communion had remained the practice of certain members of the elite, Utraquism became the cement of the whole Hussite community. Consequently, the one could easily be dissociated from the other. Jean Gerson may well have acquiesced to the views of Matthew of Cracow, yet he showed himself to be an implacable opponent of communion under both kinds. Conversely, in post-revolutionary Bohemia, there were numerous Utraquists who did not take communion as frequently as their pastors would have liked.

The case of Gerson, just cited, further illustrates the diversity of outcomes from the Early Bohemian Reform. It has long been known that the writings of Konrad of Waldhausen, Milíč, and the other Prague clerics circulated at an early date in Poland, by means of the Silesian connection. The teaching of theology at Cracow University, in particular, owed much to this phenomenon.[60] It is tempting to surmise that Polish ecclesiology shows what Bohemian reformism might have become had Wycliffism not interfered from the 1390s onward. But there were other important (and often paradoxical) areas of influence as well, two of which have recently come to light. First, the Dominican Heinrich of Bitterfeld, in addition to intervening in the controversy over frequent communion, devised in his treatise *De formatione and reformatione ordinis fratrum predicatorum* a policy for reviving study and preaching within his order. The reformed convent that was to have been founded near Roudnice never came to

---

Rejchrtová, vol. 1 (Prague: 1994), 287–97. The sermon collection in question was edited as having been "attributed" to Jan Hus: Hus, *Dicta de tempore*, ed. Zachová (Turnhout: 2011).

59 Helena Krmíčková, *Studie a texty k počátkům kalicha v Čechách* (Brno: 1997), 86–119.
60 Useful clarification in Thomas Wünsch, *Konziliarismus und Polen* (Paderborn: 1998), 33–47.

pass, but the decree issued in 1390 by the Minister-General Raymond of Capua repeated Bitterfeld's views. Dominican Observance thus finds some of its origins in Prague. Second, when one considers the preaching benefices which multiplied in south Germany from the late 14th century, the geography of their distribution, and the way their institutions were organized, one is led to believe that they were inspired by the Bohemian precedent.[61]

To use the metaphor of a stream, a diagram of the course of the Early Bohemian Reform would resemble a sort of delta: its waters divide into a tangle of tributaries with moving and interlinked branches. Palacký was therefore correct in considering that Hussitism did not come from nowhere, even if he was wrong in concluding that it represented the only possible outlet.

7 Historiographic Survey

The emergence of the historiographical concept of the "forerunners of Hus" in the work of František Palacký and the historians of the following two generations, as well as the persistence and critique of this concept in more recent scholarship, has been outlined above.[62] A starting point for research into the Bohemian Reform is now provided by František Šmahel's *Die Hussitische Revolution*, to be supplemented by the synoptic works by Zdeňka Hledíková and Olivier Marin.[63] Anthologies and reference material include the literary history by Jana Nechutová which offers a panorama of Latin sources that predate 1400, and the repertory compiled by Pavel Spunar, which lists the texts and manuscript records, but restricts itself to Czech authors exclusively.[64]

Articles by Zdeňka Hledíková, compiled in her volume *Svět české středověké církve* (The world of the Czech medieval church), have thrown considerable new light on the subject of diocesan administration. For a comparative perspective, see also the collective volume *Kirchliche Reformimpulse des 14./15.*

---

61 Bernhard Neidiger, "Wortgottesdienst vor der Reformation. Die Stiftung eigener Predigtpfründen für Weltkleriker im späten Mittelalter," *Rheinische Vierteljahrsblätter* 66 (2002): 142–89.

62 See the introductory section of this chaper.

63 Šmahel, *Die Hussitische Revolution*, vol. 2, 717–88; Zdeňka Hledíková, "Der Weg der geistlichen Entwicklung und Reformbewegung in Böhmen," in *Kunst als Herrschaftsinstrument. Böhmen und das Heilige Römische Reich unter den Luxemburgern im europäischen Kontext*, eds. Jiří Fajt and Andrea Langer (Berlin and Munich: 2009), 354–64; Marin, *L'archévêque*.

64 Jana Nechutová, *Die lateinische Literatur des Mittelalters in Böhmen* (Cologne, Weimar, and Vienna: 2007); Pavel Spunar, *Repertorium auctorum Bohemorum provectum idearum post universitatem Pragensem conditam illustrans*, 2 vols. (Studia Copernicana) 25 and 35 (Wrocław and Warsaw: 1985–995).

Jahrhunderts in Ostmitteleuropa (Eberhard and Machilek, eds.). As for edited sources, the statutes of Prague synods are now accessible, as is the record of the pastoral visit of 1379–1382.[65] In the area of spiritual literature, the spiritual dialogue by Matthew of Cracow has been edited. The *Malogranatum*, on the contrary, has not yet been the subject of a critical publication, with the exception of the section concerning communion.[66] The situation is better with the numerous *vitae* of prominent figures of the Bohemian Reform produced in the period. Various Lives have been devoted to the archbishops Arnošt of Pardubice and Jan of Jenštejn.[67] The *Vita* of Milíč of Kroměříž is problematic, since the form in which it has been preserved has probably been retouched by the Jesuit Bohuslav Balbín, as shown by David Mengel.[68] Visionary literature has recently attracted the attention of historians and editors. The vision of Bridget of Sweden is now well known, thanks to the study of its Old-Czech translation and the publication of the relevant treatises by Matthew of Cracow.[69]

As noted above, the question of Bohemian *devotio moderna* is contested among scholars.[70] There is no doubt, on the contrary, about the influence of preachers within the Czech Reform movement. The main homiletic sources have been described by F.M. Bartoš.[71] Synodal sermons are the least well known, since no synthesis of the subject has been published; some sermon texts have nevertheless been edited.[72] Much remains to be done with the great

---

65   Jaroslav V. Polc and Zdeňka Hledíková, *Pražské synody a koncily předhusitské doby* (Prague: 2002); Pavel of Janovice, *Protocollum visitationis*.

66   Matthew of Cracow, Dialogus rationis et conscientiae de crebra communione," in *Mateusza z Krakowa Opuscula theologica dotyczące spowiedzi i komunii*, eds. Władysław Seńko and Adam Ludwik Szafrański (Warsaw: 1974), 354–409; Pawel Krupa, "La communion fréquente à Prague au XIVe siècle. Malogranatum III, 1, 26: ses précurseurs et ses continuateurs," in *Crisi mendicante e crisi della chiesa. Encomia sancti Thomae e riforma savonaroliana* (Memorie domenicane) 30 (Pistoia: 1990).

67   Vilém of Lestkov, "Vita Arnesti"; Petrus Clarificator, "Vita domini Iohannis." See Pavlína Rychterová, "Charisma und charismatische Legitimation in der Vita von Johannes von Jenstein," in *Kunst als Herrschaftsinstrument. Böhmen und das Heilige Römische Reich unter den Luxemburgern im europäischen Kontext*, eds. Jiří Fajt and Andrea Langer (Berlin and Munich: 2009), 346–53.

68   Josef Emler (ed.), *Fontes rerum Bohemicarum*, vol. 1 (Prague: 1873), 401–30; David C. Mengel, "A Monk, a Preacher, and a Jesuit. Making the Life of Milíč," in *The Bohemian Reformation*, eds. David and Holeton, vol. 5, 1 (Prague: 2004), 33–55.

69   *Matthaeus de Cracovia: Tractatus Birgittini*, ed. Drahomíra Breedveld-Báránková (Fontes Latini Bohemorum) 7 (Prague: 2008); Rychterová, *Die Offenbarungen*.

70   One should begin with Derwich and Staub (eds.), *Die "Neue Frömmigkeit" in Europa*; see the discussion above, n. 25.

71   Bartoš, František Michálek, *Dvě studie o husitských postilách* (Prague: 1955).

72   Vojtěch Raňkův of Ježov: Kadlec, *Leben und Schriften*, 182–96; Milíč of Kroměříž, *Iohannis Milicii de Cremsir Tres sermones synodales*, eds. Vilém Herold and Milan Mráz (Prague:1974);

collections of sermons produced in Bohemia in the 14th century, which, with one exception, the *Quadragesimale Admontense*, remain unedited. Waldhauser's *Postilla studentium* is currently only accessible in its partial Czech adaptation.[73] The postils of Milíč, *Abortivus* and *Gratiae Dei*, unpublished, have been analysed in detail by Peter C. Morée; those attributed to Matthew of Cracow are of doubtful authenticity, as has been shown by Matthias Nuding.[74] As for the rest, extracts can be gleaned from the *Postilla Zderasiensis* by Johlín of Vodňany and the postil entitled *Consolatio spiritus*.[75] Concerning the techniques of preaching *ad clerum*, Pavel Soukup's thesis is indispensable.[76] A new account of the early history of the Bethlehem Chapel remains to be written.[77]

The theological output of the Prague masters has been reviewed by Jaroslav Kadlec in the *History of Charles University*.[78] The 1390s generation remains relatively unknown. The great Czech masters were listed by Václav Flajšhans; Štěpán of Kolín, who had been Hus's teacher, was treated in a monograph by Otakar Odložilík.[79] The German masters are even more poorly served. The Silesian Matthew of Legnica is one of several who has been brought out of obscurity

---

Kuneš of Třebovle, "Sermones synodales," in Miroslav Černý, *Kuneš z Třebovle. Středověký právník a jeho dílo* (Pilsen: 1999), 83–135; Matthew of Cracow, "Sermones synodales," in *Mateusza z Krakowa De praxi romanae curiae*, ed. Wladysław Seńko (Wrocław, Warsaw, and Cracow: 1969), 123–85.

[73] Konrad Waldhauser, *Staročeské zpracování Postily studentů svaté university pražské Konráda Waldhausera*, ed. František Šimek (Prague: 1947).

[74] Morée, *Preaching in Fourteenth-Century Bohemia*; Nuding, *Matthäus von Krakau*.

[75] Augustin Neumann (ed.), Výbor z předhusitských postil," *Archiv literární. Příloha k revui Archa* 2 (1922), 60–376 passim.

[76] Soukup, *Reformní kazatelství*.

[77] As an initial approach, see: Otakar Odložilík, "The Chapel of Bethlehem in Prague," in *Studien zur älteren Geschichte Osteuropas. Festschrift für H.F. Schmidt*, ed. Günther Stökl, vol. 1 (Graz and Cologne: 1956), 125–41, and especially Jindřich Marek, *Jakoubek ze Stříbra a počátky utrakvistického kazatelství v českých zemích. Studie o Jakoubkově postile z let 1413–1414* (Prague: 2011), 55–63. Otherwise, František Michálek Bartoš, "První století Betléma," in *Betlémská kaple. O jejích dějinách a dochovaných zbytcích* (Prague: 1923), 9–21, remains the most complete work.

[78] Jaroslav Kadlec, "Teologická fakulta," in *Dějiny Univerzity Karlovy*, vol. 1, ed. Michal Svatoš (Prague: 1995), especially 142–55. See also the studies by Jana Nechutová, "Autorita Bible a její překlady podle kvestie Jana z Mýta Utrum dictis sanctorum patrum," *Česká literatura* 47 (1999): 510–14; eadem, "Konrad von Soltau. Lectura super caput Firmiter," in *Schriften im Umkreis mitteleuropäischer Universitäten um 1400*. eds. Knapp et al. (Leiden: 2004), 3–19.

[79] Václav Flajšhans, "Předchůdcové Husovi," *Věstník České akademie* 13 (1904): 812–19; 14 (1905): 157–75 and 437–43; idem, "Pražští theologové kolem r. 1400," *Časopis Musea Království českého* 89 (1905): 16–31; Otakar Odložilík, *M. Štěpán z Kolína* (Prague: 1924).

in the wake of the study by Adolph Franz.[80] Matěj of Janov occupies a special place. The publication of his masterwork *Regulae Veteris et Novi Testamenti* is now complete. The summary of his life and work by Vlastimil Kybal has not yet been replaced, although useful indications can be found in more recent articles.[81] The Bohemian sources concerning the Schism have not yet been sufficiently studied; their doctrinal challenges have recently been pointed out by Zdeněk Uhlíř.[82] Other controversies concerned the liturgy (the introduction of the Feast of the Visitation), indulgences, and the relationship between the laity and the ecclesiastical powers.[83] The corpus dealing with polemic over frequent communion was enriched by Pavel Černuška.[84] Finally, some reformers were the target of polemical treatises and they sometimes took up their pens to defend themselves. Mention should be made, above all, of Konrad of Waldhausen's *Apologia*, which deserves to be published in a critical edition.[85]

Translated by Andrew Morris

---

80   Adolph Franz, "Matthias von Liegnitz und Nicolaus Stör von Schweidnitz," *Der Katholik* 1 (1898): 1–25.
81   Vlastimil Kybal, *M. Matěj z Janova. Jeho život, spisy a učení* (Prague: 1905); Jan B. Lášek and Karel Skalický (eds.), *Mistr Matěj z Janova ve své a v naší době* (Brno: 2002).
82   Zdeněk Uhlíř, "Eklesiologie v českém sporu o Urbana VI.," *Teologická reflexe* 8 (2002): 17–40; for an edition of sources, see Franz Bliemetzrieder; "Eine von den Kreisen des Hofes Kaiser Karls IV. inspirierte Verteidigung der Wahl Urbans VI. (1379)," *Mitteilungen des Vereines für Geschichte der Deutschen in Böhmen* 47 (1909): 382–405; František Michálek Bartoš (ed.), *Tetragonus Aristotelis. Konciliaristický projev z počátku velikého církevního rozkolu* (Prague: 1916); Jan of Jenštejn, "De veritate Urbani," in Jan Sedlák, *M. Jan Hus* (Prague: 1915), 4*-20*; idem, "Tractatulus de potestate clavium," "Tractatulus de potestate clavium," in Paul De Vooght, *Hussiana* (Leuven: 1960), 161–85.
83   Jaroslav V. Polc, *De origine festi Visitationis B.M.V.* (Rome: 1967); Eva Doležalová et al., "The Reception and Criticism of Indulgences in the Medieval Late Czech Lands," in *Promissory Notes on the Treasury of Merits. Indulgences in Late Medieval Europe*, ed. Robert N. Swanson (Leiden and Boston: 2006), 101–45; Otakar Odložilík, "Leták M. Štěpána z Kolína o pronásledování kněží," *Věstník Královské české společnosti nauk* (1926), no. 1.
84   Heinrich of Bitterfeld, *Jindřich z Bitterfeldu. Eucharistické texty*, ed. Pavel Černuška (Brno: 2006).
85   While awaiting this, reference should be made to Konstantin Höfler (ed.), *Geschichtschreiber der hussitischen Bewegung in Böhmen*, 3 vols. (Fontes rerum Austriacarum, 1. Abteilung: Scriptores) 2, 6, and 7 (Vienna: 1856–1866), vol. 2, 17–39. For this source, see Mengel, *Bones, Stones and Brothels*; and Nechutová, "Raně reformní prvky."

Bibliography

Editions of Sources

Bartoš, František Michálek (ed.), *Tetragonus Aristotelis. Konciliaristický projev z počátku velikého církevního rozkolu* [*Tetragonus Aristotelis*. A conciliarist statement from the beginnings of the Great Schism] (Prague: 1916).

Emler, Josef (ed.), *Fontes rerum Bohemicarum*, vol. 1 (Prague: 1873).

Florianová, Hana, Dana Martínková, Zuzana Silagiová, and Hana Šedinová (eds.), *Quadragesimale Admontense* (Fontes Latini Bohemorum) 6 (Prague: 2006).

Heinrich of Bitterfeld, *Jindřich z Bitterfeldu: Eucharistické texty* [Heinrich of Bitterfeld. Eucharistic Texts], ed. Pavel Černuška (Brno: 2006).

Höfler, Konstantin (ed.), *Geschichtschreiber der husitischen Bewegung in Böhmen*, 3 vols. (Fontes rerum Austriacarum, 1. Abteilung: Scriptores) 2, 6, and 7 (Vienna: 1856–1866).

Hus, Jan, *Dicta de tempore magistro Iohanni Hus attributa*, ed. Jana Zachová (Magistri Iohannis Hus Opera omnia) 26 (Corpus christianorum. Continuatio mediaevalis) 239, 2 vols. (Turnhout: 2011).

Jan of Jenštejn, "De veritate Urbani," in Jan Sedlák, *M. Jan Hus* (Prague: 1915), 4*–20*.

Jan of Jenštejn, "Tractatulus de potestate clavium," in Paul De Vooght, *Hussiana* (Leuven: 1960), 161–85.

Kuneš of Třebovle, "Sermones synodales," in Miroslav Černý, *Kuneš z Třebovle. Středověký právník a jeho dílo* (Pilsen: 1999), 83–135.

Matěj of Janov, *Regulae Veteris et Novi Testamenti*, vols. 1–4, ed. Vlastimil Kybal (Innsbruck: 1908–1913); vol. 5, eds. Vlastimil Kybal and Otakar Odložilík (Prague: 1913); vol. 6, eds. Jana Nechutová and Helena Krmíčková (Munich: 1993).

Matthew of Cracow, "Sermones synodales," in *Mateusza z Krakowa De praxi romanae curiae*, ed. Władysław Seńko (Wrocław, Warsaw, and Cracow: 1969), 123–85.

Matthew of Cracow, "Dialogus rationis et conscientiae de crebra communione," in *Mateusza z Krakowa Opuscula theologica dotyczące spowiedzi i komunii*, eds. Władysław Seńko and Adam Ludwik Szafrański (Warsaw: 1974), 354–409.

Matthew of Cracow, *Matthaeus de Cracovia. Tractatus Birgittini*, ed. Drahomíra Breedveld-Baránková (Fontes Latini Bohemorum) 7 (Prague: 2008).

Milíč of Kroměříž, *Iohannis Milicii de Cremsir Tres sermones synodales*, eds. Vilém Herold and Milan Mráz (Prague: 1974).

Milíč of Kroměříž, "Epistula ad papam Urbanum V," in Milíč of Kroměříž, *The Message for the Last Days. Three Essays from the Year 1367*, eds. Milan Opočenský and Jana Opočenská (Geneva: 1998), 18–31.

Neumann, Augustin (ed.), "Výbor z předhusitských postil" [A digest of pre-Hussite postils], *Archiv literární. Příloha k revui Archa* 2 (1922): 60–376 passim.

Pavel of Janovice, *Protocollum visitationis archidiaconatus Pragensis annis 1379–1382 per Paulum of Janowicz archidiaconum Pragensem factae*, eds. Ivan Hlaváček and Zdeňka Hledíková (Prague: 1973).

Petrus Clarificator, "Vita domini Iohannis," in Helena Krmíčková, "Petri Clarificatoris Vita domini Iohannis, Pragensis archiepiscopi tercii," in *Querite primum regnum Dei. Sborník příspěvků k poctě Jany Nechutové*, eds. Helena Krmíčková, Anna Pumprová, Dana Růžičková, and Libor Švanda (Brno: 2006), 441–61.

Tadra, Ferdinand (ed.), *Soudní akta konsistoře pražské. Acta judiciaria consistorii Pragensis*, 7 vols. (Prague: 1893–1901).

Vilém of Lestkov, "Vita Arnesti," in *Fontes rerum Bohemicarum*, ed. Josef Emler, vol. 1 (Prague: 1873), 385–400.

Waldhauser, Konrad, *Staročeské zpracování Postily studentů svaté university pražské Konráda Waldhausera* [The Old Czech adaptation of the *Postilla studentium sanctae universitatis Pragensis* of Konrad Waldhauser], ed. František Šimek (Prague: 1947).

Secondary Sources

Bartoš, František Michálek, "První století Betléma" [The first century of the Bethlehem Chapel], in *Betlémská kaple. O jejích dějinách a dochovaných zbytcích* (Prague: 1923), 9–21.

Bartoš, František Michálek, *Dvě studie o husitských postilách* [Two studies on Hussite postils] (Prague: 1955).

Bliemetzrieder, Franz, "Eine von den Kreisen des Hofes Kaiser Karls IV. inspirierte Verteidigung der Wahl Urbans VI. (1379)," *Mitteilungen des Vereines für Geschichte der Deutschen in Böhmen* 47 (1909): 382–405.

Bylina, Stanisław, "František Palacký a české reformní hnutí 14. století" [František Palacký and the Bohemian Reform movement of the 14th century], in *František Palacký 1798/1998. Dějiny a dnešek*, eds. František Šmahel and Eva Doležalová (Prague: 1999), 123–37.

Bylina, Stanisław, "La catéchisation du peuple en Bohême aux XIVe et XVe siècles" in *The Bohemian Reformation and Religious Practice*, eds. Zdeněk V. David and David R. Holeton, vol. 3 (Prague: 2000), 25–33.

Bylina, Stanisław, "La dévotion nouvelle et le problème de la communion fréquente en Europe centrale, XIVe–XVe siècles," in *The Bohemian Reformation and Religious Practice*, eds. Zdeněk V. David and David R. Holeton, vol. 4 (Prague: 2002), 31–42.

Bylina, Stanisław, "Devotio moderna et dévotion des masses chrétiennes en Europe centrale aux XIVe–XVe siècles," in *Die "Neue Frömmigkeit" in Europa im Spätmittelalter*, eds. Marek Derwich and Martial Staub (Göttingen: 2004), 211–24.

Cardelle de Hartmann, Carmen, *Lateinische Dialoge 1200–1400. Literarhistorische Studie und Repertorium* (Leiden and Boston: 2007).

Dekarli, Martin, "*Regula generalis, principalis, prima veritas*. The Philosophical and Theological Principle of *Regulae Veteris et Novi Testamenti* of Matěj of Janov," in *The*

Bohemian Reformation and Religious Practice, eds. Zdeněk V. David and David R. Holeton, vol. 8 (Prague: 2011), 30–41.

Derwich, Marek, and Martial Staub (eds.), *Die "Neue Frömmigkeit" in Europa im Spätmittelalter* (Göttingen: 2004).

Doležalová, Eva, Jan Hrdina, František Šmahel, and Zdeněk Uhlíř, "The Reception and Criticism of Indulgences in the Late Medieval Czech Lands," in *Promissory Notes on the Treasury of Merits. Indulgences in Late Medieval Europe*, ed. Robert N. Swanson (Leiden and Boston: 2006), 101–45.

Eberhard, Winfried, and Franz Machilek (eds.), *Kirchliche Reformimpulse des 14./15. Jahrhunderts in Ostmitteleuropa* (Cologne, Weimar, and Vienna: 2006).

Flajšhans, Václav, "Pražští theologové kolem r. 1400" [Prague theologians ca. 1400], *Časopis Musea Království českého* 89 (1905): 16–31.

Flajšhans, Václav, "Předchůdcové Husovi" [The forerunners of Hus], *Věstník České akademie* 13 (1904): 812–19, 14 (1905): 157–75 and 437–43.

Franz, Adolph, *Der Magister Nikolaus Magni de Jawor. Ein Beitrag zur Literatur- und Gelehretengeschichte des 14. und 15. Jahrhunderts* (Freiburg im Breisgau: 1898).

Franz, Adolph, "Matthias von Liegnitz und Nicolaus Stör von Schweidnitz," *Der Katholik* 1 (1898): 1–25.

Gerwing, Manfred, *Malogranatum oder der dreifache Weg zur Vollkommenheit. Ein Beitrag zur Spiritualität des Spätmittelalters* (Munich: 1986).

Gerwing, Manfred, "Heinrich von Bitterfeld als Reformer," *Theologie und Glaube* 95 (2005): 409–22.

Halama, Ota, *Otázka svatých v české reformaci. Její proměny od doby Karla IV. do doby České konfese* [The question of saints in the Bohemian Reformation. Its transformations from the time of Charles IV to the *Confessio Bohemica*] (Brno: 2002).

Hamm, Berndt, "Was ist Frömmigkeitstheologie? Überlegungen zum 14.–16. Jahrhundert," in *Praxis pietatis. Festschrift für Wolfgang Sommer*, eds. Hans-Jörg Nieden and Marcel Nieden (Stuttgart: 1999), 9–45.

Harvánek, Kamil, "Traktát Largum sero Jana z Holešova. Příspěvek k lidové zbožnosti ve středověku" [The treatise *Largum sero* of Jan of Holešov. A contribution to popular devotion in the Middle Ages], *Studia historica Brunensia* 56 (2009): 105–20.

Hlaváček, Ivan, "Zur böhmischen Inquisition und Häresiebekämpfung um das Jahr 1400," in *Häresie und vorzeitige Reformation im Spätmittelalter*, ed. František Šmahel (Munich: 1998), 109–31.

Hlaváček, Ivan, "Kodikologisch-bibliotheksgeschichtliche Bemerkungen zu den Provinzialstatuten Ernsts von Pardubitz von 1349," in *Partikularsynoden im späten Mittelalter*, eds. Nathalie Kruppa and Leszek Zygner (Göttingen: 2006), 331–50.

Hledíková, Zdeňka, "Die Visitationen des weltlichen Klerus im vorhussitischen Böhmen," *Mediaevalia Bohemica* 1 (1969): 249–74.

Hledíková, Zdeňka, *Biskup Jan IV. z Dražic (1301–1343)* [Bishop Jan IV of Dražice (1301–1343)] (Prague: 1992).

Hledíková, Zdeňka, "Úpadek nebo růst? K situaci církve v Čechách ve 14. století" [Decline, or growth? On the situation of the church in Bohemia in the 14th century], in *Traditio et cultus. Miscellanea historica Bohemica Miloslao Vlk archiepiscopo Pragensi ab eius collegis amicisque ad annum sexagesimum dedicata*, ed. Zdeňka Hledíková (Prague: 1993), 51–62.

Hledíková, Zdeňka, "Církev v českých zemích na přelomu 14. a 15. století" [The church in the Czech Lands at the turn of the 15th century], in *Jan Hus na přelomu tisíciletí*, eds. Miloš Drda, František J. Holeček, and Zdeněk Vybíral (Husitský Tábor. Supplementum) 1 (Tábor: 2001), 35–58.

Hledíková, Zdeňka, "Synoden in der Diözese Prag 1280–1417," in *Partikularsynoden im späten Mittelalter*, eds. Nathalie Kruppa and Leszek Zygner (Göttingen: 2006), 307–329.

Hledíková, Zdeňka, *Arnošt z Pardubic. Arcibiskup, zakladatel, rádce* [Arnošt of Pardubice. Archbishop, founder, advisor] (Prague: 2008).

Hledíková, Zdeňka, "Der Weg der geistlichen Entwicklung und Reformbewegung in Böhmen," in *Kunst als Herrschaftsinstrument. Böhmen und das Heilige Römische Reich unter den Luxemburgern im europäischen Kontext*, eds. Jiří Fajt and Andrea Langer (Berlin and Munich: 2009), 354–64.

Hledíková, Zdeňka, *Svět české středověké církve* [The world of the medieval Czech church] (Prague: 2010).

Holinka, Rudolf, *Církevní politika arcibiskupa Jana z Jenštejna za pontifikátu Urbana VI.* [The ecclesiastical politics of Archbishop Jan of Jenštejn during the pontificate of Urban VI] (Bratislava: 1933).

Kadlec, Jaroslav, *Leben und Schriften des Prager Magisters Adalbert Rankonis de Ericinio* (Münster: 1971).

Kadlec, Jaroslav, "Reformní postila a synodální kázání mistra Ondřeje z Brodu" [The reform postil and synodal sermons of Master Ondřej of Brod], *Studie o rukopisech* 16 (1977): 13–26.

Kadlec, Jaroslav, "Začátky kláštera augustiniánských kanovníků v Roudnici" [The beginnings of the monastery of Augustinian canons at Roudnice], *Studie o rukopisech* 20 (1981): 65–86.

Kadlec, Jaroslav, "Teologická fakulta" [The faculty of theology], in *Dějiny Univerzity Karlovy*, vol. 1, ed. Michal Svatoš (Prague: 1995), 135–61.

Kadlec, Jaroslav, "Petr Klarifikátor, duchovní vůdce a životopisec arcibiskupa Jana z Jenštejna" [Petrus Clarificator, spiritual leader and biographer of Archbishop Jan of Jenštejn], *Sborník Katolické teologické fakulty* 1 (1998): 101–50.

Kejř, Jiří, "Žalobní články proti Milíčovi z Kroměříže" [The prosecution articles against Milíč of Kroměříž], *Husitský Tábor* 10 (1991): 181–89.

Koudelka, Vladimír J., "Heinrich von Bitterfeld († c. 1405), Professor an der Universität Prag," *Archivum Fratrum Praedicatorum* 23 (1953): 5–65.

Krmíčková, Helena, *Studie a texty k počátkům kalicha v Čechách* [Studies and texts on the beginnings of the chalice in Bohemia] (Brno: 1997).
Krupa, Pawel, "La communion fréquente à Prague au XIVe siècle. Malogranatum III, 1, 26: ses précurseurs et ses continuateurs," in *Crisi mendicante e crisi della chiesa. Encomia sancti Thomae e riforma savonaroliana* (Memorie domenicane) 30 (Pistoia: 1990).
Kybal, Vlastimil, *M. Matěj z Janova. Jeho život, spisy a učení* [Master Matěj of Janov. His life, writings, and teachings] (Prague: 1905).
Lášek, Jan B., and Karel Skalický (eds.), *Mistr Matěj z Janova ve své a v naší době* [Master Matěj of Janov in his time and ours] (Brno: 2002).
Marek, Jindřich, *Jakoubek ze Stříbra a počátky utrakvistického kazatelství v českých zemích. Studie o Jakoubkově postile z let 1413–1414* [Jakoubek of Stříbro and the beginnings of Utraquist preaching in the Bohemian lands. A study of Jakoubek's postil from 1413–1414] (Prague: 2011).
Marin, Olivier, *L'archevêque, le maître and le dévot. Genèses du mouvement réformateur pragois. Années 1360–1419* (Paris: 2005).
Marin, Olivier, "Aux origines médiévales de la slavistique. L'Expositio cantici Hospodine pomiluj ny (1397)," *Mélanges de l'Ecole française de Rome* 117 (2005): 615–39.
Menčík, Ferdinand, *Konrád Waldhauser, mnich řádu svatého Augustina* [Konrad Waldhauser, a monk from the order of St. Augustine] (Prague: 1881).
Mengel, David C., *Bones, Stones and Brothels. Religion and Topography in Prague under Emperor Charles IV (1346–1378)* (PhD dissertation, University of Notre Dame: 2003).
Mengel, David C., "From Venice to Jerusalem and Beyond. Milíč of Kroměříž and the Topography of Prostitution in Fourteenth-Century Prague," *Speculum* 79 (2004): 407–42.
Mengel, David C., "A Monk, a Preacher and a Jesuit. Making the Life of Milíč," in *The Bohemian Reformation and Religious Practice*, eds. Zdeněk V. David and David R. Holeton, vol. 5, 1 (Prague: 2004), 33–55.
Morée, Peter C.A., *Preaching in Fourteenth-Century Bohemia. The Life and Ideas of Milicius de Chremsir († 1374) and his Significance in the Historiography of Bohemia* (Heršpice: 1999).
Morée, Peter C.A., "The Role of the Preacher According to Milicius de Chremsir," in *The Bohemian Reformation and Religious Practice*, eds. Zdeněk V. David and David R. Holeton, vol. 3 (Prague: 2000), 35–48.
Mossman, Stephen, *Marquard von Lindau and the Challenges of Religious Life in Late Medieval Germany* (Oxford: 2010).
Nechutová, Jana, "Raně reformní prvky v 'Apologii' Konráda Waldhausera" [Early reform elements in the "Apologia" of Konrad Waldhauser], *Sborník prací Filozofické fakulty brněnské univerzity* E 25 (1980): 241–48.
Nechutová, Jana, "Autorita Bible a její překlady podle kvestie Jana z Mýta Utrum dictis sanctorum patrum" [The authority of the Bible and its translations according to the

quaestio Utrum dictis sanctorum patrum of Jan of Mýto], *Česká literatura* 47 (1999): 510–14.

Nechutová, Jana, "Konrad von Soltau. *Lectura super caput Firmiter*," in *Schriften im Umkreis mitteleuropäischer Universitäten um 1400. Lateinische und volkssprachige Texte aus Prag, Wien und Heidelberg. Unterschiede, Gemeinsamkeiten, Wechselbeziehungen*, eds. Fritz Peter Knapp, and Jürgen Miethke, and Manuela Niesner (Leiden: 2004), 3–19.

Nechutová, Jana, "Reform- und Bußprediger von Waldhauser bis Hus," in *Kirchliche Reformimpulse des 14./15. Jahrhunderts in Ostmitteleuropa*, eds. Winfried Eberhard and Franz Machilek (Cologne, Weimar, and Vienna: 2006), 239–54.

Nechutová, Jana, *Die lateinische Literatur des Mittelalters in Böhmen* (Cologne, Weimar, and Vienna: 2007).

Neidiger, Bernhard, "Wortgottesdienst vor der Reformation. Die Stiftung eigener Predigtpfründen für Weltkleriker im späten Mittelalter," *Rheinische Vierteljahrsblätter* 66 (2002): 142–89.

Nodl, Martin, "Mezi laickou a učeneckou zbožností. Katechetické příručky pro faráře v českém a slezském prostředí pozdního středověku" [Between lay and learned piety. Catechetical handbooks for parish priests in the Bohemian and Silesian *milieux* of the late Middle Ages], in *Náboženský život a církevní poměry v zemích Koruny české ve 14.–17. století*, eds. Lenka Bobková and Jana Konvičná (Prague: 2009), 176–91.

Novotný, Václav, *Náboženské hnutí české ve 14. a 15. stol. Část 1. Do Husa* [The Bohemian Reform movement in the 14th and 15th centuries. Part 1: Before Hus] (Prague: 1915).

Nový, Rostislav, "Ženské řeholní a laické komunity v předhusitské Praze" [Female regular and lay communities in pre-Hussite Prague], *Documenta Pragensia* 13 (1996): 41–6.

Nuding, Matthias, *Matthäus von Krakau. Theologe, Politiker, Kirchenreformer in Krakau, Prag und Heidelberg zur Zeit des Großen Abendländischen Schismas* (Tübingen: 2007).

Odložilík, Otakar, *M. Štěpán z Kolína* [Master Štěpán of Kolín] (Prague: 1924).

Odložilík, Otakar, "Leták M. Štěpána z Kolína o pronásledování kněží" [The pamphlet of Master Štěpán of Kolín on the persecution of the clergy], *Věstník Královské české společnosti nauk* (1926): no. 1, 1–48.

Odložilík, Otakar, "The Chapel of Bethlehem in Prague," in *Studien zur älteren Geschichte Osteuropas. Festschrift für H.F. Schmidt*, ed. Günther Stökl, vol. 1 (Graz and Cologne: 1956), 125–41.

Palacký, František [under the pseudonym J.P. Jordan], *Die Vorläufer des Hussitenthums in Böhmen* (Leipzig: 1846).

Polc, Jaroslav V., *De origine festi Visitationis B.M.V.* (Rome: 1967).

Polc, Jaroslav V., *Svatý Jan Nepomucký* [Saint John Nepomuk] (Rome: 1972).

Polc, Jaroslav V., "Kapitoly z církevního života Čech podle předhusitského zákonodárství" [Chapters from Bohemia's church life according to pre-Hussite legislation], in *Pražské arcibiskupství 1344–1994*, eds. Zdeňka Hledíková and Jaroslav V. Polc (Prague: 1994), 30–57.

Polc, Jaroslav V., *Česká církev v dějinách* [The Bohemian church in history] (Prague: 1999).

Polc, Jaroslav V., and Zdeňka Hledíková, *Pražské synody a koncily předhusitské doby* [Prague synods and councils in the pre-Husite period] (Prague: 2002).

Rouse, Mary A. and Richard H. Rouse, *Preachers, Florilegia and Sermons. Studies on the Manipulus Florum of Thomas of Ireland* (Toronto: 1979).

Rychterová, Pavlína, *Die Offenbarungen der heiligen Birgitta von Schweden. Eine Untersuchung zur alttschechischen Übersetzung des Thomas von Štítné* (Cologne, Weimar, and Vienna: 2004).

Rychterová, Pavlína, "Charisma und charismatische Legitimation in der *Vita* von Johannes von Jenstein," in *Kunst als Herrschaftsinstrument. Böhmen und das Heilige Römische Reich unter den Luxemburgern im europäischen Kontext*, eds. Jiří Fajt and Andrea Langer (Berlin and Munich: 2009), 346–53.

Schmidtke, Dietrich, "Pastoraltheologische Texte des Matthäus von Krakau," in *Schriften im Umkreis mitteleuropäischer Universitäten um 1400. Lateinische und Volkssprachige Texte aus Prag, Wien und Heidleberg: Unterschiede, Gemeinsamkeiten, Wechselbeziehungen*, eds. Fritz Peter Knapp, Jürgen Miethke, and Manuela Niesner (Leiden and Boston: 2004), 178–96.

Šmahel, František, *Die Hussitische Revolution*, trans. Thomas Krzenck (Monumenta Germaniae Historica. Schriften) 43, 3 vols. (Hannover: 2002).

Soukup, Pavel, "Die Waldenser in Böhmen und Mähren im 14. Jahrhundert," in *Friedrich Reiser und die "waldensisch-hussitische Internationale,"* eds. Albert de Lange and Kathrin Utz Tremp (Heidelberg, Ubstadt-Weiher, and Basel: 2006), 131–60.

Soukup, Pavel, "'Ne verbum Dei in nobis suffocetur...' Kommunikationstechniken von Predigern des frühen Hussitismus," *Bohemia* 48 (2008): 54–82.

Soukup, Pavel, *Reformní kazatelství a Jakoubek ze Stříbra* [Reform preaching and Jakoubek of Stříbro] (Prague: 2011).

Spunar, Pavel, "Neznámé pražské nápisy v kodexu ÖNB 4550" [Unknown Prague inscriptions in codex ÖNB 4550], *Studie o rukopisech* 12 (1973): 175–90.

Spunar, Pavel, *Repertorium auctorum Bohemorum provectum idearum post universitatem Pragensem conditam illustrans*, vol. 1 (Studia Copernicana) 25 (Wrocław: 1985).

Tomek, Václav Vladivoj, *Dějepis města Prahy*, vol. 3, 2nd ed. [A History of the city of Prague] (Prague: 1893).

Uhlíř, Zdeněk, "Eklesiologie v českém sporu o Urbana VI." [Ecclesiology in the Bohemian dispute over Urban VI], *Teologická reflexe* 8 (2002): 17–40.

Valasek, Emil, *Das Kirchenverständnis des Prager Magisters Matthias von Janow (1350/55–1393). Ein Beitrag zur Geistesgeschichte Böhmens im 14. Jahrhundert* (Rome: 1971).

Välimäki, Reima, *Heresy in Late Medieval Germany. The Inquisitor Petrus Zwicker and the Waldensians* (York, York Medieval Press: 2019).

Van Dussen, Michael, "Aristotle's Tetragon. Compilation and Consensus during the Great Schism," in *Religious Controversy in Europe, 1378–1536. Textual Transmission and Networks of Readership*, eds. Michael Van Dussen and Pavel Soukup (Turnhout: 2013), 187–210.

Weltsch, Ruben E., *Archbishop John of Jenstein (1348–1400). Papalism, Humanism and Reform in Pre-Hussite Prague* (The Hague and Paris: 1968).

Winter, Eduard, *Frühhumanismus. Seine Entwicklung in Böhmen und deren europäische Bedeutung für die Kirchenreformbestrebungen im 14. Jahrhundert* (Berlin: 1964).

Wünsch, Thomas, *Konziliarimus und Polen* (Paderborn: 1998).

Zachová, Jana, "Waldhauser a Hus" [Waldhauser and Hus], in *Husitství – reformace – renesance. Sborník k 60. narozeninám Františka Šmahela*, eds. Jaroslav Pánek, Miloslav Polívka and Noemi Rejchrtová, vol. 1 (Prague: 1994), 287–97.

Zelený, Rostislav, *The Questiunculae of Stephan of Roudnice* (Rome: 1966).

Wyclif in Bohemia

Stephen E. Lahey

1   Why Wyclif?

Bohemia was known for its willingness to question and criticize ecclesiastical teachings and practice well before Wyclif began writing. Charles IV was deeply interested in fostering an atmosphere of clerical reform, encouraging Prague's first archbishop, Arnošt of Pardubice, to begin a reformative program in 1344. The most important result of this imperial openness to the improvement of the church in Bohemia was the activity of Konrad Waldhauser, an Austrian Augustinian, who preached in German and Latin. Konrad was an enthusiastic critic of his fellow friars, attacking the hypocrisy with which his fellows preached the Christian ideal, yet lived comfortable lives in the world. When his fellow Augustinian friars attacked his preaching, his indictment of their impious criticism was bitter, and apparently very well received by his Bohemian admirers.[1] Foremost among these was Milíč of Kroměříž, who had begun his ordained life with a hunger for advancement, but was thunderstruck by Konrad's preaching in 1364. He renounced his position as canon at St. Vitus Cathedral and began to preach enthusiastically against clerical abuses and, increasingly, of the urgent need to prepare for the coming of Antichrist.[2] Milíč's career is discussed elsewhere in this volume, but his example is important for understanding the kindling of interest in reform among the scholars in the Bohemian nation at Prague University in the 1360s.

---

1   Konstantin Höfler (ed.), *Geschichtschreiber der hussitischen Bewegung in Böhmen* (Fontes rerum Austriacarum, 1. Abteilung: Scriptores) 2, 6, and 7 (Vienna: 1856–1866), vol. 2, 17–39. For an overview of this period, see Paul De Vooght, *L'hérésie de Jean Huss* (Leuven: 1960), 2–40; Howard Kaminsky, *A History of the Hussite Revolution* (Berkeley and Los Angeles: 1967), 5–35; Gordon Leff, *Heresy in the Later Middle Ages. The Relation of Heterodoxy to Dissent c. 1250–c. 1450* (Manchester and New York: 1967), vol. 2, 606–12; František Šmahel, *Die Hussitische Revolution*, trans. Thomas Krzenck (Monumenta Germaniae Historica. Schriften) 43, (Hannover: 2002), vol. 2: 717–88. Thomas Fudge warns against undue connection between figures like Konrad and Jan Milíč and Hus, criticizing the anachronistic practice of perceiving Hussite tendencies in the Bohemian reformers of the mid-14th century: see Thomas A. Fudge, *Jan Hus. Religious Reform and Social Revolution in Bohemia* (London: 2010), 20–6. De Vooght is typical of what Fudge criticizes, suggesting that all of Hus is contained within the preaching of Jan Milíč (p. 14).
2   See Höfler (ed.), *Geschichtschreiber*, vol. 2, 40–7.

Wyclif developed a detailed theological program in the 1360s, which he later assembled into the two volumes of his *Summa de ente*. He again developed a comprehensive political and ecclesiological reform program in the 1370s, which he grouped into a collection of treatises called the *Summa theologie*. During his last years at Lutterworth, he seems to have revised several of the treatises in the latter collection to serve as the basis for a program of preaching the Christian life among the laity, which he supplemented with sustained Gospel commentaries (*Opus evangelicum*), two collections of Latin sermons, and a simplified *summa* he called the *Trialogus*.[3] The result is a tremendously large body of work. It includes detailed studies of ontology, modal metaphysics, the semantics underlying scriptural hermeneutics, political and legal theory, ecclesiology, spatiotemporal physics, and christological and trinitarian metaphysics, in addition to a complete *postilla* of Scripture, and a host of polemical works directed against friars, the papacy, and specific abuses such as simony and absenteeism. His eucharistic theology had been condemned almost immediately upon its publication in 1381, and both Canterbury and Avignon had compiled lists of the many errors to be found in his works before his death in 1384. It is reasonable, then, to ask why anyone would risk associating with such teachings, and why certain of them figured so importantly at Prague University, while others were generally ignored. For example, only the most radical of the Taborites were ready to embrace his remanentist eucharistic theology, while the general Hussite tendency was to reject it. Again, his theory of grace-founded dominion was largely ignored by the Bohemians, despite its theoretical suitability for the participation of the nobility in the Hussite movement. It is not sufficient to declare Wyclif's philosophical realism as a gauntlet to be thrown in the face of the German nations at Prague University, given the cafeteria-style approach with which the Bohemians appeared to have selected from Wyclif's philosophical works.[4] The aspect of Wyclif's theology that

---

3 Williel R. Thomson, *The Latin Writings of John Wyclyf* (Toronto: 1983) remains the definitive catalogue of Wyclif's Latin works. Earlier collections of his English works cannot be regarded as Wyclif's, as Anne Hudson argued in *The Premature Reformation. Wycliffite Texts and Lollard History* (Oxford: 1988). For analysis of the composition of the collections of Wyclif's works, see Hudson's *Studies in the Transmission of Wyclif's Writings* (Aldershot and Burlington: 2008), which gathers all her essays published elsewhere on the topic. See also Ivan Müller's essay in Wyclif, *De ideis,* eds. Vilém Herold and Ivan Müller (Auctores Britannici Medii Aevi) (Oxford: forthcoming); and Stephen E. Lahey's in John Wyclif, *Trialogus*, trans. Stephen E. Lahey (Cambridge: 2013).

4 This explanation is the general tenor of the arguments summarized in Leff, *Heresy*, vol. 2, 622–23, garnered from the scholarship of the period. Kaminsky, *A History*, distinguishes between the appeal of Wyclif's realism and his theological reform (p. 23), but perceives the appeal of the former to be grounded in anti-nominalism. In 1970, Šmahel raised this issue in his

appears to have had the greatest impact on Bohemian scholars in the years prior to the formal condemnation of Wyclif in 1409 was less his realism about universals than his doctrine of the divine ideas.[5]

It is important to distinguish between the two subjects, because universals are creatures, while the divine ideas are not. Wyclif carefully delineates the relation between the two in his treatises *De universalibus* and *De ideis*, in Parts 1 and 2 of the *Summa de ente* respectively. The relation of universal to particular describes the ordering of creation, and is central to Wyclif's conception of how human beings are interrelated as members of a species, to his description of the metaphysics of the Incarnation, and especially to his understanding of the centrality of Holy Scripture to the Christian religion.[6] Aside from the analyses of Stanislav of Znojmo and Štěpán Páleč, to be discussed below, there is relatively little evidence for sustained arguments about universals, although there are plenty of shorter philosophical pieces available that show it to have been of real interest in Prague.[7] The doctrine of divine ideas, on the other hand, is entirely about the ontological status of the knowledge God has of creation, and its identity with the eternal divine essence. In short order, the divine ideas became associated with an archetypal world in the *quaestiones* that were popular at Prague University in the early 1400s. While the doctrine was generally dismissed by theologians as completely foreign to the Aristotelian metaphysical worldview before the time of Wyclif, it flourished in Prague, and became the philosophical *sine qua non* for Bohemian Wycliffism. Why?

Edouard Jeauneau suggests that there had been a strong Latin Neoplatonist inclination among the Bohemian scholars at Prague University, originating in the first generation of theologians who returned to Prague from the University of Paris. There they appear to have become acquainted with the tradition of the School of Chartres, inspiring them to bring several important philosophical works back with them as they established themselves at Prague University.[8] Along with several copies of the Latin translation of Plato's *Timaeus* and

---

"Wyclif's Fortune in Hussite Bohemia," in idem, *Die Prager Universität im Mittelalter. The Charles University in the Middle Ages* (Leiden and Boston: 2007), 467–89.

5 See Vilém Herold, *Pražská univerzita a Wyclif. Wyclifovo učení o ideách a geneze husitského revolučního myšlení* (Prague: 1985) for a thorough account of the prevalence of *disputationes* on this subject. See also František Šmahel, *Alma Mater Pragensis. Studie k počátkům Univerzity Karlovy* (Prague: 2016), 229–408, for a detailed overview.
6 Ian C. Levy, *John Wyclif. Scriptural Logic, Real Presence, and the Parameters of Orthodoxy* (Milwaukee: 2003); Stephen E. Lahey, *John Wyclif* (Oxford: 2009).
7 František Šmahel, *Verzeichnis der Quellen zum Prager Universalienstreit 1348–1500* (Mediaevalia Philosophica Polonorum) 25 (Wrocław: 1980) provides a detailed list of the many brief treatments of issues of interest to realist metaphysics.
8 Edouard Jeauneau, "Plato apud Bohemos," *Mediaeval Studies* 41 (1979): 161–214.

Chalcidius's commentary on it, the most popular figure appears to have been William of Conches. Four manuscripts of his *Dragmaticon*, four of his *Glosae super Platonem*, and 17 of the florilegium *Parvi flores* remain in Prague, all dating to the late 14th and early 15th centuries. Vilém Herold noted that the foremost advocate of reform in Bohemia, Milíč's follower Matěj of Janov, incorporates a strong element of the School of Chartres in his *Regulae Veteris et Novi Testamenti*, particularly in book 3, treatise 1.[9] Here Matěj presents a description of the universal law that binds creatures in perfect order as having its basis in the divine ideas assembled eternally in the Word. His argument is based largely on Scripture and citations from Augustine, Bernard, and Anselm; of the important scholastics, only Bonaventure figures among Matěj's authorities.[10]

Another important figure whose voice echoed in the words of Wyclif was Vojtěch Raňkův of Ježov (Adalbertus Ranconis de Ericinio). Vojtěch had also studied in Paris in the 1360s, after spending time in Oxford in the 1350s. He appears to have become friendly with Richard Fitzralph of Armagh at some point and developed an antimendicant position which led him to bring a copy of Fitzralph's *De pauperie Salvatoris* back to Prague in 1365. In Prague he associated with Waldhauser and Milíč, and sponsored Matěj's trip to Paris. While little of his formal philosophical work remains (he is reputed to have engaged in a disputation with Heinrich Totting of Oyta in 1369 and again in 1372 at Prague), there is enough theological work to show a sharp philosophical mind with interests ranging across ecclesiological and political matters that would be familiar to readers conversant with Fitzralph and his relation to Wyclif.[11]

---

9   See Herold, *Pražská univerzita a Wyclif*, 230–33, and his "The University of Paris and the Foundations of the Bohemian Reformation," in *The Bohemian Reformation and Religious Practice*, eds. Zdeněk V. David and David R. Holeton, vol. 3 (Prague: 2000), 15–24. R.R. Betts had made this connection in 1951, but at a more general level. See Betts, "The Influence of Realist Philosophy on Jan Hus and His Predecessors in Bohemia," in idem, *Essays in Czech History* (London: 1969), 42–62.

10 The most in-depth study of Matěj remains Vlastimil Kybal's *M. Matěj z Janova. Jeho život, spisy a učení* (Prague: 1905). Kybal began editing the *Regulae* in 1908 and completed up to volume 5 in 1926. More recently, Jana Nechutová has completed this project. See her "Matěj of Janov and His Work Regulae Veteris et Novi Testamenti: The Significance of Volume VI and Its Relation to the Previously Published Volumes," in *The Bohemian Reformation*, eds. David and Holeton, vol. 2 (Prague: 1998), 15–24.

11 Katherine Walsh, "Die Rezeption der Schriften des Richard Fitzralph (Armachanus) im lollardisch-hussitischen Milieu," in *Das Publikum politischer Theorie im 14. Jahrhundert*, ed. Jürgen Miethke (Munich: 1992), 237–53. For Vojtěch, see Jaroslav Kadlec, *Leben und Schriften des Prager Magisters Adalbert Rankonis de Ericinio* (Münster: 1971), and Vilém Herold, "Vojtěch Raňkův of Ježov (Adalbertus Rankonis de Ericinio) and the Bohemian Reformation," in *The Bohemian Reformation*, eds. David and Holeton, vol. 7 (Prague: 2009), 72–9.

2   Stanislav of Znojmo, Štěpán Páleč, and Jerome of Prague

The three most important figures in understanding Wyclif's reception in Prague are Stanislav of Znojmo (d. 1413), Štěpán Páleč (1367–1423), and Jerome of Prague (1378/80–1416). All were enthusiastic in their adoption of Wycliffism in the 1390s, and Stanislav and Štěpán were equally enthusiastic in their renunciation of their Wycliffite errors (though they were never asked formally to abjure them) sometime between 1409 and 1412, and in their subsequent activites against their erstwhile students.[12] Jerome remained a confirmed disciple until he was compelled to renounce Wyclif while imprisoned at Constance in September 1415. Instead of being released, Jerome was put back in prison, and nearly a year later, he publicly renounced his recantation, and was burned on 30 May 1416.[13] Their work represents the fullest exploration of Wyclif's metaphysics at Prague University, and gives clear evidence of the philosophical sophistication of the Bohemian scholars' approach to Wyclif's thought.

Almost nothing is known of Stanislav before his matriculation at Vienna in 1382, other than the likelihood that he came from the Moravian town of Znojmo and that he had limited means at his disposal. He moved to Prague the next year, and after completing the prescribed course of studies in the Faculty of Arts, he incepted in theological studies in 1388, which he completed in 1400. At some point, he became acquainted with Wyclif's philosophical works, and is reported to have published a work on Aristotle's categories (now lost), as well as a treatise on *insolubilia* that followed Wyclif's approach. Stanislav Sousedík suggests that Stanislav completed a commentary on *De anima* in the early 1390's, also lost, evidence for which may lie in the later chapters of his long commentary on Wyclif's *De universalibus*, which explores the relation of soul to body with some care. He finished his long commentary in 1400, and a shorter version in 1408, and wrote a treatise on the relation of truth and falsity in propositions to truths about reality (*De vero et falso*) before 1404.[14] These works have attracted little scholarly attention, but provide the most complete picture of the first Bohemian reading of Wyclif's philosophy.[15]

---

12   See Stanislav Sousedík, "Stanislaus von Znaim († 1414). Eine Lebensskizze," *Mediaevalia Philosophica Polonorum* 17 (1973): 49–50.

13   See Thomas A. Fudge, *Jerome of Prague and the Foundations of the Hussite Movement* (New York: 2016), 214–53.

14   Stanislav of Znojmo, "Tractatus de universalibus (maior)"; idem, "Tractatus de universalibus realibus (minor)," in Jan Sedlák, *M. Jan Hus* (Prague: 1915), 81*-93*; idem, *De vero et falso*, ed. Vilém Herold (Prague: 1971).

15   Stanislav Sousedík, "Pojem *distinctio formalis* u českých realistů v době Husově," *Filosofický časopis* 18 (1970): 1024–29; Gabriel Nuchelmans, "Stanislaus of Znaim (d. 1414) On

Tensions escalated in the first years of the fifteenth century, and Stanislav's Wycliffism opened him to criticism from the German nations at Prague. The main problem was Wyclif's remanentism, the denial of transubstantiation that had led to the Blackfriars condemnation of 1382 in London. Stanislav argued that one could embrace Wyclif's metaphysics without endorsing his position on the physics of the Eucharist, and Archbishop Zbyněk ultimately supported Stanislav in his attempt to create a *via media* Wycliffism. While this set the tenor for Bohemian Wycliffism at Prague University, with Hus and Jakoubek following Stanislav's lead, Gregory XII ordered an investigation of the matter, which led to Stanislav being called to Rome in 1408. Zbyněk then distanced himself from Wycliffism, and on 24 May 1408, 45 articles defining Wyclif's errors were proclaimed at Prague University. The ongoing papal schism prompted the college of cardinals to call for a council at Pisa in 1408, and Stanislav traveled there in October to explain his position and distance himself from Wycliffite heresies. Stanislav returned in 1409 to find Prague University completely rearranged following the Decree of Kutná Hora.

His attempt at compromise had failed; Stanislav found himself on the outside of the growing number of Bohemian theologians who had embraced Wycliffism, and his acquaintance with the *magisterium* seems to have convinced him that solid orthodoxy was likely the best response to the growing tendency to combine Wyclif's philosophy with his reformative theology. By 1412 he had become an active opponent of Wycliffism, but only after having written a treatise on moral theology, *De gracia et peccato*, which contains several long, albeit uncited, sections from *Trialogus* III in its catalogue of the deadly sins.[16] From 1412 to 1414, Stanislav composed a treatise attacking Wyclif's ecclesiology, another attacking Hus's position, an indictment of Jakoubek's teachings on Antichrist, an overview of Wycliffite heresies, and an extensive, point-by-point refutation of them that would later be used at Constance.[17] His position at Prague University grew increasingly intolerable, and he left for Jindřichův Hradec in south Bohemia in 1413, where he died in early 1414.[18]

Truth and Falsity," in *Mediaeval Semantics and Metaphysics. Studies dedicated to L.M. de Rijk*, ed. Egbert Peter Bos (Nijmegen: 1985), 313–38.

16   Stanislav of Znojmo, *De gracia et peccato*, ed. Zuzana Silagiová (Fontes Latini Bohemorum) 1 (Prague: 1997), 14–20.

17   Stanislav of Znojmo, "Tractatus de Romana ecclesia" (1412); idem, "Tractatus de Anticristo contra mgr Jacobellum de Misa" (1412–13), not edited; idem, "Alma et venerabilis" (1412); idem, "Tractatus contra XLV articulos Joannis Wiclef."

18   Jan Sedlák, "Stanislav ze Znojma na Moravě," in *Miscellanea husitica Ioannis Sedlák*, eds. Jaroslav V. Polc and Stanislav Přibyl (Prague: 1996), 126–32.

De vero et falso illustrates Stanislav's mastery of Wyclif's unique understanding of the relation of words and concepts to objects in the world. This position, dubbed "pan-propositionalism" or "propositional realism," recognizes an isomorphism between the subject-predicate structure of mental and linguistic propositions and what we would call "facts" about reality.[19] While most medieval thinkers embraced the natural tie between conceptual and linguistic propositional structure, few made the jump to there being actual structure to the facts we perceive to be in the world. Wyclif embraced Adam Wodeham's idea of a complex significable to conceive of the whole of created being as a complex set of truths, arrangements that we accurately identify in a subject-predicate structure. For instance, if I correctly say, "The cat is on the mat," I am speaking truth because there is a cat sitting on a mat. The cat doing the sitting is bespeaking, or ontologically expressing that same truth in its sitting. There is not simply a being acting in the world – there is a cat engaged in mat-sitting, which itself is a real thing that is expressed by a subject like a cat. Wyclif takes this propositional realism and applies it to the knowing relation of God to creation: every structured matter of fact throughout all creation is something individually known by God precisely as it is in creation. That is, if the cat sits on the mat at Location N at Time p, God eternally knows that. Leaving aside the vexed question of the causal relation between God's eternal knowing and the created act, a topic that occupies Wyclif throughout the *Summa de ente*, Stanislav explores the complexities defining our understanding of what is and is not so, and God's understanding of this, in *De vero et falso*.[20]

Gabriel Nuchelmans explored this treatise in 1985, and concluded that Stanislav was reasoning about concepts, words, and objects according to the rudimentary description above. He incorporated Wyclif's doctrine of the divine ideas, his modal theories, and his understanding of how privative and negative knowledge claims function in logical discourse into his discussion of how to understand truth and falsity in propositions about the world. Therefore, the treatise is a primer for those wanting an accessible introduction to Wyclif's knotty logic. Wyclif's own writings are frequently opaque, while Stanislav expresses his ideas in a relatively simple manner, allowing his analysis of the problems he poses to explain the nature of the ideas involved. In a sense, *De vero et falso* serves as an *Isagoge* for Wyclif's logic. It may lack the formal

---

19   Laurent Cesali, "Le 'pan-propositionalisme' de Jean Wyclif," *Vivarium* 43 (2005): 124–55. See also his *Le réalisme propositionnel. Sémantique et ontologie des propositions chez Jean Duns Scot, Gauthier Burley, Richard Brinkley et Jean Wyclif* (Paris: 2007).
20   Stanislav of Znojmo, *De vero et falso*.

complexity of Wyclif's writings, but it explains the overall scope of Wyclif's theory very clearly.

De felicitate begins with the familiar distinction between use and enjoyment but moves speedily to analysis of mental and physical acts, and to the manner in which change occurs in agents as they act, particularly when the act has moral value. Does the change occur continuously as agents act, or is the change a series of sudden, successive alterations? What properties are necessary for change for the better or worse in the human soul, and is a habitus such as love a constant force, or one involving successive loving acts? This analysis has its base in Wyclif's *De actibus anime,* Chapter 3, along with *De logica* III, and shows evidence of Wyclif's delineation of kinds of predication in *De universalibus*. The treatise appears to be an attempt to bring the disparate elements of Wyclif's understanding of mental acts and states, mental and spiritual change over time, and the language we use to describe this, in relation to the nature of morality. For the theologian, special difficulties arise when we discuss Christ's happiness: did his assumed nature experience the fluctuations we experience? What was the relation between Christ's human and divine natures, and did the Passion alter this relation? At this point, Stanislav has moved into questions that result from Wyclif's *De incarnacione*, but which Wyclif did not explore sufficiently. The later chapters of the treatise move to changes in the nature of the blessed who experience the joys of paradise. There are sections from *Trialogus* in this latter section, as Stanislav considers the relation that will obtain between the intellect and the resurrected body.[21] Wyclif's conviction that space, time, and bodies are not continuous, but made up of "atoms" or indivisible quanta, comes up occasionally in Stanislav's reasoning, but he does not make a special effort to defend this idea. Like *De vero et falso, De felicitate* is a showpiece of Wycliffite philosophy, incorporating elements from many of the treatises of *Summa de ente* and *De logica*, but almost nothing from *Summa theologie* aside from passing reference to the nature of the church as the body of the Elect as an example of a truth that is knowable as time passes.

Jerome of Prague was famous for championing Wyclif across Europe. He began his career as Wyclif's apostle in Paris in 1403, defending his master's metaphysics and angering Jean Gerson, the chancellor of the university. He made a similar defense at the University of Cologne in 1406, and again in Heidelberg later that year. 1407 found Jerome back in Prague, where he continued to proselytize for Wyclif. He was pivotal in a famous quodlibetal disputation in 1409 on Wycliffism, when Archbishop Zbyněk condemned it. He traveled throughout Central Europe, landing in a prison in Vienna for heresy in 1410.

---

21 Ibid., 107, 111.

After he escaped from prison, his reputation as a freelance Wycliffite troublemaker grew until he was arrested and tried for heresy at Constance in April 1415. Unlike Stanislav of Znojmo and Štěpán Páleč, though, he appears to have written very little. What remains are *Quaestiones* and a record of a disputation with Blasius Lupus, all on problems his opponents found with the contents of Wyclif's *De universalibus* and *De ideis*. These are representative of the very many short pieces that remain, mostly unedited, from the period in which Wyclif's metaphysics was the chief topic of debate in the Theological Faculty in Prague.[22]

3 The 45 Articles and the Beginning of Arguments about Wycliffism

Condemning Wyclif's thought had become a regular activity by the time Hus faced his opponents at Constance in 1415. During Wyclif's lifetime, his errors elicited papal ire in 1377, when Gregory XI issued several bulls against his thought on dominion, and they expanded into a list of 24 at the so-called Earthquake Synod at the London Blackfriars' in 1382.[23] After his works arrived in Prague, Johannes Hübner, a German Dominican, spearheaded the German scholars' opposition to Wycliffism with a list of 21 errors to be added to the 1382 list. On 28 May 1403, the 45 Articles gave formal shape to the Wycliffite position by which both anti-Hussites and Hussites would measure error.[24] The Theological Faculty of Prague University condemned them again on 10 July 1412 at Žebrák Castle, when the king attempted to mediate a compromise between the opposing university factions, and added four additional erroneous positions. In 1409, Thomas Arundel, Archbishop of Canterbury, had initiated the compilation of a list that would eventually total 267 errors culled from fourteen of Wyclif's Latin works, which was completed in 1411. By now, cataloging Wycliffite error had become complicated, so Thomas Netter began to assemble

---

22 See Jerome of Prague, *Magistri Hieronymi de Praga Quaestiones, polemica, epistulae*, eds. František Šmahel and Gabriel Silagi (Corpus christianorum. Continuatio mediaevalis) 222 (Turnhout: 2010).

23 The best overall treatment of Wyclif's errors during his lifetime remains Joseph H. Dahmus, *The Prosecution of John Wyclyf* (New Haven: 1952); See also Mishtooni Bose, "The Opponents of John Wyclif," in *A Companion to John Wyclif, Late Medieval Theologian*, ed. Ian Christopher Levy (Brill's Companions to the Christian Tradition) 4 (Leiden and Boston: 2006), 407–56.

24 See František Palacký (ed.), *Documenta Mag. Joannis Hus vitam, doctrinam, causam in Constantiensi concilio actam et controversias de religione in Bohemia annis 1408–1413 motas illustrantia* (Prague: 1869), 327–31.

the definitive account in his *Doctrinale* in the 1420's, and finished it by the time he died in 1430. The 45 articles can be divided into eight groups. The largest contains the errors concerning the papacy and the church's possession of property. The remaining sets or errors pertain to monks and friars; the moral quality of the clergy in general; the efficacy of prayer; excommunication; transubstantiation; simony; and finally, Wyclif's philosophy.

The contemporary literature that accumulated in response to this list of 45 errors became voluminous, and much of the squabbling between Prague and Tábor that would injure the movement's chances for success arose from arguments about these errors. For our purposes, it will be most useful to turn to two sermons delivered during the summer of 1412. Stanislav and Páleč composed brief sermons attacking errors they themselves had endorsed not long before: these constituted the opening salvo of the quarrels over Wycliffism that would characterize Hussite debate for the next two decades.[25] Stanislav delineated five articles worth special attention. The first, Stanislav begins, that no one in mortal sin can be either a civil or ecclesiastical lord, is not simply heretical so much as it is crazy. If this were so, hereditary succession would vanish, and society would simply end. Since we all share in original sin, no one could really own anything, and all government would be impossible. No one would know whether his lord governed justly, judges would not be entitled to adjudicate, and chaos would reign.[26] The next error disrupts the balance of power between clergy and laity, because it would provide for civil lords carrying away temporal goods from churches.[27] There is no real justification for this, Stanislav reflects: the goods of God are for God to distribute, and if God decrees that some should be held by the church to further its ministry, then the king is no more suited to take these than is a peasant to take away the king's crown. The two orders of *ius*, priestly and royal, have been delineated to provide for the smooth functioning of society, as Alexander of Hales and Hugh of Saint-Victor have explained. It is interesting that Stanislav uses these two authorities here; both were established as important figures for Prague theology before Wyclif's thought had arrived.

Stanislav continues by arguing against claims that Scripture does not require tithing, and by rejecting arguments holding that the Donation of

---

25 *Mgri Stanislav de Znoyma Sermo contra quinque articulos Wiklef*, in Sedlák, *Miscellanea*, 323–34; *Mgri Stephani de Páleč Sermo contra aliquos articulos Wiklef*, in Sedlák, *Miscellanea*, 335–53.

26 "Nullus est dominus civilis, nullus est prelatus, nullus est episcopos, dum est in peccato mortali"; see Sedlák, *M. Jan Hus*, 325*.

27 "[D]omini temporales possunt ad arbitrium suum auferre bona temporalia ab ecclesiasticis habituatis i.e. possessionatis deliquentibus"; see Sedlák, *M. Jan Hus*, 329*.

Constantine is unjustified. Finally, he turns on the argument that paying the clergy runs against Christ's law. The divine law, he says, is not contrary to Christ's law, and the Old Testament is filled with cases in which the priestly class takes payment for service. For three centuries, he reflects, the church was compelled to live in penury, humble in ignominy, chaste in anguish, and poor in poverty, while the world did its best to stamp it out of existence. Now the church dominates the world, and the clergy may be humble in their glory, chaste in their enjoyment, and poor in their riches. St. Wenceslas himself exemplifies this, he concludes.

Páleč's sermon addresses two more errors, that excommunication can only come from God, and that any priest may preach God's Word without permission from a bishop, as rooted in a misunderstanding of the purpose of ecclesiastical authority. The witness of the book of Acts shows that disobedience to apostolic authority elevates the self over the Truth that governs the church, thereby rendering oneself unable to preach the Word. Were episcopal governance destroyed, Páleč concludes, chaos would quickly overcome the church. Páleč's sermon, based in Galatians 5, is interesting less for its rather weak arguments than for its castigation of the moral hypocrisy of the Wycliffites. They only pretend to walk in the spirit, but in their impugning of authority and misinterpretation of the place of the sacraments, they run counter to the centuries of wisdom that have preceded them. Wyclif and his followers overlook the wisdom of Bernard and the Victorines, not to mention Augustine himself, in their pretense at reform. Walking in the spirit, Páleč insists, means never to bring scandal to one's neighbor, which scandal the 45 articles clearly delineate. Páleč, like Stanislav, restricts his use of authority to the Victorines, Bernard, and Augustine.

4   The 1410 Defense of Wyclif's Treatises

When Archbishop Zbyněk ordered that Wyclif's books be burned on 16 July 1410, Hus responded to this by organizing a public defense of Wyclif's works that he believed had been completely innocent of objectionable ideas.[28] The result was an articulation of Hus's *De libris hereticorum legendis*, which he had written in June to ridicule the practice of banning heretical books.[29] Hus

---

28   Matthew Spinka, *John Hus' Concept of the Church* (Princeton: 1966), 79–99; Kaminsky, *A History*, 60–73.

29   *Magistri Iohannis Hus Polemica*, ed. Jaroslav Eršil (Magistri Iohannis Hus Opera omnia) 22 (Prague: 1966), 19–37.

defended *De Trinitate* on 27 July; Jakoubek took up *De mandatis divinis* the next day; Šimon of Tišnov *De probacione proposicionis* on the 29th; Jan of Jičín *De materia et forma* on the 30th; Prokop of Plzeň *De ideis* on the 31st; and Zdislav of Zvířetice defended *De universalibus* on 6 August. The defenses range from the apparently furious to the outright satirical, and it is easy to imagine the delight with which they were received by the assembled reformists.

Hus's defense is little more than a recapitulation of the argument he presents in *De libris hereticorum legendis*, in which he argues that destroying heretical books is a monstrous crime against education, destroying the intellectual wheat with the chaff in order simply to stir up the common people. He comments that the church has been attempting to silence his own preaching, an act which flies in the face of Christ's commission to preach the Gospels across the world. Augustine, he reflects, believed that heretical works should be publicized as such, the better to instruct the people in the dangers that follow from particular paths of thought. One might as well burn Aristotle's *De caelis*, since it does not agree with Genesis. His opponents may say that it is folly to argue with heretics, but Hus points out that Jesus argued regularly with those who believed him to be a blasphemer or a liar. Finally, Hus notes that no specific error is associated with Wyclif's philosophical analysis of the Trinity and wonders why the council has not bothered to list any. The treatise is not one of Wyclif's easier texts, and it is certainly likely that Hus intimates that his opponents simply lacked the intellectual firepower to understand it.[30]

The next day, Jakoubek delivered a rousing defense of Wyclif's *De mandatis divinis*, a treatise which contains Wyclif's detailed commentary on the Decalogue. Jakoubek says almost nothing at all about the treatise, but instead mentions that it was intended to nurture the blood and flesh of the Body of Christ. This, he continues, is a direct threat against the forces of darkness who lurk in the church's shadows like serpents and scorpions – which is why Christ wept for Jerusalem. He laments that the carnal priests and the laity they have seduced have forgotten the humility, poverty, and surrender of the life of Christ, leaving the house of God empty and forsaken, "a house of demons."[31] Why does Jesus permit schism and evil in the body of his mystic bride? Only those who truly have Christ within them are the church, and he must be allowing this to

---

30 Ibid., 41–56. For discussion of the contents of *De Trinitate*, see Stephen E. Lahey, "Wyclif's Trinitarian and Christological Theology," in *A Companion to John Wyclif*, ed. Levy (Brill's Companions to the Christian Tradition), 127–98.

31 See Jan Sedlák, "Husův pomocník v evangeliu," *Studie a texty k náboženským dějinám českým* 1, Part 2 (1915): 316–28. Johann Loserth, *Hus und Wiclif. Zur Genesis der husitischen Lehre* (Prague and Leipzig: 1884), which contains most of the other defenses, includes only a paragraph from Jakoubek's defense.

show the difference between the man-made institution that calls itself the church and what he knows to be the true church. The true priests of Christ must preach to the faithful and turn them from pharisaical ferment. Readers familiar with the style of Matěj of Janov will recognize the tenor of the defense, and Jakoubek was certainly fond of mining Matěj in his preaching.[32] Stanislav had returned to Prague University by summer 1410, but does not seem to have been involved in this defense, although Jakoubek may well have been having fun with his reputation, because the language of his defense mirrors Stanislav's *Vos testimonium perhibebitis* sermon delivered in 1405, equally imbued with the spirit of Matěj.[33]

Jakoubek had shifted the defense from scholastic disputation to street theater, and Šimon of Tišnov did not disappoint his audience on the 29th. The object of his defense was *De probacionibus proposicionum*, a work not in the accepted canon of Wyclif's Latin works. W.R. Thomson guesses that this may be Wyclif's *De insolubilibus*, or perhaps an introductory text attributed to Jerome in Prague, National Library, VIII F 16. I believe it to be a defense of Wyclif's brief *De logica*, a 22-chapter logic primer meant to introduce beginners to the main elements of scholastic logic.[34] Šimon begins by suggesting that his audience recall that Aristotle describes understanding in the *Sophistic Refutations* as being able to uncover lies, and refusing to lie about what one knows. The Bohemian people, he continues, is regarded throughout the world as heretical, and included in this accusation is this little book on introductory logic. "Oh, my little treatise, innocent and just, what have your persecutors and other prelates brought against you? Have you corrupted their ambitious pride?" "No," says the little treatise: "that is the work of *De civili dominio*." "Have you attempted to correct their insatiable greed?" "No, the yearly cycle of Sermons is meant to do that." "Have you demanded that the clergy embrace evangelical poverty?" "No, that is what is in the *Dialogue* and the *Trialogue*." At last the treatise speaks for itself:

> My defender, I ask that you not trouble yourself in these questions. I acknowledge my crime ... I touch upon nothing of which you accuse me. I am given to the innocent children most dear to me, with faces like lilies and roses, that they may know how to prove propositions, as my

---

32 Pavel Soukup, *Reformní kazatelství a Jakoubek ze Stříbra* (Prague: 2011), 14–9, 105–6.
33 Prague, Národní knihovna, VIII F 2, fols. 15r-21r.
34 Thomson, *The Latin Writings*, 305; see also Wyclif, *Iohannis Wyclif Tractatus De logica*, ed. Michael Henry Dziewicki (Wyclif's Latin Works) 21–3 (London: 1893–1899), vol. 1, 1–74.

introduction clearly states ... doubtless I have unjustly been sent innocent to this place of damnation and burning.[35]

Šimon finishes by wondering why the archbishop would bother having a logic primer burned and concludes that the best answer is most likely His Grace's ignorance.

Jan of Jičín's defense of *De materia et forma* on 30 July simply asks whether those who condemn Wyclif's works are to be believed. After all, they assert boldly that Wyclif burns in hell, and yet none of them can possibly be a witness to this; why then should anyone believe their testimony about his works? Prokop of Plzeň followed on the 31st with a defense of Wyclif's *De ideis*. Prokop also composed a brief treatise on Wyclif's doctrine of the divine ideas in which he examined the relation of contingency and necessity holding between eternal ideas and contingent creatures. He mentions Wyclif not at all in the treatise, but refers to as many other authorities as possible, including Aquinas, Scotus, Anselm, Grosseteste, Bacon, and even Seneca.[36] This suggests a date after the condemnation, and Herold believes it to have been 1411; he suggests that Prokop was engaged in disputation with Prokop of Kladrub on the same topic in 1417.[37] Prokop of Plzeň's defense returns to the scholastic mode, beginning by arguing that while wrong in some ideas, Wyclif's works are true in others. Why condemn someone for this? Otherwise, we would have to reject Aristotle, not to mention Averroes, Avicenna, and the writings of the rabbis. Prokop turns to an overview of Wyclif's treatise, which contains absolutely no heretical material and only explores a topic long respected by scholastics. If the treatise's persecutors understand this topic, then they must also be ready to condemn Augustine or Aquinas. If they do not understand it, they are fools condemning what they do not understand. If they do understand the divine ideas, and condemn the treatise, they blaspheme,

> for ideas and truths have a fourfold being, one real being in the divine mind, the other three in mental, created, spoken, and written signs. And because these who would condemn extend not only their mouths into heaven, but also their arms into the mind of God and to his ideas, the co-creators, and do not prevail in ripping their real being from the mind of

---

35 Loserth, *Hus und Wiclif*, 271–76. It is difficult to read this and not imagine Simon giving vent to his most theatrical impulses.
36 Prague, Národní knihovna, X E 24, fols. 150v-155r, see 153r.
37 Herold, *Pražská univerzita a Wyclif*, 142–43; Jaroslav Prokeš, *M. Prokop z Plzně. Příspěvek k vývoji konservativní strany husitské* (Prague: 1927) does not list X E 24 in his catalogue of Prokop's works.

God ... they prevent them from being spoken of, preached about, and burn them in written text. If an image of the crucifix were burned ... this would be blasphemy ... so by condemning these same divine reasons, their exemplary creators, to be burned in written form is the same contemptible blasphemy.[38]

Zdislav of Zvířetice finished the program on 6 August with a defense of *De universalibus*. Zdislav echoes Hus's opening argument, wondering whether all works that contain errors should be burned. Scripture is filled with people speaking falsely, calling Jesus a blasphemer and a fraud. Ought those to be burned? Or is it the position that is perilous? Are only Buridan and Ockham and their followers capable of sound philosophy? Would we throw away the strong learning grounded in the seven liberal arts that gives rise to Wyclif's criticisms in *De ipocritis* and *De attributis*? What profit is there from burning books? Knowledge of universals is the sure path to understanding the divine, and any who would turn readers from this path must advocate ignorance over understanding.[39]

5   Hus and the Church

Hus had been Wyclif's advocate from early on. He defended several condemned positions in a public disputation in August 1412: one on Wyclif's assertion that the only person capable of excommunicating someone is the person himself, that one may preach without permission of a bishop, that temporal lords may divest delinquent priests of their material goods, that tithing is only for alms-giving, and that no one is a civil lord or prelate or bishop who is in mortal sin.[40] Hus's *Sentences* Commentary also contains a recognizably Wycliffite position on the divine ideas, even if he adroitly steps past other areas in which he and Wyclif might have agreed with one another.[41] The most famous instance of the Hussite use of Wyclif's thought is Hus's appropriation of Wyclif's definition of the church as the community of the Elect. This definition

---

38   Loserth, *Hus und Wiclif*, 283–84.
39   Ibid., 285–89. The two works of Wyclif may be *De apostasia* and *De ente predicamentali*; he never wrote works with the titles Zdislav mentions.
40   Hus, *Polemica*, 141–232.
41   Jan Hus, *Super IV Sententiarum*, eds. Václav Flajšhans and Marie Komínková, 3 vols. (Spisy M. Jana Husi) 4–6 (Prague: 1904–1906); see also Stephen E. Lahey, "The *Sentences* Commentary of Jan Hus," in *A Companion to Jan Hus*, eds. Frantisek Šmahel and Ota Pavlíček (Brill's Companions to the Christian Tradition) 54 (Leiden and Boston: 2015), 130–69.

in itself is perfectly orthodox; Augustine had defined the church as those whom God eternally knows to be members of the Body of Christ. The difficulty comes in differentiating between those whom God eternally knows to be Elect and those who claim membership in the church. Augustine had been content to allow a veil to separate the class of people God knows, and those who believe themselves to be in the class God knows. After all, who can claim to know anyone as well as God knows them? So while the true church as God understands it may contain only the Elect, and the earthly institution we call the church may contain some whom God eternally knows to be damned, the faithful are expected to obey its leadership, trusting that Christ will guide his bride even if some within her are not truly of her.

Wyclif's interpretation of Augustine's doctrine was far less sanguine. While the church militant may have been largely free of the taint of the damned in the time of the Apostles, by now it was overcome with it. Hypocrisy, greed, and selfishness had flourished following the Donation of Constantine, and the church was shot through with corruption nurtured by those who would use its goods for their own ends. Wyclif was especially keen to probe into the moral laxity of the clergy, who were encouraged to use the power they had been given to their own ends by a papal monarchy that aped secular power. In Augustine's time, Donatus had claimed that the sacraments administered by errant clergy were invalid; Wyclif stopped just short of saying this, but elsewhere had argued that preaching and exemplifying the Gospel life was equal in salvific power to any sacrament.[42] So when he warned that clerics who were morally wanting ought not to be heeded when they preached, he was functionally a Donatist. This, at any rate, was the general reaction to his *De ecclesia*, both while he lived and at Constance.

The problem was that there was a certain truth to what Wyclif had been saying. Schoolmen and holy doctors had insisted throughout church history that clergy should embody Gospel truth and serve as moral exemplars for their flocks. Further, there had been an increasing tendency among theologians opposed to the *moderni* movement to read Augustine's doctrine of God's eternal foreknowledge to have a determinist effect on the nature of the church. Thomas Bradwardine had argued famously against the "semi-Pelagian" position of

---

42   John Wyclif, *Iohannis Wyclif Tractatus De ecclesia*, ed. Johann Loserth (Wyclif's Latin Works) 8 (London: 1886); idem, *Johannis de Wiclif Tractatus de officio pastorali*, ed. Gotthard Viktor Lechler (Leipzig: 1863). See Takashi Shogimen, "Wyclif's Ecclesiology and Political Thought," in *A Companion to John Wyclif*, ed. Levy, 199–240; Ian C. Levy, "John Wyclif and the Primitive Papacy," *Viator* 38 (2007): 159–89; Lahey, *John Wyclif*, 169–98. See also Wyclif, *Trialogus*, 320–59, which would have been Wyclif's treatment of the church most commonly read in Bohemia.

the *moderni*, holding that God alone determined who was saved and who was not. Wyclif had simply knit together the reformist tendencies lingering from Lateran IV and Archbishop Pecham with the theology of Bradwardine into an argument that nicely meshed with the preaching of Milíč of Kroměříž and Matěj of Janov in Bohemia. Street posters juxtaposing Christ and the pope soon appeared. One side showed Christ riding a humble donkey into Jerusalem, while on the other was a richly ornamented pope prancing about on a white stallion. The imagery was unmistakable: the divide between the body of the Elect and the false church could be identified by the hypocrisy of those who claimed authority in Christ's earthly body.

The canard that Hus had done little beyond plagiarizing Wyclif's *De ecclesia* in his own treatise of that name has long been laid to rest. De Vooght thought that Hus had shifted his position from a more conventional one to one resembling Wyclif later in his life, but Spinka and Fudge subsequently argued against this.[43] Hus embraced Wyclif's Augustinian definition of the church, but backed away from the functional Donatism that had come to be associated with Wyclif's version of it. He had already rejected Wyclif's eucharistic theology and was in the more traditional position of emphasizing the need for the sacraments while calling for the moral reform of the clergy, without implying that their morality affected the efficacy of the sacraments. Their morality had a bearing, though, on whether the laity might heed and obey their sermons and direction; in this, Hus agreed with Wyclif, although Hus did not cry for the secular power's correction of the clergy the way Wyclif did. Like Wyclif, Hus argued that a pope can be Antichrist, if by Antichrist we understand someone claiming Christ's mantle of authority whilst working against Christ's ends. Simply occupying an office does not make the occupant morally superior, and any occupant supposing otherwise is Antichrist.[44]

A good way to understand what was at issue in Hus's *De ecclesia* is to compare what he says to his chief critics in the period following October 1412, when Hus marshalled his arguments into the treatise we have now. He had been making his case since at least 1410, and by the summer of 1412 his erstwhile colleagues Stanislav and Páleč had each composed critiques of the general elements of Hus's position.[45] Hus spent the latter part of 1412 and early 1413

---

43   De Vooght, *L'hérésie de Jean Huss*; Spinka, *John Hus' Concept of the Church*; Fudge, *Jan Hus*.
44   Hus, *Tractatus de ecclesia*, 115.
45   Stanislav's short response to Hus on the Church, *Tractatus de Romana ecclesia* (Spunar 785), was edited by Sedlák, *Miscellanea*, 312–23. Páleč composed the treatise *De aequivocatione nominis ecclesia*: ibid., 356–65. The long *Tractatus de ecclesia* (*Contra hereses et errores Iohannis Hus*), dating to 1413–14, partly edited by Sedlák, *M. Jan Hus*, 202*-304*, was ascribed to Stanislav by Sousedík, "Stanislaus von Znaim," 56, and Spunar, *Repertorium*,

responding to these criticisms; the completed *De ecclesia* is half his own position and half his response to his critics. While Páleč was his chief critic, and each wrote additional criticisms of the other on the nature of the church, we will use Stanislav's shorter *De ecclesia* to highlight Hus's reliance on Wyclif.

Both Hus and his critics agree that the church is the body of the elect, and that it is more feasible to describe it as a body made of varying members. The disagreement lies in identifying body parts. Following Wyclif, Hus pointed out material in the body that is not really of the body, like phlegm, pus, and waste. This is how to understand the way God foreknows the damned: they may be present in the body now, but will be evacuated when the time comes.[46] Stanislav argues that there is simply no way for anyone to know who might be in the body but not of it, and warns that dwelling on such matters will only lead to further division and discontent. Gregory famously compared the church to a fishing boat, catching both edible and inedible fish in its nets, and carrying the whole catch back to port, where the fish are sorted for the market. Hus takes this as clear evidence that when the church reaches its goal, heaven, the evil will be cast away, even if it is mixed with the good now. To this, Stanislav responds that this does not mean that there are two churches now; the fish cannot recognize one another, and all make up one Catholic Church.[47] Hus describes the Elect as members of Christ's Body, while the damned are from Satan's body. The Body of Christ is mystical, while Satan's is hidden; nevertheless, the damned can be seen by God as foreknown, and have an internal deformity. This comparison, which Hus takes from Wyclif's *De ecclesia,* Chapter 18, would become popular in Tábor.[48]

A particularly important aspect of Hus's arguments in *De ecclesia* is his interpretation of obedience to clerical authority. Obedience to God's commands is every Christian's duty, and when he obeys a human law that countermands God's law, Hus declares, this is sin, and inadmissible.[49] Wyclif's position begins with the same identification of the priority of God's commands to human

---

vol. 1, no. 788; however, Páleč's authorship was proven by Sedlák, *Miscellanea*, 143–45, and Jiří Kejř, "Protihusovský traktát De ecclesia a jeho autor," in idem, *Z počátků české reformace* (Brno: 2006), 182–86.

46 Josef Macek, *Jan Hus. Studie s ukázkami z Husova díla* (Prague, 1961), 15; see Wyclif, "De fide catholica," in *Johannis Wyclif Opera minora*, ed. Johann Loserth (Wyclif's Latin Works) 34 (London: 1913), 112, for the distinction but not the analogy, which is suggested in Wyclif, *Tractatus de ecclesia*, 62 and again 75.

47 Macek, *Jan Hus*, 31; Stanislav of Znojmo, "Tractatus contra XLV articulos Joannis Wiclef," in *Magnum oecumenicum Constantiense concilium*, ed. Hermann von der Hardt, vol. 3 (Frankfurt and Leipzig: 1698), 316.

48 See Wyclif, *De ecclesia*, 424.

49 Macek, *Jan Hus*, 152.

commands. We must obey a human command that embodies a divine command, but what of a command that runs against God's commands? Since it is Luciferian pride to put one's own will above God's, resistance of such a command is meritorious.[50] But there is a difference between the merit that follows resistance of an unjust command and holding that obedience of such a command is sinful. Wyclif's discussion of the duty of Christians to obey just commands in *De officio regis* arises from his arguments against excommunication. A papal command of excommunication is not in itself just but can be just only when the subject of the command has already excommunicated himself. Therefore, resisting a papal command that someone be excommunicated can indeed be meritorious, if the subject has not excommunicated himself. But Wyclif does not say that obeying such a command is sinful; an unjust excommunication is really nothing but a false assertion and has no jussive force. Wyclif then explores five ways one might consent to a command that runs against God's commands and holds that only voluntary cooperation with such a command is sinful. But not all obedience need be voluntary, and the moral value of obedience arises from the will of the one obeying. Someone who is compelled to obey an evil command, Wyclif argues, does not sin thereby.[51]

Stanislav is well aware of this distinction, which Aquinas delineates in *Summa theologiae* (IIa IIae, Q. 104, a. 5). If a priest commands something that is forbidden, say if he gives a layman a sum of money and tells him to do something with it, the layman is obliged to consider whether the sum is the priest's to give. If it is not, the layman is bound to point this out to the priest. If the priest insists, the subject is not bound to obey, but the priest does not thereby lose his authority to give commands.[52] If the layman is coerced, his obedience is not thereby to be held against him. This distinction is particularly important given Hus's later behavior at Constance; he held that, given the council's claim to authority that it did not have, its command that he recant was unlawful, and that to obey it would be sinful. Had he recognized what Wyclif and Stanislav both had argued, he could easily have escaped death by proclaiming that his obedience was coerced.[53]

---

50   John Wyclif, *Iohannis Wyclif Tractatus De officio regis*, eds. Alfred W. Pollard and Charles Sayle (Wyclif's Latin Works) 15 (London: 1887), 234.
51   Ibid., 89–104.
52   Stanislav of Znojmo, "Tractatus contra XLV articulos Joannis Wiclef," 320–21.
53   See Fudge, *The Trial of Jan Hus*, 310.

6   Biskupec and Wyclif

Wyclif had ceased to be the main focus of debate when Hus was forced to flee Prague in 1412. The ideology of the revolution was now in the hands of the Bohemians, and while not forgotten, Wyclif had become relevant largely as an authoritative source to support Czech ideas. One of the last figures to conceive of Wyclif as more than this was Mikuláš of Pelhřimov, known as Biskupec, the leading theologian of Tábor.[54] For Mikuláš, Wyclif provided the model for a Christian state that would withstand the fiery trials of war with Antichrist, and Hus had been his worthy acolyte. The Taborite ideology is discussed elsewhere in this volume; here we will explore the role Wyclif played in Biskupec's writings. It is worth remembering that by 1421, Biskupec's opponents in Prague, notably Jan Příbram and Jan Rokycana, were already equating what they viewed as Tábor's impossible quest for a recovery of the primitive church with Wyclif's errors. This is telling; as the endless squabbling that defined the relations between Prague and Tábor continued, the Prague masters increasingly distanced themselves from Wyclif while Biskupec and Peter Payne stood by their master.[55]

Aside from the sermons and formal addresses he gave in defence of Tábor, Biskupec wrote four major works. He articulated Tábor's theology in the 1431 *Confessio Taboritarum*, and chronicled its history in the *Chronicon Taboritarum* (1434–1444), two of the chief resources for understanding Tábor's history.[56] He compiled two Scripture commentaries, one on the Apocalypse of John, and the

---

[54]   For Biskupec in Czech, see František Michálek Bartoš, *Mikuláš z Pehřimova* (Tábor: 1939); Bohuslav Souček, "*Veritas super omnia*. Z biblických studií a odkazu Mikuláše Biskupce z Pelhřimova," *Theologická příloha Křesťanské revue* 28 (1961): 73–90. In English, see Howard Kaminsky, "The Religion of Hussite Tábor," in *The Czechoslovak Contribution to World Culture*, ed. Miloslav Rechcígl (London: 1964), 210–33; idem, "Nicholas of Pelhřimov's Tabor. An Adventure into the Eschaton," in *Eschatologie und Hussitismus*, eds. Alexander Patschovsky and František Šmahel (Prague: 1996), 139–67; Thomas A. Fudge, "Crime, Punishment and Pacifism in the Thought of Bishop Mikuláš of Pelhřimov, 1420–1452," in *The Bohemian Reformation,* eds. David and Holeton, vol. 3 (Prague: 2000), 69–102. See also Erhard Peschke, "Zur Theologie des Taboriten Nikolaus von Pilgram," *Wissenschaftliche Zeitschrift der Universität Halle-Wittenberg* 19 (1970): 153–70; Paul De Vooght, "Nicolas Biskupec de Pelhřimov et son apport á l'évolution de la méthodologie théologique hussite," *Recherches de théologie ancienne et médiévale* 40 (1973): 175–207.

[55]   Mikuláš Biskupec of Pelhřimov, "Chronicon Taboritarum," in *Geschichtschreiber der husitischen Bewegung in Böhmen*, ed. Konstantin Höfler, vol. 2 (Fontes rerum Austriacarum, 1. Abteilung: Scriptores) 6 (Vienna: 1865), 590–96.

[56]   Idem, *Confessio Taboritarum*, eds. Amedeo Molnár and Romolo Cegna (Rome: 1983); idem, "Chronicon Taboritarum."

other on the Harmony of the Four Gospels.[57] In each of these, Wyclif's spirit dominates. In the *Confessio*, Wyclif's works are cited more often than any other authority, save Scripture itself. In the *Chronicon*, he details every instance of his or Peter Payne's defense of the works and ideals of Wyclif against the criticisms of Prague and Rome. In the Scripture commentaries, Wyclif features importantly in both. Biskupec prepared the Gospels commentary with an eye to the preacher, collecting brief selections from authoritative commentators for each pericope. His taste in commentary is Wyclif's: we find citations from Augustine, Origen, the *Opus imperfectum*, Nicholas of Lyra, and of Wyclif himself. Of other contemporary commentators, though, there is not a trace.

The best place to find Biskupec's appropriation of Wyclif's arguments is in the *Confessio*, which is both a summary of Tábor's theology as of 1430 (Chapters 1–22) and a refutation of Rokycana's criticisms of Tábor of 1431 (Chapters 22–51.) The first section has five parts: eight suppositions forming the foundation of Taborite theology, a survey of the seven sacraments, a section on liturgy, and a section each on purgatory and the practice of praying to the saints. Our purposes will be served best by an overview of the first two sections.

The first of the eight suppositions holds Christ to be the supreme legislator, defining justice in his Gospels. Thus the Gospel law is alone sufficient for governing the church, "since in its perfect execution it teaches most properly how all injustice should be extirpated from the republic, and how those offending against the law should be castigated, and how all Christian justice should be fostered and rewarded."[58] While this is consonant with the Prague article that mortal sins and laws opposed to God's laws are to be exposed and punished, the stipulation that Christ's law is sufficient for the governance of the church is a departure from the standard Hussite position that laws governing the church should be consonant with the Gospels. Wyclif's position was somewhere in between the two. Had private property not been introduced into the church, Wyclif believed that the law of the Gospel would have been sufficient for governing it, because it is the perfect exemplar for any moral code.[59] The true church, for Wyclif, is like a house whose foundation is eternal and whose walls

---

57   Vienna, Österreichische Nationalbibliothek, 4520 contains the Apocalypse commentary up to Rev. 18:5; Prague, Knihovna Národního muzea, XIII F 7 contains the Gospel Harmony in three codices. Kaminsky reports Souček's attempts at an edition of the former between 1939 and 1959, and Pavlína Cermanová is engaged in this project as well. There is no edition of the Gospel commentary.

58   Mikuláš Biskupec, *Confessio Taboritarum*, 69, 3–5.

59   *John Wyclif's De veritate Sacrae scripturae*, ed. Rudolf Buddensieg (Wyclif's Latin Works) 29–31 (London: 1905–1907), vol. 2, 142–44; see *On the Truth of Holy Scripture*, trans. Ian C. Levy (Kalamazoo: 2001), 272–73. Also, *Johannis Wyclif Tractatus De mandatis divinis*.

are made of stones, each stone a law of Moses. Its roof is the law of love and grace, embodied in the law of the Gospels, and both walls and roof are in a continual state of construction. When they are completed, Christ's law will be complete, and time will end.[60] While Wyclif has little time for manmade laws, he does not see the church as being in a position to be governed solely by the laws of Christ. This, his analogy for the stone house suggests, will be possible when time ends. Until then, Wyclif holds that human laws are best tolerated in the church for their utility, even if they fall short of the ideal of Christ's law. "The church would be better ruled purely by the law of the Lord as such, or with human laws added on to the law of God … [I]n the antichristian heresy, it appears that the law of God is not in itself sufficient nor equally sufficient as are human laws for stamping out injustices that crop up in the church …"[61]

Regarding Christian belief, Biskupec continues, only those things to be found in Scripture, or deducible from it, should be articles of faith. This is certainly commensurate with Wyclif's arguments with fellow theologians, whom Wyclif accuses of allowing their science to creep into their preaching, edging aside scriptural truths.[62] When the pope speaks, he is to be believed only if his words agree with Scripture, and to follow any man rather than Scripture is the very definition of blasphemy.[63] The teachings of the holy doctors and church fathers have their place, though; insofar as they further Christian teachings and what they say is grounded in the Gospels, they are beneficial for learning how to live. Sometimes, though, what they say can wander from the certainty we find in Scripture, in which case we must remember that they are only giving their opinions.[64]

The remaining four suppositions address Christian ritual and the sacraments. The veneration of the consecrated host was a well-established practice, and Biskupec admits that there was a time when having a perceptible sign for the people's instruction was useful. Still, this, or any, image of Christ, should have a lesser place in the Christian life than it does in contemporary Christian

---

Tratatus De statu innocencie, eds. Johann Loserth and F.D. Matthew (Wyclif's Latin Works) 35 (London: 1922)., 29.

60 Wyclif, *De mandatis divinis*, 48.
61 Wyclif, *De potestate pape*, 339.
62 Wyclif, *De veritate Sacrae scripturae*, vol. 2, 375–90; see Wyclif, *On the Truth of Holy Scripture*, 197–205.
63 *Iohannis Wyclif Tractatus De blasphemia*, ed. Michael Henry Dziewicki (Wyclif's Latin Works) 20 (London: 1893), 44.
64 *Iohannis Wyclif Tractatus De apostasia*, ed. Michael Henry Dziewicki (Wyclif's Latin Works) 16 (London: 1889), 221; Biskupec quotes Wyclif here: see Mikuláš Biskupec, *Confessio Taboritarum*, 69.

culture, and should only be used to instruct the faithful in the law of Christ. All the other human inventions that have cropped up after the time of the early church, Biskupec continues, are neither appropriate nor permissible. The sixth supposition stops there, leaving an opening for every sort of objection that can be made against representation or imagery and their use in worship, including clerical vestments, veneration of relics, or even conceiving of the church building itself as somehow sacred. This sentiment runs throughout Wyclif's thought; for example, he suggests that the stones of the church might well be used to strengthen the castle walls in times of national peril.[65] Priests who dispense with these things, Biskupec concludes, all other things being equal, do not sin.

The final supposition amplifies the universal applicability of the Gospel law for salvation regarding the sacraments. If a sacrament is expressly enjoined in the Gospel, it is necessary; but ritual introduced over the centuries should be recognized as invented, and not necessary. This leads to the second part of the first section of the *Confessio*, the analysis of the sacraments, which follows Wyclif's survey in *Trialogus* IV. Eucharist and baptism are certainly necessary and are commanded for all Christians in the Gospels. But the other five have only partial utility and are nowhere said to be necessary for salvation. Confirmation is nowhere in Scripture, and Biskupec stops just short of counselling that it be dropped altogether.[66] Confession and penitence are likewise prefigured in the Gospels, but not enjoined; John of God holds that Innocent III invented auricular confession, which means it is unnecessary for salvation.[67] Holy orders and matrimony are both mentioned in Scripture, but nowhere are they deemed to be sure means whereby one might receive salvific grace.[68]

These positions were very far from the Prague masters, and from Hus himself. De Vooght notes that Biskupec plunges headlong into a literal reading of Scripture, thereby eliminating any sense of nuance in his analysis of the relation of Holy Writ to sacramental theology.[69] Peschke is slightly more forgiving, attributing to Biskupec the recognition that a simple reading of Scripture will lead to confusion; one must search diligently for the sense of the law of the Gospel, always avoiding the possibility that one's understanding of one part of

---

65   Wyclif, *De officio regis*, 185.
66   He cites *Trialogus*, lib. 4, cap. 14, and *Opus evangelicum*, lib. 3, cap. 13; see Mikuláš Biskupec, *Confessio Taboritarum*, 179–82.
67   Wyclif makes this point in *Trialogus*, lib. 4, cap. 23, and also in "De eucharistia et poenitentia" in idem, *Iohannis Wyclif De eucharistia tractatus maior*, ed. Johann Loserth (Wyclif's Latin Works) 18 (London: 1892), 331.
68   *Trialogus*, lib. 4, cap. 4–5, 20, cited by Mikuláš Biskupec, *Confessio Taboritarum*, 83–4.
69   De Vooght, "Nicolas Biskupec de Pelhřimov," 205.

Scripture will conflict with another part.[70] The four Latin doctors, Augustine, Jerome, Ambrose, and Gregory, serve one well in piecing together the coherence and total applicability of Scripture to the Christian life, as Biskupec's massive Gospel commentary shows. This follows Wyclif's instructions to preachers of the Gospel to learn what he called the "logic of Christ," which he teaches in the first eight chapters of *De veritate Sacrae scripturae*. It seems that Biskupec believed himself to be Wyclif's best advocate in Bohemia, vigorously championing his master's positions against the almost continuous compromise with what he viewed as Antichrist.

The two areas in which Biskupec departed from Wyclif were the chiliastic view of history and the need for violent opposition to the enemies of Christ. Biskupec appears to have been convinced that the end of history was at hand, and conceived of Tábor as the vehicle by which Christ would begin to establish his new kingdom.[71] The consequence of this appears to have been Biskupec's growing self-conception as being above the need to restrict himself to rational consistency in his arguments, which made him an impossible person in a formal dispute. Rokycana once called Biskupec out for misusing Scripture, to which Biskupec is reported as having responded, "I take what I need."[72] The other important divergence from Wyclif was his willingness to countenance violence in effecting Taborite ends. This he articulated most clearly in his defense of the public punishment of sinners at the Council of Basel on 20–21 January 1433. He argues zealously for the need of every Christian to be continually on the lookout for his neighbors' misdeeds, and that their punishment be both public and harsh. He warns that the danger of sin is so terrible that its mere presence in a society is so toxic as to pervert all citizens, and argues that civil lords and priests who grow lax in their vigilance, or soft in their correction, may justly be overthrown by the laity.[73] This goes far beyond Wyclif, who not only refused to countenance the common correction of civil lords, but also left the correction of the clergy to the nobility. Further, it has recently been argued that Wyclif was a determined pacifist, and so would have been horrified by Tábor's readiness to translate Biskupec's arguments onto a national scale.[74]

---

70 Peschke, "Zur Theologie des Taboriten Nikolaus von Pilgram," 156–57.
71 Kaminsky, "Nicholas of Pelhřimov's Tabor," 144.
72 Kaminsky, "The Religion of Hussite Tábor," 215.
73 Mikuláš Biskupec, "Oratio pro Bohemorum articulo de peccatis publicis puniendis," in *Orationes, quibus Nicolaus de Pelhřimov, Taboritarum episcopus, et Ulricus de Znojmo, Orphanorum sacerdos, articulos de peccatis publicis puniendis et libertate verbi Dei in concilio Basiliensi anno 1433 ineunte defenderunt*, ed. František Michálek Bartoš (Tábor: 1935), 3–32.
74 See Rory Cox, *John Wyclif on War and Peace* (London: 2014).

7 Peter Payne, the English Hussite

Among the most remarkable of the leading Hussites, at least for Anglophone scholars, is Peter Payne (c. 1380–1456). Payne was born at Hough on the Hill in Lincolnshire, and began studies at Oxford in the late 1390s, where he quickly became captivated by Wyclif's thought.[75] Payne may have been responsible for stealing Oxford's seal to affix to a letter attesting to Wyclif's orthodoxy, which later led to some controversy after Mikuláš Faulfiš and Jiří of Kněhnice likely brought it back with them to Prague after a visit in 1407. Eventually, he could remain at Oxford no longer, and found his way to Prague in 1414, shortly after Hus had left for Constance. He entered into the defense of Wyclif with great zeal, and soon became known as one of the most articulate and philosophically adept advocates of the Bohemian Wycliffite cause. He appears to have written four pieces during this period: *De iuramento*, against taking oaths, *De imaginibus*, endorsing Wyclif's position on the veneration of statues and icons, and two treatises on predestination, *De predestinacione* and *De necessitate absoluta evenientium*.[76] Payne's interest in the latter two treatises is in showing how to avoid the determinism associated with the doctrine of divine omniscience that was increasingly causing Wyclif's critics to accuse his supporters of double predestination. In these, he explains the relation of the absolute necessity with which God understands all created events to the contingency inherent in human decision making, a theme fully developed in Wyclif's *De universalibus*, and discussed in briefer terms in Stanislav's *De universalibus*, Chapter 17. It is possible that Stanislav's defection had led to a decrease in interest in his description of Wyclif's thought by 1413–1417, the period in which he wrote these treatises.

Payne then became increasingly active in Hussite delegations meeting to debate internal politics, especially taking up the side of Tábor against Prague. He actively defended the Hussite position through the 1420s and went on to

---

[75] See František Šmahel, "Peter Payne," in *Oxford Dictionary of National Biography*, vol. 43 (Oxford: 2004), 208–13; S.H. Thomson, "A Note on Peter Payne and Wyclyf," *Medievalia et Humanistica* 16 (1964): 60–4; R.R. Betts, "Peter Payne in England," in idem, *Essays in Czech History* (London: 1969), 236–46. For a catalogue of his works, see František Michálek Bartoš, *Literární činnost M. Jana Rokycany, M. Jana Příbama, M. Petra Payna* (Prague: 1928), 90–113.

[76] *De imaginibus* in Prague, Národní knihovna, X E 9, fols. 210v-214r, see Jana Nechutová, "Traktát De ymaginibus připisovaný Petru Paynovi," *Husitský Tábor* 9 (1987): 325–35; *De iuramento* in Prague, Národní knihovna, V F 2, fols. 88r-94v; *De predestinacione* in Prague, Národní knihovna, V G 15, fols. 16r-21r; *De necessitate absoluta evenientium* in Prague, Národní knihovna, V F 9, fols. 68r-75r.

serve in the Hussite embassy with the Polish court, and finally, to represent the Hussites at Basel in 1433. His performance at Basel shows the extent to which he had incorporated Wyclif's thought into his defense of the Hussites. Payne's defense, and his response to his disputant, Juan Palomar, Archdeacon of Barcelona, is indicative of his brazen willingness to twist facts to suit his purposes.[77] He began by explaining that Henry of Ghent and Thomas Aquinas had defined possession as secular, evangelical, or heavenly, intimating that these authorities were reasonable starting points for his argument that none of the clergy should have any civil dominion whatsoever. Henry would defend the clergy's possession of temporal goods in the section Payne cites (*Quodlibet* VIII), and the section of the *Summa theologiae* (Ia, Q.10, a.1; IIa IIae, Q.36, a.2) he cites refers not at all to the topic. This is of no matter, though, for the issue is dominion, which entails both *proprietas* and *iurisdictio*. Several definitions are possible: Richard Fitzralph's from *De pauperie Salvatoris* (book IV, Chapter 3) suggests that dominion is a power of a mortal creature, while somebody else says that it is a relative *habitus*; the latter, he reflects, is substantially better, because a power is something that can be granted or bestowed, while a *habitus* is developed. Fitzralph's definition actually rejects the idea that dominion is a power; Payne is simply excising what he needs from Armachanus to suit his argument.[78] The other definition is much more to the point; Payne does not mention that he derives it from Wyclif's *De civili dominio*.[79] Later in his defense, he cites Fitzralph again to suggest that all clergy, in following Christ, must absolutely renounce all civil ownership or authority just as they vow to remain chaste, not to return evil for evil and to follow Christ in the example of his life. This, he explains, is from *De pauperie* (book VI, Chapter 34). In fact, what he lifts from Armachanus is a position he distinctly rejects, which he begins by saying in effect: "I suppose one might say ... but I've never found it in Scripture."[80]

When Payne responded to Juan Palomar, he cuttingly described his opponent as warping and twisting Hugh of Saint-Victor's words to suit his ends, intimating that this is precisely the sort of dishonesty to be expected from priests scrambling to preserve their ill-gotten and unjustly held civil lordship. He then

---

77 *Petri Payne Anglici Positio, replica et propositio in concilio Basiliensi a. 1433 atque oratio ad Sigismundum regem a. 1429 Bratislaviae pronunciatae. Peter Payne pro Bohemis*, ed. František Michálek Bartoš (Tábor: 1949), 1–78.
78 See Richard Fitzralph, *De pauperie Salvatoris* IV, cap. 3, in Wyclif, *De dominio divino*, 440.
79 See Wyclif, *De civili dominio*, 178.
80 R.O. Brock, *An edition of Richard Fitzralph's De Pauperie Salvatoris books V, VI, and VII* (Ph.D. dissertation, University of Colorado: 1954), in preparation for digitization.

goes on to reiterate the coherence of Fitzralph's arguments for divesting the clergy of this civil lordship, boldly citing positions that Fitzralph mentions only to reject, all the while advancing Wyclif's arguments.[81] It is certain, though, that his auditors at Basel were not even slightly fooled by Payne's tactics. That November, a delegation from Basel went to Prague, where they arranged a compromise position on the four articles. As to the fourth, the record of the agreement contains a large chunk of language that Fitzralph had used, but that Payne had glossed over, in his arguments, suggesting that someone had been following Payne's arguments with a copy of Fitzralph's work ready to hand, and easily distinguished between Armachanus and Wyclif.[82]

Payne was not finished with Wyclif after 1433. Even after the battle of Lipany in 1434, when Tábor and radical Hussitism ceased to be a political power, Payne represented Wycliffism in disputes with more conservative Hussites. He remained active in Bohemian politics for another twenty years thereafter, although his Wycliffism increasingly led to him being seen as anachronistic. Among the works connected to him is a large index to the works of Wyclif, in which he is listed as compiler of about fifteen sets of indices to Wyclif's Latin works. Many scholars have accepted the ascribed attribution to Payne, but recently Anne Hudson has pointed out the likelihood that these attributions are copiers' guesses, rather than reliable evidence.[83] With Payne's death in 1456, though, we can be certain that Bohemia had lost its final great advocate of Wycliffism.

8 Historiographic Survey

While 15th-century sources such as Netter's *Doctrinale* had associated Wyclif with Hussitism, it was Johann Loserth's now infamous 1884 monograph *Hus und Wiclif* which argued that Hus had done nothing more than plagiarize Wyclif that sparked modern scholarly interest in studying the role Wyclif played in the Hussite movement. The Wyclif Society had begun publishing modern editions of Wyclif's Latin works in the late 19th century, instilling interest in

---

81 For subsequent confusion of Wyclif and Fitzralph, see Stephen E. Lahey, "Richard Fitzralph and John Wyclif. Untangling Armachanus from the Wycliffites," in *Richard Fitzralph. His Life, Times and Thought*, eds. Michael Dunne and Simon Nolan (Dublin: 2013), 159–85.

82 František Palacký and Ernst Birk (eds.), *Monumenta conciliorum generalium seculi decimi quinti. Concilium Basileense*, Scriptores: vol. 1 (Vienna: 1857), 490–91.

83 Anne Hudson, "*Accessus ad auctorem*. The Case of John Wyclif," *Viator* 30 (1999), 323–44.

Wyclif as a theologian. While Palacký had begun editing documents concerning Hus in 1869,[84] the work of assessing and analyzing Hussite theology owes much to F.M. Bartoš, whose catalogues of the works of Jakoubek, Hus, Rokycana, Příbram, and Payne,[85] among many others, defined Czech scholarship on Hussite thought well into the second half of the 20th century. Otakar Odložilík likewise wrote influential essays on the role Wyclif played in Bohemia,[86] but the dominant figure for the second half of the 20th century, and as of this writing, is František Šmahel, who, in addition to composing the magisterial three-volume narrative of the Hussite movement, has contributed dramatically to our understanding of the Prague University reception of Wyclif in numerous articles and other works.[87] Had his monograph survived the Blitz, R.R. Betts would be remembered today for revolutionizing Anglophone understanding of the relation of Wyclif to Hussite thought; as it stands, his collected articles show a nuanced mid-20th-century understanding of the complexity of the relationship.[88] For Anglophone readers, Howard Kaminsky remains unequalled in his description of the relation of Wyclif to the genesis of Hussitism; his 1967 *A History of the Hussite Revolution*, and his landmark article "Wycliffism as Ideology of Revolution," remain indispensable. For understanding the role that Wycliffite literature played in Hussitism, Michael Van Dussen's *From England to Bohemia* and Anne Hudson's collected articles in her *Studies in the Transmission of Wyclif's Writings* are likewise necessary points of departure.

Vilém Herold's *Pražská univerzita a Wyclif* remains the most important scholarly engagement with Wyclif's philosophy and its impact on philosophical thought in Prague. More recently, Ota Pavlíček has engaged with Jerome of Prague's philosophical *quaestiones*.[89] Martin Dekarli has likewise begun to publish analysis of the use Bohemian thinkers made of Wyclif's logic and metaphysics.[90] As students of Herold, both scholars are likely to build on his

---

84 *Documenta Mag. Joannis Hus*.
85 *Literární činnost M. Jana Rokycany, M. Jana Příbrama, M. Petra Payna*.
86 Otakar Odložilík, *Wyclif and Bohemia. Two Essays* (Prague: 1937).
87 See *Die Hussitische Revolution* and the items listed in the bibliography below.
88 R.R. Betts, *Essays in Czech History* (London: 1969).
89 Ota Pavlíček "Wyclif's Early Reception in Bohemia and His Influence on the Thought of Jerome of Prague," in *Europe after Wyclif*, eds. J. Patrick Hornbeck II and Michael Van Dussen (New York: 2017), 89–114.
90 See, for example, his "Prague Nominalist Master John Arsen of Langenfeld and His Quaestio on Ideas from Around 1394/1399," in *The Bohemian Reformation*, eds. David and Holeton, vol. 9 (Prague: 2014), 35–53.

foundation. Thomas Fudge has recently published the first English-language study of Jerome of Prague,[91] thereby introducing a figure on which incredibly little has been written in English. The recent edition of Jerome's collected works prepared by František Šmahel and Gabriel Silagi, and containing Šmahel's thorough biographical introduction in German,[92] represent a solid foundation for any further research into Jerome. Also recently, a Bohemian commentary on Wyclif's *De universalibus*, ascribed to Štěpán Páleč, has been edited by Ivan Müller.[93] Stanislav of Znojmo and Štěpán Páleč nevertheless remain relatively unknown outside a small circle of scholars, despite the Wyclif Society's publication of Stanislav's *De universalibus tractatus maior* in 1905.[94] I hope to establish this treatise's importance in the understanding of Wyclif's metaphysical realism in the coming years.

Bibliography

Manuscripts

Prague, Národní knihovna České republiky [National Library of the Czech Republic], V F 2.

Prague, Národní knihovna České republiky [National Library of the Czech Republic], V F 9.

Prague, Národní knihovna České republiky [National Library of the Czech Republic], V G 15.

Prague, Národní knihovna České republiky [National Library of the Czech Republic], VIII F 2.

Prague, Národní knihovna České republiky [National Library of the Czech Republic], X E 9.

Prague, Národní knihovna České republiky [National Library of the Czech Republic], X E 24.

Prague, Národní knihovna České republiky [National Library of the Czech Republic], XIII F 7.

Vienna, Österreichische Nationalbibliothek, 4520.

---

91 *Jerome of Prague.*
92 Jerome of Prague, *Quaestiones, polemica, epistulae.*
93 Páleč, *Commentarius.*
94 "Tractatus contra XLV articulos Joannis Wiclef."

Editions of Sources

Höfler, Konstantin (ed.), *Geschichtschreiber der husitischen Bewegung in Böhmen*, 3 vols. (Fontes rerum Austriacarum, 1. Abteilung: Scriptores) 2, 6, and 7 (Vienna: 1856–1866).

Hus, Jan, *Super IV Sententiarum*, eds. Václav Flajšhans and Marie Komínková, 3 vols. (Spisy M. Jana Husi) 4–6 (Prague: 1904–1906).

Hus, Jan, *Magistri Johannis Hus Tractatus de ecclesia*, ed. S. Harrison Thomson (Cambridge, Eng., and Boulder, CO.: 1956; repr. Prague: 1958).

Hus, Jan, *Magistri Iohannis Hus Polemica*, ed. Jaroslav Eršil (Magistri Iohannis Hus Opera omnia) 22 (Prague: 1966) (Corpus christianorum. Continuatio mediaevalis) 238 (2nd ed. Turnhout: 2010).

Jerome of Prague, *Magistri Hieronymi de Praga Quaestiones, polemica, epistulae*, ed. František Šmahel and Gabriel Silagi (Corpus christianorum. Continuatio mediaevalis) 222 (Turnhout: 2010).

Juan Palomar, "Oratio," in *Sacrorum conciliorum nova et amplissima collectio*, ed. Joannes Dominicus Mansi, vol. 29 (Venice: 1788), 1105–1168.

Matěj of Janov, *Regulae Veteris et Novi Testamenti*, vols. 1–4, ed. Vlastimil Kybal (Innsbruck: 1908–1913); vol. 5, eds. Vlastimil Kybal and Otakar Odložilík (Prague: 1913); vol. 6, eds. Jana Nechutová and Helena Krmíčková (Munich: 1993).

Mikuláš Biskupec of Pelhřimov, "Chronicon Taboritarum," in *Geschichtschreiber der husitischen Bewegung in Böhmen*, ed. Konstantin Höfler, vol. 2 (Fontes rerum Austriacarum, 1. Abteilung: Scriptores) 6 (Vienna: 1865), 475–820.

Mikuláš Biskupec of Pelhřimov, "Oratio pro Bohemorum articulo de peccatis publicis puniendis," in *Orationes, quibus Nicolaus de Pelhřimov, Taboritarum episcopus, et Ulricus de Znojmo, Orphanorum sacerdos, articulos de peccatis publicis puniendis et libertate verbi Dei in concilio Basiliensi anno 1433 ineunte defenderunt*, ed. František Michálek Bartoš (Tábor: 1935), 3–32.

Mikuláš Biskupec of Pelhřimov, *Confessio Taboritarum*, eds. Amedeo Molnár and Romolo Cegna (Rome: 1983).

Palacký, František (ed.), *Documenta Mag. Joannis Hus vitam, doctrinam, causam in Constantiensi concilio actam et controversias de religione in Bohemia annis 1408–1413 motas illustrantia* (Prague: 1869).

Palacký, František, and Ernst Birk (eds.), *Monumenta conciliorum generalium seculi decimi quinti. Concilium Basileense*, Scriptores: vol. 1 (Vienna: 1857).

Páleč, Štěpán, *Commentarius in I–IX capitula tractatus De universalibus Iohannis Wyclif Stephano de Palecz ascriptus*, ed. Ivan Müller (Prague: 2009).

Payne, Peter, *Petri Payne Anglici Positio, replica et propositio in concilio Basiliensi a. 1433 atque oratio ad Sigismundum regem a. 1429 Bratislaviae pronunciatae. Peter Payne pro Bohemis*, ed. František Michálek Bartoš (Tábor: 1949).

Stanislav of Znojmo, "Tractatus contra XLV articulos Joannis Wiclef," in *Magnum oecumenicum Constantiense concilium*, ed. Hermann von der Hardt, vol. 3 (Frankfurt and Leipzig: 1698), 212–335.

Stanislav of Znojmo, "Tractatus de universalibus (maior)," in *Johannis Wyclif Miscellanea philosophica*, ed. Michael Henry Dziewicki (Wyclif's Latin Works) 28 (London: 1905), vol. 2, 1–151.

Stanislav of Znojmo, "Tractatus de Romana ecclesia," ed. Jan Sedlák, *Hlídka* 28, 11–12 (1911): appendix, 83–95; repr. Jan Sedlák, *Miscellanea husitica Ioannis Sedlák*, eds. Jaroslav V. Polc and Stanislav Přibyl (Prague: 1996), 312–322.

Stanislav of Znojmo, "Alma et venerabilis," ed. Johann Loserth, "Beiträge zur Geschichte der husitischen Bewegung 4. Die Streitschriften und Unionsverhandlungen zwischen den Katholiken und Husiten in den Jahren 1412 und 1413," *Archiv für österreichische Geschichte* 75 (1889): 361–413.

Stanislav of Znojmo, *Mistra Stanislava ze Znojma De vero et falso*, ed. Vilém Herold (Prague: 1971).

Stanislav of Znojmo, *Stanislaus de Znoyma: De gracia et peccato*, ed. Zuzana Silagiová (Fontes Latini Bohemorum) 1 (Prague: 1997).

Wyclif, John, *Iohannis Wyclif Tractatus De ecclesia*, ed. Johann Loserth (Wyclif's Latin Works) 8 (London: 1886).

Wyclif, John, *Johannis de Wiclif Tractatus de officio pastorali*, ed. Gotthard Viktor Lechler (Leipzig: 1863).

Wyclif, John, *Iohannis Wyclif De civili dominio*, ed. Johann Loserth, 4 vols. (Wyclif's Latin Works) 3–6 (London: 1885–1904).

Wyclif, John, *Iohannis Wyclif Tractatus De officio regis*, eds. Alfred W. Pollard and Charles Sayle (Wyclif's Latin Works) 15 (London: 1887).

Wyclif, John, *Iohannis Wyclif Tractatus De apostasia*, ed. Michael Henry Dziewicki (Wyclif's Latin Works) 16 (London: 1889).

Wyclif, John, *Iohannis Wycliffe De dominio divino*, ed. Reginald Lane Poole (Wyclif's Latin Works) 17 (London: 1890).

Wyclif, John, *Iohannis Wyclif De eucharistia tractatus maior*, ed. Johann Loserth (Wyclif's Latin Works) 18 (London: 1892).

Wyclif, John, *Iohannis Wyclif Tractatus De blasphemia*, ed. Michael Henry Dziewicki (Wyclif's Latin Works) 20 (London: 1893).

Wyclif, John, *Iohannis Wyclif Tractatus De logica*, ed. Michael Henry Dziewicki, 3 vols. (Wyclif's Latin Works) 21–23 (London: 1893–1899).

Wyclif, John, *Johannis Wyclif Tractatus De potestate pape*, ed. Johann Loserth (Wyclif's Latin Works) 32 (London: 1907).

Wyclif, John, *John Wyclif's De veritate Sacrae scripturae*, ed. Rudolf Buddensieg, 3 vols. (Wyclif's Latin Works) 29–31 (London: 1905–1907).

Wyclif, John, *Johannis Wyclif Opera minora*, ed. Johann Loserth (Wyclif's Latin Works) 34 (London: 1913).

Wyclif, John, *Johannis Wyclif Tractatus De mandatis divinis. Tratatus De statu innocencie*, eds. Johann Loserth and F.D. Matthew (Wyclif's Latin Works) 35 (London: 1922).

Wyclif, John, *On the Truth of Holy Scripture*, trans. Ian C. Levy (Kalamazoo: 2001).

Wyclif, John, *Trialogus*, trans. Stephen E. Lahey (Cambridge: 2013).

Wyclif, John, *De ideis*, eds. Vilém Herold and Ivan Müller (Auctores Britannici Medii Aevi) (Oxford: forthcoming).

Secondary Sources

Bartoš, František Michálek, *Literární činnost M. Jana Rokycany, M. Jana Příbama, M. Petra Payna* [The literary activity of Master Jan Rokycana, Master Jan Příbram, Master Peter Payne] (Prague: 1928).

Bartoš, František Michálek, *Mikuláš z Pehlřimova* [Mikuláš of Pelhřimov] (Tábor: 1939).

Betts, Reginald Robert, *Essays in Czech History* (London: 1969).

Betts, Reginald Robert, "The Influence of Realist Philosophy on Jan Hus and His Predecessors in Bohemia," in idem, *Essays in Czech History* (London: 1969), 42–62.

Betts, Reginald Robert, "Peter Payne in England," in idem, *Essays in Czech History* (London: 1969), 236–46.

Bose, Mishtooni, "The Opponents of John Wyclif," in *A Companion to John Wyclif, Late Medieval Theologian*, ed. Ian Christopher Levy (Brill's Companions to the Christian Tradition) 4 (Leiden and Boston: 2006), 407–56.

Brock, R.O., *An edition of Richard Fitzralph's De pauperie Salvatoris books V, VI, and VII* (Ph.D. dissertation, University of Colorado: 1954).

Cesali, Laurent "Le 'pan-propositionalisme' de Jean Wyclif," *Vivarium* 43 (2005): 124–55.

Cesali, Laurent, *Le réalisme propositionnel. Sémantique et ontologie des propositions chez Jean Duns Scot, Gauthier Burley, Richard Brinkley et Jean Wyclif* (Paris: 2007).

Cox, Rory, *John Wyclif on War and Peace* (London: 2014).

Dahmus, Joseph H., *The Prosecution of John Wyclyf* (New Haven: 1952).

De Vooght, Paul, *L'hérésie de Jean Huss* (Leuven: 1960).

De Vooght, Paul, "Nicolas Biskupec de Pelhřimov et son apport á l'évolution de la méthodologie théologique hussite," *Recherches de théologie ancienne et médiévale* 40 (1973): 175–207.

Dekarli, Martin, "Prague Nominalist Master John Arsen of Langenfeld and His Quaestio on Ideas from Around 1394/1399," in *The Bohemian Reformation and Religious Practice*, eds. Zdeněk V. David and David R. Holeton, vol. 9 (Prague: 2014), 35–53.

Dekarli, Martin, "The Law of Christ (Lex Christi) and the Law of God (Lex Dei) – Jan Hus's Concept of Reform," in *The Bohemian Reformation and Religious Practice*, eds. Zdeněk V. David and David R. Holeton, vol. 10 (Prague: 2015), 49–69.

Fudge, Thomas A., "Crime, Punishment and Pacifism in the Thought of Bishop Mikuláš of Pelhřimov, 1420–1452," in *The Bohemian Reformation and Religious Practice*, eds. Zdeněk V. David and David R. Holeton, vol. 3 (Prague: 2000), 69–102.

Fudge, Thomas A., *Jan Hus. Religious Reform and Social Revolution in Bohemia* (London and New York: 2010).

Fudge, Thomas A., *The Trial of Jan Hus. Medieval Heresy and Criminal Procedure* (Oxford: 2013).

Fudge, Thomas A., *Jerome of Prague and the Foundations of the Hussite Movement* (New York: 2016).

Herold, Vilém, *Pražská univerzita a Wyclif. Wyclifovo učení o ideách a geneze husitského revolučního myšlení* [Prague University and Wyclif. Wyclif's teaching on ideas and the genesis of Hussite revolutionary thought] (Prague: 1985).

Herold, Vilém, "The University of Paris and the Foundations of the Bohemian Reformation," in *The Bohemian Reformation and Religious Practice*, eds. Zdeněk V. David and David R. Holeton, vol. 3 (Prague: 2000), 15–24.

Herold, Vilém, "Vojtěch Raňkův of Ježov (Adalbertus Rankonis de Ericinio) and the Bohemian Reformation" in *The Bohemian Reformation and Religious Practice*, eds. Zdeněk V. David and David R. Holeton, vol. 7 (Prague: 2009), 72–9.

Hudson, Anne, *The Premature Reformation. Wycliffite Texts and Lollard History* (Oxford: 1988).

Hudson, Anne, "*Accessus ad auctorem*. The Case of John Wyclif," *Viator* 30 (1999): 323–44.

Hudson, Anne, *Studies in the Transmission of Wyclif's Writings* (Aldershot and Burlington: 2008).

Jeauneau, Edouard, "Plato apud Bohemos," *Mediaeval Studies* 41 (1979): 161–214.

Kadlec, Jaroslav, *Leben und Schriften des Prager Magisters Adalbert Rankonis de Ericinio* (Münster: 1971).

Kaminsky, Howard, "Wycliffism as Ideology of Revolution," *Church History* 32 (1963): 57–74.

Kaminsky, Howard, "The Religion of Hussite Tábor," in *The Czechoslovak Contribution to World Culture*, ed. Miloslav Rechcígl (London: 1964), 210–33.

Kaminsky, Howard, *A History of the Hussite Revolution* (Berkeley and Los Angeles: 1967).

Kaminsky, Howard, "Nicholas of Pelhřimov's Tabor. An Adventure into the Eschaton," in *Eschatologie und Hussitismus*, eds. Alexander Patschovsky and František Šmahel (Prague: 1996), 139–67.

Kejř, Jiří, "Protihusovský traktát *De ecclesia* a jeho autor" [The anti-Hus tract *De ecclesia* and its author], in idem, *Z počátků české reformace* (Brno: 2006), 182–86.

Kybal, Vlastimil, *M. Matěj z Janova. Jeho život, spisy a učení* [Master Matěj of Janov. His life, writings, and teachings] (Prague: 1905).

Lahey, Stephen E., "Wyclif's Trinitarian and Christological Theology," in *A Companion to John Wyclif, Late Medieval Theologian*, ed. Ian Christopher Levy (Brill's Companions to the Christian Tradition) 4 (Leiden and Boston: 2006), 127–98.

Lahey, Stephen E., *John Wyclif* (Oxford: 2009).

Lahey, Stephen E., "Richard Fitzralph and John Wyclif: Untangling Armachanus from the Wycliffites," in *Richard Fitzralph. His Life, Times and Thought*, eds. Michael Dunne and Simon Nolan (Dublin: 2013), 159–85.

Lahey, Stephen E., "The *Sentences* Commentary of Jan Hus," in *A Companion to Jan Hus*, eds. Frantisek Šmahel and Ota Pavlíček (Brill's Companions to the Christian Tradition) 54 (Leiden and Boston: 2015), 130–69.

Leff, Gordon, *Heresy in the Later Middle Ages. The Relation of Heterodoxy to Dissent c. 1250–c. 1450*, 2 vols. (Manchester and New York: 1967).

Levy, Ian C., *John Wyclif. Scriptural Logic, Real Presence, and the Parameters of Orthodoxy* (Milwaukee: 2003).

Levy, Ian C., "John Wyclif and the Primitive Papacy," *Viator* 38 (2007): 159–89.

Loserth, Johann, *Hus und Wiclif. Zur Genesis der husitischen Lehre* (Prague and Leipzig: 1884).

Macek, Josef, *Jan Hus. Studie s ukázkami z Husova díla* [Jan Hus. A study with examples of Hus's works] (Prague, 1961).

Nechutová, Jana, "Traktát *De ymaginibus* připisovaný Petru Paynovi" [The tract *De ymaginibus* attributed to Peter Payne], *Husitský Tábor* 9 (1987): 325–35.

Nechutová, Jana, "Matěj of Janov and His Work *Regulae Veteris et Novi Testamenti*. The Significance of Volume vi and Its Relation to the Previously Published Volumes," in *The Bohemian Reformation and Religious Practice*, eds. Zdeněk V. David and David R. Holeton, vol. 2 (Prague: 1998), 15–24.

Nuchelmans, Gabriel, "Stanislaus of Znaim (d. 1414) On Truth and Falsity," in *Mediaeval Semantics and Metaphysics. Studies dedicated to L.M. de Rijk*, ed. Egbert Peter Bos (Nijmegen: 1985), 313–38.

Odložilík, Otakar, *Wyclif and Bohemia. Two Essays* (Prague: 1937).

Pavlíček, Ota, "Wyclif's Early Reception in Bohemia and His Influence on the Thought of Jerome of Prague," in *Europe after Wyclif*, eds. J. Patrick Hornbeck II and Michael Van Dussen (New York: 2017), 89–114.

Peschke, Erhard, "Zur Theologie des Taboriten Nikolaus von Pilgram," *Wissenschaftliche Zeitschrift der Universität Halle-Wittenberg* 19 (1970): 153–70.

Prokeš, Jaroslav, *M. Prokop z Plzně. Příspěvek k vývoji konservativní strany husitské* [Master Prokop of Plzeň. A contribution to the development of the Hussite conservative party] (Prague: 1927).

Sedlák, Jan, "Husův pomocník v evangeliu" [Hus's assistant in the Gospel], *Studie a texty k náboženským dějinám českým* 1 (1914): 362–428; 2 (1915), 302–50, 446–77; 3 (1919), 24–74.

Sedlák, Jan, *M. Jan Hus* (Prague: 1915).

Sedlák, Jan, *Miscellanea husitica Ioannis Sedlák*, eds. Jaroslav V. Polc and Stanislav Přibyl (Prague: 1996).

Sedlák, Jan, "Stanislav ze Znojma na Moravě" [Stanislav of Znojmo in Moravia], in *Miscellanea husitica Ioannis Sedlák*, eds. Jaroslav V. Polc and Stanislav Přibyl (Prague: 1996), 126–32.

Shogimen, Takashi, "Wyclif's Ecclesiology and Political Thought," in *A Companion to John Wyclif, Late Medieval Theologian*, ed. Ian Christopher Levy (Brill's Companions to the Christian Tradition) 4 (Leiden and Boston: 2006), 199–240.

Šmahel, František, *Verzeichnis der Quellen zum Prager Universalienstreit 1348–1500*, (Mediaevalia Philosophica Polonorum) 25 (Wrocław: 1980).

Šmahel, František, *Die Hussitische Revolution*, trans. Thomas Krzenck (Monumenta Germaniae Historica. Schriften) 43, 3 vols. (Hannover: 2002).

Šmahel, František, "Peter Payne," in *Oxford Dictionary of National Biography*, vol. 43 (Oxford: 2004), 208–13.

Šmahel, František, "Wyclif's Fortune in Hussite Bohemia," in idem, *Die Prager Universität im Mittelalter. The Charles University in the Middle Ages* (Leiden and Boston: 2007), 467–89.

Šmahel, František, *Alma Mater Pragensis. Studie k počátkům Univerzity Karlovy* [*Alma Mater Pragensis*. Studies on the beginnings of Charles University] (Prague: 2016).

Souček, Bohuslav, "*Veritas super omnia*. Z biblických studií a odkazu Mikuláše Biskupce z Pelhřimova" [*Veritas super omnia*. From the biblical studies and legacy of Mikuláš Biskupec of Pelhřimov], *Theologická příloha Křestanské revue* 28 (1961): 73–90.

Soukup, Pavel, *Reformní kazatelství a Jakoubek ze Stříbra* [Reform preaching and Jakoubek of Stříbro] (Prague: 2011).

Sousedík, Stanislav, "Pojem *distinctio formalis* u českých realistů v době Husově" [The notion of *distinctio formalis* in Czech realists in the time of Hus], *Filosofický časopis* 18 (1970): 1024–29.

Sousedík, Stanislav, "Stanislaus von Znaim († 1414). Eine Lebensskizze," *Mediaevalia Philosophica Polonorum* 17 (1973): 37–56.

Spinka, Matthew, *John Hus' Concept of the Church* (Princeton: 1966).

Spunar, Pavel, *Repertorium auctorum Bohemorum provectum idearum post universitatem Pragensem conditam illustrans*, vol. 1 (Studia Copernicana) 25 (Wrocław: 1985).

Thomson, S.H., "A Note on Peter Payne and Wyclyf," *Medievalia et Humanistica* 16 (1964): 60–4.

Thomson, Williel R., *The Latin Writings of John Wyclyf* (Toronto: 1983).

Van Dussen, Michael, *From England to Bohemia. Heresy and Communication in the Later Middle Ages* (Cambridge: 2012).

Walsh, Katherine, "Die Rezeption der Schriften des Richard Fitzralph (Armachanus) im lollardisch-hussitischen Milieu" in *Das Publikum politischer Theorie im 14. Jahrhundert*, ed. Jürgen Miethke (Munich: 1992), 237–53.

PART 2

Major Figures

∴

Major Hussite Theologians before the *Compactata*

Petra Mutlová

The study of theology was deemed the most prestigious among academic pursuits at the end of the 14th and beginning of the 15th century. Upon the successful completion of its foundation process between 1347 and 1349, the university in Prague became the first true medieval university in Central Europe since it contained a theological faculty from the very beginning.[1] Nevertheless, this enterprise also owed its success to the existence of the *studia generalia* of several monastic orders that had already existed in Prague since the 13th century. The most important among these were the Dominicans, who granted their privilege of a *studium generale* to the newly established university. Master Johannes of Dambach was entrusted with the task of preparing its organization.[2] The activities of the founding members and first professors of theology stimulated discussions over a number of theological issues, and in consequence large numbers of works survive from Bohemia at that time.[3] This chapter presents theologians who were active in Bohemia up until 1436 and who played the most important roles in the religious developments of that period. As many aspects of the formation of Hussite ideology are covered elsewhere in this volume, the following chapter concentrates primarily on the biographical data and literary activities of the chosen figures. The survey is therefore highly selective and considers only the most substantial contributions.

1   The Predecessors of Hus and Hussitism

The development of Hussite theology can be fully appreciated only in the context of the previous generation of theologians, who are traditionally called "the

---

[1] For a general overview of the history of the university, see Michal Svatoš (ed.), *Dějiny Univerzity Karlovy*, vol. 1 (Prague: 1995); the English version was published as *A History of Charles University*, eds. František Kavka and Josef Petráň, vol. 1 (Prague: 2001).

[2] Dambach is the author of the *De consolatione theologiae*, a prime example of the medieval consolation genre that encourages deeper and more genuine piety and that echoes the influence of Rhineland mysticism.

[3] An overview of Czech authors and their works is available in Pavel Spunar, *Repertorium auctorum Bohemorum provectum idearum post universitatem Pragensem conditam illustrans*, vol. 1 (Studia Copernicana 25) (Wrocław: 1985).

predecessors of Hus and Hussitism."[4] Labelling the generation that inspired the ideological world of Hussite theologians as Hus's predecessors was to a large extent the result of the historiographical emphasis on indigenous tradition and development. As a reaction to later attempts to seek the dependence of the Bohemian Reformation on the English reformer John Wyclif, the connecting line between Hus and his predecessors was even more firmly accentuated.[5] Yet, the generation of Hussite theologians was influenced by Wyclif as well as by various heretical systems. One of the problems that hinders the accurate evaluation of the origins of Hussite ideology lies in the inaccessibility of relevant treatises, because many of them still lack critical editions. Moreover, no modern synthesis of Hussite literature (apart from catalogues or repertories) is available.[6]

Three authors are traditionally counted among the predecessors of Hussitism: Konrad Waldhauser, Matěj of Janov, and Milíč of Kroměříž.[7] Links between Hussite theologians and a number of other influential theoreticians of previous generations were also sought, including Vojtěch Raňkův of Ježov (Adalbertus Ranconis de Ericinio), Heinrich of Bitterfeld, or Matthew of Cracow, one of the most influential reformist theologians in Europe at that time. Nevertheless, the Hussite theologians did not refer to the works of their predecessors often. There are a few exceptions. Konrad Waldhauser's *Postilla studentium sanctae Pragensis universitatis*, composed around 1367–1368, was already highly popular at the time of its origin and was subsequently exploited by another popular collection of sermons, the *Dicta de tempore*, a work that was

---

4 The origins of the Czech Reform and the problematic concept of the precursors of Hus put forward by František Palacký are analyzed in full detail in the chapter by Olivier Marin in this volume.
5 The long-lasting debate on this topic was stipulated by a study of Johann Loserth, *Hus und Wiclif. Zur Genesis der husitischen Lehre* (Prague and Leipzig: 1884). See František Šmahel, "Wyclif's Fortune in Hussite Bohemia," in idem, *Die Prager Universität im Mittelalter. The Charles University in the Middle Ages* (Leiden and Boston: 2007), 467–89; Vilém Herold, "Ideové kořeny reformace v českých zemích," in *Dějiny politického myšlení*, vol. 2/2: *Politické myšlení pozdního středověku a reformace*, eds. Vilém Herold, Ivan Müller, and Aleš Havlíček (Prague: 2011), 161–91.
6 The only relevant study is Jana Nechutová, *Die lateinische Literatur des Mittelalters in Böhmen* (Cologne, Weimar, and Vienna: 2007), which deals only with literary production connected with the beginnings of Prague University (i.e. to 1400).
7 Sometimes Tomáš of Štítné is also included in this group. Tomáš was an intriguing layman, a prolific author, and a translator of numerous treatises into the vernacular. His theoretical contribution to Hussite theology is discussed in the chapter by Pavlína Rychterová in this volume.

until recently erroneously ascribed to Hus.[8] The works of Jan Milíč of Kroměříž were more often used in the Hussite milieu.[9] In his treatises, Milíč worked out an elaborate system of biblical and patristic quotations and his intricate argumentation was later used by many Hussite theologians.[10] Similarly, the work of Matěj of Janov is often seen as an influential element in the religious developments in late medieval Bohemia.[11] His most important treatise, the *Regulae Veteris et Novi Testamenti*, is the first systematic treatment of Czech reform theology.[12] In this large treatise, he placed the primary stress on the Bible, while patristic and other standard scholarly authorities are mostly absent. Matěj conceived the term *regula principalis*, a set of obligatory rules for Christians, and criticized everything that overreached this *regula* as *adinventiones hominum* (human inventions). The genetic relations of his concept of the *lex Christi* with the definitions expressed by Wyclif and Hus have been demonstrated.[13] For Matěj, daily communion was the only remedy for all sins. His treatment of the Antichrist and frequent lay communion, as well as his criticism of the cult of the saints and the abuse of images, had a major impact on Hussite theologians. Matěj also influenced this generation by his interpretation of Plato's ideas.[14]

2   The First Generation of Prague Theologians and Their Reformist Tendencies

The social impact of the foundation of Prague University was closely connected to one of the central issues of the previous reformist efforts, namely the role

---

8   Konrad's *Postilla* is as yet unedited. The *Dicta* were edited as *Dicta de tempore magistro Iohanni Hus attributa*, ed. Jana Zachová (Magistri Iohannis Hus Opera omnia) 26 (Corpus christianorum. Continuatio mediaevalis) 239, 2 vols. (Turnhout: 2011).

9   Peter C.A. Morée, *Preaching in Fourteenth-Century Bohemia. The Life and Ideas of Milicius de Chremsir (d. 1374) and his Significance in the Historiography of Bohemia* (Heršpice: 1999). Morée saw in Milíč a prime representative of gothic piety and the *devotio moderna*.

10 Milíč's most important collections of sermons include *Abortivus, Gratiae Dei*, and *Tres sermones synodales*. His other popular works are *Libellus de Antichristo* and *Sermo de die novissimo*, or the *Epistula ad papam Urbanum V*.

11 Vlastimil Kybal, *M. Matěj z Janova. Jeho život, spisy a učení* (Prague: 1905; repr. Brno: 2000).

12 Matěj of Janov, *Regulae Veteris et Novi Testamenti*, 6 vols. (1908–1993). For further publication details see the Bibliography.

13 Jana Nechutová, "Kategorie zákona božího a M. Matěj z Janova," *Sborník prací Filozofické fakulty brněnské univerzity* E 12 (1967): 211–21.

14 Herold, "Ideové kořeny reformace," 179–81.

of the Eucharist as a means of salvation for Christians and its frequent celebration. The university debates were naturally influenced by this discussion, a topic that also resonated among the Prague theologians because of the spread of Wyclif's teachings in the city. Partly due to the heated discussions of these issues, many of the founding members of the Prague Theological Faculty soon moved on to neighboring universities, including the newly founded ones in Vienna and Cracow. Yet many of them left a lasting imprint on the formation of Hussite ideology, not least because the emerging generation of reformers read and used their commentaries and expositions.

Heinrich Totting of Oyta was one of the most prolific authors of philosophical and theological treatises[15] and is the author of several commentaries on Lombard's *Sentences* (*Lectura textualis super libros sententiarum, Quaestiones super libros sententiarum*). Heinrich taught many of the subsequent reformist theologians, including Johannes of Marienwerder/Kwidzyn, who wrote a widely circulated treatise against Wycliffism, the *Exposicio symboli apostolici*.

Konrad of Soltau was one of Totting's disciples.[16] His *Quaestiones super libros sententiarum*, written around 1385, became a standard textbook at the universities of Prague and Cracow. This work shows an inclination towards reformist theology and is in part the reason why he was accused of heresy. Konrad was well versed in Wyclif's concept of universals and challenged his views on remanence.

The most famous author among the first theologians in Prague was Jenek Václavův (Iohannes Wenceslai) of Prague, a respected professor of theology, renowned philosopher and mathematician. His literary legacy includes several commentaries on Aristotle, as well as biblical exegesis. Jenek's commentaries influenced Hussite ideology significantly, and he was likely behind the Hussite insistence on the primacy of the law of God.[17]

---

15   Albert Lang, "Heinrich Totting von Oyta," in *Neue Deutsche Biographie*, vol. 8 (Berlin: 1969), 426.
16   Hans Jürgen Brandt, "Universität, Gesellschaft, Politik und Pfründen am Beispiel Konrad von Soltau (†1407)," in *The Universities in the Late Middle Ages*, eds. Jozef Ijsewijn and Jacques Paquet (Leuven: 1978), 614–27; Jana Nechutová,"Konrad von Soltau. *Lectura super caput Firmiter*," in *Schriften im Umkreis mitteleuropäischer Universitäten um 1400. Lateinische und volkssprachige Texte aus Prag, Wien und Heidelberg. Unterschiede, Gemeinsamkeiten, Wechselbeziehungen*, eds. Fritz Peter Knapp, and Jürgen Miethke, and Manuela Niesner (Leiden: 2004), 3–19.
17   Herold, "Ideové kořeny reformace," 201–10; idem, "Commentarium Magistri Johannis Wenceslai de Praga super octo libros 'Politicorum' Aristotelis," *Mediaevalia Philosophica Polonorum* 26 (1982): 53–77.

Lecturers in theology from the monastic orders formed another influential group.[18] These included the Dominican Heinrich of Bitterfeld, who harshly criticized simony and argued in favor of frequent communion;[19] and the Cistercian Jan Štěkna, who debated with Stanislav of Znojmo over issues connected to the Eucharist and Wyclif's teachings. Two other Cistercian theologians entered the polemic surrounding Wyclif's teachings: the prolific author Konrad of Ebrach, and Matouš of Zbraslav, a well-known figure who attended the Council of Constance, where he preached a reformist sermon (*Estote misericordes*, 1417).

A strong criticism of the church as well as reformist tendencies can also be discerned among the representatives of the Polish university nation, who were active at Prague University. Widely circulated were the treatises of Matthew of Cracow, who criticized simony and argued for the precedence of the council over the pope.[20] Of the works that are ascribed to him, the most influential for Hussite theologians is the *De praxi Romanae curiae* (also known as *De squaloribus Romanae curiae*). Similarly significant was the *Speculum aureum*, a highly popular treatise whose authorship was ascribed to Piotr Wysz of Radolin.[21] This literary dialogue harshly criticized simony; it showed that the pope must face the consequences of his simoniacal practices, and therefore his removal by the council is possible and necessary if he is convicted of this sin.

A number of Hus's teachers and colleagues also had a marked influence on the formation of Hussite theology.[22] Hus's teacher Štěpán of Kolín was a skilful preacher and a supporter of Wyclif's doctrines. In 1403, he delivered a synodal sermon, *Homo quidam fecit magnam cenam*, which dealt with the question of communion, and his largest work, *Lectura super Yzaiam prophetam* (1406), displays distinct reformist tendencies.[23]

---

18 For an overview of these theologians, see Jaroslav Kadlec, "Řeholní generální studia při Karlově universitě v době předhusitské," *Acta Universitatis Carolinae – Historia Universitatis Carolinae Pragensis* 7, 2 (1966): 63–108.

19 In the Czech milieu, Heinrich's treatises dealing with the question of frequent communion have been traditionally deemed the most important; see Heinrich of Bitterfeld, *Eucharistické texty*, ed. Pavel Černuška (Brno: 2006). Yet Heinrich's most important work is his *Tractatus de vita contemplativa et activa*, written for the Polish Queen Hedwig and attesting to the growing lay piety.

20 On Matthew of Cracow, see the chapter by Olivier Marin in this volume.

21 Władysław Seńko, *Piotr Wysz z Radolina (*ok. 1354 – †1414) i jego dzieło "Speculum aureum"* (Warsaw: 1995).

22 Michal Svatoš, "Hussens Freunde," in *Jan Hus. Zwischen Zeiten, Völkern, Konfessionen*, ed. Ferdinand Seibt (Munich: 1997), 67–72.

23 The *Confessionale*, a widely circulated tract on confession whose authorship has also been ascribed to Štěpán, is most probably the work of a different author; see E. Weidenhiller,

3 The Dispute over Universals

The influence of John Wyclif on the reformist circle in Prague has been mentioned above and is discussed in detail elsewhere in this volume.[24] Interest in Wyclif's teachings in Prague rose sharply from the last decade of the 14th century, and conflicts over Wyclif culminated at Prague University in the first two decades of the 15th. An early piece of evidence of the acquaintance with Wyclif's teachings in Prague is presented by the work of Mikuláš Biceps, one of the lecturers of the Dominican order at Prague University.[25] Further research is still needed to reveal the full significance of the debate on universals and its impact on the formation of Hussite ideology. The principal focus here is on how the debate manifested itself in writing and on the individuals who took part in this debate. The turn of the 14th century was marked by diligent copying of Wyclif's texts by Czech students, including Jan Hus, who himself copied Wyclif's philosophical tracts in 1398.[26] As far as the textual outcomes of the *causa Wyclif* are concerned, one moment should be mentioned from the start: the initiative of the Dominican Johannes Hübner, who successfully instigated the anti-Wyclif campaign by compiling the notorious 45 articles attributed to Wyclif and enforcing their rejection by University Act on 28 May 1403. In direct consequence, the text of these articles was the subject of many polemics that will be mentioned below. However, Hübner's endeavor had a double-edged effect: his theses proved to be a very efficient tool for spreading the most compelling elements of Wyclif's teaching.

The most important author in the early dispute over universals was Stanislav of Znojmo. Stanislav was initially one of the leading members of the reformist party who introduced Wyclif's teachings in Prague, yet he later abandoned this circle and became Hus's opponent. Stanislav started his studies at Vienna University but continued in Prague, where he became a professor of theology.[27] Stanislav's initial support of Wyclif resulted in his accusation of

---

"Stephan von Kolín," in Kurt Ruh et al. (eds.), *Die deutsche Literatur des Mittelalters. Verfasserlexikon*, 14 vols., 2nd ed. (Berlin and New York: 1978–2008), vol. 2, 4–5.

24 See the chapter by Stephen E. Lahey in this volume. See also Šmahel, *Die Prager Universität im Mittelalter*, 467–598; Herold, *Pražská univerzita a Wyclif*; idem, "Zum Prager philosophischen Wyclifismus."

25 Biceps argued against Wyclif's opinions on the Eucharist before 1380. Šmahel, "Wyclif's Fortune," 469–70, showed that Wyclif's philosophical works were known in Prague already in the 1360s.

26 The extant autograph of Hus contains Wyclif's tracts *De materia et forma*, *De tempore*, *De ideis*, and *De universalibus*.

27 Stanislav Sousedík, "Stanislaus von Znaim († 1414). Eine Lebensskizze," *Mediaevalia Philosophica Polonorum* 17 (1973): 37–56.

heresy and citation to Rome. On his way there Stanislav was captured in Bologna and arrested along with Štěpán of Páleč, who accompanied him. After months of imprisonment that preceded the final verdict, Stanislav and Štěpán returned to Prague in the summer of 1409. This ordeal turned out to be a life-changing experience for both men, and between 1410 and 1412 Stanislav gradually withdrew from the Wycliffite circle in Prague, finding refuge in Moravia in 1413. He died on his way to Constance in Jindřichův Hradec on 10 October 1414.

Stanislav's primary interest in universals is reflected in a large tract *De universalibus* (after 1394) and a shorter treatise *De universalibus realibus* (1408).[28] He wrote other philosophical treatises, such as *De felicitate* (1400), which addresses the question of true happiness, and *De vero et falso* (before 1404), which treats ontological truth. His theological treatises, such as the *De gracia et peccato* (1410), mostly deal with topical issues. In the eucharistic treatise *De corpore Christi* (1403–1406), Stanislav declared his belief in consubstantiation as opposed to Wyclif's theory of remanence; due to the subsequent accusation of heresy, he supplied an orthodox ending, in which he argued for transubstantiation. Towards the end of his life Stanislav composed two ecclesiological treatises, *Tractatus de Romana ecclesia* (1412) and *De Anticristo contra magistrum Iacobellum de Misa* (1412–1413).[29] One of his final replies to Hus and his party concerning the philosophical-theological controversies is the tract *Alma et venerabilis* (1412–1413), in which he clarified his attitude toward Wyclif's teachings. In his Moravian exile, Stanislav wrote his most important criticism of Wyclif's teachings, the widely circulated *Tractatus contra XLV articulos Ioannis Wiclef* (1413) that was part of his preparation for the Council of Constance.

In many aspects, Stanislav was greatly aided by Štěpán of Páleč. Štěpán was an influential theologian among the reformist circle in Prague, as well as a colleague and friend of Hus, with whom he shared his original enthusiasm for Wyclif's teachings. His later shift to the opposition deeply disappointed Hus. The actual reasons behind this split are unknown and were undoubtedly intricate. Štěpán became a Master of Theology in 1411 and dean of the Faculty of Theology in 1412. The indulgence riots of 1412 and imprisonment (with Stanislav) in Bologna caused Štěpán to reassess his position, and he became an

---

28   The *De universalibus* with the incipit "Cum multis in philosophia prima famosis" was printed by the Wyclif Society as Wyclif's authentic work; Stanislav of Znojmo, "Tractatus de universalibus (maior)"; the shorter treatment with the incipit "Quia nonnulli modernorum" was edited by Jan Sedlák, *M. Jan Hus* (Prague: 1915), 81*-93*.

29   Another ecclesiological text, the *Tractatus de ecclesia* (*Contra hereses et errores Iohannis Hus*), has been ascribed to Stanislav as well as to Štěpán of Páleč. The prevailing opinion maintains that it was authored by Štěpán of Páleč; see Jiří Kejř, "Protihusovský traktát *De ecclesia* a jeho autor," in idem, *Z počátků české reformace* (Brno: 2006), 182–86.

ardent opponent of Hus. Following his banishment from Prague in 1413, Štěpán left for Cracow, whence he set out for the Council of Constance. There he played an important role as the fiercest opponent in the case against Hus. After the council ended, Štěpán returned to Poland, staying there until his death in 1423.

Štěpán wrote several treatises on universals during his early period of zeal for Wyclif's doctrine. In all probability, he commented on Wyclif's *De universalibus* before 1397,[30] and he took part in the famous *quodlibet* disputation organized by Hus in 1411. On this occasion he solved the question *Utrum Deus, qui creavit mundum sensibilem*.[31] This text was later printed as Wyclif's own work, as was the case with Štěpán's other *quodlibet* question on *Utrum universalia habeant* (before 1398).[32] These and a number of other texts attest to Štěpán's active role in spreading Wyclif's doctrines in Prague.

Following upon his split from Hus, Štěpán engaged in ecclesiological theory and gradually shifted from antipapalism to conciliarism. His opinions on this matter are best illustrated in his contribution to the polemic between eight Doctors of Theology and Hus in 1413 (*Replicatio contra quidamistas*). Before that, in 1412, Štěpán wrote a *Tractatulus de ecclesia* (*De aequivocatione nominis ecclesia*). His *Antihus* (c. 1414) and *Tractatus de ecclesia* (*Contra hereses et errores Iohannis Hus*) (1413–1414)[33] were also aimed against Hus. Around 1420 Štěpán composed a highly popular *Tractatus contra quattuor articulos Hussitarum*. Several texts also stem from his actions at the Council of Constance (e.g. the sermon *Resistite fortes in fide* from 1417). It is undeniable that Štěpán was a proficient theologian and made good use of Hus's legal position and the complexities of procedural law. The outcome of the process against Hus in Constance can be attributed to a large extent to Štěpán's leverage. However, Štěpán's life and work still await full appreciation.[34]

Many theological questions were discussed during the disputations *de quolibet* at the university In Prague the *quodlibet* disputation had a fully developed

---

30   Štěpán Páleč, *Commentarius in I–IX capitula tractatus De universalibus Iohannis Wyclif Stephano de Palecz ascriptus*, ed. Ivan Müller (Prague: 2009).

31   *Johannis Wyclif De ente librorum duorum excerpta*, ed. Michael Henry Dziewicki (Wyclif's Latin Works) 33 (London: 1909), 223–32.

32   Printed partially in *Johannis Wyclif Miscellanea philosophica*, ed. Michael Henry Dziewicki (Wyclif's Latin Works) 28 (London: 1905), vol. 2, 173–87. For the complete edition, see "Positio de universalibus," ed. Ryszard Palacz: "La 'Positio de universalibus' d'Étienne de Palecz," *Mediaevalia Philosophica Polonorum* 14 (1970): 113–29.

33   See above, note 29.

34   Jana Nechutová, "M. Štěpán von Páleč und die Hus-Historiographie," *Mediaevalia Bohemica* 3 (1970): 87–122.

late-medieval form in that it had been transferred from the Theological Faculty to the Faculty of Arts. This meant that the disputations also covered a wide range of philosophical topics. The disputations *de quolibet* had been regularly organized from the last decade of the 14th century, and the source material indicates that between about 1394 and 1417 there were thirteen such occasions.[35] Among the best documented disputations are the *quodlibet* of Matěj of Knín in 1409 and that of 1411, held by Jan Hus.[36] In the 1409 disputation, Jerome of Prague delivered his *Recommendatio artium liberalium*, where he energetically praised and recommended the study of Wyclif's books and called openly for the disobedience of ecclesiastical bans.[37] Jerome's speech served as a prelude to the Kutná Hora Decree that was issued on 18 January 1409, which resulted in the withdrawal of German masters and students from Prague.[38] The consequences were also reflected in the textual discourse, as many complaints were written by professors that seceded from Prague. In the meantime, the discussion about universals continued in Prague, and archbishop Zbyněk initiated a re-examination of Wyclif's books, which resulted in a proclamation of June 1410 that ordered Wyclif's books to be burnt. In answer to this, Hus himself wrote *De libris hereticorum legendis*, and a number of defenses came from a university disputation in honor of Wyclif's books that were burnt: Hus compiled a selection of authoritative arguments in his *Defensio libri de Trinitate Iohannis Wiclif*; Jacoubek of Stříbro composed a sharp *Defensio libri Decalogi Magistri Johannis Wiklef*, in which he exploited the *Regulae* by Matěj of Janov; Šimon of Tišnov composed an ironic defense of Wyclif's *De probatione propositionum*; Prokop of Plzeň wrote *Defensio tractatus De ideis magistri Iohannis Wiclef* – to name only the most famous speakers.

A frequent topic of the *quodlibet* disputations was the question of Plato's ideas. This metaphysical debate had political consequences in Prague as it was

---

35 Jiří Kejř, *Kvodlibetní disputace na pražské univerzitě* (Prague: 1971); František Šmahel, "Die Verschriftlichung der Quodlibet-Disputationen an der Prager Artistenfakultät bis 1420," in idem, *Die Prager Universität im Mittelalter*, 359–86.

36 Material from Hus's *quodlibet* is edited in *Magistri Iohannis Hus Quodlibet. Disputationis de quolibet Pragae in facultate artium mense Ianuario anni 1411 habitae enchiridion*, ed. Bohumil Ryba (Magistri Iohannis Hus Opera omnia 20) (Prague: 1948), 2nd ed. (Corpus christianorum. Continuatio mediaevalis) 211 (Turnhout: 2006).

37 Printed in Jerome of Prague, *Quaestiones, polemica, epistulae*, 199–222; see František Šmahel, "Die Quelle der *Recommendacio arcium liberalium* des Mag. Hieronymus von Prag," in idem, *Die Prager Universität im Mittelalter*, 387–404.

38 František Šmahel, "The Kuttenberg Decree and the Withdrawal of the German Students from Prague in 1409. A Discussion," in idem, *Die Prager Universität im Mittelalter*, 159–171; Martin Nodl, *Das Kuttenberger Dekret von 1409. von der Eintracht zum Konflikt der Prager Universitätsnationen* (Cologne, Weimar, and Vienna: 2017).

aimed at the improvement of social order.[39] It formed part of the debate on Wyclif's theory of universals and most of the theologians of that time took a stand on the theme at some point. Apart from the principal treatment of the topic by Stanislav of Znojmo (*De universalibus*) and a couple of others, most of these texts remain unedited.

In 1412 the dispute over Wyclif's teachings flared up anew. This was triggered by an announcement of indulgences that Hus sharply criticized; but it turned out to have much graver consequences since more general matters of papal authority and the definition of the church were discussed in this context.[40] In consequence, the professors at the theology faculty condemned Wyclif's 45 articles again. As a reaction, a new defence of Wyclif took place at the university in August 1412. Both Štěpán of Páleč and Stanislav of Znojmo preached against these defenses, aided probably by other professors. Despite the efforts of Jan of Jesenice, the situation was still not resolved by 1413; the two parties disagreed on several dogmatic points, above all the concept of the church. A number of treatises on various aspects of systematic ecclesiology were the outcome of this controversy. Hus wrote the *De ecclesia*, in which he presented his concept of the church as the *praedestinatorum universitas*. Stanislav and Štěpán emphasized the institutional aspect of the church and its authority; Stanislav gathered evidence from Canon Law, while Štěpán enumerated six different expositions of the concept of the church and established the concept that all christened people united in the Catholic faith constitute the only true church.

Subsequently, Jan of Jesenice, together with Hus, criticized the memorandum of the professors of theology presented to the synod (*Consilium doctorum theologiae*); in reaction to which Ondřej of Brod replied to Hus (*Contra obiecciones Hussonitarum*) and Štěpán of Páleč to Jan of Jesenice (*Replicatio contra quidamistas*). Stanislav of Znojmo reacted to both in the name of the Faculty of Theology (*Alma et venerabilis*). The difficult situation resulted in the removal of four professors of theology in 1414 (Stanislav of Znojmo, Štěpán of Páleč, Jan Eliášův [Iohannes Eliae] of Horšovský Týn, and Petr of Znojmo), leaving only four professors at the faculty, which in turn hamstrung its operation. It was in this situation that Hus accepted the invitation to Constance in order to publicly defend his views.[41]

---

39   Vilém Herold, "Platonic Ideas and 'Hussite' Philosophy," in *The Bohemian Reformation and Religious Practice*, eds. Zdeněk V. David and David R. Holeton, vol. 1 (Prague: 1996), 13–23.

40   Pavel Soukup, "Jan Hus und der Prager Ablassstreit von 1412," in *Ablasskampagnen des Spätmittelalters. Luthers Thesen von 1517 im Kontext*, ed. Andreas Rehberg (Berlin and Boston: 2017), 485–500.

41   For more, see Matthew Spinka, *John Hus' Concept of the Church* (Princeton: 1966); Alexander Patschovsky, "Ekklesiologie bei Johannes Hus," in *Lebenslehren und Weltentwürfe im*

4   Hus and His Generation

Born in the small south Bohemian town of Husinec around 1370, Jan Hus started his career at Prague University sometime in the 1380s. He was promoted to Bachelor of Arts in 1393 and attained the Master of Arts degree in 1396.[42] In 1401 he became dean of the Arts Faculty and for 1409–1410 was elected rector of the entire university. Hus also continued with his studies at the Faculty of Theology, where he received the Bachelor's degree in 1409. After an initial intermezzo as a preacher in St. Michael's Church in 1401, Hus associated his career as a popular preacher with the Bethlehem Chapel (1402–1412). Jan Hus is renowned as the most famous leader of the reformist party, taking the place of Stanislav of Znojmo after his withdrawal. During his exile from Prague between 1412 and 1414, Hus continued to preach in the countryside with only exceptional visits to Prague. Responding to the aggravated political situation in Bohemia, Hus accepted the invitation of the Council of Constance, where he hoped to defend his views. He set off to Constance in the autumn of 1414, and his life ended there at the stake on 6 July 1415. Hus's literary legacy contains more than three hundred items, from long tracts to short letters scattered in hundreds of manuscripts all over Europe. His writings are grouped into twenty-six volumes of the *Magistri Iohannis Hus Opera Omnia* series.[43]

The Bethlehem Chapel in Prague is connected not only with Hus's vernacular preaching, but with a number of Czech treatises stemming from his activity there. Apart from the Bethlehem sermons and Sunday and feast day postils in Czech, Hus wrote several systematic expositions of the Credo, the Decalogue, and the Pater Noster, in which he strove to explain the basics of religious

---

Übergang vom Mittelalter zur Neuzeit, eds. Hartmut Boockmann, Bernd Moeller, and Karl Stackmann (Göttingen: 1989), 370–99.

42 The basic studies on Hus's life and teachings are Václav Novotný, *M. Jan Hus. Život a učení*, Part 1: *Život a dílo*, 2 vols. (Prague: 1919–1921); Vlastimil Kybal, *M. Jan Hus. Život a učení*, Part 2: *Učení*, 3 vols. (Prague: 1923–1931); Paul De Vooght, *L'hérésie de Jean Huss* (Leuven: 1960); Matthew Spinka, *John Hus. A Biography* (Princeton: 1968). See also Peter Hilsch, *Johannes Hus (um 1370–1415). Prediger Gottes und Ketzer* (Regensburg: 1999); Šmahel, *Jan Hus*; Soukup, *Jan Hus*; Šmahel and Pavlíček (eds.), *A Companion to Jan Hus*.

43 Only Hus's Czech treatises are edited completely. Out of the 22 Latin volumes of the series less than one half is edited critically. Many of Hus's Latin texts are available only in an early modern printed edition: Hus and Jerome, *Historia et monumenta*. An overview of the series can be found in Vidmanová, *Základní vydání spisů M. Jana Husi*, 1–11. A complete list of Hus's Latin and Czech writings is available in Bartoš and Spunar, *Soupis pramenů k literární činnosti M. Jana Husa*, 62–277.

instruction to the laity.[44] Some of them were very popular, such as *O manželství* (On matrimony), *Dcerka* (Daughter), *Knížky o svatokupectví* (Books on simony), *O šesti bludiech* (On the six errors) and others. Hus also composed a number of letters in Czech from Constance to his friends in Bohemia.[45]

As a frequent preacher, Hus composed a wide range of sermons and sermon collections in Latin. One of the earliest collections is the *Puncta*. Among his latter works the *Sermones de tempore (Collecta*, 1404–1405), *Sermones de sanctis* (1407–1408?), *Passio Domini nostri Iesu Cristi* (1407), *Leccionarium bipartitum* (1408–1409), and *Quadragesimale* (1410) were widely circulated. The sermons Hus preached in the Bethlehem Chapel in 1410–1411 (*Sermones in Bethlehem*) are based on his expositions, but the final form in which they are preserved is the product of Hus's students and not his authentic work. Hus preached twice at synods, and six of his university sermons survive, two of which were delivered on commemorative occasions (*Abiciamus opera tenebrarum*, 1404; *Confirmate corda vestra*, 1409) – both are full of criticism and attest to Hus's growing influence in the reformist circle. As a preacher, Hus was primarily concerned with the morals of the clergy rather than with doctrinal questions.

A number of Latin treatises are related to Hus's activity at the university. As a *cursor biblicus*, Hus commented on the canonical epistles (*Super canonicas*, 1404–1405) and the Psalms (*Enarratio Psalmorum 109–118*, 1405–1409). In 1409 he finished the commentary on Lombard's Sentences (*Super quatuor Sententiarum*, 1407–1409), and the last evidence for his studies at the theological faculty is a short explication of the first seven chapters of the first letter to Corinthians (*Explicacio I Cor.*, 1411). A large group of treatises is represented by university *quaestiones*, recommendations and disputations that Hus composed and delivered during his university period. Hus's preparations for the *quodlibet* disputation of January 1411, over which he presided, have also survived.

A number of smaller tracts dating to the period between 1408 and 1412 deal with the hotly debated issues of the Eucharist, the priestly office, original sin, and simony. Hus's participation in the defence of Wyclif's doctrine has been mentioned above. Nevertheless, Hus also discussed problems appealing to the laity, such as matrimony, parsimony, and various kinds of anger. Apart from this series of *Tractatus annorum 1408–1412*, several polemical treatises ensued from Hus's replies to his opponents (*Polemica*).

---

44   *Magistri Iohannis Hus Opera omnia* volumes 1–4, which comprise Hus's Czech treatises, were critically edited by Jiří Daňhelka between 1975 and 1995.
45   Hus, *Korespondence a dokumenty*.

Resulting from the announcement of indulgences in Prague in 1412 and the riots it had caused, a process against Hus was initiated at the papal curia. After an intricate series of legal actions, an aggravated anathema was promulgated over Hus in late July 1412, and he was summoned to appear before the papal court to plead his case. Hus, however, decided not to appeal to the pope and instead made an appeal to Christ on 18 October 1412.[46] As elsewhere in his works, Hus expressed his belief in the supreme authority of the *lex Dei* and its superiority over other laws, the church, or any human actions. For Hus, the law of God was not only a moral standard, but the key determining factor in all his beliefs. He also formulated this position explicitly in one of his later tracts, written shortly before his departure to Constance, the *De sufficiencia legis Cristi*.

At the end of 1412 Hus was exiled from Prague, and this period, lasting until 1414, marked a turning point in his writings. Isolated from the developments in Prague, he plunged into ardent literary activity. Most of his works from this time were composed in Czech, such as *Knížky o svatokupectví* (Books on simony) and the Czech *Postil*. However, his seminal Latin work, *De ecclesia*, was written during this time, too. One of Hus's most famous treatises, *De sex erroribus*, in which he accused the church of six sins, was written sometime at the end of 1412 or the beginning of 1413 (Hus translated the text into Czech in 1413). Selected quotations of authorities from this tract were inscribed on the walls of the Bethlehem Chapel, which has made the text the subject of immense interest.

Hus's *De ecclesia* has a central place among his Latin treatises.[47] It explains his views on the concept and power of the church, its subordination to the pope, and the status of the cardinals. By understanding the church as the community of the predestined, Hus adhered to Wyclif's position even though he also drew on St. Augustine and other orthodox authorities. The older opinion that Hus was plainly dependent on Wyclif in his ecclesiology has been revised, yet this issue still attracts scholarly attention.[48] Hus's ecclesiology played an important role in his condemnation at the Council of Constance not least because of its alleged similarity to Wyclif's.

The last phase of Hus's life is connected to his trial at the Council of Constance, where he stayed from autumn 1414 until his death at the stake on 6 July 1415. A number of Czech and Latin letters offer a unique insight into Hus's case and his personal and often emotional responses to the situation. Moreover,

---

46 Fudge, *The Trial of Jan Hus*, 188–214.
47 Herold, "Wyclif's Ecclesiology and its Prague Context."
48 For an overview of the debate, see Patschovsky, "Ekklesiologie bei Johannes Hus."

while jailed in Constance, Hus composed several shorter treatises: the so-called *Constantiensia* present valuable evidence of Hus's final treatment of contested issues, such as his explanation of faith, a sermon on peace, an explanation of love for God, penitence, his position concerning Wyclif's teachings, and the emerging question of the lay chalice.

Jerome of Prague studied in Prague, where he earned the Bachelor of Arts degree; he then proceeded to study at Oxford (ca. 1399–1401), where he copied some of Wyclif's books. The inspiration of Wyclif's teachings and desire to defend them became a life-long and indeed fatal project for Jerome. He subsequently enrolled at the universities of Paris, Cologne, and Heidelberg between 1404 and 1406, inciting animated public disputations in each location. His vigorous defenses of Wyclif and provocative disputations were always followed by accusations of heresy against Jerome, ultimately requiring him to flee. These short academic sojourns had benefits for Jerome, too, allowing him (for example) to acquire a direct knowledge of Plato's writings. On his return to Prague, Jerome first finished his studies at the Arts Faculty and took an active part in the debate over Wyclif's teachings – his role at the *quodlibet* disputation of Matěj of Knín and his *Recommendatio artium liberalium* (1409) have been mentioned above. Later on, Jerome undertook numerous travels, and his last trip to Constance in April 1415 was intended to help his friend Hus. Jerome followed the martyrdom of his friend on 30 May 1416.[49]

Jerome's extant writings are mostly connected with the teachings of Wyclif. Several *quaestiones*, polemical treatises, and letters related to this topic are preserved.[50] Jerome often treated philosophical aspects of Wyclif's teachings, especially the question of universals and ideas, possibly because he never engaged in a formal study of theology. Nevertheless – also in accordance with Wyclif – Jerome never separated theology from philosophy on formal grounds and argued that *scientia* is the common property of all. His writings include a famous graphical representation of the Trinity, the *Scutum fidei christianae* (1406), which Jerome used to illustrate the ability of Wyclif's philosophical doctrine to explain the trinitarian mystery.[51] A number of Jerome's treatises are lost, which is especially regrettable in the case of his theoretical treatment of the Eucharist and of his Prague *quodlibet quaestiones*.

A contemporary of Hus, and one of his closest friends and colleagues, Jakoubek of Stříbro justly holds the prominent place among Hussite theologians

---

49 See Šmahel's "Leben und Werk des Hieronymus von Prag," in Jerome of Prague, *Quaestiones, polemica, epistulae*, xi–cxxviii; Fudge, *Jerome of Prague*.
50 Jerome of Prague, *Quaestiones, polemica, epistulae*.
51 Ibid., 193–98.

that was suggested by Paul De Vooght.[52] Jakoubek studied at Prague University almost simultaneously with Hus: both of them were promoted to Bachelor of Arts in 1393, and Jakoubek received his Master's degree one year after Hus (1397). Jakoubek also enrolled at the Theological Faculty, and in 1410 he already held a Bachelor's degree in theology. Even though he successfully progressed through the university hierarchy, Jakoubek was never assigned a leading rank in the university administration. As an intellectual-idealist, Jakoubek enthused about evangelical poverty and criticized even his colleagues for their academic careerism.[53]

Until 1414, Jakoubek functioned as an active preacher and an eminent theologian of the reformist party. He held a benefice at St. Stephen's Church in the New Town of Prague; later he was connected with St. Michael's Church in the Old Town; and finally, he succeeded Hus as a preacher in the Bethlehem Chapel (ca. 1420). Jakoubek's cooperation with Hus was significant: he had an important role in the defence of Wyclif organized by Hus in 1410, where he defended the only theological work, the *Decalogus*. In Hus's *quodlibet* disputation of 1411, Jakoubek was assigned to solve one of the most important questions, concerning God. He is also one of the most frequent addressees of Hus's letters from Constance, a man whom Hus included among the most faithful friends of the truth.

The year 1415 was a turning point not only for Jakoubek, but also for other university masters who were now officially credited with an authority that was superior to the bishops and other church officials. This fact made Jakoubek's high position in the reformist party official.[54] Between 1415 and 1420, Jakoubek played a significant role in the spread of Utraquism and in the formulation of the Hussite political program, the so-called Four Articles of Prague. Another twist came in 1421, when Jakoubek was elected to the official hierarchy of the Hussite Church. After 1420, and until his death in 1429, he strove to maintain the doctrinal specifics of Utraquism.

As mentioned above, Jakoubek was active at the university and his theoretical work revolved mostly around Wyclif and his teachings.[55] Jakoubek was also a prolific preacher. His literary legacy consists largely of university sermons

---

52   De Vooght, *Jacobellus de Stříbro*.
53   Zilynská, "Jakoubek ze Stříbra a dobová církevní správa."
54   Kejř, *Mistři pražské univerzity a kněží táborští*, 7–18.
55   Jakoubek's writings are registered by Bartoš, *Literární činnost M. Jakoubka ze Stříbra*; Spunar, *Repertorium*, vol. 1, 214–50, 371. Zilynská, "Jakoubek ze Stříbra a dobová církevní správa," 37–38, points out that due to his position among the Hussite party, a number of testimonials, public notices and the like are traditionally ascribed to Jakoubek despite the problematic authorship.

and postils, including those composed in Czech. Jakoubek paid some attention to eschatology, especially to the Antichrist. For this purpose, he exploited the *Regulae* of Matěj of Janov,[56] but his Antichrist is more extreme. For Jakoubek the Antichrist was identical with the pope and represented the origin of all evil in the church and society, as he argued in his *Posicio de Antichristo*. The condemnation of Jan Hus was also the Antichrist's doing, as was the "recent" deprivation of the lay chalice for the laity. The eucharistic topic was by far the most important issue for Jakoubek, and his literary legacy is devoted mostly to this theme. Details will be mentioned later, but it should be underlined here that Jakoubek was the prime theologian to justify the necessity of the lay chalice (*Pius Iesus, Magna cena, Salvator noster, De communione parvulorum*), a matter in which he was considerably aided by Nicholas of Dresden. Unlike treatises on other topics, Jakoubek's eucharistic writings circulated widely, as the high numbers of extant copies testify. In his later writings from the 1420s, Jakoubek argued against the radical Hussite faction, the Taborites, in questions concerning wars or rites: for example, Jakoubek did not approve of the secular rule of the clergy and was against physical fighting. All of his extant treatises provide unique evidence of the challenges brought about by his contemporary situation.

Jan of Jesenice should be mentioned among Hussite theologians, too, even though he is more famous as the most important legal advisor and diplomat of the reformist party. Jan of Jesenice was one of Hus's students and originally a supporter of Wyclif's teachings, who took an active role in the enactment of the Decree of Kutná Hora in 1409.[57] He is most probably the author of the *Defensio mandati regis Wenceslai* – a treatise supporting King Wenceslas's decree in favor of the Bohemian university nation related to the Decree of Kutná Hora. He is also the author of the *Ordo procedendi* (1414), a text that sketches out the prosecution's case against Hus in Bohemia and at the papal curia up until 1414, when Hus left for Constance.[58] Apart from legal treatises, Jan discussed the question *Utrum iudex sciens testes*, dealing with the problem of false testimony and rooted in Wyclif's doctrine. His most widely circulated treatise is *Auctoritates pro communione sub utraque specie*, a collection of authorities that he sent to the Council of Constance in 1417. Jan engaged in a debate over the communion of children that captivated Hussite theologians in

---

56   Jakoubek was influenced by Janov in a number of other points, too, such as frequent sacramental reception of the Eucharist, or criticism of the use of images.
57   Kejř, *Husitský právník M. Jan z Jesenice*.
58   The treatise has also been ascribed to Hus, but the most recent analysis convincingly proved Jan of Jesenice's authorship; see Kejř, "K pramenům Husova procesu."

February 1417, criticizing Jakoubek's approval of the practice in his *Contra M. Iacobellum de communione parvulorum*.

5   Opponents and Internal Criticism

Many of the originally zealous supporters with reformist tendencies later became opponents of Hus, Jakoubek, and their colleagues.[59] This had much to do with the dispute over Wyclif and universals at Prague University. Nevertheless, the traditional explanation that this split was connected with the conflict between the nominalists – generally represented by the German masters – on the one hand, and the Czech masters as realists on the other hand, is to a large extent oversimplified and inaccurate. Still, some animosities were present at the university, and apart from the undeniable reasons for Czech-German antagonism, the shifting emphases of the young generation of Czech masters and their doctrinal challenging of the previous generation certainly played some role.

A case in point is the career of Ondřej of Brod. Upon finishing at the Arts Faculty, Ondřej enrolled at the Faculty of Law (1398), but his career is connected primarily with the Faculty of Theology, where he earned his doctorate (1408). Ondřej had the reputation of a distinguished scholar at Prague University and was also honored with high ranks in the university hierarchy (e.g. rector, 1407). Ondřej sincerely shared certain reformist tendencies, but he rejected Wyclif's teachings as heterodox from the very beginning. He also rebutted Jakoubek's tenet of remanence and his opinions on Utraquism. Ondřej turned into an enemy of Hus, but he did not testify against him at the Council of Constance. The end of Ondřej's career was spent at the University of Leipzig, where he worked until his death in 1427.[60]

Ondřej's substantial literary legacy includes university questions, preparations for *quodlibet* disputations, and sermons. A number of his polemical writings relate to the question of the Eucharist (*De sumpcione* and *Epistula ad Zbynconem cum tractatu contra errorem remanentiae* circulated most widely),[61] and some directly oppose Hus. While living outside Bohemia, Ondřej composed *Planctus super civitatem Pragensem* (ca. 1421) and *Tractatus de origine*

---

59   Hledíková, "Hussens Gegner und Feinde."
60   Kadlec, *Studien und Texte*.
61   The *Tractatus contra communionem calicis* (*De oboedientia*), previously ascribed to Ondřej, was written by an anonymous author before July 1415; see Krmíčková, "Paběrky z rukopisů univerzitních," 192–93, 209.

Hussitarum (1420–1422), both of which convey his anxiety over exile and bitterness towards the Hussites.

Somewhat outside the circle of Prague theologians, yet a very important figure among the adversaries of the Hussites, is Štěpán of Dolany. Štěpán was a prior of the Carthusian monastery in Dolany in Moravia, but evidence related to his life is scanty.[62] In his writings, which were frequently copied and excerpted, he stridently opposed the Hussites. Štěpán criticized Hus's and Wyclif's teachings on the matter of obedience (*Medulla tritici seu Antiwiclef*, 1408; *Antihuss*, 1412). In 1414 he composed an intricate polemic in the form of a dialogue between a goose and a sparrow (*Dialogus volatilis inter aucam et passerem*), mocking Hus's ideas and his name at the same time. His *Liber epistolaris ad Hussitas* (1417) criticized Hussite doctrines, but it is also famous for providing evidence of the work of a female Hussite author.[63] It has been observed that Štěpán was not primarily influential as a theologian, but for the literary qualities of his writings. A formal analysis of his *Dialogus volatilis*, for instance, shows that Štěpán's theological tracts fulfil the high requirements of medieval poetry and rhetoric.[64]

Šimon of Tišnov is an example of someone who fell out with his reformist colleagues fairly quickly. After his studies in the Arts and Law Faculties in Prague, Šimon obtained the Bachelor of Theology (1414) and later was elected rector of the University (1411). Initially a friend and adherent of the reformist circle in Prague, he participated in the defense of Wyclif's teachings (*De probationibus propositionum*). Šimon also took part in several *quodlibet* disputations and personally held the dispute in 1416 which was among those that most radically criticized the church, the institution of papacy, and papal power. Nevertheless, he turned against Hus and his party sometime around 1419 and subsequently polemicized on the communion of infants, baptism, the use of images, and on more general ecclesiological questions (*Contra hereses Wiclefistarum et Hussitarum*; *Tractatus de communione sub utraque, de baptismo parvulorum, de imaginibus etc. adversus Hussitas*; *De ecclesie catholice unitate*). The outcomes of his public activities include sermons as well as a widely circulated declaration against the Four Articles of Prague (*Contra quatuor articulos Bohemorum tractatus quidam*).[65]

---

62 Hikl, *Štěpán z Dolan*, 5. Spunar, *Repertorium*, vol. 1, 363–67.
63 Nechutová, "Frauen um Hus."
64 Nechutová, "K literární morfologii husitské polemiky," 216–18.
65 Odložilík, *Z počátků husitství na Moravě*; Loserth, "Simon von Tischnow."

6 The Dispute over Utraquism

As the most central issue of early Hussitism, the Utraquist dispute aptly illustrates the developments among Hussite theologians. Older historiographical tradition linked the Hussite requirement of communion under both kinds with the growing eucharistic piety that can be traced in Bohemia already in the 14th century, above all in Matěj of Janov's emphasis on frequent communion. Even though a direct connection between frequent communion and Utraquism can be disputed, the Hussite reformers did read and copy texts of their predecessors, including Janov. The most widespread story has it that Jakoubek of Stříbro – based on a close reading of Janov and in accordance with the biblical command *Nisi manducaveritis* (John 6:54) – had a "revelation" about the necessity of the lay chalice.[66] Between 1414 and 1417, a debate developed among Hussite theologians in Prague concerning this topic.[67] Initially Jakoubek presented his arguments about the necessity of the lay chalice in his sermons and at a university disputation with the question *Quia heu in templis*. Subsequently, he instigated a renewal of this abandoned practice.[68] What followed was a heated discussion among several theologians in Prague. Apart from Jakoubek, Jan of Jesenice, Peter Payne, and Nicholas of Dresden, Ondřej of Brod also took part, together with Brikcí of Žatec and Havlík (Gallus), to mention the principal names.

It is likely that the idea of the lay chalice already resonated in the Hussite milieu by the first half of 1414. After some hesitation among Hussite theologians, as expressed by Jan of Jesenice and Prokop of Plzeň, the chalice was approved by the "supreme authority" of Jan Hus. Hus was first asked to determine on the administration of the lay chalice only when in Constance, even though he was still in Bohemia when the practice commenced. Following the accusation of his support for Utraquism, Hus composed the question *De sanguine Christi sub specie vini a laicis sumendo* sometime in November 1414, in which he confirmed the beneficial effect of the Eucharist. His line of argument was based on the works of his colleagues that he had at his disposal, namely Jakoubek's *Quia heu in templis*, *Pius Iesus* and *Quod non solum sacerdotes*, and the *Collecta* by Nicholas of Dresden. However, Hus was much more moderate on the issue than Jakoubek and declared that the chalice is only beneficial and not necessary for salvation. Later on, in his eucharistic treatise *De sacramento*

---

66 Seibt, "Die revelatio des Jacobellus von Mies."
67 Krmíčková, *Studie a texty*; eadem, "Utraquism in 1414."
68 Jakoubek's oldest Utraquist work *Articulus pro communione sub utraque specie* was composed in August 1414; the university question was delivered in September 1414.

corporis et sanguinis Domini (*Sepius rogasti*), which he composed in jail in March 1415, Hus did not mention communion under both species at all.

Jakoubek of Stříbro and Nicholas of Dresden were the two most important theoreticians who stood at the beginnings of Hussite Utraquism. An early period of Utraquism, during which Jakoubek and Nicholas excerpted long passages from authorities that argued for the necessity of the lay chalice and adjusted them for their needs, is represented by Jakoubek's treatises *Quia heu in templis* (with its adjoining *Auctoritates*) and *Quod non solum sacerdotes*, as well as Nicholas's *Collecta*. In subsequent stages, only succinct and key parts from these were used by the reformers.

The practice of Utraquism had spread in Bohemia by the early autumn of 1414. We know this because Nicholas of Dresden's sermon on *Nisi manducaveritis*, which can be dated to September 1414, contains a valuable reference to the incipient practice.[69] Another witness to this practice is a synodal decree of 18 October 1414, which banned the administration of the Eucharist in both kinds to the laity under the threat of excommunication. Among those who polemicized on a theoretical level with the Utraquists in the second half of 1414 were Štěpán of Páleč (who in his *Responsa* interpreted the biblical *Nisi manducaveritis* spiritually), Brikcí of Žatec (*Utrum venerabile sacramentum eukaristie*), and possibly Petr of Uničov and Jan of Hradec, whose texts do not survive. Nevertheless, the leading opponent of Jakoubek in this matter was Ondřej of Brod: their duel of words during September and October 1414 stood at the very outset of the theoretical justification of the lay chalice.[70] Jakoubek's now lost text entitled *Remissius fiet Sodomitis* provoked an answer from Ondřej (*Utrum licitum sit*), in which he stressed that communion *sub utraque* was commanded only for priests and is redundant for the laity. The exchange of opinions continued in Jakoubek's *Pius Iesus* and Ondřej's subsequent tract *De sumpcione*, where he discussed at length the possible dangers of communion *sub utraque*. In his response Ondřej pointed out problems surrounding communion for the ill and for those with beards. Jakoubek's subsequent *Responsio* in turn solves the possible obstacles of communion of the ill and the bearded and also deals with the danger of pouring out the blood of Christ. The *Responsio* was written either at the very end of 1414 or early 1415. After the *Responsio*, possibly in February or March 1415, Jakoubek composed a long Czech tract on the same matter (*O Boží krvi* [On God's blood]). This was largely a translation of his *Quod non solum*

---

69 "Non resistamus, sed pareamus et incipiamus!" (Let us not resist, but obey and begin!); see Nicholas of Dresden, *Puncta*, 184.
70 Kadlec, "Literární polemika"; idem, *Studien und Texte*, 21–67.

sacerdotes whereby he provided the laity with arguments for the necessity of the lay chalice.

In the meantime, a sceptical voice was also to be heard amidst the reformers. Havlík (Gallus), a successor to Hus in the Bethlehem Chapel, made a stand against the lay chalice in a text entitled *Asserunt quidam*. Havlík argued against Jakoubek's *Magna cena* and stressed that communion *sub utraque* was not ordered by God but rather left to choice. Moreover, Havlík also understood communion spiritually. In this respect he held the same position as Hus, who – in a letter of 19 January 1415 – tried to soothe Havlík and forestall the emerging rift in the reformist party. Two prominent members of the reformist party opposed Havlík, namely Peter Payne (*Quia nostri temporis homines*) and Nicholas of Dresden (*Contra Gallum*). Nicholas of Dresden turned out to be the most important supporter and colleague of Jakoubek on this issue. Apart from the sermon *Nisi manducaveritis* and the *Collecta* attached to it, Nicholas wrote a number of other Utraquist treatises (e.g. *Quod fuit ab initio*, *Replica rectori scholarum in Corbach*, *Sermo ad clerum*, 1416) and complemented Jakoubek's arguments on many points. The cooperation between Jakoubek and Nicholas is well illustrated in the case of infant communion, another novelty of Hussite Utraquism.[71] Firstly, Jakoubek argued for the necessity of infant communion in his *Responsio*, in an answer to Ondřej's *De sumpcione*. In the *Contra Gallum*, written during late summer or early autumn 1415, Nicholas collected and presented relevant authorities that justified this requirement for the first time. At any rate, Utraquism proved to be a pivotal theme of Nicholas's literary legacy. Among his Utraquist treatises, the most popular and widespread treatise is the *Apologia*, Nicholas's sharp reaction to the official condemnation of the lay chalice by the Council of Constance.[72]

The official prohibition of the lay chalice was declared by the Council of Constance on 15 June 1415 by the decree *Cum in nonnullis*. The condemnation came approximately a year after this issue had come to the fore of Hussite theology, and the path leading to it was even more intricate than sketched above. The text of the prohibition ensued from the polemic represented above all by Jakoubek and Ondřej and was modelled mostly on the work of Viennese theologian Peter of Pulkau (who for this purpose undertook a thorough analysis of Jakoubek's *Pius Iesus*, resulting in his *Confutatio Iacobi de Misa*) with Pierre d'Ailly operating as the *éminence grise* in the case.[73]

---

71   Holeton, "The Communion of Infants and Hussitism"; idem, *La communion des tout-petits enfants*.
72   Nicholas of Dresden, *Apologia*.
73   Girgensohn, *Peter von Pulkau und die Wiedereinführung des Laienkelches*.

7 Hussite Theologians and the Council of Constance

The issue of the lay chalice continued to stir emotions among Catholic and Hussite theologians at the Council of Constance. Reactions to the prohibition of the lay chalice were naturally manifold. In one of the first responses, Jan Hus addressed a letter to Václav of Dubá and Jan of Chlum in which he called the council's decision simply "dementia." He also admonished Havlík to refrain from opposing the Utraquist rite.[74] The most widely circulated treatise to argue with the prohibition was a tract entitled *Apologia* by Nicholas of Dresden. Jakoubek reflected on the situation in a Czech treatise (*Zpráva, jak sněm konstantský o svátosti večeře Kristovy nařídil* [Account on the Council of Constance's decision about the sacrament of Christ's supper]). In consequence, several counter-attacking voices were heard from Constance. Jean Gerson argued that councils had the right to accept and decree even things that are not substantiated by the Bible. Johannes Hildessen defended the general authority of councils and stressed the need to accept the council's decisions. His short tract *Sacro concilio non est detrahendum* was written in the second half of 1415 and provoked an answer from Jakoubek (*Utrum omnem sentenciam cuiuslibet concilii*). The debate now took on another important aspect – the general authority of councils, a question that proved to bear significant consequences. The outcomes of this debate included singular items composed by the Hussite reformers as well as by Constance theologians.[75]

None of the official bans and threats concerning the Utraquist rite had any real impact on the situation in Bohemia. The famous chronicler Vavřinec of Březová observed that within two years after the official prohibition the supporters of the lay chalice took over almost all of the parish churches in Prague and were followed by people in the countryside. Moreover, he noted that the Eucharist was also administered in both kinds to infants.[76] As mentioned above, the communion of infants was indeed a new element in the Utraquist discussion. By the end of 1415, two Catholic reactions opposing this novelty were written: *Eloquenti viro*, ascribed to Nicholas of Dinkelsbühl, and the anonymous *Estote sine offensione*, sometimes attributed to Štěpán of Páleč and recently to Ondřej of Brod.[77] Both of them were highly popular, as dozens of extant copies prove.

---

74 Hus, *Korespondence a dokumenty*, 289, 294–95.
75 Coufal, *Polemika o kalich*, 42–101.
76 Vavřinec of Březová, "Kronika husitská," 334–35.
77 The attribution to Ondřej of Brod was suggested most recently by Traxler, "Früher Antihussitismus."

Between 1417 and 1418 another sharp polemic between the Constance theologians and the Hussites transpired. The roots of this debate lay in the attempt of Prague University to achieve a re-examination of the *Cum in nonnullis* decree (1415), possibly in connection with the officially declared support of the lay chalice announced by the university on 10 March 1417. The impulse came from Jan of Jesenice and the Utraquist masters who excerpted the most significant authorities in favor of communion in both kinds and sent them to the Council of Constance. These *Auctoritates pro communione sub utraque specie* were refuted by Jean de Roque, Nicholas of Dinkelsbühl, Jean Gerson, and Mařík Rvačka.

Master Mařík Rvačka became one of the most famous enemies of Jan Hus at the Council of Constance. Mařík studied in Prague and joined the Penitent Order of the Holy Martyrs (the Cyriacists).[78] Following the duties of his order, he traveled to Rome around 1400, where he obtained a doctorate in theology. Pope Boniface IX named him a monastic *visitator* of his order in Bohemia, Poland, and Silesia. Mařík took part in the Council of Constance as a member of the Polish delegation and during his active presence there he composed more than twenty treatises and preached on several occasions.[79] The seven extant sermons deal with ecclesiastical reform, and in them we can trace a special interest in accusing the clergy of simony. He also critically answered the *Auctoritates pro communione sub utraque* by Jan of Jesenice in his *Apostolica docet sententia*. Surviving in more than thirty medieval copies, this treatise is one of the most widely circulated from Mařík's literary legacy. Later copies of this text attest to the fact that the lay chalice was still topical more than a hundred years after its origin. A number of further treatises by Mařík dealt with various questions concerning communion *sub utraque*, but not all of the attributions to him are justified.[80] After the end of the council, Mařík traveled to Poland where he worked for the bishop of Poznan, *Andrzej Łaskarz*, to help suppress the spread of Hussite doctrines.

Many of the ex-supporters of the reformist party in Bohemia who had close ties to Prague University participated in the Council of Constance.[81] They were naturally biased by local animosities, yet it was above all their input that contributed to the "fame" of the "Czech question" at Constance. As a result, some

---

78   Mařík's biography is still obscure: Soukup, "Mařík Rvačka's Defense of Crusading Indulgences."
79   Kadlec, "Literární činnost Mistra Maříka Rvačky."
80   For instance, Mařík's authorship of the *De corpore Cristi M. Mauricii*, which was considered to demonstrate a link between Matěj of Janov and the Hussites, has been refuted; see Nechutová, "De 'Tractatus de corpore Christi' M. Mauritio adscripti fonte Janoviano."
81   Soukup, "Die böhmischen Konzilsteilnehmer."

questions discussed by the Hussite theologians were brought to the attention of the most distinguished theoreticians of the time, a fact that in turn affected the development of Hussite doctrines.

8 Radical Theologians and the Hussite Factions

Following the proceedings at the Council of Constance, a new phase in the history of the Hussite movement commenced.[82] A series of turbulent actions resulted in the development of radical Hussite ideology and several Hussite factions. The period of the Hussite wars is characterized by a number of more and less important disputes, legacies, negotiations, manifestos, notices, leaflets and the like, often surviving in single copies and seldom preserved in their original form.[83] Only a few theologians took an active part in the momentous occasions of the period and were recognized in the theoretical discourse.

During the early stages of the movement's radicalization, an important role was played by Jan Želivský, a radical preacher in the New Town of Prague.[84] Preparatory notes for his sermons delivered in 1419 have survived which aptly illustrate the mounting tensions in Prague and the reasons behind the radicalization of the poor.[85] The year 1419 is traditionally considered to mark the outbreak of the actual war period. The theoretical discussion about the legitimacy of a just war and killing in general that commenced among Prague theologians in the autumn of 1419 continued for some time after the pope announced the First Crusade against the Hussites in March 1420. Opposition to all killing was voiced by many of the radical Hussite theologians, including Nicholas of Dresden. On the other hand, the conservative theologian Jan of Příbram resolutely denied any doubts in this matter and called for defense by force of arms (*Tractatus de bello*; *De conditionibus iusti belli*). The determining moment in this matter was the testimonial of Prague University issued after Jakoubek of Stříbro and Křišťan of Prachatice had been asked about the legitimacy of wars. Together with other university masters, they elaborated an answer to this in February 1420, in which they placed conditions on the legitimacy of *bellum*

---

82   Howard Kaminsky in his synthesis of the Hussite revolution marked this as "the establishment of Hussitism"; see his *A History*, 141.
83   For theoretical remarks about the material, see Hruza, "'Audite et cum speciali diligencia attendite.'"
84   Kopičková, *Jan Želivský*.
85   Želivský, *Dochovaná kázání*; however, Marek, *Jakoubek ze Stříbra*, 72–74, raises doubts about Želivský's authorship of the material.

iustum but gave an overall positive answer.[86] Moreover, the foundation of Tábor at the beginning of 1420, a new centre for radical Hussites who strove to live according to a strict application of the *lex Dei*, is also a milestone in the development of Hussite ideology. The ongoing debates between Prague theologians and the representatives of Tábor were a source of numerous frictions, and certain tensions between these two groups persisted throughout the Hussite wars.[87]

The prolific theologian Jan of Příbram studied at Prague University and after Želivský's death in 1422 became the most influential theologian in Prague next to Jakoubek of Stříbro.[88] Both men were involved in the radicalization of Hussite ideology. After his initial support of the radical party, Příbram became a representative of the conservative wing. From the 1420s, he participated in the polemics between the Prague theologians and Tábor, in which he fervently criticized the novelties of the Taborites, endorsed the good tradition of the Catholic Church, and did not fear to play a patriotic note. During the period that he was exiled from Prague (1427–1436), Příbram composed most of his Czech treatises as well as a number of polemics criticizing Wyclif (as the supreme authority for the Taborites) and arguing with Peter Payne. Příbram's demand to return to the indigenous tradition (Janov, Hus) and his belief in a local reformed church that would return to the Christian community is considered to have been driven by his genuine concern for the Kingdom of Bohemia. Příbram was also an active member of the Hussite delegation to the Council of Basel in 1437, and the failure of the Hussites to convince the council of the necessity of the chalice for salvation was a source of bitter disappointment to him. During the subsequent disputes between various Utraquist factions, Příbram was the leader of the moderate Utraquists until his death in 1448.

The pivotal themes of Příbram's large literary legacy, comprising approximately forty items, are the issues of the Eucharist and the rites concerning the Mass.[89] A number of his polemics were aimed against Peter Payne (*Proposicio*; *Quia plerique*; *Tractatus de erroribus Wiclifi contra Petrum Payne*) and the doctrines of Wyclif (*Quia istis novissimis temporibus*; *Apologia*) or the radical Hussites (*Contra articulos Picardorum*; *De ritibus misse*; *Ad occurendum homini insano*; *Surge domine*). Among his Czech treatises, the longest is the popular

---

86   Seibt, *Hussitica*, 16–57.
87   Kaminsky, "Hussite Radicalism and the Origins of Tábor"; Kejř, *Mistři pražské univerzity a kněží táborští*; Soukup, "The Masters and the End of the World."
88   Příbram, *Život kněží táborských*, 1–11.
89   Bartoš, *Literární činnost M. Jana Rokycany, M. Jana Příbrama, M. Petra Payna*, 56–89; Spunar, *Repertorium*, vol. 2, 154–74.

Knížky o zamúceniech velikých cierkve svaté (Books on the great sadness of Holy Church). However, the most influential among his Czech writings (and even his oeuvre as a whole) is *Život kněží táborských* (The life of the Taborite priests), a large antithetical diptych written around 1430. The first part criticizes a resolution of the synod of Tábor of 1430, while the second, which fiercely and at length describes the flaws and sins of the Taborite clergy, is a sort of supplement to the first. The text – albeit tendentious and full of venom – is valuable not only for its topical details regarding the radical Hussites, but also because it contains excerpts from otherwise lost Taborite treatises. A number of Příbram's texts also survive from his activities at the Council of Basel (*Posicio Przibram in concilio Basiliensi contra auditorem*; *Replica in concilio Basiliensi contra auditorem Iohannem de Palomar*).

In Tábor, a faction of moderate Hussites gradually prevailed whose most prominent representative was Mikuláš Biskupec of Pelhřimov. Mikuláš studied in Prague and in 1420 he was elected an elder of the Taborites. He functioned as their spokesman and was active in the polemics with Prague University as well as in the negotiations leading to the Council of Basel. After the Hussite wars, Mikuláš continued to defend the ideological positions of the Taborites and clashed with Aeneas Silvius Piccolomini. He gradually fell into isolation and his opinions were finally condemned at a diet in 1444.

Mikuláš's literary legacy comprises a number of polemics with the radical Hussites, with Petr Chelčický, and others. A polemic concerning the Eucharist among the Taborites, especially the most radical factions in 1421, resulted in several texts by Mikuláš (e.g. *Ad magnificacionem*). Mikuláš also authored several tracts on biblical topics (*Commentarius super Apocalypsin*; *Scriptum super quatuor evangelia in unum concordata*). His lengthy commentary on the Apocalypse, in which he instructed the Taborite priests on how to perceive this apocalyptic vision, is especially noteworthy.[90] However, his most important treatise is the *Confessio et apologia Taboritarum* (c. 1431),[91] composed in connection with a university disputation of 30 April 1431. In an attempt to resolve the conflict between the Prague theologians and the Taborite priests, Mikuláš, as a representative of the Tábor party, disputed with Jan Rokycana. Mikuláš focused on the question of whether all sacraments were instituted by Christ and are necessary for salvation. His negative answer represented the belief of the Taborites that only baptism, the Eucharist and matrimony are necessary. In

---

90   Kaminsky, "Nicholas of Pelhřimov's Tabor"; Cermanová, *Čechy na konci věků*, 129–41 and passim.
91   Mikuláš Biskupec, *Confessio Taboritarum*.

his emphasis on the primitive church and its practices as well as on the *lex Christi*, Mikuláš largely followed the opinions of Nicholas of Dresden, even though he drew on other authorities as well (including Hus). *Confessio et apologia Taboritarum* is the most significant and comprehensive manifestation of radical Hussite ideology. It had a substantial impact not only on the formation of Taborite ideology but was influential outside Bohemia as well – it was translated, for instance, by the Romance Waldensians in Piedmont in the 16th century.[92] Mikuláš composed a number of additional texts in connection with his participation at the Council of Basel and the negotiations leading to it. He is also the author of an important chronicle describing the cause of the Taborite priests in three volumes (*Chronica causam sacerdotum Thaboriensium continens*).

As already mentioned, in the university disputation of 1431 the university party was represented by the skilful politician Jan Rokycana, a follower of Hus and friend of Jakoubek of Stříbro.[93] Rokycana was in charge of the Utraquist Church in Prague after Jakoubek's death in 1429 and was an influential preacher who also played a significant role at the Council of Basel in 1433 (*Collacio M. Johannis de Rokyczana in concilio Basiliensi*). In 1435 Rokycana was elected archbishop of Prague, but the election was not officially recognized. His expansive literary legacy includes around fifty mostly short items that comprise polemics, letters, and postils.[94] At the university disputation of 1431, Rokycana delivered a speech on *De quinque prioribus sacramentis* and criticized the Taborites by pointing out seven of their deviations from the doctrines of the Prague Utraquists (*De septem culpis Taboritarum*).

An important figure among the Hussites was the Englishman Peter Payne.[95] He was educated at Oxford, where he became closely acquainted with the doctrines of Wyclif. His activities in spreading Wyclif's tenets ran afoul of English church authorities, and it was likely the imminent charges that compelled Payne to flee England around 1413.[96] He traveled through Germany, reaching

---

[92] A Waldensian adaptation of the *Confessio* is known as the *Tresor e lume de fe* and, together with a Waldensian translation of the *De quadruplici missione* by Nicholas of Dresden and Hus's *De matrimonio*, represents a direct link between the Hussites and the Waldensians; see Molnár, "Hus's *De matrimonio* and Its Waldensian Version"; idem, "Tresor e lume de fe."

[93] Boubín and Zachová (ed.), *Žaloby katolíků na Mistra Jana z Rokycan*.

[94] Bartoš, *Literární činnost M. Jana Rokycany, M. Jana Příbrama, M. Petra Payna*, 14–55. For Rokycana's activities after the *Compactata*, see Jindřich Marek's chapter in this volume.

[95] Šmahel summarized Payne's life in *The Oxford Dictionary of National Biography*, vol. 43, 208–13; a full German biography is available in Šmahel, "Magister Peter Payne."

[96] The date of his departure ranges from 1413 to 1416; see Šmahel, "Magister Peter Payne," 243–44.

Prague c. 1414, and spent the rest of his life in Bohemia. Payne was admitted to the board of masters of Prague University only in 1417, and this late acceptance has sometimes been considered the result of his connections with the so-called Dresden School in Prague, a center of German nonconformists who gathered around Nicholas of Dresden.[97] Payne subsequently became a chief diplomat of many Hussite legations, and he participated in all major negotiations during the war period between 1420 and 1434. In the Slavonic Monastery (*Na Slovanech*) in the New Town of Prague, he initiated work on a catalogue of Wyclif's writings and their indexes that were to serve as quick reference guides at the upcoming theological disputations at the Council of Basel.[98] Payne's chief position among Hussite theologians was demonstrated by the decision of the diet of October 1434 that elected him arbiter of the doctrinal disputes between the two most important Hussite wings, the Prague and the Taborite parties. His turbulent destiny moreover involved several attempts to make him face charges from Oxford, including imprisonment and ransoming. Efforts to identify him with Konstantinos Anglikos, an envoy of the Bohemian Utraquist consistory who appeared in Constantinople in 1452, are presently rejected by most scholars.[99] After 1452 Payne lived again in the monastery *Na Slovanech* in Prague, where he probably died in 1456.

Payne's rich literary legacy originated in Bohemia and dealt with the most important issues of the day.[100] His first contribution to the early Utraquist dispute of the Hussite theologians with Havlík was a tract *Quia nostri temporis homines*, and his determined defence of the lay chalice soon won him recognition among the Hussites. Payne also dealt with the problem of taking oaths,[101] the theory of predestination and free will, and the worship of images. A number of his works polemicize with Jan of Příbram mostly over Wyclif's doctrines (*Posicio M. Petri Anglici contra Przibram*; *Tractatus M. Petri Anglici contra errores circa sacramentum altaris venerabile*). In 1433 at the Council of Basel, Payne skilfully defended clerical poverty against Juan Palomar (*Petri Payne Anglici Posicio, replica et proposicio in concilio Basiliensi*).

---

97 Mutlová, "Die Dresdner Schule in Prag."
98 Hudson, "*Accessus ad auctorem*," 333–37; eadem, "The Hussite Catalogue of Wyclif's Works"; eadem, "From Oxford to Bohemia."
99 Šmahel, "Magister Peter Payne," 259–60.
100 Bartoš, *Literární činnost M. Jana Rokycany, M. Jana Příbrama, M. Petra Payna*, 93–111.
101 On his denial of taking oaths and its possible Lollard origin, see Hudson, *The Premature Reformation*, 371.

9 Historiographic Survey

Interest in Hussite theologians is closely connected with the beginnings of Prague University. A volume on the general history of the university, *A History of Charles University*,[102] provides a useful starting point with a succinct overview of the founding masters of the Theological Faculty and their treatises. More details can be found in the literary history of medieval Latin literature that covers the period until 1400,[103] or in repertories of authors connected with Prague University – either Czech authors,[104] or those who were active in the pre-Hussite period until 1409.[105] The so-called *Verfasserlexikon* remains an indispensable guidebook for a number of authors with lesser-known oeuvres.[106] An anthology of Hussite literature with Czech translations of selected texts is also available.[107]

Research into the development of Hussite theology has been triggered, among other things, by the concept of the "forerunners of Hus and Hussitism," a term coined by Zitte in 1786 and Palacký in 1846.[108] The origins of the Bohemian Reformation continue to attract scholarly attention,[109] and a summary of this debate can be found in Šmahel,[110] or in a recent work by Marin.[111] The influence of John Wyclif was of central importance for Hussite theology at the turn of the 14th and 15th centuries. A profound assessment of this issue is provided by Herold[112] and Šmahel.[113] A list of relevant treatises composed in connection with the dispute over universals was compiled by Šmahel;[114] lists of university *quaestiones* and disputations *de quolibet* are also available.[115] Research into textual transmission between England and Bohemia has brought

---

102 Svatoš (ed.), *Dějiny Univerzity Karlovy*; English version: Kavka and Petráň (eds.), *A History of Charles University*.
103 Nechutová, *Die lateinische Literatur*.
104 Spunar, *Repertorium*.
105 Tříška, *Literární činnost předhusitské univerzity*; idem, *Životopisný slovník*.
106 Ruh et al. (eds.) *Die deutsche Literatur des Mittelalters. Verfasserlexikon*.
107 Havránek et al. (eds.), *Výbor*.
108 Zitte, *Lebensbeschreibungen*; Palacký, *Die Vorläufer des Hussitenthums in Böhmen*.
109 For example, Eberhard and Machilek (eds.), *Kirchliche Reformimpulse*.
110 *Jan Hus. Život a dílo*.
111 *L'archevêque*.
112 *Pražská univerzita a Wyclif*; "Zum Prager philosophischen Wyclifismus"; "Wyclif's Ecclesiology"; and "Ideové kořeny reformace."
113 *Die Prager Universität im Mittelalter*, 467–598.
114 *Verzeichnis der Quellen zum Prager Universalienstreit*.
115 Herold, *Pražská univerzita a Wyclif*; Šmahel, *Die Prager Universität im Mittelalter*.

about valuable insights into this matter, too.[116] Modern syntheses on Wyclif also reflect subsequent theological developments associated with Hus and the Hussites.[117] The central role of the Eucharist in the Hussite movement has been subject to a number of studies, and the situation up to the rejection of Utraquism issued by the Council of Constance in 1415 has been mapped out minutely.[118] Developments in the subsequent stages of Hussitism, including the question of infant communion,[119] await further research. Recently the role of preachers in the Czech Reformation, and particularly that of Jakoubek of Stříbro, has received significant attention.[120]

Major Hussite theologians have been treated in scholarly literature profusely. However, many of their treatises are not available in critical editions, which remains the most limiting factor in appraising the period. This applies to Hus himself: his treatises appear in the *Magistri Iohannis Hus Opera omnia* series at a pace that can hardly be described as satisfactory.[121] Hus's Czech treatises are completely edited, but his Latin works have been treated much more poorly. The same holds true for even more important theologians, such as Jakoubek of Stříbro, Štěpán of Páleč, Jan of Příbram, and many others. A fortunate exception is now Jerome of Prague, whose treatises have recently been edited[122] and whose biography is available in English.[123]

The lack of critical editions is particularly surprising given the ideological distortion of the Hussite period during the era of communism and the plethora of studies on radical Hussite theologians. A general context of the history of the Hussite revolution is provided by Betts,[124] Kaminsky,[125] and Šmahel.[126] For the subsequent period, the history of Tábor has received some attention.[127] Features of sources that originated during the Hussite wars have been

---

116 Hudson, *Premature Reformation*; eadem, *Studies in the Transmission of Wyclif's Writings*; Van Dussen, *From England to Bohemia*.
117 Levy (ed.), *A Companion to John Wyclif*; Hornbeck and Van Dussen (eds.), *Europe After Wyclif*.
118 Krmíčková, *Studie a texty*.
119 See Holeton, *La communion des tout-petits enfants*.
120 Soukup, *Reformní kazatelství*; Marek, *Jakoubek ze Stříbra*.
121 See Vidmanová, *Základní vydání*.
122 Jerome of Prague, *Quaestiones, polemica, epistulae*.
123 Fudge, *Jerome of Prague*.
124 *Essays in Czech History*.
125 *History of the Hussite Revolution*.
126 *Die Hussitische Revolution*.
127 Šmahel, *Dějiny Tábora*.

examined, as have some of the most common textual sources – manifestos, satirical treatises, etc.[128] Nonetheless, the period of the Hussite wars deserves further attention as far as the source material is concerned.

Bibliography

Repertories

Bartoš, František Michálek, *Literární činnost M. Jakoubka ze Stříbra* [The literary activity of Master Jakoubek of Stříbro] (Prague: 1925).

Bartoš, František Michálek, *Literární činnost M. Jana Rokycany, M. Jana Příbrama, M. Petra Payna* [The literary activity of Master Jan Rokycana, Master Jan Příbram, Master Peter Payne] (Prague: 1928).

Bartoš, František Michálek, and Pavel Spunar, *Soupis pramenů k literární činnosti M. Jana Husa a M. Jeronýma Pražského* [An inventory of sources concerning the literary activity of Master Jan Hus and Master Jerome of Prague] (Prague: 1965).

Nechutová, Jana, *Die lateinische Literatur des Mittelalters in Böhmen* (Cologne, Weimar, and Vienna: 2007).

Ruh, Kurt, et al. (eds.), *Die deutsche Literatur des Mittelalters. Verfasserlexikon*, 14 vols., 2nd ed. (Berlin and New York: 1978–2008).

Šmahel, František, *Verzeichnis der Quellen zum Prager Universalienstreit 1348–1500*, (Mediaevalia Philosophica Polonorum) 25 (Wrocław: 1980).

Šmahel, František, "Die Verschriftlichung der Quodlibet-Disputationen an der Prager Artistenfakultät bis 1420," in idem, *Die Prager Universität im Mittelalter. The Charles University in the Middle Ages* (Leiden and Boston: 2007), 359–86.

Spunar, Pavel, *Repertorium auctorum Bohemorum provectum idearum post universitatem Pragensem conditam illustrans*, 2 vols. (Studia Copernicana) 25 and 35 (Wrocław and Warsaw: 1985–1995).

Tříška, Josef, *Literární činnost předhusitské univerzity* [The literary activity of the pre-Hussite university] (Prague: 1967).

Tříška, Josef, *Životopisný slovník předhusitské pražské univerzity 1348–1409* [A biographical dictionary of pre-Hussite Prague university 1348–1409] (Prague: 1981).

Vidmanová, Anežka, *Základní vydání spisů M. Jana Husi. Le principali edizioni degli scritti del maestro Jan Hus* (Prague: 1999).

---

128 Molnár (ed.), *Husitské manifesty*; Svejkovský (ed.), *Veršované skladby doby husitské*. Hruza also discusses manifestos and satires specifically: see "Audite et cum speciali diligencia attendite" and "Audite celi!"

Editions of Sources

Havránek, Bohuslav, Josef Hrabák, and Jiří Daňhelka (eds.), *Výbor z české literatury doby husitské* [An anthology of Czech literature of the Hussite period], 2 vols. (Prague: 1963–1964).

Heinrich of Bitterfeld, *Henricus Bitterfeld de Brega OP. Tractatus de vita contemplativa et activa*, eds. Bruno Mazur, Władysław Seńko, and Richard Tatarzyński (Warsaw: 2003).

Höfler, Konstantin (ed.), *Geschichtschreiber der husitischen Bewegung in Böhmen*, 3 vols. (Fontes rerum Austriacarum, 1. Abteilung: Scriptores) 2, 6, and 7 (Vienna: 1856–1866).

Hus, Jan, *M. Jana Husi Korespondence a dokumenty* [Master Jan Hus's Correspondence and documents], ed. Václav Novotný (Spisy M. Jana Husi) 9 (Prague: 1920).

Hus, Jan, *Sermones in Bethlehem 1410–1411*, ed. Václav Flajšhans, 6 vols. (Věstník Královské české společnosti nauk) (Prague: 1938–1945).

Hus, Jan, *Magistri Iohannis Hus Quodlibet. Disputationis de quolibet Pragae in facultate artium mense Ianuario anni 1411 habitae enchiridion*, ed. Bohumil Ryba (Magistri Iohannis Hus Opera omnia 20) (Prague: 1948); 2nd ed. (Corpus christianorum. Continuatio mediaevalis) 211 (Turnhout: 2006).

Hus, Jan, "De sex erroribus," in *Betlemské texty*, ed. Bohumil Ryba (Prague: 1951), 39–63, 167–183, 225–230.

Hus, Jan, *Magistri Johannis Hus Tractatus de ecclesia*, ed. S. Harrison Thomson (Cambridge, Eng., and Boulder, CO.: 1956; repr. Prague: 1958).

Hus, Jan, *Positiones, recommendationes, sermones*, ed. Anežka Schmidtová (Prague: 1958).

Hus, Jan, *Magistri Iohannis Hus Sermones de tempore qui Collecta dicuntur*, ed. Anežka Schmidtová (Magistri Iohannis Hus Opera omnia) 7 (Prague: 1959).

Hus, Jan, *Magistri Iohannis Hus Passio Domini nostri Iesu Cristi*, ed. Anežka Vidmanová-Schmidtová (Magistri Iohannis Hus Opera omnia) 8 (Prague: 1972).

Hus, Jan, *Magistri Iohannis Hus Postilla adumbrata*, ed. Bohumil Ryba (Magistri Iohannis Hus Opera omnia) 13 (Prague: 1975); 2nd ed. (Corpus christianorum. Continuatio mediaevalis) 261 (Turnhout: 2015).

Hus, Jan, *Leccionarium bipartitum. Pars hiemalis*, ed. Anežka Vidmanová-Schmidtová, (Magistri Iohannis Hus Opera omnia) 9 (Prague: 1988).

Hus, Jan, *Magistri Iohannis Hus Questiones*, ed. Jiří Kejř (Magistri Iohannis Hus Opera omnia) 19a (Corpus christianorum. Continuatio mediaevalis) 205 (Turnhout: 2004).

Hus, Jan, *Magistri Iohannis Hus Polemica*, ed. Jaroslav Eršil (Magistri Iohannis Hus Opera omnia) 22 (Prague: 1966); 2nd ed. (Corpus christianorum. Continuatio mediaevalis) 238 (Turnhout: 2010).

Hus, Jan, *Magistri Iohannis Hus Enarratio Psalmorum (Ps. 109–118)*, eds. Jana Nechutová, Helena Krmíčková, Dušan Coufal, Jana Fuksová, Petra Mutlová, Anna Pumprová,

Dana Stehlíková, and Libor Švanda (Magistri Iohannis Hus Opera omnia) 17 (Corpus christianorum. Continuatio mediaevalis) 253 (Turnhout: 2013).
Hus, Jan, *Magistri Iohannis Hus Constantiensia*, eds. Helena Krmíčková, Jana Nechutová, Dušan Coufal, Jana Fuksová, Lucie Mazalová, Petra Mutlová, Libor Švanda, Soňa Žákovská, and Amedeo Molnár (Magistri Iohannis Hus Opera omnia) 24 (Corpus christianorum. Continuatio mediaevalis) 274 (Turnhout: 2016).
Hus, Jan, and Jerome of Prague, *Ioannis Hus et Hieronymi Pragensis confessorum Christi Historia et monumenta*, ed. Matthias Flacius Illyricus, 2 vols. (Nuremberg: 1558; repr. Frankfurt: 1715).
Jakoubek of Stříbro, "Defensio libri Decalogi Magistri Johannis Wiklef," ed. Jan Sedlák, "Husův pomocník v evangeliu" [Hus's assistant in the Gospel], *Studie a texty k náboženským dějinám českým* 2 (1915): 316–328.
Jakoubek of Stříbro, *Výklad na Zjevenie sv. Jana* [Exposition of the Revelation of St. John], ed. František Šimek, 2 vols. (Prague: 1932–1933).
Jakoubek of Stříbro, "Salvator noster," in *Betlemské texty*, ed. Bohumil Ryba (Prague: 1951), 105–139, 209–216, 231–234.
Jerome of Prague, *Magistri Hieronymi de Praga Quaestiones, polemica, epistulae*, eds. František Šmahel and Gabriel Silagi (Corpus christianorum. Continuatio mediaevalis) 222 (Turnhout: 2010).
Matěj of Janov, *Regulae Veteris et Novi Testamenti*, vols. 1–4, ed. Vlastimil Kybal (Innsbruck: 1908–1913); vol. 5, ed. Vlastimil Kybal and Otakar Odložilík (Prague: 1913); vol. 6, eds. Jana Nechutová and Helena Krmíčková (Munich: 1993).
Mikuláš Biskupec of Pelhřimov, "Chronicon Taboritarum," in *Geschichtschreiber der husitischen Bewegung in Böhmen*, ed. Konstantin Höfler, vol. 2 (Fontes rerum Austriacarum, 1. Abteilung: Scriptores) 6 (Vienna: 1865), 475–820.
Mikuláš Biskupec of Pelhřimov, *Confessio Taboritarum*, eds. Amedeo Molnár and Romolo Cegna (Rome: 1983).
Mikuláš Biskupec of Pelhřimov, *Mikuláš z Pelhřimova: Vyznání a obrana Táborů* [Confession and defense of the Taborites], trans. František M. Dobiáš and Amedeo Molnár (Prague: 1972).
Molnár, Amedeo (ed.), *Husitské manifesty* [Hussite Manifestos] (Prague: 1980).
Nicholas of Dresden, *Nicolai (ut dicunt) de Dresda vulgo appellati de Čerruc (De Černá růže id est de Rosa Nigra [†1418?]) Puncta*, ed. Romolo Cegna (Mediaevalia Philosophica Polonorum) 33 (Warsaw: 1996), 55–156.
Nicholas of Dresden, *Nicolai Dresdensis Apologia. De conclusionibus doctorum in Constantia de materia sanguinis*, ed. Petra Mutlová (Brno: 2015).
Ondřej of Brod, "Contra obiecciones Hussonitarum," ed. Johann Loserth, "Beiträge zur Geschichte der husitischen Bewegung 4. Die Streitschriften und Unionsverhandlungen zwischen den Katholiken und Husiten in den Jahren 1412 und 1413," *Archiv für österreichische Geschichte* 75 (1889): 342–44.

Palacký, František (ed.), *Documenta Mag. Joannis Hus vitam, doctrinam, causam in Constantiensi concilio actam et controversias de religione in Bohemia annis 1408–1413 motas illustrantia* (Prague: 1869).

Páleč, Štěpán, "Replicatio contra quidamistas," ed. Johann Loserth, "Beiträge zur Geschichte der husitischen Bewegung 4. Die Streitschriften und Unionsverhandlungen zwischen den Katholiken und Husiten in den Jahren 1412 und 1413," *Archiv für österreichische Geschichte* 75 (1889): 344–61.

Páleč, Štěpán, "De aequivocatione nominis ecclesia," ed. Jan Sedlák, *Hlídka* 29, 1–2 (1912), appendix, 97–106; repr. Jan Sedlák, *Miscellanea husitica Ioannis Sedlák*, eds. Jaroslav V. Polc and Stanislav Přibyl (Prague: 1996), 356–63.

Páleč, Štěpán, "Tractatus de ecclesia (Contra hereses et errores Iohannis Hus)," in Jan Sedlák, *M. Jan Hus* (Prague: 1915), 202*–304* (selected parts).

Páleč, Štěpán, "Positio de universalibus," ed. Ryszard Palacz, "La 'Positio de universalibus' d'Étienne de Palecz," *Mediaevalia Philosophica Polonorum* 14 (1970): 113–29.

Páleč, Štěpán, *Commentarius in I–IX capitula tractatus De universalibus Iohannis Wyclif Stephano de Palecz ascriptus*, ed. Ivan Müller (Prague: 2009).

Příbram, Jan, *Jan z Příbramě. Život kněží táborských* [The life of the Taborite priests], ed. Jaroslav Boubín (Příbram: 2000).

Prokop of Plzeň, "Defensio tractatus De ideis magistri Iohannis Wiclef," in Johann Loserth, *Hus und Wyclif. Zur Genesis der husitischen Lehre* (Prague and Leipzig: 1884), 277–85.

Ryba, Bohumil (ed.), *Betlemské texty* [Bethlehem texts] (Prague: 1951).

Sedlák, Jan, *Miscellanea husitica Ioannis Sedlák*, eds. Jaroslav V. Polc and Stanislav Přibyl (Prague: 1996).

Stanislav of Znojmo, "Tractatus contra XLV articulos Joannis Wiclef," in *Magnum oecumenicum Constantiense concilium*, ed. Hermann von der Hardt, vol. 3 (Frankfurt and Leipzig: 1698), 212–335; repr. *Sacrorum conciliorum nova et amplissima collectio*, ed. Giovanni Domenico Mansi, vol. 28 (Venice: 1785, repr. Paris: 1903), 83–157.

Stanislav of Znojmo, "Alma et venerabilis," ed. Johann Loserth, "Beiträge zur Geschichte der husitischen Bewegung 4. Die Streitschriften und Unionsverhandlungen zwischen den Katholiken und Husiten in den Jahren 1412 und 1413," *Archiv für österreichische Geschichte* 75 (1889): 361–413.

Stanislav of Znojmo, "Tractatus de universalibus (maior)," in *Johannis Wyclif Miscellanea philosophica*, ed. Michael Henry Dziewicki, vol. 2 (Wyclif's Latin Works) 28 (London: 1905), 1–151.

Stanislav of Znojmo, "Tractatus de Romana ecclesia," ed. Jan Sedlák, *Hlídka* 28, 11–12 (1911): appendix, 83–95; repr. Jan Sedlák, *Miscellanea husitica Ioannis Sedlák*, eds. Jaroslav V. Polc and Stanislav Přibyl (Prague: 1996), 312–322.

Svejkovský, František (ed.), *Veršované skladby doby husitské* [Versified compositions of the Hussite period] (Prague: 1963).

Wyclif, John, *Johannis Wyclif Miscellanea philosophica*, ed. Michael Henry Dziewicki, vol. 2, (Wyclif's Latin Works) 28 (London: 1905).

Wyclif, John, *Johannis Wyclif De ente librorum duorum excerpta*, ed. Michael Henry Dziewicki (Wyclif's Latin Works) 33 (London: 1909).

Želivský, Jan, *Dochovaná kázání z roku 1419* [Preserved sermons from 1419], ed. Amedeo Molnár, vol. 1 (Prague: 1953).

Secondary Sources

Betts, Reginald Robert, *Essays in Czech History* (London: 1969).

Brandmüller, Walter, *Das Konzil von Konstanz 1414–1418*, 2 vols. (Paderborn: 1997–1999).

Brandt, Hans Jürgen, "Universität, Gesellschaft, Politik und Pfründen am Beispiel Konrad von Soltau (†1407)," in *The Universities in the Late Middle Ages*, eds. Jozef Ijsewijn and Jacques Paquet (Leuven: 1978), 614–27.

Coufal, Dušan, *Polemika o kalich mezi teologií a politikou 1414–1431. Předpoklady basilejské disputace o prvním z pražských artikulů* [Polemic about the chalice between theology and politics 1414–1431. Preconditions of the Basel disputation on the first Prague article] (Prague: 2012).

De Vooght, Paul, *Jacobellus de Stříbro (†1429), premier théologien du hussitisme* (Leuven: 1972).

De Vooght, Paul, *L'hérésie de Jean Huss*, 2 vols., 2nd ed. (Leuven: 1975).

Eberhard, Winfried, and Machilek, Franz (ed.), *Kirchliche Reformimpulse des 14./15. Jahrhunderts in Ostmitteleuropa* (Cologne, Weimar, and Vienna: 2006).

Fudge, Thomas A., *Jan Hus. Religious Reform and Social Revolution in Bohemia* (London: 2010).

Fudge, Thomas A., *The Trial of Jan Hus. Medieval Heresy and Criminal Procedure* (Oxford: 2013).

Fudge, Thomas A., *The Memory and Motivation of Jan Hus, Medieval Priest and Martyr* (Turnhout: 2013).

Fudge, Thomas A., *Jan Hus Between Time and Eternity. Reconsidering a Medieval Heretic* (Lanham, MD.: 2016).

Fudge, Thomas A., *Jerome of Prague and the Foundations of the Hussite Movement* (New York: 2016).

Girgensohn, Dieter, *Peter von Pulkau und die Wiedereinführung des Laienkelches. Leben und Wirken eines Wiener Theologen in der Zeit des Großen Schismas* (Götingen: 1964).

Herold, Vilém, "Commentarium Magistri Johannis Wenceslai de Praga super octo libros 'Politicorum' Aristotelis," *Mediaevalia Philosophica Polonorum* 26 (1982): 53–77.

Herold, Vilém, *Pražská univerzita a Wyclif. Wyclifovo učení o ideách a geneze husitského revolučního myšlení* [Prague University and Wyclif. Wyclif's teaching on ideas and the genesis of Hussite revolutionary thought] (Prague: 1985).

Herold, Vilém, "Platonic Ideas and 'Hussite' Philosophy," in *The Bohemian Reformation and Religious Practice*, eds. Zdeněk V. David and David R. Holeton, vol. 1 (Prague: 1996), 13–23.

Herold, Vilém, "Zum Prager philosophischen Wyclifismus," in *Häresie und vorzeitige Reformation im Spätmittelalter*, ed. František Šmahel (Munich: 1998), 133–46.

Herold, Vilém, "Wyclif's Ecclesiology and Its Prague Context," in *The Bohemian Reformation and Religious Practice*, eds. Zdeněk V. David and David R. Holeton, vol. 4 (Prague: 2002), 15–30.

Herold, Vilém, "Ideové kořeny reformace v českých zemích" [Ideological roots of the Reformation in the Czech Lands], in *Dějiny politického myšlení, vol. 2/2: Politické myšlení pozdního středověku a reformace*, eds. Vilém Herold, Ivan Müller, and Aleš Havlíček (Prague: 2011), 161–236.

Hikl, Rudolf, *Štěpán z Dolan* (Olomouc: 1966).

Hledíková, Zdeňka, "Hussens Gegner und Feinde," in *Jan Hus. Zwischen Zeiten, Völkern, Konfessionen*, ed. Ferdinand Seibt (Munich: 1997), 91–102.

Holeton, David R., *La communion des tout-petits enfants. Étude du mouvement eucharistique en Bohême vers la fin du Moyen-Âge* (Rome: 1989).

Hornbeck II, J. Patrick and Michael Van Dussen (eds.), *Europe After Wyclif* (New York: 2017).

Hruza, Karel, "'Audite et cum speciali diligencia attendite verba litere huius.' Hussitische Manifeste: Objekt – Methode – Definition," in *Text – Schrift – Codex. Quellenkundliche Arbeiten aus dem Institut für Österreichische Geschichtsforschung*, eds. Christoph Egger and Herwig Weigl (Vienna and Munich: 2000), 345–84.

Hruza, Karel, "Audite celi! Ein satirischer hussitischer Propagandatext gegen König Sigismund," in *Propaganda, Kommunikation und Öffentlichkeit (11.-16. Jahrhundert)*, ed. Karel Hruza (Vienna: 2002), 129–51.

Hudson, Anne, *The Premature Reformation. Wycliffite Texts and Lollard History* (Oxford: 1988).

Hudson, Anne, "The Hussite Catalogue of Wyclif's Works," in *Husitství – reformace – renesance. Sborník k 60. narozeninám Františka Šmahela*, eds. Jaroslav Pánek, Miloslav Polívka, and Noemi Rejchrtová, vol. 1 (Prague: 1994), 401–17.

Hudson, Anne, "*Accessus ad auctorem*. The Case of John Wyclif," *Viator* 30 (1999): 323–44.

Hudson, Anne, *Studies in the Transmission of Wyclif's Writings* (Aldershot and Burlington: 2008).

Hudson, Anne, "From Oxford to Bohemia. Reflections on the Transmission of Wycliffite Texts," *Studia mediaevalia Bohemica* 2 (2010): 25–37.

Kadlec, Jaroslav, "Řeholní generální studia při Karlově univerzitě v době předhusitské" [Regular *studia generalia* at Charles University in the pre-Hussite period], *Acta*

Universitatis Carolinae – Historia Universitatis Carolinae Pragensis, 7, 2 (1966): 63–108.

Kadlec, Jaroslav, "Literární činnost Mistra Maříka Rvačky" [The literary activity of Master Mařík Rvačka], in *Pocta dr. Emmě Urbánkové*, ed. Pavel R. Pokorný (Prague: 1979), 152–63.

Kadlec, Jaroslav, *Studien und Texte zum Leben und Wirken des Prager Magisters Andreas von Brod* (Münster: 1982).

Kaminsky, Howard, "Hussite Radicalism and the Origins of Tábor 1415–1418," *Medievalia et Humanistica* 10 (1956): 102–30.

Kaminsky, Howard, *A History of the Hussite Revolution* (Berkeley and Los Angeles: 1967).

Kejř, Jiří, *Husitský právník M. Jan z Jesenice* [The Hussite Lawyer Master Jan of Jesenice] (Prague: 1965).

Kejř, Jiří, *Kvodlibetní disputace na pražské universitě* [Quodlibet disputations at Prague University] (Prague: 1971).

Kejř, Jiří, *Mistři pražské univerzity a kněží táborští* [The masters of Prague university and the Taborite priests] (Prague: 1981).

Kejř, Jiří, *Z počátků české reformace* [From the beginnings of the Bohemian Reformation] (Brno: 2006).

Kejř, Jiří, "K pramenům Husova procesu: tzv. *Ordo procedendi*" [On the sources of Hus's trial: the so-called *Ordo procedendi*], in idem, *Z počátků české reformace* (Brno: 2006), 132–45.

Kopičková, Božena, *Jan Želivský* (Prague: 1990).

Krmíčková, Helena, *Studie a texty k počátkům kalicha v Čechách* [Studies and texts on the beginnings of the chalice in Bohemia] (Brno: 1997).

Krmíčková, Helena, "Utraquism in 1414," in *The Bohemian Reformation and Religious Practice*, eds. Zdeněk V. David and David R. Holeton, vol. 4 (Prague: 2002), 99–105.

Krmíčková, Helena, "Paběrky z rukopisů univerzitních" [Gleanings from university manuscripts], in *Campana codex civitas. Miroslao Flodr octogenario* (Brno: 2009), 178–211.

Krzenck, Thomas, *Johannes Hus. Theologe, Kirchenreformer, Märtyrer* (Gleichen: 2011).

Kybal, Vlastimil, *M. Matěj z Janova, jeho život, spisy a učení* [Master Matěj of Janov. His life, writings, and teachings] (Prague: 1905; repr. Brno: 2000).

Kybal, Vlastimil, *M. Jan Hus. Život a učení* [Master Jan Hus. Life and teachings], Part 2: *Učení* [Teachings], 3 vols. (Prague: 1923–1931).

Lang, Albert, "Heinrich Totting von Oyta," in *Neue Deutsche Biographie*, vol. 8 (Berlin: 1969), 426.

Lášek, Jan B., and Karel Skalický (eds.) *Mistr Matěj z Janova ve své a v naší době* [Master Matěj of Janov in his time and ours] (Brno: 2002).

Levy, Ian Christopher (ed.), *A Companion to John Wyclif, Late Medieval Theologian* (Brill's Companions to the Christian Tradition) 4 (Leiden and Boston: 2006).

Loserth, Johann, *Hus und Wyclif. Zur Genesis der husitischen Lehre* (Prague and Leipzig: 1884), 2nd ed. (Munich and Berlin: 1925).

Loserth, Johann, "Simon von Tischnow. Ein Beitrag zur Geschichte des böhmischen Wiclifismus," *Mittheilungen des Vereines für Geschichte der Deutschen in Böhmen* 26 (1888): 221–45.

Marek, Jindřich, *Jakoubek ze Stříbra a počátky utrakvistického kazatelství v českých zemích. Studie o Jakoubkově postile z let 1413–1414* [Jakoubek of Stříbro and the beginnings of Utraquist preaching in the Bohemian lands. A study of Jakoubek's postil from 1413–1414] (Prague: 2011).

Marin, Olivier, *L'archevêque, le maître et le dévot. Genèses du mouvement réformateur pragois. Années 1360–1419* (Paris: 2005).

Molnár, Amedeo, "Hus's De matrimonio and Its Waldensian Version," *Communio viatorum* 1 (1958): 142–57.

Molnár, Amedeo, "Tresor e lume de fe. En marge du traité de dogmatique vaudoise," *Communio viatorum* 7 (1964): 285–89.

Morée, Peter C.A., *Preaching in Fourteenth-Century Bohemia. The Life and Ideas of Milicius de Chremsir (†1374) and his Significance in the Historiography of Bohemia* (Heršpice: 1999).

Nechutová, Jana, "M. Štěpán von Páleč und die Hus-Historiographie," *Mediaevalia Bohemica* 3 (1970): 87–122.

Nechutová, Jana, "De 'Tractatus de corpore Christi' M. Mauritio adscripti fonte Janoviano," *Listy filologické* 93 (1970): 262–70.

Nechutová, Jana, "K literární morfologii husitské polemiky. Štěpán z Dolan, Diagolus volatilis," *Sborník prací Filozofické fakulty brněnské univerzity* E 29 (1984): 209–18.

Nechutová, Jana, "Frauen um Hus. Zu den frauenfeindlichen Satiren der Hussitenzeit," in *Jan Hus. Zwischen Zeiten, Völkern, Konfessionen*, ed. Ferdinand Seibt (Munich: 1997), 73–79.

Nechutová, Jana, "Konrad von Soltau. Lectura super caput Firmiter," in *Schriften im Umkreis mitteleuropäischer Universitäten um 1400. Lateinische und volkssprachige Texte aus Prag, Wien und Heidelberg. Unterschiede, Gemeinsamkeiten, Wechselbeziehungen*, eds. Fritz Peter Knapp, Jürgen Miethke, and Manuela Niesner (Leiden: 2004), 3–19.

Novotný, Václav, *M. Jan Hus. Život a učení* [Master Jan Hus. Life and teachings], Part 1: *Život a dílo* [Life and works], 2 vols. (Prague: 1919–1921).

Odložilík, Otakar, *Z počátků husitství na Moravě. Šimon z Tišnova a Jan Vavřincův z Račic* [From the beginnings of Hussitism in Moravia. Šimon of Tišnov and Jan Vavřincův of Račice] (Brno: 1925).

Palacký, František [under the pseudonym J.P. Jordan], *Die Vorläufer des Hussitenthums in Böhmen* (Leipzig: 1846).

Sedlák, Jan, *M. Jan Hus* (Prague: 1915).
Seibt, Ferdinand, *Hussitica. Zur Struktur einer Revolution* (Cologne and Graz: 1965).
Seibt, Ferdinand (ed.), *Jan Hus. Zwischen Zeiten, Völkern, Konfessionen* (Munich: 1997); Czech version: *Jan Hus mezi epochami, národy a konfesemi*, ed. Jan B. Lášek (Prague: 1995).
Seńko, Władysław, *Piotr Wysz z Radolina (*ok. 1354 – †1414) i jego dzieło "Speculum aureum"* [Piotr Wysz of Radolina (ca. 1354–1414) and his work *Speculum aureum*] (Warsaw: 1995).
Šmahel, František, *Dějiny Tábora* [A history of Tábor], 2 vols. (České Budějovice: 1988–1990).
Šmahel, František, *Die Hussitische Revolution*, trans. Thomas Krzenck (Monumenta Germaniae Historica. Schriften) 43, 3 vols. (Hannover: 2002).
Šmahel, František, *Die Prager Universität im Mittelalter. The Charles University in the Middle Ages* (Leiden and Boston: 2007).
Šmahel, František, "The Kuttenberg Decree and the Withdrawal of the German Students from Prague in 1409. A Discussion," in idem, *Die Prager Universität im Mittelalter. The Charles University in the Middle Ages* (Leiden and Boston: 2007), 159–71.
Šmahel, František, "Die Quelle der *Recommendacio arcium liberalium* des Mag. Hieronymus von Prag," in idem, *Die Prager Universität im Mittelalter. The Charles University in the Middle Ages* (Leiden and Boston: 2007), 387–404.
Šmahel, František, *Jan Hus. Život a dílo* [Jan Hus. Life and work] (Prague: 2013).
Šmahel, František, and Pavlíček, Ota (ed.), *A Companion to Jan Hus* (Brill's Companions to the Christian Tradition) 54 (Leiden and Boston: 2015).
Soukup, Pavel, *Reformní kazatelství a Jakoubek ze Stříbra* [Reform preaching and Jakoubek of Stříbro] (Prague: 2011).
Soukup, Pavel, "Mařík Rvačka's Defense of Crusading Indulgences from 1412," in *The Bohemian Reformation and Religious Practice*, eds. Zdeněk V. David and David R. Holeton, vol. 8 (Prague: 2011), 77–97.
Soukup, Pavel, *Jan Hus* (Stuttgart: 2014).
Soukup, Pavel, "Die böhmischen Konzilsteilnehmer zwischen Häresiebekämpfung und Kirchenreform. Die Konstanzer Predigten von Mauritius Rvačka, Stephan Páleč und Matthäus von Königsaal," in *Das Konstanzer Konzil als europäisches Ereignis. Begegnungen, Medien und Rituale*, eds. Gabriela Signori and Birgit Studt (Ostfildern: 2014), 173–217.
Soukup, Pavel, "Jan Hus und der Prager Ablassstreit von 1412," in *Ablasskampagnen des Spätmittelalters. Luthers Thesen von 1517 im Kontext*, ed. Andreas Rehberg (Berlin and Boston: 2017), 485–500.
Spinka, Matthew, *John Hus. A Biography* (Princeton: 1968).
Svatoš, Michal, "Hussens Freunde," in *Jan Hus. Zwischen Zeiten, Völkern, Konfessionen*, ed. Ferdinand Seibt (Munich: 1997), 67–72.

Svatoš, Michal (ed.), *Dějiny Univerzity Karlovy* [A history of Charles University], vol. 1, 1347/48–1622 (Prague: 1995); English version: Kavka, František, and Josef Petráň (eds.), *A History of Charles University*, vol. 1 (Prague: 2001).

Traxler, Christina, "Früher Antihussitismus. Der Traktat *Eloquenti viro* und sein Verfasser Andreas von Brod," *Archa Verbi* 12 (2015): 130–77.

Van Dussen, Michael, *From England to Bohemia. Heresy and Communication in the Later Middle Ages* (Cambridge: 2012).

Zitte, Augustin, *Lebensbeschreibungen der drey auszeichnetsten Vorläufer des berühmten M. Johannes Hus von Hussinecz, benanntlich: des Konrad Stiekna, Johannes Milicz und Mathias von Janow; nebst einer kurzen Uebersicht der böhmischen Religionsgeschichte bis auf seine Zeit* (Prague: 1786).

Major Figures of Later Hussitism (1437–1471)

Jindřich Marek

The Hussite wars were formally ended in 1436 by the *Compactata*, an agreement concluded between the representatives of the Hussite parties and the universal church council in Basel.[1] These *church Compactata* were later solemnly announced in Jihlava, at the border of Bohemia and Moravia.[2] At the same time, there were *imperial Compactata* negotiated between the Estates and the Roman Emperor, Sigismund of Luxembourg. An accord with Sigismund, the legal heir of the crown and brother of the deceased Bohemian king, Wenceslas IV, became the law of the land and allowed Sigismund's ascension to the Bohemian throne. With the privileges designated for Bohemia and Moravia, as well as for the city of Prague, the king was above all bound to respect the religious freedoms of the Utraquists. The essence of both *Compactata* was the acceptance of the Hussite program of the Four Articles of Prague, though the form of these was significantly weaker than their original formulation at the beginning of the Hussite wars; they were now primarily restricted to the acceptance of the option of administering the chalice to the laity during the mass.

1 Social and Cultural Background

The purpose of the agreements derived from the religious program was the renewal of order, but with the implementation of new elements–namely, changes in the status of particular social classes of Bohemian society, or comprehensive changes in land-holdings.[3] Over time, the *Compactata* were supplemented by the other regulations, adopted through the participation of both the Bohemian ruler and representatives of the Catholic Church. After Sigmund's death, the *Compactata* were confirmed by the successors to the Bohemian throne, up until the end of the Poděbrad era of Bohemian history: Albrecht II of Habsburg (1438–1439), Ladislas Posthumous (1453–1457), and

---

[1] This chapter was created at Charles University under the PROGRES program Q09: History – The Key to Understanding the Globalized World.
[2] František Šmahel, *Die Basler Kompaktaten mit den Hussiten (1436). Untersuchung und Edition* (Monumenta Germaniae Historica, Studien und Texte) 65 (Wiesbaden: 2019).
[3] Josef Válka, "Kompaktáta a kapitulace. Charta stavovských svobod?," *Časopis Matice moravské* 129 (2010): 19–43.

George of Poděbrady (1458–1471). The last of these attempted to build a kingdom of two peoples, where the two faiths would co-exist, but his efforts were undermined by the endeavors of the Roman curia, Bohemian Catholics, and even some Utraquists.[4]

Once the agreement was reached, each party understood it in its own way. Catholics perceived the *Compactata* at most as an act of appeasement in the realm of church rite, where the church felt authorized to enact concessions. Yet for the majority that now formed the Utraquist Church – which understood the chalice not only as a matter of rite, but as a necessity of faith – the tolerance of Utraquist practice was insufficient on its own because the majority of Utraquists believed that *all* Christians should take the Eucharist in both kinds. Moreover, Catholics and Utraquists were unable to agree even on principal rules of mutual co-existence. Each party was convinced that it represented the true church and denied the claims of the other party. In their faith and church practice, Utraquists relied exclusively on Scripture, while Catholics also incorporated church tradition. In addition, the notion of the *Compactata* assumed a uniform church authority, which was impossible to enforce due to the resistance of both rival camps.

Even the Bohemian Utraquists, however, were not internally unified, as there existed among them several main factions distinguished by ideological and political orientation, even if the borders between factions were fluid and allowed for transgression. Except for the chalice-extremists, all factions were supported by the institutional bodies of the Prague towns and by the Bohemian and Moravian nobility. The spokesmen of these groups, who were all active authors, were foremost the masters of the Faculty of Arts of Prague University, as well as the priests in Prague and the provinces. The oldest among them were born in the 1380s, mostly in the second half of that decade. They graduated from Prague University even before instruction was confined to one faculty, the Faculty of Arts. The group whose members born in the second half of the 1390s was numerous, studying at the university after the secession of about seven hundred students and teachers to Leipzig, while some of their members obtained higher degrees only after the renewal of the university's activity in 1430. Utraquists active in the later years of the Poděbrad period were often born in the 1420s or later. If they studied at the university, they knew it only in its regionalized and confined, single-faculty form. They usually became Masters of Liberal Arts, virtually unable to receive a theological education. When the *Compactata* were concluded, the Hussite leaders were in their early 40s

---

4 Jaroslav Boubín, *Česká "národní" monarchie. K domácím zdrojům a evropskému kontextu království Jiřího z Poděbrad* (Prague: 1992).

and possibly 50s and divided into factions. These distinguished themselves according to the radicalism with which they held to the original Hussite program, or to political views regarding the organization of society and the desired level of economic peace or personal freedom. Thus, with a degree of simplification, the modern notions of "left" and "right" may be applied.

Under Hussitism, the alternation of political power among the parties in Prague had an exceptional influence on countrywide development. Thus Hussitism was called by one researcher as "a revolution of the Bohemian cities with Prague at the head."[5] After the coup of 1427, the political groups in power in the Prague towns were made up of more radical Utraquists gathered around Jan Rokycana, who were in turn replaced by the conservatives in 1437. The more radical Utraquists returned to power, this time permanently, after the conquest of Prague by George of Poděbrady in 1448.[6]

It is possible to characterize the years 1437–1448 as a period in which an attempt was made to calm domestic relations after the previous radical regime. The main representatives of the restorative regime were the "minimalists" at Sigismund's court in Prague, who would be satisfied with the minimal achievements of the revolution in the religious and political spheres so as not to threaten their social gains, and the conservative nobles. The city council supported the "minimalists," and the burghers and nobles once again took the reins of practical politics from the priests and preachers. Meanwhile, the changes in land ownership that had occurred during the wars were preserved and codified. The national Utraquist Church distinguished itself from the Catholic Church in the matters of the lay chalice, the communion of infants, the singing and reading at masses in Czech, and the veneration of the memory of Jan Hus and Jerome of Prague.[7] The cult of saints and reliquaries were restored, as were religious pilgrimages. Moreover, it is possible to observe an argumentative shift of the main representatives of Utraquism, from the reliance on Scripture alone to the citation of the church fathers and doctors.[8]

In addition to Catholics, the spokesmen of this regime from the beginning were primarily Jan Příbram and Prokop of Plzeň, who began to assume functions within church administration. Conversely, Jan Rokycana had to leave Prague and operate in eastern Bohemia, where in 1441 he became the head of

---

5 Jan Slavík, *Husitská revoluce* (Prague: 1934), 43.
6 Karel Hrubý, "Sociologický model husitské revoluce v hranicích politického systému pražských měst," *Sociologický časopis* 3 (1967): 575–90.
7 Renáta Modráková and Zdeněk Uhlíř, *Law and Scripture. Manuscripts of the Czech Reformation of the 14th–16th Centuries* (Prague: 2009), 43–58.
8 Ota Halama, *Otázka svatých v české reformaci. Její proměny od doby Karla IV. do doby České konfese* (Brno: 2002), 29–64.

the clergy in that region, which was controlled by the opposition politician Hynce Ptáček of Pirkštejn. Rokycana's party agreed with Příbram's to work together to isolate and eliminate Tábor. The politically skilled Jan Rokycana had a greater role in the success of this project than the grim Jan Příbram. In 1447, a delegation was sent to Rome, attempting to achieve the confirmation of an archbishop. Though this mission failed, the efforts of the delegates succeeded in confirming the privilege of the University of Prague. In its one faculty, instruction began in the spirit of the popular teaching of John Versor, under the direction of the conservative Hussites and with considerable assistance from the professors arriving from the University of Vienna.[9] Along with other trends at this time, we can also observe the growth of nationalist-leaning propaganda.[10]

The conquest of Prague in 1448 returned the "maximalists" of Poděbrad's party to power, those who wanted to maintain the maximum number of achievements of the revolution in both the socio-political and the religious spheres. In Prague, it was especially members of the patrician elite tied to this party who came to govern, but the community in general, including the congregation of all burghers (*velká obec*), was also strengthened. Jan Rokycana and his supporters returned to Prague and immediately took back the church offices from which they were earlier evicted. They also continued to build up the Utraquist Church. In 1452, Tábor capitulated to the army of the kingdom's governor, George of Poděbrady, and the unique social experiment it represented came to an end. In the second half of the 1450s, the university was marred by the struggle between the Utraquists and Catholics, which later led to the administrative displacement of the Catholics and the strengthening of the university's regional character.[11] In 1458 George of Poděbrady became the Bohemian king. In 1462, Bohemian ambassadors traveled to Rome to express, in the names of the king and the kingdom, the desire to confirm the *Compactata*. Instead, Pope Pius II's reaction was to unilaterally abolish them. In 1471 both George of Poděbrady and Jan Rokycana, the leading representatives of secular and church power, respectively, died. After the Utraquist uprising of 1483, only the Kutná Hora peace agreement of 1485 brought peace to the situation. Nevertheless, Catholics and Utraquists henceforth remained irreconcilably divided, representing the "two peoples" of the kingdom, divided by faith.[12]

---

9   Michal Svatoš, "Kališnická univerzita (1419–1556)," in *Dějiny Univerzity Karlovy*, vol. 1, ed. Michal Svatoš (Prague: 1995), 207–08.
10 František Šmahel, *Idea národa v husitských Čechách*, 2nd ed. (Prague: 2000), 198.
11 Svatoš, "Kališnická univerzita," 208–09.
12 In addition to the Czech-language compendia, see František Šmahel, *Die Hussitische Revolution*, trans. Thomas Krzenck (Monumenta Germaniae Historica. Schriften) 43, 3 vols. (Hannover: 2002), vol. 3, 1691–2015.

Literature under the Hussites underwent great changes.[13] The eruption of the Hussite wars introduced alterations, both to the prevailing genres as such and to the emergence of literature in the vernacular language.[14] In this sense, the period after the *Compactata* represented a return to the pre-Hussite status of genres, even if some genres completely disappeared and were not reintroduced. This was especially true of versified chivalric epics, chivalric prose, and secular lyric poetry. Similarly, romances and dramatic legends in verse ceased. Nevertheless, some works belonging to some of these genres continued to be spread by copying among the nobility. Legends and religious songs were transformed, and the pamphlet and the manifesto which emerged at the time of radical Hussitism endured. Chronicle texts (such as the *Old Czech Annals*) were written just as in the previous period, as were versified monologues or dialogues. University texts, in comparison to the pre-Hussite era, were decreasing, while preaching and polemical tractates had a greater role. This shift was linked to the polemics between the individual parties and to their propagation. It was also based on the Hussite preference for ascetic life and an orientation toward spiritual values.

Literature had to conform to the new religious, social, and political situation. Thus, the political writings which emerged concerned themselves with the significance and interpretation of the *Compactata*, and a special type of these were the various ceremonial discourses delivered at political negotiations. Various manifestos and addresses to foreign churches had similar purposes. The endless polemics often addressed the questions of the Eucharist, the veneration of saints, and pilgrimages. In the 1440s, in the disputes between the masters of the Prague University and the priests of Tábor, even older writings were in use which addressed sacraments other than the Eucharist. Similarly, the sacramentals (*sacramentalia*) were discussed, especially the *aspergillum*. Also, questions regarding the rite of the mass were dealt with, for instance whether the kiss of peace should be maintained at masses. Due to the disputes between Catholics and Utraquists regarding the authority of the pope and church hierarchy, many works were concerned with ecclesiology and obedience to the church. Others deconstructed indulgences and the existence of purgatory or were committed to the social practice of the church, especially with priestly property, priestly lordship, and the Donation of Constantine.

---

13   A concise overview of medieval Czech literature by genre can be found in Winfried Baumann, *Die Literatur des Mittelalters in Böhmen. Deutsch-lateinisch-tschechische Literatur vom 10. bis zum 15. Jahrhundert* (Munich: 1978).

14   Jaroslav Kolár, "K transformaci středověkého žánrového systému v literatuře husitské doby," *Husitský Tábor* 5 (1982): 135–44. Kolár's impulses were furthered by Petr Čornej and Milena Bartlová, *Velké dějiny zemí Koruny české*, vol. 6 (Prague and Litomyšl: 2007), 304–05.

Biblical commentaries and sermons, including synodal sermons, maintained their traditional significance, as did interpretations of the Ten Commandments. There also emerged new translations of the Bible into Czech. Some writings addressed secular themes, such as the organization of society or social obligations. Certain politicians and officials of the Poděbrad period were also active as authors. The Governor and Chief Justice of Moravia, Ctibor Tovačovský of Cimburk (1438–1494), wrote the *Disputation between Truth and Lies on Clerical Properties and their Lordship*, in which he defended Utraquism and the political ideas of George of Poděbrady and propagated the Hussite idea of clerical poverty. The councillor of the Old Town of Prague, Vaněk Valečovský of Kněžmost (ca. 1400–1472), is the author of a tractate against Jan Rokycana that rebuked the priesthood for egotism and domineering.[15]

2 The Conservative Utraquists

The conservative Utraquists were probably the group that was most content with the *Compactata*. Having acknowledged the doctrinal specificity of the Hussites, the agreement assumed that the Czech and Moravian church would be integrated into the Catholic Church without obstruction. Thus, conservative Utraquists who held important church offices resumed older efforts especially aimed at the elimination of Tábor, fearing that the radicals tainted the image of a unified Bohemian church. The main problem for the conservatives was the Taborites' adherence to the teachings of the English reformer John Wyclif, who admittedly was also favored by the earlier Bohemian reformers Jan Hus and Jakoubek of Stříbro. The marginalization of Tábor, however, was only achieved by the centrist party, who began to work with the conservatives toward this end. Příbram and his conservative party subsequently paid for their political inflexibility and the dwindling of their power base. This decrease of influence was partially conditioned by the fact that the conservatives remained dedicated to the enactment of two contradictory ideas until the end: unification with the Roman Church and the chalice. It would seem that conservative

---

15   Editions: Ctibor Tovačovský of Cimburk, *Hádání Pravdy a Lži o kněžské zboží a panování jich* (Prague: 1539); Jaromír Čelakovský, "Traktát podkomořího Vaňka Valečovského proti panování kněžstva," *Věstník Královské české společnosti nauk* 36 (1881): 325–45. Cf. Pavel Spunar, "Literární činnost utrakvistů doby poděbradské a jagellonské," in *Acta reformationem Bohemicam illustrantia*, vol. 1: *Příspěvky k dějinám utrakvismu*, ed. Amedeo Molnár (Prague: 1978), 225–31; Eduard Petrů, "Paradox Hádání Pravdy a Lži Ctibora Tovačovského z Cimburka," *Listy filologické* 95 (1972): 221–28; Rudolf Urbánek, *Věk poděbradský*, 4 vols. (České dějiny) 3 (Prague: 1915–1962), vol. 3, 72–85.

Utraquists, who maintained in their writings that receiving the Eucharist under one kind was sufficient for the Christian believer, leaned toward the Catholics. In fact, however, they upheld the *Compactata*, as these acknowledged Utraquist and Catholic ritual practice as equal.

Jan Příbram was the main representative of the Hussite conservatives.[16] He received his baccalaureate in 1409, became a Master of Liberal Arts at Prague University in 1413, and from the 1420s was one of the administrators in the Utraquist Church. From 1437 until his death in 1448 he worked as a parish priest in the church of St. Giles in Prague's old town. In his youth, he worked with Jakoubek of Stříbro, the "first Hussite theologian,"[17] collecting arguments for communion under both kinds, and for the legitimacy of secular warfare. Concerning the latter, and in contrast with Jakoubek, his tractates emphasized the concept of homeland and the necessity of defence.[18] Even his oldest writings are marked by the author's hot-headed temperament and patriotism. From early on, he was dedicated to the polemics against the Taborites, whom he criticized for doctrinal excesses, especially for their rites of the mass and the Eucharist.[19] After the coup in Prague in 1427, he was forced to flee to the countryside, paradoxically to the estates of the Taborite nobility in southwest Bohemia, where he remained until 1436. In his exile he wrote pointed polemical works against the Taborites. The target of his rebukes became John Wyclif and his English defender in Bohemia, Peter Payne.

As revealed by Příbram's 1423 polemical tractate against Tábor on the Eucharist, with the incipit *Surge Domine*, its author was a very astute thinker.[20] Příbram engaged in polemics with obsessive diligence and energy, refuting Taborite ideas and compiling an extensive and systematic catalogue of Wyclif's errors. In the introduction of another tractate he complained that instead of collecting the treasures of the Holy Church, he began to collect the repulsive

---

16 Biography: Jan Příbram, *Život kněží táborských*, ed. Jaroslav Boubín (Příbram: 2000), 7–11. Repertories of works: František Michálek Bartoš, *Literární činnost M. Jana Rokycany, M. Jana Příbrama, M. Petra Payny* (Prague: 1928), 56–89; Pavel Spunar, *Repertorium auctorum Bohemorum provectum idearum post universitatem Pragensem conditam illustrans*, vol. 2 (Studia Copernicana) 35 (Warsaw: 1995), vol. 2, 153–74.

17 See Paul De Vooght, *Jacobellus de Stříbro (†1429), premier théologien du hussitisme* (Leuven: 1972).

18 Ferdinand Seibt, *Hussitica. Zur Struktur einer Revolution*, 2nd ed. (Cologne: 1990), 48–52.

19 Jan Příbram, "De ritibus misse," in Konstantin Höfler (ed.), *Geschichtsschreiber der husitischen Bewegung in Böhmen*, 3 vols. (Fontes rerum Austriacarum, 1. Abteilung: Scriptores) 2, 6, and 7 (Vienna: 1856–1865), vol. 2, 501–45.

20 Edited in Jan Sedlák, *Táborské traktáty eucharistické* (Brno: 1918), 36–106.

filth of the Wycliffite errors by necessity, in order to purify the church of them.[21] From his other statements, it is clear that he intentionally avoided sophisticated scholastic arguments in these tractates, relying primarily on Scriptural evidence.[22]

In the apocalyptic work *Knížky o zarmúceních velikých církve svaté* (The books of the great sorrows of the Holy Church, 1427–1429) he analyzed (under the influence of current events and perhaps his own personal fate) the afflictions which the church and every faithful soul will suffer from the dragon in the last days, and the seven wounds with which the Antichrist will crucify God's faithful. Here he relied on biblical apocalyptic texts, namely the prophecy of Daniel, the book of Job, and the Revelation of John.[23] In his *Vyznání věrných Čechů* (Confession of faithful Czechs), which concerned his 1429 disputes with Peter Payne on Wyclif's articles, Příbram hides his opinion behind a claim to objectivity; the work gives the impression that it was written by the "faithful Czechs," who issue an impartial testimony of the disputes.[24]

One of the best-known works of Jan Příbram is his extensive *Život kněží táborských* (The life of the Taborite priests), written in Czech around 1430 and preserved in a later, slightly altered version.[25] The introduction expressly derives the source of Taborite teachings from the devil himself, and is followed by an exposition of the false prophets and then the Taborite errors regarding the rite of the mass and the Eucharist. The life of the Taborite priests is here analyzed in sharp contrast with the life of Christ and the apostles. Příbram uses Wyclif himself to argue against the opinions of the Taborite priests by extracting orthodox formulations from Wyclif's works. Immediately after this work Příbram wrote his *Professio fidei*, apparently in reaction to the decree of the priests of Tábor that every priest in their territory should give a confession of faith.[26] This decree was perhaps aimed directly at Příbram, who, by preparing

---

21 Jana Zachová and Jaroslav Boubín, "Monumentální soupis Viklefových bludů z kapitulního sborníku D 49," *Mediaevalia Historica Bohemica* 7 (2000): 138.
22 Kamil Krofta, "O některých spisech M. Jana z Příbramě," *Časopis Musea Království českého* 73 (1899): 212.
23 Jan Příbram, *Knihy o zarmutceních velikých církve svaté* (Prague: 1542). The work was printed under Milíč's name; cf. Ladislav Klicman, "Studie o Milíčovi z Kroměříže I. Kdo je spisovatelem 'Knížek o zarmouceních velikých církve svaté i každé duše věrné'?," *Listy filologické* 17 (1890): 29–44, 114–25, 256–68, 347–62.
24 Jaroslav Boubín and Alena Míšková, "Spis M. Jana Příbrama Vyznání věrných Čechů," *Folia Historica Bohemica* 5 (1983): 239–87 (with an edition of the text).
25 Příbram, *Život kněží táborských*.
26 Edited in Johannes Cochlaeus, *Historiae Hussitarum libri duodecim* (Mainz: 1549), 503–47.

this original manifesto, reacted entirely differently than the Taborite priests expected.[27]

In the first half of the 1430s, Příbram produced a work called *Processus cause*, which is preserved along with his other works in a bulky manuscript volume.[28] He further expanded it in the 1440s, during the disputes between the Prague masters and the priests of Tábor. In it he addresses the teachings of three English "heretics": John Wyclif, William Thorpe, and their follower, Peter Payne. In 430 chapters, Příbram assembles the most expansive inventory of Wyclif's errors with reference to the respective works of the English scholar. He overlooked only Wyclif's philosophical works, and although he complained that he had only a few of his works at his disposal while writing, he cited a remarkably large number of them. To the plea that he finally leave Wyclif in peace from his accusations of heresy, Příbram answered that he is concerned with Wyclif's followers, of whom there are still many. While in his earlier *The Life of the Taborite Priests* Příbram combatted his enemies with those theses of Wyclif which could be judged orthodox, here Wyclif emerges as a thinker infected with heresy.[29] It is interesting that Příbram here also comes out against those ideas which were held by Jan Hus, and along with Wyclif he reproaches not only the Taborites, but, covertly, also their "spiritual father" and devoted Wycliffite, Jakoubek of Stříbro, who had died not long before (1429).

Příbram's tractate *De usura*, apparently from 1432, is based on the older scholastic work of Theodoric de Ehrlich.[30] In contradiction to earlier assumptions, Příbram defined usury only in terms of financial transactions based on fraud, and he did not challenge the collection of interest. The tractate is thus a testament to his liberal conviction. From the preserved fragment of a tractate on the authority of the church from the period around 1430, it is clear that Jan Příbram, at least at that time, conceived of the church in a purely Hussite, rather than Catholic, manner.[31] In the 1430s he was involved in the negotiations

---

27 Jaroslav Boubín, "K protipikartským traktátům Petra Chelčického a M. Jana Příbrama," *Folia Historica Bohemica* 4 (1982): 144.
28 Prague, Archiv Pražského hradu, Knihovna Metropolitní kapituly, D 49. Partial editions: Höfler (ed.), *Geschichtschreiber*, vol. 2, 822–27; Jaroslav Goll (ed.), *Quellen und Untersuchungen zur Geschichte der Böhmischen Brüder*, vol. 2: *Peter Chelčický und seine Lehre* (Prague: 1882), vol. 2, 61–64; Jana Zachová and Jaroslav Boubín, "Z největšího latinského spisu Jana Příbrama proti Viklefovi a táborům," *Mediaevalia Historica Bohemica* 6 (1999): 143–59; eidem, "Monumentální soupis."
29 Zachová and Boubín, "Monumentální soupis," 136–37.
30 Zdeněk Uhlíř, "Traktát Jana z Příbrami De usura," in *O felix Bohemia! Studie k dějinám české reformace*, ed. Petr Hlaváček (Prague: 2013), 105–18.
31 Jindřich Marek, "Die 'Quaestio' des Magisters Prokops von Pilsen über die kirchliche Autorität," in *Roma – Praga. Praha – Řím: Omaggio a Zdeňka Hledíková*, eds. Kateřina

with the legates from the Council of Basel, and in 1437 he was sent to Basel, along with Prokop of Plzeň, to defend and promote the lay chalice even for small children. The result of this unsuccessful mission, along with his response to the objections of Juan Palomar, is preserved as one of his tractates. Příbram is credited in the manuscripts with a collection of sermons on saints' days and few sermons *de tempore*. In addition, a synodal sermon from 1441 and a sermon to the clergy from 1444 have been preserved.[32] At the end of his life's work, Jan Příbram could be described, in a manner of speaking, as both a conservative and a liberal. After his early improvisations with Tábor, during which his hotheaded temperament emerged, he promoted tolerance toward Catholics and the preservation of the *Compactata*.

Similar to Příbram, both in his life-trajectory and his views, was Prokop of Plzeň.[33] A few years older than Příbram, he received his baccalaureate in 1403 and became a Master of the Faculty of Arts at Prague University in 1408. In 1410, he actively participated in the famous defenses of Wyclif's books. In the 1420s he, like Jan Příbram, was one of the administrators in the Utraquist Church. After 1437 he acted as a rector at St. Henry's in the New Town of Prague, and from 1448 until his death in 1457 he functioned as the provost of the chapter of All Saints at Prague Castle.

Prokop's talent is attested by his early philosophical writings on Platonic ideas, in which he proposed original solutions.[34] Though his thoughts were based in Augustinianism, on which Wyclif also relied, he was also able to move beyond it. In the long course of his life, he went from defending Wyclif's books to fighting against Wycliffism. Although he was among the most conservative Hussites, his works on the authority of the church – written in the later part of his life – do not forsake his inspiration from Wyclif. This is particularly clear in his argument that the authority of the church is subordinate to the Gospel because God's law is superior to all other laws.[35]

Bobková-Valentová, Eva Doležalová, Eva Chodějovská, Zdeněk Hojda, and Martin Svatoš (Prague: 2009), 166–67.

32   Spunar, *Repertorium*, vol. 2, 165–66.

33   Jaroslav Prokeš, *M. Prokop z Plzně. Příspěvek k vývoji konservativní strany husitské* (Prague: 1927).

34   Vilém Herold, "Magister Procopius von Pilsen, ein Schüler und Anhänger Hussens, und seine frühen philosophischen Schriften," in *Historia Philosophiae Medii Aevi. Studien zur Geschichte der Philosophie des Mittelalters. Festschrift für Kurt Flasch zu seinem 60. Geburtstag*, eds. Mojsisch Burkhard and Olaf Pluta (Amsterdam and Philadelphia: 1991), 363–85.

35   Marek, "Die 'Quaestio'" (with an edition of the text).

In 1437, Prokop left with Jan Příbram for the Council of Basel to defend the reception of the lay chalice for children. His tractate on this topic has been preserved, along with a rejoinder to Juan Palomar, who polemicized against him.[36] In his manuscript collection of small tractates, called *Collectura*, we find discussions of contemporary questions, including ecclesiology, the ordination of priests, the livelihood of priests, usury, oaths, purgatory, indulgences, the veneration of the cross, saints and their relics, images, and the rite of the mass.[37] In these matters, Prokop usually supported the opinion of the Catholic Church.

Prokop's work *De malo regimine et abhominacionibus in Bohemia* likely originated in the post-*Compactata* period.[38] In it, Prokop reacted to the actual social and religious situation in Bohemia. According to him, people in Bohemia live outside the Christian regulations and without Christian discipline. The faith is weakened, and what is spread instead are errors and heresies. The rite has been drastically reduced, and many monasteries have been destroyed. Moreover, robbery is widespread and there is little enforcement of the law. In another work, *De communione et compactatis*, he explains that the biblical authority "*nisi manducaveritis*" (John 6:54) should be interpreted only in the spiritual sense. Therefore, Utraquism is not necessary; it is possible to take the Eucharist under one kind only, and to assert the opposite would be forbidden and sacrilegious. Moreover, it is a question of rite, which is decided by the church. In a tractate *De communione*, he contested the necessity of small children to receive the lay chalice, which he earlier defended officially before church representatives. He repeated his opinions again in the work *De compactatis*, dated to 1447. All of these works may be regarded as polemics with the "centrist" Hussites, who by then had come to dominate Utraquism.[39]

Prokop's two collections of sermons expounding the Sunday and feast day Gospels and epistles come from the same period. The character of these collections is somewhat heterogeneous, and only one sermon, which probably comes from the earlier period, is markedly anti-papal. The rest of the sermons propagate ordinary conservative Hussite ideas, and thus constitute a counterpart to Prokop's writings intended for an educated public. It is interesting that Prokop wavers between the traditional Catholic and the radical Hussite notion

---

36   Prokeš, *M. Prokop z Plzně*, 147–48.
37   Jaroslav Kadlec, "Collectura M. Prokopa z Plzně," *Listy filologické* 80 (1957): 237–45.
38   Prokeš, *M. Prokop z Plzně*, 105–06, 148–49. Edition: Prokop of Plzeň, "De malo regimine et abhominacionibus in Bohemia," ed. Jan Sedlák, "Drobné texty k dějinám husitství," *Studie a texty k náboženským dějinám českým* 3 (1918): 126–27.
39   Prokeš, *M. Prokop z Plzně*, 106–07, 134–35, 148–49.

of the church.[40] From the authorities favored by Hussites, he cites Matěj of Janov.

Although Prokop of Plzeň distanced himself from the original radical Hussite ideals, his ideas, together with those of Jan Příbram, offered a coherent program for the Hussite church as a part of the universal church, founded on the inclusivist adoption of the agreements reached at the Council of Basel. This program, however, was not taken up.

3 The Utraquist Mainstream

The main representative of the centrist party, overshadowing all others in his political and literary activities, was Jan Rokycana.[41] The son of a smith from Rokycany, he apparently entered into the local Augustinian monastery and received his Baccalaureate of Liberal Arts at Prague University in 1415. He became a master only in 1430, shortly after the renewal of university activity that had been interrupted in 1422. He worked at the university until 1465. In 1427, he is documented as a rector in the Týn church in Prague. In the autumn of 1435, the Diet of Bohemia elected him the Archbishop of Prague, though he was never confirmed in this position by the pope. He participated in the negotiations with the Council of Basel, where he defended the reception of Utraquist communion. In 1437 he left Prague and went into exile at Hradec Králové in eastern Bohemia, whence he returned and resumed his function as rector in the Týn church in 1448, after Prague's conquest by George of Poděbrady. He died at the very end of the Poděbrad era in 1471, leaving behind literary works which are among the most extensive in medieval Bohemia, and the most interesting in content.

Soon after the death of Jakoubek of Stříbro, Jan Rokycana established himself as a critic of Tábor. His polemic against the Taborite notion of the Eucharist is already included in his sermons to the clergy in October 1429. He continued on this path with his influential tractates *De quinque prioribus sacramentis*

---

40   Ibid., 105–06, 155–57.
41   Biography: Jaroslav Boubín and Jana Zachová (eds.), *Žaloby katolíků na Mistra Jana z Rokycan* (Rokycany: 1997), 5–19; Frederick G. Heymann, "John Rokycana. Church Reformer between Hus and Luther," *Church History* 28 (1959): 240–80. From the older scholarship, see especially Zdeněk Nejedlý, "Mládí M. Jana z Rokycan," *Časopis Musea Království českého* 73 (1899): 517–34. Repertory of works: Bartoš, *Literární činnost M. Jana Rokycany, M. Jana Příbrama, M. Petra Payna*, 14–55.

and *De septem culpis Taboritarum*.⁴² Both probably come from 1431 and are concerned with defending the views of the Prague Hussite party regarding church sacraments. Not long after, he participated in the negotiations of the *Compactata* with the Council of Basel. He held various formal speeches before the plenary council in the name of the Bohemian delegation, and he primarily defended the Eucharist in both kinds. His defense of the chalice included his response to the objections of John Stojković, thus he also addressed such matters as infant communion and the concept of the church.⁴³

After the agreement of the *Compactata*, Rokycana turned his attention to the building-up and unification of the Utraquist Church. It was especially necessary to deal with Taborite teachings and church practice. Thus, with the co-operation of the conservative Hussite wing, he initiated synods which met at Kutná Hora and were to decide on the doctrinal disputes between the Prague masters and the priests of Tábor.⁴⁴ In this context, Rokycana wrote his *Tractatus de existentia corporis Christi in sacramento eucharistiae* of 1443, which primarily disputed the views of the Taborite Mikuláš of Pelhřimov. The political and dogmatic defeat of Tábor, which was completed with the decision of the Bohemian Land Diet in January 1444, was mainly Rokycana's doing. Here, the view of the Prague masters on the Eucharist was acknowledged as superior, and the priests of Tábor were ordered to align themselves with the former in matters of faith.⁴⁵

Later, Rokycana exercised the title of his office to defend the Utraquist notion of the Eucharist against both Catholics and the Unity of Brethren. He wrote and exchanged several letters in the first half of the 1450s with the prominent Catholic proselytizer John of Capistrano (1386–1456). In these, Rokycana defended Utraquism and proposed a disputation, though this never came about. Two other letters from the same period were written to the Greek Church in Constantinople, sent in the context of negotiations regarding a Hussite union with the Greek Church. In the middle of the 1450s Rokycana delivered two synodal sermons, the purpose of which was to remind the clergy to

---

42 Bartoš, *Literární činnost M. Jana Rokycany, M. Jana Příbrama, M. Petra Payna*, 22–23. The first of the tracts is edited in Cochlaeus, *Historiae hussitarum libri duodecim*, 445–500. See also Ota Halama, *Otázka svatých v české reformaci. Její proměny od doby Karla IV. do doby České konfese* (Brno: 2002), 42–43.

43 Bartoš, *Literární činnost M. Jana Rokycany, M. Jana Příbrama, M. Petra Payna*, 25–33.

44 Zdeněk Nejedlý (ed.), *Prameny k synodám strany Pražské a Táborské. Vznik husitské konfesse v létech 1441–1444* (Prague: 1900); Blanka Zilynská, *Husitské synody v Čechách 1418–1440. Příspěvek k úloze univerzitních mistrů v husitské církvi a revoluci* (Prague: 1985), 63–65, 67–71.

45 Zilynská, *Synody v Čechách 1440–1540*, 72–75.

hold to Utraquism. Rokycana's tractate *Contra sex proposiciones frivolas doctorum apostatarum* was composed for the purpose of the lengthy disputation before the king in February 1465, regarding the reception of the chalice. Here, he sets himself against six theses of his opponents, Hilarius Litoměřický (ca. 1430–1468) and Václav Křižanovský (1427/1428–ca. 1470). This tractate, which primarily defends communion in both kinds, also survives in a vernacular translation.[46] At some point at the end of his public role, Rokycana issued several letters opposing the teachings of the Brethren, especially their teachings on the Eucharist.[47]

All of Rokycana's extant sermon collections come from the 1450s and 1460s.[48] Some of them explain the pericopes of the church year, while others systematically interpret the books of the Bible. Rokycana's commentaries on all but one of the Gospels (Mark) have been preserved.[49] The exegesis of the Gospel of John also has a Czech version. Rokycana additionally interpreted the letters of Paul and the canonical epistles. His postils on the church year, whether the Latin collection of 1457 or the Latin-Czech homilies of 1468–1469, reveal that Rokycana venerated saints' days, though some of his opponents asserted the opposite.[50] In his older postils he used Wyclif's sermons on the saints, and referred to the English scholar directly in one of the texts.[51] The Czech-language postil on Gospel readings for Sundays and saints' days was apparently composed in the 1460s.[52] The oldest texts entered in the postil probably come from the period of King Ladislas (i.e. not after 1457), though the final version of the whole postil was written later. The work characterizes the living language, which imitates spoken address.

Ideologically, Rokycana was an advocate of the "middle way" between the Catholics and conservative Utraquists on the one hand, and the radical

---

46   Edition: Jan Rokycana, "O přijímání krve," ed. František Šimek, "Traktát mistra Jana Rokycany O přijímání krve. České zpracování latinského traktátu Contra sex proposiciones frivolas doctorum apostatarum," *Věstník Královské české společnosti nauk*, třída pro filosofii, historii a filologii (Prague: 1941), no. 2.
47   For all the works mentioned in this paragraph, see Bartoš, *Literární činnost M. Jana Rokycany, M. Jana Příbrama, M. Petra Payna*, 38–44.
48   Ibid., 45–50.
49   Ibid., 46 (commentaries on the Gospels of Matthew and John); František Michálek Bartoš, "Nová postila M. Jana Rokycany," *Reformační sborník* 5 (1934): 94–96 (commentary on the Gospel of Luke).
50   Ota Halama, "Utrakvistická úcta k českým světcům," in *Světci a jejich kult ve středověku*, ed. Petr Kubín (České Budějovice: 2006), 189–99.
51   Prague, Archiv Pražského hradu, Knihovna Metropolitní kapituly, F 59, fol. 359v.
52   Edition: Jan Rokycana, *Postilla Jana Rokycany*, ed. František Šimek, 2 vols. (Prague: 1928–1929).

Utraquists on the other.[53] After Jakoubek of Stříbro, he assumed the leadership of the centrist party and tried to construct a national church. Aside from the ideas of his teachers, he emerged from the legacy of Matěj of Janov, Jan Hus, and John Wyclif. However, he had a broad theological perspective and he also drew from the church fathers. Rokycana remained faithful to the notions of his teachers, and he did not arrive at any radical change during his ideological development. His theology, in contrast to his politics, was uncompromising, and took the apostolic and primitive church as a model. Like other reformers, he emerged from the mendicant model of devotion, and his views on the world are surprisingly close to the ideas of the Franciscans and reformed Augustinianism.[54]

Rokycana's attempts at the construction of a national Utraquist Church over time conflicted with the attempts of George of Poděbrady to internally consolidate the kingdom and stabilize its European relations. While George wanted to maintain conditions in which there existed two parties, Catholic and Utraquist, *de facto* within the kingdom and exclude any third party as sectarian, Rokycana sought to unite the church country-wide during the Basel negotiations, with the whole country receiving the chalice. He later modified this approach so that unity was to be preserved at least in individual locales. Although he sought papal confirmation for his title of Archbishop, he continued to attack the Catholic Church, and he believed that Catholics should also arrive unconditionally at the practice of Utraquism. His notion of the church was a compromise between Catholic concepts and Hussite traditions.[55] Though he acknowledged the pope and church hierarchy and never dared to disturb apostolic succession, he also understood the church – according to the Wycliffite-Hussite conception – as the community of the predestined.

Jan Rokycana acknowledged seven sacraments, even though he believed that the sacraments are ineffective in and of themselves. He placed the main emphasis on the moral state of a person, on his works and responsibility, not on the community of the church. A consistent biblicism is characteristic of his theoretical thought, and moral puritanism is significant for his practical theology. He acknowledged the intercession of the saints, but certainly did not overvalue it. The Eucharist had an important place in Rokycana's theology; he emphasized that the sacrament should be taken often and – from his view – in the

---

53 Kamil Krofta, "Mistr Jan Rokycana," in idem, *Listy z náboženských dějin českých* (Prague: 1936), 222–39 (reprinted lecture from 1911).
54 Heymann, "John Rokycana," 245, 257–58.
55 František Šimek, *Učení M. Jana Rokycany* (Prague: 1938), 35; Heymann, "John Rokycana," 253–54, 266.

complete form, namely, bread and wine, even by small children.[56] His disputes with Tábor and the assertions in his postils prove that he held to the real presence of Christ in the sacrament, which the Taborites denied.[57] That does not mean, however, that he could not simultaneously hold to remanence, as his opponents accused him.[58] He avoided questions on the nature of consecration, so we know little of his views on the matter other than what he imparted in his sermons.

Paradoxically, and to a large extent unwillingly, the leader of Utraquism's middle way was simultaneously one of the founding fathers of the radical splinter sect, the Unity of Brethren. Like Jakoubek, he had sympathy for the provincial radicals, and he maintained close relations not only with the idiosyncratic thinker Petr Chelčický – from whose ideas the Unity of Brethren later emerged – but also with his close relative Řehoř Krajčí, who was another of the Brethren's direct founders. Historians have already appreciated a certain degree of tolerance in Rokycana, and although the Hussite archbishop worked to prosecute heresy, he did this without the use of force. With his authority, he protected Peter Payne and later, to an extent, the Unity of Brethren, even while he issued letters against them.[59]

Václav of Dráchov shared many of Rokycana's experiences and ideological focus.[60] He similarly received his baccalaureate in 1415 and became a Master of Liberal Arts at Prague University in 1430. He participated in the discussions of the Prague masters with Tábor and in the negotiations on the *Compactata* with the council. Already in 1433 he was acting as preacher in Bethlehem Chapel and later became its administrator. After the negotiations on the *Compactata*, he unsuccessfully ran in 1437 for the office of administrator of the Utraquist priesthood on Rokycana's side against the more conservative Křišťan of Prachatice. In 1440 he had to abandon Prague. Dráchov mostly remained in exile in Louny in northwest Bohemia in the years before the conquest of Prague by George of Poděbrady in 1448, after which he returned to his benefices, dying in 1469.

---

56 Heymann, "John Rokycana," 250, 260, 269. See also Halama, *Otázka svatých v české reformaci*, 56–64.
57 Šimek, *Učení M. Jana Rokycany*, 221–25.
58 Boubín and Zachová (ed.), *Žaloby katolíků na Mistra Jana z Rokycan*, 22, 36, 44.
59 Heymann, "John Rokycana," 251, 269.
60 František Michálek Bartoš, "Václav z Dráchova," *Jihočeský sborník historický* 4 (1935): 78–86; Jindřich Marek, "Husitské postily připisované mistru Václavovi z Dráchova," *Miscellanea oddělení rukopisů a starých tisků* 18 (2003–2004): 4–144.

Dráchov's oldest known work is a Latin Sunday postil on the Gospels and epistles whose manuscript copy can be dated to around 1437.[61] A simplified and shortened version of the summer sermons also survives, which was likely written twenty years later.[62] The postil, as is standard for second-generation Utraquist preaching, offers few specifics. The sermons highlight morals for the listeners and references to the practice of the primitive church. Matěj of Janov is directly cited. The preacher criticizes worldly learning and generally defines himself against errors about Christ's divinity. On Sundays after the Trinity the book of Judges is expounded, with emphasis on spiritual battle, opposition to the wealthy, and criticism of simoniacs. In the summer portion of the postil we find texts with apocalyptic elements.

An extensive commentary on Psalms 109–118, which were understood christologically in the medieval exegetical tradition, was apparently created during the period of Dráchov's exile.[63] The colophon of one of the surviving manuscripts places it in Louny in 1444.[64] The compiler of the commentary eclectically draws from the previous exegetical tradition, defends the chalice and the poverty of the priesthood, accepts oaths, purgatory, and intercession of the saints, and cites an entire paragraph from Wyclif's *De veritate Sacrae scripturae*.

In the 1447 text *De confessione*, Václav of Dráchov propagates the Catholic notion of confession, arguing, in conformity with the canons, that a sinner should confess to his own priest, and not to another suitable priest, as the previous tradition of Hussitism believed.[65] The fact that the author was a Hussite is attested only by the rare citations of Wyclif. His views are perhaps influenced by those of Jan Rokycana, with whom they adhere closely. In 1448, a colophon credits Václav of Dráchov with a commentary on the Ten Commandments which has its basis in the older work of Jakoubek of Stříbro from the 1420s.[66] Dráchov's Latin postil on the gospels and epistles from 1457, *De tempore et de sanctis*, is preserved in two manuscripts with various levels of redaction,[67] one

---

61   Prague, Národní knihovna České republiky, III E 31.
62   Spunar, *Repertorium*, vol. 2, 130.
63   Jindřich Marek, "Husitský výklad Žalmů v rukopise Národní knihovny ČR XIII G 25," *Studie o rukopisech* 37–38 (2007–2008): 3–23.
64   Prague, Národní knihovna České republiky, XIV F 3, fol. 208r.
65   Jiří Kejř, *Summae confessorum a jiná díla pro foro interno v rukopisech českých a moravských knihoven* (Prague: 2003), 116–17; Jiří Kejř, "Teaching on Repentance and Confession in the Bohemian Reformation," in *The Bohemian Reformation and Religious Practice*, eds. Zdenek V. David and David R. Holeton, vol. 5, 1 (Prague: 2004), 114–15.
66   František Michálek Bartoš, "Husitský sborník novoříšský," *Jihočeský sborník historický* 21 (1952): 67–68.
67   Marek, "Husitské postily," 51–68.

of which contains interpolated articles from the *Golden Legend*. Just as in the preaching works of Jan Rokycana, here we find the standard saints' days included, as well as the sermon for the day of Jan Hus.[68] Hus's letters are even directly cited in the text.

Jan Rokycana and Václav of Dráchov became the founders of the Utraquist style of preaching.[69] Their texts often presented a re-working of exegetical commentaries from the earlier stage of Utraquism. The first theologian of Hussitism, Jakoubek of Stříbro, accentuated in his writings that the end times have come, and that people must primarily fulfill neglected commandments of Christ, including communion from the chalice. Because he did not distinguish between the church and society, he wanted to change society according to his utopian image of the relations among early Christians. In contrast, Rokycana and his companions of the same generation turned away from Jakoubek's eschatological vision to some extent and attempted to address the "common man" in the framework of pastoral care. They continued to use the works of John Wyclif and Matěj of Janov, but also returned to traditional positions on a number of issues.

Martin Lupáč, "the most radical Praguer," or "the most conservative Taborite," is also connected to the Utraquist centrist party.[70] Until 1437 he worked as a rector in Chrudim in eastern Bohemia, after which he apparently resided in Moravia. He participated in the negotiations of the Hussites with the Council of Basel, and in 1435 he was chosen by the Land Diet to be Rokycana's suffragan. From the beginning of the 1450s he worked as a rector in Klatovy in southwest Bohemia, and after 1456 he resided in various places in Bohemia (Německý Brod, Běstvina, Chotěboř, Žatec), dying in 1468.

The oldest preserved work of Martin Lupáč is his postil, which survives in an autograph manuscript from 1428–1431.[71] It contains Sunday and feast day sermons and three *quadragesimalia* on the Gospel and epistle pericopes. Lupáč did not avoid contemporary themes with a wider social relevance, and a certain degree of anti-Taborite sentiment is discernible. He emphasized that only some may kill in wars, namely those who are specially commanded by God. He

---

68   Edition: Václav Novotný (ed.), *Fontes rerum Bohemicarum*, vol. 8 (Prague: 1932), 373–76; cf. ibid., ci-ciii.

69   Zdeněk Uhlíř, "Středověké kazatelství v českých zemích. Nástin problematiky," *Almanach historyczny* 7 (2005): 88–89.

70   Repertory of works: Spunar, "Literární činnost utrakvistů," 171–84. The older annotated overview of Lupáč's life and works is still valuable: František Michálek Bartoš, "Martin Lupáč a jeho spisovatelské dílo," *Reformační sborník* 7 (1939): 115–40.

71   František Michálek Bartoš, "Postilový sborník Martina Lupáče z let 1428–31," *Reformační sborník* 5 (1935): 92–93. It is now preserved in Prague, Národní knihovna, I F 50.

acknowledged the veneration of the Virgin Mary and other saints. His stance against avarice and wealth belongs to the rhetoric of Utraquist preaching literature. It is evident from the second manuscript of Lupáč's sermons, which was edited in the 1450s by his assistant, that he propagated a simple belief in the real presence of Christ in the Eucharist; he considered further theological speculation superfluous, especially for the common people.[72] His sermons demonstrate theological erudition and moderation; he was – in the context of radical Hussitism – dogmatically liberal yet morally rigorous. He defended processions on Rogation Days but expressed himself to be radically against the *aspergillum*. It may be said that Martin Lupáč stood at the cradle of the second generation of Utraquist preaching, but at the same time harbored more radical positions than Rokycana and Dráchov and favored the exegetical homily.[73]

His polemic against an unknown convert to Catholicism, *De quinque sedibus*, copes with the results of the unsuccessful delegation to Rome in 1447.[74] Lupáč connected the ideas introduced in this work to the tractate *De ecclesia*, strongly condemning the contemporary church. The source of all knowledge, according to Lupáč, is Scripture, not the authority of the church. From the 1450s, Lupáč devoted himself to interpreting the *Compactata*. His first impetus for this was the preparation of Cardinal Nicholas of Cusa's journey to Bohemia in 1452, when the latter issued a challenge to the Bohemian Estates in which he explained his view on the Bohemian question. Cusanus stated, among other things, that the *Compactata* no longer have effect, because the Hussite clergy do not hold to them. Responding to him, Martin Lupáč said that the Cardinal desired a simple answer in the matter of obedience to the pope. Yet, according to Lupáč, it is necessary first to obey the Scripture, since the pope idolatrously and blasphemously usurps obedience, while the Hussites, in compliance with the *Compactata*, are obedient only to Scripture.[75] In Lupáč's *Sensus seu intellectus compactatorum*, a polemic with the conservative Jan Papoušek of Soběslav, which comes from the period 1449–1462 (most likely from the 1450s), he recalls his memories of the negotiations of the Cheb Judge in 1432.[76] The

---

72 Josef Truhlář, "Paběrky z rukopisů Klementinských: XI. Kázání kněze Martina Lupáče," *Věstník České akademie* 7 (1898): 409–10.
73 Uhlíř, "Středověké kazatelství," 88.
74 Ota Halama, "Spis 'De ecclesia' Martina Lupáče z doby poděbradské," *Theologická revue* 75 (2004): 420–35 (with an edition of the text).
75 František Michálek Bartoš, "Cusanus and the Hussite Bishop Martin Lupáč," *Communio viatorum* 5 (1962): 35–46 (with an edition of the text).
76 Adam Pálka, "Papoušek versus Lupáč. Polemika o výklad basilejských kompaktát z poloviny 15. století," *Studia mediaevalia Bohemica* 8 (2016): 41–87 (with an edition of the text).

most significant work on this theme is the extensive tractate *Super responso Pii pape* from 1462, which responds to the arguments used by the Catholics at the cancellation of the *Compactata*.[77] It notes that the Hussites did not feel the need to confirm the chalice with the *Compactata*, because it is an evangelical truth, but they confirmed it only because the Catholic Church wished them to do so. Adjoined to the tractate is a short text *Contra papam*, which asserts that the pope is the Antichrist.[78]

In Lupáč's private letters, his radicalism is expressed through his recommendation that the Utraquist Church secede from Rome. In 1467 this idea was realized, also on his initiative, by the decision of the Unity of Brethren to elect its own priests. In another letter, which its editor names *Modus disputandi pro fide*, Lupáč spoke out against the participation of young graduates of the Faculty of Arts, non-priests, in disputations with Catholics.[79] One should argue not with eloquence or scholastic argumentation, but with Holy Scripture. According to him, it followed from the *Compactata* that communion should not be taken in Prague in one kind. Lupáč spoke out many times in favor of infant communion from the chalice in various places in his writings. According to his work *Probacio preceptorum minorum*, Christ's Sermon on the Mount is not to be taken as mere advice, but as actual commands to be upheld.[80]

Lupáč's polemics against the Catholic administrator of the Prague Archbishopric, Hilarius Litoměřický, come from the years 1465–1467. The first, *Contra sex proposiciones doctoris bullati Hilarii*, is a reaction to the disputation before the king from 1465, and the second, *Replica in tractatum Loquencii Hilarii, doctoris bullati, veritatum Christi emuli*, reacts to Hilarius's rendering of the disputation.[81] In the first of his tractates, Lupáč calls communion in one kind only "half a sacrament," and he dismisses the authority of the church doctors. In the second, he claims that the cancellation of the *Compactata* is a violation

---

77   Spunar, "Literární činnost utrakvistů," 176–77. Older partial edition: Beda Dudík, *Forschungen in Schweden für Mährens Geschichte* (Brno: 1852), 458–66. See also Adam Pálka, "*Super responso Pii pape* Martina Lupáče jako pramen k jednáním husitů s basilejským koncilem," *Časopis Matice moravské* 134 (2015): 29–54. For the Czech version of the writing that appeared in the 16th century under the name of Lupáč, see Martin Lupáč, *Hádání o kompaktátech*, ed. Anna Císařová-Kolářová (Prague: 1953). Cf. also Urbánek, *Věk poděbradský*, vol. 4: 556–59.

78   Spunar, "Literární činnost utrakvistů," 177. Cf. Urbánek, *Věk poděbradský*, vol. 4, 559.

79   Amedeo Molnár, "Martin Lupáč. *Modus disputandi pro fide*," *Folia Historica Bohemica* 4 (1982): 161–77 (with an edition of the text).

80   Amedeo Molnár, "'Probacio preceptorum minorum' de Martin Lupáč," *Communio viatorum* 9 (1966): 55–62 (with an edition of the text).

81   Spunar, "Literární činnost utrakvistů," 174–75.

of the agreement with the Hussites at Cheb and is the filthiest stain that has tarnished the Roman Church.

The opinions of Martin Lupáč are interesting in their radicalism and the consistency with which he rejected the institutional Roman Church, and thus the pope and the church hierarchy. He interpreted the *Compactata* in much the same way as did Jan Rokycana, writing at the same time; he emphasized that, in those places where communion is taken in both kinds, namely in almost all of Bohemia, Catholics should not be tolerated. Similarly, he also did not accept that communion under one kind was sufficient for any Christian.

Václav Koranda the Younger, who also called himself "of New Plzeň," richly benefitted from the intellectual legacy of Jan Rokycana and Martin Lupáč.[82] He held a leading role in the University of Prague (he was the rector three times, in 1462–1463, 1470–1471, and 1513), and was also a distinguished member of the Bohemian delegation sent to pope Pius II in Rome in 1462. Between 1471 and 1489 he was a lay administrator of the Utraquist Church, and he died in 1519. Here we will only deal with his works published up to 1471.

In his 1462 speech before the pope in Rome, in the name of the king and kingdom, Koranda presented the views of the Utraquists on the Hussite wars and primarily defended the chalice and the *Compactata*.[83] He complained that Catholics did not uphold the *Compactata* and vilified Bohemians and Moravians, thus disturbing the peace of the land. Moreover, he asserted, they did this with the permission of the papacy. It was necessary, therefore, that the pope officially recognize the *Compactata*. Václav Koranda's argumentation took place more on the political than the religious level. This was related to the fact that Bohemian Utraquism was no longer developing theologically in the Poděbrad era, and the *Compactata* were understood as a privilege which confirmed the special status of the Bohemian Estates. Koranda's speech was understood by Catholic listeners as a fierce attempt to hold to the doctrines unacknowledged by the church. The pope reacted unfavorably to the request of the Bohemian delegation, cancelling the *Compactata* entirely.

The year 1464 witnessed a literary polemic between Václav Koranda and Hilarius Litoměřický.[84] It was sparked by two questions from Koranda; in clear reference to the Catholics and Utraquists he asked: which birds are superior, those who only eat, or those who eat and drink. The second question sought to

---

82 Jindřich Marek, *Václav Koranda mladší. Utrakvistický administrátor a literát* (Prague: 2017), a list of Koranda's works is on pp. 214–24.
83 Spunar, "Literární činnost utrakvistů," 205–06. Edition: Josef Kalousek (ed.), *Archiv český čili Staré písemné památky české i moravské*, vol. 8 (Prague: 1888), 321–64. On the embasssy to Rome, see Urbánek, *Věk poděbradský*, vol. 4, 520–38.
84 Cf. Urbánek, *Věk poděbradský*, vol. 4, 729–37.

understand why birds who only eat harbor a grudge against the others. Hilarius answered his questions in a Latin writing referred to as *Argute, augur*. Some birds, writes Hilarius, apparently can survive on food alone, so they do not drink, and others are subordinate to them; and thus, those who only eat are superior. Koranda then replied to Hilarius with the Czech writing *Nenie ptáčníkuov* (There are no fowlers). He attacked his opponent and accused him of choosing Latin so that he would not understand. He does not think that the birds who only eat, and rule over the others, are superior, but that rather they are worse because they harm the other birds. The response enraged Hilarius, and so he prepared a rejoinder called *De avibus responsum*. He reproached his opponent for confusing the meaning of two Latin words and because he began his text as an allegory but did not hold to it. He mocked the former rector of the Prague University, saying that he studied in Latin, not Slavic schools, and thus he should write in Latin. In his conclusion he asks his opponent to write in Latin next time and promises to reply. Koranda did indeed answer him, but probably only after a long delay. He said he wrote to teach the laity and wanted to turn not only Hilarius to the truth, but also the members of his party, namely Catholics. After a Latin introduction he shifted to Czech, because he wanted to address primarily that section of society which did not understand Latin.

Koranda wrote many polemical letters, especially in the 1460s. All these letters contain personal invectives and are often based on rhetorical figures, while also deconstructing and negating Catholic doctrine and propagating Utraquist practice. Moreover, they define themselves sharply against monks. In 1465, when King George's opposition was formed, the Bishop of Wrocław, Jošt of Rožmberk, sent tracts to queen Johana of Rožmitál and to the king himself. Václav Koranda responded to the second of these, in which the author addressed doctrinal matters.[85] At the end of the same year, Jošt sent King George the text *Třinácte šprochuov vagovských* (Thirteen sayings of the jongleurs), in which he glossed contemporary events in gnomic form. Koranda replied with his own writing. Perhaps from the end of the 1460s comes Koranda's letter against the "Pikarts," addressed to the king.[86] In it he reacts in an official capacity to one of the writings of the Bohemian Brethren that no longer survives, and he positions himself against the errors it contains.

As for all Utraquists, Scripture was for Koranda the basic starting point. It represented God's law, by which the teaching of the true church was revealed,

---

85   Spunar, "Literární činnost utrakvistů," 203; Josef Truhlář (ed.), *Manualník M. Vácslava Korandy* (Prague: 1888), 207–10.
86   Spunar, "Literární činnost utrakvistů," 199; Truhlář (ed.), *Manualník*, 121.

and which, above all, was the essential distinctive characteristic of Utraquism.[87] According to the so-called Cheb Judge, he also recognized the tradition of the apostolic church and the church fathers and doctors, insofar as they did not contradict Scripture. We do not find theological innovations in his writings but rather an attempt to overwhelm his opponent with rhetorically based arguments. While he still used Latin in the 1460s, with the notable exception of his correspondences with Hilarius Litoměřický, he later wrote to a domestic public almost exclusively in Czech. The scholastic method is limited in his works to the refutation of the arguments of his opponents and the affirmation of his own views, the conclusions of which are given in advance. Earlier researchers have described him fittingly as a more radical actor but less original thinker than his predecessors.

4 The Hussite Radicals

Radical Hussitism comprised a wide range of figures who did not conform with the ideas of the conservative or moderate parties. Until 1452 this included the entire party of Tábor, which, to a certain extent, stood for the dazzling military and diplomatic successes of Hussitism on the international stage, but in 1434, along with the Orphans, was militarily defeated by a Catholic-Utraquist alliance and remained idle in the following years. Several other personalities joined themselves to Tábor; some of them were on the border between the centrist party and the left, and thus they have already been discussed above.

Tábor's prominent representative was Peter Payne, called "English."[88] Coming from England, he received the title of Master of Liberal Arts from Oxford University in 1408. He came to Prague in 1415 and began working as a professor at Prague University two years later. He participated in the disputes between the Prague masters and the priests of Tábor, as well as in the negotiations with the Council of Basel. At the council, he defended the article concerning the poverty of the priesthood and the secular dominion of the church. Until 1437,

---

87 Jindřich Marek, "Václav Koranda ml. a mediální strategie obrany utrakvismu: autorita bible," in *Amica – sponsa – mater. Bible v čase reformace*, ed. Ota Halama (Prague: 2014), 143–53.

88 Biography: František Michálek Bartoš, *M. Petr Payne, diplomat husitské revoluce* (Prague: 1956); František Šmahel, "Magister Peter Payne. Curriculum vitae eines englischen Nonkonformisten," in *Friedrich Reiser und die "waldensisch-hussitische Internationale,"* eds. Albert de Lange and Katherine Utz Tremp (Heidelberg, Ubstadt-Weiher, and Basel: 2006), 241–60. Repertory of works: Bartoš, *Literární činnost M. Jana Rokycany, M. Jana Příbrama, M. Petra Payna*, 90–111.

and after 1448, he was the head of the Prague monastery Na Slovanech, and he likely died in 1455 or 1456.

Peter Payne was more of a politician than a writer. From the beginning of his activity in Bohemia he dedicated himself to the defense of communion in both kinds and the polemics against defenders of oaths.[89] Later, he worked on useful subject indexes to Wyclif's works. His defense of the article on clerical poverty and an exposition on the secular dominion of the priesthood come from the period of the Basel Council, as does Payne's response to Juan Palomar's remarks on his writings submitted to the council. Already in the 1420s he had entered into disputes with Jan Příbram concerning the doctrine of the Eucharist (as seen in the work *Tripes*, as well as in the acts of the disputation with Příbram), which later climaxed in his 1441 tractate against Příbram.[90]

The foremost Taborite figure was Mikuláš of Pelhřimov, called Biskupec. He became a Bachelor of Liberal Arts at Prague University in 1409[91] and later acted as a clergyman in southern Bohemia, after which he was elected the Bishop of Tábor in 1420. He participated in the negotiations with the Council of Basel, defending the article on the punishing of public sins and responding to the objections of Giles Charlier.[92] After the defeat of Tábor in 1452, he was imprisoned for the rest of his life, dying probably in 1460.

Beginning in the 1420s Mikuláš wrote tractates on the Eucharist.[93] In his opinion, Christ is not really present anywhere on earth, and thus not even in the Eucharist. His best known and most significant work, *Confessio Taboritarum*, is a confession and defense of the Taborite faith. It was written in the period around 1431 but is preserved in a version redacted after 1434.[94] The *Confessio* is a reaction to the writings that Rokycana aimed at the Taborites during this period (*De quinque prioribus sacramentis, De septem culpis Taboritarum*). Mikuláš found it important to recall the principles of the Cheb Judge of 1432, the negotiations for which the Taborites offered significant contributions. He declared a return to the primitive church and drew his arguments from the

---

89 Bartoš, *Literární činnost M. Jana Rokycany, M. Jana Příbrama, M. Petra Payna*, 95–97.

90 Ibid., 101–08. For more on Payne as an advocate of Wyclif, see Stephen E. Lahey's chapter in this volume.

91 Spunar, *Repertorium*, vol. 2, 71–80. Cf. also Howard Kaminsky, "Nicholas of Pelhřimov's Tabor. An Adventure into the Eschaton," in *Eschatologie und Hussitismus*, eds. Alexander Patschovsky and František Šmahel (Prague: 1996), 139–67.

92 Spunar, *Repertorium*, vol. 2, 77–78.

93 Ibid., 72–73; Mikuláš Biskupec of Pelhřimov, *O zvelebené v pravdě svátosti těla a krve pána našeho Jezu Krista*, ed. Vojtěch Sokol (Tábor: 1929).

94 Mikuláš Biskupec of Pelhřimov, *Confessio Taboritarum*, eds. Amedeo Molnár and Romolo Cegna (Rome: 1983).

Bible and from the old church fathers. He cited Thomas Aquinas as the most qualified representative of Catholic theology, though he naturally distanced himself from him in matters of the Eucharist.[95] He defined himself against the Catholic Church, which he saw as failing in its mission. Mikuláš decidedly rejected the teachings of the Catholic Church regarding the sacraments because, according to him, the Catholic ceremonies were established without biblical support and for financial gain. Following Jan Hus and especially Jakoubek of Stříbro, he emphasized the motif of the resurrected Christ in his conception of the Eucharist, in contrast to the ritual observance which is found, he argued, in the Catholic Church. Regarding consecration, however, his understanding conformed completely with the Taborite conception, and thus he was convinced that Christ is not really present in the sacrament. He stood against purgatory and the cult of saints, and on the matter of confession he followed Jakoubek of Stříbro, relying on Wyclif's *Trialogus*, to argue that people should confess silently to God and that auricular confession is not necessary for salvation.

Mikuláš's description of the argument between the priests of Tábor and the masters of Prague, called *Chronica causam sacerdotum Thaborensium continens et magistororum Pragensium eiusdem impugnationes*, adheres to his work on the sacraments in its temperament and tendencies.[96] Its three parts were written gradually over the years 1435, 1442, and 1444. After the introduction, which deals with Jan Hus and the beginnings of reform attempts in Bohemia, explaining the basis of the dispute, the text includes or paraphrases documents which were created by the Taborites and the Prague party.

By all accounts, his extensive commentary on Revelation was written at the end of the 1420s and is preserved in a single manuscript attributed to Jakoubek of Stříbro. Historians believe that the medieval owner of the manuscript was in fact mistaken in the attribution, and that the author of the commentary is in fact Mikuláš.[97] The work exhibits a significant number of similarities with Jakoubek's Czech commentary on Revelation. When compared to Jakoubek's text, we find in Mikuláš's a great many references to the Antichrist.[98] Another of

---

95 De Vooght, "Nicolas Biskupec de Pelhřimov," 179.
96 Spunar, *Repertorium*, vol. 2, 74–75. Edition: Höfler (ed.), *Geschichtschreiber*, vol. 2, 475–820.
97 František Michálek Bartoš, "Táborské bratrstvo z let 1425–1426 na soudě svého biskupa Mikuláše z Pelhřimova," *Časopis Společnosti přátel starožitností českých* 29 (1922): 102–22; idem, "Kdy vznikl Biskupcův výklad na Zjevení Janovo?," *Časopis Společnosti přátel starožitností českých* 67 (1959): 11–13.
98 Pavlína Cermanová, "Jakoubkův a Biskupcův Výklad na Apokalypsu. Porovnání s důrazem na interpretaci antikristovského mýtu," in *Jakoubek ze Stříbra. Texty a jejich působení*, eds. Ota Halama and Pavel Soukup (Prague: 2006), 218.

Mikuláš's exegetical works is the extensive postil on the Gospel harmony (*Scriptum super quatuor evangelia in unum concordata*), created between 1435 and 1448 and preserved in three redactions.[99] One of its components is the *Questio de divisione Scripture sacre multiplici*, which highlights the importance of the New Testament.[100] The postil is an aid for preachers which offers explanations regarding the circumstances and nature of biblical texts extracted from patristic and more recent literature, primarily from the works of John Wyclif, whom the Taborites held as the "fifth evangelist."[101]

On the side of the radical Hussites, though isolated, stood Petr Chelčický.[102] It is apparent from his works that he was influenced by Taboritism and also by the Hussite centrist party, and he personally knew the representatives of both parties. We know little about Chelčický's life; he has been identified most convincingly with the nobleman Petr Záhorka of Záhorčí, and he probably died in 1460.

Thanks to his connection with Tábor, his early work acts as the single source for our knowledge of ideas which were current in the first half of the 1420s in the Taborite commune. In his writings from this period, he deals with the problem of whether it is possible to defend the truth with physical war and whether it is possible to organize a Christian society according to the example of the Gospels. Finally, his early works reflect Chelčický's position on Taborite eucharistic doctrine.[103] From the end of the 1420s and beginning of the 1430s, Chelčický turned his polemical efforts to the Prague party. Later, in the 1430s and beginning of the 1440s, he was concerned about the movement of the Utraquists toward the Catholic Church, as reflected in his tractate cycles on the Antichrist. In his writings, which are permeated by eschatological awareness, we find elements of popular Waldensianism, as well as the conviction that the true faith has been preserved only by a small, exclusive group of the faithful.

---

99 Spunar, *Repertorium*, vol. 2, 76–77.
100 Edition: Amedeo Molnár, "Réformation et Révolution. Le cas du senior taborite Nicolas Biskupec de Pelhřimov," *Communio viatorum* 13 (1970): 154–70.
101 Bohuslav Souček, "*Veritas super omnia*. Z biblických studií a odkazu Mikuláše Biskupce z Pelhřimova," *Theologická příloha Křesťanské revue* 28 (1961): 75.
102 Biography: Urbánek, *Věk poděbradský*, vol. 3, 882–980; Matthew Spinka, "Peter Chelčický. The Spiritual Father of the Unitas Fratrum," *Church History* 12 (1943): 271–91; Howard Kaminsky, "Peter Chelčický's Place on the Hussite Left," *Studies in Medieval and Renaissance History* 1 (1964): 107–36; Murray L. Wagner, *Petr Chelčický. A Radical Separatist in Hussite Bohemia* (Scottsdale, PA. and Kitchener, ON.: 1983); Jaroslav Boubín, *Petr Chelčický. Myslitel a reformátor* (Prague: 2005).
103 Kaminsky, "Peter Chelčický's Place," 116.

He applied a consistent biblicism throughout his works, though occasionally he also cited patristic and scholastic authors extracted from Wyclif.[104]

In the tractate *O boji duchovním* (On spiritual battle), Chelčický declared that battle should only be carried out spiritually.[105] The Taborites, just as the Praguers, justified their right to armed resistance as the defense of the truth against invading armies. Chelčický did not agree with this, taking from the discussions of 1420–1421 the idea of non-violence, founded on biblical, especially New Testament, principles. To kill is a sin, and the reason why Christians do not realize this lies in the fact that some warriors self-righteously proclaim themselves the instruments of God. Though he understood social matters only as aspects of moral problems, he maintained that society is corrupted from top to bottom.[106] In the treatise *O rotách českých* (On the Bohemian parties), preserved only in fragments, he discussed the religious situation in Bohemia, naming four parties: the papalists, the Prague masters and priests, the Taborite priests, and everyone else.[107]

In the work *O těle božím* (On the body of God), he reacts to the Taborite rejection of the significance of the Eucharist from the beginning of the 1420s, and to the tractate on remanence by Jan Němec of Žatec – the teacher of Mikuláš of Pelhřimov and of Petr Chelčický himself – who denied the real presence of Christ in the sacrament.[108] The Taborites believed that Christ is in heaven in his natural, not his glorified body, and thus cannot be present in the sacrament. They anxiously awaited his arrival, which was to occur soon, and thus the Eucharist was not even a reunion with Christ. Contrarily, Petr believed in the real presence, which should not be speculated on but simply believed, because of the words of Christ in the Gospel.[109] The most extensive discussion of the Eucharist by Petr Chelčický is in his *Reply to Mikuláš Biskupec*. Here, he gives voice to his disappointment with teachings of the Taborites. Consistent with the views of John Wyclif and Jan Hus, he proclaims his allegiance to the

---

104 Jaroslav Boubín, "Dílo Petra Chelčického a současný stav jeho edičního zpřístupnění," *Český časopis historický* 102 (2004): 278.
105 Edition: Petr Chelčický, *Drobné spisy*, ed. Eduard Petrů (Prague: 1966), 28–98.
106 Kaminsky, "Petr Chelčický's Place," 119–20.
107 Edition: Petr Chelčický, *Zprávy o svátostech. O rotách českých. O nejvyšším biskupu Pánu Kristu*, eds. Amedeo Molnár, Milan Opočenský, and Noemi Rejchrtová (Acta reformationem Bohemicam illustrantia) 2 (Prague: 1980).
108 Edition: Petr Chelčický, "Traktát o těle Božím," ed. Milan Opočenský, "Traktát Petra Chelčického o těle Božím," *Theologická příloha Křesťanské revue* 25 (1958): 138–43.
109 Pavel Kolář, "'Neb novým angelským obyčejem krmeni budou.' O chiliastickém pozadí sporu o svátostné přijímání v Chelčického Replice proti Mikuláši Biskupci Táborskému," *Husitský Tábor* 17 (2012): 131.

idea of remanence, but also emphasizes the real presence of Christ in the Eucharist.

In the treatise *O církvi svaté* (On the Holy Church), Chelčický states that the true church is not an institution but the mystical Body of Christ, the body of the elect. The work *O trojím lidu* (On the three estates) rejects the notion that human society is divided into three estates by necessity – on the basis of whether they pray, work, or rule – and he offers therein an analysis of political power.[110]

Chelčický's *Zprávy o svátostech* (Instructions on the sacraments) was written in the context of polemics with the Prague masters in 1432–1433.[111] The first instigation probably came from the two tractates of Jan Rokycana written against the Taborites, to which Mikuláš of Pelhřimov reacted. With slight variations, Chelčický supported the Taborite conception of the sacraments; he acknowledged only baptism, the Eucharist, and partially confession and the consecration of priests, while completely rejecting marriage, confirmation, and last unction as sacraments. He was against the baptism of infants, which he regarded as influenced by the priests' desire for money. His idea of the Eucharist, however, entirely distinguished him from Tábor since he continued to insist on the real presence of Christ in the sacrament. He opposed obligatory confession as imposed by Innocent III and dedicated a relatively large amount of space to this in his discussion, on the basis of the tractate of Jakoubek of Stříbro titled *De confessione*.

Chelčický's *Reply to Rokycana* is clearly a reaction to a letter by the addressee,[112] and is characterized by a sharp polemical tone. The main theme of the work is purgatory, which Petr rejects in accord with the Taborites, while also rejecting the doctrinal authority of the priests and masters. He acknowledges only God's law as contained in the words and deeds of Christ. Petr's *Postil* is the most acrimonious of all his works against the Catholics, an approach which he explains is due to their wealth and their complete corruption.[113] His model and inspiration was Hus's Czech postil of 1413, and more generally the Czech postil of Tomáš Štítný of Štítný, who was also a layman. The extensive work, from which only an abridged version is preserved, was written after the mid-1430s, and is characteristic in its rigorous biblicism.

---

110 These works are edited in Chelčický, *Drobné spisy*, 132–210, 99–104, and 105–31.
111 Chelčický, *Zprávy o svátostech*. Cf. also Amedeo Molnár, "Petr Chelčický's 'Instructions on the Sacraments,'" *Communio viatorum* 19 (1976): 177–93.
112 Petr Chelčický, *Spisy z Pařížského sborníku*, ed. Jaroslav Boubín (Sbírka pramenů k náboženským dějinám) 1 (Prague: 2008), 51–92.
113 Petr Chelčický, *Petra Chelčického Postilla*, ed. Emil Smetánka, 2 vols. (Prague: 1900–1903). A new edition is being prepared by Jaroslav Boubín.

From this period come three tractate cycles by Chelčický.[114] The first is the so-called cycle on the beast, the second is on the Antichrist, and the third cycle deals with human law and purgatory. The first cycle was widely read at the turn of the 15th and 16th centuries, when it was also released in print. The contemporary lay readers for whom the work was intended were surely intrigued by the concise rejection of contemporary Christianity. In the tractate cycles, Petr expresses the notion that the Antichrist imposed his laws on people in the form of fallen Christianity, and that contemporary Christianity is in fact idolatry. Instead, people should live according to the law of God, and every Christian who professes Christ only in words is the Antichrist.

Chelčický's radical eschatology reached a peak sometime between 1440 and 1443 with the work *Síť víry* (The net of faith), which was also printed in 1521, probably by the so-called "Minor Party" (*malá stránka*) of the Unity of Brethren.[115] Petr's starting point for his pessimistic and eschatologically urgent exposition comes from a part of the pericope from Luke's Gospel on the miraculous catch and the net torn by the abundance of fish. The net of faith was torn by two giant fish, Chelčický says – the pope and the emperor, who want to rule and command. Whereas Jan Hus or Jan Rokycana had explained this pericope morally, emphasizing the practical impacts on their listeners' conduct, Chelčický explains it allegorically, and is inspired by the image of torn nets.[116] In the first part of his work, he places the law of God in sharp contrast with the practice of contemporary society, and in the second part he offers a "sociological" explanation of the current state of affairs. He sharply condemns both groups (*roty*), the secular order, namely the nobility and cities, and the spiritual order, comprised of monks, university masters, and priests.[117] In comparison to other thinkers, Chelčický accentuated the notion of freedom, though he understood it in a negative sense, much like the puritanical Rokycana, primarily as the freedom of the body or the freedom to sin.[118] Society is governed according to human laws, not the law of God; it is fraudulent and completely controlled by lies. In accordance with Wyclif, he regarded the Constantinian Donation as the beginning of this state, when a voice from heaven proclaimed

---

114 Boubín, *Petr Chelčický*, 114–24. More on editing these writings in Boubín, "Dílo Petra Chelčického," 286.
115 Edition: Petr Chelčický, *Siet viery*, ed. Jaroslav Boubín (Sbírka pramenů k náboženským dějinám) 3 (Prague: 2012).
116 Eduard Petrů, "Dvě studie o Petru Chelčickém," *Listy filologické* 89 (1966): 394–402.
117 Boubín, *Petr Chelčický*, 125–31.
118 Jaroslav Boubín, "Pojem svobody u Petra Chelčického," in *Od knížat ke králům. Sborník u příležitosti 60. narozenin Josefa Žemličky*, eds. Eva Doležalová and Robert Šimůnek (Prague: 2007), 454–65.

that on that day, poison was poured into the Holy Church. The Antichrist thereby took control of the church and society.[119]

To follow Petr's ideas to their conclusion meant to form a parallel polis and transform social relations within its borders; to remove oneself from this world and found a society that governs itself according to God's law, as was later done by Chelčický's followers who founded the Unity of Brethren. Contrary to the Prague masters who sought a national reformation, Chelčický, like the Taborites, was closer to the Waldensians, who founded sectarian communities. Chelčický not only rejected society but also physical battle, and thus became one of the few medieval pacifists.[120] In approximately half of its occurrences, the word "power" referred to political or authoritarian power. As historians have noted, Petr – as a "medieval sociologist" – appreciated the reality that in society, fear rules rather than respect, compulsion rather than agreement, force rather than right. Powers are only here so that Christians suffer, and the state and authority cannot exist without force and fear.[121]

Regarding exegesis, which was the basic method of most of his works,[122] it has been proven that he often only vaguely knew the sophisticated argumentation of his predecessors, and that he used them only to the extent that he thought they did not oppose Scripture.[123] This gave him a certain stamp of originality and strengthened the element of discontinuity with previous tradition in his thought. In some cases, the addressees of his writings were priests, in others, laymen, and it is often unclear which text is intended for which. Part of Chelčický's contribution is also the fact that he wrote systematically in Czech about religious issues.[124]

In his originality of thought, Waldensian influences were synthesized with a learned reformation. As he sought to understand the complex issues of faith for himself, he searched through the works of Jan Hus, Jakoubek of Stříbro, and Jan Příbram, as well as the writings of the Taborites, and he maintained personal contacts with all of them.[125] It seems that their explanations of the

---

119 Spinka, "Peter Chelčický," 274; Boubín, *Petr Chelčický*, 125–31.
120 Kaminsky, "Peter Chelčicky's Place," 112 and 130.
121 Josef Macek, "Sémantická analýza slova 'moc' ve slovníku P. Chelčického," *Listy filologické* 115, supplementum 2 (1992): 101 and 108.
122 Boubín, "Dílo Petra Chelčického," 276.
123 Pavel Soukup, "Metaphors of the Spiritual Struggle Early in the Bohemian Reformation: The Exegesis of Arma Spiritualia in Hus, Jakoubek, and Chelčický," in *The Bohemian Reformation and Religious Practice*, eds. Zdenek V. David and David R. Holeton, vol. 6 (Prague: 2007), 107.
124 Boubín, *Petr Chelčický*, 66–7.
125 Jaroslav Boubín, "Petr Chelčický a mistři pražské univerzity," in *Jakoubek ze Stříbra. Texty a jejich působení*, eds. Ota Halama and Pavel Soukup (Prague: 2006), 241–55.

complex issues of the Eucharist drew him closer to the views of Jakoubek and Příbram, whom he warned of Taborite Pikartism.[126] The degree to which he distinguished the secular from the sacred remains an open question.[127] To a certain extent, he desacralized the world around him by rejecting certain sacraments, yet he simultaneously insisted that people should live according to the law of God, and that the state is ideally not required. In his anarchism and separatism, he did not acknowledge society as an independent entity, but rather regarded it, in ideal circumstances, as the secular part of the church.[128] He spoke about the state, society, and the contemporary institutionalized church in heavily ironic terms, and he understood human life above all from his eschatological perspective, without distinguishing between its religious and social aspects.[129]

5   Conclusion

From the beginning, the Bohemian Reform movement criticized the contemporary church and society from moral standpoints. The target of attack became simony and the corruption that was seen to permeate the entire system of the Roman Church and, along with it, all of society. Emphasis was placed on personal devotion and frequent communion of the Eucharist. The lay celebration of the Eucharist from the chalice soon became the visible symbol of the movement. This practice was esteemed as a command from God and, for a large section of society, expressed the notion that all are equal before God, and that no one should be privileged in any way. The contemporary ecclesiastical and in part social order was replaced with a new one, reformed according to the example of the primitive church. In the second third of the 15th century, and after undisputable Hussite military and diplomatic victories, came the negotiation of the *Compactata*, an agreement of the Hussite parties with the Council of Basel and Emperor Sigismund. At their enactment, the emperor, sixteen years after his coronation in Prague, actually sat on the Bohemian throne, and the newly formed Utraquist Church received religious freedoms. After the chalice, the *Compactata* became the symbol of a new era.

This postwar period brought new conflicts not only between Utraquists and Catholics, but also between individual Hussite parties. After the elimination of

---

126   Kaminsky, "Peter Chelčický's Place," 134–35.
127   Macek, "Sémantická analýza slova 'moc,'" 112.
128   Spinka, "Peter Chelčický," 286–87.
129   Kaminsky, "Peter Chelčický's Place," 126–28.

the Taborites in the 1440s, the Hussite centrist party became the integral actor in the Utraquist Church, and gradually dominated it. The Eucharist was often discussed at the gathering of the parties and at their learned disputations, but a more hidden struggle was brewing regarding the distinction between church and society. While the representatives of the Hussite left were convinced that society was merely the secular part of the church and should be arranged according to God's law, the Hussite right and centrist parties had a greater appreciation of the social changes that occurred in late-medieval Bohemian society, including those inspired by reformist intentions, and therefore did not merge church and society conceptually. The centrist party created a "low church" socio-religious doctrine that was more appropriate for the urban milieu. They were actually distinguished from the conservative party only in their emphasis on doctrine, the difference of interpretation of the *Compactata*, and by their position on the Catholic minority. The inclination of the left toward eschatological visions and narratives of the Antichrist were, apart from reactions to a distressing age, a reflection of the rapid acculturation which contemporary Bohemian society underwent not long before but was unable to absorb. For this reason, radical theses appeared that inherently rejected contemporary society and the use of force. This rejection encouraged the urgent movement away from the church and society and toward the creation of autarchic communities in regions which had not yet experienced a more pronounced agricultural and urban expansion.

During the Jagellonian period, Hussitism was to a certain degree radicalized, completely overcome by the centrist party that was originally the party of Rokycana. Disputes with Catholics eventually led to a peaceful agreement in 1485. In this period, the Utraquist Church in principle no longer developed either organizationally or intellectually. Such potential development was blocked on the one hand by Utraquist doctrinarism, and on the other by the steps taken by foreign and local Catholics against Utraquism. The later Bohemian Utraquist Church absorbed influences from the wider Reformation, and as a result was significantly transformed internally.

6   Historiographic Survey

Research on the main figures of Hussitism between 1437 and 1471 is fragmentary and convoluted. At the beginning of the critical historiography, František Palacký used the known sources for his overview of Czech history,[130] sketching

---

130   František Palacký, *Dějiny národu českého v Čechách a v Moravě*, 6 vols. (Prague: 1968–1973), vol. 4.

the profiles of significant Hussite personalities. At the beginning of the 20th century, newly available catalogues of Czech manuscript libraries – especially those of today's National Library of the Czech Republic[131] and the Metropolitan Chapter of St. Vitus[132] – afforded a better understanding of Hussite history. The first catalogue of these collections, in which codices from the college libraries of Prague University were preserved, was accompanied by the exploratory studies of Josef Truhlář, who also edited Koranda's *Manuálník*.[133] Also important was the collection of the Dietrichstein Library in Mikulov, part of which is today kept in the Moravian Library in Brno. Besides the catalogues, overviews of important authors' literary works were also produced that include information on previous research.[134]

At the end of the 19th and beginning of the 20th century, the Czech historian Jaroslav Goll devoted himself to the study of later Hussitism.[135] Notable among his students were Zdeněk Nejedlý, with his monographs on the Prague and Taborite synods and on Hussite chant;[136] the works of Kamil Krofta on Příbram and Koranda;[137] and the study of Hynek Hrubý on Czech-language postils.[138] Catholic historiography was represented by Jan Sedlák and his works on the eucharistic tractates of the Taborites and their opponents.[139] The works of Petr Chelčický attracted a great deal of attention; Emil Smetánka published several of them, including the expansive *Postilla*.[140] Rudolf Urbánek attended in great detail to Chelčický, Rokycana, and other figures in his magnum opus on the Poděbrad era (esp. in volume 3).[141] Apart from editing Rokycana's Czech-language works (especially his postils), František Šimek also prepared a systematic summary of Rokycana's teachings based on thorough excerpts from

---

131 Josef Truhlář, *Catalogus codicum manu scriptorum latinorum qui in C. R. bibliotheca publica atque Universitatis Pragensis asservantur*, 2 vols. (Prague: 1905–1906).
132 Antonín Podlaha, *Soupis rukopisů Knihovny metropolitní kapitoly Pražské*, 2 vols. (Prague: 1910–1922).
133 Cf. Jindřich Marek, "Josef Truhlář a středověká bohemikální literatura," *Studie o rukopisech* 44 (2014): 305–18.
134 In the bibliography below, see the works of F.M. Bartoš on the works of Rokycana, Příbram, and Payne; the catalogues of the second- and third-generation Utraquists from Pavel Spunar, and the works of Eduard Petrů and Jaroslav Boubín on Petr Chelčický.
135 See, for example, his Jaroslav Goll, "Rokycanova Postilla," *Časopis Musea Království českého* 53 (1879): 59–70, 199–211 and idem, *Chelčický a Jednota v xv. století* (Prague: 1916).
136 Nejedlý (ed.), *Prameny k synodám*; Zdeněk Nejedlý, *Dějiny husitského zpěvu*, 6 vols., 2nd ed. (Prague: 1954–1956).
137 See, for example, his "O některých spisech M. Jana z Příbramě" and the several relevant entries in the bibliography below.
138 Hynek Hrubý, *České postilly. Studie literárně a kulturně historická* (Prague: 1901).
139 Sedlák, *Táborské traktáty eucharistické*.
140 Chelčický, *Postilla*.
141 Urbánek, *Věk poděbradský*.

his works.[142] The monograph of Jaroslav Prokeš on Prokop of Plzeň provided an important inspiration for a better understanding of the conservative Hussites.[143] František M. Bartoš published many contributions to the religious history of Hussitism over the course of the first half of the 20th century: among other things, he prepared a catalogue of the works of Jan Rokycana, Jan Příbram, and Peter Payne, and to Payne Bartoš devoted a monograph while also editing his speeches.[144] Bartoš also published a foundational study of Martin Lupáč.[145] In the postwar era, Palacký's positive appraisal of Jan Rokycana as the representative of the national church persisted, a view also shared by Zdeněk Nejedlý,[146] while Marxist historiography gave preference to the radical Hussites, resulting in a stagnation in research on the Hussite "right."

The current state of research varies depending on the individual Hussite author. In the case of Jan Příbram, researchers have predominantly dealt with his views on war;[147] more recently, many studies by Jana Zachová and Jaroslav Boubín have been published, often including selectective editions of Příbram's texts,[148] and Boubín also published Příbram's work *The Life of the Taborite Priests*.[149] Most recently, we may mention the studies of Thomas A. Fudge and Zdeněk Uhlíř on Příbram,[150] and the work of Vilém Herold and Jindřich Marek on Prokop of Plzeň.[151] Following the studies of Frederick G. Heymann, who assessed the Utraquist archbishop as a theologian comparable with Jan Hus or Martin Luther,[152] Jan Rokycana's modern biography was presented by Jaroslav Boubín and Jana Zachová in the introduction to the edition of

142 Šimek, *Učení M. Jana Rokycany*.
143 Prokeš, *M. Prokop z Plzně*.
144 Bartoš, *Literární činnost M. Jana Rokycany, M. Jana Příbrama, M. Petra Payna*; *Petri Payne Anglici Positio*.
145 Bartoš, "Martin Lupáč a jeho spisovatelské dílo."
146 Nejedlý, *Dějiny husitského zpěvu*, vol. 5, 98–100.
147 Seibt, *Hussitica*; Howard Kaminsky, *A History of the Hussite Revolution* (Berkeley and Los Angeles: 1967).
148 See, for example, Jana Zachová and Jaroslav Boubín, "Drobné spisky Jana Příbrama na obranu katolické víry," in *Facta probant homines. Sborník příspěvků k životnímu jubileu prof. dr. Zdeňky Hledíkové*, ed. Ivan Hlaváček (Prague: 1998), 521–34, together with the other relevant publications in the bibliography below.
149 Příbram, *Život kněží táborských*.
150 Thomas A. Fudge, "Václav the Anonymous and Jan Příbram, Textual Laments on the Fate of Religion in Bohemia (1424–1429)," in *The Bohemian Reformation and Religious Practice*, eds. Zdeněk V. David and David R. Holeton, vol. 8 (Prague: 2011), 115–32; Uhlíř, "Traktát Jana z Příbrami De usura."
151 Herold, "Magister Procopius von Pilsen"; Marek, "Die 'Quaestio' des Magisters Prokops von Pilsen."
152 Heymann, "John Rokycana. Church Reformer."

Catholic grievances against him,[153] and Blanka Zilynská dealt with Rokycana in her studies on the development of church administration.[154] The postils and expositions of Václav of Dráchov have recently been assessed in several articles by Jindřich Marek,[155] while Martin Lupáč has received the attention of Ota Halama and most recently Adam Pálka.[156] Following several partial studies, Jindřich Marek has prepared the first monograph on Václav Koranda the Younger.[157] Currently, the thought and apocalyptic expositions of Mikuláš Biskupec have also enjoyed greater attention (following the older studies of F.M. Bartoš, Amedeo Molnár, Paul De Vooght, and Howard Kaminsky) in the works of Pavlína Cermanová and Thomas A. Fudge.[158] Following the older studies and editions of Eduard Petrů and Murray L. Wagner,[159] contemporary research on Petr Chelčický is represented by Jaroslav Boubín, who published his biography and is systematically editing his works,[160] while Pavel Kolář devotes himself to Chelčický's sacramental theology.[161]

Translated by Martin Pjecha

Bibliography

Manuscripts

Prague, Archiv Pražského hradu, Knihovna Metropolitní kapituly [Prague Castle Archives, Library of the Metropolitan Chapter], F 59.

Prague, Národní knihovna České republiky [National Library of the Czech Republic], I F 50.

---

153 Boubín and Zachová (eds.), *Žaloby katolíků na Mistra Jana z Rokycan*.
154 Zilynská, *Husitské synody*; eadem, *Synody v Čechách 1440–1540*.
155 See the entries in the bibliography below.
156 Halama, "Spis 'De ecclesia' Martina Lupáče"; Pálka, "*Super responso Pii pape* Martina Lupáče" and "Papoušek versus Lupáč."
157 Marek, *Václav Koranda mladší*.
158 Cermanová, "Jakoubkův a Biskupcův Výklad na Apokalypsu"; Thomas A. Fudge, "Crime, Punishment and Pacifism in the Thought of Bishop Mikuláš of Pelhřimov, 1420–1452," in *The Bohemian Reformation and Religious Practice*, eds. Zdeněk V. David and David R. Holeton, vol. 3 (Prague: 2000), 69–103.
159 For example, Petrů, "Dvě studie o Petru Chelčickém"; Wagner, *Petr Chelčický*.
160 See the several relevant entries in the bibliography below.
161 See, for example, Pavel Kolář, "Petr Chelčický's Defense of Sacramental Communion. Response to Mikuláš Biskupec of Tábor," in *The Bohemian Reformation and Religious Practice*, eds. Zdenek V. David and David R. Holeton, vol. 6 (Prague: 2007), 133–42.

Prague, Národní knihovna České republiky [National Library of the Czech Republic], III E 31.
Prague, Národní knihovna České republiky [National Library of the Czech Republic], XIV F 3.

Manuscript Catalogues

Podlaha, Antonín, *Soupis rukopisů Knihovny metropolitní kapitoly Pražské* [A catalogue of manuscripts of the library of the Prague metropolitan chapter], 2 vols. (Prague: 1910–1922).

Truhlář, Josef, *Catalogus codicum manu scriptorum latinorum qui in C. R. bibliotheca publica atque Universitatis Pragensis asservantur*, 2 vols. (Prague: 1905–1906).

Editions of Sources

Boubín, Jaroslav, and Jana Zachová (eds.), *Žaloby katolíků na Mistra Jana z Rokycan* [Grievances of the Catholics against Master Jan Rokycana] (Rokycany: 1997).

Chelčický, Petr, *Petra Chelčického Postilla* [Peter Chelčický's *Postilla*], ed. Emil Smetánka, 2 vols. (Prague: 1900–1903).

Chelčický, Petr, "Traktát o těle Božím [Treatise on the Corpus Christi]," ed. Milan Opočenský, "Traktát Petra Chelčického o těle Božím," *Theologická příloha Křesťanské revue* 25 (1958): 138–43.

Chelčický, Petr, *Drobné spisy* [Minor writings], ed. Eduard Petrů (Prague: 1966).

Chelčický, Petr, *Zprávy o svátostech. O rotách českých. O nejvyšším biskupu Pánu Kristu* [Instructions on sacraments. On Bohemian sects. On the highest bishop Lord Christ], eds. Amedeo Molnár, Milan Opočenský, and Noemi Rejchrtová (Acta reformationem Bohemicam illustrantia) 2 (Prague: 1980).

Chelčický, Petr, *Siet viery* [The net of the faith], ed. Jaroslav Boubín (Sbírka pramenů k náboženským dějinám) 3 (Prague: 2012).

Chelčický, Petr, *Spisy z Olomouckého sborníku* [Writings from the Olomouc manuscript], ed. Jaroslav Boubín (Sbírka pramenů k náboženským dějinám) 4 (Prague: 2016).

Chelčický, Petr, *Spisy z Kapitulního sborníku* [Writings from the Chapter manuscript], ed. Jaroslav Boubín (Sbírka pramenů k náboženským dějinám) 5 (Editiones, B) 14 (Prague: 2008).

Cochlaeus, Johannes, *Historiae Hussitarum libri duodecim* (Mainz: 1549).

Ctibor Tovačovský of Cimburk, *Hádání Pravdy a Lži o kněžské zboží a panování jich* [A Disputation between Truth and Lies on clerical properties and their lordship] (Prague: 1539).

Goll, Jaroslav (ed.), *Quellen und Untersuchungen zur Geschichte der Böhmischen Brüder*, vol. 2: *Peter Chelčický und seine Lehre* (Prague: 1882).

Höfler, Konstantin (ed.), *Geschichtschreiber der husitischen Bewegung in Böhmen*, 3 vols. (Fontes rerum Austriacarum, 1. Abteilung: Scriptores) 2, 6, and 7 (Vienna: 1856–1865).

Kalousek, Josef (ed.), *Archiv český čili Staré písemné památky české i moravské* [The Czech Archive, or Ancient written documents from Bohemia and Moravia], vol. 8 (Prague: 1888).

Lupáč, Martin, *Hádání o kompaktátech* [Disputation on the *Compactata*], ed. Anna Císařová-Kolářová (Prague: 1953).

Mikuláš Biskupec of Pelhřimov, *O zvelebené v pravdě svátosti těla a krve pána našeho Jezu Krista* [On the venerable and truthful sacrament of the body and blood of our Lord Jesus Christ], ed. Vojtěch Sokol (Tábor: 1929).

Mikuláš Biskupec of Pelhřimov, *Confessio Taboritarum*, eds. Amedeo Molnár and Romolo Cegna (Rome: 1983).

Nejedlý, Zdeněk (ed.), *Prameny k synodám strany Pražské a Táborské. Vznik husitské konfesse v létech 1441–1444* [Sources of the synods of the Prague and Tábor parties. The rise of the Hussite confession in the years 1441–1444] (Prague: 1900).

Novotný, Václav (ed.), *Fontes rerum Bohemicarum*, vol. 8 (Prague: 1932).

Payne, Peter, *Petri Payne Anglici Positio, replica et propositio in concilio Basiliensi a. 1433 atque oratio ad Sigismundum regem a. 1429 Bratislaviae pronunciatae. Peter Payne pro Bohemis*, ed. František Michálek Bartoš (Tábor: 1949).

Příbram, Jan, *Knihy o zarmutceních velikých církve svaté* [Books on the great tribulations of the holy church] (Prague: 1542).

Příbram, Jan, *Život kněží táborských* [The life of the Taborite priests], ed. Jaroslav Boubín (Příbram: 2000).

Prokop of Plzeň, "De malo regimine et abhominacionibus in Bohemia," ed. Jan Sedlák, "Drobné texty k dějinám husitství," *Studie a texty k náboženským dějinám českým* 3 (1918): 126–27.

Rokycana, Jan, *Postilla Jana Rokycany* [The postil of Jan Rokycana], ed. František Šimek, 2 vols. (Prague: 1928–1929).

Rokycana, Jan, "O přijímání krve" [On the reception of the blood], ed. František Šimek, "Traktát mistra Jana Rokycany O přijímání krve. České zpracování latinského traktátu Contra sex proposiciones frivolas doctorum apostatarum," *Věstník Královské české společnosti nauk*, třída pro filosofii, historii a filologii (Prague: 1941), no. 2.

Truhlář, Josef (ed.), *Manualník M. Vácslava Korandy* [The Manual of Master Václav Koranda] (Prague: 1888).

Secondary Sources

Bartoš, František Michálek, "Táborské bratrstvo z let 1425–1426 na soudě svého biskupa Mikuláše z Pelhřimova" [The Taborite brotherhood of 1425–1426 under the judgement of their bishop, Mikuláš of Pelhřimov], *Časopis Společnosti přátel starožitností českých* 29 (1922): 102–22.

Bartoš, František Michálek, *Literární činnost M. Jana Rokycany, M. Jana Příbrama, M. Petra Payna* [The literary activity of Master Jan Rokycana, Master Jan Příbram, Master Peter Payne] (Prague: 1928).

Bartoš, František Michálek, "Nová postila M. Jana Rokycany" [A new postil of Master Jan Rokycana], *Reformační sborník* 5 (1934): 94–96.

Bartoš, František Michálek, "Václav z Dráchova," *Jihočeský sborník historický* 4 (1935): 78–86.

Bartoš, František Michálek, "Postilový sborník Martina Lupáče z let 1428–31" [The postil manuscript of Martin Lupáč from the years 1428–1431], *Reformační sborník* 5 (1935): 92–93.

Bartoš, František Michálek, "Martin Lupáč a jeho spisovatelské dílo"[Matin Lupáč and his authorial work], *Reformační sborník* 7 (1939): 115–40.

Bartoš, František Michálek, "Husitský sborník novoříšský" [The Hussite miscellany from Nová Říše], *Jihočeský sborník historický* 21 (1952): 67–68.

Bartoš, František Michálek, *Dvě studie o husitských postilách* [Two studies on Hussite postils] (Prague: 1955).

Bartoš, František Michálek, *M. Petr Payne, diplomat husitské revoluce* [Master Peter Payne, diplomat of the Hussite revolution] (Prague: 1956).

Bartoš, František Michálek, "Kdy vznikl Biskupcův výklad na Zjevení Janovo?" [When was Biskupec's exposition on John's Revelation created?], *Časopis Společnosti přátel starožitností českých* 67 (1959): 11–13.

Bartoš, František Michálek, "Cusanus and the Hussite Bishop Martin Lupáč," *Communio viatorum* 5 (1962): 35–46.

Baumann, Winfried, *Die Literatur des Mittelalters in Böhmen. Deutsch-lateinisch-tschechische Literatur vom 10. bis zum 15. Jahrhundert* (Munich: 1978).

Boubín, Jaroslav, "K protipikartským traktátům Petra Chelčického a M. Jana Příbrama" [On the anti-Pikart treatises of Petr Chelčický and Master Jan Příbram], *Folia Historica Bohemica* 4 (1982): 127–59.

Boubín, Jaroslav, *Česká "národní" monarchie. K domácím zdrojům a evropskému kontextu království Jiřího z Poděbrad* [The Czech "national" monarchy. On the domestic sources and European context of George of Poděbrady's kingship] (Prague: 1992).

Boubín, Jaroslav, "Dílo Petra Chelčického a současný stav jeho edičního zpřístupnění" [The work of Petr Chelčický and the current state of its editing], *Český časopis historický* 102 (2004): 273–96.

Boubín, Jaroslav, *Petr Chelčický. Myslitel a reformátor* [Petr Chelčický. Thinker and reformer] (Prague: 2005).

Boubín, Jaroslav, "Petr Chelčický a mistři pražské univerzity" [Petr Chelčický and the masters of Prague university], in *Jakoubek ze Stříbra. Texty a jejich působení*, eds. Ota Halama and Pavel Soukup (Prague: 2006), 241–55.

Boubín, Jaroslav, "Pojem svobody u Petra Chelčického" [The notion of freedom in Petr Chelčický], in *Od knížat ke králům. Sborník u příležitosti 60. narozenin Josefa Žemličky*, eds. Eva Doležalová and Robert Šimůnek (Prague: 2007), 454–65.

Boubín, Jaroslav, and Alena Míšková, "Spis M. Jana Příbrama Vyznání věrných Čechů" [Master Jan Příbram's Confession of the faithful Czechs], *Folia Historica Bohemica* 5 (1983): 239–87.

Čelakovský, Jaromír, "Traktát podkomořího Vaňka Valečovského proti panování kněžstva" [The treatise of the subchamberlain Vaněk Valečovský against clerical dominion], *Věstník Královské české společnosti nauk* 36 (1881): 325–45.

Cermanová, Pavlína, "Jakoubkův a Biskupcův Výklad na Apokalypsu. Porovnání s důrazem na interpretaci antikristovského mýtu" [Jakoubek's and Biskupec's expositions of the Apocalypse. A comparison with emphasis on the interpretation of the Antichrist myth], in *Jakoubek ze Stříbra. Texty a jejich působení*, eds. Ota Halama and Pavel Soukup (Prague: 2006), 209–28.

Cermanová, Pavlína, "*Antichristus avarus contra pauperes Christi*. Chudoba a její význam v apokalyptickém diskurzu" [Poverty and its significance in the apocalyptic discourse], in *Zbožnost středověku*, ed. Martin Nodl (Colloquia meadiaevalia Pragensia) 6 (Prague: 2007), 111–34.

Cermanová, Pavlína, "Funkce rituálu v apokalyptických textech husitského věku" [The function of the ritual in apocalyptic texts of the Hussite age], in *Rituály, ceremonie a festivity ve střední Evropě 14. a 15. století*, eds. Martin Nodl and František Šmahel (Colloquia mediaevalia Pragensia) 12 (Prague: 2009), 319–37.

Čornej, Petr, and Milena Bartlová, *Velké dějiny zemí Koruny české* [A comprehensive history of the lands of the Bohemian Crown], vol. 6 (Prague and Litomyšl: 2007).

De Vooght, Paul, *Jacobellus de Stříbro (†1429), premier théologien du hussitisme* (Leuven: 1972).

De Vooght, Paul, "Nicolas Biskupec de Pelhřimov et son apport a l'évolution de la méthodologie théologique hussite," *Recherches de théologie ancienne et médiévale* 40 (1973): 176–207.

Dudík, Beda, *Forschungen in Schweden für Mährens Geschichte* (Brno: 1852).

Fudge, Thomas A., "Crime, Punishment and Pacifism in the Thought of Bishop Mikuláš of Pelhřimov, 1420–1452," in *The Bohemian Reformation and Religious Practice*, eds. Zdeněk V. David and David R. Holeton, vol. 3 (Prague: 2000), 69–103.

Fudge, Thomas A., "Václav the Anonymous and Jan Příbram, Textual Laments on the Fate of Religion in Bohemia (1424–1429)," in *The Bohemian Reformation and Religious Practice*, eds. Zdeněk V. David and David R. Holeton, vol. 8 (Prague: 2011), 115–32.

Goll, Jaroslav, "Rokycanova Postilla" [Rokycana's Postil], *Časopis Musea Království českého* 53 (1879): 59–70, 199–211.

Goll, Jaroslav, *Chelčický a Jednota v XV. století* [Chelčický and the Unity in the 15th century] (Prague: 1916).

Halama, Ota, *Otázka svatých v české reformaci. Její proměny od doby Karla IV. do doby České konfese* [The question of saints in the Bohemian Reformation. Its transformations from the time of Charles IV to the *Confessio Bohemica*] (Brno: 2002).

Halama, Ota, "Spis 'De ecclesia' Martina Lupáče z doby poděbradské" [The work "De ecclesia" of Martin Lupáč from the Poděbrad period], *Theologická revue* 75 (2004): 420–35.

Halama, Ota, "Utrakvistická úcta k českým světcům" [The Utraquist cult of Czech saints], in *Světci a jejich kult ve středověku*, ed. Petr Kubín (České Budějovice: 2006), 189–99.

Herold, Vilém, "Magister Procopius von Pilsen, ein Schüler und Anhänger Hussens, und seine frühen philosophischen Schriften," in *Historia Philosophiae Medii Aevi. Studien zur Geschichte der Philosophie des Mittelalters. Festschrift für Kurt Flasch zu seinem 60. Geburtstag*, eds. Mojsisch Burkhard and Olaf Pluta (Amsterdam and Philadelphia: 1991), 363–85.

Heymann, Frederick G., "John Rokycana. Church Reformer between Hus and Luther," *Church History* 28 (1959): 240–80.

Hrubý, Hynek, *České postilly. Studie literarně a kulturně historická* [Czech postils. A study in literary and cultural history] (Prague: 1901).

Hrubý, Karel, "Sociologický model husitské revoluce v hranicích politického systému pražských měst" [A sociological model of the Hussite revolution within the borders of the political system of the Prague towns], *Sociologický časopis* 3 (1967): 575–90.

Kadlec, Jaroslav, "*Collectura* M. Prokopa z Plzně" [The *Collectura* of Master Prokop of Plzeň], *Listy filologické* 80 (1957): 237–45.

Kaminsky, Howard, "Peter Chelčický's Place on the Hussite Left," *Studies in Medieval and Renaissance History* 1 (1964): 107–36.

Kaminsky, Howard, *A History of the Hussite Revolution* (Berkeley and Los Angeles: 1967).

Kaminsky, Howard, "Nicholas of Pelhřimov's Tabor. An Adventure into the Eschaton," in *Eschatologie und Hussitismus*, eds. Alexander Patschovsky and František Šmahel (Prague: 1996), 139–67.

Kejř, Jiří, *Summae confessorum a jiná díla pro foro interno v rukopisech českých a moravských knihoven* (Prague: 2003).

Kejř, Jiří, "Teaching on Repentance and Confession in the Bohemian Reformation," in *The Bohemian Reformation and Religious Practice*, eds. Zdenek V. David and David R. Holeton, vol. 5, 1 (Prague: 2004), 89–116.

Klicman, Ladislav, "Studie o Milíčovi z Kroměříže I. Kdo je spisovatelem 'Knížek o zarmouceních velikých církve svaté i každé duše věrné'?" [Studies on Milíč of Kroměžíž I. Who is the author of the "Books on the great tribulation of the holy church"?], *Listy filologické* 17 (1890): 29–44, 114–25, 256–68, 347–62.

Kolár, Jaroslav, "K transformaci středověkého žánrového systému v literatuře husitské doby" [On the transformation of the medieval genre system in the literature of the Hussite period], *Husitský Tábor* 5 (1982): 135–44.

Kolář, Pavel, "Petr Chelčický's Defense of Sacramental Communion: Response to Mikuláš Biskupec of Tábor," in *The Bohemian Reformation and Religious Practice*, eds. Zdenek V. David and David R. Holeton, vol. 6 (Prague: 2007), 133–42.

Kolář, Pavel, "'Neb novým angelským obyčejem krmeni budou.' O chiliastickém pozadí sporu o svátostné přijímání v Chelčického Replice proti Mikuláši Biskupci Táborskému" [For they will be fed according to a new angelic custom. On the chiliastic background of the argument concerning holy communion in Chelčický's Response to Mikuláš Biskupec of Tábor], *Husitský Tábor* 17 (2012): 105–52.

Krofta, Kamil, "O některých spisech M. Jana z Příbramě" [On some writings of Master John of Příbram], *Časopis Musea Království českého* 73 (1899): 209–20.

Krofta, Kamil, "O spisech Václava Korandy mladšího z Nové Plzně" [On the writings of Václav Koranda the Younger of Nová Plzeň], *Listy filologické* 39 (1912): 122–38, 215–32.

Krofta, Kamil, "Mistr Jan Rokycana" [Master Jan Rokycana], in idem, *Listy z náboženských dějin českých* (Prague: 1936), 222–39.

Krofta, Kamil, "Václav Koranda ml. a jeho názory náboženské" [Václav Koranda the Younger and his religious views], in idem, *Listy z náboženských dějin českých* (Prague: 1936), 240–87.

Macek, Josef, "Sémantická analýza slova 'moc' ve slovníku P. Chelčického" [A semantic analysis of the word "moc" (power) in the vocabulary of P. Chelčický], *Listy filologické* 115, supplementum 2 (1992): 96–119.

Marek, Jindřich, "Husitské postily připisované mistru Václavovi z Dráchova" [Hussite postils attributed to Master Václav of Dráchov], *Miscellanea oddělení rukopisů a starých tisků* 18 (2003–2004): 4–144.

Marek, Jindřich, "Betlémský kazatel Václav z Dráchova. Kazatelské rukopisy a otázky jejich zpracování" [The Bethlehem preacher Václav of Dráchov. Sermon manuscripts and the questions of their treatment], in *Jakoubek ze Stříbra. Texty a jejich působení*, eds. Ota Halama and Pavel Soukup (Prague: 2006), 257–71.

Marek, Jindřich, "Husitský výklad Žalmů v rukopise Národní knihovny ČR XIII G 25" [The Hussite exposition of the Psalms in National Library of the Czech Republic MS XIII G 25], *Studie o rukopisech* 37–38 (2007–2008): 3–23.

Marek, Jindřich, "Die 'Quaestio' des Magisters Prokops von Pilsen über die kirchliche Autorität," in *Roma – Praga. Praha – Řím: Omaggio a Zdeňka Hledíková*, eds. Kateřina Bobková-Valentová, Eva Doležalová, Eva Chodějovská, Zdeněk Hojda, and Martin Svatoš (Prague: 2009), 159–72.

Marek, Jindřich, "Josef Truhlář a středověká bohemikální literatura" [Josef Truhlář and medieval literature from Bohemia], *Studie o rukopisech* 44 (2014): 305–18.

Marek, Jindřich, "Václav Koranda ml. a mediální strategie obrany utrakvismu: autorita bible" [Václav Koranda the Younger and the media strategy of defending Utraquism.

The authority of the Bible], in *Amica – sponsa – mater. Bible v čase reformace*, ed. Ota Halama (Prague: 2014), 143–53.

Marek, Jindřich, *Václav Koranda mladší. Utrakvistický administrátor a literát* [Václav Koranda the Younger. Utraquist administrator and man of letters] (Prague: 2017).

Modráková, Renáta and Zdeněk Uhlíř, *Law and Scripture. Manuscripts of the Czech Reformation of the 14th–16th Centuries* (Prague: 2009).

Molnár, Amedeo, "'Probacio preceptorum minorum' de Martin Lupáč," *Communio viatorum* 9 (1966): 55–62.

Molnár, Amedeo, "Réformation et Révolution. Le cas du senior taborite Nicolas Biskupec de Pelhřimov," *Communio viatorum* 13 (1970): 137–70.

Molnár, Amedeo, "Petr Chelčický's 'Instructions on the Sacraments,'" *Communio viatorum* 19 (1976): 177–93.

Molnár, Amedeo, "Martin Lupáč. *Modus disputandi pro fide*," *Folia Historica Bohemica* 4 (1982): 161–77.

Nejedlý, Zdeněk, "Mládí M. Jana z Rokycan" [Master Jan Rokycana's youth], *Časopis Musea Království českého* 73 (1899): 517–34.

Nejedlý, Zdeněk, *Dějiny husitského zpěvu* [The history of Hussite chant], 6 vols., 2nd ed. (Prague: 1954–1956).

Palacký, František, *Dějiny národu českého v Čechách a v Moravě* [A history of the Czech nation in Bohemia and Moravia], 6 vols. (Prague: 1968–1973).

Pálka, Adam, "*Super responso Pii pape* Martina Lupáče jako pramen k jednáním husitů s basilejským koncilem" [*Super responso Pii pape* of Martin Lupáč as a source for the negotiations between the Hussites and the Council of Basel], *Časopis Matice moravské* 134 (2015): 29–54.

Pálka, Adam, "Papoušek versus Lupáč. Polemika o výklad basilejských kompaktát z poloviny 15. století" [Papoušek vs. Lupáč. The polemic over the interpretation of the Basel *Compactata* from the mid-15th century], *Studia mediaevalia Bohemica* 8 (2016): 41–87.

Petrů, Eduard, *Soupis díla Petra Chelčického a literatury o něm* [A catalogue of the works of Petr Chelčický and literature about him] (Prague: 1957).

Petrů, Eduard, "Dvě studie o Petru Chelčickém" [Two studies of Petr Chelčický], *Listy filologické* 89 (1966): 394–402.

Petrů, Eduard, "Paradox Hádání Pravdy a Lži Ctibora Tovačovského z Cimburka" [The paradox of the Disputation between Truth and Lies of Ctibor Tovačovský of Cimburk], *Listy filologické* 95 (1972): 221–28.

Prokeš, Jaroslav, *M. Prokop z Plzně. Příspěvek k vývoji konservativní strany husitské* [Master Prokop of Plzeň. A contribution to the development of the Hussite conservative party] (Prague: 1927).

Sedlák, Jan, *Táborské traktáty eucharistické* [Taborite eucharistic tracts] (Brno: 1918).

Seibt, Ferdinand, *Hussitica. Zur Struktur einer Revolution*, 2nd ed. (Cologne: 1990).

Šimek, František, *Učení M. Jana Rokycany* [The teachings of Master Jan Rokycana] (Prague: 1938).
Slavík, Jan, *Husitská revoluce* [The Hussite revolution] (Prague: 1934).
Šmahel, František, *Idea národa v husitských Čechách* [The idea of the nation in Hussite Bohemia], 2nd ed. (Prague: 2000).
Šmahel, František, *Die Hussitische Revolution*, trans. Thomas Krzenck, (Monumenta Germaniae Historica. Schriften) 43, 3 vols. (Hannover: 2002).
Šmahel, František, "Magister Peter Payne. *Curriculum vitae* eines englischen Nonkonformisten," in *Friedrich Reiser und die "waldensisch-hussitische Internationale,"* eds. Albert de Lange and Katherine Utz Tremp (Heidelberg, Ubstadt-Weiher, and Basel: 2006), 241–60.
Šmahel, František, *Die Basler Kompaktaten mit den Hussiten (1436). Untersuchung und Edition* (Monumenta Germaniae Historica, Studien und Texte) 65 (Wiesbaden: 2019).
Souček, Bohuslav, "*Veritas super omnia*. Z biblických studií a odkazu Mikuláše Biskupce z Pelhřimova" [*Veritas super omnia*. From the biblical studies and legacy of Mikuláš Biskupec of Pelhřimov], *Theologická příloha Křesťanské revue* 28 (1961): 73–90.
Soukup, Pavel, "Metaphors of the Spiritual Struggle Early in the Bohemian Reformation. The Exegesis of Arma Spiritualia in Hus, Jakoubek, and Chelčický," in *The Bohemian Reformation and Religious Practice*, eds. Zdenek V. David and David R. Holeton, vol. 6 (Prague: 2007), 87–109.
Spinka, Matthew, "Peter Chelčický. The Spiritual Father of the *Unitas Fratrum*," *Church History* 12 (1943): 271–91.
Spunar, Pavel, "Literární činnost utrakvistů doby poděbradské a jagellonské" [The literary activity of Utraquists of the Poděbrad and Jagellonian periods], in *Acta reformationem Bohemicam illustrantia*, vol. 1: *Příspěvky k dějinám utrakvismu*, ed. Amedeo Molnár (Prague: 1978), 165–269.
Spunar, Pavel, *Repertorium auctorum Bohemorum provectum idearum post universitatem Pragensem conditam illustrans*, vol. 2 (Studia Copernicana) 35 (Warsaw: 1995).
Svatoš, Michal, "Kališnická univerzita (1419–1556)" [The Utraquist university (1419–1556)], in *Dějiny Univerzity Karlovy*, vol. 1, ed. Michal Svatoš (Prague: 1995), 205–217.
Truhlář, Josef, "Paběrky z rukopisů Klementinských: XI. Kázání kněze Martina Lupáče" [Gleanings from Clementinum manuscripts XI. A sermon of the priest Martin Lupáč], *Věstník České akademie* 7 (1898): 409–10.
Uhlíř, Zdeněk, "Středověké kazatelství v českých zemích. Nástin problematiky [Medieval preaching in the Czech Lands. An outline]," *Almanach historyczny* 7 (2005): 57–94.
Uhlíř, Zdeněk, "Traktát Jana z Příbrami *De usura* [Jan Příbram's treatise *De usura*]," in *O felix Bohemia! Studie k dějinám české reformace*, ed. Petr Hlaváček (Prague: 2013), 105–18.

Urbánek, Rudolf, *Věk poděbradský* [The Poděbrad era] 4 vols. (České dějiny) 3 (Prague: 1915–1962).

Válka, Josef, "Kompaktáta a kapitulace. Charta stavovských svobod?" [The *Compactata* and the capitulation. A charter of Estates' liberties?], *Časopis Matice moravské* 129 (2010): 19–43.

Wagner, Murray L., *Petr Chelčický. A Radical Separatist in Hussite Bohemia* (Scottsdale, PA. and Kitchener, ON.: 1983).

Zachová, Jana and Jaroslav Boubín, "Drobné spisky Jana Příbrama na obranu katolické víry" [Minor works of Jan Příbram in defense of the Catholic faith], in *Facta probant homines. Sborník příspěvků k životnímu jubileu prof. dr. Zdeňky Hledíkové*, ed. Ivan Hlaváček (Prague: 1998), 521–34.

Zachová, Jana and Jaroslav Boubín, "Z největšího latinského spisu Jana Příbrama proti Viklefovi a táborům" [From the largest Latin writing of Jan Příbram against Wyclif and the Taborites], *Mediaevalia Historica Bohemica* 6 (1999): 143–59.

Zachová, Jana and Jaroslav Boubín, "Monumentální soupis Viklefových bludů z kapitulního sborníku D 49" [A monumental list of Wyclif's errors from Chapter manuscript D 49], *Mediaevalia Historica Bohemica* 7 (2000): 133–74.

Zachová, Jana and Jaroslav Boubín, "Příbramova excerpta z táborských traktátů z kapitulního sborníku D 49" [Příbram's excerpts from Taborite tracts in Prague Chapter manuscript D 49], *Mediaevalia Historica Bohemica* 8 (2001): 139–67.

Zilynská, Blanka, *Husitské synody v Čechách 1418–1440. Příspěvek k úloze univerzitních mistrů v husitské církvi a revoluci* [Hussite synods in Bohemia 1418–1440. A contribution to the role of the university masters in the Hussite church and revolution] (Prague: 1985).

Zilynská, Blanka, *Synody v Čechách 1440–1540. Proměny synodální praxe v Čechách v kontextu vývoje synodality v Evropě* [Hussite synods in Bohemia 1440–1540. Transformations of synodal practice in Bohemia in the context of the development of synods in Europe], Ph.D. dissertation, Charles University, Faculty of Arts, Insititute of Czech History (Prague: 2008).

PART 3

Religious Politics

∴

The Apocalyptic Background of Hussite Radicalism

Pavlína Cermanová

Apocalypticism played an essential role in pre-Hussite and Hussite thought, shaping and contributing to the dynamic course of events.[1] Pre-Hussite and Hussite authors often relied on apocalyptic terminologies and imagery in defining their self-identity, their enemies, and in declaring the necessity of reform or revolution. Moreover, Hussite theologians employed an apocalyptic narrative in explaining and legitimizing current events, their positions, and their actions. Hussite discourses of the end of the world, or the end of an age – based on Christian eschatological concepts – provided new impulses to the reformist movement in its various expressions and equipped it with political and above all ideological tools to shape a religiously-defined society. The focal message of medieval apocalyptic texts emphasized the necessity of change and correction before the world's end and the judgement of sins. This basic founding premise naturally resounded strongly within the context of Hussite radicalism, both among those who expected an imminent Last Judgement, and among those who awaited a transition into a millennial age. The medieval apocalyptic tradition, including that in the Hussite context, provided a flexible hermeneutical framework which could potentially and simultaneously structure, explain, and legitimize current events. Prophetic texts essentially related to the future, yet their interpretation primarily referred to the present and its place in salvation history.[2]

Apocalyptic interpretations of the present and the identification of current events with apocalyptic symbols is a phenomenon which occurs particularly in eras that contemporaries understand as critical – moments perceived as transitions between two ages, when the continuity of history is disturbed, but is nevertheless understood as proceeding according to God's providential plan. While in purely universalistic eschatological prophecies salvation is meant to play out in the continuity of one age, there is a necessary discontinuity in apocalyptic schemas, a catastrophic division in which the old world is destroyed and replaced by the new within the framework of the world's history. In the gradual formation of Hussite apocalyptic thought – and in its individual

---

1 This study was supported by a grant from the Czech Science Foundation (GA ČR): "Cultural Codes and Their Transformations in the Hussite Period" (P405/12/G148).
2 Jakoubek of Stříbro, for example, says this explicitly in *Výklad na Zjevenie sv. Jana*, ed. František Šimek, 2 vols. (Prague: 1932–1933), vol. 1, 150.

layers – this discontinuity was described in a number of ways and with varying degrees of radicalism. These variations converged in the fact that they all characterized this division as a contemporary battle of the true church against the greatest apocalyptic enemy, the Antichrist.

1   The Antichrist

The concept of the Antichrist was a fundamental instrument for the formulation of reformist thought during the Hussite period. For Hussite theologians, the Antichrist was the power behind the pathetic state of the church, and also that which prevented the Hussite warriors from enacting a purification in Christ's name and from bringing the church into a state of perfection. According to the Hussites, the Antichrist took many forms; generally, he was identified as the main representative of evil, sin, and an enemy of God's law. In interpreting the Antichrist, Hussite authors largely avoided the historicizing method which was still found among previous authors, including Milíč of Kroměříž in his *Sermo de die novissimo* (1367).[3] Hussite theologians did not describe the Antichrist merely as one of those particular sons of perdition whose biography unfolds as an inverse copy of Christ's – a tradition that the Middle Ages inherited particularly from Adso of Montier-en-Der's *De ortu et tempore Antichristi*.[4] John Wyclif, a significant influence on Hussite thought, also avoided the historical reading of the figure of the Antichrist, and explicitly rejected the relevance of the received Antichrist narrative – namely that he will come from the line of Dan, rule for a particular period, enact miracles, and so on. Wyclif mentions, sarcastically, that according to these conventions, the Antichrist should come equipped with a fiery horse and carriage, along with other nonsensical fantasies. For the purpose of reform, Wyclif unambiguously preferred the

---

3 Jan Milíč of Kroměříž, "Sermo de Die novissimo Domini," in Milíč of Kroměříž, *The Message for the Last Days. Three Essays from the Year 1367*, eds. Milan Opočenský and Jana Opočenská (Geneva: 1998), 32–55.

4 Adso of Montier-en-Der, *De Ortu et Tempore Antichristi*, ed. Daniel Verhelst (Corpus christianorum. Continuatio mediaevalis) 45 (Turnhout: 1976). Adso's work represents a synthesis of imagery coming from writings of St. Jerome and some 6th- to 9th-century sources (Haimo of Auxerre, Alcuin, as well as the Byzantine Prophecy of the Tiburtine Sibyl and Ps.-Methodius), see Daniel Verhelst, "La préhistoire des conceptions d'Adson concernant l'Antichrist," *Recherches de théologie ancienne et médiévale* 40 (1973): 52–103. The Tiburtine Sibyl describes Antichrist as someone who will turn the world upside down, seduce many and expose Christendom to tyranny, to be eventually defeated by the Archangel Michael on the Mount of Olives: Richard K. Emmerson, "Antichrist as Anti-Saint," *American Benedictine Review* 30 (1979): 183–85.

allegorical-tropological interpretation, understanding the Antichrist as adherence to sin and the aggregate of the foreknown (*praesciti*), the worst among whom was to be Antichrist's head.[5] This interpretation is also echoed in the works of Jan Hus and other Hussite thinkers.

Hussite authors understood the Antichrist primarily as the amorphous, personified agent of all evil, sin, and corruption which dominated the church, against whom it was necessary to lead an active battle. This did not mean, however, that they avoided searching for signs of the Antichrist among their contemporaries. In this regard, they found support and great inspiration in Matěj of Janov and his exposition on the Antichrist, to which he dedicated the third book of his monumental *Regulae Veteris et Novi Testamenti*.[6] For Matěj, the Antichrist was every Christian who did not live in the spirit of Christ.[7] In addition to this composite body, Matěj also expected the coming of a specific, individual Antichrist who would be the head of the entire antichristian society. He interpreted the papal schism as a premonition of the great Antichrist's arrival and saw the two bodies – that of Christ (the true church) and the Antichrist (the collection of sinners, hypocrites, the avaricious, etc.) – as fundamentally opposed. Just as he counterposed Christ and Antichrist (*maximus Antichristus*), on another level he opposed the entire principle by which the Antichrist dominated, namely, "antichristianity" (*antichristeitas*), to the truth and values of Christ.[8] This concept of "antichristianity" was thereafter established in the Czech reformist context, and is also found among other Hussite authors who worked on expositions of John's Revelation.[9] The explicit identification of the pope with the Antichrist – which Matěj thought to be so obvious that "it must be clear to everyone who is not asleep"[10] – and reflections on the figure and presence of the Antichrist in the world not only acquired great currency, but also served to radicalize reform.

Hussite theologians drew a great deal from Matěj's exposition of the Antichrist. At the beginning of the 1420s, Jakoubek of Stříbro wrote a vast

---

5   John Wyclif, *Johannis Wyclif Tractatus De potestate pape*, ed. Johann Loserth (Wyclif's Latin Works) 32 (London: 1907), 118. On this topic, see Alexander Patschovsky, "'Antichrist' bei Wiclif," in *Eschatologie und Hussitismus*, eds. Alexander Patschovsky and František Šmahel (Prague: 1996), 92.
6   Matěj of Janov, *Regulae Veteris et Novi Testamenti*, ed. Vlastimil Kybal (Innsbruck: 1908–1913), vols. 1–4.
7   For example, *Regulae*, vol. 1, 263.
8   *Regulae*, vol. 3, 3–4.
9   Jakoubek of Stříbro, *Výklad na Zjevenie*, vol. 1, 268; Vienna, Österreichische Nationalbibliothek, 4520, fols. 65v-66r.
10 Matěj of Janov, *Regulae*, vol. 3, 30.

exposition of John's Revelation which, less than a decade later, was used by the foremost theologian of the Taborite faction, Mikuláš Biskupec of Pelhřimov, as the basis of his own work from the perspective of Hussite radicalism (though written in Latin, unlike Jakoubek's).[11] Both of these authors located the core concept of the Antichrist in the moral antithesis to Christ, and both worked with an allegorical-tropological method of exposition, reflecting the reformist context of their works. Jakoubek and Biskupec placed Christ, the head of the church, against the Antichrist, the head of all wickedness and evil (*caput iniquorum, caput reproborum, caput omnium malorum*).[12] This was based on the New Testament premise that the Antichrist is he who places himself in contradiction to Christ and his law. Following late-medieval church reformers, particularly John Wyclif, Hussite authors combined two levels of exposition in their approach to the Antichrist: the tropological and anagogical plane of interpretation, standing outside the category of time, and the historical exposition, referring to particular events and individuals. Both Jakoubek and Mikuláš Biskupec included all secular and spiritual estates standing in opposition to Christ and Christian values in their definition of the Antichrist.[13] Biskupec went even further in his spiritual exposition, identifying the Antichrist with the whole sinful, physical world; he conceived of him not only as the composite enemy of the true faith, but also as the figure personifying evil in general, as the principle driving the material world, and thereby sin. He brought the common topoi of theological-pastoral literature – linking the world, the body, and the devil – into the framework of Hussite apocalyptic thought and the image of the Antichrist. Sin, the world, material embodiment, and the desire for wealth formed a unity which stood in opposition to spiritual values and expressed the apocalyptic binary model of good and evil.[14]

---

11 Jakoubek of Stříbro, *Výklad na Zjevenie*; Mikuláš Biskupec of Pelhřimov, *Super Apocalypsim*, Vienna, Österreichische Nationalbibliothek, 4520, fols. 1r-297v.
12 From the previous tradition, see e.g. Rupert of Deutz, who wrote: "Antichristus, id est Christo contrarius (...) Antichristus, quod vere non Christus, sed secundum nomen suum Christo contrarius. Hic est Christus, qui sanguinem suum fudit, hic est Antichristus, qui sanguinem fudit alienum." Rupert of Deutz, "Commentaria in Apocalypsim," in *Patrologiae cursus completus. Series Latina*, ed. Jacques-Paul Migne, vol. 169 (Paris: 1894), 1083. Matěj of Janov describes the Antichrist in similar terms.
13 Vienna, Österreichische Nationalbibliothek, 4520, fol. 69v: "et est Antichristus, secundum modum loquendi scripture, quicunque Christo aut legi sue est contrarius"; fol. 179r: "Antichristus, id est status spiritualis et secularis, qui erunt contrarii Christo verbo et opera."
14 Vienna, Österreichische Nationalbibliothek, 4520, fol. 236v. Cf. Jan Hus, *Magistri Johannis Hus Tractatus de ecclesia*, ed. S. Harrison Thomson (Cambridge, Eng., and Boulder, CO.: 1956; repr. Prague: 1958), 9; idem, *Sermo de pace*, eds. František M. Dobiáš and Amedeo

This broad definition of the apocalyptic Antichrist – whom Hussite authors sought not only in the future, nor described exclusively as one particular individual – was among those theses which enemies of the Hussites later brought against them at the Council of Basel. For instance, in his speech *De ecclesia militanti catholica* from 1432, Heinrich Toke explicitly labeled as an *error wickleffitarum* the argument that the Antichrist, who enacts the events of the apocalypse, will not be one particular person, but is already now everyone who stands in opposition to the law of Christ in mores and teaching.[15] According to Toke, Hussite interpretations were thus opposed to the patristic expositions that were valid in the church, which placed the coming of the apocalyptic Antichrist in the future – even if, in the spirit of John's epistles (1 John 2:18), these expositions acknowledged the presence of many Antichrists in the world.[16]

2   Hussite Apocalyptic Spirituality

Insofar as radical Hussite theologians reflected on contemporary events in Bohemia, they linked the church's degradation and the general decline of Christian mores with the interference of the Antichrist in the world. They insisted that the "purifying" work of the Hussite armies, who violently rid the church of property and correct sinners, was not the only necessary condition for perfect order and the destruction of the Antichrist; also required was each individual's personal introspection and conversion from sin. Already in the eleventh chapter of Jan Hus' tractate *De ecclesia*, speaking of the power which allowed the predestined to conquer the beast and the dragon, Hus referred to the ability of each individual to internally defeat sin and worldly affection. This power from predestination is then complemented by the "completed" power (*potestas comsumata*) which God gives the blessed in heaven.[17] In this passage, Hus expresses the basic framework of his eschatological understanding of the church: in the final battle, the predestined, as the true church, defeat Satan's church governed by the Antichrist, represented by the apocalyptic dragon and the beast. In that decisive time of the final battle, the most important virtues will be those of poverty, meekness, humility, patience, and purity, through which Christ should be followed in the actions of every believer.

Molnár (Prague: 1963), 3; idem, *Výklady*, ed. Jiří Daňhelka (Magistri Iohannis Hus Opera omnia) 1 (Prague: 1975), 323.
15   Munich, Bayerische Staatsbibliothek, Clm 28255, fol. 168r-v.
16   Cf. Roberto Rusconi, "Antichrist and Antichrists," in *The Encyclopedia of the Apocalypticism*, ed. Bernard McGinn, vol. 2 (New York: 1999).
17   Hus, *Tractatus de ecclesia*, 92.

Jakoubek of Stříbro, in his exposition of the letters to Philadelphia (Rev. 3:7–13), described the spiritually mature person as one who contributes to the destruction of the Antichrist and to eschatological perfection. Chronologically, he assigned this passage from Revelation to his own time, namely the sixth age of the church and the "current final period" of great grief and suffering, which was nevertheless marked by the defeat of the Antichrist and the beginning of the progress toward rest and the perfection of the seventh age.[18] In his pastoral addresses, Jakoubek encouraged the faithful to love God and one's neighbor, listen to the Word of the Lord, repent, and take communion frequently. Only in this way could one be reborn, reaching the unity of spirit and understanding of God's Word. In his exposition of Revelation, Jakoubek assigned the Utraquist Eucharist an important role in individual and collective eschatology, perceiving it as one of the main defenses of the faithful against the Antichrist and his power. At the same time, he referenced the coming union with Christ, salvation and damnation, and the eschatological battle between good and evil.[19] This overarching explication, related both to the eschatological battle and to the *caelestia mysteria ventura*, gives us an understanding of the integral role of the Eucharist in Hussite apocalyptic thought. For Jakoubek, the Eucharist was a path upon which the believer could approach and accomplish spiritual perfection in the coming age: "For those things in the coming age are all spiritual and for the enjoyment of the Lord, and thus we must also be spiritual. And therefore we take the body and blood of the Lord, so that we may be spiritualized."[20]

Already in the pre-Hussite period with Milíč of Kroměříž and especially Matěj of Janov, it is possible to observe this emphasis on the Eucharist as a powerful tool of rebirth in the apocalyptic-theological concepts of history. Matěj expressed himself in clear terms on this matter with an appeal to Matthew 24:28: "'Wherever the body lies, there, too, will the eagles gather.' And then Sodom will return in its old dignity, and omega will move back to alpha, and Elijah will come and renew everything."[21] Matěj of Janov, like Jakoubek after him, identified a clear connection between the beginning of the Antichrist's worldly interference and the abandonment of the practice of frequent

---

18   Jakoubek of Stříbro, *Výklad na Zjevenie*, vol. 1, 151.
19   This notion is to be seen in connection with the concept of the Church. Already some patristic authors, in their anagogical interpretations, identified the terrestrial church of Christ with the Heavenly Church. The Hussite authors, including Jakoubek, enriched this interpretation with the eucharistic theme. Cf. Henri de Lubac, *Exégèse médiévale. Les quatre sens de l'Écriture*, 4 vols. (Paris: 1959–1964), vol. 2, 623–24.
20   Jakoubek of Stříbro, *Výklad na Zjevenie*, vol. 1, 214.
21   Matěj of Janov, *Regulae*, vol. 1, 100.

communion among the laity,[22] an idea he probably adopted from Paris, as a similar understanding was found among the works of John Quidort of Paris.[23]

The emphasis on the Eucharist meant that not only was the salvation of the individual at stake, but so was the life of the community, under threat by Antichrist and the devil. The eucharistic reminder of the suffering of Christ served as both a corrective to individual behavior and a means to strengthen the body of the Christian faithful.[24] For Jakoubek, Utraquist communion was an expression of one's adherence to the true church, as well as a way of defeating the enemy,[25] namely the sinful sect of the Antichrist.[26] In the context of actual warfare, Utraquist communion assumed the role of a "weapon" with which victory over "sin, the world, and the body" may be achieved: "Taking the communion of the blood of the Lord from the chalice is the sword of Gideon, with which the enemy is defeated."[27] Here, Hussite authors referred to one of the foundational elements upon which Christian apocalyptic thought was built, namely that the worldly church is already in its current state the Body of Christ and participates in his new life in God's kingdom.[28] It was this membership in the eternal church of Christ which Jakoubek directly linked to Utraquist communion: "Heaven, those living in heaven, rejoice, for those dwelling on earth are defeating Satan with the proper Eucharist, the body and blood of the Lord. There are surely people dwelling bodily here on earth, and living in heaven."[29] According to the works of apocalyptically minded authors in Bohemia in the first decade of the 15th century, Hussite society should aim for perfection, spiritual fulfillment, and sinlessness. Naturally bound to this rhetoric was the idea

---

22 The dependence of Jakoubek's eucharistic teaching on Matěj of Janov was shown by Helena Krmíčková, "Vliv Matěje z Janova na utrakvismus Jakoubka ze Stříbra a Mikuláše z Drážďan," in *Mistr Matěj z Janova ve své a v naší době*, eds. Jan B. Lášek and Karel Skalický (Brno: 2002), 78–81; Helena Krmíčková, *Studie a texty k počátkům kalicha v Čechách* (Brno: 1997), 86–119. Matěj of Janov, *Regulae*, vol. 3, 168, 215.

23 Quidort's work corresponds with that of Bohemian authors in calculations of the exact date of the Antichrist's coming. They may all have used same sources, above all works by Arnald of Villanova and John Rupescissa; Milíč of Kroměříž uses the same calculations as these authors. See John Quidort of Paris, *The Tractatus de Antichristo of John of Paris. A Critical Edition, Translation, and Commentary*, ed. Sara Peters Clark (Ithaca: 1981), 53. See also Manfred Gerwing, *Vom Ende der Zeit. Der Traktat des Arnald von Villanova über die Ankunft des Antichrist in der akademischen Auseinandersetzung zu Beginn des 14. Jahrhunderts* (Münster: 1996), 397.

24 Jakoubek of Stříbro, *Výklad na Zjevenie*, vol. 1, 482; see also 595.

25 Ibid., vol. 2, 605.

26 Ibid., vol. 1, 594.

27 Ibid., vol. 1, 116.

28 Thomas Forsyth Torrance, "Liturgie et Apocalypse," *Verbum Caro* 11 (1957): 31.

29 Jakoubek of Stříbro, *Výklad na Zjevenie*, vol. 1, 172.

of election and the identity of Christ's Body, which stood opposed to the Antichrist and his servants. Within the framework of the vision of apocalyptic battle, Hussite authors – especially Jakoubek of Stříbro, and Mikuláš Biskupec after him – again defined the distinguishing signs of the church of Christ and the Antichrist. The main indices of belonging included one's support for the Hussite reformist program; the rejection of material property, bodily pleasure, and sin more generally; the hearing of preaching; and naturally, as we have seen, participation in Utraquist communion.[30]

Both of the aforementioned authors understood the events occurring in Hussite Bohemia to be part of an eschatologically defined course of history. Crises, described as and attributed to the free reign of the Antichrist, were to be followed by a general change for the better, a rebirth into perfection and a new order that was modeled on the primitive church. The distinction between the past ideal and the contemporary state of the church, emphasized in both word and image, was used instructively to highlight the current reign of sin. This idea of the contemporary church as the antithesis to the primitive church was expressed graphically, for instance, in Nicholas of Dresden's *Tabulae veteris et novi coloris*.[31] For Hussite authors, one's conformity to the practice and tradition of the early church was one of the foundational signs of belonging either to Christ's church or to those serving the Antichrist. For the originators of the vastly heterogeneous Hussite ideology, the primitive church served as a symbolic and rhetorical figure through which they maintained a stark contrast with the contemporary church ruled by errors, and thus by the Antichrist. Both Jakoubek of Stříbro and Mikuláš Biskupec expressed this thought in their exposition of Revelation 17:1, where the whore set above the waters represents the contemporary, sinful church. Opposite her stands the apocalyptic woman dressed in the sun (Rev. 12), identified with the primitive church of the apostles that successfully suppressed all sins and the power of the Antichrist.[32]

Jakoubek conceived of the primitive church as an ideal from the past, the exemplary model from which the contemporary church strayed due to the iniquity of the Antichrist, but to which it would again return. Mikuláš Biskupec further developed this idea, understanding the primitive church as a living

---

30 Ibid.
31 Petra Mutlová, "Communicating Texts through Images. Nicholas of Dresden's *Tabulae*," in *Public Communication in European Reformation. Artistic and other Media in Central Europe 1380–1620*, eds. Milena Bartlová and Michal Šroněk (Prague: 2007), 29–37. See also František Šmahel, "Die hussitische Kommune von Tábor 1420–1422," in *Jan Hus und die Hussiten in europäischen Aspekten* (Trier: 1987), 95–105.
32 Jakoubek of Stříbro, *Výklad na Zjevenie*, vol. 2, 54. Österreichische Nationalbibliothek 4520, fols. 184v, 265v.

model toward which Taborite society already actively strove and was to fulfill in the age after the defeat of the Antichrist. The primitive church, therefore, was not only an ideal from the past, but also a goal set in the future. Biskupec described the Taborite community as a society of "holy warriors" who carried the burden of battle in the final stage of history against the apocalyptic enemy, renewing the ideal of the apostolic church in themselves. Here we can hear the echoes of similar claims of exceptionalism and election, as made in the early Hussite movement by different authors – whether in the sermons of Jan Želivský,[33] or the early, chiliastically focused Taborite radicals (see below). Biskupec himself, however, was forced to admit that despite all attempts at reform, the Taborite community constantly struggled with evil and sin, traits which either did not affect the primitive church, or were immediately suppressed therein.[34] Repeatedly, he called upon the community to struggle against sins and turn itself toward the spiritual life, repentance, and prayer. Since it was not merely the individual who was meant to turn himself toward salvation, but rather the entire Hussite community (the true *societas christiana* governed by Christ and the apostles),[35] we also hear appeals to share responsibility for sins and their extirpation.[36]

The basic activities which, according to Biskupec, led to spiritual serenity and rigor in the primitive church were pious prayer and fervent preaching. As he reflected on the relationship between the Taborite community and the primitive church, Biskupec drew (among other sources) from the Wycliffite exposition of Revelation known by its incipit as *Opus arduum valde*, a popular text in Hussite Bohemia.[37] Following the *Opus arduum*, he outlined the path which the contemporary church must take to achieve the level of its apostolic forebear, the means being similar to those attested in the age of Christ and the apostles: the path should be narrow, uncomfortable, and full of suffering. Here, Biskupec had in mind the pure path of individual, spiritual maturation by

---

33   Jan Želivský, *Dochovaná kázání z roku 1419*, ed. Amedeo Molnár (Prague: 1953), 49–50.
34   Vienna, Österreichische Nationalbibliothek, 4520, fols. 184v, 273v. More on this in Howard Kaminsky, "Nicholas of Pelhřimov's Tabor. An Adventure into the Eschaton," in *Eschatologie und Hussitismus*, eds. František Šmahel and Alexander Patschovsky (Prague: 1996), 157.
35   Vienna, Österreichische Nationalbibliothek, 4520, fols. 57r-v, 89v, 190v.
36   This also applies to other religious and reform movements, for example the Wycliffites in England; see Patrick J. Hornbeck, Stephen E. Lahey, and Fiona Somerset (eds.), *Wycliffite Spirituality* (New York and Mahwah, NJ.: 2013), 15–18.
37   See Anne Hudson, "A Neglected Wycliffite Text," *Journal of Ecclesiastical History* 29 (1978): 257–59, Curtis V. Bostick, *The Antichrist and the Lollards. Apocalypticism in Late Medieval and Reformation England* (Leiden, Boston, and Cologne: 1998); Romolo Cegna, "*Ecclesia Primitiva*. Dall'*Opus arduum valde* a Nicolaus de Drazna (de Rosa Nigra)," *Archa Verbi* 9 (2012): 66–88.

means of long fasts, prayers, preaching, study, and the subduing of bodily passions. Most important was the gift of the Holy Spirit, in which the Taborite community was to be spiritually rejuvenated.[38] Thus, again borrowing from the *Opus arduum*, the goal would be reached, a new doctrine would pour out over all the faithful, and the darkness of the Antichrist would be dispelled and replaced by the light of evangelic truth.[39] This vision of a sinless society also corresponded to one of the main points of the Hussite program, the punishment of public sins, which was the article defended by Mikuláš Biskupec in 1433 at the Council of Basel.

3 An Apocalyptic Theology of History

The medieval perception of history was founded on the teleological conviction that time is progressing toward a goal according to God's preordained plan. History since the original Fall led inevitably to redemption, and thus the eschatological, apocalyptic element necessarily entered into theological speculations on history. At the same time, history was not understood as a continuum, as one flowing whole, but rather as a sequence of individual ages, which led to schemas of explanation and periodization.[40] Hussite thinkers sought from the Revelation of John and other biblical prophecies, among other sources, answers to the problem of positioning their own tumultuous times within the flow of history. Here they followed the sequential scheme of seven ages, which corresponded to the seven parts into which John's Revelation was traditionally divided. According to this model, first developed by the Venerable Bede in the 8th century, the church experienced a series of dangers, each connected to a specific group of enemies and defenders of the faith: in the first age, the Jews and apostles stood opposed, followed by the age of pagans and martyrs, and then heretics and church fathers, while the fourth was the age of hypocrites who had overpowered the monks. The fifth age belonged to the forerunners of the Antichrist, who prepared the path for him to take over the world in the

---

38 Vienna, Österreichische Nationalbibliothek, 4520, fols. 156r-156v.
39 Ibid., fol. 156v; cf. Prague, Archiv Pražského hradu, Knihovna metropolitní kapituly, A 163, fol. 68v.
40 The fundamental study of these issues is Roderich Schmidt, "*Aetates mundi*. Die Weltalter als Gliederungsprinzip der Geschichte," *Zeitschrift für Kirchengeschichte* 67 (1955–1956): 288–317; see also Hans Werner Goetz, "Endzeiterwartung und Endzeitvorstellung im Rahmen des Geschichtsbildes des früheren 12. Jahrhunderts," in *The Use and Abuse of Eschatology in the Middle Ages*, eds. Werner Verbeke, Daniel Verhelst, and Andries Welkenhuysen (Leuven: 1988), 312–13.

sixth. After the defeat of the Antichrist was the anticipated seventh age, bringing rest before the Final Judgement.[41] It was this age which, following the defeat of the Antichrist, signaled for both patristic and many medieval authors the path of return to the age of perfection after the Antichrist, without actually turning to open millenarianism.[42] As we shall see, the Hussites entertained both alternatives.

Following this model of periodization, Jakoubek of Stříbro and Mikuláš Biskupec assigned the reign of the Antichrist to the sixth age, which was to end with his defeat.[43] Although both placed themselves in the fifth age – which was to precede and prefigure the full coming of the Antichrist – they did not feel themselves at all bound by this assignment, and both spoke of their own age as existing contemporaneously with that of the Antichrist's open reign.[44] They did not necessarily describe the sixth age in terms of chronological succession, but qualitatively: it was not an age in itself, but rather an escalation of the dangers of the fifth age. Following Jakoubek, Biskupec described his own time as corresponding to both the fifth and sixth ages, as shown by the terms he used for both periods: "temporibus nostris novissimis," "temporibus novissimis in adventu Antichristi," "ex his igitur ad destruendum regnum Antichristi temporibus novissimis," "et nunc temporibus Antichristi," etc.[45]

What is particularly striking from the Hussite apocalyptic expositions discussed here is their conviction to confront the eschatological enemy, who is already openly present in the world. After all the trials and sufferings of history – that is, after the defeat of the Antichrist – the seventh age was expected to establish in the church a renewed organization and foundation in the primitive church, and this was to last until the Final Judgement. Both Jakoubek and Biskupec (though at least rhetorically opposed to Hussite

---

41   Bede's periodization is summarized by Gerald Bonner, "Saint Bede in the Tradition of Western Apocalyptic Commentary," in *Church and Faith in the Patristic Tradition*, ed. Gerald Bonner (London: 1996), 14. Jakoubek of Stříbro followed Bede's model.
42   Robert E. Lerner, The Medieval Return to the Thousand-Year Sabbath," in *The Apocalypse in the Middle Ages*, eds. Richard K. Emmerson and Bernard McGinn (Ithaca and London: 1992), 51–71; idem, "Refreshment of the Saints. The Time after Antichrist as a Station for Earthly Progress in Medieval Thought," *Traditio* 32 (1976): 97–144.
43   Vienna, Österreichische Nationalbibliothek, 4520, fol. 112r: "Sermo igitur nobis erit de sexto ordine predicatorum, vel de predicatoribus sexte etatis, tempore Antichristi regni, que etas sive status incipiet ab adventu Antichristi cum suis percursoribus, et durabit usque ad diem iudicii." Jakoubek of Stříbro, *Výklad na Zjevenie*, vol. 1, 267–68.
44   Vienna, Österreichische Nationalbibliothek, 4520, fol. 97r; Jakoubek of Stříbro, *Výklad na Zjevenie*, vol. 1, 335–36.
45   Vienna, Österreichische Nationalbibliothek, 4520, fols. 77r, 82r, 228r a 65v. More on this in Kaminsky, "Nicholas of Pelhřimov's Tabor," 156, n. 64.

chiliasm)[46] developed visions of the perfect age after the Antichrist's defeat within the framework of the Hussite program. Both authors similarly described the last age of history in terms of the Eucharist, the age of free preaching, and the suppression of sin; a time when the body and blood of the Lord would be taken in abundance.[47] With these visions of the age of perfection in worldly history, Jakoubek's and Biskupec's expositions of Hussite events within the framework of an apocalyptic theology of history reached their consummation.

4 Practicing the Fulfilment of Biblical Prophecies

The vision of an imminent battle with the Antichrist and the establishment of a perfect age found its most striking expression in the wave of Hussite chiliasm at the beginning of the 1420s, when theories expounding the prophecies shifted into practice. According to the radical Hussite preachers, the beginning of the Hussite wars marked the beginning of the fulfillment of apocalyptic prophecies. In 1419, preachers in Prague and the Bohemian countryside called upon people to abandon their homes and make way "to the mountains" in search of their salvation and the reformation of society.[48] These calls to congregate on the mountains were infused with a strong apocalyptic charge. They spoke of battle with the Antichrist but did not yet envision God's kingdom on earth – which would bring blessedness, abundance, and social equality – as they did several months later. The model and instructions for the faithful and their leaders were found not only in the Gospels (especially Mt 28:16–20, describing the revelation of Jesus on the mountain in Galilee), but also in Old Testament stories that spoke of battle for the true faith. From among the latter, these apocalyptic exhortations often made reference to the Maccabees and their preparedness to fight and sacrifice their lives. At the core of this new message introduced by the pilgrimages to the mountains stood the sacrament of the Eucharist; yet the form of these gatherings was to a great extent related to the

---

46 Jakoubek of Stříbro, *Výklad na Zjevenie*, vol. 1, 295–96, 527; Vienna, Österreichische Nationalbibliothek, 4520, fol. 80r.

47 The motif of free preaching in an age defined in apocalyptic terms was not of Hussite origin; it rather originated in the expositions of Dominican authors around Hugh of Saint-Cher. See Robert E. Lerner, "Poverty, Preaching, and Eschatology in the Revelation Commentaries of Hugh of St Cher," in *The Bible in the Medieval World. Essays in Memory of Beryl Smalley*, eds. Katherine Walsh and Diana Wood (Oxford: 1985), 157–91.

48 For example, František Palacký (ed.), *Dějiny národu českého v Čechách a v Moravě*, 6 vols. (Prague: 1848–1876), vol. 6, 41–43.

orthodox religious practice emerging from the sacramental life of parishes and processions.[49] The external appearance of such congregations was not necessarily distinct from the previous practice of religious life in any significant way: here the faithful also made pilgrimages in crowds behind priests with monstrances, heard preaching, repented, and took the sacrament of the Body – and now blood – of the Lord. Those who were learned and eloquent took the stage and, from the early morning, preached to the congregated faithful. Most often those gathered heard admonitions against pride, greed, and the arrogance of the clergy, emphasized by numerous references to apocalyptic events, through language of an impending decisive moment in the apocalyptic battle, and by encouragement for active participation in this final struggle. This rhetoric, along with the sacrament of the Eucharist, established the mountaintop congregations within a transformed religious context and endowed them with a new spiritual and symbolic character. The fact that the faithful made pilgrimage to the mountains already bears witness to a strong belief in the fulfillment of eschatological events, as many Old Testament eschatological narratives were notably set on mountains (Is. 2:2; Is. 25:6–7; Ez. 34:13–15, Mich. 4:1).[50] The association with biblical events also inspired the naming of individual mountains as "Tábor," which referred not only to the christological tradition of the Lord's transfiguration, but also to the Old Testament story from the books of Judges. Here, the prophet Debora ordered Barak, the leader of Israel, to ascend with an army to the mountain of Tábor according to the Lord's will, and from Tábor Barak then decisively defeated the Canaanite army (Judges 4:6).[51] Although the sources emphasize above all the spiritual sense of these congregations, the *Old Czech Annals* also mention the exhortation of the radical priest

---

49 Mikuláš Biskupec describes the form and religious aspect of the movement to the hills in his "Chronicon Taboritarum," 478; cf. Vavřinec of Březová, "Kronika husitská," in *Fontes rerum Bohemicarum*, eds. Josef Emler, Jan Gebauer, and Jaroslav Goll, vol. 5 (Prague: 1893), 400–01. See František Šmahel, *Dějiny Tábora*, 2 vols. (České Budějovice: 1988–1990), vol. 1, 229–30. On the hilltop congregations, see also Stanisław Bylina, "Husyckie pouťe na hory i ich uczestnici," in *Wspólnoty małe i duże w społeczeństwach Czech i Polski w średniowieczu i w czasach wczesnonowożytnych*, eds. Wojciech Iwańczak and Janusz Smołucha (Cracow: 2010), 337–52, who sees a continuity between this movement and the pre-Hussite Bohemian tradition of preaching. See also Jan Hrdina, Aleš Mudra, and Marcella K. Perett, "Re-use and Reinvent. The Function of Processions in Late Medieval and Early Modern Bohemia," *Studia mediaevalia Bohemica* 7 (2015): 289–312.

50 Amedeo Molnár, "Eschatologická naděje české reformace," in *Od reformace k zítřku* (Prague: 1956), 29.

51 František Michálek Bartoš, "Do čtyř pražských artykulů. Z myšlenkových i ústavních zápasů let 1415–1420," *Sborník příspěvků k dějinám hlavního města Prahy* 5 (1932): 511.

Václav Koranda (the Elder) for the faithful to make the pilgrimage armed with scythes, lances, flails, and swords.[52]

The mountaintop congregation movement was also tied with events occurring in Prague. There, the radical preacher Jan Želivský in particular found common ground with the Taborites. Just as in the countryside, in Prague the otherworldly images from John's Revelation were invigorated, used by Želivský to encourage battle against the enemies of the faith and Sigismund of Luxembourg, whom he compared to the apocalyptic red dragon.[53] Nor did Želivský renounce chiliastic visions, which proved their mobilizing potential in the Prague context. He thus employed the image of the ideal society, one that espoused social equality and sinlessness as its main characteristics. Upon Želivský's initiative in Prague, and in support of the Taborite radicals, gambling was prohibited, prostitution outlawed, and there was an attempt to prevent licentiousness by forbidding women from adorning themselves. During this period, therefore, we can observe in Prague the vision of a sinless community moving toward an apocalyptically defined concept of perfection.

By autumn 1419, the situation in Bohemia intensified, and it became clear that an open confrontation could not be avoided.[54] The idea that a perfect age of God's elect could be established now took clearer shape. The complexity of contemporary society and events was greatly simplified with the employment of apocalyptic explanatory schema. This meant that the new spirituality, which had already reached a broad social spectrum within a short time, became at least superficially more comprehensible, and thus more effective and radical. In one of the circulating letters to a certain Hussite community, we read of the inevitability of physical battle, which was argumentatively endorsed and legitimized by reference to biblical prophecies.[55] The text continues by distinguishing false Christians from those who battled in the Lamb's name, referring to Revelation 17:14. The elect were to congregate in five fortified cities, where they would withstand God's vengeance with prayer and repentance and find their salvation.[56]

The expectation of vengeance, the annihilation of all injustice from the world, and the inauguration of Christ's kingdom went hand in hand with the

---

[52] František Šimek (ed.), *Staré letopisy české z vratislavského rukopisu* (Prague: 1937), 23.
[53] Howard Kaminsky, *A History of the Hussite Revolution* (Berkeley and Los Angeles: 1967), 366.
[54] Šmahel, *Dějiny Tábora*, vol. 1, 227–28.
[55] Palacký (ed.), *Archiv český*, vol. 6, 41.
[56] Ibid., 43.

self-perception of the radical Hussites as the elect warriors of God. Another surviving circular letter bears witness to this self-confidence, speaking in clear terms – again mostly referring to prophecies from the Old and New Testaments[57] – about a historical shift that will usher in a dramatic annihilation of all sinners and then bring an "open paradise, the spread of goodness, and the establishment of perfect love."[58] This letter, with its explicit chiliastic motifs, shows that hopes for the renewal of a perfect age were already expressed at the turn of 1419/1420, and thus before the traditional starting-point of the more markedly chiliastic phase of radical Hussitism, namely, February 1420.[59]

The expositions of apocalyptic prophecies proved to be important mobilizing stimulants for contemporary events, and yet not everyone was granted authority to properly comprehend them. The Hussites held to the traditional premise that only the one who lives in conformity with Christ, in repentance and humility, can properly understand the biblical messages. Hussite theologians added to these conditions the practice of proper (Utraquist) communion, though the matter was still not so simple. The wave of chiliasm, founded on the literal exposition of biblical prophecies, called received concepts of authority and the legitimate exposition of prophetic texts into question, even among the Hussites themselves. This problem became an important theme in writings that appeared from the beginning of the 1420s, when the potential danger that apocalyptic prophecies could possess if enacted as catalysts to events became clear. The theologians of the Utraquist Prague University in particular, with Jakoubek of Stříbro at their head, rejected the validity of the literalist expositions of the Taborite radicals, charging them with false prophecies and the spread of dangerous errors.[60]

---

57 On biblical argumentation in millenarist texts, see Norman Housley, *Religious Warfare in Europe, 1400–1536* (Oxford: 2002), 106–07; Šmahel, "Die hussitische Kommune"; Franz Machilek, Heilserwartung und Revolution der Taboriten 1419/21," in *Festiva Lanx. Studien zum mittelalterlichen Geistesleben Johannes Spörl dargebracht aus Anlass seines sechzigsten Geburtstages*, ed. Karl Schnith (Munich: 1966), 82–83.

58 Bartoš, "Do čtyř pražských artykulů," 576–77.

59 Cf. Stanisław Bylina, "Dwa nurty proroctw chiliastycznych," in idem, *Hussitica. Studia* (Warsaw: 2007), 76.

60 Also recorded by Vavřinec of Březová, "Kronika husitská," 355, 417. Jakoubek spoke about radical interpretations much as he spoke about phantasies: he was sceptical of them and cautioned against them. See Bartoš, "Do čtyř pražských artykulů," 563, 577. More on this in Pavel Soukup, "The Masters and the End of the World. Exegesis in the Polemics with Chiliasm," in *The Bohemian Reformation and Religious Practice*, eds. Zdeněk V. David and David R. Holeton, vol. 7 (Prague: 2009), 98–105.

5 Hussite Chiliasm: Awaiting the Kingdom of God

According to the radical Hussite preachers, the apocalyptic expectation of the final battle with the Antichrist, the second coming of Christ on earth, and the establishment of his kingdom had begun to be fulfilled between 1419 and 1420. The dominant authority in the Hussite vision of a new, sinless, and blessed world after the termination of the old, sinful one was the Bible, particularly those passages which called for the physical separation of the elect from sinners (Dn 2:44; Iz 52:11; Rev. 18:4; Jr 51:6). Chiliast concepts became the foundation of the most radical contemporary ideas of social change, since they included the most extreme attitudes toward political, economic, and religious transformation, and the newly distinct group of the "elect" defined itself in completely different terms than those of the contemporary elite. In their most extreme form, the Hussite chiliasts did not aim for a reform of the previous or contemporary order, but rather its destruction and replacement by another.

Radical Hussite eschatology gradually passed through several phases,[61] the boundaries of which were created by the radical preachers themselves. They claimed the turning point to be the carnival week from 10 to 14 February 1420, during which the merciless prophecies regarding the coming day of Judgement were to be fulfilled. Christ was to personally step down to earth to exterminate all sinners from its surface and thus establish a kingdom of God in the world.[62]

The sources from which we learn of the events and teachings of Hussite chiliasm, however, were written *ex post facto*, once it was already evident that Christ's expected intervention and establishment of a kingdom would not be fulfilled. As a result, the records of events and expectations related to the pivotal week in February 1420 are mixed with an alternative chiliast visionary plan which began to spread only thereafter. The first of the set of chiliast articles, on which disputations were held in December 1420 in the house of Petr Zmrzlík of Svojšín, announced "that already now in this year, which is the year 1420, there will be and there is a fulfilment of the age, namely the destruction of all wicked things."[63] His formulation suggests that the anticipation was not of the Final Judgement and the utter destruction of the world (*consummacio mundi*), but

---

61 Kaminsky, *A History*; Šmahel, *Die Hussitische Revolution*, vol. 2, 1049–60; Alexander Patschovsky, "Der taboritische Chiliasmus: seine Idee, sein Bild bei den Zeitgenossen und die Interpretation der Geschichtswissenschaft," in *Häresie und vorzeitige Reformation im Spätmittelalter*, ed. František Šmahel (Munich: 1998), 169–95.
62 We know this term from Jakoubek's letter to master Jan of Jičín: Kaminsky, *A History*, 540.
63 Vavřinec of Březová, "Kronika husitská," 454. Vavřinec also included another twenty articles in his chronicle. See ibid., 413–16. Chiliastic articles survive in several accounts listed by Soukup, "The Masters and the End of the World," 93.

rather the end of one age and the beginning of a new one. Still in 1420, in the days of anticipated vengeance, the chiliasts held that, according to the reference to the seven plagues in Sirach (Sir. 39:35–36), "all the sinners of the world and enemies of God's law were to perish by fire, sword, hunger, the teeth of beasts, scorpions and snakes, hail, and death" (art. 2).[64] The age of vengeance knew of neither mercy nor pity (art. 3). In this age, all the faithful were supposed to follow Christ, not in his mercy but in his zeal, cruelty, and just vengeance (art. 4). Thus "every faithful person who withheld his sword from the blood of the enemy of Christ's law was damned. Every faithful person was to wash his hands in the blood of Christ's enemies" (art. 5). All of the faithful, including priests, were to "fight, injure, and kill sinners and strike them with the sword and other weapons and arms" (art. 6). Salvation was found on the mountains and in mountain caves (art. 10 and 11). Those who congregated on the mountains were the angels of vengeance, "the body to which eagles also congregated," and "the hosts sent by God to enact all the plagues and vengeance upon all the world, upon the nations; and they should destroy and burn their cities, towns, villages, fortresses, and castles" (art. 12). The concept of finding salvation on the mountains gradually shifted to finding salvation in cities. At the end of 1419, the priests of the radical eschatological movement revived the Old Testament prophecy of Isaiah regarding the five cities (Is. 19:18) that were to provide refuge to all the good and the elect at the time of their greatest persecution (art. 8). From among the Bohemian cities, the five they finally decided upon were Plzeň, Žatec, Klatovy, Louny, and Slaný or Písek. Prague, likened to Babylon, was to be completely destroyed and burned (art. 9). Everyone who did not accept the four articles was to be considered Satan and the apocalyptic dragon, and as such was to be killed and his property seized (art. 13). In addition, there followed articles relating to religious and liturgical habits, fasting, holidays, purgatory, funerary offerings, and rulings imposing a simplification of mass ceremonies, condemning liturgical vestments and verbal confession, among other things. Great attention was also paid to the sacrament of the Eucharist (art. 44–50).

Chiliast articles referring to the end of the old age and the destruction of sinners were often expressed militantly, proclaiming it the task of all the faithful to stand at Christ's side and destroy all evil and sinners with weapon in hand. Also bound to pass away was everything which, according to the Taborite priests, did not adhere to the traditional practice of the apostolic church.[65]

---

64 Unless indicated otherwise, the numbers refer to the articles in Vavřinec of Březová, "Kronika husitská," 454–62.
65 Patschovsky, "Der taborische Chiliasmus," 174.

According to an account on the last phase of Taborite chiliasm left by Jan Žižka and passed on by Vavřinec of Březová, the most radical preachers proclaimed that the seventh apocalyptic angel had already poured out his vessel and that the time had come when "blood will flow over the whole earth, up to the bridles of horses."[66] Chiliast extremists supposedly felt themselves summoned to fulfil their role in the apocalyptic scenario, a task which, according to chroniclers' accounts, they assumed with fanatical determination. As they cast out sin from the surface of the earth, they referred to themselves as God's angels.[67] Jan Příbram, a moderate Utraquist and avowed opponent of the Hussite radicals, expressed his deep skepticism as he recorded the promise of the Taborite priests, that whoever dies in battle with the sinful enemy will "in that very hour (…) be sure of Christ's kingdom."[68] Yet the value of these cited sources is problematized by the circumstances of their origin. One cannot forget that, as Žižka contributed to the liquidation of the Hussite extremist radicals in 1421, his account was undoubtedly biased. Similarly, Jan Příbram did not hide his negative opinions regarding Hussite radicalism.

According to the visions of the Hussite chiliasts, the renewed kingdom of Christ was to be established after the closure of the current age and the destruction of sin. This is a concept already present before February 1420, namely in the period when the concept of Christ's immediate intervention on earth was spreading in Bohemia. The image of the destruction of the old and the establishment of a new, more perfect, and sinless age did not disappear even after the enigmatic prophecy was not fulfilled; rather the assumption regarding the nature of Christ's return and his presence in the world had to change. It makes sense, therefore, to divide the development of the radical period of Taborite apocalyptic expectations into two periods, the adventist and the chiliast, as is done by the foundational historiographical works on Hussite chiliasm.[69] Yet it is necessary to add that both periods were chiliastically oriented, as they both expected the destruction of the old and establishment of the new age within the frame of temporal history.[70] What changed was the character of Christ's coming: until February 1420, chiliast priests excitedly and urgently preached that Christ will step down personally to the earth; but when this vision was not fulfilled a new notion was spread, that Christ had indeed

---

66 Vavřinec of Březová, "Kronika husitská," 518.
67 Ibid.
68 Jan Příbram, *Život kněží táborských*, ed. Jaroslav Boubín (Příbram: 2000), 44.
69 Kaminsky, *A History*, 336–51.
70 Pavlína Cermanová, "V zajetí pojmu: definice husitského chiliasmu," in *Heresis seminaria. Pojmy a koncepty v bádání o husitství*, eds. Pavel Soukup and Pavlína Rychterová (Prague: 2013), 160–61.

come down to earth, but "secretly," as a thief in the night (Mt 24:43).[71] The dual coming of Christ, one secret and the other at the Last Judgement, was a distinction made even by one of the redactions of the chiliast articles themselves.[72] The old age was to be entirely destroyed in all its wickedness by means of the Taborite brothers, and the elect were then meant to enjoy the bliss of the new age. The sinful world was to be renewed by fire, just as in the time of Noah's flood it was destroyed and renewed by water.

6 Tábor: The Society of God's Elect

During the carnival week of February 1420, when Christ was to personally intervene to destroy the wicked, nothing extraordinary occurred, at least from the apocalyptic perspective. Thereafter, events proceeded in their own direction. As Vavřinec of Březová records, the southern Bohemian Hussites used the carnival period not only to contemplate the end of the world, but also to prepare for the recapture of the city of Sezimovo Ústí. They exploited the fact that the city's guard was distracted by the celebrations, and so were able to capture the city on the morning of Ash Wednesday. Shortly thereafter they also took the nearby castle of Hradiště, which from a strategic perspective seemed to be a better choice for refuge. Once they burned the city of Ústí, therefore, the Utraquist Hussite faithful made for this castle. They came with their wives and children and built houses in the remains of the previous city, fortifying the area and naming it after the biblical Tábor.[73] Here the Hussite faithful, under the leadership of their priests, envisaged the creation of a perfect Christian community and awaited the imminent transformation of Christ's secret presence into a corporeal one. They expected that once the old age was entirely destroyed by the Taborite brothers, Christ would also arrive corporally to fully rule his empire in the new age.[74] This was to occur in several years' time.

The spiritual elite of the Hussite radicals were soon concentrated in Tábor: the preachers Václav Koranda and Jan of Jičín worked here from the beginning, and Mikuláš Biskupec of Pelhřimov came from Písek. Also present was the most radical visionary of the new perfect age, Martin Húska. Tábor's beginnings entirely matched the atmosphere of chiliastic tension in which this

---

71 Palacký (ed.), *Archiv český*, vol. 3, 220.
72 František Michálek Bartoš, "Španělský biskup proti Táboru a Praze," *Jihočeský sborník historický* 11 (1938): 69–70.
73 Vavřinec of Březová, "Kronika husitská," 357.
74 Palacký (ed.), *Archiv český*, vol. 3, 220.

community was founded, and Hussite preachers maintained both their prophetic enthusiasm and their vision of God's worldly kingdom. With Christ's secret presence among them, the Hussites not only assumed his punitive role as Christ's army, but, with the founding of the Taborite model community, they also drew nearer to that order in which the elect were to rule with Christ. Thereafter, it was reform, conversion from sin, and not least the sword by which the Antichrist was to be defeated. These were to fulfill the ideal of the apocalyptic age, where all would be able to preach the Word of God and take the Utraquist communion uninhibited, as at a great eucharistic feast. The Holy Spirit would illuminate the elect with God's secrets and the age of equality and abundance would begin. It is into this context that we should understand the initial social and economic egalitarianism of Tábor: all were brothers and sisters, donating their property into common chests.

Thus, from the extreme chiliast wing emerged the idea that Taborite society would surpass even the primitive church in its perfection and would reach a sinless state.[75] Just as it was in the time of Adam and Eve, here, too, there would be no sin, wickedness, or deceit; secular and ecclesiastical power were to vanish completely, and tithes and other levies along with them (art. 22);[76] there would be no persecution among people (art. 21), or bodily death; there would be no need for women to be inseminated by male semen, nor for children to be conceived through bodily lust, and women would give birth without pain (art. 29–32). The conclusion which the radicals drew from these points was dangerous, namely, that they were no longer bound to obey the contemporary church. The conscious efforts to reach a utopian state of innocence was also combined with a pantheistic belief in a complete unity with God. With this, the Hussite chiliasts could be categorized alongside other medieval heresies, such as that of the Free Spirit.[77] The latter's teachings were supposedly introduced into

---

75 Ibid., 221.
76 The numbering of articles is taken from Vavřinec of Březová, "Kronika husitská," 413–16.
77 Cf. Robert E. Lerner, *The Heresy of the Free Spirit in the Later Middle Ages* (Berkeley, Los Angeles, and London: 1972); Patschovsky, "Der taborische Chiliasmus," 178. Patschovsky considers both cases to be imagined heresies. A connection between the two teachings is advocated by Howard Kaminsky, "K dějinám chiliastického Tábora. O traktátu Ad occurendum homini insano," *Československý časopis historický* 8 (1960): 901–02. Cf. the juxtaposition of articles in Rudolf Holinka, "Sektářství v Čechách před revolucí husitskou," *Sborník Filozofické fakulty Univerzity Komenského v Bratislavě* 6, 52 (1929): 292–97. Howard Kaminsky, "The Free Spirit in the Hussite Revolution," in *Millennial Dreams in Action*, ed. Sylvia L. Thrupp (The Hague: 1962), 166–86, remains the fundamental study; see also Krista Feigl-Procházková, "Frei sollen sie sein, die Söhne und Töchter Gottes. Chiliastisches Gerüst, gnostisches Fundament des Táborischen Radikalismus?," *Husitský Tábor* 13 (2002): 9–30.

Bohemia in 1418 by a group of heretics expelled from distant Picardy (thus the label of "Pikart" ascribed to this Taborite sect and its teachings).[78]

7 The Hussite Age of the Holy Spirit

Related to the concepts of the extreme Hussite chiliasts, which were emphasized by Martin Húska, was the belief that a new age of the Holy Spirit had begun, in which the elect would be enlightened and would no longer need the Holy Scriptures since they would fully comprehend even without instruction, study, or reading. According to master Příbram, Húska – whom his followers called an angel of God's hosts and another Daniel because of his illuminated spirit – maintained that "Christ is the Holy Spirit," and in this sense is present with the faithful on earth.[79] Húska's group soon clashed with the rest of the Taborite theologians, the cardinal point of contention being the sacrament of the Eucharist and the antagonistic opinions regarding the presence of Christ therein. While contemplating questions such as whether Christ's Body could simultaneously exist in multiple places, or whether Christ's Body was large enough for all believers, Húska came to the conclusion that Christ cannot be present in the sacrament of the Eucharist in any way. He thought of priests as conjurors who tried in vain to lure Christ into the host by pretending to change the bread into his Body, and deceitfully claimed to change the worse into the better while behaving like idolaters themselves.[80] Disagreement on this point resulted in the expulsion of the Pikarts from Tábor, and in part their later liquidation. Húska's understanding of the Eucharist, combined with his pantheism, stood in a causal relationship with his chiliastic determination of Christ's presence on earth. He allegedly expressed it this way in his own words: that Christ already "feasts with his faithful during every meal, not only in a small piece of bread and a sip of wine."[81]

According to some sources, the Pikart heresy arrived at its decadent peak – and its fall – in the form of the so-called Adamites.[82] Members of this group,

---

[78] This group raises many questions; the term "Pikart" might be a version of the German "Beghard" rather than geographical reference. See Lerner, *The Heresy of the Free Spirit*, 122–23.

[79] Příbram, *Život kněží táborských*, 66–67. See also Stanisław Bylina, *Na skraju lewicy husyckiej* (Warsaw: 2005), 52–89, Molnár, "Eschatologická naděje," 33–34.

[80] Příbram, *Život kněží táborských*, 67.

[81] Vavřinec of Březová, "Kronika husitská," 517; Příbram, *Život kněží táborských*, 67.

[82] Howard Kaminsky even suggested that the Hussite Revolution would never have occurred, were it not for the heresy of the Free Spirit, whose medieval phase culminated in Bohemia: Kaminsky, "The Free Spirit."

already expelled by the decision of the leading Taborite theologians, were said to have taken refuge in the forest and fallen into a perverse lifestyle: like Adam and Eve in the nude, they danced wildly around fires, and they also gave themselves to sexual pleasures and sodomy, "fornicating by day and murdering by night."[83] They apparently held the conviction that they lived in a sinless age, that they were illuminated by the Holy Spirit, and that Christ was already among them. However, there is reason to doubt that such characterizations applied to the entire group of sectarians that were expelled from Tábor. Martin Húska and his followers conducted themselves with extreme moral rigor, and thus any tendencies toward promiscuous behavior among them was highly unlikely. The sources also record that the Adamites or Pikarts expelled and decapitated a certain Mary for spending the night with a man.[84] Thus, if the heretical group expelled from Tábor fell into orgiastic behavior, it was only after the leaders of the Pikart puritans were burned or had abandoned the group.

The main source which provides thorough information on the chaos caused by the Adamite sect is the chronicle of Vavřinec of Březová, specifically one letter copied therein, apparently sent by Žižka to Prague after he cruelly crushed and burned the nudists.[85] This letter includes a series of accusations of acts supposedly committed by the Adamites. Due to its similarity with contemporary stereotypes, such as those found in inquisitorial handbooks and protocols, the description of Adamite activities evokes a degree of suspicion.[86] It also raises the question of where the Hussite military leader could have acquainted himself with heresiological literature, according to which he could construct a similar text. It is further necessary to consider Žižka's primary motivation. What led a man who burned villages and cities and had no pity for his enemies to justify his intervention in a letter to the Praguers by portraying the Taborite sectarians as amoral monsters? It is possible to understand Žižka's letter, with its dramatic description of Adamite perversity and cruelty, as an *exemplum*, authored by someone (not necessarily Žižka himself) who placed the proper practice of Utraquist communion and reverence toward the

---

83   Vavřinec of Březová, "Kronika husitská," 519.
84   Ibid.
85   A different version of this text (without any indication that it was Žižka's letter) is in the Wrocław manuscript of the Old Czech Annals: Šimek (ed.), *Staré letopisy české z vratislavského rukopisu*, 30–31.
86   Lerner, *The Heresy of the Free Spirit*, 119–24; Patschovsky, "Der taboritische Chiliasmus," 182–91; Kaminsky, "Free Spirit," 180–82, has no doubt about the existence and excesses of the Adamites. Kaminsky's theses were taken up by Bylina, *Na skraju*, 165–86. The question of the Adamites was problematized by Petr Čornej, "Ráj je na ostrově aneb prostor pro adamity," *Táborský archiv* 13 (2007): 37–46, who nevertheless admits they existed.

eucharistic sacrament at the center of his conceptual world. The description of the sexual perversity and bloodthirstiness of the Adamites, therefore, would have functioned as a lesson on the types of decadent consequences that result from disrespect to the eucharistic sacrament.[87] This interpretation is also suggested by the fact that the letter was probably meant to be read aloud publicly, which explains its literary form.[88]

Although some of the sources require a cautious approach, it is not possible to completely reject the existence of Taborite Adamitism. It is a fact that, in the first months of 1421, a group of heretics who entered into irreconcilable disputes with the Taborite spiritual leaders were expelled from the city. The bone of contention was none other than an unacceptable approach to the sacrament of the Eucharist, namely its abolition. Also justified is the claim that the Taborite sectarians then took refuge in the forest around Příběnice, whence the survivors then moved to an undesignated nearby island under the leadership of the self-proclaimed messiah, Rohan. Meanwhile, a group around Petr Kániš probably took shelter in the settlement on the right bank of the Lužnice.[89] Martin Húska separated from these groups; after his release from the dungeon where he was held in January 1421, he left for Moravia, where he spread his teachings for several months. In the second half of April 1421, Jan Žižka departed on a disciplinary expedition against these sectarians, slaying some and capturing others, sending them to Klokoty to be burned. A purge then followed within Tábor itself, where twenty-five brothers and sisters suspected of sympathizing with the Pikart heresy were burned. Those sectarians who survived were crushed by Žižka in October of that year near the river Nežárka. Earlier, in the summer of the same year, Húska was again imprisoned in Chrudim and was later burned in a sealed barrel in Roudnice nad Labem. The Pikart heresy also found its way into Prague in this period, where the religious life was shaped from the pulpits not only of the university masters, but of Jan Želivský, who was prone to the temptations of chiliast visions. Thus, in July 1421, the community of Prague adopted a decree which not only regulated the functioning of uncertified preachers, but also established an investigatory body which was meant to reveal Pikart heretics and punish them (at the very least) with imprisonment.[90]

---

87   On this, see especially Patschovsky, "Der taboritische Chiliasmus," 190–91.
88   Petr Čornej, "Adamité – tabu 15. i 19. století?," in *Sex a tabu v české kultuře 19. století*, ed. Václav Petrbok (Prague: 1999), 147.
89   Šmahel, *Dějiny Tábora*, vol. 1, 288.
90   Palacký (ed.), *Archiv český*, vol. 1, 204–05.

One important point that speaks against the rejection of the Adamites' existence is the fact that they did not disappear from the sources. The fact that Žižka's letter was meant for transmission certainly played a role here, since news of bloodthirsty and morally perverse heretics quickly spread even in societies with limited means of communication. Nevertheless, we must allow for the possibility that these rumors, however exaggerated, were founded in some degree of truth. This possibility is supported by the fact that some of the sources come from a close proximity to the events themselves. We find an assault on Adamite values in the words of Mikuláš Biskupec, who recalls in his exposition of Revelation those who were led away from preaching truth and toward a life of Sodomy.[91] Another important account comes from Petr Chelčický, who was himself in Tábor at the time of the Pikart crisis. In 1425, Chelčický recorded how "they turned themselves in their horrid fornication toward the forests and lairs, and so some were killed on an island, others elsewhere."[92] Other sources which provide information on the Adamites do so selectively. Vavřinec's chronicle has already been noted; Jakoubek also mentions the fornication and fleshly abominations which are "in darkness called light and blessings."[93] The unspeakable customs of the Pikarts expelled from Tábor were also mentioned, for instance, in the so-called *Versed Annals*.[94] The first to speak of the Taborite sectarians as "Adamites" was Ondřej of Brod, in the tractate *De origine hussitarum*.[95] An especially important source for the creation of what would come to be an accepted characterization of the Adamite sect is the *Locustarium*, a work attributed to Jan Vodňanský, written in the early 1520s.[96] The story of the Adamite sectarians also spread abroad: in 1426, the Viennese preacher Oswald Reinlein mentioned the sexual promiscuity of the Hussites, claiming that they went around nude and took any woman they pleased. The Adamites were even spoken of at the Council of Basel; Juan Palomar mentioned them in his speech, and John Stojković also referred to them in the negotiations at the council.[97]

---

91 Vienna, Österreichische Nationalbibliothek, 4520, fol. 175v.

92 Petr Chelčický, "Replika proti Mikuláši Biskupcovi," in idem, *Drobné spisy*, ed. Eduard Petrů (Prague: 1966), 156.

93 Jakoubek of Stříbro, *Výklad na Zjevenie*, vol. 2, 366.

94 František Svejkovský (ed.), *Veršované skladby doby husitské* (Prague: 1963), 162–63.

95 Ondřej of Brod, *Traktát mistra Ondřeje z Brodu o původu husitů. Visiones Ioannis, archiepiscopi pragensis, et earundem explicaciones* (*alias Tractatus de origine Hussitarum*), ed. Jaroslav Kadlec (Tábor: 1980), 17, 23.

96 Vatican City, Biblioteca Apostolica, Ottob. Lat. 1518.

97 References to Reinlein and Palomar in Pavel Soukup, "Wiener Predigten Oswald Reinleins als Quelle zur Geschichte des Hussitenkrieges," in *Zwischen Feinden und Freunden. Kommunikation im spätmittelalterlichen Krieg*, eds. Petr Elbel, Alexandra Kaar, and Robert Novotný (forthcoming). Stojković's remark is mentioned by Dušan Coufal, "Jan Hus na

The nude Bohemian sectarians were also mentioned in the historiographical works of Thomas Ebendorfer and Aeneas Silvius Piccolomini.[98]

•••

The liquidation of the extreme Taborite chiliasts meant an end to Hussite apocalyptic thinking in its most radical and revolutionary form. Nevertheless, Taborite theologians never abandoned the idea of the exceptionality of the Taborite community and their role in the battle against the Antichrist. Still, images of the complete annihilation of the current order and its replacement with a new one, defined in spiritual and utopian terms, never fully made their way back into their teachings. Though the apocalyptic exposition of Mikuláš Biskupec from between the end of the 1420s and the beginning of the 1430s speaks of the establishment of a more perfect age after the defeat of the Antichrist, it distances itself from open chiliasm. His text reflects the complex ideas of Hussite radicalism and Hussite apocalyptic thought once it was liberated from the extreme revolutionary content carried by the chiliastic visions. Visions condemning institutionalized power, secular and ecclesiastical, as the source and seat of evil, complemented by powerful moralizing images and appeals to warfare against the apocalyptic beasts, especially the Antichrist, were preserved in their purest form in the works of Petr Chelčický up until the 1440s. It was from these radical ideas that the Unity of Brethren drew.[99]

Apocalyptically defined theological-historical concepts and models were found in a number of discourses during the Hussite movement, where they served self-identifying, legitimizing, and mobilizing roles. The intricate complex of apocalyptic expositions and prophecies was no longer only a part of the academic, ecclesiastic, and Latinate environments; it also spread into lay and vernacular contexts where it took on different functions. As shown by the example of Hussite chiliasm and its extreme manifestations, the inescapable question which arose here was that of interpretative authority: who was authorized and qualified to expound the biblical prophecies so as not to overstep the thin line between heresy and orthodoxy, including "Hussite orthodoxy"?

---

basilejském koncilu," in *Jan Hus 1415 a 600 let poté*, eds. Jakub Smrčka and Zdeněk Vybíral (Husitský Tábor. Supplementum) 4 (Tábor: 2015), 61.

[98] Thomas Ebendorfer, *Chronica Austriae*, ed. Alphons Lhotsky (Monumenta Germaniae Historica. Scriptores rerum Germanicarum, Nova series) 13 (Berlin and Zurich: 1967), 362; Aeneas Silvius Piccolomini, *Aeneae Silvii Historia Bohemica. Enea Silvio: Historie česká*, eds. Dana Martínková, Alena Hadravová, and Jiří Matl (Prague: 1998), 116, 118.

[99] Jaroslav Boubín, *Petr Chelčický. Myslitel a reformátor* (Prague: 2005), 27. On the Brethren, see the chapter by Ota Halama in this volume.

The exposition of the Revelation of John, along with the alignment of prophecies with current events, informed the main points of the Hussite program. Moral maxims were transmitted to the whole community, and the obligatory model for individuals and society was the apostolic church of the first Christians. The Hussites insisted that Utraquist communion, the free spread of God's Word, the disendowment of the church, and the appeal for individual introspection and repudiation of sin were essential to bringing about the fulfillment of the apocalyptic prophecies.

8 Historiographic Survey

Over the last few decades, apocalyptic concepts within various spheres of medieval thought have represented an important topic of research. The apocalyptic theology of history, the structure of apocalyptic interpretations, but also the social situations that produced apocalyptic interpretation and rhetoric, have attracted attention. Apocalyptic thought has been analyzed as an important component of the discourses of reform and power, as well as an interpretative category of human history and social process. Research on Hussite apocalyptic thought, however, has taken different paths in the past. From the whole range of apocalyptic ideology, the focus has been primarily on chiliasm and its practical impact. In Czech historiography of the 20th century, which was influenced by various ideologies, analysis of the sources was often subordinated to ideological positions. Evaluation of the apocalyptic component of Hussite radicalism has ranged from total rejection in the works of Catholic (Jan Sedlák) or conservative authors (Josef Pekař) before World War II,[100] to the celebration of Hussite chiliasm as the manifestation of a historical process directed by class struggle (Josef Macek in the mid-20th century).[101] Religious concepts and terminology were regarded as the utilitarian propaganda of social revolution. Despite the prevailing official Marxist discourse after World War II, varied interpretations emerged once again. Robert Kalivoda understood Hussite apocalypticism as a "philosophy of history" that provides popular heresy with an ideology of revolutionary social change.[102] From his

---

100 Jan Sedlák, *Táborské traktáty eucharistické* (Brno: 1918); Josef Pekař, *Žižka a jeho doba*, 4 vols. (Prague: 1927–1933).
101 Josef Macek *Tábor v husitském revolučním hnutí*, 2 vols. (Prague: 1952–1956), vol. 1.
102 Robert Kalivoda, *Revolution und Ideologie. Der Hussitismus*, trans. Heide Thorwart and Monika Gletter (Cologne: 1976).

Protestant point of view, Amedeo Molnár emphasized the positive elements in the eschatological expectations of Hussite apocalypticists.[103]

However, the most important works analyzing those phenomena of the Hussite period that were influenced by apocalyptic ideology were written outside Czechoslovakia. Howard Kaminsky's *A History of the Hussite Revolution* is a brilliant analysis of Taborite radicalism, based on a thorough examination of Hussite doctrine. Five years after Kaminsky, Robert E. Lerner's *The Heresy of the Free Spirit in the Later Middle Ages* shed new light on the sources of radical Hussite apocalypticism through an analysis of Hussite chiliasm in the context of other medieval heresies, primarily the teaching of the Free Spirit. Lerner also raised new questions concerning Hussite Adamitism. This line of research was taken further in the late 1990s by Alexander Patschovsky, who challenged the historicity not only of the sect of the Free Spirit but also of the Hussite Adamites by identifying both as heresiological constructs of the time.[104] Despite the skepticism of some authors abroad, however, Czech historiography has not given up the historicity of the most radical branch of Taborite apocalypticism (František Šmahel, Petr Čornej).[105]

Translated by Martin Pjecha

Bibliography

Manuscripts

Munich, Bayerische Staatsbibliothek, Clm 28255, fols. 168r-214r (Heinrich Toke, *De ecclesia militanti catholica*).

Prague, Archiv Pražského hradu, Knihovna Metropolitní kapituly [Prague Castle Archives, Library of the Metropolitan Chapter], A 163, fols. 1r-128v (*Opus arduum valde*).

Vatican City, Biblioteca Apostolica Vaticana, Ottob. Lat. 1518 (Jan Vodňanský, *Locustarium*).

Vienna, Österreichische Nationalbibliothek, 4520, fols. 1r-297v (Mikuláš Biskupec of Pelhřimov, *Super Apocalypsim*).

---

103   Molnár, "Eschatologická naděje."
104   Patschovsky, "Der taboritische Chiliasmus."
105   See František Šmahel, *Die Hussitische Revolution*, trans. Thomas Krzenck, (Monumenta Germaniae Historica. Schriften) 43, 3 vols. (Hannover: 2002), vol. 2, 1032–70; Čornej, "Ráj je na ostrově"; and other relevant entries by these authors in the bibliography below.

Editions of Sources

Adso of Montier-en-Der, *De Ortu et Tempore Antichristi*, ed. Daniel Verhelst (Corpus christianorum. Continuatio mediaevalis) 45 (Turnhout: 1976).

Aeneas Silvius Piccolomini, *Aeneae Silvii Historia Bohemica. Enea Silvio. Historie česká*, eds. Dana Martínková, Alena Hadravová and Jiří Matl (Prague: 1998).

Chelčický, Petr, "Replika proti Mikuláši Biskupcovi" [The *Replica* against Mikuláš Biskupec], in idem, *Drobné spisy*, ed. Eduard Petrů (Prague: 1966), 132–210.

Ebendorfer, Thomas, *Chronica Austriae*, ed. Alphons Lhotsky (Monumenta Germaniae Historica. Scriptores rerum Germanicarum, Nova series) 13 (Berlin and Zurich: 1967).

Hus, Jan, *Magistri Johannis Hus Tractatus de ecclesia*, ed. S. Harrison Thomson (Cambridge, Eng., and Boulder, CO.: 1956; repr. Prague: 1958).

Hus, Jan, *Sermo de pace*, eds. František M. Dobiáš and Amedeo Molnár (Prague: 1963).

Hus, Jan, *Výklady* [Expositions], ed. Jiří Daňhelka (Magistri Iohannis Hus Opera omnia) 1 (Prague: 1975).

Jakoubek of Stříbro, *Výklad na Zjevenie sv. Jana* [Exposition of the Revelation of St. John], ed. František Šimek, 2 vols. (Prague: 1932–1933).

Matěj of Janov, *Regulae Veteris et Novi Testamenti*, vols. 1–4, ed. Vlastimil Kybal (Innsbruck: 1908–1913); vol. 5, eds. Vlastimil Kybal and Otakar Odložilík (Prague: 1913); vol. 6, eds. Jana Nechutová and Helena Krmíčková (Munich: 1993).

Mikuláš Biskupec of Pelhřimov, "Chronicon Taboritarum," in *Geschichtschreiber der husitischen Bewegung in Böhmen*, ed. Konstantin Höfler, vol. 2 (Fontes rerum Austriacarum, 1. Abteilung: Scriptores) 6 (Vienna: 1865), 475–820.

Milíč of Kroměříž, "Sermo de Die novissimo Domini," in Milíč of Kroměříž, *The Message for the Last Days. Three Essays from the Year 1367*, eds. Milan Opočenský and Jana Opočenská (Geneva: 1998), 32–55.

Ondřej of Brod, *Traktát mistra Ondřeje z Brodu o původu husitů. Visiones Ioannis, archiepiscopi pragensis, et earundem explicaciones (alias Tractatus de origine Hussitarum)* [The treatise of Master Ondřej of Brod on the origins of the Hussites], ed. Jaroslav Kadlec (Tábor: 1980).

Příbram, Jan, *Jan z Příbramě. Život kněží táborských* [The life of the Taborite priests], ed. Jaroslav Boubín (Příbram: 2000).

Quidort of Paris, John, *The Tractatus de Antichristo of John of Paris. A Critical Edition, Translation, and Commentary*, ed. Sara Peters Clark (Ithaca: 1981).

Rupert of Deutz, "Commentaria in Apocalypsim," in *Patrologiae cursus completus. Series Latina*, ed. Jacques-Paul Migne, vol. 169 (Paris: 1894), 827–1214.

Šimek, František (ed.), *Staré letopisy české z vratislavského rukopisu* [Old Czech annals from the Wrocław manuscript] (Prague: 1937).

Svejkovský, František (ed.), *Veršované skladby doby husitské* [Versified compositions of the Hussite period] (Prague: 1963).

Vavřinec of Březová, "Kronika husitská [The Hussite Chronicle]," in *Fontes rerum Bohemicarum*, eds. Josef Emler, Jan Gebauer and Jaroslav Goll, vol. 5 (Prague: 1893), 327–534.

Wyclif, John, *Johannis Wyclif Tractatus De potestate pape*, ed. Johann Loserth (Wyclif's Latin Works) 32 (London: 1907).

Želivský, Jan, *Dochovaná kázání z roku 1419* [Preserved sermons from 1419], ed. Amedeo Molnár (Prague: 1953).

Secondary Sources

Bartoš, František Michálek, "Do čtyř pražských artykulů. Z myšlenkových i ústavních zápasů let 1415–1420" [Toward the Four Articles of Prague. From the ideological and constitutional struggles of 1415–1420], *Sborník příspěvků k dějinám hlavního města Prahy* 5 (1932): 481–591.

Bartoš, František Michálek, "Španělský biskup proti Táboru a Praze" [A Spanish bishop against Tábor and Prague], *Jihočeský sborník historický* 11 (1938): 67–70.

Bonner, Gerald, "Saint Bede in the Tradition of Western Apocalyptic Commentary," in *Church and Faith in the Patristic Tradition*, ed. Gerald Bonner (London: 1996), 1–28.

Bostick, Curtis V., *The Antichrist and the Lollards. Apocalypticism in Late Medieval and Reformation England* (Leiden, Boston, and Cologne: 1998).

Boubín, Jaroslav, *Petr Chelčický. Myslitel a reformátor* [Petr Chelčický. Thinker and reformer] (Prague: 2005).

Bylina, Stanisław, *Na skraju lewicy husyckiej* [On the margin of the Hussite left] (Warsaw: 2005).

Bylina, Stanisław, "Dwa nurty proroctw chiliastycznych" [Two strands of chiliast prophecies], in idem, *Hussitica. Studia* (Warsaw: 2007), 65–85.

Bylina, Stanisław, "Husyckie poutě na hory i ich uczestnici" [The Hussite peregrinations to the mountains and their participants], in *Wspólnoty małe i duże w społeczeństwach Czech i Polski w średniowieczu i w czasach wczesnonowożytnych*, eds. Wojciech Iwańczak and Janusz Smołucha (Cracow: 2010), 337–52.

Cegna, Romolo, "*Ecclesia Primitiva*: Dall'*Opus arduum valde* a Nicolaus de Drazna (de Rosa Nigra)," *Archa Verbi* 9 (2012): 66–88.

Cermanová, Pavlína, "V zajetí pojmu. Definice husitského chiliasmu" [Captured by concepts. Definitions of Hussite chiliasm], in *Heresis seminaria. Pojmy a koncepty v bádání o husitství*, eds. Pavel Soukup and Pavlína Rychterová (Prague: 2013), 139–70.

Čornej, Petr, "Adamité – tabu 15. i 19. století?" [The Adamites, a taboo of the 15th and the 19th centuries?], in *Sex a tabu v české kultuře 19. století*, ed. Václav Petrbok (Prague: 1999), 142–59.

Čornej, Petr, "Ráj je na ostrově aneb prostor pro adamity" [Paradise is on an island, or a space for the Adamites], *Táborský archiv* 13 (2007): 37–46.

Coufal, Dušan, "Jan Hus na basilejském koncilu" [Jan Hus at the Council of Basel], in *Jan Hus 1415 a 600 let poté*, eds. Jakub Smrčka and Zdeněk Vybíral (Husitský Tábor. Supplementum) 4 (Tábor: 2015), 41–68.

Emmerson, Richard K., "Antichrist as Anti-Saint," *American Benedictine Review* 30 (1979): 175–90.

Feigl-Procházková, Krista, "Frei sollen sie sein, die Söhne und Töchter Gottes. Chiliastisches Gerüst, gnostisches Fundament des Táborischen Radikalismus?," *Husitský Tábor* 13 (2002): 9–30.

Gerwing, Manfred, *Vom Ende der Zeit. Der Traktat des Arnald von Villanova über die Ankunft des Antichrist in der akademischen Auseinandersetzung zu Beginn des 14. Jahrhunderts* (Münster: 1996).

Goetz, Hans Werner, "Endzeiterwartung und Endzeitvorstellung im Rahmen des Geschichtsbildes des früheren 12. Jahrhunderts," in *The Use and Abuse of Eschatology in the Middle Ages*, eds. Werner Verbeke, Daniel Verhelst and Andries Welkenhuysen (Leuven: 1988), 307–32.

Holinka, Rudolf, "Sektářství v Čechách před revolucí husitskou" [Sectarianism in Bohemia before the Hussite revolution], *Sborník Filozofické fakulty Univerzity Komenského v Bratislavě* 6, 52 (1929): 125–313.

Hornbeck II, Patrick J., Stephen E. Lahey, and Fiona Somerset (eds.), *Wycliffite Spirituality* (New York and Mahwah, NJ.: 2013).

Housley, Norman, *Religious Warfare in Europe, 1400–1536* (Oxford: 2002).

Hrdina, Jan, Aleš Mudra, and Marcella K. Perett, "Re-use and Reinvent: The Function of Processions in Late Medieval and Early Modern Bohemia," *Studia Mediaevalia Bohemica* 7 (2015): 289–312.

Hudson, Anne, "A Neglected Wycliffite Text," *Journal of Ecclesiastical History* 29 (1978): 257–79.

Kalivoda, Robert, *Revolution und Ideologie. Der Hussitismus*, trans. Heide Thorwart and Monika Gletter (Cologne: 1976).

Kaminsky, Howard, "Chiliasm and the Hussite Revolution," *Church History* 26 (1957): 43–71.

Kaminsky, Howard, "K dějinám chiliastického Tábora. O traktátu *Ad occurendum homini insano*" [On the history of chiliast Tábor. The treatise *Ad occurendum homini insano*], *Československý časopis historický* 8 (1960): 895–904.

Kaminsky, Howard, "The Free Spirit in the Hussite Revolution," in *Millennial Dreams in Action*, ed. Sylvia L. Thrupp (The Hague: 1962), 166–86.

Kaminsky, Howard, *A History of the Hussite Revolution* (Berkeley and Los Angeles: 1967).

Kaminsky, Howard, "Nicholas of Pelhřimov's Tabor: An Adventure into the Eschaton," in *Eschatologie und Hussitismus*, eds. František Šmahel and Alexander Patschovsky (Prague: 1996), 139–67.

Krmíčková, Helena, *Studie a texty k počátkům kalicha v Čechách* [Studies and texts on the beginnings of the chalice in Bohemia] (Brno: 1997).

Krmíčková, Helena, "Vliv Matěje z Janova na utrakvismus Jakoubka ze Stříbra a Mikuláše z Drážďan" [The influence of Matěj of Janov on the Utraquism of Jakoubek of Stříbro and Nicholas of Dresden], in *Mistr Matěj z Janova ve své a v naší době*, ed. Jan B. Lášek and Karel Skalický (Brno: 2002), 78–87.

Lerner, Robert E., *The Heresy of the Free Spirit in the Later Middle Ages* (Berkeley, Los Angeles, and London: 1972).

Lerner, Robert E., "Refreshment of the Saints. The Time after Antichrist as a Station for Earthly Progress in Medieval Thought," *Traditio* 32 (1976): 97–144.

Lerner, Robert E., "Poverty, Preaching, and Eschatology in the Revelation Commentaries of Hugh of St Cher," in *The Bible in the Medieval World. Essays in Memory of Beryl Smalley*, eds. Katherine Walsh and Diana Wood (Oxford: 1985), 157–91.

Lerner, Robert E., "The Medieval Return to the Thousand-Year Sabbath," in *The Apocalypse in the Middle Ages*, eds. Richard K. Emmerson and Bernard McGinn (Ithaca and London: 1992), 51–71.

Lubac, Henri de, *Exégèse médiévale. Les quatre sens de l'Écriture*, 4 vols. (Paris: 1959–1964).

Macek, Josef, *Tábor v husitském revolučním hnutí* [Tábor in the Hussite revolutionary movement], 2 vols. (Prague: 1952–1956).

Machilek, Franz, "Heilserwartung und Revolution der Taboriten 1419/21," in *Festiva Lanx. Studien zum mittelalterlichen Geistesleben Johannes Spörl dargebracht aus Anlass seines sechzigsten Geburtstages*, ed. Karl Schnith (Munich: 1966), 67–94.

Molnár, Amedeo, "Eschatologická naděje české reformace" [The eschatological hope of the Bohemian Reformation], in *Od reformace k zítřku* (Prague: 1956), 11–101.

Mutlová, Petra, "Communicating Texts through Images. Nicholas of Dresden's *Tabulae*," in *Public Communication in European Reformation. Artistic and other Media in Central Europe 1380–1620*, eds. Milena Bartlová and Michal Šroněk (Prague: 2007), 29–37.

Palacký, František, *Dějiny národu českého v Čechách a v Moravě* [A history of the Czech nation in Bohemia and Moravia], 6 vols. (Prague: 1848–1876).

Patschovsky, Alexander, "'Antichrist' bei Wiclif," in *Eschatologie und Hussitismus*, eds. Alexander Patschovsky and František Šmahel (Prague: 1996), 83–98.

Patschovsky, Alexander, "Der taboritische Chiliasmus. Seine Idee, sein Bild bei den Zeitgenossen und die Interpretation der Geschichtswissenschaft," in *Häresie und vorzeitige Reformation im Spätmittelalter*, ed. František Šmahel (Munich: 1998), 169–95.

Pekař, Josef, *Žižka a jeho doba* [Žižka and his time], 4 vols. (Prague: 1927–1933).

Rusconi, Roberto, "Antichrist and Antichrists," in *The Encyclopedia of the Apocalypticism*, ed. Bernard McGinn, vol. 2 (New York: 1999).

Schmidt, Roderich, "*Aetates mundi*. Die Weltalter als Gliederungsprinzip der Geschichte," *Zeitschrift für Kirchengeschichte* 67 (1955–1956): 288–317.

Sedlák, Jan, "Spis Stanislava ze Znojma 'de Antichristo'" [The writing of Stanislav of Znojmo 'de Antichristo'], *Hlídka* 24 (1907): 1–6.

Sedlák, Jan, *Táborské traktáty eucharistické* [Taborite eucharistic tracts] (Brno: 1918).

Šmahel, František, "Die hussitische Kommune von Tábor 1420–1422," in *Jan Hus und die Hussiten in europäischen Aspekten* (Trier: 1987), 9–28.

Šmahel, FrantišekŠmahel, František, *Dějiny Tábora* [A history of Tábor], 2 vols. (České Budějovice: 1988–1990).

Šmahel, František, "Die *Tabule veteris et novi coloris* als audiovisuelles Medium hussitischer Agitation," *Studie o rukopisech* 29 (1992): 95–105.

Šmahel, František, *Die Hussitische Revolution*, trans. Thomas Krzenck (Monumenta Germaniae Historica. Schriften) 43, 3 vols. (Hannover: 2002).

Soukup, Pavel, "The Masters and the End of the World: Exegesis in the Polemics with Chiliasm," in *The Bohemian Reformation and Religious Practice*, eds. Zdeněk V. David and David R. Holeton, vol. 7 (Prague: 2009), 91–114.

Soukup, Pavel, "Wiener Predigten Oswald Reinleins als Quelle zur Geschichte des Hussitenkrieges," in *Zwischen Feinden und Freunden. Kommunikation im spätmittelalterlichen Krieg*, eds. Petr Elbel, Alexandra Kaar, and Robert Novotný (forthcoming).

Torrance, Thomas Forsyth, "Liturgie et Apocalypse," *Verbum Caro* 11 (1957): 28–40.

Verhelst, Daniel, "La préhistoire des conceptions d'Adson concernant l'Antichrist," *Recherches de théologie ancienne et médiévale* 40 (1973): 52–103.

The Utraquist Church after the *Compactata*

Blanka Zilynská

At the turn of the 14th century, ecclesiastic organization in the Czech lands had reached a high level, and in many ways exceeded the European standard. In the six decades of its existence (it had only been elevated to an archiepiscopal see in 1344), the independent province of Prague – with its two suffragan bishoprics in Olomouc and Litomyšl – not only reached the organizational level of the older metropoles, but also aspired to exercize its influence in other regions. In 1365, Emperor Charles IV successfully convinced the pope to designate the Archbishop of Prague a permanent papal legate, holding power in the dioceses of Regensburg, Bamberg, and Meissen.[1] The ecclesiastical administration of the metropolis and both its subordinate dioceses was managed by established, permanent authorities (*officia*) who, on behalf of the archbishop or bishops, carried out administrative, judicial, inquisitorial, and correctional tasks.[2] The province was administered according to the codifying work of Arnošt of Pardubice, whose provincial statute from 1349 was a unique and significant legislative achievement[3] that was popular not only among Arnošt's followers, but also affected the legislation of other dioceses which did not fall under the authority of Prague. The province of Prague maintained a rich synodal life with regular diocesan synods held twice annually, in the spring and autumn terms.[4] The presence of a university in Prague, the center of the province, helped to preserve the juristic and general cultural standards of church administrators.[5]

Despite this ideal institutional status of the Bohemian church, or perhaps as a result of it, a series of critical voices arose even before the end of the 14th century, making more rigorous demands of the clergy, calling for deeper individual devotion, and unveiling the darker side of this impressive church

---

1 On medieval Church administration, see Zdeňka Hledíková, Jan Janák, and Jan Dobeš, *Dějiny správy v českých zemích od počátků státu po současnost* (Prague: 2005), 172–201.
2 Zdeňka Hledíková, *Svět české středověké církve* (Prague: 2010).
3 Zdeňka Hledíková, *Arnošt z Pardubic. Arcibiskup, zakladatel, rádce* (Prague: 2008).
4 Jaroslav V. Polc and Zdeňka Hledíková, *Pražské synody a koncily předhusitské doby* (Prague: 2002); Zdeňka Hledíková, "Synoden in der Diözese Prag 1280–1417," in *Partikularsynoden im späten Mittelalter*, eds. Nathalie Kruppa and Leszek Zygner (Göttingen: 2006), 307–29; Pavel Krafl, *Synody a statuta olomoucké diecéze období středověku* (Prague: 2003; 2nd ed. 2014).
5 Michal Svatoš, (ed.), *Dějiny Univerzity Karlovy*, vol. 1: 1347/48–1622 (Prague: 1995).

organization.[6] After the eruption of revolution and war in 1419–1420, the province of Prague found itself in crisis and, from April 1421, when the Prague Ordinary Konrad of Vechta accepted the chalice, on the verge of collapse. Although the archbishop's seat was formally filled initially, the archbishop himself – as an apostate – lost all power over the Catholic clergy. The Litomyšl diocese disappeared in the chaos of the first war years,[7] and only the diocese of Olomouc fully maintained its continuity, its representatives even temporarily assuming the tasks of the Prague archbishop as administrators of the province. Over decades of war, the foundations of a modified, Utraquist church structure began to form, and two faiths were formally codified in the land after the *Compactata* agreement.[8]

Ecclesiastical conditions in the Czech lands were very complex in the period following the Hussite wars. The Prague church province suffered great losses in terms of property, people, and prestige, and its territorial and structural foundations were seriously disrupted. From this context a new institution emerged, built on the ideas of the Hussite reformers: the Utraquist Church.[9]

It is very difficult to define this church in terms of origin and form. The name "Utraquist" itself is a modern one which attempts to distinguish a certain church community from the Catholic, Roman Church, on the one hand, and from the more radical movement arising from Hussitism – namely the Taborite "Church" and the Unity of Brethren – on the other. Thus, we refer to the Utraquist Church as that part of the Utraquist clergy which, with the support of the king and the Estates, was able to attain an official status in the 1430s, form an administrative structure, and, as an officially consolidated institution,

---

6   Franz Machilek, "Die Frömmigkeit und die Krise des 14. und 15. Jahrhunderts," *Mediaevalia Bohemica* 3 (1970): 209–27; Jana Nechutová, "Konfesionalizace před konfesionalizací? Víra a společnost v husitské epoše," in *Heresis seminaria. Pojmy a koncepty v bádání o husitství*, eds. Pavlína Rychterová and Pavel Soukup (Prague: 2013), 233–66; Jaroslav V. Polc, *Česká církev v dějinách* (Prague: 1999); Olivier Marin, *L'archevêque, le maître et le dévot. Genèses du mouvement réformateur pragois. Années 1360–1419* (Paris: 2005).

7   Zdeňka Hledíková, "Litomyšlské biskupství," in *Litomyšl. Duchovní tvář českého města*, ed. Milan Skřivánek (Litomyšl: 1994), 29–52.

8   A survey of Church administration and an assessment of the state of the clergy on the eve of the Hussite Revolution is provided in František Šmahel, *Die Hussitische Revolution*, trans. Thomas Krzenck (Monumenta Germaniae Historica. Schriften) 43, 3 vols. (Hannover: 2002), vol. 1: 168–219. On the fates of the Catholic Church organization under Hussitism, see František Šmahel, "Pražská církevní provincie ve víru husitské revoluce," *Acta Universitatis Carolinae – Historia Universitatis Carolinae Pragensis* 31 (1991): 107–15; Jaroslav Kadlec, *Katoličtí exulanti čeští doby husitské* (Prague: 1990); idem, *Přehled českých církevních dějin*, 2 vols. (Prague: 1991).

9   The impact of Hussitism on ecclesiastical life is assessed by Petr Čornej and Milena Bartlová, *Velké dějiny zemí Koruny české*, vol. 6 (Prague and Litomyšl: 2007), 11–19.

claim uniquely to represent Utraquism in the Czech lands. During the period of the Hussite brotherhoods, Utraquism was represented by the centrist, moderate party that was embodied primarily by the "Praguers" as one of the Hussite parties. Although the Utraquists never conclusively ruptured from the universal church, as Martin Luther would later advise them, they took a completely independent path and functioned as a church divorced from Rome.[10] The term "Utraquist Church," therefore, can itself be challenged, since it both was and was not an independent church.[11] We know very little of its structure and operation, since its oldest documents, which interest us here, were destroyed with only minor exceptions.[12]

1 Ideological Foundations and the Emergence of the Utraquist "Confession"

The foundations of the Hussite concept of the church were established by Master Jan Hus,[13] who conspicuously relied on the thought of John Wyclif. Hus conceived of the church as the community of those predestined to salvation (*communitas praedestinatorum*). Since the identity of the predestined is unknown to all, the role of the visible church is obscured, and its organizational principle, its power over secular affairs, and especially its divine establishment and authority in matters of salvation are thrown into question. The essence of the church was thereby threatened, as it lost its legitimacy and its salvific role. The teaching of predestination was therefore deemed heretical. Hus's important tractate *De ecclesia* was among his most controversial works and

---

[10] Pavel Soukup, "Kauza reformace. Husitství v konkurenci reformních projektů," in *Heresis seminaria. Pojmy a koncepty v bádání o husitství*, eds. Pavlína Rychterová and Pavel Soukup (Prague: 2013), 208.

[11] See for example Frederick G. Heymann, "The Hussite-Utraquist Church in the Fifteenth and Sixteenth Centuries," *Archiv für Reformationsgeschichte* 52 (1961): 1–16; Soukup, "Kauza reformace," 210, speaks of a "provincial Church" and its "potential for confessionalization."

[12] The archives of the lower consistory before 1525 do not survive. For records after that date, see Klement Borový (ed.), *Akta konsistoře utrakvistické* (Prague: 1868); older fragments were published by Jindřich Marek and Renáta Modráková, *Zlomky rukopisů v Národní knihovně České republiky* (Prague: 2006).

[13] Václav Novotný, *M. Jan Hus. Život a učení*, Part 1: *Život a dílo*, 2 vols. (Prague: 1919–1921), remains the foundational biographical study. A systematic analysis of Hus's works was done by Vlastimil Kybal, *M. Jan Hus. Život a učení*, Part 2: *Učení*, 3 vols. (Prague: 1923–1931). Recent biographies include: Peter Hilsch, *Johannes Hus (um 1370–1415). Prediger Gottes und Ketzer* (Regensburg: 1999); František Šmahel, *Jan Hus. Život a dílo* (Prague: 2013); František Šmahel and Ota Pavlíček (eds.), *A Companion to Jan Hus* (Brill's Companions to the Christian Tradition) 54 (Leiden and Boston: 2015); Pavel Soukup, *Jan Hus* (Stuttgart: 2014).

was used by his enemies as the main argument for his citation and the prosecutorial articles against him. While there was no precise, official definition of the church in Hus's period, the various theological works on the church's foundation recognized its organizational structure. Hus obviously understood that the church functioned in the form of an institutional hierarchy, but for him this external appearance had lost its meaning. Hus did not seek to attack the contemporary church organization, nor did he have revolutionary intentions, but some of his opinions could be deemed to have revolutionary potential. In his discussion of the foundation of the church and the immutability of the status of salvific predestination by any efforts on its part, Hus established himself distinctly outside the recognized principles of the Catholic faith.[14]

Certain favorable intellectual, confessional, and political conditions were necessary for the emergence of the new Utraquist Church.[15] Intellectually, its roots may be found much earlier, prior to the Hussite wars; its foundation was established, among other things, by the introduction of the lay chalice, which distinguished those who longed for the realization of reformist thought from those who upheld the established order and lacked the motivation to abandon it. From the beginning, therefore, the Utraquist Church was liturgically distinct in that it administered the Eucharist to the laity in both its forms, bread and wine. In the 15th century, approximately two-thirds of Bohemia's inhabitants adhered to the chalice.[16]

Intellectually, the structure of the Utraquist Church was also prepared by the numerous meetings of the Hussite clergy, though the Hussites never created a document which could be called a "confession" in the later sense of the word;[17] the Four Articles of Prague, which formed the foundation of the later *Compactata*, were the expression of the whole movement's program, but they were still far from comprising a confessional document. They governed the liturgical, authoritative, and societal aspects of Christian life (the chalice, preaching the Word of God, the punishment of sins, church property). Specific matters of faith, however, were dealt with differently, by the congregated Hussite clergy and via learned disputations that formulated positions on contentious points of faith. Even the resolutions of these synods did not represent a

---

14   For a summary of Hus's ecclesiology, see Jiří Kejř, *Jan Hus známý i neznámý. Resumé knihy, která nebude napsána* (Prague: 2009; 2nd ed., 2015), 36–37.
15   Similarly, Soukup, "Kauza reformace," 209.
16   On the beginnings of Utraquism, see Šmahel, *Die Hussitische Revolution*, vol. 2, 604–24, 913–18; Helena Krmíčková, *Studie a texty k počátkům kalicha v Čechách* (Brno: 1997); Dušan Coufal, *Polemika o kalich mezi teologií a politikou 1414–1431. Předpoklady basilejské disputace o prvním z pražských artikulů* (Prague: 2012).
17   Novotný, "Konfesionalizace před konfesionalizací," 233–40.

true confession, but were rather its foundations, mere expressions of that which distinguished the Hussites from the "Romans," and of what distinguished the two main factions of the Hussites themselves – the Praguers and the Taborites.[18] Nevertheless, awareness of their difference, expressed by the enumeration of distinct articles of faith and the "basic truths" of the new church entity, presented certain confessional features. Post-*Compactata* society was divided confessionally, not by state but rather estate confessionalization, permeating all layers of society: confessional lines crossed boundaries of estates and societal organizations.[19]

The cornerstone for the construction of the new church was Wyclif and Hus's definition of authority in the church,[20] which gave it a distinct character despite its similarity to the Catholic Church in other matters of doctrine and practice. Thus, there were few structural differences between the Utraquists and existing institutions. The Utraquists' critique of individual popes and of the papacy in general did not at all imply their interest in a collective solution to problems of authority across the whole church in the form of a general council; rather, their critique pointed to the presumed state of the primitive church. The rejection of an earthly arbiter complicated the possibility of an accord, though Utraquists continued to regard themselves as part of the universal church, which they strove to correct by applying their own principles that were formulated on the foundation of biblical and theological study. After the initial revolutionary phase, a period of discussion and deliberation set in, whereby militant zeal gave way to a defensive stance, compromise, and regression into exclusivity. Hussitism and Utraquism thus remained halfway between medieval reform and modern Reformation.[21] This exclusivity was defended not only against the Roman Church, but also against "dissidents" of the movement – the Taborites and the Unity of Brethren.

2   The Formation of the Utraquist Church's Institutional Structure

The institutional dimension of the Utraquist Church had been taking shape since at least the beginning of the Hussite revolution. The competence of the

---

18   František Šmahel, *Basilejská kompaktáta. Příběh deseti listin* (Prague: 2011); Blanka Zilynská, *Husitské synody v Čechách 1418–1440. Příspěvek k úloze univerzitních mistrů v husitské církvi a revoluci* (Prague: 1985).
19   On the persistence of social and cultural norms across confessions, see Soukup, "Kauza reformace," 211; Novotný, "Konfesionalizace před konfesionalizací."
20   Soukup, "Kauza reformace," 215.
21   A broad consideration of this matter is Soukup, "Kauza reformace."

church administration, fixed by canonical law, was disturbed by the interventions of the king, the actions of the nobility, and the activity of the university masters. Up until 1412, King Wenceslas IV supported Hus's reform party, and did not stand firmly against it even after the indulgence affair. It is difficult to say whether this was the result of personal sympathies or pragmatic politics. At any rate, the king's pressure against the archbishop weakened, or even inhibited, the efforts of church dignitaries against the Wycliffite faction. A hint of Václav's Gallican behavior can be found in his initiatives calling for extraordinary synods in 1408, 1412, and 1414, which he pressured to resolve disputes over Wyclif's teachings, particularly the concept of remanence, and other contemporary problems.[22]

Some among the nobility also acted in the benefit of the reform party, expressing material support through the commission of the Corpus Christi Chapel in Prague's New Town and the Bethlehem Chapel in the Old Town to the Czech university nation. Intellectual support for the movement was provided in those dominions where the lay chalice was adopted by the will of the noble lords. Of fundamental importance, however, was the step taken by the pro-reform noblemen in September 1415, when the recently established Utraquist union of nobles granted exceptional powers to the University of Prague, thus introducing a new actor into the drama.[23] The University partially earned this extraordinary position itself, as its intellectuals worked in the service of the reform movement as "learned advisors" and important theoreticians. More important for the formation of a new church, however, was the recognition of the University as arbiter in matters of faith. In instances where the bishop was seen to have decided unfairly regarding a clergyman accused of heresy, appeals were to be made to the rector, doctors, and Masters of Theology. This principle was formulated on 5 September 1415, during a congress called by nobles who were sympathetic to the reform movement and Hus's ideas. From 1415 to 1420, we know of a series of reports in which the University resolved matters of faith to the benefit of the Hussites. Given the fact that the Theological Faculty was paralyzed during the formulation of this document, the masters of the Arts

---

22   Blanka Zilynská, "Hussitische Synoden – die Vorläufer der reformatorischen Synodalität," in *Die Hussitische Revolution. Religiöse, politische und regionale Aspekte*, ed. Franz Machilek (Cologne, Weimar, and Vienna: 2012), 60–64.

23   Czech text from 5 September 1415 (with the editor's Latin translation) in František Palacký (ed.), *Documenta Mag. Joannis Hus vitam, doctrinam, causam in Constantiensi concilio actam et controversias de religione in Bohemia annis 1408–1413 motas illustrantia* (Prague: 1869), 590–95, esp. 591 and 594; cf. Bohdan Zilynskyj, "Stížný list české a moravské šlechty proti Husovu upálení. Otázky vzniku a dochování," *Folia Historica Bohemica* 5 (1983): 205–06.

Faculty took over the respective tasks without hesitation. Their most significant task was the express approval of the lay chalice in March 1417. Thus, the University and its masters became the organizational core around which other structures began to form.[24]

The vague legal status of the acting group formed by university masters and parts of the clergy is expressed by the terminology used first in the autumn of 1418, when "convocatio magistrorum et aliorum seniorum fratrum et sacerdotum plurimorum" (a collection of masters, other senior brothers, and many priests) on the feast of St. Wenceslas issued the first extensive doctrinal document defining the emerging position of the Utraquist Church toward certain matters of church practice.[25] Thereafter, the functioning of the university masters is traceable throughout the entire revolutionary period, in the resolution on the *Compactata*, and in the structures of the Utraquist Church in the post-*Compactata* period.

The conversion of Archbishop Konrad of Vechta to the Hussite party in April 1421 gave the Utraquist Church a certain legality, though this also led to the destruction of existing local infrastructures of the universal church. A part of the clergy decided to emigrate, primarily the metropolitan chapter and the communities of friars. The archbishop's officials settled and presided in Zittau, which was then already a part of Upper Lusatia. As an apostate, the archbishop lost all power over the Catholic clergy, which immediately renounced him. He was also placed under anathema, though his excommunication was announced only five years later. The Prague diocese was temporarily administered by the bishop of Olomouc, and later administrators were appointed from among the canons of St. Vitus Cathedral.[26]

Vechta, who left Prague for Roudnice nad Labem, acted as the "Hussite Archbishop" for the entire decade. He was present in various political situations (for instance, the Diet of Čáslav in 1421, and the diplomatic negotiations with Sigismund Korybut), though his own activity within the church was

---

24　František Šmahel, *Die Prager Universität im Mittelalter. The Charles University in the Middle Ages* (Leiden and Boston: 2007); Jiří Kejř, *Mistři pražské univerzity a kněží táborští* (Prague: 1981), 9–12, 21–22; Svatoš, *Dějiny Univerzity*, vol. 1, 85–99, 205–07; Zilynská, *Husitské synody*, 81–83; Howard Kaminsky, "The University of Prague in the Hussite Revolution. The Role of Masters," in *Universities in Politics. Case Studies from the Late Middle Ages and Early Modern Period,* eds. John W. Baldwin and Richard A. Goldthwaite (Baltimore and London: 1972), 79–106; Martin Nodl, *Dekret kutnohorský* (Prague: 2010), 309–23.

25　Edited in Palacký (ed.), *Documenta Mag. Joannis Hus*, 677–81, no. 118; for a study of its transmission, see Zilynská, *Husitské synody*, 15, 31–39.

26　Zdeňka Hledíková, "Administrace pražské diecéze na sklonku prvé poloviny 15. století," *Acta Universitatis Carolinae – Historia Universitatis Carolinae Pragensis* 31 (1991): 117–28.

limited. In fact, Vechta merely acted as a figurehead, lending his name and title to decisions made by the true power-holders, the administrators of the Hussite clergy, who were mostly university masters, some of whom were connected to the archbishop. Vechta occasionally named his proxies (for instance, the chairmen of the St. Prokop Synod in 1421) or established his officials with traditional titles (e.g. *vicarius, officialis*). While seriously ill toward the end of his life, Konrad still continued to ordain some masters (the report named Jan Rokycana and Martin Lupáč), though these were later challenged, given the severity of the archbishop's medical condition. Konrad died in 1431, but the officials established by him did not abandon their posts.[27] Vicar Jan Rokycana kept the seal of the consistory in his hand and remained at the head of the Utraquist clergy. A certain bond, therefore, existed between the emerging church and the existing one.[28]

In many regards, the Utraquist Church mimicked the existing church institution, though its support from the archbishop and his newly named officials and delegated authorities was not the sole element leading to the establishment of the new local church. The office for the prosecution of public sins represented a revolutionary novelty. Its establishment in 1421 was a response to an older demand included in the Four Prague Articles for the eradication of deadly sins. On 21 July 1421, the community of Prague ordered the formation of an office of honest citizens, over fifty from each town, who would search for people suspected of Pikart errors, and those disloyal to the masters who had been appointed as clerical administrators.[29] The later activity of this office is a matter for debate: was it also established in other cities? Did it function in various degrees of intensity for decades, or only in the revolutionary moment? We have no sources that reveal how it functioned, only critical polemics regarding

---

27 Ivan Hlaváček, "Konrad von Vechta. Ein Niedersachse im spätmittelalterlichen Böhmen," *Beiträge zur Geschichte der Stadt Vechta* 4 (1974): 5–35; Ferdinand Seibt, "Konrad von Vechta," in idem, *Hussitenstudien. Personen, Ereignisse, Ideen einer frühen Revolution* (Munich: 1987), 241–52; Jiří Stočes, "Původ a studium bratří Konráda a Konstantina z Vechty," *Mediaevalia Historica Bohemica* 14, 2 (2011): 91–112.

28 Surveys of Utraquist Church administration are listed below in the historiographical survey.

29 The community's order is edited by Palacký (ed.), *Archiv český*, vol. 1, 205. On the office for the prosecution of public sins, see Rudolf Urbánek, *Věk poděbradský*, 4 vols. (České dějiny) 3 (Prague: 1915–1962), vol. 3, 817–19; Blanka Zilynská, "Utrakvistická církevní správa a možnosti jejího studia," *Acta Universitatis Carolinae*, Philosophica et historica 2, Z pomocných věd historických 15 (1999): 45–47; and recently František Šmahel, "Drobné záhady rejstříku Rečkovy koleje," *Acta Universitatis Carolinae – Historia Universitatis Carolinae Pragensis* 53, 2 (2013): 14.

the intrusion of uneducated laymen into matters that were until then resolved by church courts.

The next reference to the existence of the office occurs only in 1427. Here we learn that after the crisis surrounding the expulsion of Sigismund Korybut, the office, which some sought to annul, was now in fact revived,[30] though we do not know for how long. The record is again silent on the matter until the tense period surrounding the Prague riots in the first half of the 1480s. A document from the three united Prague towns from 6 October 1483 mentions the restoration of the spiritual offices in all Prague town councils, indicating that these were to have the same authority as they had had in the early 1420s. The enumeration of deadly sins, which was attached to the document, mostly dealt with the morals of the citizenry (pertaining particularly to their clothing, entertainment, visits to taverns, and relations between the sexes), and there is no mention of their orthodoxy of belief.[31] After the agreement of the religious settlement in 1485, the situation calmed and, apparently, the functions of this office also ceased.

Yet the course of the Utraquist Church's development seems primarily to have been influenced by the archbishop's officers, by Jan Rokycana himself, and by the involvement of the University. The Hussite clergy elected their first four administrators at the St. Prokop's Synod of 1421. Their position oscillated somewhere between that of an independent administration and the exercise of the office on behalf of Archbishop Vechta, who promised at his conversion to accept university masters into his council. The sources label them as *directores cleri sub utraque*, or administrators of the Utraquist clergy. Three of them, Jan of Příbram, Jakoubek of Stříbro, and Prokop of Plzeň, were recruited from the ranks of the university masters, and the fourth, Jan Želivský, represented the radicals. After the partial personnel change in the fall of 1421 when, following pressure from Želivský, Příbram and Prokop were replaced by two other masters (Jan Kardinál and the Englishman Peter Payne) who were to be set at the head of the church, these administrators functioned until the first months of 1422.[32] After Želivský's death, this four-member leadership evidently fell apart. From that point forward, the main figure was Jakoubek of Stříbro, though

---

30 Palacký (ed.), *Archiv český*, vol. 3, 263.
31 The document was edited by František Šmahel, "Pražské povstání 1483," *Pražský sborník historický* 19 (1986): 94–99.
32 Zilynská, *Husitské synody*, 16–17, 45–46; on the consistory, see Kamil Krofta, "Boj o konsistoř pod obojí v letech 1562–1575 a jeho historický základ," *Český časopis historický* 17 (1911): 30–57.

we know nothing of his election or confirmation.[33] Only in 1428–1429 is the restored title of the official and general vicar documented: it was granted by Archbishop Konrad to two university masters – Jan Kardinál and Jan of Rokycana.[34]

Jan of Rokycana's star began to rise after the fall of Sigismund Korybut in 1427. He first served at the side of his teacher Jakoubek of Stříbro, and after the latter's death in 1429 he gained the directorship of the Utraquist clergy (*director cleri*).[35] At Konrad of Vechta's death (1431), there arose discussion in favor of granting Rokycana twelve aids. Although we do not know if this ever happened, we can assume that the administrator had people surrounding him who performed necessary official tasks. The form this office took, however, remains unclear: were there only individual officials, as was then common, or did the consistory take on a new shape, as we know from the later period? During his administration of the Utraquist clergy, therefore, Rokycana apparently relied on the Office of Spiritual Law, an institution that had no fixed form and whose title only appeared at the close of the Hussite wars. Its members were decided either by the will of the clergy or chosen by Rokycana himself. Beside this office, Rokycana may have allowed the continuation of the office for the prosecution of sins, a board which included laymen and operated at the town hall (though some scholars suggest that both offices were merged). The Office of Spiritual Law probably broadened its jurisdiction over matrimonial affairs as well, and in 1435 it was supposedly confirmed by Sigismund, inclusive of this agenda.[36]

Aside from his political activities, what we mainly know of Jan Rokycana's administration of the Utraquist clergy pertains to his congregation of the clergy and chairing of synods, including the delivery of synodal sermons. In addition, he cared for the network of provincial deans and performed judicial tasks in relation to the Utraquist clergy. We know that the king directed disputing

---

33   Blanka Zilynská, "Jakoubek ze Stříbra a dobová církevní správa," in *Jakoubek ze Stříbra. Texty a jejich působení*, eds. Ota Halama and Pavel Soukup (Prague: 2006), 9–48.

34   The document that mentions Jan Kardinál as official (dated 4 May 1428) and Jan Rokycana as general vicar (dated 19 October 1429) is quoted by Václav Vladivoj Tomek, *Dějepis města Prahy*, 12 vols. (Prague: 1855–1901), vol. 4, 437. Later on, Václav of Dráchov was mentioned as official (ibid., 692).

35   Jaroslav Boubín, "Mistr Jan z Rokycan. Stručný náčrt jeho životních osudů," in *Žaloby katolíků na M. Jana z Rokycan*, eds. Jaroslav Boubín and Jana Zachová (Rokycany: 1997), 5–19; Frederick G. Heymann, "John Rokycana. Church Reformer between Hus and Luther," *Church History* 28 (1959): 240–80; Šmahel, *Die Hussitische Revolution*, vol. 3, 1868–78.

36   Urbánek, *Věk poděbradský*, vol. 3, 812; Krofta, "Boj o konsistoř," 36; Palacký (ed.), *Archiv český*, vol. 3, 433 (the edition of a document that Sigismund issued for the Prague towns relies on a very late record from 1618).

parties to him in cases that fell under the authority of the church court. On the other hand, he was well aware that he had not been confirmed as a bishop, and thus did not perform tasks relegated to the jurisdiction of this office, especially acts of ordination.[37]

Rokycana's position as the administrator of the Utraquist clergy was not as strong as we might expect. Firstly, his authority was challenged by the New Town radical Jakub Vlk, who temporarily placed himself at the head of the New Town clergy after the rift between the Prague towns in 1428.[38] Rokycana's position was strengthened by his election to the candidacy of the Prague Archbishopric on 21 October 1435, along with two suffragans, Václav of Vysoké Mýto (from Choceň) and Martin Lupáč (from Chrudim).[39] However, although Jan Rokycana worked to strengthen his hold on the administration of church matters, his position was greatly complicated after the agreement on the *Compactata* and the arrival of Emperor Sigismund and the council legate Philibert to Prague.

Philibert de Montjeu (d. 1439), the Bishop of Coutance in Normandy, was the head of all delegations sent by the Council of Basel to the Hussites in the period between 1433 and 1436. After the announcement of the *Compactata* in Jihlava, this native Burgundian settled in Prague with the status of plenipotentiary legate (*legatus a latere*), developing wide-ranging efforts for the restoration of the church's status in the Czech lands. He was not made administrator, nor was he given another function, but rather proceeded as a fully empowered legate and ordained bishop: he consecrated clergy and church buildings, summoned congregations of the clergy, and worked to improve the administrative conditions of parishes and provincial deaneries. Moreover, he performed liturgical duties for Sigismund's court, oversaw the coronation of Queen Barbara, and assisted in the coronation of King Albrecht. Philibert's legation and dwelling in Prague were financed by the income of his Norman diocese, from which he also supported the renewal of the functions of the Prague metropolitan chapter. As legate, he had relations with both sides – Catholic and Utraquist – and clearly strove for a renewal of the pre-Hussite status quo in Bohemia. Nevertheless, he was regarded as an authority by the Utraquists as well, who still referred to him in the later period. His synodal provision from 1437 was

---

37   Josef Kalousek (ed.), *Archiv český čili Staré písemné památky české i moravské* (Prague: 1888), vol. 14, 100–101, no. 1715. A number of details concerning Rokycana can be found in Urbánek, *Věk poděbradský*.

38   On Jakub Vlk and the events in the New Town of Prague in 1428, see Tomek, *Dějepis města Prahy*, vol. 4, 412, 574–75, 608, 635–40.

39   A record of the election is in Palacký (ed.), *Archiv český*, vol. 3, 436–37, no. 15; Sigismund's consent is found in ibid., 429, 445–46. Cf. Krofta, "Boj o konsistoř," 40–43.

included among the acknowledged legal texts of the Utraquists, who apparently were also grateful for his ordination of a certain number of new priests. Philibert's mission in Bohemia was prematurely interrupted by a plague epidemic in June 1439.[40] In reaction to his death, the Council of Basel sent to Bohemia the Prague canon Mikuláš Jindřichův as the designated Prague Archbishop and council legate. He arrived in Prague in January 1441 but was unsuccessful in his bid for confirmation by the Land Diet, the metropolitan chapter, and the Utraquist community that included the University.[41]

Although he was elected by the diet commission and confirmed by Sigismund, Jan Rokycana was forced to give way to Philibert and instead chose to leave Prague (1437). Křišťan of Prachatice was elected administrator in his place. After the latter's death, the Prague Utraquist clergy elected two administrators – Jan Příbram and Prokop of Plzeň. The Utraquist Church thus temporarily split into two factions: the more conservative under the leadership of Příbram and Prokop, who maintained ties with the metropolitan chapter, which represented the Catholic clergy; and the centrists under the leadership of Rokycana. Rokycana settled in Hradec Králové in eastern Bohemia, from where he tried to assert his jurisdiction over the entire Utraquist Church by means of Utraquist synods congregated at Kutná Hora. These synods formulated the Utraquist doctrinal stance (1441) and the positions of Tábor (1443). The disunity was mitigated in 1442 by negotiations between Příbram and Rokycana and was overcome as a result of the military actions of George of Poděbrady, who occupied Prague in early September 1448 and brought Jan Rokycana back to the capital city.

The Utraquist archbishop-elect took administrative control of his church and remained its head for over twenty years (1448–1471). Spiritual law was also renewed in the form of Rokycana's consistory. References to it in the sources

---

40 Christian Kleinert, *Philibert de Montjeu (ca. 1374–1439). Ein Bischof im Zeitalter der Reformkonzilien und des Hundertjährigen Krieges* (Ostfildern: 2004); Blanka Zilynská, "Biskup Filibert a české země," *Jihlava a Basilejská kompaktáta* (Jihlava: 1992), 56–94; Blanka Zilynská, "Z Burgundska až do husitských Čech: životní pouť Filiberta de Montjeu. Opožděná reflexe biografické knihy," *Historie – Otázky – Problémy* 3, 2 (2011): 127–42; Kateřina Horníčková, "Bishop Phillibert of Coutances and Catholic Restoration in Hussite Prague," in *Culture of Memory in East-Central Europe in the Late Middle Ages and the Early Modern Period (1000–1600)*, ed. Rafał Wójcik (Poznań: 2008), 255–64; eadem, "Memory, Politics and Holy Relics. Catholic Tactics amidst the Hussite Reformation," in *Materializing Memory. Archaeological Material Culture and the Semantics of the Past*, eds. Irene Barbiera, Alice M. Choyke, and Judith A. Rasson (Oxford: 2009), 97–103; reprinted in *The Bohemian Reformation and Religious Practice*, eds. Zdeněk V. David and David R. Holeton, vol. 8 (Prague: 2011), 133–42.

41 Kleinert, *Philibert de Montjeu*, 427, n. 2; Urbánek, *Věk poděbradský*, vol. 1, 652–75, 687–99; Čornej, *Velké dějiny*, vol. 6, 83–84.

are found only sporadically, but repeatedly, over the 1450s and 1460s, though we find clear information on the form and functioning of the Utraquist consistory only in the later period. It was reorganized in 1478 with the appointment of eight clergymen and four notable laymen, namely, university masters.[42] The administrator – often the current or retiring rector of the university – chaired the twelve-member college. From official records, which are available only from the 1530s, it seems that the consistory (labeled the "lower" consistory, as opposed to the "higher" Catholic one based in Prague Castle) probably met every week to manage administrative and judicial matters. It served as the highest authority for Utraquists, and there was no appeal above it. The office resided in the Karolinum, the largest Prague University college, and as such was linked to the University by personnel and locale. The extent to which these facts can be projected back to the period before 1478 remains an open question, as is that of whether, and how, the office overseeing public morals functioned beside this consistory.[43]

3   Administrative Functioning

Church administration in Bohemia, therefore, was split from 1421. The *Compactata* supported this state of affairs with their legalization of the lay chalice, even if they did not necessarily foresee the establishment of a dual institution. The *Compactata* only dealt with the matter of ordaining clerical novices and the dual forms of performing the Eucharist but were silent on the construction of individual administrative institutions, and thus the matter was dealt with in an ad hoc manner. As a result, both administrative structures functioned similarly in many regards: at the head of both systems were the administrators; officials were appointed and given common titles; and the system of lower administrators (deaneries and parishes) was more or less preserved. The Catholic minority was subordinated to the administrator elected or appointed by the council of the metropolitan chapter. From 1437 to 1440, the latter returned to Prague along with its chancery, which until then had functioned provisionally in Zittau.[44] Over the course of the 15th century it abandoned Prague two more

---

42 Older sources of varying credibility were listed by Krofta, "Boj o konsistoř," 47–50; for further interpretations, see Šmahel, "Drobné záhady," 15; Zikmund Winter, *Život církevní v Čechách. Kulturně-historický obraz z XV. a XVI. století*, 2 vols. (Prague: 1895–1896), vol. 1, 319–99; Josef Macek, *Víra a zbožnost jagellonského věku* (Prague: 2001), 102–18.
43 Šmahel, "Drobné záhady," 15; Urbánek, *Věk poděbradský*, vol. 3, 821–24.
44 In addition to the literature listed above, works on the Catholic Church in Bohemia include Anton Frind, *Die Kirchengeschichte Böhmens*, 4 vols. (Prague: 1864–1878), vols. 3–4;

times, once in fear of George of Poděbrady's army in September 1448, and again during a state of war at the end of the 1460s. Both periods of forced exile from Prague were spent in Plzeň in west Bohemia,[45] and the see of Prague only received its ordinary in 1561.

The parallel church structures also had their differences. Among these was the extraordinarily strong influence of the laity in the affairs of the Utraquist Church, as well as the latter's far greater collective agency, expressed by its repeated gatherings that decided on doctrinal and political issues. Regarding their disruption of certain canonical norms, the Utraquists faced their greatest problems in the matter of electoral practice, namely, in determining how to choose their representatives and ensure their recognition and legality when the preservation of existing procedures was impossible. This especially affected administrators of the clergy, who were first elected by a congregation of the clergy, a practice which was employed several times during the Hussite wars. A special election of "Archbishop" Rokycana also took place in the commission of the diet, in which laymen were naturally also represented. After the death of Rokycana, this manner of electing a Utraquist archbishop was not repeated, and the church was only managed thereafter by administrators.

After 1471, the election of administrators passed to the assembly of Estates, which became an institution superior to the Utraquist Church and decided matters of faith.[46] An administrator's term in office was not of a set length, but rather depended on developments in the political sphere. The first

---

Václav Vladivoj Tomek, "Rozdíly v náboženství a v církevním zřízení v Čechách v xv. století," *Časopis Musea Království českého* 65 (1891): 145–64; Hledíková, "Administrace pražské diecéze"; Wojciech Iwańczak, "Katolicy i husyci w czasach Jerzego z Podiebradu," in *Stosunki miedzywyznaniowe w Europie Środkowej i Wschodniej w XIV–XVII wieku*, ed. Marian Dygo, Sławomir Gawlas, and Hieronim Grala (Warszawa: 2002), 25–37; idem, "Kościól w Czechach w xv w. – dezintegracja i łączność," *Przegląd humanystyczny* 3 (2006): 21–30.

45 Antonín Mařík, "K postavení katolické církve v Čechách v době poděbradské. Činnost katolických administrátorů za Jiřího z Poděbrad," *Folia Historica Bohemica* 7 (1984): 101–96; idem, "Administrátoři a svatovítská kapitula v době poděbradské. Úřad administrátorů pod jednou a jeho představitelé," *Sborník archivních prací* 51, 2 (2001): 313–58; idem, "Svatovítská kapitula za vlády Jiřího z Poděbrad," *Documenta Pragensia* 20 (2002): 25–53; idem, "Teritoriální rozsah katolické církevní správy v době Jiřího z Poděbrad na základě administrátorských akt," in *Církevní správa a její písemnosti na přelomu středověku a novověku*, ed. Ivan Hlaváček (Acta Universitatis Carolinae – Philosophica et historica) 1999, 2; (Z pomocných věd historických) 15 (Prague: 2003), 213–40; Veronika Macháčková, "Církevní správa v době jagellonské (na základě administrátorských akt)," *Folia Historica Bohemica* 9 (1985): 235–90; Macek, *Víra a zbožnost*, 173–88.

46 Jiří Rak, "Vývoj utrakvistické správní organizace v době předbělohorské," *Sborník archivních prací* 31 (1981): 179–80.

administrator after Jan Rokycana was Václav Koranda the Younger (d. 1519), another distinctive figure in the Utraquist mileu – a university master, man of letters, and probably an unordained layman. His priesthood is a disputed matter, and the fact that he could become the head of the Utraquist clergy (until 1497) demonstrated the loosening of rules which, until then, were ingrained with taboos.[47]

The superiority of the laity is also documented by the institute of secular defensors of the Estates, which from 1531 were elected by the assembly of Estates from the nobility.[48] They were meant to be the patrons of the Utraquist Church and had the authority to call Utraquist assemblies. After a century of the official Utraquist Church's existence, it was already clear that the episcopal form of the church establishment would not return, and the model of the Estates' political body was imposed in this realm as well: the assembly of the Utraquist Estates became the top authority for the national church (*Landeskirche*). The means of choosing members of the lower consistory changed as well, as this election also passed from the clerical congregation to the assembly of Estates, which from about 1497 regularly passed this task on to the Old Town council. These "lords of Prague" knew the Prague priests better and stipulated which among them would stand at the head of the Utraquist clergy.[49]

The connection between urban self-government and church authorities also developed in the second largest Bohemian city, Kutná Hora. It was there that, during the residence of Bishop Filippo de Villanuova (on whom, more below) following his conflict with the Utraquist consistory and his withdrawal from Prague, the so-called Kutná Hora consistory was formed.[50] This mixed body, formed of clerics and laymen, and established from the first decade of the sixteenth century, usurped a portion of the jurisdiction of the central authority, but in the first decades of its existence, it essentially functioned

---

47   Kamil Krofta, *Václav Koranda mladší z Nové Plzně a jeho názory náboženské* (Pilsen: 1914).
48   Rak, "Vývoj utrakvistické správní organizace," 181–82. Another form of secularization was to replace the canon law by secular provincial (land) law, as shown by Petr Elbel, "Správa utrakvistické církve na Moravě mezi husitskou revolucí a reformací," in *Náboženský život a církevní poměry v zemích Koruny české ve 14.-17. století*, eds. Lenka Bobková and Jana Konvičná (Korunní země v dějinách českého státu) 4 (Prague: 2009), 141–42.
49   Blanka Zilynská, "Město Praha a utrakvistická církev. Role konšelů při obsazování 'dolní konsistoře' (do r. 1547)," *Documenta Pragensia* 33 (2014): 85–94.
50   Its archives from 1515 to 1619 survive at Kutná Hora; see Lubomír Vaněk and Marie Kapavíková, "Církevní správa," in *Průvodce po archivních fondech a sbírkách OA v Kutné Hoře* (Kutná Hora: 1970), 250–52; František Trnka, "Náboženské poměry při kutnohorské konsistoři r. 1464–1547," *Věstník Královské české společnosti nauk* (1934), Třída filosoficko-historicko-jazykozpytná, no. 5, 1–92. On the delegation of powers, see Hledíková, "Administrace pražské diecéze," 126–27.

according to an understanding with Prague and possessed a sort of delegated authority. Along with the archdean at the head, the Kutná Hora consistory exercised its authority over twenty-six parishes in the surrounding region, in addition to the city in which it was based.

The authority of the lower consistory over Moravia is also a matter relevant to the territorial jurisdiction of the Utraquist consistory. Although the Prague administrators claimed jurisdiction over the Utraquists in Moravia, the reality was more complex. Some sources suggest that Utraquist officials held a degree of influence over certain Moravian cities, but they also indicate that the bishopric of Olomouc practiced the chief administrative tasks of the Utraquists in Moravia.[51]

Apart from the administrator and the Utraquist consistory, an important organ of the Utraquist Church was the assembly of clerics from various ranks. Independent synods of Utraquist clergy were organized from the beginning of the Hussite era, with increasing frequency after the revolution, since they were supposed to pronounce on doctrinal matters.[52] Closest to the existing practice of the diocesan synod were the synods of the Praguers, the moderate branch of Hussites. Among them, some were summoned to include the Hussite priests from the whole land, and their resolutions were meant to be valid for everyone. Among these, we may cite the St. Prokop Synod of 1421 and the St. Jacob Synod of 1434. The third collection of doctrinal articles that were widely accepted was announced in Kutná Hora in October 1441. The priests of Tábor met independently, and their resolutions from 1421–1424 and 1430 reacted primarily to the attacks of the Praguers. The Taborite clergy maintained a doctrinally independent status until 1444. The consultations of Taborite priests from the 1440s can only be problematically labeled synods, however, since the number of Taborite priests was reduced over the course of the wars to only a few individuals. Direct doctrinal discussions between Prague and Tábor also occurred in the framework of disputations, open debates in which the only judge could be Holy Scripture or an agreed-upon commission, often formed by laymen. The collective resolution of spiritual matters during the Hussite revolution was a distinct novelty compared to the earlier state of affairs, and revolutionary

---

51 Josef Válka, *Husitství na Moravě. Náboženská snášenlivost. Jan Amos Komenský* (Brno: 2005); Elbel, "Správa utrakvistické církve na Moravě"; idem, "Zlomek olomoucké konfirmační knihy z let 1452–1455. Předběžné výsledky rozboru opomíjeného pramene k poznání církevní topografie, diecézní správy a konfesního soužití na Moravě po polovině 15. století," in *Církevní topografie a farní síť pražské církevní provincie v pozdním středověku*, eds. Jan Hrdina and Blanka Zilynská (Colloquia mediaevalia Pragensia) 8 (Prague: 2007), 91–137.

52 Zilynská, *Husitské synody*; Zdeněk Nejedlý (ed.), *Prameny k synodám strany Pražské a Táborské. Vznik husitské konfesse v létech 1441–1444* (Prague: 1900).

conditions were favorable to this innovation. Conditions changed after the agreement of the *Compactata* and the stabilization of the situation. The legate Philibert was first to try to take matters into his own hands, and from among his activities we know of three assemblies of all the clergy of the land in 1437. After his death older practices returned, but slowly these were modified along with developments on the political scene.

During the reigns of Ladislas Posthumous and George of Poděbrady, the organization of synods was reduced. The king did not want disruptive discussions which only led, he argued, to further disturbances rather than the settling of conflicts. Ladislas, and later George, called only two large assemblies of the clergy, which were comprised of both confessions and tasked with replying to the king's provision and supporting his church politics. Thus, the doctrinal and legal role of the clerical assembly gave way to the primacy of politically demonstrative proceedings.[53]

With the arrival of the Jagellonians, a new means of assembly began to take shape among the Utraquist clergy, one which reflected the culmination of the kingdom's ruling estate system: the Utraquist clergy would assemble simultaneously with the assembly of Estates, and thus the spiritual synod became a part of the Estates' assembly.[54] The assembly's "clerical curia" either expressed itself on the resolutions of the assembly, or had on its agenda the administrative problems of the Utraquist Church. For the Jagellonian period, there are thirty clerical assemblies documented. Though the Utraquist clergy possibly met every year, it now only exceptionally dealt with matters of doctrine (in 1524), in contrast to the revolutionary era.

The lower administrative structure of both the Utraquist and the Catholic Churches remained systematically identical as before Hussitism, but in many locales it was disturbed by the interventions of laymen (e.g. with regard to the secularization of property) or by personnel problems (e.g. the lack of novice priests, problems with the ordination of Utraquists). In the case of several archdeaneries, we read of Catholic representatives, while Utraquists apparently did not employ this level of the administrative system. However, the structure of provincial deaneries continued to function on both sides, and was the main element linking the center and the lower clerical ranks. In principle, the system of patronage was not disturbed either, even if attempts of laymen

---

53   For the synods of 1454 and 1462, see Urbánek, *Věk poděbradský*, vol. 3, 243–49, 570–72.
54   Blanka Zilynská, "Synoden im utraquistischen Böhmen 1418–1531," in *Partikularsynoden im späten Mittelalter*, eds. Nathalie Kruppa and Leszek Zygner (Göttingen: 2006), 377–86; eadem, "Les nouvelles formes de la synodalité à la fin du Moyen Âge. La Bohême dans le contexte de la Réforme européenne," in *Religious Space of East-Central Europe in the Middle Ages*, eds. Krzysztof Bracha and Paweł Kras (Warsaw: 2010), 79–100.

to interfere in church matters influenced the application of the bishop's (or his representatives') right, and there were clearly local variations. From the repeated demands of the Utraquist consistory that the candidates for individual parishes be submitted for their approval, we can assume that this process was not always maintained.[55]

These changes even affected the most basic unit: the parish. We can observe a more marked self-assertion of the communities, especially in the urban sphere, which took over the administration of chantry endowments, even temporarily assuming the right and responsibility of paying priests, and in some places procuring the election of parish priests themselves.[56] Hussitism thus notably accelerated the transfer of the administration of church properties from individual priests to lay church wardens. The function of these wardens (*vitrici*) gained significance, and such clerks elected by the city council or the parish community began to enforce one of the Four Articles of Prague: that priests should hold no secular dominion. From the beginning of the revolution, lay church wardens seized any property connected with churches and benefices. Priests were thus paid from chantry funds as "wage laborers," a practice which is reflected both in Catholic propaganda and in critiques from within as a form of simony.[57] Yet the payment of priests and school officials by the city or funerary funds was not a practice exercised everywhere uniformly. Local variations ranged from weekly to quarterly payments through single contributions, and in some cases priests did not even figure into urban or chantry accounts.[58]

Over the course of the 15th century and later, those properties that were tied to the parish church and used exclusively by the priest (the benefice) were re-established, through gifts from wills[59] or from the remnants of the original

---

55 On patronage, see Urbánek, *Věk poděbradský*, vol. 3, 761, 843; Winter, *Život církevní*, vol. 2, 499–530.

56 Winter, *Život církevní*, vol. 2, 533–37; Urbánek, *Věk poděbradský*, vol. 3, 855–56; Pavel B. Kůrka, *Kostelníci, úředníci, měšťané. Samospráva farností v utrakvismu* (Prague: 2010).

57 Jan Papoušek ze Soběslavě, "Querele de motibus Bohemie," in: *Výbor z české literatury doby husitské*, eds. Bohuslav Havránek, Josef Hrabák, and Jiří Daňhelka, vol. 2 (Prague: 1964), 132–36, here lines 82–83; Jaromír Čelakovský, "Traktát podkomořího Vaňka Valečovského proti panování kněžstva," *Věstník Královské české společnosti nauk* 36 (1881): 325–45.

58 Winter, *Život církevní*, vol. 2, 538–95; Urbánek, *Věk poděbradský*, vol. 3, 849–58; Jaroslav Vaniš (ed.), *Liber rationum civitatis Lunae ad annos 1450–1472 et 1490–1491 pertinens* (Prague: 1979).

59 Zdeňka Hledíková, "Donace církevním institucím v Čechách v prvém dvacetiletí 15. stol. (Statistický přehled)," in *Husitství – reformace – renesance. Sborník k 60. narozeninám Františka Šmahela*, eds. Jaroslav Pánek, Miloslav Polívka, and Noemi Rejchrtová, vol. 1

church endowments. Thus, in time, the priest became financially independent even in Hussite Bohemia. Gradually, older forms of priestly revenue were restored as well, including tithes, which had been temporarily annulled under Hussitism.[60] Apart from the benefice, the chantry endowment became a financial source of church construction, maintenance, and holy services; it remained a separate part of the parish revenue, administered by the local laity.[61] For this purpose, the lay administrators acquired their own books of office (e.g. account books), the oldest of which survives from 1431 in Jičín. From then until the end of the Middle Ages, we have about ten such individual books, as well as account records in other town books from places where city councils gained a fundamental influence over the economies of their parishes.[62] Similar developments can be found in cities that were not exclusively controlled by Utraquists. Thus, it is clear that the participation of the laity in parish administration was not only a matter of Hussite ideology, but rather that Hussitism accelerated trends which were also present elsewhere in Europe. Within the Czech lands, this development permeated into Catholic regions as well.

Apart from the priest, the chaplain also participated in the parish administration, though under Utraquism he was not an administrator of a chapel with an independent benefice, but an assistant to the priest from among the clerical novices. The emphasis on practical experience was also a result of the limitations on educational opportunities. Prague University, reduced to only one faculty – the Faculty of Arts – may have provided higher education, but it did not train students to be specialists in theology or canon law. According to contemporary accounts, the chaplaincy was a tedious stage in which the novice entirely depended on the will and material support of his priest. Though his powers were regulated by the provisions of the synod, this regulation was not always effective. The newly ordained were obliged to stay in the chaplaincy for

  (Prague: 1994), 251–60; Bohdan Zilynskyj, "Postavení utrakvistické a katolické konfese na Novém Městě pražském v letech 1436–1459 (Úvodní poznámky)," *Documenta Pragensia* 9, 2 (1991): 389–405; Kateřina Jíšová, "Spása duše a očistec u novoměstských měšťanů. K religiozitě novoměstského měšťanstva v pozdním středověku," in *Evropa a Čechy na konci středověku. Sborník příspěvků věnovaných Františku Šmahelovi*, eds. Eva Doležalová, Robert Novotný, and Pavel Soukup (Prague: 2004), 253–68.
60 Winter, *Život církevní*, vol. 2, 543–45.
61 Blanka Zilynská, "Záduší," in *Facta probant homines. Sborník příspěvků k životnímu jubileu prof. dr. Zdeňky Hledíkové*, ed. Ivan Hlaváček (Prague: 1998), 535–48; Kůrka, *Kostelníci*.
62 Church accounts are listed in Rostislav Nový, *Městské knihy v Čechách a na Moravě 1310–1526. Katalog* (Prague: 1963). Some books were found since; see Jindřich Francek, "Úřad kostelníků v Jičíně a jejich kniha záduší z let 1431–1508," *Sborník archivních prací* 31 (1981): 75–104. We can add the books of three churches in Kutná Hora (St. Barbara, Our Lady in Náměť, and St. Bartholomew) and the re-discovered book of St. Castulus in Prague.

three years, and thus a novelty was established as a result of the unresolved status of semi-legal Utraquism.[63]

4 Other Features of the Utraquist Church

Hussitism strongly affected the life of the chapters and monastic orders, which were the primary sources of the Catholic clerical emigration, and the type of church institutions which the process of secularization particularly targeted.[64] Thus, the renewal of chapter and, in some cases, monastic activities faced not only the intellectual resistance of the Hussites, but also material realities. The Utraquists themselves did not develop a monastic life, the only exception being the Na Slovanech (Emmaus) Monastery in Prague, whose abbot converted to Utraquism. The monastery then served to safeguard some administrators and remained in the hands of Utraquists until nearly the end of the 16th century.[65] Another form of religious community, to a certain extent specific to the Czech lands, were religious brotherhoods. They provided liturgical music, performed dignified funerals for their members, and cared for their own altars (similar to some guilds). Among other things, illuminated songbooks (graduals and hymnals) bear witness to the endeavors of these brotherhoods.[66]

A new phenomenon appeared at the end of the 15th century which soon would be employed for religious agitation, church administration, and the dissemination of news: print technology. The Catholic Church employed print for the spread of its own legislation and liturgical books and other handbooks very early; Latin editions of the provincial *Statuta Arnesti*, agenda, and missals, as well as the Holy Scriptures (the New Testament) and the lives of saints in Czech (the *Passionale*) appeared in the 1470s. The Czech Bible was repeatedly printed

---

63   Winter, *Život církevní*, vol. 1, 461–63, vol. 2, 569–70; and Noemi Rejchrtová, *Studie k českému utrakvismu, zejména doby jagellonské*, unpublished habilitation thesis, Charles University, Protestant Theological Faculty (Prague: 1984).

64   Kadlec, *Katoličtí exulanti*. For a survey of secularized ecclesiastical property, see Milan Moravec, "Zástavy Zikmunda Lucemburského v českých zemích z let 1420–1437," *Folia Historica Bohemica* 9 (1985): 89–175.

65   Pavel B. Kůrka, "Slovanský klášter mezi husitstvím a katolicismem. Dějiny klášterní komunity v letech 1419–1592," in *Emauzy. Benediktinský klášter Na Slovanech v srdci Prahy*, eds. Klára Benešovská and Kateřina Kubínová (Prague: 2007), 107–24.

66   Martina Šárovcová, "*Cantate domino canticum novum*. Iluminované hudební rukopisy české reformace," in *Umění české reformace*, eds. Kateřina Horníčková and Michal Šroněk (Prague: 2010), 413–67; Jaroslav Kolár, Anežka Vidmanová, Hana Vlhová-Wörner and David R. Holeton (eds.), *Jistebnický kancionál. MS. Praha, Knihovna Národního muzea, II C 7. Kritická edice*, vol. 1: *Graduale* (Brno: 2005).

from the 1480s onward. The Utraquists used print on a smaller scale. Notable here was Václav Koranda the Younger's *Tractate on the Glorious and Holy Sacrament of the Altar, and How It Should Be Received*, printed in 1493. It propagated Utraquism, infant communion, and Czech singing during the mass. The repeated reprinting of the *Compactata* can be interpreted not only as the publicization of one part of the land's laws, but also as the propagation of the Utraquist position. The first documented use of print for clerical statutes were the articles of the assembly of the Utraquist Estates, printed in 1521, containing the administrator Václav of Litomyšl's regulation of the priesthood.[67]

The official Utraquist Church also gradually defined itself against its own radical elements, or against non-conformist groups, such that we may speak of "Utraquist heresies." Various smaller groups of sectarians, peculiar thinkers and their followers appeared in the land, the most famous being Petr Chelčický, who wrote Czech theological works criticizing the contemporary church, but also attacking Taborite or official Prague Utraquism.[68] Chelčický's thought later contributed to the formation of the Unity of Brethren.[69]

How, then, did this "new" Utraquist Church compare to its Catholic counterpart more generally? Though it had marked particularities in its theoretical foundations (e.g. Wyclif's definition of the church), doctrinal distinctiveness (the repeated formulation of articles of faith), and its ethical dimension (a strongly moralizing context), both were formally similar. Its creation came in part from social pressures: the demand of a poor church subjected to strong lay influence, and the participation of the laity in the administration of the church, corresponded to ideas forming in the community of the Estates. The Utraquist Church ceased to be subject to the papal curia, whose centralized ecclesiastical authority was replaced by a local secular one – the assembly of Estates. The Utraquists' dependence on secular power was even deepened at the beginning of the 16th century, with the institution of the Estates' defensor. The institutional system of the Utraquist Church was shaped by compromise insofar as it was usually impossible to replicate the model of the primitive

---

67   Petr Voit, *Český knihtisk mezi pozdní gotikou a renesancí: severinsko-kosořská dynastie 1488–1557*, vol. 1 (Prague: 2013); Blanka Zilynská, "From Learned Disputation to the Happening. The Propagation of Faith through Word and Image," in *Public Communication in European Reformation. Artistic and other Media in Central Europe 1380–1620*, eds. Milena Bartlová and Michal Šroněk (Prague: 2007), 60; Šmahel, *Basilejská kompaktáta*, 115–22.

68   Jaroslav Boubín, *Petr Chelčický. Myslitel a reformátor* (Prague: 2005).

69   Joseph Theodor Müller, *Geschichte der Böhmischen Brüder*, vol. 1: *1400–1528*; vol. 2: *1528–1576*; vol. 3: *Die polnische Unität 1548–1793. Die böhmisch-mährische Unität 1575–1781* (Herrnhut: 1922–31); Rudolf Říčan, *Dějiny Jednoty bratrské* (Prague: 1957); Tabita Landová, *Liturgie Jednoty bratrské (1457–1620)* (Prague: 2014).

church. Nevertheless, certain novel or necessitated solutions anticipated developments in the European Reformation.[70]

5 The Position of the Czech Utraquist Church in Relation to the Catholic Church

The Utraquist Church did not emerge and exist in a vacuum. In was very much part of its European context, even when it stood in opposition to certain contemporary intellectual currents. Though its legality was supposed to be ensured by the *Compactata*, the status of the Utraquist Church remained vague: it never abandoned its relationship with the Roman Church, but neither was it a typical component of it. This ambivalence affected the Utraquists' policy, limited their possibilities for action and also caused the hesitant reception of the European Reformation in the following century.

The relations of Hussite Bohemia with the pope and the council were those which most urgently required regulation, and representatives of the Utraquist Church continually alternated between the two. They used the rivalries between the conciliarists and the papalists without pronouncedly engaging in the conciliar discourse.[71] Over the course of the 15th century, they approached the council and the pope in turns in an attempt to gain a confirmation of the *Compactata* and an archbishop. The *Compactata* – an agreement between the representatives of the Bohemian kingdom and the church represented by the Council of Basel – were the common foundation of the relationship between the Hussites and the church.[72] The council approved of the results of the negotiations between their legates and the Bohemians, though no pope ever ratified them. Pius II thus gave the final verdict on the matter on 31 March 1462, when he announced that the *Compactata* were no longer valid. Although the *Compactata* were nullified on the international stage, Bohemian society

---

70 Soukup, "Kauza reformace," 212, describes the Utraquist Church as "an institution capable of surviving, with an identity of its own, rooted in distinctive teachings, the support of the populace and public cult practice."

71 Wycliffite ecclesiology did not deal with the superiority of the pope or the council; only a few individuals from the Czech lands pronounced on conciliar theory. Cf. Josef Macek, "Le mouvement conciliaire, Louis XI et Georges de Poděbrady (en particulier dans la période 1466–1468)," *Historica* 15 (1968): 5–63; Mario Fois, "Eklesiologie konciliarismu," in *Jan Hus na přelomu tisíciletí*, eds. Miloš Drda, František J. Holeček, and Zdeněk Vybíral (Husitský Tábor. Supplementum) 1 (Tábor: 2001), 181–207.

72 Šmahel, *Basilejská kompaktáta*; Šmahel, *Die Hussitische Revolution*, vol. 1, 604–74; Čornej, *Velké dějiny*, vol. 5, 250–54, vol. 6, 11–19, 452–57.

elevated them to the law of the land, and they remained the foundation of the kingdom's legal order until the mid-16th century. The *Compactata* thus became the core of the agreement concluded between Bohemian Catholics and Utraquists in 1485 at Kutná Hora, which was founded on the freedom of choice both for lords and their subjects between the two official confessions (thus distinct from the later Reformation agreement of *cuius regio, eius religio*).[73]

The basis of the *Compactata* was the program behind the Hussite movement – the Four Prague Articles, which were announced in the summer of 1420, and defended via military campaigns and public disputes.[74] They demanded the free preaching of the Word of God, the communion of the Eucharist for the laity in both kinds, the punishment of deadly sins in all estates, and the rejection of the secular dominion of the clergy. The distinctiveness of Utraquist church practice, both liturgically and organizationally, can be derived from the content of the Four Prague Articles that were included in the *Compactata* in a moderated form. In international relations, as well as domestic relations with local Catholics, the *Compactata* were meant to guarantee that Utraquists would not be accused of heresy for Utraquist practice, and that their status in the land would be respected. Yet the formulation of the *Compactata* was not unambiguous; both sides argued for their own interpretation of their contents, and thus the *Compactata* remained a source of controversy between Hussites and Catholics both within the kingdom and abroad.

The matter of determining who would occupy the seat of the Prague Archbishopric also forced Utraquist Church representatives to negotiate with the council and the papal curia. For the Utraquists, only one solution would be acceptable: the confirmation of their elected candidate, Jan Rokycana. Since this proved unacceptable to the church, the assertion of demands from the one side and indifference from the other led to a stalemate. After the death of Archbishop Konrad of Vechta, conciliar and curial diplomats made several attempts to properly fill this important position over the course of the century, though none of them were successful. The first attempt at replacement was the confirmation of the plenipotentiary legate of the Council of Basel, Philibert de Montjeu, the Bishop of Coutances. Václav of Krumlov was also suggested in the search to fill the archbishopric at the end of the 1450s,[75] as was the Polish

---

73   Macek, *Víra a zbožnost*, 394–99; Winfried Eberhard, *Konfessionsbildung und Stände in Böhmen 1478–1530* (Munich and Vienna: 1981), 56–60.
74   Luboš Lancinger, "Čtyři artikuly pražské a podíl universitních mistrů na jejich vývoji," *Acta Universitatis Carolinae – Historia Universitatis Carolinae Pragensis* 3, 2 (1962): 3–61.
75   Mařík, "Administrátoři a svatovítská kapitula," 317–18; Urbánek, *Věk poděbradský*, vol. 3, 55–61, 463.

prelate and chronicler Jan Długosz;[76] among other candidates there was even the son of King George of Poděbrady, Jindřich (the Elder).[77] Both sides wanted to see a new archbishop commanding the clergy of both confessions, yet the irreconcilability of the situation meant that the Prague archbishopric was left vacant for nearly a century and a half.[78]

6 Apostolic Succession

The long vacancy of the Prague Archbishopric had one fundamental consequence: the shortage of clerical novices. This problem affected the Utraquists more acutely, as their candidates were faced with considerable opposition internationally, but it also affected Catholic applicants due to the general negative reputation of Bohemian heretics throughout Europe. It was necessary to find an emergency solution, then, among which several possibilities were considered.

The Catholics maintained canonical procedures both in the organization of local ordinations from the authority of the administrator, and in granting dimissory letters to candidates leaving to pursue university studies and ordination abroad. Administrators occasionally confirmed the ordination of bishops present in Bohemia, but more commonly, ordained bishops in surrounding dioceses were charged with ordaining Bohemian candidates.[79] It remains unclear from surviving sources whether Utraquist clerics could also be ordained in this way. Perhaps only with Bishop Philibert – whose authority as plenipotentiary legate of the council allowed him to perform ordinations between 1437 and 1439 – is it highly likely that a portion of ordained clergy were adherents of the chalice.[80]

---

76   Čornej, *Velké dějiny*, vol. 6, 409.
77   Ondřej Felcman and Radek Fukala (eds.), *Poděbradové. Rod českomoravských pánů, kladských hrabat a slezských knížat* (Prague: 2008), 106–10.
78   František Kavka and Anna Skýbová, *Husitský epilog na koncilu tridentském a původní koncepce habsburské rekatolizace Čech. Počátky obnoveného pražského arcibiskupství 1561–1580* (Prague: 1969).
79   A summary appraisal of the Catholic party's situation is found in Zdeňka Hledíková, *Svět české středověké církve* (Prague: 2010); Eva Doležalová, "Ways of clerics to ordination in the post-Hussite Bohemia – an outline," in *Roma – Praga. Praha – Řím: Omaggio a Zdeňka Hledíková*, eds. Kateřina Bobková-Valentová, Eva Doležalová, Eva Chodějovská, Zdeněk Hojda, and Martin Svatoš (Prague: 2009), 145–58.
80   František Štědrý, "Rejstřík svěcenců na kněžství legáta sněmu basilejského Filiberta, biskupa kostnického," *Sborník Historického kroužku* 5 (1904): 92–98, 139–43; Blanka Zilynská,

Until the beginning of the European Reformation, Utraquists did not consider breaking apostolic succession. They continued to see themselves as part of the universal church, a part which underwent reform and thus could act as a model and a more perfect component of what they regarded to be the corrupt contemporary church. Yet because these messianic ideas were not generally accepted, a difficult dilemma arose: although the Utraquist Church was practically divorced from the Roman curia, it remained dependent on the Catholic Church in the matters of ordination and the administration of sacraments as vehicles of grace.[81] There was no one among the local clergy who could help with ordination – the bishops of Olomouc and Litomyšl refused, and Hussite candidates for bishoprics were themselves not ordained. Utraquists therefore usually chose to send their priests abroad, most often to Italy. These trips were connected with financial incentives and a dual oath: first, for the sake of appearances, an oath to renounce the chalice, and secondly an oath of obedience to the representatives of the Utraquist Church and faithfulness to the chalice upon return. These attempts did not always succeed; in Stolpen in 1446, the Bishop of Meissen, Johannes IV Hoffmann, refused to ordain certain pupils who he was warned were Utraquists.[82] After such experiences, several candidates decided to convert to Catholicism. The best-known cases were the two pupils of Jan Rokycana, Hilarius of Litoměřice and Václav of Křižanov, who made impressive careers for themselves after their conversions and became firm opponents of their teacher from within their new position in the Catholic Church.[83]

Another option was to invite a foreign bishop into the kingdom.[84] His acceptance of this invitation would gain him the status of an apostate, with all

---

"Svěcení kněžstva biskupem Filibertem v Praze v letech 1437–1439," *Documenta Pragensia* 9 (1991): 361–88.

[81] Soukup, "Kauza reformace," 207–08, 216. On the ordination of Utraquists, see Urbánek, *Věk poděbradský*, vol. 4 (following the register).

[82] Franz Machilek, "Johannes Hoffmann aus Schweidnitz und die Hussiten," *Archiv für schlesische Kirchengeschichte* 26 (1968): 114; Urbánek, *Věk poděbradský*, vol. 2, 76, 272; Blanka Zilynská, "Johann Hoffmann. Prager Student, antihussitischer Repräsentant und Bischof von Meißen," in *Universitäten, Landesherren und Landeskirchen. Das Kuttenberger Dekret von 1409 im Kontext der Epoche von der Gründung der Karlsuniversität 1348 bis zum Augsburger Religionsfrieden 1555*, ed. Blanka Zilynská (Acta Universitatis Carolinae – Historia Universitatis Carolinae Pragensis) 49, 2 (Prague: 2010), 81–98.

[83] Jaroslav Kadlec, "Hilarius Litoměřický v čele duchovenstva podjednou," in *In memoriam Josefa Macka*, eds. Miloslav Polívka and František Šmahel (Prague: 1996), 187–94; Tomáš Kalina, "Hilarius Litoměřický," *Český časopis historický* 5 (1899): 311–21; idem, "Václav Křižanovský," *Český časopis historický* 5 (1899): 333–59.

[84] The most complete account of the auxiliary bishops is Macek, *Víra a zbožnost*, 118–38; for surviving documents, see Vaněk and Kapavíková, "Církevní správa," with bibliography. Cf.

the accompanying revulsion, since aid to the Utraquists of this kind was prohibited. Nevertheless, two bishops subsequently set upon this path: the first to arrive in Prague was Agostino Luciani, Bishop of Santorini, who essentially acted as an ordaining bishop between 1482 and 1493. The second was Bishop Filippo de Villanuova, who resided in Bohemia between 1504–1507. Though aiding the Utraquists significantly, both encountered difficulties cohabitating with local representatives of the Utraquist Church, with whom they competed for authority.

The third possible solution – though it was never realized for practical reasons – was to pursue closer ties with the Orthodox Church, particularly in Constantinople.[85] Orthodox Church circles were contacted via a secret envoy of the Utraquists, named Konstantinos Anglikos in the sources, and thus identified by some Czech historians as the English master and companion of the Czech Hussites, Peter Payne. However, the fall of Constantinople to the Ottomans after the first exchange of letters interrupted any kind of further negotiation.

7 Conclusion

At the beginning of the 1430s, contrary to all existing traditions, a dialogue developed between the Roman Church and the "Bohemian heretics," the Hussites. Members of the Council of Basel used the Bohemian question as an argument against Pope Eugene IV, who wanted to dissolve the council. The Hussites, on the other hand, courted both the council and the pope in their attempt to gain recognition. The repeated negotiations on the confirmation of the *Compactata* and the approval of an archbishop did not result in any agreement regarding the status of the Utraquist Church within the universal church. Nevertheless, throughout the period in question, Utraquists did not abandon apostolic succession and, until the assertion of the Lutheran Reformation in the Czech lands, maintained a fruitless dialogue with Rome. Although a clear separation of the Utraquists from the universal church never occurred, the Utraquist Church organization functioned more or less independently. Yet we

---

also Šmahel, *Husitské Čechy*, 77–176; Winter, *Život církevní*, vol. 1, 322–26; Tomek, *Dějepis města Prahy*, vol. 10, 113–15, 208–09, 222–27, 239–41; Eberhard, *Konfessionsbildung*.

85 Urbánek, *Věk poděbradský*, vol. 2, 542–46, 594–617; Milada Paulová, "Styky českých husitů s cařihradskou církví," *Časopis Musea Království českého* 92 (1918): 1–20, 111–21, 215–28; Antonín Salač, *Constantinople et Prague en 1452* (Prague: 1958); Robin Baker, "'Constantine from England and the Bohemians.' Hussitism, Orthodoxy, and the End of Byzantium," *Central Europe* 5 (2007): 23–46.

can reasonably assume that, had there been no new reformist impulse, their opposition would have been difficult to maintain for another century, given their concern to preserve apostolic succession, together with the marked shortage of clerical novices. As things did unfold, however, the Czech attempt at reform was largely successful, and the Utraquist Church found a way to survive and provide sanctuary for its believers.

8 Historiographic Survey

The issue of ecclesiastical administration in post-Hussite Bohemia lacks a modern monograph. Contemporary authors still rely on the older works of V.V. Tomek, who developed a broad overview of the Utraquist ecclesiastical establishment.[86] Still in the nineteenth century, Jan Herben also provided a survey,[87] while Klement Borový concentrated on the issue of the illicit ordination of the Utraquist clergy.[88] Zikmund Winter has collected documents on matters of everyday affairs in the church over a broad timespan – from the 15th to the beginning of the 17th century – though the core of his interests lay in the 16th century, given the surviving sources available to him.[89] In the following generation Rudolf Urbánek drew on new sources, primarily polemical literature. In the third volume of his work *Věk poděbradský* (The age of Poděbrad) he focused extensively on the ecclesiastical and religious conditions of 15th-century Bohemia, and he returned to the subject in a collective work on Czechoslovak culture and national history.

A number of surveys appeared in postwar historiography, notably by Ferdinand Hrejsa and, slightly later, the (not entirely reliable) attempt of Vladimír Sakař to survey lay participation in ecclesiastical administration.[90] A more recent outline is provided by Noemi Rejchrtová in her unpublished habilitation thesis.[91] František Šmahel summarized the development of ecclesiastical structures during the Hussite wars in 1991.[92] Thomas A. Fudge has also focused

---

86   See the last version in his *Dějepis města Prahy*, vol. 9, 29–51, 324–61.
87   Jan Herben, "Církevní zřízení strany pod obojí," *Jednota* 1, 1–6 (1892).
88   Klement Borový, *Die Utraquisten in Böhmen* (Vienna: 1866).
89   Winter, *Život církevní v Čechách*.
90   Ferdinand Hrejsa, *Dějiny křesťanství v Československu*, vols. 2–4 (Prague: 1947–1948); Vladimír Sakař, "O účasti laiků na správě církve v husitství," *Theologická revue Církve československé husitské* 11, 6 (1978): 161–68.
91   Rejchrtová, *Studie k českému utrakvismu*.
92   Šmahel, "Pražská církevní provincie."

on the lower consistory.[93] In a focused study from 1999, Blanka Zilynská summarized the older views on the problem of church administration and the situation of the sources.[94] Consideration of church institutions also appears in Zdeňka Hledíková's contribution to the collective history of administration in the Czech lands.[95] Josef Macek's monograph on the Jagellonian period discussed the complex situation between Utraquists and Catholics, though the description of the administrative system is only one aspect of his study.[96]

Detailed investigations based on analyses of source materials from the period after 1526 are found in a number of master's theses (which are unfortunately not always accessible – one exception is the study by Jiří Rak[97]). These often build upon older studies by Kamil Krofta, which focused on the development of the lower consistory and the system of appointing administrators (though Krofta partially relied on certain later, less reliable sources coming from the second half of the 16th century).[98] Winfried Eberhard focused on the political aspects of the religious situation in the country at the turn of the 15th century, though he also touched upon developments within the consistory.[99] The works of Blanka Zilynská are devoted to the transformation of synodal practice.[100] From among earlier studies, Zdeněk Nejedlý published a small monograph on the topic of the synod of the Praguers and Taborites in the 1440s.[101] František Šmahel provided a condensed summary and new considerations on the Taborite clergy in his comprehensive history of Tábor.[102]

Equally worth mentioning are the works focused on the situation of the Catholic Church in the country. Zdeňka Hledíková, Antonín Mařík, and Veronika Macháčková drew upon the administrative acts of the Catholic consistory.[103]

---

93 Thomas A. Fudge, "Reform and the Lower Consistory in Prague 1437–1497," in *The Bohemian Reformation and Religious Practice*, eds. Zdeněk V. David and David R. Holeton, vol. 2 (Prague: 1998) 67–96.
94 Zilynská, "Utrakvistická církevní správa."
95 Hledíková, Janák, and Dobeš, *Dějiny správy*, 172–201.
96 Macek, *Víra a zbožnost*, 41–159; there is a useful annotated bibliography on the subject compiled by Martin Nodl and Jan Hrdina in the same volume at pp. 460–72.
97 Rak, "Vývoj utrakvistické správní organizace."
98 Krofta, "Boj o konsistoř."
99 Eberhard, *Konfessionsbildung*.
100 Zilynská, *Husitské synody*; "Synoden im utraquistischen Böhmen"; "Les nouvelles formes de la synodalité"; "Hussitische Synoden – die Vorläufer."
101 Nejedlý (ed.), *Prameny k synodám*.
102 František Šmahel, *Dějiny Tábora*, 2 vols. (České Budějovice: 1988–1990), vol. 2, 521–30.
103 Hledíková, "Administrace pražské diecéze"; eadem, "*Registrum perceptorum a sigillo*. Z agendy pražských administrátorů na konci 15. století," *Acta Universitatis Carolinae*. Philosophica et historica 1 (1975): 89–104; Mařík, "K postavení katolické církve"; idem, "Teritoriální rozsah"; Macháčková, "Církevní správa."

In her recent monograph, Zdeňka Hledíková also discussed the complex problem of clerical ordination in Hussite and post-Hussite Bohemia.[104] In a series of studies, Hana Pátková and Jan Hrdina uncovered various forms of religiosity held by believers of both faiths.[105] New research trends on the religious situation in 15th-century Bohemia focus on tractate literature, which is undoubtedly one way to broaden our knowledge, especially considering that official records have already been exhausted. The sources on ecclesiastical administration in the post-Hussite period are not as complex as those of the pre-Hussite era. Official acta of the Utraquist administration in the 15th century are mostly lost, though smaller fragments have been collected by Jindřich Marek and Renáta Modráková.[106] Acta from the Utraquist consistory are only available from the 1520s,[107] and the collection of the Kutná Hora consistory begins only a decade earlier.[108] The acta of the Unity of Brethren also provide information on the Utraquists.[109] The remaining references are thus scattered throughout municipal books, narrative sources, and correspondences, whose editions and archival locations cannot be included here.

Bibliography

Editions of Sources

Bidlo, Jaroslav (ed.), *Akty Jednoty bratrské* [Acts of the Unity of Brethren], 2 vols. (Brno: 1915–1923).

Borový, Klement (ed.), *Akta konsistoře utrakvistické* [*Acta* of the Utraquist consistory] (Prague: 1868).

Kalousek, Josef (ed.), *Archiv český čili Staré písemné památky české i moravské* [The Czech Archive, or Ancient written documents from Bohemia and Moravia], vol. 14 (Prague: 1895).

Kolár, Jaroslav, Anežka Vidmanová, Hana Vlhová-Wörner and David R. Holeton (eds.), *Jistebnický kancionál. MS. Praha, Knihovna Národního muzea, II C 7. Kritická edice.*

---

104   Zdeňka Hledíková, *Svěcení duchovenstva v církvi podjednou. Edice pramenů z let 1438–1521* (Prague: 2014).
105   E.g. Hana Pátková, *Bratrstvie ke cti Božie. Poznámky ke kultovní činnosti bratrstev a cechů ve středověkých Čechách* (Prague: 2000); Jan Hrdina, "Die Topographie der Wallfahrtsorte im spätmittelalterlichen Böhmen," in *Geist, Gesellschaft, Kirche im 13.-16. Jahrhundert*, ed. František Šmahel (Colloquia mediaevalia Pragensia) 1 (Prague: 1999), 191–206.
106   Modráková, *Zlomky rukopisů*.
107   Borový (ed.), *Akta konsistoře utrakvistické*.
108   Trnka, "Náboženské poměry při kutnohorské konsistoři."
109   Jaroslav Bidlo (ed.), *Akty Jednoty bratrské*, 2 vols. (Brno: 1915–1923).

Jistebnice kancionál. MS. Prague, National Museum Library II C 7, vol. 1: *Graduale* (Brno: 2005).

Nejedlý, Zdeněk (ed.), *Prameny k synodám strany Pražské a Táborské. Vznik husitské konfesse v létech 1441–1444* [Sources of the synods of the Prague and Tábor parties. The rise of the Hussite confession in 1441–1444] (Prague: 1900).

Palacký, František (ed.), *Archiv český čili Staré písemné památky české i moravské* [The Czech Archive, or Ancient written documents from Bohemia and Moravia], vol. 1 (Prague: 1840); vol. 3 (Prague: 1844).

Palacký, František (ed.), *Documenta Mag. Joannis Hus vitam, doctrinam, causam in Constantiensi concilio actam et controversias de religione in Bohemia annis 1408–1413 motas illustrantia* (Prague: 1869).

Papoušek ze Soběslavě, Jan, "Querele de motibus Bohemie," in: *Výbor z české literatury doby husitské*, eds. Bohuslav Havránek, Josef Hrabák, and Jiří Daňhelka, vol. 2 (Prague: 1964), 132–36.

Vaniš, Jaroslav (ed.), *Liber rationum civitatis Lunae ad annos 1450–1472 et 1490–1491 pertinens* (Prague: 1979).

Secondary Sources

Baker, Robin, "'Constantine from England and the Bohemians.' Hussitism, Orthodoxy, and the End of Byzantium," *Central Europe* 5 (2007): 23–46.

Borecký, František, *Mistr Jakoubek ze Stříbra* (Prague: 1945).

Borový, Klement, *Die Utraquisten in Böhmen* (Vienna: 1866).

Boubín, Jaroslav, "Mistr Jan z Rokycan. Stručný náčrt jeho životních osudů" [Master Jan of Rokycany. A brief outline of his fate], in *Žaloby katolíků na M. Jana z Rokycan*, eds. Jaroslav Boubín and Jana Zachová (Rokycany: 1997), 5–19.

Boubín, Jaroslav, *Petr Chelčický. Myslitel a reformátor* [Petr Chelčický. Thinker and reformer] (Prague: 2005).

Čelakovský, Jaromír, "Traktát podkomořího Vaňka Valečovského proti panování kněžstva" [The treatise of the subchamberlain Vaněk Valečovský against clerical dominion], *Věstník Královské české společnosti nauk* 36 (1881): 325–45.

Čornej, Petr, *Velké dějiny zemí Koruny české* [A comprehensive history of the lands of the Bohemian Crown], vol. 5 (Prague and Litomyšl: 2000).

Čornej, Petr, and Milena Bartlová, *Velké dějiny zemí Koruny české* [A comprehensive history of the lands of the Bohemian Crown], vol. 6 (Prague and Litomyšl: 2007).

Coufal, Dušan, *Polemika o kalich mezi teologií a politikou 1414–1431. Předpoklady basilejské disputace o prvním z pražských artikulů* [The polemic on the chalice between theology and politics, 1414–1431. Preconditions of the Basel disputation on the first Prague article] (Prague: 2012).

Doležalová, Eva, "Ways of clerics to ordination in the post-Hussite Bohemia – an outline," in *Roma – Praga. Praha – Řím: Omaggio a Zdeňka Hledíková*, eds. Kateřina Bobková-Valentová, Eva Doležalová, Eva Chodějovská, Zdeněk Hojda, and Martin Svatoš (Prague: 2009), 145–58.

Eberhard, Winfried, *Konfessionsbildung und Stände in Böhmen 1478–1530* (Munich and Vienna: 1981).

Elbel, Petr, "Zlomek olomoucké konfirmační knihy z let 1452–1455. Předběžné výsledky rozboru opomíjeného pramene k poznání církevní topografie, diecézní správy a konfesního soužití na Moravě po polovině 15. století" [A fragment of the Olomouc confirmation book from 1452–1455. Preliminary results of the analysis of a neglected source for church topography, diocese administration and confessional coexistence in Moravia in the mid-fifteenth century], in *Církevní topografie a farní síť pražské církevní provincie v pozdním středověku*, eds. Jan Hrdina and Blanka Zilynská (Colloquia mediaevalia Pragensia) 8 (Prague: 2007), 91–137.

Elbel, Petr, "Správa utrakvistické církve na Moravě mezi husitskou revolucí a reformací [Administration of the Utraquist Church in Moravia between the Hussite revolution and the Reformation]," in *Náboženský život a církevní poměry v zemích Koruny české ve 14.-17. století*, eds. Lenka Bobková and Jana Konvičná (Korunní země v dějinách českého státu) 4 (Prague: 2009), 126–44.

Felcman, Ondřej, and Radek Fukala (eds.), *Poděbradové. Rod českomoravských pánů, kladských hrabat a slezských knížat* [The Poděbrads. A lineage of Bohemian-Moravian lords, earls of Kłodsko and princes of Silesia] (Prague: 2008).

Fois, Mario, "Eklesiologie konciliarismu" [The ecclesiology of conciliarism], in *Jan Hus na přelomu tisíciletí*, eds. Miloš Drda, František J. Holeček, and Zdeněk Vybíral (Husitský Tábor. Supplementum) 1 (Tábor: 2001), 181–207.

Francek, Jindřich, "Úřad kostelníků v Jičíně a jejich kniha záduší z let 1431–1508" [The office of church wardens in Jičín and their book of chantry endowment from the years 1431–1508], *Sborník archivních prací* 31 (1981): 75–104.

Frind, Anton, *Die Kirchengeschichte Böhmens*, 4 vols. (Prague: 1864–1878).

Fudge, Thomas A., "Reform and the Lower Consistory in Prague 1437–1497," in *The Bohemian Reformation and Religious Practice*, eds. Zdeněk V. David and David R. Holeton, vol. 2 (Prague: 1998), 67–96.

Havránek, Bohuslav, Josef Hrabák, and Jiří Daňhelka (eds.), *Výbor z české literatury doby husitské* [An anthology of Czech literature of the Hussite period], 2 vols. (Prague: 1963–1964).

Herben, Jan, "Církevní zřízení strany pod obojí" [The church constitution of the Utraquist party], *Jednota* 1, 1–6 (1892), passim.

Heymann, Frederick G., "John Rokycana. Church Reformer between Hus and Luther," *Church History* 28 (1959): 240–80.

Heymann, Frederick G., "The Hussite-Utraquist Church in the Fifteenth and Sixteenth Centuries," *Archiv für Reformationsgeschichte* 52 (1961): 1–16.

Hilsch, Peter, *Johannes Hus (um 1370–1415). Prediger Gottes und Ketzer* (Regensburg: 1999).

Hlaváček, Ivan, "Konrad von Vechta. Ein Niedersachse im spätmittelalterlichen Böhmen," *Beiträge zur Geschichte der Stadt Vechta* 4 (1974): 5–35.

Hledíková, Zdeňka, *"Registrum perceptorum a sigillo.* Z agendy pražských administrátorů na konci 15. století" [*Registrum perceptorum a sigillo.* The agenda of Prague administrators at the end of the 15th century], *Acta Universitatis Carolinae. Philosophica et historica* 1 (1975): 89–104.

Hledíková, Zdeňka, "Administrace pražské diecéze na sklonku prvé poloviny 15. století" [The adminitration of Prague diocese at the end of the first half of the 15th century], *Acta Universitatis Carolinae – Historia Universitatis Carolinae Pragensis* 31 (1991): 117–28.

Hledíková, Zdeňka, "Donace církevním institucím v Čechách v prvém dvacetiletí 15. stol." (Statistický přehled) [Donation to church institutions in Bohemia in the first twenty years of the fifteenth century], in *Husitství – reformace – renesance. Sborník k 60. narozeninám Františka Šmahela*, eds. Jaroslav Pánek, Miloslav Polívka, and Noemi Rejchrtová, vol. 1 (Prague: 1994), 251–60.

Hledíková, Zdeňka, "Litomyšlské biskupství" [The bishopric of Litomyšl], in *Litomyšl. Duchovní tvář českého města*, ed. Milan Skřivánek (Litomyšl: 1994), 29–52.

Hledíková, Zdeňka, "Synoden in der Diözese Prag 1280–1417," in *Partikularsynoden im späten Mittelalter*, eds. Nathalie Kruppa and Leszek Zygner (Göttingen: 2006), 307–329.

Hledíková, Zdeňka, *Arnošt z Pardubic. Arcibiskup, zakladatel, rádce* [Arnošt of Pardubice. Archbishop, founder, advisor] (Prague: 2008).

Hledíková, Zdeňka, *Svět české středověké církve* [The world of the medieval Czech Church] (Prague: 2010).

Hledíková, Zdeňka, *Svěcení duchovenstva v církvi podjednou. Edice pramenů z let 1438–1521* [The ordination of clerics in the church *sub una.* An edition of the sources from the years 1438–1521] (Prague: 2014).

Hledíková, Zdeňka, Jan Janák, and Jan Dobeš, *Dějiny správy v českých zemích od počátků státu po současnost* [A history of administration in the Czech Lands from the origins of the state to the present] (Prague: 2005).

Horníčková, Kateřina, "Bishop Phillibert of Coutances and Catholic Restoration in Hussite Prague," in *Culture of Memory in East-Central Europe in the Late Middle Ages and the Early Modern Period (1000–1600)*, ed. Rafał Wójcik (Poznań: 2008), 255–64.

Horníčková, Kateřina, "Memory, Politics and Holy Relics. Catholic Tactics amidst the Hussite Reformation," in *Materializing Memory. Archaeological material culture and the semantics of the past*, eds. Irene Barbiera, Alice M. Choyke, and Judith A. Rasson

(Oxford: 2009), 97–103; reprinted in *The Bohemian Reformation and Religious Practice*, eds. Zdeněk V. David and David R. Holeton, vol. 8 (Prague: 2011), 133–42.

Hrdina, Jan, "Die Topographie der Wallfahrtsorte im spätmittelalterlichen Böhmen," in *Geist, Gesellschaft, Kirche im 13.-16. Jahrhundert*, ed. František Šmahel (Colloquia mediaevalia Pragensia) 1 (Prague: 1999), 191–206.

Hrejsa, Ferdinand: *Dějiny křesťanství v Československu* [A history of Christianity in Czechoslovakia], vols. 2–4 (Prague: 1947–1948).

Iwańczak, Wojciech, "Katolicy i husyci w czasach Jerzego z Podiebradu" [Catholics and Hussites in the time of George of Poděbrady], in *Stosunki międzywyznaniowe w Europie Środkowej i Wschodniej w XIV–XVII wieku*, eds. Marian Dygo, Sławomir Gawlas, and Hieronim Grala (Warszawa: 2002), 25–37.

Iwańczak, Wojciech, "Kościół w Czechach w XV w. – dezintegracja i łączność" [The Church in Bohemia in the fifteenth century – disintegration and communication], *Przegląd humanystyczny* 3 (2006): 21–30.

Jíšová, Kateřina, "Spása duše a očistec u novoměstských měšťanů. K religiozitě novoměstského měšťanstva v pozdním středověku" [The salvation of the soul and purgatory among citizens of Prague's New Town. On the piety of New Town citizens in the late Middle Ages], in *Evropa a Čechy na konci středověku. Sborník příspěvků věnovaných Františku Šmahelovi*, eds. Eva Doležalová, Robert Novotný, and Pavel Soukup (Prague: 2004), 253–68.

Kadlec, Jaroslav, *Katoličtí exulanti čeští doby husitské* [Czech Catholic exiles of the Hussite period] (Prague: 1990).

Kadlec, Jaroslav, *Přehled českých církevních dějin* [A survey of Czech church history], 2 vols. (Prague: 1991).

Kadlec, Jaroslav, "Hilarius Litoměřický v čele duchovenstva podjednou" [Hilarius of Litoměřice leading the clergy *sub una*], in *In memoriam Josefa Macka*, eds. Miloslav Polívka and František Šmahel (Prague: 1996), 187–94.

Kalina, Tomáš, "Hilarius Litoměřický," *Český časopis historický* 5 (1899): 311–21.

Kalina, Tomáš, "Václav Křižanovský," *Český časopis historický* 5 (1899): 333–59.

Kaminsky, Howard, "The University of Prague in the Hussite Revolution. The Role of Masters," in *Universities in Politics. Case Studies from the Late Middle Ages and Early Modern Period*, eds. John W. Baldwin and Richard A. Goldthwaite (Baltimore and London: 1972), 79–106.

Kavka, František, and Anna Skýbová, *Husitský epilog na koncilu tridentském a původní koncepce habsburské rekatolizace Čech. Počátky obnoveného pražského arcibiskupství 1561–1580* [The Hussite epilogue at the Council of Trent and the original concept of the Habsburg recatholicization of Bohemia. The beginnings of the renewed Prague archbishopric 1561–1580] (Prague: 1969).

Kejř, Jiří, *Mistři pražské univerzity a kněží táborští* [The masters of Prague university and the Taborite priests] (Prague: 1981).

Kejř, Jiří, *Jan Hus známý i neznámý. Resumé knihy, která nebude napsána* [Jan Hus known and unknown. A summary of a book that will not be written] (Prague: 2009; 2nd ed. 2015).

Kleinert, Christian, *Philibert de Montjeu (ca. 1374–1439). Ein Bischof im Zeitalter der Reformkonzilien und des Hundertjährigen Krieges* (Ostfildern: 2004).

Krafl, Pavel, *Synody a statuta olomoucké diecéze období středověku* [Synods and statutes of the Olomouc diocese in the medieval period] (Prague: 2003; 2nd ed. 2014).

Krmíčková, Helena, *Studie a texty k počátkům kalicha v Čechách* [Studies and texts on the beginnings of the chalice in Bohemia] (Brno: 1997).

Krofta, Kamil, "Boj o konsistoř pod obojí v letech 1562–1575 a jeho historický základ" [The struggle for the Utraquist consistory in the years 1562–1575 and its historical foundation], *Český časopis historický* 17 (1911): 28–57, 178–99, 283–303, 383–420.

Krofta, Kamil, *Václav Koranda mladší z Nové Plzně a jeho názory náboženské* [Václav Koranda the Younger of Nová Plzeň and his religious views] (Pilsen: 1914).

Kůrka, Pavel B., "Slovanský klášter mezi husitstvím a katolicismem. Dějiny klášterní komunity v letech 1419–1592" [The Slavonic monastery between Hussitism and Catholicism. The history of the monastic community in the years 1419–1592], in *Emauzy. Benediktinský klášter Na Slovanech v srdci Prahy*, eds. Klára Benešovská and Kateřina Kubínová (Prague: 2007), 107–24.

Kůrka, Pavel B., *Kostelníci, úředníci, měšťané. Samospráva farností v utrakvismu* [Church wardens, clercs, citizens. The self-administration of parishes under Utraquism] (Prague: 2010).

Kybal, Vlastimil, *M. Jan Hus. Život a učení* [Master Jan Hus. Life and teachings], Part 2: *Učení* [Teachings], 3 vols. (Prague: 1923–1931).

Lancinger, Luboš, "Čtyři artikuly pražské a podíl universitních mistrů na jejich vývoji" [The Four Articles of Prague and the role of university masters in their development], *Acta Universitatis Carolinae – Historia Universitatis Carolinae Pragensis* 3, 2 (1962): 3–61.

Landová, Tabita, *Liturgie Jednoty bratrské (1457–1620)* [The liturgy of the Unity of Brethren (1457–1620)] (Prague: 2014).

Macek, Josef, "Le mouvement conciliaire, Louis XI et Georges de Poděbrady (en particulier dans la période 1466–1468)," *Historica* 15 (1968): 5–63.

Macek, Josef, *Víra a zbožnost jagellonského věku* [The faith and piety of the Jagellonian period] (Prague: 2001).

Macháčková, Veronika, "Církevní správa v době jagellonské (na základě administrátorských akt)" [Church adminstration in the Jagellonian period (based on the administrators' acts)], *Folia Historica Bohemica* 9 (1985): 235–90.

Machilek, Franz, "Johannes Hoffmann aus Schweidnitz und die Hussiten," *Archiv für schlesische Kirchengeschichte* 26 (1968): 96–123.

Machilek, Franz, "Die Frömmigkeit und die Krise des 14. und 15. Jahrhunderts," *Mediaevalia Bohemica* 3 (1970): 209–27.

Marek, Jindřich, and Renáta Modráková, *Zlomky rukopisů v Národní knihovně České republiky* [Manuscript fragments in the National Library of the Czech Republic] (Prague: 2006).

Mařík, Antonín, "K postavení katolické církve v Čechách v době poděbradské. Činnost katolických administrátorů za Jiřího z Poděbrad" [On the position of the Catholic Church in Bohemia in the Poděbrad period. The activity of Catholic administrators in the time of George of Poděbrady], *Folia Historica Bohemica* 7 (1984): 101–96.

Mařík, Antonín, "Administrátoři a svatovítská kapitula v době poděbradské. Úřad administrátorů pod jednou a jeho představitelé" [Administrators and the St. Vitus chapter in the Poděbrad period. The office of the administrators *sub una* and its representatives], *Sborník archivních prací* 51, 2 (2001): 313–58.

Mařík, Antonín, "Svatovítská kapitula za vlády Jiřího z Poděbrad" [The St. Vitus chapter under the rule of George of Poděbrady], *Documenta Pragensia* 20 (2002): 25–53.

Mařík, Antonín, "Teritoriální rozsah katolické církevní správy v době Jiřího z Poděbrad na základě administrátorských akt" [The territorial extent of the Catholic church administration in the time of George of Poděbrady based on the administrators' acts], in *Církevní správa a její písemnosti na přelomu středověku a novověku*, ed. Ivan Hlaváček (Acta Universitatis Carolinae – Philosophica et historica) 1999, 2; (Z pomocných věd historických) 15 (Prague: 2003), 213–40.

Marin, Olivier, *L'archevêque, le maître et le dévot. Genèses du mouvement réformateur pragois. Années 1360–1419* (Paris: 2005).

Moravec, Milan, "Zástavy Zikmunda Lucemburského v českých zemích z let 1420–1437" [The pledges of Sigismund of Luxembourg in the Czech Lands from the years 1420–1437], *Folia Historica Bohemica* 9 (1985): 89–175.

Müller, Joseph Theodor, *Geschichte der Böhmischen Brüder*, vol. 1: *1400–1528*; vol. 2: *1528–1576*; vol. 3: *Die polnische Unität 1548–1793. Die böhmisch-mährische Unität 1575–1781* (Herrnhut: 1922–31).

Nechutová, Jana, "Die charismatische Spiritualität in Böhmen in der Vorreformatorischen Zeit," *Österreichische Osthefte* 39, 3 (1997): 411–19.

Nodl, Martin, *Dekret kutnohorský* [The Decree of Kutná Hora] (Prague: 2010).

Novotný, Robert, "Konfesionalizace před konfesionalizací? Víra a společnost v husitské epoše" [Confessionalization before confessionalization? Faith and society in the Hussite era], in *Heresis seminaria. Pojmy a koncepty v bádání o husitství*, eds. Pavlína Rychterová and Pavel Soukup (Prague: 2013), 233–66.

Novotný, Václav, *M. Jan Hus. Život a učení* [Master Jan Hus. Life and teachings], Part 1: *Život a dílo* [Life and works], 2 vols. (Prague: 1919–1921).

Nový, Rostislav, *Městské knihy v Čechách a na Moravě 1310–1526. Katalog* [Town books in Bohemia and Moravia 1310–1526. A catalogue] (Prague: 1963).

Pátková, Hana, *Bratrstvie ke cti Božie. Poznámky ke kultovní činnosti bratrstev a cechů ve středověkých Čechách* [Brotherhood in honor of God. Remarks on the cult activity of brotherhoods and guilds in medieval Bohemia] (Prague: 2000).

Paulová, Milada, "Styky českých husitů s cařihradskou církví" [Contacts of Czech Hussites with the Constantinople Church], *Časopis Musea Království českého* 92 (1918): 1–20, 111–21, 215–28.

Polc, Jaroslav V., *Česká církev v dějinách* [The Bohemian church in history] (Prague: 1999).

Polc, Jaroslav V., and Zdeňka Hledíková, *Pražské synody a koncily předhusitské doby* [Prague synods and councils in the pre-Husite period] (Prague: 2002).

Rak, Jiří, "Vývoj utrakvistické správní organizace v době předbělohorské" [The development of the Utraquist administrative organization before 1620], *Sborník archivních prací* 31 (1981): 179–206.

Rejchrtová, Noemi, *Studie k českému utrakvismu, zejména doby jagellonské* [Studies in Czech Utraquism, especially of the Jagellonian period], unpublished habilitation thesis, Charles University, Protestant Theological Faculty (Prague: 1984).

Říčan, Rudolf, *Dějiny Jednoty bratrské* [A history of the Unity of Brethren] (Prague: 1957).

Sakař, Vladimír, "O účasti laiků na správě církve v husitství" [On the participation of the laity in church administration under Hussitism], *Theologická revue Církve československé husitské* 11, 6 (1978): 161–68.

Salač, Antonín, *Constantinople et Prague en 1452* (Prague: 1958).

Šárovcová, Martina, "Cantate domino canticum novum. Iluminované hudební rukopisy české reformace" [Illuminated musical manuscripts of the Bohemian Reformation], in *Umění české reformace*, eds. Kateřina Horníčková and Michal Šroněk (Prague: 2010), 413–67.

Seibt, Ferdinand, "Konrad von Vechta," in idem, *Hussitenstudien. Personen, Ereignisse, Ideen einer frühen Revolution* (Munich: 1987), 241–52.

Šmahel, František, "Pražské povstání 1483" [The Prague insurrection of 1483], *Pražský sborník historický* 19 (1986): 35–102.

Šmahel, František, *Dějiny Tábora* [A history of Tábor], 2 vols. (České Budějovice: 1988–1990).

Šmahel, František, "Pražská církevní provincie ve víru husitské revoluce" [The Prague church province in the turbulence of the Hussite revolution], *Acta Universitatis Carolinae – Historia Universitatis Carolinae Pragensis* 31 (1991): 107–15.

Šmahel, František, "Die Prager Universität und Hussitismus," in *Die Universität in Alteuropa*, eds. Alexander Patschovsky and Horst Rabe (Konstanz: 1994), 111–28, reprinted in Franrtišek Šmahel, *Die Prager Universität im Mittelalter. The Charles University in the Middle Ages* (Leiden and Boston: 2007), 172–95.

Šmahel, František, *Husitské Čechy. Struktury, procesy, ideje* [Hussite Bohemia. Structures, processes, ideas] (Prague: 2001).

Šmahel, František, *Die Hussitische Revolution*, trans. Thomas Krzenck (Monumenta Germaniae Historica. Schriften) 43, 3 vols. (Hannover: 2002).

Šmahel, František, *Basilejská kompaktáta. Příběh deseti listin* [The Basel Compactata. A story of ten charters] (Prague: 2011).

Šmahel, František, *Jan Hus. Život a dílo* [Jan Hus. Life and work] (Prague: 2013).

Šmahel, František, "Drobné záhady rejstříku Rečkovy koleje" [Small mysteries of the Reček College register], *Acta Universitatis Carolinae – Historia Universitatis Carolinae Pragensis* 53, 2 (2013): 11–21.

Šmahel, František, and Ota Pavlíček (eds.), *A Companion to Jan Hus* (Brill's Companions to the Christian Tradition) 54 (Leiden and Boston: 2015).

Soukup, Pavel, "Kauza reformace. Husitství v konkurenci reformních projektů" [The case of the Reformation. Hussitism among competing reform projects], in *Heresis seminaria. Pojmy a koncepty v bádání o husitství*, eds. Pavlína Rychterová and Pavel Soukup (Prague: 2013), 171–217.

Soukup, Pavel, *Jan Hus* (Stuttgart: 2014).

Štědrý, František, "Rejstřík svěcenců na kněžství legáta sněmu basilejského Filiberta, biskupa kostnického" [A register of candidates for ordination of the Basel Council legate Philibert, bishop of Coutance], *Sborník Historického kroužku* 5 (1904): 92–98, 139–43.

Stočes, Jiří, "Původ a studium bratří Konráda a Konstantina z Vechty" [The origin and study of the brothers Konrad and Konstantin of Vechta], *Mediaevalia Historica Bohemica* 14, 2 (2011): 91–112.

Svatoš, Michal (ed.), *Dějiny Univerzity Karlovy* [A History of Charles University], vol. 1: 1347/48–1622 (Prague: 1995).

Tomek, Václav Vladivoj, "O církevní správě strany pod obojí v Čechách od r. 1415 až 1622" [On church administration of the Utraquist party in Bohemia from 1415 to 1622], *Časopis Českého museum* 22 (1848): 365–83, 441–68.

Tomek, Václav Vladivoj, "Rozdíly v náboženství a v církevním zřízení v Čechách v XV. století" [Differences in religion and church constitution in Bohemia in the 15th century], *Časopis Musea Království českého* 65 (1891): 145–64.

Tomek, Václav Vladivoj, *Dějepis města Prahy* [A history of the city of Prague], 12 vols. (Prague: 1855–1901).

Trnka, František, "Náboženské poměry při kutnohorské konsistoři r. 1464–1547" [The religious situation at the Kutná Hora consistory in the years 1464–1547], *Věstník Královské české společnosti nauk* (1934), Třída filosoficko-historicko-jazykozpytná, no. 5: 1–92.

Urbánek, Rudolf, *Věk poděbradský* [The Poděbrad era], 4 vols. (České dějiny) 3 (Prague: 1915–1962).

Urbánek, Rudolf, "Prvních sto let utrakvismu" [The first hundred years of Utraquism], in *Československá vlastivěda: Dějiny*, eds. Václav Novotný and Václav Dědina, vol. 4 (Prague: 1932), 163–340.

Válka, Josef, *Husitství na Moravě. Náboženská snášenlivost. Jan Amos Komenský* [Hussitism in Moravia. Religious Tolerance. Jan Amos Komenský] (Brno: 2005).

Vaněk, Lubomír, and Kapavíková, Marie, "Církevní správa" [Church administration], in *Průvodce po archivních fondech a sbírkách OA v Kutné Hoře* (Kutná Hora: 1970), 250–52.

Voit, Petr, *Český knihtisk mezi pozdní gotikou a renesancí: severinsko-kosořská dynastie 1488–1557* [Bohemian printing between Late Gothic and Renaissance. The Severin-Kosoř dynasty 1488–1557], vol. 1 (Prague: 2013).

Winter, Zikmund, *Život církevní v Čechách. Kulturně-historický obraz z XV. a XVI. století* [Church life in Bohemia. A cultural-historical picture from the 15th and 16th centuries], 2 vols. (Prague: 1895–1896).

Zilynská, Blanka, "Svěcení kněžstva biskupem Filibertem v Praze v letech 1437–1439" [The ordination of clergy by Bishop Philibert in Prague in the years 1437–1439], *Documenta Pragensia* 9 (1991): 361–88.

Zilynská, Blanka, "Biskup Filibert a české země" [Bishop Philibert and the Czech Lands], *Jihlava a Basilejská kompaktáta* (Jihlava: 1992), 56–94.

Zilynská, Blanka, "Záduší" [Chantry endowment], in *Facta probant homines. Sborník příspěvků k životnímu jubileu prof. dr. Zdeňky Hledíkové*, ed. Ivan Hlaváček (Prague: 1998), 535–48.

Zilynská, Blanka, "Utrakvistická církevní správa a možnosti jejího studia" [Utraquist church administration and the perspectives of its study], *Acta Universitatis Carolinae*, Philosophica et historica 2, Z pomocných věd historických 15 (1999): 29–53.

Zilynská, Blanka, "Jakoubek ze Stříbra a dobová církevní správa" [Jakoubek of Stříbro and the church administration of his time], in *Jakoubek ze Stříbra. Texty a jejich působení*, eds. Ota Halama and Pavel Soukup (Prague: 2006), 9–48.

Zilynská, Blanka, "Synoden im utraquistischen Böhmen 1418–1531," in *Partikularsynoden im späten Mittelalter*, eds. Nathalie Kruppa and Leszek Zygner (Göttingen: 2006), 377–86.

Zilynská, Blanka, "From Learned Disputation to the Happening. The Propagation of Faith through Word and Image," in *Public Communication in European Reformation. Artistic and other Media in Central Europe 1380–1620*, eds. Milena Bartlová and Michal Šroněk (Prague: 2007), 55–67.

Zilynská, Blanka, "Johann Hoffmann. Prager Student, antihussitischer Repräsentant und Bischof von Meißen," in *Universitäten, Landesherren und Landeskirchen. Das Kuttenberger Dekret von 1409 im Kontext der Epoche von der Gründung der Karlsuniversität 1348 bis zum Augsburger Religionsfrieden 1555*, ed. Blanka Zilynská (Acta Universitatis Carolinae – Historia Universitatis Carolinae Pragensis) 49, 2 (Prague: 2010), 81–98.

Zilynská, Blanka, "Les nouvelles formes de la synodalité à la fin du Moyen Âge. La Bohême dans le contexte de la Réforme européenne," in *Religious Space of East-Central Europe in the Middle Ages*, eds. Krzysztof Bracha and Paweł Kras (Warsaw: 2010), 79–100.

Zilynská, Blanka, "Z Burgundska až do husitských Čech. Životní pouť Filiberta de Montjeu. Opožděná reflexe biografické knihy" [From Burgundy to Hussite Bohemia. The life journey of Philibert de Montjeu. A belated reflection on a biography], *Historie – Otázky – Problémy* 3, 2 (2011): 127–142.

Zilynská, Blanka, "Hussitische Synoden – die Vorläufer der reformatorischen Synodalität," in *Die Hussitische Revolution. Religiöse, politische und regionale Aspekte*, ed. Franz Machilek (Cologne, Weimar, and Vienna: 2012), 57–75.

Zilynská, Blanka, "Město Praha a utrakvistická církev. Role konšelů při obsazování 'dolní konsistoře' (do r. 1547)" [The city of Prague and the Utraquist Church. The role of the councillors in appointing the "lower consistory" (to 1547)], *Documenta Pragensia* 33 (2014): 85–94.

Zilynská, Blanka, *Husitské synody v Čechách 1418–1440. Příspěvek k úloze univerzitních mistrů v husitské církvi a revoluci* [Hussite synods in Bohemia 1418–1440. A contribution to the role of the university masters in the Hussite church and revolution] (Prague: 1985).

Zilynská, Blanka: "Kališnická církev" [The Utraquist Church], in *Husitské století*, eds. Pavlína Cermanová, Robert Novotný, and Pavel Soukup (Prague: 2014), 586–605.

Zilynskyj, Bohdan, "Stížný list české a moravské šlechty proti Husovu upálení. Otázky vzniku a dochování" [The letter of complaint of the Bohemian and Moravian nobility against the immolation of Hus. The question of its origin and transmission], *Folia Historica Bohemica* 5 (1983): 195–237.

Zilynskyj, Bohdan, "Postavení utrakvistické a katolické konfese na Novém Městě pražském v letech 1436–1459 (Úvodní poznámky)" [The position of the Utraquist and Catholic confessions in the New Town of Prague in the years 1436–1459 (introductory remarks)], *Documenta Pragensia* 9, 2 (1991): 389–405.

PART 4

Theology and Religious Practice

∴

Key Issues in Hussite Theology

Dušan Coufal

Scholarship on Hussite theology admits three main intellectual sources for Hussite thought: John Wyclif,[1] the Czech reform tradition of the 14th century (most commonly referring to the so-called forerunners of Hus: Konrad Waldhauser, Milíč of Kroměříž, and Matěj of Janov), and, to a limited extent, Waldensianism.[2] Given that the focus of our attention here is the formation of Hussite theological doctrine in the period after Jan Hus's death, a fourth source of inspiration may also be added, namely, Hus's works themselves.[3]

The relationship between Hus and Hussitism, as well as the presumed influence of the first three intellectual inspirations on Hussite thought, is unclear. It is generally true that the most ardent defender of Wyclif in Bohemia after 1415 was his countryman Peter Payne, and that over the course of the 1420s and early 1430s there were numerous disputations related to Wyclif between the Taborite radicals and the Prague masters.[4] Jan Hus's direct relationship to the legacy of preachers that have been called his predecessors is today viewed more and more critically; conversely, the influential reception of Matěj of Janov's works by Jakoubek of Stříbro – from 1408 at the latest – is indisputable,[5] and thus we will give increased attention to them here. A clear connection

---

[1] This study was supported by a grant from the Czech Science Foundation (GA ČR): "Cultural Codes and Their Transformations in the Hussite Period" (P405/12/G148).

[2] These sources of inspiration were recently assessed from the perspective of reformist strategies by Pavel Soukup, *Reformní kazatelství a Jakoubek ze Stříbra* (Prague: 2011), 44–120, and from the perspective of the history of political thought by Vilém Herold, "Ideové kořeny reformace v českých zemích," in *Dějiny politického myšlení*, vol. 2/2: *Politické myšlení pozdního středověku a reformace*, eds. Vilém Herold, Ivan Müller, and Aleš Havlíček (Prague: 2011), 161–236.

[3] See Amedeo Molnár, "Husovo místo v evropské reformaci," *Československý časopis historický* 14 (1966): 4–5. On Hus see František Šmahel and Ota Pavlíček (ed.), *A Companion to Jan Hus* (Brill's Companions to the Christian Tradition) 54 (Leiden and Boston: 2015).

[4] William R. Cook, "John Wyclif and Hussite Theology 1415–1436," *Church History* 42 (1973): 335–49; Jiří Kejř, *Mistři pražské univerzity a kněží táborští* (Prague: 1981); František Šmahel, "Wyclif's Fortune in Hussite Bohemia," in idem, *Die Prager Universität im Mittelalter. The Charles University in the Middle Ages* (Leiden and Boston: 2007), 484–89.

[5] The concept of "forerunners" comes from František Palacký [under the pseudonym J.P. Jordan], *Die Vorläufer des Hussitenthums in Böhmen* (Leipzig: 1846); followed by Václav Novotný, *Náboženské hnutí české ve 14. a 15. stol. Část 1. Do Husa* (Prague: 1915); and more recently, by Vilém Herold, "The Spiritual Background of the Czech Reformation. Precursors of Jan Hus," in *A Companion to Jan Hus*, eds. Franti̇sek Šmahel and Ota Pavlíček (Brill's Companions to the

between Waldensianism and the emergence of the Hussite movement is as yet unproven. The German group of masters in the Prague University circle *U černé růže* (At the Black Rose) (the so-called Dresden School) is often mentioned as supporting evidence, though current research indicates that the influence may have gone the other way.[6]

The intellectual sources of Hussite thought certainly determined its character. The Prague reformist preaching movement of the 14th century was particularly oriented toward the moral reform of the church and society rather than the reform of doctrine,[7] and so the improvement of church practice was emphasized over refined theological speculation. This kind of practically oriented theology remained characteristic for the later Hussites as well. It is natural, therefore, that the main media of Hussite thought were not only university *quaestiones*, but also occasional polemical tractates, individual sermons to the clergy, as well as popular preaching collections and rhymed satirical compositions, including songs. The thought of the Hussite masters, priests, and preachers was openly communicated to both clerical and lay audiences.[8] This was also expressed by the fact that theological reflections, originally in Latin, were made available in the vernacular.[9] The social dimension of Hussite theology is also significant for any consideration of Hussitism as a heresy or reformist movement, or of the movement more generally as bringing about a

---

Christian Tradition) 54 (Leiden and Boston: 2015), 69–95. The discussion was summarized by Soukup, *Reformní kazatelství*, 11–21.

6 The scholarship on this topic is summarized in the volume edited by Albert de Lange and Kathrin Utz Tremp, (eds.), *Friedrich Reiser und die "waldensisch-hussitische Internationale"* (Heidelberg, Ubstadt-Weiher, and Basel: 2006), esp. by Petra Mutlová, "Die Dresdner Schule in Prag. Eine waldensische 'Connection'?," 261–76; cf. Soukup, *Reformní kazatelství*, 64–66.

7 Thomas A. Fudge, "The 'Law of God.' Reform and Religious Practice in Late Medieval Bohemia," in *The Bohemian Reformation and Religious Practice*, ed. David R. Holeton, vol. 1 (Prague: 1996), 50.

8 Amedeo Molnár, "K otázce reformační iniciativy lidu. Svědectví husitského kázání," in *Acta reformationem bohemicam illustrantia*, vol. 1: *Příspěvky k dějinám utrakvismu*, ed. Amedeo Molnár (Prague: 1978), 5–44.

9 See Pavlína Rychterová, "Theology Goes to the Vernaculars. Jan Hus, 'On simony,' and the Practice of Translation in Fifteenth-Century Bohemia," in *Religious Controversy in Europe, 1378–1536. Textual Transmission and Networks of Readership*, eds. Michael Van Dussen and Pavel Soukup (Turnhout: 2013), 231–50; eadem, "The Vernacular Theology of Jan Hus," in *A Companion to Jan Hus*, eds. Frantisek Šmahel and Ota Pavlíček (Brill's Companions to the Christian Tradition) 54 (Leiden and Boston: 2015), 170–213; Marcela K. Perett, "John Příbram and his Vernacular Treatises. Equipping the Laity in Battle against Hussite Radicals," in *Christianity and Culture in the Middle Ages. Essays to honor John Van Engen*, eds. David C. Mengel and Lisa Ann Wolverton (Notre Dame: 2015), 419–35.

reformation.[10] The link between Hussite intellectuals, preachers, priests, and other social strata does not, however, mean that the consideration of the problems of church practice and morality lacked deeper theoretical considerations.[11]

In what follows, particular attention is given to the thought of Matěj of Janov and Jakoubek of Stříbro, though texts by Nicholas of Dresden, Jan Želivský, Peter Payne, Jan Rokycana, and Mikuláš of Pelhřimov will also be considered.[12] While existing attempts to form a synthetic understanding of Hussite theological thought – beginning with the writings of Amedeo Molnár – more or less approach this material as biographically and chronologically structured within a framework of the "Bohemian" or "First" Reformation,[13] here the material is approached differently, according to four logically connected thematic sections. The first two focus on important normative or prescriptive concepts such as *lex* (*Dei*), *regula* (*Christi*), *Sacra scriptura*, and *ecclesia primitiva* in the texts of the aforementioned authors. This conceptual background further reflects the theoretical basis of the key aspect of contemporary religious practice, and our third thematic focus, the eucharistic

---

10   Amedeo Molnár, "Husovo místo v evropské reformaci," *Československý časopis historický* 14 (1966): 7; Robert Kalivoda, "K otázkám myšlenkového modelu tzv. první a druhé reformace," in *Bratrský sborník*, eds. Rudolf Říčan, Amedeo Molnár, and Michal Flegl (Prague: 1967), 120–26; Pavel Soukup, "Kauza reformace. Husitství v konkurenci reformních projektů," in *Heresis seminaria. Pojmy a koncepty v bádání o husitství*, ed. Pavlína Rychterová and Pavel Soukup (Prague: 2013), 171–217; Wolf-Friedrich Schäufele, "'Vorreformation' und 'erste Reformation' als historiographische Konzepte. Bestandsaufnahme und Problemanzeige," in *Jan Hus. 600 Jahre Erste Reformation*, eds. Andrea Strübind and Tobias Weger (Munich: 2015), 209–31.

11   Marxist historiography emphasized the social dimension of Hussite thought at the expense of the religious one; see Robert Kalivoda, *Revolution und Ideologie. Der Hussitismus*, trans. Heide Thorwart and Monika Gletter (Cologne: 1976); Miloslav Ransdorf, *Kapitoly z geneze husitské ideologie* (Prague: 1986). A methodologically more balanced study is Howard Kaminsky, *A History of the Hussite Revolution* (Berkeley and Los Angeles: 1967), esp. 1–3, who considers Hussite teachings in a broad context, as does František Šmahel, *Die Hussitische Revolution*, trans. Thomas Krzenck (Monumenta Germaniae Historica. Schriften) 43, 3 vols. (Hannover: 2002), vol. 2: 717–1006.

12   A basic overview of relevant figures and their works can be found in Amedeo Molnár, "Über Quellen zur Theologiegeschichte des Hussitentums," *Communio viatorum* 30 (1987): 253–69.

13   See Amedeo Molnár, "Eschatologická naděje české reformace," in *Od reformace k zítřku* (Prague: 1956), 11–101; idem, "L'évolution de la théologie hussite," *Revue d'histoire et de philosophie religieuses* 43 (1963): 133–71; idem, *Pohyb teologického myšlení* (Prague: 1982), 150–295; idem, "The Ideological Significance of Hussitism," *Communio viatorum* 31 (1988): 103–25; following Molnár, see Martin Wernisch, *Husitství. Raně reformační příběh* (Brno: 2003); Ota Halama, "Husitské teologické myšlení," in *Husitské století*, eds. Pavlína Cermanová, Robert Novotný, and Pavel Soukup (Prague: 2014), 401–14.

communion in both kinds. The final section deals with the intellectual background of the Four Articles of Prague as the programmatic common denominator of all Hussite parties.

1   *Lex, Regula, Scriptura, Iudex* – A Search for Norms

A key theological concept in Hussite thought was *lex Dei* (or *divina, Christi, evangelica*),[14] a topic to which Jan Hus himself dedicated two independent works. In the *quaestio De lege divina* (1408?), Hus distinguished between three laws: God's law, natural law, and human law (*lex divina, naturalis*, and *humana*). God's law was partially uncreated, eternal, and pre-existing in the mind of God, and partially created, the truth leading man to the proper service of God.[15] In the *quaestio De sufficiencia legis Cristi* (1414) – which he intended to present at the Council of Constance – Hus expressed himself on the topic of law in greater detail. Here he also maintained that the law, in the true sense of the word, is the truth leading one to the attainment of blessedness. He understood the concept abstractly on the one hand, as the first truth, and concretely on the other, as a specific kind of truth; the former referred to God's law, the latter to human law, though these were not contradictory. God's law, and thus the law of Christ, primarily referred to the law of God expressed in Scripture, but more broadly speaking, every true law somehow contained in Scripture could also be called the law of God. Only that human law contained in Scripture, however – whether explicitly or implicitly – is true.[16] With this theocratic approach to law, Hus was a proper Wycliffite, as was Mikuláš Biskupec, for instance. As long as it was perfectly fulfilled, it would be the law of Christ which, according to Wyclif, regulated the proper administration of the state ("lex Christi plene iusticiam docet rempublicam regulare").[17]

---

14 On the notion of God's law in general, see Theo Mayer-Maly, "Rechtsphilosophie und Rechtstheologie im Mittelalter," in *Theologische Realenzyklopädie*, vol. 28 (Berlin and New York: 1997), 216–27.

15 Jan Hus, "Questio de lege divina," in *Magistri Iohannis Hus Questiones*, ed. Jiří Kejř (Magistri Iohannis Hus Opera omnia) 19a (Corpus christianorum. Continuatio mediaevalis) 205 (Turnhout: 2004), 19.

16 Jan Hus, "De sufficiencia legis Cristi," in *Magistri Iohannis Hus Constantiensia*, eds. Helena Krmíčková, Jana Nechutová, Dušan Coufal, Jana Fuksová, Lucie Mazalová, Petra Mutlová, Libor Švanda, Soňa Žákovská, and Amedeo Molnár (Magistri Iohannis Hus Opera Omnia) 24 (Corpus christianorum. Continuatio mediaevalis) 274 (Turnhout: 2016), 48.

17 On the concept of God's law in Wyclif, see Howard Kaminsky, "Wycliffism as Ideology of Revolution," *Church History* 32 (1963): 66–67 (here also a quote from Wyclif's *De civili dominio*). The reception of this passage by Biskupec has not been recognized: see Mikuláš

In regard to Hus's *quaestiones* and their intellectual foundation, the connection of the Hussite concept of *lex Dei* with John Wyclif's metaphysics has recently been rightly emphasized,[18] although this was only one source of Hussite thought. Another was the extensive *Regulae Veteris et Novi Testamenti* by Matěj of Janov from the turn of the 1380s and 1390s, which approached the concept of church and societal improvement according to thirteen rules. The first and second books introduced four rules for the discretion of spirits (*discretio spirituum*) and eight rules for the assessment of hypocrisy and false holiness. Immediately in the first tractate of the third book, *De regula in se*, Matěj introduced the thirteenth, and most important, rule, which he called the general, principal rule (*regula generalis, principalis*), or the first truth (*veritas prima*). This rule was fundamentally distinct from the others, for it contained an ontological character; it was simultaneously the second person of the Trinity, Christ the Son, which bound divinity to creation. According to the Book of Revelation, this "first truth" was inscribed three times into the history of the created world: as a natural law (*lex naturalis*), containing all creation; as a written law (*lex scripta*), namely the Ten Commandments; and finally as the law of grace (*lex gratiae*) of Jesus Christ. Its content was the commandment of love, and for mankind the new inscription of this law meant, on the one hand, the renewal of internal self-knowledge, and on the other, the opportunity to see God's image in oneself more clearly. Aided by this rule, mankind was to conform to the unchangeable exemplar of all being, Jesus Christ, with an important role being played by the Eucharist and its proper reception as frequently as possible, as this was the path to mystical union with Christ and to union among people.[19]

In the scholarship, the normative concepts of *regula generalis* (Matěj of Janov) and *lex Dei* (Jan Hus) have been labeled as both identical and distinct.[20] In particular, it has recently been noted that in his naming of the first truth, Hus did not use the term "rule" (*regula*), but rather the stronger, firmer, and

---

Biskupec of Pelhřimov, *Confessio Taboritarum*, eds. Amedeo Molnár and Romolo Cegna (Rome: 1983), 66–67, where Mikuláš combines Wyclif with Hus's "De sufficiencia."

18 Stephen E. Lahey, "Wyclif, the 'Hussite Philosophy,' and the Law of Christ," in *The Bohemian Reformation and Religious Practice*, eds. Zdeněk V. David and David R. Holeton, vol. 9 (Prague, 2014), 54–71.

19 Matěj of Janov, *Regulae Veteris et Novi Testamenti*, vols. 1–4, ed. Vlastimil Kybal (Innsbruck: 1908–1913). See also Martin Dekarli, "Od pravidla (*regula*) k zákonu (*lex*), od nápravy k reformě. Doktrinální analýza transformace principů myšlení rané české reformace (1392–1414)," in *O felix Bohemia! Studie k dějinám české reformace*, ed. Petr Hlaváček (Prague: 2013), 44–50.

20 See Jana Nechutová, "Kategorie zákona božího a M. Matěj z Janova," *Sborník prací Filozofické fakulty brněnské univerzity* E 12 (1967): 211–21.

more prescriptive term, "law" (*lex*).[21] Nevertheless, we should note that, in his *Regulae*, Matěj of Janov used not only the term *regula*, but also the category of *lex*, even if less frequently. Immediately in his first rule on the discretion of spirits, he maintained that human acts, considerations, and counsels should be scrutinized to correspond to God's law.[22] Most of all, as mentioned above, Matěj identified the first truth with the three laws, and also maintained that the thirteenth rule, Christ, was "the law of life and the rule of all truth and teachings."[23] Thus, although *regula* stood conceptually at the forefront of Matěj's thought, there already existed a certain christocentric connection between *regula* and *lex*.

In any case, such a connection anticipated the thinking of Jakoubek of Stříbro, who was among the first known readers of Matěj's works after his death and also knew the works of John Wyclif.[24] At Prague University in August 1412, Jakoubek defended Wyclif's article on church property, and in the introduction to his *quaestio* stated that he would decide on the matter of clerical poverty according to the precept of Christ (*regula Christi*). He understood the *regula Christi* to be the truth of Christ's life, teachings, and preaching – none other than the evangelical law (*lex evangelica*) – that led believers to blessedness.[25] Twenty years later, at the introduction to the negotiations with the Council of Basel, Jakoubek's successor Jan Rokycana expressed the matter similarly: the evangelic and apostolic teaching is an immaculate law, a means, a rule, and a word to order human thought and feeling (*intellectum hominis et affectum*). Once we subordinate our judgement (*iudicium*) to it, we will realize who is a heretic and who a Catholic, what is correct and what is false. Moreover, according to Rokycana, since the Hussites wanted to live piously and appropriately, they worked with all of their being, actions, and thought to subordinate themselves to this evangelical teaching, the law of perfect freedom, like the infallible precept of 2 Cor. 10:5.[26]

---

21   See Dekarli, "Od pravidla (*regula*) k zákonu (*lex*)," 56, where Hus's reception of John Wyclif is considered to be responsible for the aforementioned change of the "conceptual field of thinking." See also Martin Dekarli, "The Law of Christ (*Lex Christi*) and the Law of God (*Lex Dei*) – Jan Hus's Concept of Reform," in *The Bohemian Reformation and Religious Practice*, eds. Zdeněk V. David and David R. Holeton, vol. 10 (Prague, 2015), 49–69.

22   Matěj of Janov, *Regulae*, vol. 1, lib. 1, cap. 3, 30.

23   Ibid., vol. 2, lib. 3, tract. 1, cap. 11, 30: "lex vite et regula omnis veritatis et discipline."

24   See Jan Sedlák, "Husův pomocník v evangeliu," *Studie a texty k náboženským dějinám českým* 1 (1914): 371 and 373–74.

25   Jakoubek of Stříbro, "Ditare clerum," in *Mistra Jana Husi Tractatus responsivus*, ed. S. Harrison Thomson (Prague: 1927), 161.

26   Jan Rokycana, "Collatio super Matth. 2,2," in *Veterum scriptorum et monumentorum historicorum, dogmaticorum, moralium amplissima collection*, ed. Edmond Martène and Ursin Durand, vol. 8 (Paris: 1733), 258C-259A.

For Jakoubek and Rokycana, *regula* and *lex* were two sides of the same coin, the same norm that simultaneously included the what (*doctrina*) and how (*vita*), or the theoretical and practical dimensions, of truth. This truth would lead one to recognize the true and the false, and thus to attain salvation. It was important, then, that this norm apply to every Christian. In a sermon from 1413/1414, Jakoubek explicitly stated that Christ's life, from the beginning to the end, had been the truest precept for a Christian's life. The most useful reminder of his suffering, therefore, was to live according to the example provided by Christ himself.[27] With their christocentric emphasis on the Christian lifestyle according to Christ's rule, Jakoubek – and Rokycana even more markedly – also conducted a latent polemic with established religious orders, whose hypocrisy had already been criticized by Wyclif, Matěj of Janov, and others. It was Wyclif who wrote that Christ was the abbot of all, and that friars should abandon their orders and become members of the free sect of Jesus Christ. Thus, the religious ideal previously reserved for the religious clergy became in Hussitism a principal for all of society.[28]

The life of Christ, however, had yet another important function in Jakoubek's and Rokycana's thought: that of hermeneutics. In 1417, Jakoubek was provoked to write a *replica* on the scathing report of Jean Gerson, the foremost theologian of the Council of Constance, on the matter of the lay chalice. Gerson formulated ten theoretical and ten practical guidelines to deal with the Hussite heresy, addressing proper biblical interpretation among the former.[29] Jakoubek postulated four of his own guidelines against Gerson, which merit further attention.

First, Jakoubek admitted the veracity of Gerson's first rule: "Holy Scripture is the rule of faith (*regula fidei*) against which, properly understood (*bene intellecta*), no human authority or argument can stand; nor does any tradition,

---

27   See Jakoubek of Stříbro, *Postilla*, Prague, Knihovna Národního muzea, XIV E 4, fol. 97r: "Vita enim Cristi, quam duxit a principio sui usque mortem, est verissima regula cristiani, secundum quam dirigi deberemus in vita nostra. Illa enim utillissima est memoria passionis: vivere sic, sicut ipse nobis exemplavit."

28   Kaminsky, "Wycliffism as Ideology of Revolution," 62–63, with references to relevant sources.

29   Gerson's tractate *De necessaria communione laicorum sub utraque specie* is edited in Jean Gerson, *Œuvres complètes*, ed. Palémon Glorieux (Paris, 1973), vol. 10, 55–68. On Gerson's hermeneutics, see recently David Zachariah Flanagin, "Making Sense of It All: Gerson's Biblical Theology," in *A Companion to Jean Gerson*, ed. Brian Patrick McGuire (Brill's Companions to the Christian Tradition) 3 (Leiden and Boston: 2006), esp. 161–63; Ian Christopher Levy, "Holy Scripture and the Quest for Authority among Three Late Medieval Masters," *Journal of Ecclesiastical History* 61 (2010): 40–68.

provision, or opinion which we can show to be contrary to Scripture."[30] This agreement between both theologians may primarily be explained by the fact that Scripture was for both men the sufficient (namely, the exclusive) source of God's theophany. The agreement of their guidelines diverged, however, in their distinct understandings of *bene intellecta*. While Gerson found the guarantor of authentic interpretation outside of Scripture, in the established tradition of the church, Jakoubek identified it in the Bible itself: "Insofar as it suffices for the salvation of humanity, the most faithful, most truthful, most reliable, and clearest expositor of Holy Scripture is the way of life (*vita practica*) of Jesus Christ, his apostles, and also his other holy followers in the church."[31] The life of Jesus Christ (and the apostles), therefore, was for Jakoubek not only the proper model for each Christian's life, but also the guarantor of the proper understanding of Scripture. Jan Rokycana was still convinced of this in the 1460s.[32]

In his third rule, Jakoubek explained why the discussion of the relevant (biblical) figures became a decisive hermeneutical principle. For him, the way of life of Christ, the apostles, and the primitive church was an infallible achievement of the Holy Spirit, and thus was a useful, effective, and living interpretation of the Bible. The criterion of the authentic Christian life also found its way into the fourth of Jakoubek's rules, in which he highlighted the expositions of the holy doctors Jerome, Ambrose, Augustine, and Gregory the Great, as they supposedly interpreted Scripture more faithfully and authentically (particularly in instances of mutual agreement) than the thousands of modern interpreters who were polluted by worldly ambitions.

Indeed, Jakoubek similarly argued that post-biblical tradition could not be attributed the same authority as Scripture, but conversely, must be subservient to it: "The expositions of the doctors, the established church, tradition, norms, and human laws which interpret and illuminate Scripture," Jakoubek said, "should be piously, humbly, and diligently subjected to it, and should serve it in all the ways a servant does a lord and a handmaiden does a mistress." They should be employed only to the extent that they are founded in Scripture and

---

30   I use Jakoubek's unedited polemical reply *Contra Gerson* from the manuscript copy in Prague, Archiv Pražského hradu, Knihovna Metropolitní kapituly, D 51, fols. 167v-176v, quote at fol. 168r.

31   Ibid. See Dušan Coufal, "Výklad a autorita bible v polemice mezi Janem Gersonem a Jakoubkem ze Stříbra z roku 1417," *Listy filologické* 131 (2008): 54–62; Pavel Spunar, *Repertorium auctorum Bohemorum provectum idearum post universitatem Pragensem conditam illustrans*, vol. 1 (Studia Copernicana) 25 (Wrocław: 1985), vol. 1, no. 610.

32   Noemi Rejchrtová, "Pravda zákona Kristova v pochopení pozdního utrakvismu," in *Epitoauto. Sborník k pětašedesátinám Petra Pokorného*, eds. Jiří Mrázek, Štěpán Brodský, and Rut Dvořáková (Prague: 1998), 15, with a quote for the source.

that could be shown by means of effective reason (*racione vivaci*).³³ In another of his tractates, Jakoubek explicitly applied the same norm to the teachings of Augustine and Jan Hus,³⁴ while Hus himself repeatedly endorsed the normativity of Scripture and reason according to the model of Wyclif.³⁵ Similarly, Nicholas of Dresden was willing only to subject himself to the truth of the Lord's law, and to those canonical and civil laws founded upon it.³⁶

In summary, *lex Christi/Dei* in Hussite thought ordered the behavior of the Christian to lead him to salvation, sufficing entirely for the conduct of the church militant (and ideally, even the state). *Lex*, of course, was included in Holy Scripture, because only Scripture was full and fully a sufficient source of God's theophany (the rules of faith and life). The life of Christ and the primitive church were the hermeneutical keys to proper scriptural understanding, since they were led by the Holy Spirit, which alone conveyed the effective and life-giving exposition of the Bible. The relation of *lex/regula Christi* (as the truths of Christ's life and teaching) to *Sacra scriptura* for Jakoubek was thus principally of a hermeneutical nature, just as for Matěj of Janov the *regula principalis*, thrice inscribed into history in the form of law, was an assurance of true Christian (self-) understanding.

After 1417, Jakoubek's normative considerations became the shared inheritance of the moderate Prague Hussites and the Taborite radicals led by Mikuláš of Pelhřimov in their collective attempt to defend the program of the Four Prague Articles in a free, public debate.³⁷ Over time, this inheritance crystallized into a prescriptive formula of faith (first appearing in its fixed form in 1429 at the Bratislava negotiations) which the Hussites were able to assert as the decisive norm of the negotiations on the Four Articles with the Council of Basel. As its adoption came during the negotiations in Cheb in May 1432, it is

---

33   Prague, Archiv Pražského hradu, Knihovna Metropolitní kapituly, D 51, fol. 172r.
34   Extracts from Jakoubek's work *Plures tractatuli pullulant* were printed in Romolo Cegna, "Początki utrakwizmu w Czechach w latach 1412–1415," *Przegląd historyczny* 69 (1978): 113.
35   See, for example, Alexander Patschovsky, "Ekklesiologie bei Johannes Hus," in *Lebenslehren und Weltentwürfe im Übergang vom Mittelalter zur Neuzeit*, eds. Hartmut Boockmann, Bernd Moeller, and Karl Stackmann (Göttingen, 1989), 393, n. 70, with references to the sources.
36   Nicholas of Dresden, "Sermo ad clerum de materia sanguinis," in *Nicolai (ut dicunt) de Dresda vulgo appellati de Čerruc (de Černá Růže id est de Rosa Nigra [† 1418?]) Puncta*, ed. Romolo Cegna (Mediaevalia Philosophica Polonorum) 33 (Warsaw: 1996), 158–59.
37   Franz Machilek, "Die hussitische Forderung nach öffentlichem Gehör und der Beheimsteiner Vertrag von 1430," in *Husitství – reformace – renesance. Sborník k 60. narozeninám Františka Šmahela*, eds. Jaroslav Pánek, Miloslav Polívka, and Noemi Rejchrtová, vol. 2 (Prague: 1994), 503–27; Dušan Coufal, *Polemika o kalich mezi teologií a politikou 1414–1431. Předpoklady basilejské disputace o prvním z pražských artikulů* (Prague: 2012), 103–275.

often called the Cheb Judge (*Iudex Egrensis*), which says: "... the law of God, the practice of Christ, the apostles, and the primitive church, together with the councils and teachers who are properly founded in them, will be adopted as the most truthful and impartial judge."[38] In other words, the judge was to be the truth which led mankind to salvation as revealed in Scripture, illustrated by the truth of the life of Christ and the primitive church, together with those traditions which complied with an understanding reached in this way.[39] It was not by chance that Jan Hus (following Wyclif), Nicholas of Dresden, Jakoubek of Stříbro, and Mikuláš of Pelhřimov repeatedly cited the words of Ps.-Chrysostom's *Opus imperfectum in Matthaeum*, that "every doctor is a servant of the law, for he cannot add to the law anything from his own head (*de suo sensu*), nor can he remove anything from it in his exposition, but can only preach that which is in the law ... For the Lord of the law is Christ ..."[40] In Hussite thought, therefore, priority was given to God's law over church tradition, which Hussites did not completely reject, but regarded with discrimination.

2 *Ecclesia primitiva* – A Noetic Instrument of Reform

As mentioned above, the Hussite search for an infallible norm was motivated by the desire to discern the true from the false, the heretic from the Catholic. One of the most important noetic tools of reform for the Hussites in this endeavor was the life of the apostolic church.[41]

---

38 Article 7 of the Cheb agreement reads as follows: "In causa quatuor articulorum, quam ut praefertur prosequuntur, lex divina, praxis Christi, apostolica et ecclesiae primitivae unacum conciliis doctoribusque fundantibus se veraciter in eadem pro veracissimo et indifferenti judice in hoc Basiliensi concilio admittentur"; see František Palacký and Ernst Birk (eds.), *Monumenta conciliorum generalium seculi decimi quinti. Concilium Basileense*, Scriptores: vol. 1 (Vienna: 1857), vol. 1, 220. Cf. Amedeo Molnár, "Chebský soudce," in *Soudce smluvený v Chebu. Sborník příspěvků přednesených na symposiu k 550. výročí* (Prague: 1982), esp. 27–28.

39 See Amedeo Molnár, "Zur hermeneutischen Problematik des Glaubensdisputs im Hussitentum," in *Studien zum Humanismus in den Böhmischen Ländern*, ed. Hans-Bernd Harder, Hans Rothe (Cologne and Vienna: 1988), esp. 96–99.

40 Ps.-Chrysostom, "Opus imperfectum in Matthaeum," in *Patrologiae cursus completus. Series Graeca*, ed. Jacques-Paul Migne, vol. 56 (Paris: 1859), 747. For citations in the works of Hussite authors, see Romolo Cegna's introduction to Nicholas of Dresden, "Sermo ad clerum de materia sanguinis," 171, n. 58.

41 The most detailed accounts of the primitive church in Hussitism are Jana Nechutová, "Ecclesia primitiva v husitských naukách," *Sborník prací Filozofické fakulty brněnské univerzity* E 33 (1988): 87–93 and Dan Török, "The Ideal of the Primitive Church in the Early Reformation," in *The Bohemian Reformation and Religious Practice*, eds. Zdeněk V. David

Already for Matěj of Janov, the primitive church of the saints (*ecclesia sanctorum primitiva*) represented sure knowledge in a time of hypocrites and great divisions in spiritual matters. He explicitly spoke of the "infinite multitude of the Antichrist," who could be revealed and identified by comparing their qualities with those of the primitive church of the saints.[42] Matěj's noetic method was the antithetical juxtaposition, and he clearly demonstrated the ways in which the contemporary church erred and where it required correction. The theme of unity was key for him, and its disturbance was a result of the cooling of mutual love. Matěj judged that a merely formal, external manner of Christian unity was insufficient, and provided Christians instead with the example of belonging with Christ and his apostles, in a unity of spirit and heart with the true primitive church.[43] The greater the internal unity of love (*unitas intrinseca dilectionis*) in the church, the greater the external unity in customs and mores, and thus the greater the sharing of all things. According to Matěj, this was why it was written of the church of the first Christians that they had everything in common and no one claimed ownership of anything.[44] This made it all the more difficult for him to endure, therefore, the fact that the uncontrolled desire of his contemporaries to claim and own earthly goods was not only judged as sinless, but honorable and wise, while those who relied solely on the poor Christ were deemed foolish.[45] Here, Matěj particularly targeted the hypocritical monks and friars who asserted a monopoly on the states of perfection, the apostles, and the primitive church,[46] while in reality they lusted for vain renown and riches over that love which esteems the order of the primitive church and is commanded for all.[47] With this, Matěj followed earlier critiques

---

and David R. Holeton, vol. 10 (Prague: 2015), 144–57. The tradition goes back to the 12th century: see Thomas J. Renna, "The Primitive Church according to Jean Gerson and the Dutch Anabaptists," *Fifteenth Century Studies* 20 (1993): 276–77. The conciliarists also worked in the same tradition, using the primitive church to justify general councils and the larger decentralization of the Church. See Louis Bernard Pascoe, "Jean Gerson: The *Ecclesia Primitiva* and Reform," *Traditio* 30 (1974): 379–410 and Thomas Prügl, "Urkirche und frühchristliche Praxis als Legitimationsstrategie im Basler Konziliarismus," *Archa Verbi* 9 (2012): 136–60.

42 Matěj of Janov, *Regulae*, vol. 3, 184.
43 Ibid., vol. 2, 185.
44 Ibid., vol. 2, 174.
45 Ibid., vol. 3, 48–49.
46 Ibid., vol. 3, 62.
47 Ibid., vol. 2, 283.

of mendicants by Konrad Waldhauser, Milíč of Kroměříž, and also William of Saint-Amour, with whose writings he became familiar in Paris.[48]

Also necessary and useful for the unity of the church would be the reduction of the number of false holy men and masters who promoted and praised only themselves, and who ought to be led back to their proper, original state in the hierarchy of the Holy Church – namely, they ought to be subordinated to their immediate superiors, such as curate priests and bishops,[49] for few in the primitive church desired positions of leadership.[50]

When faced with the biblical state of the primitive church, however, Matěj observed not only the fatal failure of the contemporary one with regard to its internal, spiritual unity – which was smashed, divided, and confused by hypocritical ambitions, the uncontrolled lust for property, renown, and status, and the false piety of pilgrimages and reliquaries – but also highlighted the contradiction between the contemporary and primitive churches' approaches to eucharistic communion, and placed his greatest hope in the correction of corrupted Christianity in overcoming this contradiction. According to Matěj, all of Scripture predicted that Christ's church would be corrected before the end of the world.[51] Those believing and expecting this could already observe its onset in those who were zealous in the spirit of the primitive church, and who enthusiastically received the eucharistic sacrament daily. As long as those who desired it were able to take daily communion openly, the adornment and glory (*decor et gloria*) of the primitive church would return and the spiritual Sodom would revert to its ancient dignity, both unachievable by means of the spiritual sacrament alone, namely by the hearing of the mass.[52] For Matěj, therefore, the importance of frequent communion lay precisely in the fact that it was a means by which the spirit of the primitive church persisted.[53]

This norm of the primitive church, understandably, was not foreign to Jan Hus, who in his *De ecclesia*, for instance, drew attention to the fact that this church's administration survived with only priests and deacons.[54] Again, however, we are particularly interested in the reflections of Jakoubek of Stříbro, who applied the ideal of the primitive church in a broad reformist

---

48   On William, see Kaminsky, *A History*, 14, and Olivier Marin, *L'archevêque, le maître et le dévot. Genèses du mouvement réformateur pragois. Années 1360–1419* (Paris: 2005), 275–84.
49   Matěj of Janov, *Regulae*, vol. 2, 303.
50   Ibid., vol. 3, 45.
51   Ibid., vol. 5, 207.
52   Ibid., vol. 5, 355.
53   Ibid., vol. 5, 206–08.
54   Jan Hus, *Magistri Johannis Hus Tractatus de ecclesia*, ed. S. Harrison Thomson (Cambridge, Eng., and Boulder, CO.: 1956; repr. Prague: 1958), 127–28.

context. In his postil from 1413/1414, he wrote that the baptized Christian ought to love the Holy Church of the old saints (*ecclesiam sanctam antiquorum sanctorum*), run to her in times of danger and find joy therein, and "gradually allow himself to be nurtured by their texts" (*nutriri eorum documentis*).[55] The primitive church was the guide and protector of Christians in their spiritual life.

Jakoubek expanded his understanding of the primitive church in detail in his Czech exposition of Revelation (1420–1421).[56] What especially fascinated him was the perfect order of the primitive church, which guided everything via Christ and the apostles.[57] It had just judges, through whom God judged fairly.[58] In it there were good pastors and humble, God-fearing priests; they were the kingdom of God.[59] Every Christian loved Christ and the Holy Spirit filled their hearts. They suffered martyrdom and God's commandments shone in them.[60] For Jakoubek, the primitive church was even the ideal for worldly rule, since according to him, wicked people and kings were not to be found in it. This was also the case in early Christian Bohemia, when good rulers like St. Wenceslas "hated the beastly life and destroyed sins."[61]

Thus for Jakoubek, as for Matěj of Janov, it was important that the modern church learn from the example of the primitive one.[62] In the time of the Antichrist, it was necessary to be in company with people who would bear witness to the practice of the primitive church – with those bearing witness to Christ's life against disorder and sin.[63] As long as people heard God's law, they would readily conform their lives to it; they would hold to it and fulfill it with the

---

55 See Jakoubek of Stříbro, *Postilla*, fol. 132v, quoted by Vlastimil Kybal, *M. Jan Hus. Život a učení*, Part 2: *Učení*, 3 vols. (Prague: 1923–1931), vol. 1, 143, n. 1. Cf. Jindřich Marek, *Jakoubek ze Stříbra a počátky utrakvistického kazatelství v českých zemích. Studie o Jakoubkově postile z let 1413–1414* (Prague: 2011), 201.

56 See Pavlína Cermanová, "Jakoubek ze Stříbra a tradice apokalyptických proroctví a jejich výkladů v husitství," in *Amica – sponsa – mater. Bible v čase reformace*, ed. Ota Halama (Prague: 2014), 131–33. In connection to the topics discussed here, see Pavlína Cermanová, "Jakoubkův a Biskupcův Výklad na Apokalypsu. Porovnání s důrazem na intepretaci antikristovského mýtu," in *Jakoubek ze Stříbra. Texty a jejich působení*, eds. Ota Halama and Pavel Soukup (Prague: 2006), 214–16, where the author points out that also Mikuláš Biskupec's Expostition on Revelation was permeated by the ideal of the primitive church, which Mikuláš considered to have been realized in the Tábor community.

57 Jakoubek of Stříbro, *Výklad na Zjevenie sv. Jana*, ed. František Šimek (Prague: 1932–1933), vol. 1, 26–27.

58 Ibid., vol. 1, 189–90.

59 Ibid., vol. 1, 592.

60 Ibid., vol. 2, 27.

61 Ibid., vol. 2, 108.

62 Ibid., vol. 1, 51–52.

63 Ibid., vol. 1, 51–53.

deeds of the saints of the primitive church, for through this conformity man came to know God.[64]

As in numerous earlier texts, Jakoubek also dealt with the relationship between spiritual and physical battle in his exposition of John's Revelation. He maintained that, just as in the first, so in the final church a difficult struggle will take place. Thus, it was important and wise for people to know the nature of this struggle and to understand spiritual battle, since the dragon (the devil) was deceptive and could transform this holy, spiritual battle of God into a satanic, beastly, and physical battle.[65] Perhaps reminiscing over the deaths of Hus, Jerome, and others, he argued that the structure of the primitive church was introduced by martyrdom, and not by the wars to which he was a witness. Even if it was permitted for some to battle for Christ's will, according to Jakoubek, it was dangerous to do so, because the whole army would suffer for any individual's sin. Only those should enter battle, therefore, who kept in mind God's law concerning love for one's enemy.[66] Already in 1413 he expressed himself in similar terms, emphasizing that it was first necessary to carry on an internal war within oneself with spiritual arms, and with the prospect of spiritual rewards according to God's law, as Christ did on earth. According to the example of the primitive church, therefore, the uprooting of public sins – namely, the power of the Antichrist – such as fornication, simony, the hypocrisy of monks, etc., should be the responsibility of secular powers informed by God's wisdom.[67] Nor did Jakoubek doubt the means of correcting the church via the secular powers in his exposition of Revelation, for kings in the primitive church greatly supported the turn to Christianity.[68]

Proper knowledge was also important because Satan, in his cleverness, was able to employ even the example of the primitive church to serve his own goals. There once had been good shepherds, spiritual and secular alike, and their subordinates had been subservient to them in obedience, love, patience, and repentance. Preachers were confirmed by elders in their faithfulness, their interest in people's salvation, and their teaching of truth. Now it was different,

---

64   Ibid., vol. 1, 407–08.
65   Ibid., vol. 1, 469. Cf. Pavel Soukup, "Metaphors of the Spiritual Struggle Early in the Bohemian Reformation. The Exegesis of Arma Spiritualia in Hus, Jakoubek, and Chelcický," in *The Bohemian Reformation and Religious Practice*, eds. Zdeněk V. David and David R. Holeton, vol. 6 (Prague: 2007), 87–109.
66   Jakoubek of Stříbro, *Výklad na Zjevenie*, vol. 1, 559.
67   Jakoubek of Stříbro, "Ad bellum," in Pavel Soukup, "Dobývání hradu Skály v roce 1413 a husitská teorie války. Ke spisku Jakoubka ze Stříbra o duchovním boji," *Mediaevalia historica Bohemica* 9 (2003): 205–06.
68   Jakoubek of Stříbro, *Výklad na Zjevenie*, vol. 1, 33.

as the "great thrones" were filled with hypocrites who asked their subordinates to obey them even in matters which were against Scripture and God; the Lord's Prayer was in their mouths, but they kneeled before the Beast in their hearts.[69]

Another of Jakoubek's antithetical juxtapositions is also noteworthy: in the primitive church there had been unity of speech, preaching, and deed, while in the modern church there was diversity in law, love, and truth.[70] Jakoubek details what he meant by unity of speech elsewhere. The great unity of the primitive church rested on the fact that it praised God together in its own language, so even the lowest people had cried "Amen" to confirm that which they heard and understood. But the language had changed to a foreign one, and someone else now answered for the people.[71] This argument also supported the Hussite emphasis on the accessibility of God's Word in the vernacular,[72] though as we have seen, the matter was not comprehension itself, but the unity which originated from it. Jakoubek not only used the primitive church as a measure for the institutional, Roman Church, but also to criticize the excesses of the Taborite radicals, especially on the matter of the Eucharist.[73] His references to the primitive church, therefore, were not primarily meant as incentives for some utopian return to the past, but rather to promote correct knowledge in his contemporaries and their self-improvement as a result.

The intellectually radical Nicholas of Dresden used the ideal of the primitive church as a tool for proper understanding, striving for the correction of the contemporary church in an illustrative way, as exemplified in two of his texts: *Tabule veteris et novi coloris* (1412) and the *Consuetudo et ritus primitive ecclesie et moderne, seu derivative* (1412?). In these writings Nicholas used collections of authorities (which he called tables) to place the primitive and modern Roman churches, as well as the lives of Christ and the Antichrist, in opposition. Like Matěj of Janov and Jakoubek, Nicholas also emphasized the spiritual character of the primitive church, in which the Holy Spirit worked visibly and no ritualization was required, though this came afterwards, once the Spirit was weakened by a slackening of faith. Nicholas fervently contrasted the power and jurisdiction of both churches, deeming the hierarchical structure of the contemporary church to be far removed from its original state. Nor did he shy away from critiques of simony, pompous dress, and the offices of mendicants

---

69   Ibid., vol. 1, 560.
70   Ibid., vol. 1, 579.
71   Ibid., vol. 1, 248–49.
72   See, in a different context, Dušan Coufal, "Výklad a autorita bible v polemice mezi Janem Gersonem a Jakoubkem ze Stříbra z roku 1417," *Listy filologické* 131 (2008): 60.
73   Ibid., vol. 2, 179.

and bishops.[74] One of the sources he drew upon for his critique was the Wycliffite exposition on John's Revelation, *Opus arduum valde*, in which the juxtaposition of the primitive and modern churches appeared frequently.[75]

The search for correct knowledge or understanding via the ideal of the primitive church later became the shared inheritance of both radical and moderate Hussites. From the end of the decade, the radical Prague preacher Jan Želivský, who was familiar with the works of Nicholas of Dresden, Jakoubek of Stříbro, Matěj of Janov, and Jan Hus, repeatedly used antithetical juxtapositions in his sermons. On one side, he described the Christian law, the Gospel, and the primitive church as in the Acts of the Apostles, and on the other he placed the law of the Antichrist with human customs that suffocated the old faith. He was similarly charmed by the charismatic primitive church, in which life was ordered according to the power of the Holy Spirit.[76]

Jan Rokycana likewise identified the victorious primitive church (*illa ecclesia primitiva jam triumphans*) as the most secure model for imitation (*exemplar tutissimum*) at the Council of Basel in 1433. In his opening speech – drawing on the words of Matěj of Janov – he elaborated one of the great contradictions between the age of the primitive church and the contemporary age, where virtue was forced to cower and hide. Thus, according to Rokycana, the truth of the primitive church's life and doctrine will reveal and judge the hypocrisy of his own time.[77] Face to face with the council, Rokycana again recalled the prescriptive conceptualizations of his chief Czech instructors, Matěj of Janov and Jakoubek of Stříbro.

---

74   Nicholas of Dresden, "Tabule veteris et novi coloris seu cortina de Anticristo," in *Master Nicholas of Dresden. The Old Color and the New. Selected Works Contrasting the Primitive Church and the Roman Church*, eds. Howard Kaminsky, Dean Loy Bilderback, Imre Boda and Patricia N. Rosenberg (Transactions of the American Philosophical Society, New Series) 55, 1 (Philadelphia: 1965), 38–65; on this work, see recently Petra Mutlová, "Communicating Texts through Images. Nicholas of Dresden's *Tabulae*," in *Public Communication in European Reformation. Artistic and other Media in Central Europe 1380–1620*, eds. Milena Bartlová and Michal Šroněk (Prague: 2007), 29–37; Nicholas of Dresden, "Consuetudo et ritus primitive ecclesie et moderne, seu derivative," in *Master Nicholas of Dresden: The Old Color and the New. Selected Works Contrasting the Primitive Church and the Roman Church*, eds. Howard Kaminsky, Dean Loy Bilderback, Imre Boda and Patricia N. Rosenberg (Transactions of the American Philosophical Society, New Series) 55, 1 (Philadelphia: 1965), 66–85.

75   See Cegna, "Ecclesia Primitiva."

76   See Jan Želivský, *Dochovaná kázání z roku 1419*, ed. Amedeo Molnár (Prague: 1953), 117. Generally, see Alberto Cadili, "*Ecclesia moderna* und *ecclesia primitiva* in den Predigten des Jan Želivský," *Archa Verbi* 9 (2012): esp. 96–99.

77   Jan Rokycana, "Collatio super Matth. 2,2," col. 259B-260D. For the quote in col. 260AB, see Matěj of Janov, *Regulae*, vol. 3, 31.

3   *Communio calicis* – Between Sacrament and Symbol

We have already discussed how closely the considerations on the structure of the primitive church, the necessity of frequent communion, and the vision of a corrected church were associated in the thought of Matěj of Janov. Even if, while in Prague in the second half of the fourteenth century, the Parisian master was not alone in seeing the path toward the internalization and strengthening of the Christian faith in the practice of frequent eucharistic communion, in 1414 in Bohemia it was principally his works that fueled the renewal of lay reception of the sacrament in both kinds, bread and wine.[78] Nor were Wyclif's writings comparably influential on this matter. Though it is undoubtable that Nicholas of Dresden was also particularly engaged in the issue,[79] the sources convincingly identify the Prague Bachelor of Theology, Jakoubek of Stříbro, as the father of the concept of Bohemian Utraquism.[80] Here, Jakoubek spoke notably of a revelation (*revelatio*), by which he meant an understanding (*modus cognoscendi*) of the relevant theological literature – which, apart from the Bible, explicitly included Augustine, Cyprian, Bernard of Clairvaux, and John Chrysostom.[81]

The notion and practice of the Hussite chalice, on the one hand, drew from the application of the prescriptive concepts discussed in the previous sections, since according to Jakoubek the practice corresponded to God's law, Christ's precept, and the use of the primitive church. Yet the intellectual background of the chalice was more complicated. Gradually, between 1414 and 1418, Jakoubek advanced and developed three main, mutually connected, theological points, which he was driven in part to elaborate under pressure from his opponents, who were not exclusively Catholics. He was convinced that the reception of the sacrament in both kinds was necessary for salvation (*necessaria*), was

---

[78]   Books 4 and 5 of Matěj's *Regulae* are especially relevant in this context. On frequent communion in Matěj, see Ondřej M. Petrů, *Matěj z Janova o častém svatém přijímání* (Olomouc: 1946); in other Prague authors, see Marin, *L'archevêque*, 486–575. For more detail, see below.

[79]   Nicholas's Utraquist writings have recently been discussed by Mutlová in *Nicolai Dresdensis Apologia. De conclusionibus doctorum in Constantia de materia sanguinis*, ed. Petra Mutlová (Brno: 2015), 29–51.

[80]   All of the theories were assessed in detail by Helena Krmíčková, *Studie a texty k počátkům kalicha v Čechách* (Brno: 1997); see also eadem, "Utraquism in 1414," in *The Bohemian Reformation and Religious Practice*, eds. Zdeněk V. David and David R. Holeton, vol. 4 (Prague: 2002), 99–105.

[81]   See Ferdinand Seibt, "Die revelatio des Jacobellus von Mies über die Kelchkommunion," *Deutsches Archiv für Erforschung des Mittelalters* 22 (1966): 618–24.

beneficial or useful (*expediens/utilis*), and was commanded by Christ (*praecepta*).[82] The oft-portrayed symbol of the Hussite chalice, therefore, was one infused with powerful theological content referring to the true church, whose members stood in close fellowship with God and the angels.[83]

To understand Jakoubek's first point on the necessity of receiving the sacrament, we must first understand his close connection to the neo-Platonic view of the world in the Christian interpretation of Ps.-Dionysius the Areopagite. Only through sensory perception of those signs which we presume to be images of heavenly beauty can our limited intellects reach spiritual reality. For Jakoubek, therefore, only perfect Christians, already essentially living in the heavenly kingdom, are able to receive spiritual sacramental grace in the same way as angels (*modo angelico*) without the mediating sacrament as such (he called it *manducatio spiritualis tantum*). The majority of Christians are incapable of such an invisible reception of Christ, and thus require a more appropriate means to attain it. In the footsteps of Matěj of Janov, Jakoubek found this in the simultaneous spiritual and sacramental communion, which was none other than a combination of the spiritual preparation for worthy communion (such as piety, repentance, etc.) with the physical, sacramental communion. Yet if Christ established the sacramental reception of the Eucharist under both kinds for all without exception (*sine acceptione personarum*), as proven, according to Jakoubek, by the evangelists and the apostle Paul (particularly in 1 Cor. 11:28), then this form of communion would be an adequate means for imperfect Christians to reach the fruits of the otherwise unattainable reception in "the angelic method." Thus, the reception of the Eucharist on earth became for Jakoubek a real image of the full participation in Christ, which occurred in heaven and was only attainable to average Christians through perceivable signs.[84]

If, however, this image would be disturbed or unfulfilled, a pact (*pactum*) would be violated which, according to Jakoubek, Christ established in his sacraments between himself and his church; there would be a violation of the general law (*lex communis*) established by Christ. Therefore, Jakoubek saw that only via this proper communion in both kinds – according to the established pact – could the sacrament be beneficial to the recipient, since only in this way did he reach eucharistic grace according to his ability, which was necessary for

---

82 For a concise account of Jakoubek's defense of the lay chalice and an overview of his relevant works, see Dušan Coufal, "*Sub utraque specie*. Die Theologie des Laienkelchs bei Jacobell von Mies (†1429) und der frühen Utraquisten," *Archa Verbi* 14 (2017): 125–68.

83 See Milena Bartlová, "Původ husitského kalicha z ikonografického hlediska," *Umění* 44 (1996): 167–83.

84 Coufal, *Polemika o kalich*, 27–28, with references to relevant sources.

the preservation of a Christian life without deadly sins. For Jakoubek, the removal of one of the sacramental forms was an unbearable sacrilege which, by violating God's precept given to the faithful on the path to spiritual reality, would rob him of the salvific power which would otherwise flow from its proper reception. Thus, although Jakoubek did not deny that Christ was present truly and completely in both forms, he maintained that both represented a specific *modus figurandi*, and that their reception was not established by Christ without cause for those who were burdened by sense perception. Following this, we may more easily understand how Jakoubek found such a complex truth – that Utraquist communion was necessary for the salvation of the faithful – best expressed in John 6:54 ("Nisi manducaveritis carnem Filii hominis et biberitis eius sanguinem non habebitis vitam in vobis" [Unless you eat the flesh of the Son of Man and drink his blood, you have no life in you]), which he could only interpret as referring to the simultaneous spiritual and sacramental communion (although Jan Hus understood its content spiritually, as did the majority of 16th-century reformers).[85]

The basis for Jakoubek's opinion on the unique benefits of communion in both kinds was an argument by Albert the Great, who stated that the sacramental blood had effects distinct from the sacramental body. While Christ gave his body *in communionem*, he gave his blood *in redemptionem*. Under the first form, therefore, the worthy communicant participated in the mystical Body of Christ and his benefits; under the second he participated in the grace of redemption. Jakoubek illustrated this in an example borrowed from Thomas Aquinas: just as one and the same craftsman performs various tasks with the help of various tools, so one and the same Christ via bread and wine performs through these two sacraments various "works." In this way, the chalice that contained Christ's blood enacts in the spirits of the faithful the increase of grace (*augmentum gratiae*), for it is a different grace than that which flows to the faithful via the reception of Christ's Body.[86]

Jakoubek's requirement of the lay chalice, therefore, naturally and consequently followed from the emphasis on the salvific quality of frequent eucharistic communion, and his emphasis on *praeceptum* came from the same intellectual background. Jakoubek took seriously the weakness of the entire Christian community, especially the priests and their propensity toward sin, and stressed the necessity of a reasonable – namely, a perceivable and also spiritual – cure. In this context, he re-read previously collected authorities,

---

85   Coufal, *Polemika o kalich*, 28–29.
86   On this crucial aspect of Jakoubek's theology of the Chalice, see Coufal, "Sub utraque specie," 145–52.

who had themselves chosen the word *praeceptum*, and came to the conclusion that Christ not only established the eucharistic communion under both kinds, but also directly commanded it, an opinion he first emphasized in his tractate *Magna cena*.[87]

This rather radical eucharistic conception faced an immediate reaction not only from Catholics (particularly from the Czech Doctor of Theology Ondřej of Brod),[88] but was also opposed by some of Hus's own followers. It fell to Jan Hus, now in Constance, to ward off a deepening conflict. With the help of his friends, he developed a written position on the topic, naming the lay chalice as beneficial, but nothing more, and thus did not bind himself to Jakoubek's and Nicholas's view of the necessity of the chalice for salvation.[89]

No more than three years after the administration of the chalice to the adult laity had begun, Jakoubek of Stříbro drew new conclusions from his eucharistic teachings, as he began to argue for the necessity of administering Utraquist communion even to infants (the first references to which occur in 1416). Here also, the inspiration was the ancient custom of the Eastern Church.[90] Yet this step also faced opposition not only from Catholics, but also from conservative Hussites, such as Jan of Jesenice.[91]

---

87   Jakoubek's tractate *Magna cena* has been edited by Krmíčková, *Studie a texty*, 131–36. On the development of his thinking on the notion of *praeceptum*, see ibid., 24–25.

88   His treatises were edited and discussed by Jaroslav Kadlec, *Studien und Texte zum Leben und Wirken des Prager Magisters Andreas von Brod* (Münster: 1982); see also idem, "Literární polemika mistrů Jakoubka ze Stříbra a Ondřeje z Brodu o laický kalich," *Acta Universitatis Carolinae – Historia Universitatis Carolinae Pragensis* 21 (1981): 71–88.

89   Jan Hus, "De sumpcione sangwinis Iesu Cristi sub specie vini," in *Magistri Iohannis Hus Constantiensia*, eds. Helena Krmíčková, Jana Nechutová, Dušan Coufal, Jana Fuksová, Lucie Mazalová, Petra Mutlová, Libor Švanda, Soňa Žákovská, and Amedeo Molnár (Magistri Iohannis Hus Opera Omnia) 24 (Corpus christianorum. Continuatio mediaevalis) 274 (Turnhout: 2016), 103–16. On this *quaestio*, see Helena Krmíčková, "K pramenům Husovy kvestie De sanguine Christi sub specie vini," *Sborník prací Filozofické fakulty brněnské univerzity* C 45 (1998): 79–102, who stressed the importance of this writing for dating other early Utraquist works, esp. those by Jakoubek of Stříbro. From a theological perspective, see recently Pavel Kolář, "Husovo učení o přijímání eucharistie a jeho vztah k učení Jakoubkovu," in *Mistra Jan Hus v proměnách času a jeho poselství víry dnešku*, eds. Zdeněk Kučera and Tomáš Butta (Prague: 2012), 93–94.

90   On the *communio parvulorum* see David R. Holeton, *La communion des tout-petits enfants. Étude du mouvement eucharistique en Bohême vers la fin du Moyen Âge* (Rome: 1989); Helena Krmíčková, "Několik poznámek k přijímání maličkých 1414–1416," *Sborník prací Filozofické fakulty brněnské univerzity* C 44 (1997): 59–69.

91   Jiří Kejř, "Auctoritates contra communionem parvulorum M. Jana z Jesenice," *Studie o rukopisech* 19 (1980): 5–21; repr. in idem, *Z počátků české reformace* (Brno: 2006), 230–44.

4   *Articuli Pragenses quattuor* – The Program of Revolution

Already in the time of Matěj of Janov, the category of so-called human innovations (*adinventiones hominum*) played a unique role in Czech reformist thought. This referred to various forms of religious practice – often of a liturgical or administrative nature – which were judged corrupt or useless and were supposedly in contradiction to God's law. These were a thorn in the side of reformers, especially because they often went hand in hand with the superstitious faith and piety of the people, as well as the financial demands of the clergy.

One such innovation, as labeled by the Hussites, was the inappropriate veneration of the saints and holy images.[92] Authors that we might call Hussite were not always united in their discussion of these controversial matters. Still in the early 1430s, second-generation Hussite theologians like Jan Rokycana (for the moderate Utraquists) and Mikuláš Biskupec of Pelhřimov (for the Taborites) continued to argue about this matter. This dispute mainly involved the intellectual inheritance from Matěj of Janov, John Wyclif, and Jakoubek of Stříbro, but was also a matter of applying the shared theological norms described above. In the third part of his tractate *De septem culpis Taboritarum*, Rokycana allowed for the proper, appropriate cult of the saints, in continuity with older reformist tradition.[93] Biskupec's response, in his *Confessio Taboritarum*, conversely found no support for it in Scripture.[94]

As the Hussite revolution progressed, numerous matters of faith – closely connected to religious practice – were up for debate, and mutual understanding between moderate and radical Hussites often faced difficulty. With the death of King Wenceslas IV and the eruption of the revolution, it was urgent

---

[92] On medieval cults of saints in general, see, e.g. Barbara Abou-el-Haj, *The Medieval Cult of Saints. Formations and Transformations* (Cambridge: 1994); in the context of the Bohemian Reformation, see Ota Halama, *Otázka svatých v české reformaci. Její proměny od doby Karla IV. do doby České konfese* (Brno: 2002).

[93] Rokycana's tractate remains unedited. See František Michálek Bartoš, *Literární činnost M. Jana Rokycany, M. Jana Příbrama, M. Petra Payna* (Prague: 1928), no. 3, 23. Here I use Brno, Moravská zemská knihovna, Mk 112, fol. 168v-187r, which contains the passage on the third Taborite offense – that they do not revere the saints – and which has hitherto been wrongly considered an independent writing, see Zdeněk Uhlíř, "Die Texte über den Aberglauben in den tschechischen Handschriftensammlungen des Mittelalters," in *Religion und Magie in Ostmitteleuropa. Spielräume theologischer Normierungsprozesse in Spätmittelalter und Früher Neuzeit*, ed. Thomas Wünsch (Münster, Berlin, and Hamburg: 2006), 117.

[94] Mikuláš Biskupec, *Confessio Taboritarum*, 227–28; cf. Amedeo Molnár and František Mrázek Dobiáš, "Předmluva," in *Mikuláš z Pelhřimova. Vyznání a obrana Táborů*, eds. Amedeo Molnár and F.M. Dobiáš (Prague: 1972), 21–8.

that the diverse followers of Jan Hus clearly and concisely share the message behind their drive to reform church and society with the surrounding world. Thus in 1420, the Four Articles of Prague were born, demanding:

1) That the Word of God be freely preached in the Kingdom of Bohemia, without disturbance,
2) That the Eucharist be freely administered to the faithful without deadly sin under both its kinds, bread and wine,
3) That the clerical rule over secular domains – which is against the command of Christ and to the detriment of their office and secular rule – cease, and the clergy be returned to the rules of the Gospel (*ad regulam evangelicam*) and the apostolic life,
4) That all deadly sins, especially public ones, and other perversities opposing God's law, be properly and wisely prohibited in each estate, and combatted by those to whom the task appropriately falls.[95]

Although these were called the Prague Articles, the Taborite brothers staying in Prague during their official announcement undoubtedly were involved in their constitution and actively defended them in the following years. Over time, the order of the articles changed: for the theologians around Jakoubek, the most important point was the chalice, which they always placed first insofar as they could influence the order. The Taborite priests, on the other hand, preferred the articles regarding the public punishment of deadly sins and church poverty.[96] The culmination of the lengthy diplomatic and military effort by all the Hussite parties to defend these articles in front of a church assembly were the negotiations on the Prague Articles with the Council of Basel from 1433 to 1436, and the agreement on the mutual settlement, the so-called *Compactata*.[97]

---

[95] In Latin, see Vavřinec of Březová, "Kronika husitská," in *Fontes rerum Bohemicarum*, eds. Josef Emler, Jan Gebauer, and Jaroslav Goll, vol. 5 (Prague: 1893), 391–95. Substantiations consisting of quotes of varying length from the Bible, church fathers, and canon law were appended to individual claims.

[96] See Luboš Lancinger, "Čtyři artikuly pražské a podíl universitních mistrů na jejich vývoji," *Acta Universitatis Carolinae – Historia Universitatis Carolinae Pragensis* 3, 2 (1962): 3–61; František Šmahel, "Die Vier Prager Artikel. Das Programm der hussitischen Reformation," in *Kirchliche Reformimpulse des 14./15. Jahrhunderts in Ostmitteleuropa*, eds. Winfried Eberhard and Franz Machilek (Cologne, Weimar, and Vienna: 2006), 329–39; Karel Hruza, "Schrift und Rebellion. Die hussitischen Manifeste aus Prag von 1415–1431," in *Geist, Gesellschaft, Kirche im 13.-16. Jahrhundert*, ed. František Šmahel (Colloquia mediaevalia Pragensia) 1 (Prague: 1999), 81–108.

[97] On the Basel period, see Ernest Fraser Jacob, "The Bohemians at the Council of Basel 1433," in *Prague Essays*, ed. Robert Seton-Watson (Oxford: 1949), 81–123; Paul De Vooght, "La confrontation des thèses hussites et romaines au concile de Bâle (Janvier–Avril 1433),"

We have already partially observed how the germs of the individual articles could be found in the thought of Jakoubek of Stříbro and Nicholas of Dresden, and even that of Jan Hus and Matěj of Janov.[98] During the Basel negotiations in 1433, the philosopher Nicholas of Cusa expressed the justified position that, while three of the articles aimed for the improvement of morals, the matter of Utraquist communion was one of faith.[99] We noted above how the chalice, and the Hussite theology associated with it, was a problematic article of faith, but even the remaining articles carried with them the genetic code of the prescriptive thought described above. There is no space to detail their ideological background here, on the one hand because they were of an ecclesiastic-administrative nature rather than one of faith, and on the other because we are missing the necessary case studies. The following discussion, therefore, should rather be understood as a stimulus for further study of Hussite thought in its broad societal aspects.

The article requiring the freedom of preaching essentially had its roots in the Prague reformist preaching movement of the 14th century. The ideal, however, was molded primarily in the disputes of Jan Hus and his followers with the Prague theologians and church hierarchy in 1410–1412. Among other things, one matter was the exposition of Romans 10:15: "How can they preach, unless they are sent?" The Hussites assumed the necessity for every priest to preach, and they understood this verse as referring to the condition for their performance, namely a higher calling, especially of a moral standard. In other words, Hus, like Wyclif, acknowledged the right of a priest to preach God's Word without special previous permission from a bishop or pope. Indeed, he worked with a higher category than that of clerical ordination, namely the law inscribed in the heart (*lex privata*), the impetus from the Spirit of God. Thus, one who lived according to Christ's commandments had God's permission to preach in the time of need. Nicholas of Dresden drew upon Hus's thought to argue for the benefits of the lay apostolate, and even interpreted Hus's description

---

Recherches de théologie ancienne et médiévale 37 (1970): 97–137; František Šmahel, *Basilejská kompaktáta. Příběh deseti listin* (Prague: 2011).

98 Šmahel, *Die Hussitische Revolution*, vol. 1, 577–78; Šmahel, "Die Vier Prager Artikel," 329–30. The study by Mathilde Uhlirz, *Die Genesis der vier Prager Artikel* (Sitzungsberichte der Kaiserlichen Akademie der Wissenschaften in Wien, Philosophisch-Historische Klasse), 175, 3 (Vienna: 1914), is outdated; a modest bibliography of further works is found in Amedeo Molnár, "'Život v dobré proměniti.' Nad čtvrtým pražským artikulem," *Theologická revue Československé církve husitské* 16 (1983): 50, n. 1.

99 "Petri Zatecensis Orphanorum sactae presbyteri Liber diurnus de gestis Bohemorum in concilio Basileensi," in *Monumenta conciliorum generalium seculi decimi quinti. Concilium Basileense*, eds. František Palacký and Ernst Birk, Scriptores: vol. 1 (Vienna: 1857), 331.

of the internal vocation as supporting female preaching. Yet the lay apostolate did not immediately imply the Waldensian heresy, as shown by the preaching of the lay master Jerome of Prague.[100]

The third article on priestly dominion is markedly Wycliffite.[101] F.G. Heymann correctly identified this article as the most important politically, with great social repercussions.[102] Wyclif's revolutionary theory of rule is well known, according to which the right to ownership and dominion is dependent upon God's grace, and thus is possessed only by those who are in a state of grace, being predestined (*praedestinati*). Conversely, he who has committed deadly sin and has not repented – the foreknown (*praescitus*) – cannot legitimately possess anything.[103] The Hussites, however, were much more concerned with the practical dimension of the matter, and thus worked with the category of the apostolic life rather than grace as the decisive norm. Even here, though, they could rely on Wyclif, according to whom the clergy were meant to reign evangelically (*evangelice*) and not secularly (*civiliter*), and thus precisely in the way in which the third article demanded.[104] As expressed by the defense of this article in Basel by Wyclif's fellow countryman, Peter Payne, Wyclif's concern was not to deny the clergy any property whatsoever, but primarily secular or political possession (*possesio saecularis civilis aut politica*). Payne defined secular dominion (*dominium civile*) as the government established by man due to sin, and as belonging to human civil law (*ius humanum civile*), the task of which was to ensure conciliation in society by preventing the usurpation of one another's property. The clergy, however, had a special character and was meant to live apostolically (*apostolice*), and thus its possessions should be possessed communally and not secularly, as that of secular lords.[105] Conservative and moderate Hussites, such as Jan Příbram and Jan Rokycana, accused the

---

100   See Pavel Soukup, "'Jak mohou zvěstovat, nejsou-li posláni?' Autorita a autorizace kazatele u Husa a jeho současníků," in *Amica – sponsa – mater. Bible v čase reformace*, ed. Ota Halama (Prague: 2014), 122–42, with references to relevant sources; see also František Šmahel, "The Hussite Critique of the Clergy's Civil Dominion," in *Anticlericalism in Late Medieval and Early Modern Europe*, eds. Peter A. Dykema and Heiko A. Oberman (Leiden: 1993), 85–86.

101   For the larger context of Hussite anti-clericalism, see Šmahel, "The Hussite Critique."

102   Frederick G. Heymann, *John Žižka and the Hussite Revolution* (Princeton: 1965), 153–54.

103   Herold, "Ideové kořeny reformace v českých zemích," 233–34.

104   Kaminsky, "Wycliffism as Ideology of Revolution," 64–66, with a citation of the source.

105   Peter Payne, "Posicio M. Petri Englici in Basilea coram concilio," in *Petri Payne Anglici Positio, replica et propositio in concilio Basiliensi a. 1433 atque oratio ad Sigismundum regem a. 1429 Bratislaviae pronunciatae. Peter Payne pro Bohemis*, ed. František Michálek Bartoš (Tábor: 1949), 1–3.

Taborite priests of disregarding exactly this article in the latter's engagement in the administration of the Taborite community.[106]

The fourth article, on the punishment of public, deadly sins, is of Taborite provenance. It dealt with a catalogue of actions and activities harmful to society, such as fornication, prostitution, gluttony, drunkenness, theft, murder, false oaths, usury, war, selfishness, simony, the sale of indulgences, various fees and taxes, and bans.[107] The Hussite understanding of sin remained traditional; public sins (*peccata publica*) were to be corrected publicly, especially if they were deadly sins, namely, those that went against God's commandments (*contra praeceptum Dei*). Yet the Hussites were distinct from the medieval church in their desire to quickly punish and eliminate such sins. The more radical the interpretation of this article, the more consistently such sins pointed to social or societal injustice. The exiled Štěpán of Páleč called the article heretical and detrimental, since it supposedly violated the entire secular and spiritual establishment.[108] Also unique was the fact that Prague Utraquists gave control over the correction of sinners to a special office in which laymen were engaged, wherein there was a marked distinction from the traditional inquisitorial organ. Jan Žižka decided to realize this article in a more extreme and violent form, while the south Bohemian layman Petr Chelčický approached it entirely conversely, rejecting any violent enforcement of virtue.[109]

5   Conclusion

As illustrated by the various contemporary Hussite approaches toward the comprehension and application of the fourth article, Hussitism essentially resists any kind of summary description and straightforward assessment. Similarly, Hussite thought was never a uniform system, since it did not emerge primarily from scholastic theories, but was formed in reaction to the concrete late-medieval problems of church and society. It cannot, therefore, be easily

---

106   On Rokycana: František Mrázek Dobiáš, "Rokycanův spis De septem culpis," *Theologická příloha Křesťanské revue* 34 (1967): 109; on Příbram: Šmahel, "The Hussite Critique," 88–89.

107   See, e.g. Vavřinec of Březová, "Kronika husitská," 394.

108   The relevant passage from Stephen's treatise against the Four Articles, *De portis inferi*, is printed in Konstantin Höfler (ed.), *Geschichtschreiber der husitischen Bewegung in Böhmen*, 3 vols. (Fontes rerum Austriacarum, 1. Abteilung: Scriptores) 2, 6, and 7 (Vienna: 1856–65), vol. 2, 480: "totius politiae spiritualis et saecularis turbativus et exterminativus."

109   See Molnár, "Život v dobré proměniti," 50–61.

understood and described as a system. Nevertheless, in the works of those authors we can call Hussite, we find general concepts such as God's law, Christ's precept, and the primitive church, which for them were of fundamental importance: they led Christians to salvation by helping them to securely distinguish true Christianity from the false antichristianity at a time of the institutional church's failure, and offered every possibility for authentic knowledge of oneself and others. As expressed especially in the works of Jakoubek of Stříbro, a reform of the church (and society) conceived in this way attracted new enthusiasm as the thought of John Wyclif, on the one hand, and Matěj of Janov, on the other, were synthesized. Yet there were those who did not arrive at this synthesis, including Jan Hus himself. Others saw it critically, such as Jan Příbram in the 1420s and 30s. Still others, like the Taborites, took this synthesis to its extreme conclusions, even if these were distasteful to Jakoubek himself. Hussitism, therefore, just like Hussite thought, was a multi-layered entity, which, in the first three decades of the fifteenth century, is fascinating for its dynamism – a dynamism that repeatedly calls for new reflections.

6 Historiographic Survey

Because a uniform Hussite ideology never existed, each researcher must choose the extent to which (if at all) he or she will work to establish a common ground for Hussite theological thinking. To date, chronologically organized surveys of important figures, works, and ideas prevail, notably those of Amedeo Molnár,[110] Martin Wernisch,[111] Vilém Herold,[112] and Ota Halama.[113] Similar overviews form part of larger synthetic works on Hussitism, such as the histories of the Hussite revolution by Howard Kaminsky[114] and František Šmahel.[115] In general, Amedeo Molnár has been alone in proposing a thesis of one central and common idea of the Bohemian Reformation, which he identified as the eschatological hope. Molnár did not elaborate this thesis further, however, after he first introduced it in 1956.[116]

---

110 Molnár, "Eschatologická naděje"; *Pohyb teologického myšlení*.
111 Martin Wernisch, *Husitství. Raně reformační příběh* (Brno: 2003).
112 Herold, "Ideové kořeny reformace."
113 Halama, "Husitské teologické myšlení."
114 Kaminsky, *A History*.
115 Šmahel, *Die Hussitische Revolution*.
116 Molnár, "Eschatologická naděje."

Besides these synthetic overviews, we must rely primarily on individual analyses of more limited topics. Naturally, the following bibliography reflects only those selected themes that have been treated above. Among other relevant issues that have been omitted for practical reasons, there are topics such as Hussite ecclesiology or the question of remanence and the real presence of Christ in the Eucharist. Another major concern in Hussite theology is eschatology, which is treated elsewhere in this book.

In contrast to existing scholarship, the present essay proposes new possibilities for grasping Hussite theological thought by focusing on key concepts and notions that recur in the texts of relevant authors and on their application in specific instances. A full application of this approach is a matter of future research, which will also depend on the study and editorial treatment of a number of hitherto unpublished sources.

Translated by Martin Pjecha

Bibliography

Manuscripts

Brno, Moravská zemská knihovna [Moravian Library], Mk 112.

Prague, Knihovna Národního muzea [National Museum Library], XIV E 4 (Jakoubek of Stříbro, *Postilla per circulum anni*).

Prague, Archiv Pražského hradu, Knihovna Metropolitní kapituly [Prague Castle Archives, Library of the Metropolitan Chapter], D 51 (Jakoubek of Stříbro, *Contra Gerson*).

Editions of Sources

Gerson, Jean, *Œuvres complètes*, ed. Palémon Glorieux, vol. 10 (Paris, 1973).

Höfler, Konstantin (ed.), *Geschichtschreiber der husitischen Bewegung in Böhmen*, 3 vols. (Fontes rerum Austriacarum, 1. Abteilung: Scriptores) 2, 6, and 7 (Vienna: 1856–1865).

Hus, Jan, *Magistri Johannis Hus Tractatus de ecclesia*, ed. S. Harrison Thomson (Cambridge, Eng., and Boulder, CO.: 1956; repr. Prague: 1958).

Hus, Jan, "Questio de lege divina," in *Magistri Iohannis Hus Questiones*, ed. Jiří Kejř (Magistri Iohannis Hus Opera omnia) 19a (Corpus christianorum. Continuatio mediaevalis) 205 (Turnhout: 2004), 19–22.

Hus, Jan, "De sufficiencia legis Cristi," in *Magistri Iohannis Hus Constantiensia*, eds. Helena Krmíčková, Jana Nechutová, Dušan Coufal, Jana Fuksová, Lucie Mazalová, Petra

Mutlová, Libor Švanda, Soňa Žákovská, and Amedeo Molnár (Magistri Iohannis Hus Opera Omnia) 24 (Corpus christianorum. Continuatio mediaevalis) 274 (Turnhout: 2016), 39–63.

Hus, Jan, "De sumpcione sangwinis Iesu Cristi sub specie vini," in *Magistri Iohannis Hus Constantiensia*, eds. Helena Krmíčková, Jana Nechutová, Dušan Coufal, Jana Fuksová, Lucie Mazalová, Petra Mutlová, Libor Švanda, Soňa Žákovská, and Amedeo Molnár (Magistri Iohannis Hus Opera Omnia) 24 (Corpus christianorum. Continuatio mediaevalis) 274 (Turnhout: 2016), 103–16.

Jakoubek of Stříbro, "Ditare clerum," in *Mistra Jana Husi Tractatus responsivus*, ed. S. Harrison Thomson (Prague: 1927), 161–62.

Jakoubek of Stříbro, *Výklad na Zjevenie sv. Jana* [Exposition of the Revelation of St. John], ed. František Šimek, 2 vols. (Prague: 1932–1933).

Jakoubek of Stříbro, "Ad bellum," in Pavel Soukup, "Dobývání hradu Skály v roce 1413 a husitská teorie války. Ke spisku Jakoubka ze Stříbra o duchovním boji," *Mediaevalia historica Bohemica* 9 (2003): 205–08.

Matěj of Janov, *Regulae Veteris et Novi Testamenti*, vols. 1–4, ed. Vlastimil Kybal (Innsbruck: 1908–1913); vol. 5, eds. Vlastimil Kybal and Otakar Odložilík (Prague: 1913); vol. 6, eds. Jana Nechutová and Helena Krmíčková (Munich: 1993).

Mikuláš Biskupec of Pelhřimov, *Confessio Taboritarum*, eds. Amedeo Molnár and Romolo Cegna (Rome: 1983).

Nicholas of Dresden, "Tabule veteris et novi coloris seu cortina de Anticristo," in *Master Nicholas of Dresden: The Old Color and the New. Selected Works Contrasting the Primitive Church and the Roman Church*, eds. Howard Kaminsky, Dean Loy Bilderback, Imre Boda and Patricia N. Rosenberg (Transactions of the American Philosophical Society, New Series) 55, 1 (Philadelphia: 1965), 38–65.

Nicholas of Dresden, "Consuetudo et ritus primitive ecclesie et moderne, seu derivative," in *Master Nicholas of Dresden: The Old Color and the New. Selected Works Contrasting the Primitive Church and the Roman Church*, eds. Howard Kaminsky, Dean Loy Bilderback, Imre Boda and Patricia N. Rosenberg (Transactions of the American Philosophical Society, New Series) 55, 1 (Philadelphia: 1965), 66–85.

Nicholas of Dresden, "Sermo ad clerum de materia sanguinis," in *Nicolai (ut dicunt) de Dresda vulgo appellati de Čerruc (de Černá Růže id est de Rosa Nigra [† 1418?]) Puncta*, ed. Romolo Cegna (Mediaevalia Philosophica Polonorum) 33 (Warsaw: 1996), 157–87.

Nicholas of Dresden, *Nicolai Dresdensis Apologia. De conclusionibus doctorum in Constantia de materia sanguinis*, ed. Petra Mutlová (Brno: 2015).

Palacký, František, and Ernst Birk (eds.), *Monumenta conciliorum generalium seculi decimi quinti. Concilium Basileense*, Scriptores: vol. 1 (Vienna: 1857).

Payne, Peter, "Posicio M. Petri Englici in Basilea coram concilio," in *Petri Payne Anglici Positio, replica et propositio in concilio Basiliensi a. 1433 atque oratio ad Sigismundum regem a. 1429 Bratislaviae pronunciatae. Peter Payne pro Bohemis*, ed. František Michálek Bartoš (Tábor: 1949), 1–40.

"Petri Zatecensis Orphanorum sactae presbyteri Liber diurnus de gestis Bohemorum in concilio Basileensi," in *Monumenta conciliorum generalium seculi decimi quinti. Concilium Basileense*, eds. František Palacký and Ernst Birk, Scriptores: vol. 1 (Vienna: 1857), 287–357.

Ps.-Chrysostom, "Opus imperfectum in Matthaeum," in *Patrologiae cursus completus. Series Graeca*, ed. Jacques-Paul Migne, vol. 56 (Paris: 1859), 611–946.

Rokycana, Jan, "Collatio super Matth. 2,2," in *Veterum scriptorum et monumentorum historicorum, dogmaticorum, moralium amplissima collection*, eds. Edmond Martène and Ursin Durand, vol. 8 (Paris: 1733), 254–62.

Vavřinec of Březová, "Kronika husitská" [The Hussite Chronicle], in *Fontes rerum Bohemicarum*, eds. Josef Emler, Jan Gebauer, and Jaroslav Goll, vol. 5 (Prague: 1893), 327–534.

Želivský, Jan, *Dochovaná kázání z roku 1419* [Preserved sermons from 1419], ed. Amedeo Molnár (Prague: 1953).

Secondary Sources

Abou-el-Haj, Barbara, *The Medieval Cult of Saints. Formations and Transformations* (Cambridge: 1994).

Bartlová, Milena, "Původ husitského kalicha z ikonografického hlediska" [The origin of the Hussite chalice from the point of view of iconography], *Umění* 44 (1996): 167–83.

Bartlová, Milena, "Ikonografie kalicha, symbolu husitství" [Iconography of the chalice, the symbol of Hussitism], in *Jan Hus na přelomu tisíciletí*, eds. Miloš Drda, František J. Holeček and Zdeněk Vybíral (Husitský Tábor. Supplementum) 1 (Tábor: 2001), 453–87.

Bartoš, František Michálek, *Literární činnost M. Jana Rokycany, M. Jana Příbrama, M. Petra Payna* [The literary activity of Master Jan Rokycana, Master Jan Příbram, Master Peter Payne] (Prague: 1928).

Cadili, Alberto, "*Ecclesia moderna* und *ecclesia primitiva* in den Predigten des Jan Želivský," *Archa Verbi* 9 (2012): 86–135.

Cegna, Romolo, "Początki utrakwizmu w Czechach w latach 1412–1415" [The beginnings of Utraquism in Bohemia in the years 1412–1415], *Przegląd historyczny* 69 (1978): 106–14.

Cegna, Romolo, "*Ecclesia Primitiva*. Dall'*Opus arduum valde* a Nicolaus de Drazna (de Rosa Nigra)," *Archa Verbi* 9 (2012): 64–85.

Cermanová, Pavlína, "Jakoubkův a Biskupcův Výklad na Apokalypsu. Porovnání s důrazem na intepretaci antikristovského mýtu" [Jakoubek's and Biskupec's expositions of the Apocalypse. A comparison with emphasis on the interpretation of the Antichrist myth], in *Jakoubek ze Stříbra. Texty a jejich působení*, eds. Ota Halama and Pavel Soukup (Prague: 2006), 209–28.

Cermanová, Pavlína, "Jakoubek ze Stříbra a tradice apokalyptických proroctví a jejich výkladů v husitství" [Jakoubek of Stříbro and the tradition of apocalyptic prophecies and their interpretations in Hussitism], in *Amica – sponsa – mater. Bible v čase reformace*, ed. Ota Halama (Prague: 2014), 122–42.

Cook, William R., "John Wyclif and Hussite Theology 1415–1436," *Church History* 42 (1973): 335–49.

Coufal, Dušan, "Výklad a autorita bible v polemice mezi Janem Gersonem a Jakoubkem ze Stříbra z roku 1417" [The interpretation and authority of the Bible in the polemic of 1417 between Jean Gerson and Jakoubek of Sříbro], *Listy filologické* 131 (2008): 45–72.

Coufal, Dušan, *Polemika o kalich mezi teologií a politikou 1414–1431. Předpoklady basilejské disputace o prvním z pražských artikulů* [Polemic on the chalice between theology and politics, 1414–1431. Preconditions of the Basel disputation on the first Prague article] (Prague: 2012).

Coufal, Dušan, "*Sub utraque specie*. Die Theologie des Laienkelchs bei Jacobell von Mies (†1429) und der frühen Utraquisten," *Archa Verbi* 14 (2017): 125–68.

Dekarli, Martin, "Od pravidla (*regula*) k zákonu (*lex*), od nápravy k reformě: doktrinální analýza transformace principů myšlení rané české reformace (1392–1414)" [From rule (*regula*) to law (*lex*), from remedy to reform: a doctrinal analysis of the transformation of the principles of thought of the early Bohemian Reformation (1392–1414)], in *O felix Bohemia! Studie k dějinám české reformace*, ed. Petr Hlaváček (Prague: 2013), 39–58.

Dekarli, Martin, "The Law of Christ (Lex Christi) and the Law of God (Lex Dei) – Jan Hus's Concept of Reform," in *The Bohemian Reformation and Religious Practice*, eds. Zdeněk V. David and David R. Holeton, vol. 10 (Prague, 2015), 49–69.

de Lange, Albert, and Utz Tremp, Kathrin (ed.), *Friedrich Reiser und die "waldensisch-hussitische Internationale"* (Heidelberg, Ubstadt-Weiher, and Basel: 2006).

De Vooght, Paul, "La confrontation des thèses hussites et romaines au concile de Bâle (Janvier–Avril 1433)," *Recherches de théologie ancienne et médiévale* 37 (1970): 97–137.

Dobiáš, František Mrázek, "Rokycanův spis *De septem culpis*" [Rokycana's writing *De septem culpis*], *Theologická příloha Křesťanské revue* 34 (1967): 106–10.

Flanagin, David Zachariah, "Making Sense of It All: Gerson's Biblical Theology," in *A Companion to Jean Gerson*, ed. Brian Patrick McGuire (Brill's Companions to the Christian Tradition) 3 (Leiden and Boston: 2006), 133–77.

Fudge, Thomas A., "The 'Law of God.' Reform and Religious Practice in Late Medieval Bohemia," in *The Bohemian Reformation and Religious Practice*, ed. David R. Holeton, vol. 1 (Prague: 1996), 49–72.

Halama, Ota, *Otázka svatých v české reformaci. Její proměny od doby Karla IV. do doby České konfese* [The question of saints in the Bohemian Reformation. Its transformations from the time of Charles IV to the *Confessio Bohemica*] (Brno: 2002).

Halama, Ota, "Husitské teologické myšlení" [Hussite theological thought], in *Husitské století*, eds. Pavlína Cermanová, Robert Novotný, and Pavel Soukup (Prague: 2014), 401–14.

Herold, Vilém, "Ideové kořeny reformace v českých zemích" [Ideological roots of the Reformation in the Czech Lands], in *Dějiny politického myšlení*, vol. 2/2: *Politické myšlení pozdního středověku a reformace*, eds. Vilém Herold, Ivan Müller, and Aleš Havlíček (Prague: 2011), 161–236.

Herold, Vilém, "The Spiritual Background of the Czech Reformation: Precursors of Jan Hus," in *A Companion to Jan Hus*, eds. Frantisek Šmahel and Ota Pavlíček (Brill's Companions to the Christian Tradition) 54 (Leiden and Boston: 2015), 69–95.

Holeton, David R., *La communion des tout-petits enfants. Étude du mouvement eucharistique en Bohême vers la fin du Moyen Âge* (Rome: 1989).

Hruza, Karel, "Schrift und Rebellion. Die hussitischen Manifeste aus Prag von 1415–1431," in *Geist, Gesellschaft, Kirche im 13.-16. Jahrhundert*, ed. František Šmahel (Colloquia mediaevalia Pragensia) 1 (Prague: 1999), 81–108.

Heymann, Frederick G., *John Žižka and the Hussite Revolution* (Princeton: 1965).

Jacob, Ernest Fraser, "The Bohemians at the Council of Basel 1433," in *Prague Essays*, ed. Robert Seton-Watson (Oxford: 1949), 81–123.

Kadlec, Jaroslav, "Literární polemika mistrů Jakoubka ze Stříbra a Ondřeje z Brodu o laický kalich" [Literary polemic of Masters Jakoubek of Stříbro and Ondřej of Brod on the lay chalice], *Acta Universitatis Carolinae – Historia Universitatis Carolinae Pragensis* 21 (1981): 71–88.

Kadlec, Jaroslav, *Studien und Texte zum Leben und Wirken des Prager Magisters Andreas von Brod* (Münster: 1982).

Kalivoda, Robert, "K otázkám myšlenkového modelu tzv. první a druhé reformace" [On the questions raised by the thought model of the so-called First and Second Reformation], in *Bratrský sborník*, eds. Rudolf Říčan, Amedeo Molnár, and Michal Flegl (Prague: 1967), 120–26.

Kalivoda, Robert, *Revolution und Ideologie. Der Hussitismus*, trans. Heide Thorwart and Monika Gletter (Cologne: 1976).

Kaminsky, Howard, "Wycliffism as Ideology of Revolution," *Church History* 32 (1963): 57–74.

Kaminsky, Howard, *A History of the Hussite Revolution* (Berkeley and Los Angeles: 1967).

Kejř, Jiří, *Mistři pražské university a kněží táborští* [The masters of Prague university and the Taborite priests] (Prague: 1981).

Kejř, Jiří, "Auctoritates contra communionem parvulorum M. Jana z Jesenice," *Studie o rukopisech* 19 (1980): 5–21; repr. in idem, *Z počátků české reformace* (Brno: 2006), 230–44.

Kolář, Pavel, "Husovo učení o přijímání eucharistie a jeho vztah k učení Jakoubkovu" [Hus's teachings on the eucharist and their relation to the teachings of Jakoubek], in *Mistra Jan Hus v proměnách času a jeho poselství víry dnešku*, eds. Zdeněk Kučera and Tomáš Butta (Prague: 2012), 83–102.

Krmíčková, Helena, *Studie a texty k počátkům kalicha v Čechách* [Studies and texts on the beginnings of the chalice in Bohemia] (Brno: 1997).

Krmíčková, Helena, "Několik poznámek k přijímání maličkých 1414–1416" [A few remarks on the communion of infants 1414–1416], *Sborník prací Filozofické fakulty brněnské univerzity* C 44 (1997): 59–69.

Krmíčková, Helena, "K pramenům Husovy kvestie *De sanguine Christi sub specie vini*" [On the sources of Hus's *quaestio De sanguine Christi sub specie vini*], *Sborník prací Filozofické fakulty brněnské univerzity* C 45 (1998): 79–102.

Krmíčková, Helena, "Utraquism in 1414," in *The Bohemian Reformation and Religious Practice*, eds. Zdeněk V. David and David R. Holeton, vol. 4 (Prague: 2002), 99–105.

Kybal, Vlastimil, *M. Jan Hus. Život a učení* [Master Jan Hus. Life and teachings], Part 2: *Učení* [Teachings], 3 vols. (Prague: 1923–1931).

Lahey, Stephen E., "Wyclif, the 'Hussite Philosophy,' and the Law of Christ," in *The Bohemian Reformation and Religious Practice*, eds. Zdeněk V. David and David R. Holeton, vol. 9 (Prague, 2014), 54–71.

Lancinger, Luboš, "Čtyři artikuly pražské a podíl univerzitních mistrů na jejich vývoji" [The Four Articles of Prague and the role of university masters in their development], *Acta Universitatis Carolinae – Historia Universitatis Carolinae Pragensis* 3 (1962): 3–61.

Levy, Ian Christopher, "Holy Scripture and the Quest for Authority among Three Late Medieval Masters," *Journal of Ecclesiastical History* 61 (2010): 40–68.

Machilek, Franz, "Die hussitische Forderung nach öffentlichem Gehör und der Beheimsteiner Vertrag von 1430," in *Husitství – reformace – renesance. Sborník k 60. narozeninám Františka Šmahela*, eds. Jaroslav Pánek, Miloslav Polívka, and Noemi Rejchrtová, vol. 2 (Prague: 1994), 503–27.

Marin, Olivier, *L'archevêque, le maître et le dévot. Genèses du mouvement réformateur pragois. Années 1360–1419* (Paris: 2005).

Marek, Jindřich, *Jakoubek ze Stříbra a počátky utrakvistického kazatelství v českých zemích. Studie o Jakoubkově postile z let 1413–1414* [Jakoubek of Stříbro and the beginnings of Utraquist preaching in the Bohemian lands. A study of Jakoubek's postil from 1413–1414] (Prague: 2011).

Mayer-Maly, Theo, "Rechtsphilosophie und Rechtstheologie im Mittelalter," in *Theologische Realenzyklopädie*, vol. 28 (Berlin and New York: 1997), 216–27.

Molnár, Amedeo, "Eschatologická naděje české reformace" [The eschatological hope of the Bohemian Reformation], in *Od reformace k zítřku* (Prague: 1956), 11–101.

Molnár, Amedeo, "L'évolution de la théologie hussite," *Revue d'histoire et de philosophie religieuses* 43 (1963): 133–71.

Molnár, Amedeo, "Husovo místo v evropské reformaci [Hus's place in the European Reformation]," *Československý časopis historický* 14 (1966): 1–14.

Molnár, Amedeo, "K otázce reformační iniciativy lidu. Svědectví husitského kázání" [On the question of the reformation initiative of the people. The witness of Hussite preaching], in *Acta reformationem bohemicam illustrantia*, vol. 1: *Příspěvky k dějinám utrakvismu*, ed. Amedeo Molnár (Prague: 1978), 5–44.

Molnár, Amedeo, *Pohyb teologického myšlení* [The movement of theological thinking] (Prague: 1982).

Molnár, Amedeo, "Chebský soudce" [The Judge of Cheb], in *Soudce smluvený v Chebu. Sborník příspěvků přednesených na symposiu k 550. výročí* (Prague: 1982), 9–37.

Molnár, Amedeo, "'Život v dobré proměniti.' Nad čtvrtým pražským artikulem" ["Turning life into something good." On the fourth Article of Prague], *Theologická revue Československé církve husitské* 16 (1983): 50–61.

Molnár, Amedeo, "Über Quellen zur Theologiegeschichte des Hussitentums," *Communio viatorum* 30 (1987): 253–269.

Molnár, Amedeo, "The Ideological Significance of Hussitism," *Communio viatorum* 31 (1988): 103–25.

Molnár, Amedeo, "Zur hermeneutischen Problematik des Glaubensdisputs im Hussitentum," in *Studien zum Humanismus in den Böhmischen Ländern*, eds. Hans-Bernd Harder and Hans Rothe (Cologne and Vienna: 1988), 93–110.

Molnár, Amedeo, and Dobiáš, František Mrázek, "Předmluva [Foreword]," in *Mikuláš z Pelhřimova: Vyznání a obrana Táborů*, eds. Amedeo Molnár and F.M. Dobiáš (Prague: 1972), 5–68.

Mutlová, Petra, "Die Dresdner Schule in Prag: eine waldensische 'Connection'?," in *Friedrich Reiser und die "waldensisch-hussitische Internationale,"* eds. Albert de Lange and Kathrin Utz Tremp (Heidelberg, Ubstadt-Weiher, and Basel: 2006), 261–76.

Mutlová, Petra, "Communicating Texts through Images: Nicholas of Dresden's *Tabulae*," in *Public Communication in European Reformation. Artistic and other Media in Central Europe 1380–1620*, eds. Milena Bartlová and Michal Šroněk (Prague: 2007), 29–37.

Nechutová, Jana, "Kategorie zákona božího a M. Matěj z Janova" [The category of divine law and Master Matěj of Janov], *Sborník prací Filozofické fakulty brněnské univerzity* E 12 (1967): 211–21.

Nechutová, Jana, "*Ecclesia primitiva* v husitských naukách" [The *Ecclesia primitiva* in Hussite doctrines], *Sborník prací Filozofické fakulty brněnské univerzity* E 33 (1988): 87–93.
Novotný, Václav, *Náboženské hnutí české ve 14. a 15. stol. Část 1. Do Husa* [The Bohemian Reform movement in the 14th and 15th centuries. Part 1. Before Hus] (Prague: 1915).
Palacký, František [under the pseudonym J.P. Jordan], *Die Vorläufer des Hussitenthums in Böhmen* (Leipzig: 1846).
Pascoe, Louis Bernard, "Jean Gerson. The *Ecclesia Primitiva* and Reform," *Traditio* 30 (1974): 379–410.
Patschovsky, Alexander, "Ekklesiologie bei Johannes Hus," in *Lebenslehren und Weltentwürfe im Übergang vom Mittelalter zur Neuzeit*, eds. Hartmut Boockmann, Bernd Moeller, and Karl Stackmann (Göttingen, 1989), 370–99.
Perett, Marcela K., "John Příbram and his Vernacular Treatises. Equipping the Laity in Battle against Hussite Radicals," in *Christianity and Culture in the Middle Ages. Essays to honor John Van Engen*, eds. David C. Mengel and Lisa Ann Wolverton (Notre Dame: 2015), 419–35.
Petrů, Ondřej M., *Matěj z Janova o častém svatém přijímání* [Matěj of Janov on frequent holy communion] (Olomouc: 1946).
Prügl, Thomas, "Urkirche und frühchristliche Praxis als Legitimationsstrategie im Basler Konziliarismus," *Archa Verbi* 9 (2012): 136–60.
Ransdorf, Miloslav, *Kapitoly z geneze husitské ideologie* [Chapters from the genesis of Hussite ideology] (Prague: 1986).
Renna, Thomas J., "The Primitive Church according to Jean Gerson and the Dutch Anabaptists," *Fifteenth Century Studies* 20 (1993): 275–90.
Rejchrtová, Noemi, "Pravda zákona Kristova v pochopení pozdního utrakvismu" [The truth of Christ's law in the understanding of late Utraquism], in *Epitoauto. Sborník k pětašedesátinám Petra Pokorného*, eds. Jiří Mrázek, Štěpán Brodský, and Rut Dvořáková (Prague: 1998), 157–62.
Rychterová, Pavlína, "Theology Goes to the Vernaculars. Jan Hus, 'On simony,' and the Practice of Translation in Fifteenth-Century Bohemia," in *Religious Controversy in Europe, 1378–1536. Textual Transmission and Networks of Readership*, eds. Michael Van Dussen and Pavel Soukup (Turnhout: 2013), 231–50.
Rychterová, Pavlína, "The Vernacular Theology of Jan Hus," in *A Companion to Jan Hus*, ed. Frantisek Šmahel and Ota Pavlíček (Brill's Companions to the Christian Tradition) 54 (Leiden and Boston: 2015), 170–213.
Sedlák, Jan, "Husův pomocník v evangeliu" [Hus's assistant in the Gospel], *Studie a texty k náboženským dějinám českým* 1 (1914): 362–428; 2 (1915): 302–350, 446–477; 3 (1919): 24–74.

Schäufele, Wolf-Friedrich, "'Vorreformation' und 'erste Reformation' als historiographische Konzepte. Bestandsaufnahme und Problemanzeige," in *Jan Hus. 600 Jahre Erste Reformation*, eds. Andrea Strübind and Tobias Weger (Munich: 2015), 209–31.

Seibt, Ferdinand, "Die revelatio des Jacobellus von Mies über die Kelchkommunion," *Deutsches Archiv für Erforschung des Mittelalters* 22 (1966): 618–24.

Šmahel, František, "The Hussite Critique of the Clergy's Civil Dominion," in *Anticlericalism in Late Medieval and Early Modern Europe*, eds. Peter A. Dykema and Heiko A. Oberman (Leiden: 1993), 83–90.

Šmahel, František, *Die Hussitische Revolution*, trans. Thomas Krzenck (Monumenta Germaniae Historica. Schriften) 43, 3 vols. (Hannover: 2002).

Šmahel, František, "Die Vier Prager Artikel. Das Programm der hussitischen Reformation," in *Kirchliche Reformimpulse des 14./15. Jahrhunderts in Ostmitteleuropa*, ed. Winfried Eberhard and Franz Machilek (Cologne, Weimar, and Vienna: 2006), 329–39.

Šmahel, František, "Wyclif's Fortune in Hussite Bohemia," in idem, *Die Prager Universität im Mittelalter. The Charles University in the Middle Ages* (Leiden and Boston: 2007), 467–89.

Šmahel, František, *Basilejská kompaktáta. Příběh deseti listin* [The Basel *Compactata*. A story of ten charters] (Prague: 2011).

Šmahel, František, and Ota Pavlíček (eds.), *A Companion to Jan Hus* (Brill's Companions to the Christian Tradition) 54 (Leiden and Boston: 2015).

Soukup, Pavel, "Metaphors of the Spiritual Struggle Early in the Bohemian Reformation. The Exegesis of Arma Spiritualia in Hus, Jakoubek, and Chelcický," in *The Bohemian Reformation and Religious Practice*, eds. Zdeněk V. David and David R. Holeton, vol. 6 (Prague: 2007), 87–109.

Soukup, Pavel, *Reformní kazatelství a Jakoubek ze Stříbra* [Reform Preaching and Jakoubek of Stříbro] (Prague: 2011).

Soukup, Pavel, "Kauza reformace. Husitství v konkurenci reformních projektů" [The case of the Reformation. Hussitism among competing reform projects], in *Heresis seminaria. Pojmy a koncepty v bádání o husitství*, eds. Pavlína Rychterová and Pavel Soukup (Prague: 2013), 171–217.

Soukup, Pavel, "'Jak mohou zvěstovat, nejsou-li posláni?' Autorita a autorizace kazatele u Husa a jeho současníků" ["How can they preach unless they are sent?" Authority and the authorization of preachers in Jan Hus and his contemporaries], in *Amica – sponsa – mater. Bible v čase reformace*, ed. Ota Halama (Prague: 2014), 122–42.

Spunar, Pavel, *Repertorium auctorum Bohemorum provectum idearum post universitatem Pragensem conditam illustrans*, vol. 1, (Studia Copernicana) 25 (Wrocław: 1985).

Török, Dan, "The Ideal of the Primitive Church in the Early Reformation," in *The Bohemian Reformation and Religious Practice*, eds. Zdeněk V. David and David R. Holeton, vol. 10 (Prague: 2015), 144–57.

Uhlíř, Zdeněk, "Die Texte über den Aberglauben in den tschechischen Handschriftensammlungen des Mittelalters," in *Religion und Magie in Ostmitteleuropa. Spielräume theologischer Normierungsprozesse in Spätmittelalter und Früher Neuzeit*, ed. Thomas Wünsch (Münster, Berlin, and Hamburg: 2006), 85–120.

Uhlirz, Mathilde, *Die Genesis der vier Prager Artikel* (Sitzungsberichte der Kaiserlichen Akademie der Wissenschaften in Wien, Philosophisch-Historische Klasse), 175, 3 (Vienna: 1914).

Wernisch, Martin, *Husitství. Raně reformační příběh* [Hussitism. An early Reformation story] (Brno: 2003).

Preaching, the Vernacular, and the Laity

Pavlína Rychterová

After the inception of the Hussite movement in the first two decades of the 15th century, Bohemia experienced an acceleration in the process of the vernacularization of written culture that decisively influenced the subsequent development of literary culture and intellectual life in Bohemia. The Hussite movement defined itself as Czech-speaking, and the Czech population of all social strata was its target audience from the very beginning. The main tribune for the dissemination of reform ideas outside of the university was the pulpit in the Chapel of the Holy Innocents (the so-called Bethlehem Chapel), founded and richly endowed by wealthy Czech-speaking burghers from Prague specifically for preaching in the Czech language. In the crucial years of the movement's formation, from 1402 until 1412, the incumbent of this pulpit was the leader of the movement, Jan Hus.

The energetic and active core of his lay, and mainly Czech-speaking, following, many of them university students, showed its resoluteness during the indulgence riots in spring 1412. During these riots, the debate on church reform held at the University of Prague during the previous decade reached its climax. Those involved in the debate were masters of the Faculty of Arts (mostly Czechs), and members of the Bohemian university nation. Their adversaries at that time (before 1409) were mainly German-speaking theologians of the other three nations (Saxon, Bavarian, and Silesian). The Czech leaders of the movement which gradually spread beyond university debates emphasized Czech, not only as a language in which they communicated with their lay adherents, but also as a symbolic means of building a group identity. The strategies of identification that the group of Czech reformist masters developed were aimed at engaging the lay adherents, especially the influential members of the Czech-speaking nobility, more deeply in the reform debate. From these efforts, a specific ideological construct of Czech identity emerged. It found its expression in 1409 at the university during a quodlibetal disputation, in the speech of one of Hus's most ardent adherents, Master Jerome of Prague. Jerome defined common language (*lingua*), common origin (*sanguis*), and common religion (*fides* – here in the sense of its Wycliffite definition) as basic markers of any community. He described the *sacrosancta communitas Boemica* as a *communitas universorum hominum*; this community should include Czech-speaking adherents of the reform party, of all social strata, whose parents should also speak Czech.[1] Although Jerome's concept did not become an official ideology in the modern sense, it clearly shows the direction in which the leaders of the reform party at the university were heading. The messianic effort of the early reformist movement, the need to involve lay sympathizers, the construction of an adversary to the reform – the German-speaking theologian, as well as the practice of allocating students and teachers at the university into university nations – were all decisive elements of the self-consciously Czech character of the reform movement. The older tradition of the political use (and misuse) of "Czechness," defined as linguistic and biological belonging, and observable in Bohemia approximately from the last decades of the 13th century, also played a role.

The Czech language as an expression of the political claims of an ethnically defined group had already been highlighted by the anonymous author of the Chronicle of the so-called Dalimil, written in Czech and composed in the second decade of the 14th century. The *Dalimil Chronicle* combined the history of the Czech *gens* (adapted from the Chronicle of Cosmas of Prague) with the story of the struggle of the Bohemian/Czech nobility against the German-dominated royal court and cities, arguing for ethnically justified rights to supremacy by Czech-speaking Bohemians. The Czech-speaking nobles of the second decade of the fourteenth century competed with German courtiers for the king's favor, and with German patricians for economic power. It would of course be simplistic to draw a direct line from these earlier expressions to the university masters formulating their reform program in ethnic or national terms a hundred years later. But it is important to point out that a politically motivated national understanding of the Czech language had surfaced recurrently from at least the second half of the 13th century, when Bohemia witnessed a significant immigration from the technologically and economically more developed German lands.

The first Czech religious writings appear at roughly the same time that the Czech language gained its function in political disputes, during the second half of the 13th century. Their number is admittedly modest (some fragments, glosses, interlinear translations, etc.), but they reveal a surprisingly high quality of translation techniques, especially concerning the problems of Latin and Czech syntactic differences. These texts also prove the capacity of the language to express complicated theological and spiritual concepts.[2] The first translations

---

1 František Šmahel, *Idea národa v husitských Čechách*, 2nd ed. (Prague: 2000), 47.
2 Dušan Šlosar, "Frühe volkssprachliche Entwicklung – Early Vernacular Development," in *Die Slavischen Sprachen. The Slavic Languages. Ein internationales Handbuch zu ihrer Struktur,*

of the Psalter into Czech were produced at the beginning of the 14th century, and the first complete Psalter translation comes from the middle of that century. The first full Czech translation of the Bible was produced at this time as well, probably commissioned by some of the leading Dominican houses or by the Prague archbishops (possibly with the knowledge and support of Emperor Charles IV), and perhaps in cooperation with the Augustinian Canons in Roudnice.[3] This impressive but – in terms of quantity – modest production of Czech religious literature would see a striking increase from the 1370s onwards.

Several Bohemian authors from the second half of the 14th century whose names and religious writings (in Latin and Czech) are known are characterized in the prevailing scholarship as predecessors of Jan Hus and the Hussites. In many respects this is a reasonable claim.[4] Certain works from the last third of the 14th century do indeed share common features with the works of Jan Hus written in Czech – criticism of the church and its immoral clergy, for example, and an emphasis on a more spiritual approach to personal devotion. But these aspects are not unique to Czech vernacular catechesis of the period; they are widespread in contemporary works from the rest of Europe, many of which sought to establish more sophisticated forms of lay religious education. However, it is unique to the works of the so-called predecessors of Hus that the Czech language and its lay speakers assume an importance which is not so remote from later Hussite concepts.

The most prominent author of catechetical and theological literature in Czech before Hus was a layman, the south Bohemian lower nobleman Tomáš of Štítné (ca. 1330–soon after 1400). The first book he wrote in the early 1370s was a theological compendium.[5] In the introduction to his translation of *De septem processibus*, a text originally written for monks by David of Augsburg, Tomáš profoundly discusses the difference between monks and nuns on the one hand, and the laity (both men and women) on the other. According to him,

---

ihrer Geschichte und ihrer Erforschung. An international Handbook of their Structure, their History and their Investigation, eds. Karl Gutschmidt and Sebastian Kempgen, vol. 2 (Berlin, Munich, and Boston: 2014), 1392.

3 Jakub Sichálek, "European Background. Czech Translations," in *The Wycliffite Bible. Origin, History and Interpretation*, ed. Elizabeth Solopova (Leiden and Boston: 2017), 78–82.

4 The concept of the so-called predecessors was developed as early as Hus's own time. He and his associates created a dignified tradition for their own reform efforts, which were rejected by their adversaries as deceptive novelty. Modern Czech historiography adopted this self-description uncritically. For an analysis of the concept as formulated by Hus, see Martin Dekarli, *Politická a morální teologie Jana Husa v kontextu pražské univerzitní tradice* (forthcoming).

5 Tomáš of Štítné, *Tomáš ze Štítného. Sborník Vyšehradský*, ed. František Ryšánek (Prague: 1960).

monks and nuns are not better human beings than laypeople who live according to biblical laws and Christ's commandments. Therefore, the texts designed for the spiritual education of monks and nuns (but also of priests and scholarly masters) were not only suitable but necessary for the spiritual education of laypeople.

In his second volume, dated to 1376,[6] Tomáš of Štítné proceeds even further: In his tract "On the nine angelic choirs and nine human choirs," he speaks of pious laypeople as belonging to the first choir of seraphim together with the biblical prophets, the apostles, and the evangelists, arguing that true religiosity and spirituality is not bound to social status (the actual topic of the tract is an exposition of the three-estates theory). Laypeople reading devotional books and living in true imitation of Christ deserve the highest status in society, thereby replacing depraved priests.[7] Only from these people will true renewal come. This concept echoes the teaching of Tomáš's contemporary, Matěj of Janov, especially his concept of the church of the elect as a community of saints led by the life and spirit of Jesus Christ.[8] However, the *Reguale Veteris et Novi Testamenti* in which Matěj developed his ideas appear some years later than Tomáš's collection, which means that Tomáš's source of inspiration may be Milíč of Kroměříž, who himself heavily influenced Matěj of Janov. In one of Milíč's three extant synodal sermons, delivered sometime between 1364 and 1373, a first step in the development of the concept of an elevated lay status may be found in a passage drawn from Ps.-Chrysostom: "Videte ergo, quomodo sedeatis super cathedram, quia cathedra non facit sacerdotem, sed sacerdos facit cathedram, non locus sanctificat hominem, sed homo sanctificat locum. Non omnis sacerdos sanctus est, sed omnis sanctus sacerdos."[9] In Tomáš's work, the new definition of the status of laypeople within the church is connected to the status of the Czech vernacular. In the preface to his second theological collection he seizes on this topic:

---

6 Prague, Národní knihovna České republiky XVII A 6, 158 fols. Tomáš of Štítné, *Tomáše ze Štítného Knížky šestery o obecných věcech křesťanských*, ed. Karel Jaromír Erben (Prague: 1852).

7 Pavlína Rychterová, "Kirchen- und Klerikalkritik im Böhmen des 14. und 15. Jahrhunderts zwischen Latein und Volkssprachen," in *Clero contro clero. Retoriche anticlericali fra medioevo e prima età moderna*, eds. Gian Luca Potestá and Roberto Rusconi, *Rivista di storia del Cristianesimo* 12 (2015): 329–49.

8 Vlastimil Kybal, *M. Matěj z Janova. Jeho život, spisy a učení* (Prague: 1905), 92, 124.

9 Milíč of Kroměříž, *Iohannis Milicii de Cremsir Tres sermones synodales*, eds. Vilém Herold and Milan Mráz (Prague: 1974), 54.

> Inspired by one homily of St. Augustine I will write more books in Czech concerning Scripture. In this homily everybody may understand how beneficial it is to read Scripture. And those who defame Czech books despite their quality with the intention that only they should be regarded as wise should be afraid of God's wrath ... Those who are wiser understand that God loves the Czech [reader] the same as he loves the Latin [one] ... So did Saint Paul. He wrote his letters in the language of their readers, for Jews in Hebrew, for Greeks in Greek. Saint Jerome translated Scripture for women from a language unknown to them. He did not say, 'The simple ones will not understand. Should we stop building bridges only because some unwise people could fall down from them?' ... Therefore I do not think it is bad to write books in Czech for Czechs, from which they may gather teaching in the Christian faith as well as instruction in good morals.[10]

The Czech language is here positioned side by side with the three sacred languages of Hebrew, Greek, and Latin and defined as their equal because all of them were (at least at one time) also vernacular languages whose speakers included laypeople, both men and women. According to Tomáš, speakers define the status of the language themselves. If, for example, the speaker is of high status (in the sense of being a true Christian imitating Christ), his language also gains that high status with him. Tomáš here emphasizes a direct connection between language, its speakers, and the true faith. This nexus returns again under different circumstances, in a different form, and with a different ideological background several years later in the debates of the Bohemian reformist leaders.

None of Tomáš's works – mostly translations and compilations, sometimes equipped with considerably long sections of his own reasoning – may be characterized as simple catechetical instruction, because he chose his models from a higher level of religious education. Their targeted recipient is a devout Christian of considerable literacy (mostly vernacular), substantial proficiency in all basic Christian rites, with a good knowledge of their biblical and theological background, and orientation in the topics and rhetoric of ordinary homiletics. Whether such recipients were common in the Czech lands at this time is not entirely clear. The modest transmission of the works of Tomáš of Štítné would militate against assuming a great number of well-educated lay readers. Nor does the research on lower and higher education in 14th-century Bohemia reveal a widespread audience of this kind. Most villages and small towns in

---

10   Tomáš of Štítné, *Knížky šestery*, 2–5.

Bohemia had either one school or no school at all. This fact would seem to suggest that illiteracy prevailed among the majority of the population. Yet almost a quarter of the students at Prague University who achieved a Bachelor's degree in the first two decades of the 15th century came from the Bohemian countryside.[11] It is therefore entirely possible that the number of literate persons who could read at least in their own language was in fact higher than research on institutionalized education of the time has led us to believe.[12]

Hus and his circle did not lean on older catechetical and theological texts in Czech, nor could they, as religious thinking in the Czech language did not produce an independent discourse at that time. Czech religious literature depended entirely on Latin models and faithfully mirrored the development of Latin written culture. As the reform movement began to radicalize at the university, its leaders operated only in the Latin theological discourse. They produced texts in Latin that were aimed at their supporters and adversaries in their own milieu – the university and the church hierarchy. However, all of them preached in Czech and used the vernacular as the most important means for the mobilization of their lay followers, who consequently grew into an important and active element of the movement.[13] Jan Hus transformed himself from a reform preacher into a tribune of the people as a result of his decision to turn to his Czech-speaking audience in the Bethlehem Chapel with his harsh critique of the papacy and its practice of indulgences.[14]

After Hus's banishment from Prague in 1412, and after his departure for Constance, the second leader of the reform party at the university, Jakoubek of Stříbro, took charge of the coordination and ideological definition of the group of reformists that came not only from the university, but also from among the burghers of Prague and the Czech-speaking nobility. The emphasis on the vernacular as a means of reform propaganda grew stronger under Jakoubek, who introduced (or, according to his own understanding, restored from ancient

---

11   Petr Čornej and Milena Bartlová, *Velké dějiny zemí Koruny české*, vol. 6 (Prague and Litomyšl: 2007), vol. 6: 286–303.

12   Stanisław Bylina, "La catéchisation du peuple en Bohême aux XIVe et XVe siècles" in *The Bohemian Reformation and Religious Practice*, eds. Zdeněk V. David and David R. Holeton, vol. 3 (Prague: 2000), 25–33, assumed a higher level of religious education in Bohemia in the pre-Hussite era in comparison with other regions of East-Central Europe.

13   Pavlína Rychterová, "Die Verbrennung von Johannes Hus als europäisches Ereignis. Öffentlichkeit und Öffentlichkeiten am Vorabend der hussitischen Revolution," in *Politische Öffentlichkeit im Spätmittelalter*, eds. Martin Kintzinger and Bernd Schneidmüller (Vorträge und Forschungen) 75 (Ostfildern: 2011), 361–83.

14   On Hus and his Czech writings, see Pavlína Rychterová, "The Vernacular Theology of Jan Hus," in *A Companion to Jan Hus*, eds. František Šmahel and Ota Pavlíček (Brill's Companions to the Christian Tradition) 54 (Leiden and Boston: 2015), 170–213.

custom) the important liturgical practice of communion under both kinds (Utraquism). This groundbreaking step provided the reform movement with a powerful symbol and transformed it thus into an independent Christian confession. Jakoubek started quickly to defend this liturgical innovation in Czech, including biblical, historical, and theological argumentation. Communion *sub utraque specie* was introduced in Prague by Jakoubek and his followers shortly before Jan Hus's departure for Constance in the autumn of 1414. Hus, as the recognized leader of the movement, wrote a treatise in support of Utraquism at Constance just after his arrival. Until that time the debate on the chalice was held in Latin, mainly between Jakoubek of Stříbro and Nicholas of Dresden on the one side, and Ondřej of Brod and Štěpán of Páleč on the other. But shortly after the practice of communion *sub utraque specie* started, the main theological arguments supporting its legitimacy were spread among lay adherents of the reform. Around the beginning of 1415, Jakoubek wrote the Czech treatise *O boží krvi* (On God's Blood). He defined his purpose as follows:

> As the Christian community has to learn of this ineffable gift which was given to it, and as it often has to drink the sacramental blood of the crucified Lord Jesus Christ, it is right and proper to present here the arguments from God's law and interpretations as well as arguments [formulated by] many holy [men], that formerly it was given and held in this way.[15]

As the first argument in favor of his opinion, Jakoubek introduces verses from Matthew 26. Detailed polemics countering the opinions of his Catholic adversaries follow in the form of comments on quotations from his sources. The exposition on the Eucharist constitutes a second, larger part of the tract. Here the older topics from early Hussite preaching prevail, for example, the critique of the declining veneration of the Eucharist and the simultaneously increasing veneration of relics; and long quotations from the authorities which at the time were quoted only briefly in the Latin treatises because those involved in the debate knew them by heart.[16] Jakoubek evidently wanted to equip his reader with a sound and detailed argumentative foundation.

It is entirely possible that the targeted readers of Jakoubek's Czech treatise were not lay adherents of the reform movement but rather members of the clergy who had reformist sympathies – Czech priests and students whose skill in Latin Jakoubek did not trust. These people needed to be provided with

---

15   Jakoubek of Stříbro, *Dvě staročeská utrakvistická díla Jakoubka ze Stříbra*, eds. Mirek Čejka and Helena Krmíčková (Brno: 2009), 32.
16   Ibid., 14–18.

material that was as detailed as possible for use in debate. But the topic was hotly discussed among the laity as well. A number of songs survive from the period (1414–1415). The texts deal with the problem of communion under both kinds from a reformist perspective and act as vehicles for argumentative propaganda. Biblical as well as later church authorities, especially Cyprian, whose works Jakoubek quoted extensively in his treatise, serve as primary proofs of the legitimacy of Utraquist practice. In other words, some of the main features of the scholastic disputation were maintained even in propagandistic street songs. These songs, as well as other vernacular tracts, appeal not only to the affect of the reader or hearer, but also – and especially – to his or her ability to discern spirits with the intellect.

The first of these texts was an ambitious macaronic "tract in verse" (a compilation of Latin quotations from the Bible and various authorities, together with their Czech verse paraphrases): *Řeč o přijímání těla božieho pod obým zpósobem* (Talk [in the sense of "sermo"] on communion under both kinds), also titled *Otázka nynie taková běží* (A question goes around). This was written by a Hussite priest and close collaborator of Jakoubek, Jan Čapek, toward the beginning of 1415. Čapek's text relies mainly on two sources: Jakoubek's Latin tract *Quod non solum sacerdotes*, which Jakoubek also translated extensively in his Czech treatise *O boží krvi*; and the *Quaestio de sanguine Cristi sub specie vini*, written by Jan Hus at Constance in November 1414.[17] Jan Čapek's Czech song maintains the form of a *quaestio*, which is likely the reason why Pavel Spunar calls it a "tract in verse":[18]

> A question goes around these days
> among the lay people and also the clergy,
> whether it is appropriate for faithful Christians,
> lay women as well as men,
> to receive God's blood from the chalice
> or whether it is reserved only for priests.[19]

---

17   The *Quaestio* and Jakoubek's tracts rely on the same authorities. Hus had several of Jakoubek's tracts in hand during his work on his *Quaestio*. See Helena Krmíčková, "K pramenům Husovy kvestie *De sanguine Christi sub specie vini*," *Sborník prací Filozofické fakulty brněnské univerzity* C 45 (1998): 79–102.

18   Pavel Spunar, *Repertorium auctorum Bohemorum provectum idearum post universitatem Pragensem conditam illustrans*, 2 vols. (Studia Copernicana) 25 and 35 (Wrocław and Warsaw: 1985–1995), vol. 2: 42.

19   František Svejkovský (ed.), *Veršované skladby doby husitské* (Prague: 1963), 90.

Jan Čapek reworked his Czech verse tract again later; it was then included in the *Jistebnický kancionál* (The Cantionale of Jistebnice), which contains Czech and some Latin texts. Here the form of a *quaestio* is abandoned and the song starts with a reference to the Last Supper. 1 Corinthians 11: 23–26 is then quoted, followed by an assertion, expressed catechetically, that communion under both kinds is necessary:

> And you should consider
> that this should be maintained and last
> until the Day of Judgement.
> Although the whole of Christ
> is in each of both kinds,
> it is not in vain to give it
> in both kinds to the people;
> rather, it is proper
> and very useful for the people
> to eat God's body
> and to drink his blood separately.
> Separate communion of the body
> serves our body for salvation,
> and to drink his blood
> serves our soul for purification.
> Therefore, beloved brothers,
> let us fulfill God's command,
> let us not oppose the Lord in this respect. ...
> Doing this,
> fulfilling his law,
> avoiding sins,
> we will reign together with him forever.
> Have mercy upon us, Lord,
> that the evil in the people may end.[20]

After the Council of Constance issued the decree *Cum in nonnullis* in June 1415, in which Utraquism was banned, another wave of polemical and apologetic texts were produced by Hussite theologians. It was again Jakoubek of Stříbro who transferred the debate into the Czech vernacular. He wrote his *Zpráva, jak sněm konstanský o svátosti večeře Kristovy nařídil* (Report, how the Council of

---

20 Bohuslav Havránek, Josef Hrabák, and Jiří Daňhelka (eds.), *Výbor z české literatury doby husitské*, 2 vols. (Prague: 1963–1964), vol. 1, 313–14.

Constance decreed on the sacrament of Christ's supper) sometime in the second half of 1415, and certainly after the death of Jan Hus, whom he mentions in the tract as deceased. The tract maintains the form of a scholastic polemic; Jakoubek quotes extensively from the work that he disputes, and counters select passages with arguments based on quotations from the New Testament and various church authorities. This is accompanied by a harsh critique of the hierarchical church and the council. In addition, subtle scholastic expositions on the Eucharist play an important role.[21] At the end of the tract, there is a shift in the argumentation, as compared to Jakoubek's previous works; here Jakoubek links the struggle for communion under both kinds directly to Jan Hus and his martyrdom: just as the council passed an unjust sentence on Hus, so did they act unjustly in the case of the lay chalice.[22]

Apart from Jan Hus, Jakoubek of Stříbro was the most important author of theological texts in the Czech vernacular during the first phase of the reform movement, until the outbreak of revolt in 1419. Besides his own works, among which the eucharistic tracts assume a prominent position, he also translated the writings of the main authority of the movement, John Wyclif. In this he was again in line with Jan Hus, who quoted extensively from Wyclif's oeuvre in his Czech writings. This translation activity was known in Bohemia and abroad. One of the Twenty-Four Articles issued by the Council of Constance at the beginning of 1418 appeals directly to the Bohemian people to hand over the books of Wyclif translated into the vernacular by Jan Hus and Jakoubek of Stříbro, as well as other vernacular texts by these authors.[23] Pope Martin V repeated the same request some weeks later.

It is not known how many individual translations of Wyclif's works may have been produced in Hussite Bohemia before these decrees were issued. We have evidence of two that do not survive – a translation of the *Trialogus*, very probably made by Jan Hus, and a translation of *De civili dominio* by an unknown author. The translation of Wyclif's *Dialogus* by Jakoubek of Stříbro is the only Czech translation of Wyclif's work extant, transmitted in two 15th-century manuscripts, one of which is almost complete, and the other fragmentary.[24] The work is unascribed, though Jakoubek is without doubt its

---

21 Jakoubek of Stříbro, *Dvě staročeská utrakvistická díla*, 23–26.
22 Ibid., 107.
23 "Viginti quatuor Articuli Constantiesis Concilii contra Hussitas & Bohemos," in *Magnum Oecumenicum Constantiense Concilium*, ed. Hermann von der Hardt, vol. 4 (Frankfurt and Leipzig: 1699), 1516.
24 Spunar, *Repertorium*, vol. 1, 245, no. 670. On Hussite translations of Wyclif's works, see Martin Dekarli, "Translating Political Theology into Vernacular. Réécriture of John Wyclif's Oeuvre in Late Medieval Bohemia," in *Pursuing a New Order II. Late Medieval*

author, judging by its language and stylistic correspondence with his other Czech vernacular works.[25] The editor of the work, Milan Svoboda, dated the work convincingly to 1411, noting the text's remarks on current events.[26] In particular, the translation refers to the conflict between the Archbishop of Prague, Zbyněk Zajíc of Házmburk, and King Wenceslas IV, which reached its peak in June 1411 when the archbishop proclaimed his interdict on Prague following the riots by Hus and his followers, who protested Zbyněk's order from June 1410 that Wyclif's books be burned. The archbishop's decision was mocked on the streets in several Czech songs, one of which is transmitted in a Hussite manuscript of later provenance. In response to Zbyněk's actions, the king then allowed the confiscation of revenues from the episcopal estates.

This date makes Jakoubek's translation of the *Dialogus* the first work of contemporary scholastic theology translated into Czech (although the *Dialogus* belongs to the more accessible works of Wyclif). In many respects Jakoubek was a pioneer, although the tradition of catechetical and spiritual Czech literature was already considerable. Even so, he is not known to have been especially interested in these earlier works. The most probable inspiration for his appreciation of vernacular religious education, the Czech writing of Matěj of Janov (only one work in Czech is mentioned in the sources), does not survive.[27] Jakoubek relied on Matěj of Janov heavily in many respects – in his emphasis on the importance of the Eucharist for the religious life of lay people, in his apocalyptic tendencies, and also in his theology. That he also drew on his paragon in appreciating the importance of vernacular theology is very probable. It is also likely that Janov's lost Czech work represents the missing link between the catechetical and educational literature of the last third of the 14th century and the more ambitious vernacular theology pursued by Jakoubek and Hus. Excerpts from the *Regulae* had already been translated into Czech by the first phase of the reform movement at the beginning of the 15th century, though it is not possible to determine if translations from the *Regulae* were common.[28]

It is unclear why Jakoubek decided to translate Wyclif's *Dialogus* in its entirety and not to use it as a source for his own exposition; we do not know if Jakoubek presented his text as a translation of Wyclif specifically: the extant

---

    Vernacularization and the Bohemian Reformation, eds. Pavlína Rychterová and Julian Ecker (Turnhout: 2019), 53–89.

25 Jakoubek of Stříbro, *Mistra Jakoubka ze Stříbra překlad Viklefova Dialogu*, ed. Milan Svoboda (Prague: 1909), xxiii-xxxiii.

26 Ibid., xxxiv-xxxvii.

27 Kybal, *M. Matěj z Janova*, 76.

28 Stanislav Souček, "Staročeský výňatek z Regulí Matěje z Janova," *Listy filologické* 54 (1927): 113–23.

text of the longer fragment is a later copy, transmitted anonymously. In any case, he systematically changed all of the passages in the text that refer specifically to English events. Nevertheless, he announces in the prologue that the text is a translation (if not from Wyclif specifically) and stresses the importance of the vernacular:

> It is proper if the exposition of Christian faith which pertains to the clerical estate more than to any other is translated into natural language from Latin and revealed to faithful Christians. Because the more God's truth concerning human salvation that is hidden in God's law is revealed, the more Christian souls who are capable of it are illuminated.[29]

Milan Svoboda, as well as Jan Sedlák, who in his work on the role of Jakoubek of Stříbro in the first phase of the Hussite movement provided the only analysis of the text until today,[30] emphasized the importance of Jakoubek's translation for the further radicalization of the lay adherents of the movement. Wyclif's treatise represents a radical critique of the papacy, the church hierarchy, the clergy in general, and their relationship to the imperative of poverty in particular. In Bohemia the treatise was widely circulated and copied (nineteen extant manuscripts of the Latin original text originate in Bohemia), but it is doubtful if Jakoubek targeted the laity as such. More likely is that he made the translation for some members of the nobility, or perhaps, through the mediation of sympathetic nobles, for the king himself. Passages in the original Latin text that contain a sharp critique of those who hold secular power – especially the Roman emperors, which according to Wyclif were co-responsible for the disintegration of the church by their "foolish donations" – were left out from the translation. For example, the passage scorning the Roman emperors who corrupted the church through wealth is translated as follows:

---

29 Jakoubek of Stříbro, *Překlad Viklefova Dialogu*, 1. Jakoubek changed the first sentences of his Latin model: "ac lingua latina plus regulariter dilatatur atque extensius, visum est quibusdam quod sentencia catholica collecta fidelibus in vulgari reseretur communius in latino. Veritas enim utilis de quanto diffusius dilatatur de tanto mentes fidelium plus illustrat." Cf. Wyclif, *Dialogus*, 1. Jakoubek defended the vernacular translations of the Bible and theological texts repeatedly, for example in his reaction to a speech Jean Gerson gave at Constance on 20 August 1417: "ceterum ex ordinacione ecclesie Slavi, in ydiomate cum Bohemis ut plurimum concordantes non solum scripturam sanctam in suo ydiomate permissi sunt habere, ymo et divina in lingua sua peragunt per orbem universum." František Micháleck Bartoš, *Literární činnost M. Jakoubka ze Stříbra* (Prague: 1925), 54.
30 Jan Sedlák, "Husův pomocník v evangeliu," *Studie a texty k náboženským dějinám českým* 1 (1914): Part 1, 314–15.

> The clergy together with the pope, because of the foolish and excessive endowment, established for themselves another, greater law that the priests and deacons may make the endowments hereditary ...[31]

Where Wyclif talks about the foolish donations of the emperors, the translator avoids attributing the action to emperors specifically. The translation is also harsher and more concrete than Wyclif's original in its critique of high clerics, and it more often draws a comparison between secular and spiritual lordship, coming close to a direct address of the reader. For example, the passage

> ... non mirum si conversantes cum illis de isto dominio tam abhominabili dedignantur. Et ideo non mirum necessitantur dicti clerici arma crudelius macabeis arripere et pugnare. Et sic officium prime partis et secunde ecclesie simpliciter est subversum.[32]

is rendered:

> Therefore, it is no wonder that common people and princes and lords and esquires also brace themselves against this revolting clerical lordship forbidden by God: because secular [lords] have a better right to it than have the clergy. It is forbidden to the clergy and it is conferred on secular [lords]. But devilish shrewdness in its hypocrisy interpreted it differently. And it is no wonder that this bossy clergy takes up the knightly garment and the arms of secular lords, and that it fights brutally and defends this ill-gotten dominion even to bloodshed, more cruelly than did the so-called Maccabee heroes. And to all those who are willing to help them, they give many false indulgences on which they rave as if they were dreaming. It's like when one [pope] damned another for his worldly dominion and one gave many indulgences to all those who helped him to shed blood against the other, and the other against him. And much of this happens now as well. And so the true office of the first state of the holy church, that is, the state of the clergy, is now completely overturned.[33]

---

31   Jakoubek of Stříbro, *Překlad Viklefova Dialogu*, 5. Cf. John Wyclif, *Iohannis Wycliffe Dialogus sive Speculum ecclesie militantis*, ed. Alfred W. Pollard (London: 1886), 8: "clerus cum papa ex concessione stulta cesaris stabilit sibi pro lege perpetua quod sacerdotes et levite habebunt capitaliter hereditatem perpetuam...."
32   Wyclif, *Dialogus*, 8.
33   Jakoubek of Stříbro, *Překlad Viklefova Dialogu*, 6.

Jakoubek enriched Wyclif's text with many concrete examples of the depraved way of life of the clergy and especially the papacy. He never marked his additions as such and (as far as the surviving copies reveal) did not declare that the author of his model text was John Wyclif. Still, it is entirely possible that the likely addressees of his work, the Czech noble adherents of Hus's reform party, knew the author of the treatise. They were well acquainted with the polemics concerning Wyclif at the university, and it is likely that Jakoubek did not need to name his model, whose objective, namely the secularization of suplerfluous church temporalities, was appreciated by English and Czech nobility alike. Jakoubek provided his readers with an excellent argumentative arsenal, including additions that the lords were unlikely to identify as such, and which they did not hesitate to use.

Jakoubek's use of the vernacular seems always to have had a concrete purpose. He turned to the vernacular whenever it was necessary to gain support from lay circles, and he differentiated among his targeted recipients according to their social status and respective interests. He never wrote a Czech text for the religious education of the "people" in general. His extensive *Exposition on the Apocalypse*, a Czech homily probably written in 1421, is an important example. Here Jakoubek addressed the difficult task of distinguishing between the individual factions of the *ecclesia militans*: the Catholics, true to Rome; his own Utraquists; and the radical factions of the Utraquist community formed in the newly founded city of Tábor. For each he sought to define a place in God's plan of salvation. He drew a more or less clear line between his own theological and ecclesiological system of the reformed "church" (defined as a community of faithful believers) and the "Roman" Church from which his reformed church had dissociated itself; and also between his church and the theory and practice of the radical Taborite faction. The text represents a superb fusion of several genres – exegetical tract, polemical treatise, moral exhortation, all in the form of a postil, the individual sermons commenting subsequently on the individual verses of the Revelation of St. John. The church of Jakoubek's own time, that is, the Roman, Utraquist and Taborite divisions, are interpreted as players in God's scheme of the history of salvation. At the same time, the polemic with the Taborites and the critique of Roman Catholics is based on a traditional moral interpretation of the relevant biblical verses:

> [God] takes anybody he likes, he takes him like a whip, good or bad, and he uses this whip rightfully: in the same way that he drove the merchants who resisted him out of the temple [John 2:15], he now drives and sweeps away hypocrites out of the monasteries with flails. But he also permits himself to strike his own people, wherefore they grumble and show

impatience. They should show humility and kiss the whip of Christ, loving him while he is visiting them in vengeance. Many, nevertheless, who count themselves among God's party, perform many things without love, but everyone must regard only God and bow only before him.[34]

In this passage, Jakoubek clearly linked the exposition to contemporary events, when he spoke about purging monsteries with a flail, the iconic weapon of the Hussite troops. By God's "own people" he meant the Hussite/Utraquist Church, whereas the "many who count themselves among God's party" were the Taborite radicals who fiercely persecuted the Roman prelates but also fought theological battles against the Utraquists. The moral lesson, in the end, should be taken by "everyone," that is, by Jakoubek's readers.

With the emphasis on the moral sense of Scripture,[35] Jakoubek countered the literal-historical interpretation of the Bible favored by the radical Taborites (the Taborites are described unmistakably as the envoys of Antichrist, as the apocalyptic people of Gog and Magog, etc.).[36] But he did not choose the genre of polemic, because he aimed at a more differentiated audience than was the case in his previous Czech writings. In the case of the *Dialogus*, the Czech-speaking noble supporters of the reform party at the University had likely been the addressees; in the case of the tracts on communion under both kinds he addressed the adherents of the reform church crystallizing around the liturgical innovation/restoration. In the *Exposition on the Apocalypse* Jakoubek addressed not only an inner circle of adherents, but rather the whole, inwardly divided Utraquist community, especially those people who did not clearly fall within any one faction. His placement of various contemporary ideological positions, religious practices, and events into a moral interpretation of the apocalyptic scheme was intended to help the reader to distinguish the church of the faithful. In Jakoubek's interpretation, it is only through a true faith and the correct devotional practice, namely Utraquist communion, that one is able to discern spirits and to learn to read one's experience in the world as set of instructions for spiritual conduct, thus leading the way to salvation.[37]

---

34 Jakoubek of Stříbro, *Výklad na Zjevenie sv. Jana*, ed. František Šimek, 2 vols. (Prague: 1932–1933), vol. 1, 23–24.
35 Amedeo Molnár, "Poslední věci v pohledu Jakoubka ze Stříbra," *Teologická příloha Křesťanské revue* 22 (1955): 39–40.
36 On Jakoubek's interpretation of the Apocalypse, see Vít Hlinka, *Erunt duo luminaria. "Restitutio" a jeho apokalyptičtí vyslanci ve františkánské a husitské perspektivě* (PhD dissertation, Olomouc: 2013), 264–78.
37 Jakoubek of Stříbro, *Výklad na Zjevenie*, lxxv–lxxix.

Jakoubek's *Exposition on the Apocalypse* is extant in a single codex and, like the translation of *Dialogus*, was transmitted anonymously.[38] This should not be taken as an indication that there was little interest in these texts, however. Jakoubek's *Dialogus* was received by Petr Chelčický, an influential lay theologian of the second phase of the Hussite movement (on whom, more below); large parts of the *Exposition* were reused in the Latin translation by the bishop of the Taborite Hussite faction, Mikuláš of Pelhřimov, in his own *Exposition on the Apocalypse*.[39] Jakoubek's vernacular Czech work initiated a new stage in theological thinking and textual production among Hussite elites, and its reception established an independent vernacular Czech theological discourse. In the time to come, the Latin and Czech languages would be regarded as equal in authority, not only among lay readers, but also among the chief university-trained theologians of the movement.

It was the fragmentation of the movement after the foundation of Tábor that accelerated this development. This can be demonstrated by the tract on the Eucharist written by Petr Chelčický, conceived as an answer to the writings of Mikuláš of Pelhřimov and other Taborite theologians. Chelčický wrote the text around 1425 as the Taborite teaching on the Eucharist became institutionalized after the crisis of 1421.[40] In his tract, he quoted at least four Taborite treatises on the problem, two of which he had likely read in Czech,[41] the other two in Latin. The main problems discussed in the text are transubstantiation and remanence – the most complicated theological questions on the Eucharist. This required a focused and terminologically differentiated argumentation that could be developed only with difficulty in the vernacular, as Chelčický's struggle for proper terminology and definitions shows. The tract describes the setting of the debate, in which it seems not only Chelčický and Taborite theologians participated, but also the moderate Utraquist theologians from the University of Prague, the foremost opponents of Taborite theology of the Eucharist. Furthermore, lay adherents of both factions participated, as well as believers who were as yet undecided. Chelčický describes the beginnings of his involvement in the debate as follows, addressing Mikuláš of Pelhřimov:

---

38   The manuscript, Prague, Archiv Pražského hradu, Knihovna Metropolitní kapituly, A 37, is dated 1528.
39   Pavlína Cermanová, *Čechy na konci věků. Apokalyptické myšlení a vize husitské doby* (Prague: 2013), 129–40.
40   Jan Sedlák, *Táborské traktáty eucharistické* (Brno: 1918).
41   The Taborite tract on the Eucharist written in Czech is extant in Prague, Archiv Pražského hradu, Knihovna Metropolitní kapituly, D 82, fols. 287r-297v. The codex also contains seveal works by Petr Chelčický. See Jaroslav Goll, *Quellen und Untersuchungen zur Geschichte der Böhmischen Brüder*, vol. 2: *Petr Chelčický und seine Lehre* (Prague: 1882), 60–65.

Now it was, I think, three years ago, when during your visit in Vodňany,[42] you, together with the priest Lukas, sent for me and asked me, resting on the dam of the fishpond, what I had heard of you, about your opinion on the Body of Christ. And I told you then that I keep hearing that some people say you were wrong, and others that you were right. And you said that you were never against [i.e. against the right doctrine], that you only followed the Scripture, and that your desire and effort was to separate from this sacrament false ideas, invented by men. And there was a lot of talk about this here. And I really quite liked what you said. Then, after a long time, you sent for me so that I might come to you [i.e. your community]. And again you talked too much in the same sense, you know where and in whose presence. I liked these talks from you. I therefore asked you to write them down for me, not because, having acquired them from you, I would think of betraying you or campaigning against you, but just because I wanted them for my own benefit as the right teaching. I did not know anything about it, being a simpleton, until I received your writings and contemplated them – I have not acquired everything directly from you.... I knew as little about these things at that time about which I am now writing as I know now about what the pope in Rome is doing these days.[43]

Chelčický was already a profound thinker and an exceptional person by the time that his contacts with Taborite theologians began,[44] and so this passage should not be taken to represent a situation that was typical of the everyday experience of an average Utraquist or lay believer in Bohemia at that time. Nevertheless, the readiness of the priestly elite to discuss difficult theological questions in the vernacular probably was a common phenomenon, practiced especially by the radical Taborite faction of the Hussite movement. Jakoubek of Stříbro interpreted this Taborite practice in the course of his exegesis of Apoc. 16:4:

The devil dug great wells during these days in Bohemia from which great streams of blasphemy and heresy against the blessed sacrament of the

---

42   A town in southern Bohemia, not far from Tábor.
43   Petr Chelčický, *Spisy z Olomouckého sborníku*, ed. Jaroslav Boubín (Sbírka pramenů k náboženským dějinám) 4 (Prague: 2016), 61–62, 69. Cf. Petr Chelčický, *Drobné spisy*, ed. Eduard Petrů (Prague: 1966), 132–35.
44   Jaroslav Boubín, *Petr Chelčický. Myslitel a reformátor* (Prague: 2005), 14–41. See also Howard Kaminsky, *A History of the Hussite Revolution* (Berkeley and Los Angeles: 1967), 464–65.

> Body of Christ flow. And these streams of Babylon and wells of stolen waters came from those Christians who communicated the Body of Christ and who had the Word of Christ. And from these wells, that is, from the heretics and hypocrites, streams flow, that is, treatises in Latin as well as in the Czech language aiming at blasphemy of the blessed sacrament.[45]

The vernacular language was explicitly refused as a language of theology and learned debate only by Catholic adversaries of Utraquism. Utraquists (the moderate ones as well as the Taborites) switched in their polemics from Latin to the vernacular and back again. In fact, they more often chose Latin, as did the major figure of the Taborite faction, Mikuláš of Pelhřimov, in whose extant oeuvre Latin texts prevail.

Nevertheless, the vernacular served as a key element of Utraquist group identity, as seen in the works of the leading Utraquist intellectual, Václav Koranda the Younger and Hilarius of Litoměřice, the Catholic administrator of the Prague archdiocese, in the course of their polemic on communion under both kinds in 1464. Two extant treatises by Hilarius were written in Latin, while Koranda's subsequent replies, as well as his opening question initiating the debate (which is not preserved, but its content may be reconstructed from the first tract by Hilarius), were written in Czech. In these texts the question of the language used in the polemic was repeatedly addressed. Hilarius maintained and defended the exclusive position of Latin as the learned language in the domain of doctrinal and theological polemic, whereas Koranda saw in the choice of language a powerful weapon in the polemical battle (or "duel," as he formulates it). Only in the vernacular, argues Koranda, can the laity (among whom he numbers himself) understand what is being discussed, for only in the vernacular can the misunderstandings caused by misleading Latin wordplay be avoided:[46]

> To my questions, short and written in Czech, you deliver lengthy answers and in Latin, in Latin colors with which I do not entertain myself; I do not know if this is because you want me to understand it less. Saint Paul chose five words to say reasonable [things], rather than a thousand to say

---

45   Jakoubek of Stříbro, *Výklad na Zjevenie*, vol. 2, 18–19.
46   On Václav Koranda the Younger, see the chapter by Jindřich Marek in the present volume.

unreasonable [things]. Or is it because [everyone] should know that your drum is tight?[47]

The extant manuscripts of the Czech translation of the Bible from this period, many of them lavishly decorated, with some even containing depictions of Jan Hus at the stake as a holy martyr, provide evidence for the high symbolic value of the Czech vernacular among the Utraquist laity. One handsome example is an illuminated Czech Bible from the second decade of the fifteenth century that was made for the noble adherent of Jan Hus, Petr Zmrzlík of Svojšín. Another, the Boskovická Bible from the first half of the 1420s, was likely commissioned by the important Utraquist nobleman Čeněk of Vartemberk. A third Bible, dated 1435 and extensively illuminated, was made for the Taborite captain Filip of Padeřov.[48]

Despite the high symbolic value of both the vernacular and the preacher's office in Hussite ideology, Czech did not dominate in the sermon literature of the 15th century. For example, Václav of Dráchov, who followed Jakoubek of Stříbro in the pulpit of Bethlehem Chapel, left no work written in Czech to posterity, though several of his postils survive.[49] Only a few Czech postils are extant from the 15th century: an anonymous collection of sermons for feast days from the first decade;[50] two of Jakoubek's Czech postils (in addition to his *Exposition on the Apocalypse*) from the second;[51] the postil written by Petr Chelčický in the 1430s–1440s, a text which was not designed for preaching but primarily for reading by the laity; and the postil of the first archbishop of the Utraquist Church, Jan Rokycana.[52] This last work, written in the late 1450s, is remarkable for its broad reception: ten manuscripts from the end of the 15th century and well into the 16th have been preserved. The text's editor, František Šimek, considers it to be a record of the Sunday and feast day sermons preached by Rokycana, recorded by his adherents and probably revised by the preacher himself. Šimek notes the lively language of the sermons as their most striking

---

47 Josef Truhlář (ed.), *Manualník M. Vácslava Korandy* (Prague: 1888), 194.
48 Václav Kyas, *Česká bible v dějinách národního písemnictví* (Prague: 1997), 66–68, 101–02.
49 Spunar, *Repertorium*, vol. 2: 89–93.
50 Władysław Wysłocki, "Kazania niedzielne i świąteczne w języku łacińskim i czeskim z początku xvgo wieku, podług kodeksiu biblijoteki hr. Tarnowskich w Dzikowie," *Rozprawy wydziału filologiczneho Akademii umiejętnośći v Krakowie* 3 (1875): 256–342.
51 Spunar, *Repertorium*, vol. 1, 246–47.
52 See also František Michálek Bartoš, *Dvě studie o husitských postilách* (Prague: 1955), 12–13.

feature.⁵³ Indeed, the character of the language is exceptional when compared with other Czech literary texts from the period, even giving the impression of recorded speech (though of course it could also be a characteristic of Rokycana's literary style), as seen in this example:

> Third, to hold the right hope: in all struggles, troubles, and sorrows find refuge in nobody and nothing else than the beloved Lord – let's expect help from nowhere but him. Are you doing it this way, Christians? Aha!? One [goes] to sorcerers and magicians, another to enchantresses and exorcists, one to this, another to that. And if there is nothing left that could help, only then let's go to God. 'Uh huh,' they say, 'now I entrust myself to the dear God.' Such are these people.⁵⁴

It is possible that the text was composed by the author primarily for reading, but the character of the extant manuscripts suggests that they were used as compendia of model sermons for preachers. Jan Rokycana used several Czech vernacular models in his texts, especially the Czech Sunday postil of Jan Hus, the Czech *Passionale* (the translation of the *Legenda aurea*, made in the 14th century and extant in several widely differing copies),⁵⁵ and also the works written by Petr Chelčický, primarily his postil.⁵⁶ In his interpretation of the pericopes, Rokycana relies heavily on the work of Matěj of Janov – particularly his spiritual interpretation of Scripture, his teaching of *imitatio Christi* through personal devotion, and his concern for the struggle of the true believers with temptation and sin, especially the sin of hypocrisy.

The text of the postil is partially based on material from about twenty years earlier and represents a unique insight into the topics of Utraquist preaching, driven by inter- as well as intra- confessional polemic. In this polemic, once again lay (vernacular) theological activity plays an important role as the cause of prevailing religious discord. Jan Rokycana regarded the translation of liturgical chants to be an important weapon against the devil;⁵⁷ at the same time, a

---

53 Jan Rokycana, *Postilla Jana Rokycany*, ed. František Šimek, 2 vols. (Prague: 1928–1929), vol. 1, xiv.
54 Ibid., 15–16.
55 Anežka Vidmanová, "La branche tchèque de la Légende dorée," in *Legenda aurea. Sept siècles de diffusion*, ed. Brenda Dunn-Lardeau (Montréal: 1986), 291–98.
56 Rokycana, *Postilla*, vol. 1, lxxvi-lxxvii.
57 Rokycana, *Postilla*, vol. 1, 482: "There, where the pericopes or devout songs are given in Czech or in the language the people understand, you will see how quickly the devil will rebel against it." See also pp. 360, 756.

self-initiated vernacular theology was a weapon that the devil used against God's elect:

> There are many people in Bohemia and Moravia who are oddly dazed and seduced from right belief in the Most Precious Body and the dearest Blood of Lord Jesus, so that they do not believe it could be his dearest Body and his holy Blood; they have fallen into such heresy. And there are also many priests who walk around clad like laymen and seduce people. They appear here and there, they daze people and strive for their souls. If the devil would come from the burning hell, he would always find mates among this folk! ... [Therefore, don't] fiddle with it, don't think it is possible to catch it with your own reason, the way in which God's Body is here [in the sacrament]. It outdoes all human reason; it should only be believed, saying: Because my Lord Jesus said: This is my Body and This is my blood, I believe him strongly; I believe that this is his real body and his holy Blood. But to fiddle with it, [to fuss over] the way in which it is here, I advise you: Let it be! ... But to measure all this, to mess about with it! Alas, wretched men, impudent and nosy! And you see that the devil mostly seduces these know-it-alls, supplying them with misgivings. Some Bartalas or a Beguine just starts to read and suddenly he or she longs to hand out their reasoning and to compose tracts and write (alas, wretched people!), and to blather about heavenly things; and they think they become 'somebody' with it.[58]

The Latin postils from the Hussite period, of which a considerable number survive, often contain Czech quotations, glosses, and insertions.[59] Although a similar practice may also be observed in pre-Hussite times, the macaronic collections of sermons from this time are much rarer. Only one such collection from the last third of the 14th century survives: the so-called *Quadragesimale Admontense*.[60] Jan Odstrčilík, the author of the first comparative analysis of this type of Latin-Czech collection,[61] observed a quality change in the Czech glosses and insertions in the postils from the second half of the 15th century, when compared with similar texts of the pre-Hussite period. For example, the

---

58   Rokycana, *Postilla*, vol. 1, 222–24.
59   Spunar, *Repertorium*, vol. 2, 96–101.
60   Hana Florianová, Dana Martínková, Zuzana Silagiová, and Hana Šedinová Hana (eds.), *Quadragesimale Admontense*, (Fontes Latini Bohemorum) 6 (Prague: 2006).
61   Jan Odstrčilík, *Analýza dvou latinských překladů Husovy české nedělní postily v rkp. Brno, Moravská zemská knihovna, Mk 56 a Mk 91 a jejich částečná edice* (PhD dissertation, Prague: 2015).

Czech passages in the postil of Michal Polák constitute an integral part of the text. The author chose them in many cases not because he would have difficulty in finding suitable Latin expressions, but because in his eyes the Czech language offered better expressions. Aside from this particular case, the presence of Czech words and sentences, as well as Czech syntactic constructions in Latin texts used by preachers, usually simplified the translation of the Latin model and its modification into new circumstances in Czech. Latin remained the primary language of the genre because it offered many stable phrases, an elaborate style, and a sophisticated system of abbreviations. All this taken together made the composition of a sermon in Latin (with or without the help of various preaching manuals) much easier than in the vernacular. But the boundaries were gradually getting blurred in this genre as well. For example, an interesting system of abbreviations can be found in some of the extant manuscripts of the Czech postil of Jan Rokycana, which was probably also used by preachers for their own work.

The boundaries were also becoming blurred between what had seemed to be the fixed ideological positions of Utraquists and Catholics. A remarkable testimony of this is found in the Latin translation of the Czech Sunday postil written by Jan Hus in 1413. This was translated sometime in the 1430s by a Roman Catholic priest (the translation survives in a single manuscript from the 1450s). By means of omissions from and modifications to the model, the translator managed to redefine the genre, purpose, and overall tenor of Hus's passionate declaration of his critical attitudes towards the church and his ideas for reform. Unlike the Czech original, the translation could be used as a preaching manual for any priest, regardless of confession, whether Utraquist or Catholic. Only the Taborites remained the target of sharp criticism, and it was for this purpose that the translator changed the original wording of selected passages in Hus's text.[62]

The struggle of the leaders of the Utraquist Church with the radical Taborite interpretations of Scripture, resulting in an idiosyncratic eucharistic practice, drove them more and more in the direction of a spiritual interpretation of Scripture, and to a lay catechesis which increasingly resembled the approaches found in the vernacular texts of the pre-Hussite period. This development is exemplified in the voluminous vernacular treatise of Jan Příbram, *Knížky o zamúceniech velikých cierkve svaté* (Books on the great tribulations of Holy Church). Aside from Jakoubek of Stříbro, Jan Příbram was the leading

---

62 Ibid. See also Jan Odstrčilík, "Translation and Transformation of Jan Hus's Czech Sunday Postil," in *Pursuing a New Order II. Late Medieval Vernacularization and the Bohemian Reformation*, ed. Pavlína Rychterová and Julian Ecker (Turnhout: 2019), 153–84.

theologian of the conservative Utraquist party. He was also one of the most important polemicists against Taborite theology, and against the Taborite interpretation of Wyclif's teaching – and eventually against Wyclif's teaching itself. He wrote in Latin as well as in the Czech vernacular:[63] his *Život kněží táborských* (The life of the Taborite priests), written at the beginning of 1430, delivers the most comprehensive information on the Taborite eucharistic teaching and practice and, as such, is significant for the historiography of the Hussite revolution.[64]

Příbram's treatise *Knížky o zamúceniech velikých cierkve svaté* survives in three manuscripts, all of them from the second half of the 15th century, and in two early prints from 1538 (now lost) and 1542.[65] The work conveys Příbram's interpretation of the events in Bohemia in the first three decades of the 15th century, leaning on the exegesis of Revelation and other biblical texts. His interpretation lacks the polemical character of Jakoubek's earlier *Exposition on the Apocalypse*. Jan Příbram's work may be described as a combination of meditation on the Cross (in the first part), exegesis of Revelation (the second part), and exposition on the Passion of Christ (the last and longest part). The author returns to the metaphoric vocabulary of Matěj of Janov, the only non-biblical authority he mentions by name,[66] drawing, for example, on Matěj's ecclesiological concepts of the Christian church as the church of the elect concentrated on the imitation of Christ in his Passion (which Jakoubek also featured in his exposition):

> We should clad ourselves in spiritual garments so that we may courageously pass through and bear these things, through worldly disgrace or praise, as seducers or liars or worthy of death, through punishments and flagellations, through grief and poverty, so that we do not deny the crucifixion of Christ but always long to emulate him and his tribulations, as did the apostles ...[67]

---

63 Interesting in this respect is his tract *Confessio fidei de corpore Christi – Vyznání o večeři páně* [Confession on the Lord's Supper] from the years 1426–1427, which is a Latin tract accompanied by an authorial Czech translation. See Jan Příbram, *Jan z Příbramě. Život kněží táborských*, ed. Jaroslav Boubín (Příbram: 2000), 12–14.
64 On Jan Příbram see the chapter by Petra Mutlová in the present volume. Cf. Příbram, *Život kněží táborských*, 7–32.
65 Spunar, *Repertorium*, vol. 2, 153–54.
66 Brno, Moravská zemská knihovna, Mk 97, fol. 50r (where his source is called Matěj of Bohemia).
67 Ibid., fol. 118v.

The events of the previous three decades, and especially the topic that concerned Příbram the most, the struggle against Taborite theology, are here embedded in Janov's concept of the "carnal" church of "hypocrites," without having to specify particular historical or theological contexts. This characteristic feature of the work likely encouraged the publisher of the 1542 printed edition to attribute the work to Milíč of Kroměříž, that is, to an author who was even older than Matěj of Janov.

Příbram's primary aim was nevertheless to put the confusion of his present time into the right perspective and to make it interpretable again: "Diligently consider this speech, and you will understand where you are, against whom you fight, and with whom you will come to the end."[68] The main explanatory tool in this work is the concept of temptation:

> Consider what Saint Judith says in the eighth chapter: You should remember that all your fathers were tempted because they had to be tried and tested, whether they rightfully venerated the Lord, their God ... Also, all those who were loved by God went through many tribulations. But those who did not accept this temptation fearfully, but fell into impatience and rumination against God, those were weeded out ... Therefore, we do not avenge the evil we suffer, but ascribing it to our sins, we say that these tribulations are less than we deserve ...[69]

Only *fuga saeculi* and endless patience in the face of many tribulations may ensure that the temptations of the devil (identified with Antichrist and vice versa) may be avoided or overcome (thus this text represents a shift away from the eschatological urgency that characterized the early Hussite and Taborite movements):

> Certainly, if anybody wants to defend himself against evil spirits, he must build his spiritual life as an ark and to stay in it with his whole heart forever, and never pour himself out into the world. And it is not enough [for him] to build the ark, but his Lord God must lock him personally into it from this world, as Noah did, so that no abysmal drop may trickle into his heart.[70]

---

68   Ibid., fol. 15v.
69   Ibid., fol. 15r-v.
70   Ibid., fol. 8r.

As an exceptional example of the evil power of the devil and the world (i.e. of the carnal church of the hypocrites) Jan Hus's fate in Constance is introduced as part of an interpretation of the Book of Job:

> How strongly [the devil] inveighs against [anybody who reveals his rage to the people] ...; so much so that he arouses against him all the secular and ecclesiastical powers, not only the evil and carnal ones but also good people, or those who seem to be the best of all ... And this [is done] so that the preacher or any good person who announces his evils would obey these many good, learned, holy people, appreciated by the community ... But the one who is good will defy all this and say with Holy Job ...: 'Have I feared the multitude, have I feared the disdain of my friends and of my people.' ... Each good man ... should expect with certainty a fierce fight with the devil, especially one who attempts to [speak] great truths and reveal great heresies and hidden ones, who announces the hidden, silent wickedness of Behemoth like Christ who often revealed priestly sins and started to admonish them. Thus he awoke the hidden Behemoth who brought him to the cross and whom the good Job defeated through great pains. Each good Christian who courageously provokes the devil may not expect any other end than Lord Jesus on the cross or festered Job, filled with pain.[71]

The passage quoted here illustrates the method Jan Příbram chose in this work for inserting current events into the overall scenario of salvation. This is not an apocalyptic scenario, *per se*, although the Apocalypse belongs to the biblical texts the author interprets. For example, the Whore of Babylon (Jezebel) is related directly to the Taborite faction of the Hussite movement, here called a "special community":

> And this woman is, you should understand, not only all the evil clergy but also other clergy from a special community, which is on the surface adorned with holiness but inside is full of horrible, merciless, and cruel heresy.[72]

---

[71] Ibid., fols. 50v-52r.
[72] Ibid., fol. 109r. The Taborite faction is also compared to the apocalyptic locusts (Mk 97, 115v), an interpretation that accords with Jakoubek's interpretation in his *Exposition on the Apocalypse*. Although there are no matches in rhetorical formulations, the interpretation of the Taborites in the salvation scenario is identical in both works.

But again, the Apocalypse is not the main interpretative model, as was the case in Jakoubek of Stříbro's exposition. The key is without doubt Christ's Passion; its description, which takes up nearly half the treatise, is the only biblical text interpreted here verse by verse to provide instruction for the pious reader for his daily Christian conduct. Everything else is subordinated to this goal. Even the namesake and founder of the movement, Jan Hus, who is never called by name but is described as the "good man" or "preacher," only serves here as a more or less general example of this achievement for which the reader must strive.

At almost the same time that Jan Příbram wrote his *Books on the Great Tribulations of Holy Church*, Thomas à Kempis, a member of the congregation of Windesheim, composed his famous book of pious instruction, *The Imitation of Christ*, a work with which Příbram's book bears comparison. Příbram's book is written in the vernacular, the targeted reader is clearly a devout lay person, and the purpose is to restore the state of the apostolic church, not in the world, but in the soul of each "elect" Christian. In Bohemia this emphasis was carried by the need to address all the small groups of devout people struggling to find their way among various spiritual offerings of the individual factions of the Hussite church. The concentration on individual lay devotion of more or less traditional tailoring presented a means of dealing with the liturgical obsession of many priests, no matter what the faction. There was indeed an audience for this kind of material in Bohemia in the second half of the fifteenth century, namely, those who were wearied by the religious and social turmoil of previous decades. It was these readers who quietly sought to return rebellious Bohemia to the paths of salvation that were less spectacular and less suited to the rapid cure of the Christian community here and now, seeking out a more stable and less bloody way. It is no coincidence that the majority of the works of Tomáš of Štítné survive in manuscripts from the last two thirds of the 15th century. Many of the Czech devotional texts from the last third of the fourteenth century survive in manuscripts from this period as well. Jan of Příbram's emphasis on the religious education of the laity, on their personal, private religious conduct, shares much in common with Tomáš of Štítné's goals. Štítné's texts, like the texts of his anonymous contemporaries, were much read a century later in Catholic as well as Utraquist milieux. The Utraquist copies were sometimes slightly modified according to the new creed, mostly in the passages where communion under one kind was mentioned in the original text.[73]

---

73 This is the case in later (15th- and 16th-century) copies of the Czech translation of the Revelations of Bridget of Sweden. See Pavlína Rychterová, *Die Offenbarungen der heiligen*

The most original examples of Hussite Czech vernacular theology, namely, those written by the lay theologian Petr Chelčický, come from the same time as Jan Příbram formulated his concept of lay religious education for postwar Bohemia. Petr had also learned from the Czech devotional literature of the pre-Hussite period, especially from the works of Tomáš of Štítné (one of Štítné's major works survives in his personal copy, annotated in his own hand).[74] Petr Chelčický interpreted anew the lay devotional message of Tomáš of Štítné. He did it in his major work, the vernacular Czech postil he wrote after 1435, emulating the so-called *Sunday and Feast Day Talks* of Tomáš of Štítné and the *Czech Sunday Postil* written by Jan Hus. In the prefaces to his individual works, Tomáš of Štítné eloquently defended his right as a lay man to write about spiritual topics: according to him, many spiritual questions should be discussed at home in a circle of devout Christians. Although he expressed more than once his skepticism towards the clergy and their moral standards, and although he held any devout lay Christian to be spiritually superior to any depraved cleric, he never questioned the role of ordained priests as intermediaries in the salvation process. The same applies to Jan Hus, who doubted only the position of depraved priests. Yet the central figure of the renewal of the church was for him not a devout layman, but the rightful preacher who was also a priest. In the eyes of Petr Chelčický, the intermediary role of the clergy had been irretrievably forfeited by the worldly greed into which the clergy had lapsed as a consequence of the personal failure of Pope Silvester, the one who baptized the pagan Emperor Constantine without teaching him Christian humility.[75] The preaching of this clergy could therefore only delude the people because it had departed from the Gospels, that is, from the Word of God himself.[76] But the pericopes which were (in Chelčický's words).

> used by this clergy for the satisfaction of their carnal desires, along with the Sunday and feast day sermons, have to be retained, that is, read and meditated upon, because these pericopes were bequeathed by Christ himself to console all those who are willing to implement them, read

---

Birgitta von Schweden. Eine Untersuchung zur alttschechischen Übersetzung des Thomas von Štítné (Cologne, Weimar, and Vienna: 2004), 216–17.

74 Tomáš of Štítné, *Tomáš ze Štítného. Řeči besední*, ed. Milada Nedvědová (Prague: 1992).

75 Here Wyclif's emphasis on the Donation of Constantine as the source of all evil in the Church finds an echo. See Takashi Shogimen, "Wyclif's Ecclesiology and Political Thought," in *A Companion to John Wyclif, Late Medieval Theologian*, ed. Ian Christopher Levy (Brill's Companions to the Christian Tradition) 4 (Leiden and Boston: 2006), in particular 207–11.

76 Boubín, *Petr Chelčický*, 105–24.

them, talk about them and to spend Sunday in this occupation ... Therefore, I will write something on these pericopes for the benefit of those who have learned the truth and who love it.[77]

From Chelčický's perspective, the true Christian is not a layperson hearing the sermon pronounced by preachers who have been "elected by God," as was the idea of the Hussite leaders of the first generation, but a lay person reading these "sermons" (that is, the expositions on biblical texts, not the whole Bible itself – there was indeed a limit to Petr Chelčický's rigorous biblicism) and discussing them, both in their vernacular and in their own circle of devout lay Christians, at home. This was also the ideal of Tomáš of Štítné and other European Christian authors from these turbulent times, laymen as well as members of the clergy who strove for the reform of the church in the heart of each individual believer. In contrast to them, Chelčický and his followers decided to pursue this goal outside the Catholic Church, and outside its Utraquist branch. Here the lay emancipation found its most remarkable expression, "vernacular" in every respect.

1 Historiographic Survey

Hussite vernacularization was approached from the beginnings of the modern humanities in the early 19th century as part of the history of a national language and literature. Modern research on vernacular literature in Bohemia started with Josef Dobrovský, with his *Geschichte der böhmischen Sprache und Literatur*. Dobrovský focused on the language, and he treated individual literary works as monuments of the six different stages that he recognized in the language's development. He regarded the Hussite period as an individual stage in the development of the Czech language and its literature, situating its beginning between the years 1410 and 1420. This chronology was nevertheless based on historical, not literary events. Dobrovský's follower, the Czech linguist and literary historian Josef Jungmann, took over this periodization.[78] He highlighted the issuing of the Decree of Kutná Hora (1409) as the Czech victory over German cultural domination and as a crucial moment of Hussite vernacularization.

---

77 Prague, Knihovna Národního muzea, XVII E 5, fols. 1r-2r. The Postil of Petr of Chelčický was edited by Smetánka: Petr Chelčický, *Petra Chelčického Postilla*, ed. Emil Smetánka, 2 vols. (Prague: 1900–1903). I quote from the fragmentary manuscript which the editor, who used an early print as his base text, did not consult.

78 Josef Jungmann, *Historie literatury české aneb Soustavný přehled spisů českých s krátkou historií národu, osvícení a jazyka* (Prague: 1825).

The subsequent overall narrative on Czech literature, written by Jaroslav Vlček at the end of the 19th century, concentrated on the ideological struggle of the Hussites against their Catholic adversaries.[79] In this study, which still carries influence, individual literary works faded into the background. The vernacular literature of the Hussite period was nevertheless the chief focus of the leading Czech linguist Jan Gebauer and his pupils, who also provided the first critical or semi-critical editions of the most important Czech vernacular texts, such as the works of Tomáš of Štítné, Jakoubek of Stříbro, Jan Rokycana, and Petr Chelčický.[80] Led by their linguistic interest, their editions and analyses usually do not provide detailed socio-cultural contextualization.

Incipient stages of this contextualization leaned on historiographic narratives, among which František Palacký's narrative dominated until the first decades of the 20th century.[81] It was then replaced by the volumes of *České dějiny* (Czech history) issued by Jan Laichter's publishing house. Among the volumes published before the communist coup d'état in 1948, the Hussite period (1415–1437) was missing. A modern positivist narrative on the decisive period of the Hussite wars (1415–1437) was therefore represented by monographs on Jan Hus, written by Jan Sedlák and Václav Novotný, and by the monograph of Josef Pekař on Jan Žižka.[82] In these books the problem of vernacularization and vernacular literature was never approached as such, and the relevant texts were regarded as evidence of lay religious activity, and as an expression of Hussite "democratization." This opinion was also shared by the literary-historical narratives of the time, for example, that of Jan Jakubec. The period of communist rule in Bohemia (1948–1989) gave strong emphasis to the revolutionary, "folkish," and anti-German character of the Hussite period. Here the process of vernacularization was regarded as an expression of political and cultural emancipation of "the people." In the four decades of communist rule, important editorial work was done, especially concerning the Czech vernacular texts written by Jan Hus, but also many other texts, particularly those which could be interpreted as more or less folkish creations or otherwise as proof of the emancipation of the people. Texts regarded as especially valuable from an aesthetic point of view were also edited. After 1989, no new narrative on the

---

79 Jaroslav Vlček, *Dějiny české literatury*, 3 vols. (Prague: 1959–1961).
80 Tomáš of Štítné, *Sborník Vyšehradský*; Jakoubek of Stříbro, *Překlad Viklefova Dialogu*; Rokycana, *Postilla*; Chelčický, *Postilla*.
81 František Palacký, *Dějiny národu českého v Čechách a v Moravě*, 6 vols. (Prague: 1848–1876).
82 Jan Sedlák, *M. Jan Hus* (Prague: 1915); Václav Novotný, *M. Jan Hus. Život a učení*, Part 1: *Život a dílo*, 2 vols. (Prague: 1919–1921); Josef Pekař, *Žižka a jeho doba*, 4 vols. (Prague: 1927–1933).

history of Czech literature (of which Hussite literature is a part) has appeared. A comprehensive exposition on the Latin, German, and Czech literature of the period, organized according to literary genre, was nevertheless published in the sixth volume of the series *Velké dějiny zemí Koruny české*.[83]

Bibliography

Manuscripts

Brno, Moravská zemská knihovna [Moravian Library], Mk 97.
Prague, Archiv Pražského hradu, Knihovna Metropolitní kapituly [Prague Castle Archives, Library of the Metropolitan Chapter], A 37.
Prague, Archiv Pražského hradu, Knihovna Metropolitní kapituly [Prague Castle Archives, Library of the Metropolitan Chapter], D 82.
Prague, Knihovna Národního muzea [National Museum Library], XVII E 5.
Prague, Národní knihovna České republiky [National Library of the Czech Republic], XVII A 6.

Editions of Sources

Chelčický, Petr, *Petra Chelčického Postilla* [Peter Chelčický's *Postilla*], ed. Emil Smetánka, 2 vols. (Prague: 1900–1903).
Chelčický, Petr, *Drobné spisy* [Minor writings], ed. Eduard Petrů (Prague: 1966).
Chelčický, Petr, *Spisy z Olomouckého sborníku* [Writings from the Olomouc manuscript], ed. Jaroslav Boubín (Sbírka pramenů k náboženským dějinám) 4 (Prague: 2016).
Florianová, Hana, Dana Martínková, Zuzana Silagiová, and Hana Šedinová Hana (eds.), *Quadragesimale Admontense* (Fontes Latini Bohemorum) 6 (Prague: 2006).
Havránek, Bohuslav, Josef Hrabák, and Jiří Daňhelka (eds.), *Výbor z české literatury husitské doby* [An anthology of Czech literature of the Hussite period], 2 vols. (Prague: 1963–1964).
Jakoubek of Stříbro, *Mistra Jakoubka ze Stříbra překlad Viklefova Dialogu* [Master Jakoubek of Stříbro's translation of Wyclif's *Dialogus*], ed. Milan Svoboda (Prague: 1909).
Jakoubek of Stříbro, *Výklad na Zjevenie sv. Jana* [Exposition of the Revelation of St. John], ed. František Šimek, 2 vols. (Prague: 1932–1933).
Jakoubek of Stříbro, *Dvě staročeská utrakvistická díla Jakoubka ze Stříbra* [Two Old Czech Utraquist works of Jakoubek of Stříbro], eds. Mirek Čejka and Helena Krmíčková (Brno: 2009).

---

83 Čornej and Bartlová, *Velké dějiny zemí Koruny české*, vol. 6, 304–39.

Milíč of Kroměříž, *Iohannis Milicii de Cremsir Tres sermones synodales*, eds. Vilém Herold and Milan Mráz (Prague: 1974).
Příbram, Jan, *Jan z Příbramě: Život kněží táborských* [The life of the Taborite priests], ed. Jaroslav Boubín (Příbram: 2000).
Rokycana, Jan, *Postilla Jana Rokycany* [The postil of Jan Rokycana], ed. František Šimek, 2 vols. (Prague: 1928–1929).
Svejkovský, František (ed.), *Veršované skladby doby husitské* [Versified compositions of the Hussite period] (Prague: 1963).
Tomáš of Štítné, *Tomáše ze Štítného Knížky šestery o obecných věcech křesťanských* [Six books on general Christian matters], ed. Karel Jaromír Erben (Prague: 1852).
Tomáš of Štítné, *Tomáš ze Štítného. Sborník Vyšehradský* [The Vyšehrad manuscript], ed. František Ryšánek (Prague: 1960).
Tomáš of Štítné, *Tomáš ze Štítného. Řeči besední* [Conversations], ed. Milada Nedvědová (Prague: 1992).
Truhlář, Josef (ed.), *Manualník M. Vácslava Korandy* [The Manual of Master Václav Koranda] (Prague: 1888).
"Viginti quatuor Articuli Constantiesis Concilii contra Hussitas & Bohemos," in *Magnum Oecumenicum Constantiense Concilium*, ed. Hermann von der Hardt, vol. 4 (Frankfurt and Leipzig: 1699), 1514–19.
Wyclif, John, *Iohannis Wycliffe Dialogus sive Speculum ecclesie militantis*, ed. Alfred W. Pollard (London: 1886).

Secondary Sources

Bartoš, František Michálek, *Literární činnost M. Jakoubka ze Stříbra* [The literary activity of Master Jakoubek of Stříbro] (Prague: 1925).
Bartoš, František Michálek, *Dvě studie o husitských postilách* [Two studies on Hussite postils] (Prague: 1955).
Boubín, Jaroslav, *Petr Chelčický. Myslitel a reformátor* [Petr Chelčický. Thinker and reformer] (Prague: 2005).
Bylina, Stanisław, "La catéchisation du peuple en Bohême aux XIVe et XVe siècles" in *The Bohemian Reformation and Religious Practice*, eds. Zdeněk V. David and David R. Holeton, vol. 3 (Prague: 2000), 25–33.
Cermanová, Pavlína, *Čechy na konci věků. Apokalyptické myšlení a vize husitské doby* [Bohemia at the end of times. Apocalyptic thought and visions of the Hussite period] (Prague: 2013).
Čornej, Petr, and Bartlová, Milena, *Velké dějiny zemí Koruny české* [A comprehensive history of the lands of the Bohemian Crown], vol. 6 (Prague and Litomyšl: 2007).
Dekarli, Martin, "Translating Political Theology into Vernacular. Réécriture of John Wyclif's Oeuvre in Late Medieval Bohemia," in *Pursuing a New Order* II. *Late*

Medieval Vernacularization and the Bohemian Reformation, eds. Pavlína Rychterová and Julian Ecker (Turnhout: 2019), 53–89.

Dekarli, Martin, *Politická a morální teologie Jana Husa v kontextu pražské univerzitní tradice* [The political and moral theology of Jan Hus in the context of Prague university tradition] (forthcoming).

Dobrovský, Josef, *Geschichte der böhmischen Sprache und Literatur* (Prague: 1791).

Goll, Jaroslav, *Quellen und Untersuchungen zur Geschichte der Böhmischen Brüder*, vol. 2: *Petr Chelčický und seine Lehre* (Prague: 1882).

Hlinka, Vít, *Erunt duo luminaria. "Restitutio" a jeho apokalyptičtí vyslanci ve františkánské a husitské perspektivě* [*Erunt duo luminaria*. "Restitutio" and its apocalyptic envoys in Franciscan and Hussite perspectives] (PhD dissertation, Olomouc: 2013).

Jakubec, Jan, *Dějiny literatury české. Od nejstarších dob do probuzení politického* [A history of Czech literature. From the earliest times to the political awakening] (Prague: 1911).

Jungmann, Josef, *Historie literatury české aneb Soustavný přehled spisů českých s krátkou historií národu, osvícení a jazyka* [A history of Czech literature, or A systematic survey of Czech writings with a brief history of the nation, enlightenment and language] (Prague: 1825).

Kaminsky, Howard, *A History of the Hussite Revolution* (Berkeley and Los Angeles: 1967).

Krmíčková, Helena, "K pramenům Husovy kvestie *De sanguine Christi sub specie vini* [On the sources of Hus's *quaestio De sanguine Christi sub specie vini*]," *Sborník prací Filozofické fakulty brněnské univerzity* C 45 (1998): 79–102.

Kyas, Václav, *Česká bible v dějinách národního písemnictví* [The Czech Bible in the history of national literature] (Prague: 1997).

Kybal, Vlastimil, *M. Matěj z Janova. Jeho život, spisy a učení* [Master Matěj of Janov. His life, writings, and teachings] (Prague: 1905).

Molnár, Amedeo, "Poslední věci v pohledu Jakoubka ze Stříbra" [The last things in the view of Jakoubek of Stříbro], *Teologická příloha Křesťanské revue* 22 (1955): 39–40.

Novotný, Václav, *M. Jan Hus. Život a učení* [Master Jan Hus. Life and teachings], Part 1: *Život a dílo* [Life and works], 2 vols. (Prague: 1919–1921).

Odstrčilík, Jan, *Analýza dvou latinských překladů Husovy české nedělní postily v rkp. Brno, Moravská zemská knihovna, Mk 56 a Mk 91 a jejich částečná edice* [An analysis of two Latin translations of Hus' Czech Sunday Postil in Mss. Brno, Moravian Library, Mk 56 and Mk 91 and their partial edition] (PhD dissertation, Prague: 2015).

Odstrčilík, Jan, "Translation and Transformation of Jan Hus's Czech Sunday Postil," in *Pursuing a New Order* II. *Late Medieval Vernacularization and the Bohemian Reformation*, eds. Pavlína Rychterová and Julian Ecker (Turnhout: 2019), 153–84.

Palacký, František, *Dějiny národu českého v Čechách a v Moravě* [A history of the Czech nation in Bohemia and Moravia], 6 vols. (Prague: 1848–1876).

Pekař, Josef, *Žižka a jeho doba* [Žižka and his time], 4 vols. (Prague: 1927–1933).
Rychterová, Pavlína, *Die Offenbarungen der heiligen Birgitta von Schweden. Eine Untersuchung zur alttschechischen Übersetzung des Thomas von Štítné* (Cologne, Weimar, and Vienna: 2004).
Rychterová, Pavlína, "Die Verbrennung von Johannes Hus als europäisches Ereignis. Öffentlichkeit und Öffentlichkeiten am Vorabend der hussitischen Revolution," in *Politische Öffentlichkeit im Spätmittelalter*, eds. Martin Kintzinger and Bernd Schneidmüller (Vorträge und Forschungen) 75 (Ostfildern: 2011), 361–83.
Rychterová, Pavlína, "Kirchen- und Klerikalkritik im Böhmen des 14. und 15. Jahrhunderts zwischen Latein und Volkssprachen," in *Clero contro clero. Retoriche anticlericali fra medioevo e prima età moderna*, eds. Gian Luca Potestá and Roberto Rusconi, *Rivista di storia del Cristianesimo* 12 (2015): 329–49.
Rychterová, Pavlína, "The Vernacular Theology of Jan Hus," in *A Companion to Jan Hus*, ed. Frantisek Šmahel and Ota Pavlíček (Brill's Companions to the Christian Tradition) 54 (Leiden and Boston: 2015), 170–213.
Sedlák, Jan, "Husův pomocník v evangeliu" [Hus's assistant in the Gospel], *Studie a texty k náboženským dějinám českým* 1 (1914): 362–428; 2 (1915): 302–350, 446–477; 3 (1919): 24–74.
Sedlák, Jan, *M. Jan Hus* (Prague: 1915).
Sedlák, Jan, *Táborské traktáty eucharistické* [Taborite eucharistic tracts] (Brno, 1918).
Shogimen, Takashi, "Wyclif's Ecclesiology and Political Thought," in *A Companion to John Wyclif, Late Medieval Theologian*, ed. Ian Christopher Levy (Brill's Companions to the Christian Tradition) 4 (Leiden and Boston: 2006), 199–240.
Sichálek, Jakub, "European Background. Czech Translations," in *The Wycliffite Bible. Origin, History and Interpretation*, ed. Elizabeth Solopova (Leiden and Boston: 2017), 66–84.
Šlosar, Dušan, "Frühe volkssprachliche Entwicklung – Early Vernacular Development," in *Die Slavischen Sprachen. The Slavic Languages. Ein internationales Handbuch zu ihrer Struktur, ihrer Geschichte und ihrer Erforschung. An international Handbook of their Structure, their History and their Investigation*, eds. Karl Gutschmidt and Sebastian Kempgen, vol. 2 (Berlin, Munich, and Boston: 2014), 1384–96.
Šmahel, František, *Idea národa v husitských Čechách* [The idea of the nation in Hussite Bohemia], 2nd ed. (Prague: 2000).
Souček, Stanislav, "Staročeský výňatek z Regulí Matěje z Janova" [An Old Czech excerpt from the *Regule* of Matěj of Janov], *Listy filologické* 54 (1927): 113–23.
Spunar, Pavel, *Repertorium auctorum Bohemorum provectum idearum post universitatem Pragensem conditam illustrans*, 2 vols. (Studia Copernicana) 25 and 35 (Wrocław and Warsaw: 1985–1995).
Vidmanová, Anežka, "La branche tchèque de la Légende dorée," in *Legenda aurea. Sept siècles de diffusion*, ed. Brenda Dunn-Lardeau (Montréal: 1986), 291–98.

Vlček, Jaroslav, *Dějiny české literatury* [A history of Czech literature], 3 vols. (Prague: 1959–1961).

Wysłocki, Władysław, "Kazania niedzielne i świąteczne w języku łacińskim i czeskim z początku xvgo wieku, podług kodeksiu biblijoteki hr. Tarnowskich w Dzikowie" [Sunday and Feast Sermons in Latin and Czech from the beginning of the 15th century in the Tarnowski Library in Dzików], *Rozprawy wydziału filologiczneho Akademii umiejętnośći v Krakowie* 3 (1875): 256–342.

Liturgy, Sacramental Theology, and Music

David R. Holeton, Pavel Kolář and Eliška Baťová

Of the various sacramental and liturgical movements that took place in Europe during the late Middle Ages and Renaissance, the events which began in mid-14th-century Bohemia are, perhaps, the most important, the least studied, and the most frequently misunderstood.

1   The Seeds of Reform: Sacramental Renewal

The beginnings of the movement were quite limited in their intent and are, on the whole, in no sense parallel to the clearly articulated liturgical reforms that characterize the churches of the Reformation of the 16th century. The Bohemian sacramental and liturgical reform movement began as a pastoral response to one very specific experiment: the "Jerusalem" community of the priest Milíč of Kroměříž.[1] Milíč gathered around himself a diverse group of followers: clerics, lay people (both married and unmarried) and a number of the sex workers who had either quit that work to begin new lives or had left because they were advancing in age and were now destitute. Here, in the chapel which was dedicated to St. Mary Magdalene (then believed to have been a repentant prostitute herself), like any priest of his time, Milíč celebrated the Eucharist daily, at which he also preached to his congregation in Czech as well as Latin. Unheard of for the time, however, was Milíč's initiative to begin giving communion to his congregation at each celebration of the mass. This was unheard of because at that time the average lay person received the sacrament rarely (often only once a year), partly out of a sense of personal unworthiness, and partly on the popular belief that the priest received communion on behalf of the congregation as a whole.[2] Milíč's motivations for this innovation were

---

[1] On the life of Milíč see: Peter C.A. Morée, *Preaching in Fourteenth-Century Bohemia. The Life and Ideas of Milicius de Chremsir († 1374) and his Significance in the Historiography of Bohemia* (Heršpice: 1999); David C. Mengel, "A Monk, a Preacher, and a Jesuit. Making the Life of Milíč," in *The Bohemian Reformation and Religious Practice*, eds. Zdeněk V. David and David R. Holeton, vol. 5, 1 (Prague: 2004), 33–55.

[2] Berthold of Regensburg (d. 1272) appears to have been the first to propose the idea: Sermon 31: "Von der Messe," in Berthold of Regensburg, *Berthold von Regensburg. Vollständige Ausgabe seiner Predigten*, eds. Franz Pfeiffer and Joseph Strobl, 2 vols. (Vienna: 1862–1880), vol. 1, 488–504. William Durandus, *Rationale divinorum officiorum* (Venice: 1599), book 4, cap. 56, 1,

mixed: in part they were a pastoral response to the community that had come to share a common life at the heart of which was the altar; in part they were a response to a renewed understanding of Jesus's command to receive communion as words addressed to all Christians and not the clergy alone; but perhaps most of all, they grew out of a renewed understanding of the Eucharist as a foretaste of the heavenly banquet at which all the redeemed will eat and drink together. This latter image was one that clearly spoke to Milíč's times: many believed that Christ would soon return to judge the world which they believed showed all the signs of the last days. This restoration of frequent communion seems to have had a transformative or revolutionary effect on the participants. The members of the "Jerusalem" community believed that, in receiving communion together often, they were experiencing a foretaste of the heavenly Jerusalem – the coming reign of God – that was *already* in their midst.

2   The Utraquist Consensus: The Chalice and the Communion of All the Baptized

This isolated experiment proved to be a catalyst for a movement that was to make Bohemia unique in late medieval Europe. Over the course of the next quarter-century the practice of frequent communion for the laity was to gain the support of important Prague theologians (Matěj of Janov, Matthew of Cracow, Heinrich of Bitterfeld) and churchmen (Vojtěch Raňkův [Adalbertus Ranconis], Archbishop Jan of Jenštejn) and also became the subject of popular textual transmission in Czech beyond university circles (Tomáš Štítný of Štítné). Thus, by the end of the 14th century, the frequent reception of the Eucharist, at least weekly, and often daily, had become common practice in Bohemia – unlike any other place in contemporary Christendom.[3]

Frequent communion led to two further steps: the restoration of the lay chalice, which took place in 1414,[4] and, two years later, the restoration of the practice of communicating all from the time of their baptism, infants included.[5]

133a, said that "while in the primitive church the faithful communicated daily ... it was decided because of human sinfulness that we receive the sacrament of communion three times a year, and the priest daily on behalf of all."

3   Miri Rubin, *Corpus Christi. The Eucharist in Late Medieval Culture* (Cambridge: 1991), names no other frequent communion movement during the medieval period.

4   Howard Kaminsky, *A History of the Hussite Revolution* (Berkeley and Los Angeles: 1967), 97–136.

5   David R. Holeton, *La communion des tout-petits enfants. Étude du mouvement eucharistique en Bohême vers la fin du Moyen Âge* (Rome: 1989); idem, "The Communion of Infants and

These were both theologically logical consequences of frequent communion. It is difficult to say why it took so long between the restoration of frequent communion and the restoration of the lay chalice. When, in early 1415, Jakoubek of Stříbro was challenged over the lay cup by Ondřej of Brod, he replied that the idea came as a *revelatio*, by which he meant through the reading and re-reading of the dossier of biblical and patristic texts that had been compiled since the time of Matěj of Janov to justify frequent communion. It took three years for the same "revelation" to be understood as applying to all the baptized and not to adults alone. That said, it is difficult to credit that it took three or four decades for the incongruity of the renewed practice of frequent communion under one species and the language of the biblical texts to become evident. The relatively modern doctrine of concomitance, which argued that each species (bread and wine) contained the entire Christ and was a primary defense for communion *sub una*, would be unconvincing among Bohemian theologians, who increasingly rejected scholastic arguments.

Needless to say, the effect of these three changes was revolutionary for the average lay person and radically changed the nature of the liturgical celebration. Participation at mass, which had been primarily an activity of the eyes as the laity observed the actions of the priest – particularly the elevation of the consecrated host and chalice – now became an activity that involved physical movement as the whole community came to the altar to receive communion, standing beside friend and neighbor (including children and babes-in-arms) to receive the sacrament. The spiritual benefits of "communion," which had been understood to be received by gazing at the sacrament rather than actually receiving the elements themselves, now became dependent upon the direct reception of the consecrated bread and wine by all of those who were baptized. As the laity once again received the chalice, there would have been a palpable sense that one of the most visible signs of the division between the clergy and the laity had been shattered.[6]

In Prague, there was also heated debate between those who chose to continue to use the traditional ceremonies and ornaments and those who would have their use discontinued. A close reading of this early (ca. 1415–17) controversy over the necessity of vestments and other ornaments reveals that the

---

Hussitism," *Communion Viatorum* 27 (1984): 207–25; idem, "The Communion of Infants. The Basel Years," *Communio Viatorum* 29 (1986): 15–40.

6 A more detailed survey of this movement can be found in David R. Holeton, "The Bohemian Eucharistic Movement in its European Context," in *The Bohemian Reformation and Religious Practice*, ed. David R. Holeton, vol. 1 (Prague: 1996), 23–48.

fundamental issue at hand was not the use or disuse of vestments; rather, it was the celebration of the mass in whatever manner that made it possible for all – rich or poor – to receive the sacrament *sub utraque* when they were sick or dying and unable to get to their parish church to receive communion.[7] Those initial controversies aside, Utraquists generally remained loyal to the use of the traditional ornaments and vessels that were in general use before the controversies over the chalice. Practical accommodations, of course, needed to be made so that flagons were provided to allow for the consecration of a sufficient quantity of wine for all the communicants and, in some parishes, spoons were provided to facilitate communicating infants and small children as well as for taking the sacrament *sub utraque* to the sick and shut-in.[8]

3   Worship in Czech

The next action that revolutionized worship during the Bohemian Reformation period was the introduction of the vernacular into the liturgy. This was the culmination of a very long process in which Czech slowly emerged as a "sacred" language on an equal footing with Latin, which had long been regarded as the sole sacred language of western theological discourse and public prayer. Over the course of several centuries Czech had slowly appeared as a language into which first portions, and then the entirety of the Bible had been translated and prayer books (Books of Hours) for the wealthy laity had been prepared; sermons were regularly preached, hymns were sung and theology was popularized (e.g. through the writings and translations of Tomáš of Štítné). In this gradual evolution of Czech as a "sacred" language, the next obvious step was to move to the final domain where Czech had yet to find a place and to begin translating portions of the liturgy into the vernacular.[9] Exactly at whose initiative

---

7   David R. Holeton, "The Role of Jakoubek of Stříbro in the Creation of a Czech Liturgy. Some Further Reflections" in *Jakoubek ze Stříbra. Texty a jejich působení*, eds. Ota Halama and Pavel Soukup (Prague: 2006), 72–86.

8   Kateřina Horníčková and Michal Šroněk (eds.), *Umění české reformace (1380–1620)* (Prague: 2010), 211–12; Kateřina Horníčková, "A Utraquist Church Treasure and Its Custodians. A Few Observations on the Lay Administration of Utraquist Churches," in *The Bohemian Reformation and Religious Practice*, eds. Zdeněk V. David and David R. Holeton, vol. 6 (Prague: 2007), 189–208; Zuzana Všetečková, "Was the Pyx of Mělnik (with the Image of Christ on the Mount of Olives) Utraquist?" in *The Bohemian Reformation and Religious Practice*, eds. Zdeněk V. David and David R. Holeton, vol. 8 (Prague: 2011), 316–31.

9   David R. Holeton, "Bohemia Speaking to God. The Search for a National Liturgical Expression" in *Public Communication in European Reformation. Artistic and other Media in Central Europe 1380–1620*, eds. Milena Bartlová and Michal Šroněk (Prague: 2007), 103–32.

and how this took place remains unknown. Our first witness to an attempt to produce a "Czech liturgy" is the well-known *Jistebnický kancionál*.[10] It is clear from the manuscript, however, that the *Kancionál* is a corporate work based on other extant texts from manuscripts which are now lost, in which the sung portions of the liturgy had already been put into Czech.

4 The Daily Office[11]

The daily office, as such, seems to have received little, if any, attention from the 14th-century members of the Bohemian Reform movement. While the Czech lands were certainly subject to the same trends towards the "privatization" of the office as elsewhere in Europe, there is every reason to believe that monasteries continued to sing the full cursus and that some offices were sung regularly in parish churches throughout the land. All energy for liturgical reform was at first entirely concentrated on the Eucharist.

The first decades of the 15th century, however, bring us an important impulse for the renewal of the Divine Office, known to us through its most important witness, the *Jistebnický kancionál*, mentioned above. Internal evidence makes it clear that the *Kancionál* contains liturgical texts drawn from various sources which were themselves copied by different scribes.[12] Approximately one third of the liturgical material contained in the *Kancionál* is intended for use in the office.[13] While it does not provide material for the entire liturgical year, it does provide copious material for the great feasts: Christmas, Easter, Ascension, Pentecost, Corpus Christi, and Trinity.[14] Interestingly, extensive material is also provided for the three offices of *Tenebrae* sung during Holy

---

10   *Jistebnický kancionál*, vol. 2: *Cantionale* is in preparation.
11   This topic is treated much more extensively in David R. Holeton, "The Evolution of the Celebration of the Daily Office in Utraquism. An Overview," in *The Bohemian Reformation and Religious Practice*, eds. Zdeněk V. David and David R. Holeton, vol. 8 (Prague: 2011), 199–202.
12   Stanislav Petr, "A Codicological and Palaeographical Analysis of the Jistebnice Kancionál," in *Jistebnický kancionál. MS. Praha, Knihovna Národního muzea, II C 7. Kritická edice. Jistebnice kancionál. MS. Prague, National Museum Library II C 7*, vol. 1: *Graduale*, eds. Jaroslav Kolár, Anežka Vidmanová, and Hana Vlhová-Wörner (Brno: 2005), 62–71.
13   Hana Vlhová-Wörner, "The Jistebnice Kancionál – its Contents and Liturgy," in *Jistebnický kancionál. MS. Praha, Knihovna Národního muzea, II C 7. Kritická edice. Jistebnice kancionál. MS. Prague, National Museum Library II C 7*, vol. 1: *Graduale*, eds. Jaroslav Kolár, Anežka Vidmanová, and Hana Vlhová-Wörner (Brno: 2005), 265–75, nos. 143–306.
14   The latter two, curiously, in that order.

Week.[15] It would be dangerous to guess what may have existed elsewhere, but here we have a witness that assumes popular participation in the offices on at least the greatest feasts and at *Tenebrae*.

Almost at the same time as the promoters of the vernacular office were doing their work, the state of the office in Bohemia lost one important dimension. After the outbreak of the "revolutionary" period of the reformist movement in 1419, the destruction of the monasteries and the exile of the religious orders saw the disappearance of the largest single constituency who had sung the office corporately on a daily basis. It is clear, however, that the mainstream reform movement in no way saw the sung office as a "monkish" affair and had no intention of abandoning the traditional patterns of daily prayer. The Prague Synod of 7 July 1421[16] and the St. James's Day Synod of 25 July 1434[17] enjoined that the Divine Office continue as it had in times past. We know that some communities continued to sing the office corporately, but how many is difficult to estimate. The decimation of the clergy (both Roman Catholic and Utraquist) during this era would have had negative consequences on the number of parishes (let alone monasteries) with sufficient human resources to sing the daily office.[18]

In the Czech lands, as elsewhere in Europe, it is virtually impossible to draw an accurate picture of the number of churches where the whole *cursus* of offices was sung daily. Certainly there were several, including the Týn Church in Prague and St. James's in Kutná Hora, in which at least matins and vespers were sung daily. We have various references, extending from the early days of the Bohemian Reform movement to its very end, to schoolboys being required to sing the offices – sometimes daily, sometimes only on Sundays and great feasts, and sometimes on an additional weekday.[19] In Moravia, we know that there were at least five churches where the office was sung daily in the 15th

---

15 Vlhová-Wörner, "The Jistebnice Kancionál – its Contents and Liturgy," nos. 194–230.
16 František Palacký (ed.), *Urkundliche Beiträge zur Geschichte des Hussitenkrieges*, 2 vols. (Prague: 1873), vol. 1, 134.
17 Blanka Zilynská, *Husitské synody v Čechách 1418–1440. Příspěvek k úloze univerzitních mistrů v husitské církvi a revoluci* (Prague: 1985), 114, article 8.
18 Šmahel estimates that during the period between 1400 and 1500 the number of prebendiary priests in Prague (i.e. those holding titles and, therefore, obliged to sing the office in the parish where they held them) dropped from about 1,200 to 200. Parishes that had a number of priests at the beginning of the 15th century had one (at most) by the end. František Šmahel, *La révolution hussite, une anomalie historique* (Paris: 1985), 110.
19 Cf. Zikmund Winter, *Život a učení na partikulárních školách v Čechách v XV. a XVI. století* (Prague: 1901), 449–50.

century.[20] The practice appears to have continued unchanged at least until the time that some of those churches became Lutheran,[21] and perhaps longer, as it appears that the singing of the office by school boys continued even in some parishes that had become Lutheran.[22]

These witnesses to the longevity of sung office throughout the Czech lands need to be set alongside other forms of praying the office. It would certainly have been very common in Prague, with its large number of university students, to take advantage of the provision to recite the office privately because they were otherwise occupied with their studies. Most of these, after all, were clerks in holy orders who held benefices in places other than Prague and thus were unable to fulfill their legal obligations to sing the office in the church to which they were beneficed.

5   The Calendar

With one significant exception, Utraquism respected the liturgical year as it had developed in the Prague Use of the Roman Rite until the late 14th century. Missals written specifically for Utraquist parishes maintained the same temporal and sanctoral cycles that could be found in missals written for Roman parishes. Over time, the number of saints' days provided for in large Utraquist musical books diminished considerably but were long maintained in printed missals. This reflects several realities. First, human resources became greatly diminished and there were fewer parishes that could maintain the musical resources necessary to sing the liturgy frequently on weekdays. Second, the production of richly illuminated graduals depended increasingly on individuals who could be called upon to underwrite *one* set of propers. These sponsors (now largely burghers) generally paid for the illumination of the major feasts in the temporal cycle (Christmas, Easter, etc.), and not for saints' days. Third, as the sixteenth century progressed, the importance of saints' days diminished in Utraquist devotional practice (as opposed to Utraquist theological belief). Quite simply, fewer people appear to have gone to church on lesser saints' days. But here we encounter one of the distinct features of Utraquist devotional

---

20   The Cathedral of St. Wenceslas and the Collegiate Church of St. Maurice in Olomouc, the collegiate churches of St. Maurice in Kroměříž and St. Peter and Paul in Brno, and, possibly the church of St. James in Brno.
21   We are grateful to our colleague Dr. Vladimír Maňas of the Department of Musicology of the Faculty of Arts in the Masaryk University in Brno for this information.
22   Winter, *Život a učení na partikulárních školách*, 145.

practice: the liturgical commemoration of "Saint" Jan Hus and the other martyrs of the Bohemian Reformation.

News of the execution of Jan Hus at Constance on 6 July 1415 came as a shock and an outrage to much of the population in Bohemia. Understandably, upon hearing the news, requiem masses were celebrated in memory of Hus. More remarkable, however, was the celebration of masses using liturgical songs and prayers normally used for the feast of a martyr. Jerome of Prague (burnt on 30 May 1416) also came to be commemorated on 6 July, as did others martyred for the Utraquist cause. These included the approximately 1,500 "martyrs of Kutná Hora" who were killed with particular cruelty in 1419–1420[23] and, later, the priests Michal Polák (pastor of St. Mary-before-Týn, the principal Utraquist parish in Prague, who died in 1480 for publicly opposing King Vladislav the Jagellonian when he turned against the chalice) and Jan Bechyňka (d. 1507, a fervent defender of the chalice and communion for the very young).[24] Thus, after their deaths, Hus and the other Bohemian "martyrs" were commemorated on a single feast day which was incorporated among the many feasts of saints traditionally kept by the church in Bohemia. Slowly, liturgical propers were composed in their honor.[25] The feast on 6 July became fundamental to Utraquism's self-identity so that the day was observed not only liturgically but also as a popular holiday marked by bonfires at night and, at times, with anti-Roman Catholic provocations.[26]

---

23 Ota Halama, "The Martyrs of Kutná Hora," in *The Bohemian Reformation and Religious Practice*, eds. Zdeněk V. David and David R. Holeton, vol. 5, 1 (Prague: 2004), 139–46.

24 Joel Seltzer, "Re-envisioning the Saint's Life in Utraquist Historical Writing," in *The Bohemian Reformation and Religious Practice*, eds. Zdeněk V. David and David R. Holeton, vol. 5, 1 (Prague: 2004), 147–63.

25 Most of the texts for the Eucharist can be found in David R. Holeton, "'*O felix Bohemia – O felix Constantia.*' The Liturgical Commemoration of Saint Jan Hus," in *Jan Hus. Zwischen Zeiten, Völkern, Konfessionen*, ed. Ferdinand Seibt (Munich: 1997), 385–403, and for the office in idem, "The Office of Jan Hus. An Unrecorded Antiphonary in the Metropolitan Library of Estergom," in *Time and Community*, ed. J. Neil Alexander (Washington: 1990), 137–52; and David R. Holeton and Hana Vlhová-Wörner, "A Remarkable Witness to the Feast of St. Jan Hus," in *The Bohemian Reformation and Religious Practice*, eds. Zdeněk V. David and David R. Holeton, vol. 7 (Prague: 2009), 156–84. A critical edition of the musical texts in the gradual are found in Jiří Žůrek, *Graduale Bohemorum. Proprium sanctorum* (Prague: 2011), 138–45. For the lections, see Ota Halama, "Biblical Pericopes for the Feast of Jan Hus," in *The Bohemian Reformation and Religious Practice*, eds. Zdeněk V. David and David R. Holeton, vol. 9 (Prague: 2014), 173–84.

26 Because the ashes of Hus and Jerome were tipped into the Rhine, there were no relics of their bodies remaining for veneration. However, a fragment of Hus's pulpit in the Bethlehem Chapel was venerated by students at the university. At Kutná Hora, a chapel was built in honor of the local martyrs, and annual pilgrimages took place there during the

6   Liturgical Music

The most basic prerequisite which influenced the music of the Utraquist liturgy was the demand for the comprehensibility of the sung words. The same demand was repeated, in many variations, among all important pre- and post-*Compactata* Hussite figures. The main purpose of scriptural citations, which were related to the comprehensibility of singing the holy service, was the vernacularization of the liturgy (this was the focus of a series of 15th-century tractates entitled *De cantu vulgari*).[27] Another basic requirement was thus the prohibition of the *fractio vocis* (in Old Czech: *lámanie hlasóv* or *prolamovanie*). Although this term describes the rhythmicized form of the melismatic monophony (*cantus fractus*) or polyphony (*contrapunctus fractus*) in contemporary musical theory, it is sometimes interpreted by researchers as denoting contemporary modern polyphonic style.[28] Yet resistance against *fractio vocis* was primarily aimed at the melisma (i.e. a group of notes sung to one syllable), complicating the understanding of the biblical lection as sung in the Czech vernacular. Hence, both demands were closely related, as is illustrated by the resolution of the St. Jacob's Synod in 1434, led by Jan Rokycana: "[p]riests may preach the epistles and gospels in the vernacular; yet in both cases, for the time being and for certain reasons, they should leave out the *discantus* with *fractio vocis* ...; the confession of faith should be read or sung in the vernacular at the appropriate time."[29] Thus, the widespread tradition of the improvised polyphonic embellishment of masses and services should not interfere with the intelligibility of the biblical words sung in the people's vernacular. The singing of the *Credo* was apparently also viewed in this way, as it was one of the most typical representations of the practice of *cantus fractus*.

Rogation Days until after the Battle of Bílá Hora. A skeletal torso, still wearing a chasuble and believed to be a relic of the priest Jan Chůdek, was found in the pits and was venerated in the chapel. Halama, "The Martyrs of Kutná Hora," 143.

27   Eliška Baťová, "'O zpievaní a čtení českém tractat' by Václav Koranda the Younger. A Contribution to the History of Czech Liturgical Language," in *The Bohemian Reformation and Religious Practice*, eds. Zdeněk V. David and David R. Holeton, vol. 8 (2011), 145–61.

28   Jaromír Černý, "Das retrospektive Organum oder Neo-organum?," *Hudební věda* 38 (2001): 3–31.

29   "Sacerdotes epistolam et ewangelium in wulgari predicent; vtrique vero discantus cum fractura vocis pro hac re certis ex causis intermittant, nisi horum postea ex racionabili causa vnanimi consensu resumendorum affuerit; symbolumque legatur aut decantetur tempore oportuno." František Palacký and Ernst Birk (eds.), *Monumenta conciliorum generalium seculi decimi quinti. Concilium Basileense*, Scriptores: vol. 1 (Vienna: 1857), 745. Cf. the slightly different version: Zilynská, *Husitské synody*, 117–18.

In the development of other forms of Czech liturgical chant, we also continue to see consistent efforts striving for a purely syllabic text setting, often ignoring the original structure of phrases and the meaningful placement of words. In the sphere of polyphony, a style influenced by these ideas gradually developed, labeled "neo-organum" due to its use of certain characters of the older compositional organum practice, which it harmonically processed according to the new style of the Low Countries.[30] Only in Václav Koranda the Younger's summary *Contra cantum mensuratum*[31] do we find a notable shift in the interpretation of the concept of *fractio vocis*. His application of this term more generally to polyphonic mensural music apparently reflected the contemporary spread of the polyphonic style of the Low Countries into Utraquist churches. The development of this repertoire – despite the noted reservations which, however, were never unanimously shared by all the principal representatives of Hussitism[32] – is also witnessed by surviving musical sources, especially the so-called *Kodex Speciálník*.[33] Organ accompaniment only gradually returned to Utraquist churches in a similar manner, after it had been rejected by radical Hussites due to their distrust of its "bare" sound which did not carry words with it.[34]

7 Czech Liturgical Singing and the *Jistebnický kancionál*

Czech singing during holy service was intellectually and practically derived from the Benedictine Slavic liturgy of the Roman rite, first permitted in Croatian dioceses by Pope Innocent IV in 1248 and 1252. Its usage in the newly founded monastery Na Slovanech (Emmaus) in Prague's New Town was based on the privilege of Clement VI from May 1346.[35] In founding this monastery, Charles IV attempted to establish conditions for the development of a Slavic center of ecclesiastic education, including a scriptorium that would produce liturgical books written in Glagolitic and – according to a reference in the

---

30 Černý, "Das retrospektive Organum," 17.
31 Prague, Knihovna Národního muzea, XIV E 7, fols. 35r-37r.
32 Petr Čornej and Milena Bartlová, *Velké dějiny zemí Koruny české*, vol. 6 (Prague and Litomyšl: 2007), vol. 6, 370.
33 Hradec Králové, Muzeum východních Čech, Hr 7. See also Lenka Mráčková, "Kodex Speciálník – eine kleine Foliohandschrift böhmischer Provenienz," *Hudební věda* 39 (2002): 163–84.
34 See Jan Frei, "Dva pokusy husitologické," *Hudební věda* 39 (2002): 129–61.
35 Emanuel Poche and Jan Krofta, *Na Slovanech. Stavební a umělecký vývoj pražského kláštera* (Prague: 1956), 11–3.

founding documents to the cultivation of *bohemice nostre lingue*[36] – eventually even in Czech.[37] The direct relation of the Czech Hussite liturgy to this practice is hinted at in the oldest version of the tractate *De cantu vulgari* by Jakoubek of Stříbro,[38] and by the later Utraquist tradition of the 16th century.[39]

Research on the *Jistebnický kancionál* has also fueled the hypothesis that Hussite vernacular liturgy built on the Czech-Glagolitic manuscript production at Emmaus.[40] The origin of this 132-folio codex is still not entirely clear, though the form of biblical texts it presents suggests that it came from circles associated with the monastery Na Slovanech,[41] which was one of the centers of Hussitism from 1419 onward. Despite its fragmentary state, the *Jistebnický kancionál*, written around the 1420s, is the most significant manuscript to contain a Czech version of the Latin liturgy from the Hussite period. The surviving share of the gradual (almost all the *ordinarium missae* and a significant portion of the *proprium de tempore*, among other passages, are missing) is followed by a significant section of songs, antiphons, and addenda. As yet, however, the question of the scope and scale of the *Jistebnický kancionál*'s influence remains unanswered. Until recently, the accepted thesis proposed two unrelated traditions – a Czech version of the liturgy written in the *Jistebnický kancionál*, and a tradition initiated over a century later by the writer and reformer of vernacular chant, Jan Táborský of Klokotská Hora (ca. 1500–1572).[42] Yet it was subsequently proven that the Czech liturgy continually developed, and that the translation of certain chants from the *Jistebnický kancionál* even permeated 16th-century sources.[43] Yet there is a series of other Czech manuscripts from the second half of the 15th and beginning of the 16th centuries which may at least partially resolve the issue surrounding the continuity of Czech liturgical

---

36 Roman Jakobson, "Úvahy o básnictví doby husitské," *Slovo a slovesnost* 2 (1936): 10.
37 See Ludmila Pacnerová, "Die tschechische Variante der kroatischen eckigen Glagolica – Die dritte Periode des Glagolitismus in Böhmen" in *Glagolitica. Zum Ursprung der slavischen Schriftkultur*, eds. Sylvia Richter, Velizar Sadovski, and Heinz Miklas (Vienna: 2000), 192–97.
38 Jakobson, "Úvahy o básnictví doby husitské," 10–1.
39 *Mikuláš Konáč z Hodíškova: Pikartské dialogy*, ed. Ota Halama (Prague: 2017), 52; Bohuslav Bílejovský, *Bohuslava Bílejovského Kronika česká. Acta Reformationem Bohemicam Illustrantia*, ed. Ota Halama (Prague: 2011), 43.
40 Prague, Knihovna Národního muzea, II C 7.
41 Žůrek, *Graduale Bohemorum*, 7. The same view is expressed by Hana Vlhová-Wörner in an analysis of biblical translations.
42 Martin Horyna, "Česká reformace a hudba," *Hudební věda* 48 (2011): 10; Čornej, *Velké dějiny*, vol. 6, 370.
43 Jiří Žůrek, "The Analogies between the Chants of the Jistebnický Kancionál and the Repertory of the Oldest Czech Graduals in the 16th Century," *Hudební věda* 48 (2011): 41–78.

music.⁴⁴ Only a detailed comparative inventory of repertoires can hope to do justice to the heterogeneity of the situation,⁴⁵ which can currently be understood only opaquely. In the second half of the 15th century, the Czech-language liturgy was always complemented by Latin components, whereas Czech singing was especially preserved in three repertory cycles: a series of chants for holy week (lections, namely passions and lamentations, non-biblical lamentations and tropes, antiphons, and responsoria);⁴⁶ a collection of prefaces to the whole church calendar, including the Our Father and liturgical greetings; and Czech songs and hymns which form the largest part of the preserved repertoire.

8   Vernacular Song

Of course, the vernacular song tradition did not begin with the Hussite movement, as vernacular singing of a para-liturgical character already existed, especially the so-called *kyriamina* (coming from the litany with repeated invocations of *Kyrie eleison*) or the *benedicamina*, songs which developed from the concluding exclamation of the mass, *Benedicamus Domino*. There was a great volume of Czech songs which originated during Hus's life, a fact documented by the prohibition of "all new songs" except four traditional ones that was issued by the Prague synod in June 1408.⁴⁷ Most Czech songs of the 15th century are preserved in codices of varying content and language, which include liturgical and para-liturgical compositions (for instance, the so-called *Roudnický sborník*).⁴⁸ The first known autonomous collection appeared only in 1501 in a printed edition called *Piesničky* (*Songs*), which includes 86 preserved texts coming mostly from the sphere of the Unity of Brethren.⁴⁹ The first extensive hymnbook of the Reformation type, however, only appeared in the *Kolínský kancionál* manuscript from 1517,⁵⁰ which summarized the musical repertoire

---

44 Eliška Baťová, "Opomíjený pramen husitského zpěvu doby poděbradské a repertoár cantiones hebdomadae sanctae," *Hudební věda* 51 (2014): 229–78.

45 Compare the statement of Rokycana's opponents in the year 1461: "Item ewangelium et epistolam, oraciones et similia in missa tenet vulgariter.... Alii de suis vulgariter tenent totam missam, alii tantum ewangelium, alii canonem, alii que placent etc." Boubín, Jaroslav, and Jana Zachová (eds.), *Žaloby katolíků na Mistra Jana z Rokycan* (Rokycany: 1997), 40.

46 See in particular Prague, Národní knihovna České republiky, XVII F 3.

47 Jaroslav V. Polc and Zdeňka Hledíková, *Pražské synody a koncily předhusitské doby* (Prague: 2002), 286.

48 Litoměřice, Státní oblastní archiv, no shelf-mark.

49 *Piesničky* (Prague: 1501).

50 Kolín, Regionální muzeum, př. č. 80/88.

of the 15th century and presents Czech vernacular song as an emancipated liturgical genre.

Just as for the *Jistebnický kancionál*, the musical content of the hymnbooks of the first half of the 16th century can be categorized as either temporal (related, as with tropes or other supplements, directly to the liturgy), as so-called "common songs," or as topical songs pertaining to contemporary events (entirely extra-liturgical). In regard to the hymnbooks, a significant section of "common songs" features most of the *preces* – a cycle of prayers including the Our Father, the *Credo*, and the Ten Commandments – which represented the common prayer practice before the holy service. A large group of doctrinal texts can also be counted among the "common songs," especially eucharistic songs, whose importance also lay in the fact that just the introduction of the chalice, and the later extension of this part of the mass, could strengthen the role of vernacular song within the liturgy.[51]

9 Users of Liturgical Manuscripts and Performers of the Song Repertoire

Much remains to be learned concerning the users of manuscripts containing Utraquist liturgical repertoire, from Latin graduals with traditional chant to manuscripts with polyphonic music, or hymnbooks with Latin or Czech songs. Groups of pupils of a parish school may have been regarded as professional choirs that were likely connected to the performance of the liturgy. Tellingly, the word *clerus* in the rubrics of some manuscripts is replaced with the words *žákovstvo* (i.e. students, pupils) or *scolares*.[52] Yet the activity of lay choirs, known as *fraternitates literatorum*, remains unclear. Older literature linked them to almost all relevant manuscripts from urban environments, but more recent interpretations have limited their musical role to the singing of the morning Marian mass, called the *matura*.[53]

Associations of *literati* (for which analogous cases may be found across Europe) functioned on a corporative principle similar to guilds. They emerged thanks to the relaxed societal situation after the 1485 Kutná Hora religious peace. The oldest *literati* hymnbooks mostly contain the Latin repertoire – chant

---

51 See Jan Kouba, "Od husitství do Bílé hory (1420–1620)," in *Hudba v českých dějinách. Od středověku do nové doby*, ed. Jaromír Černý, 2nd ed. (Prague: 1989), 100.
52 See also Prague, Národní knihovna České republiky, XVII F 3, fol. 142r. The "omnemque clerum" passage is here translated as "all pupils."
53 Martin Horyna, "Vícehlasá hudba v Čechách v 15. a 16. století a její interpreti," *Hudební věda* 43 (2006): 118.

addenda and songs (especially the popular Marian *cantiones*) and polyphonic compositions in the archaic as well as the *ad voces aequales* styles.[54] Rather than the result of the Hussite emphasis on lay participation in the liturgy, these guilds may be understood as expressions of the emerging Utraquist burgher class. The overly ostentatious emphasis on burghers' representation had already been the target of critique by Hus and his predecessors.[55] Thus, it is necessary to distinguish the significant monuments of urban musical patronage, such as the *Kodex Franus*,[56] from manuscripts that emphasize Hussite doctrine more explicitly, such as the *Kolínský kancionál*.

The issue of participation by the "people" or community in the liturgical singing in Utraquist churches remains another open question; it is only possible to speak in general about lay participation in the holy service, particularly in urban settings (in rural contexts less is known about lay participation).[57] The label *vulgares cantilenas hereticas*, which summarily expressed the Catholic position on Czech songs,[58] should be understood linguistically, as "heretical songs in the vulgar tongue," rather than descriptively, referring to the performers of these songs as "common people" (*vulgus*). This linguistic aspect, as well the didactic character of the songs, illustrates the fundamental significance of song for the laity, though we need not assume that the entire content of hymnbooks was designed for communal singing.

10 The Place of Liturgical Tradition in Utraquism

Faithfulness to the tradition of the liturgy as it was inherited by the church in Bohemia was close to the heart of Utraquism. Many of the theological debates invoked the historic liturgical texts of the Prague Use of the Roman Rite, and Utraquists continued to point to their fidelity to that tradition. The claim that Utraquism remained faithful to this tradition was asserted in the many debates over such issues as frequent communion, the chalice, and the communion of

---

54 For example, Hradec Králové, Muzeum východních Čech v Hradci Králové, Hr 7, or Prague, Národní knihovna České republiky, 59 R 5116.

55 Hana Pátková, *Bratrstvie ke cti Božie. Poznámky ke kultovní činnosti bratrstev a cechů ve středověkých Čechách* (Prague: 2000), 96–9.

56 Hradec Králové, Muzeum východních Čech v Hradci Králové, Hr 6. Hlávková, "Codex Franus."

57 Kouba, "Od husitství do Bílé hory," 116. František Šmahel, *Die Hussitische Revolution*, trans. Thomas Krzenck (Monumenta Germaniae Historica. Schriften) 43, (Hannover: 2002), vol. 3, 2010.

58 Boubín and Zachová (ed.), *Žaloby katolíků na Mistra Jana z Rokycan*, 40.

infants. In claiming adherence to an established tradition, Utraquists undeniably had history on their side. Consequently, Utraquism was liturgically very conservative, and the Lower (Utraquist) Consistory continued to enjoin a strict observance of the Prague Use. Over time, particularly with the appearance of Lutheranism, the same observance was not always practicable, and there is evidence that some Utraquists took liberties in their adherence to the Prague Use, for which the Consistory tried to discipline them.[59]

While slavishly faithful to what they understood to be the tradition of the Bohemian church, the Utraquists were also able to introduce apparent innovations which had not been part of Bohemian practice, such as the liturgy in Czech, on the grounds of consistency with the ancient tradition of the churches in general. While it would have been virtually impossible to find a "western" liturgy in a language other than Latin, the Utraquists knew that other ancient churches used their own vernacular languages as the language of the liturgy, and so justified their own practice as remaining consistent with the tradition of the church as a whole.

How worship was experienced would have varied tremendously over the period of the Bohemian Reformation. The 14th-century frequent communion movement had already made a substantial change in the way worship was experienced: the ocular (gazing at and adoring the elevated host and chalice) had been replaced by the gustatory (eating and drinking the consecrated elements of bread and wine). The reintroduction of the lay chalice and the communion of all the baptized (regardless of age) would have had a great social leveling effect within the worshiping assembly. Ecclesiastical status (lay or ordained), so important in the medieval church, was relativized when the laity could once again receive from the chalice, thereby shattering an important symbol of the gulf between the clergy and the laity. Differences of age and education were also effaced when baptism became the sole requirement for admission to communion. Every celebration of the Eucharist made clear that the rules that governed the Christian community, where divisions of social status, class and age were not ultimate, were at variance with the rules by which civil society governed itself. From the time of Milíč's "Jerusalem" experiment it became clear that the Eucharist was the venue *par excellence* for inclusion, incorporating, as

---

59   Pavel Kolář, "Utraquist Liturgical Practice in the Later Sixteenth Century," in *The Bohemian Reformation and Religious Practice*, eds. Zdeněk V. David and David R. Holeton, vol. 8 (Prague: 2011), 225–36.

it did, in its central act of communion, social classes (clergy, laity, men, women, former prostitutes) that otherwise had little interaction.[60]

The gradual introduction of Czech into the liturgy also would have had an inclusive effect on the communities that chose to use the vernacular for worship. From the second decade of the 15th century Czech was legally enjoined for the readings and the Creed. For the first time in centuries, the lay person could understand the biblical readings. From the time of the *Jistebnický kancionál*, it would indeed have been possible for the laity to understand every word that was sung or addressed to them in the liturgy. What may seem odd, however, is that there is relatively little evidence to suggest that many Utraquist communities availed themselves of this early possibility of using Czech as the medium of worship until the second quarter of the 16th century.

In sum, Utraquist worship was in visible continuity with the uses elsewhere (so that foreign visitors could comment that they found themselves "at home"), but also in radical discontinuity in some important ways. As far as liturgical texts and rites, vestments, vessels, art, and music were concerned, Utraquism stood solidly in the tradition of the use of the Bohemian church;[61] when it came to frequent communion, the chalice, the communion of all the baptized, and the use of the vernacular, Utraquism stood solidly in the a much more ancient tradition, but one that had long since died out in western Europe.

That said, it is important to remember that the "Utraquist consensus" did not include the entirety of Bohemia. While the reforms described in the preceding pages were the foundation of Utraquism and were followed by a significant majority of the Bohemian population, there were those who, from the earliest years, pressed for more radical reforms, as well as those who thought that even the relatively modest reforms of the 14th century (i.e. frequent communion) had probably gone too far. Still later, the advent of Lutheranism was to change further the mosaic of liturgical life in Bohemia.

11   Southern Bohemian Radicalism

The outbreak of the Hussite revolution in 1419 saw the appearance of a theological movement that was in no sense content with the relatively modest reforms that constituted the Utraquist consensus. The first we know of the worship of these radicals is to be found in the various accounts of the great

---

60   David R. Holeton, "Revelation and Revolution in Medieval Bohemia," *Communio Viatorum* 36 (1994): 32.

61   Horníčková and Šroněk (eds.), *Umění české reformace*; Horníčková, "A Utraquist Church Treasure and Its Custodians," 189–208.

"movement to the hills" in 1419. The context in which this worship took place – at first out-of-doors and, later, in private houses – encouraged a rejection of more recent traditions or, to put it positively, encouraged a greater domesticity in worship. Both in the open air and in private houses the vestments, vessels, ornaments and even liturgical books which were used in Utraquist worship would have seemed out of place, if not absurd.[62] While this liturgical puritanism never gained the upper hand in Bohemian religious life, it did remain an important undercurrent even after the defeat of the armies of Tábor and eventually resurfaced with the emergence of the Unity of Brethren, which constituted the one, ongoing, organized church of the liturgical left in Bohemia.

The majority of the theological polemics between conservative and radical proponents of reform took place within the University of Prague, making it an institution which protected against even greater theological and practical radicalism in the capital. Outside of Prague, radical reformism received greater support and spread via a number of smaller founts in Plzeň, Žatec, and eastern Bohemia. The strongest among them gradually became Sezimovo Ústí and its surroundings in southern Bohemia, which was hit by a plague epidemic in 1414–1415. The radicalization of the southern Bohemian region was fueled not only by the long presence of Christian heterodox movements there (Waldensians), but also by the fact that Ústí had been one of Hus's host cities during his forced exile from Prague (Kozí Hrádek). Nevertheless, information on the beginnings of radical liturgical practices comes to us mostly from the reports of the conservative masters of the Prague University, which are thus markedly negative and polemical in character, and of debatable value as sources. References to the liturgical practices of the radical preachers and clergy in the university reports, for instance, could represent reactions to the apparent "temerity" of these practices, rather than their wide dissemination in radical circles.

12 The Pilgrimages to the Mountains and the Fundamental Structure of Taborite Liturgy

The oldest document on the influence of reformist radicalism upon liturgical practice in Bohemia is a polemical and anonymous report, probably from the

---

62   This rejection of images, vesture, etc. has often been categorized as iconoclasm. Recently, it has been suggested that there are relatively few examples of genuine Hussite iconoclasm and that the destruction wrought was primarily a means of venting rage against monastic wealth. See Milena Bartlová, "Understanding Hussite Iconoclasm," in *The Bohemian Reformation and Religious Practice*, eds. Zdeněk V. David and David R. Holeton, vol. 7 (Prague: 2009), 115–26.

turn of 1416–1417, which mentions various offenses (*delicta*) which certain priests in the south-Bohemian city of Sezimovo Ústí committed against the established practice of the church.[63] Certain issues which appear in the report were later to become permanent trends of the radical liturgical practice of the Taborites, such as the presbyterianism and laicization of holy services (the critique of traditional bishops' ceremonies, calling for their abolition or performance by priests; preaching performed by the laity), the de-consecration of liturgical practice (challenging the significance of traditional vestments, altars, baptistries, and consecrated spaces), and the abandonment of the traditional Roman rite in the celebration of the Eucharist. Although we cannot eliminate the possible inspiration of certain Christian heterodox groups (for instance, the Waldensians) which hid in the south-Bohemian region from the church's inquisitorial investigators, it is impossible to prove a direct relationship between their activities and the radical liturgical practice of Utraquism. Indeed, a direct relationship is unlikely. The beginnings of radical liturgical practices are illuminated by the polemics between certain Prague University masters and adherents of the radical reform. These began with a letter from master Křišťan of Prachatice addressed to Václav Koranda in Plzeň at the beginning of 1417,[64] and ended with a list of nineteen articles[65] that were probably part of the preparations of conservative university masters for the St. Wenceslas Synod,[66] held in autumn 1418.[67] In their list, the masters reacted negatively to the liturgical practices they held to be noteworthy: giving the Eucharist in both kinds to infants and children; the rejection of prayers and other acts performed for the dead; abolishing prayers to the saints; neglecting established holidays and fasts; the celebration of a shortened mass without chasubles and a consecrated altar; singing the mass in Czech; preaching by the laity or women; rejecting the traditional ceremonies of blessing; carrying consecrated wine to the ill; the rejection of the usage of the chrism and oil; practicing confession

---

[63] František Palacký (ed.), *Documenta Mag. Joannis Hus vitam, doctrinam, causam in Constantiensi concilio actam et controversias de religione in Bohemia annis 1408–1413 motas illustrantia* (Prague: 1869), 636–38, no. 104.

[64] Ibid., 633–36, no. 103.

[65] František Palacký (ed.), *Archiv český čili Staré písemné památky české i moravské*, vol. 6 (Prague: 1872), 37–8.

[66] Palacký (ed.), *Documenta Mag. Joannis Hus*, 677–81, no. 118.

[67] Zilynská, *Husitské synody*, 15 and 31–9.

without the participation of a priest; and challenging the validity of ceremonies performed by priests in deadly sin.

From the perspective of the radical priests, only the mass celebrated *ex integro* was deemed to be proper holy service. *The Books* of the priest Jan Čapek from 1417 – which Zdeněk Nejedlý first showed to be significant for an understanding of Taborite liturgical development – illustrate the importance of this distinction.[68] Among other things, *The Books* contain a brief commentary on the traditional practice of receiving the Eucharist on Good Friday, as well as a proposed alternative order of celebrating the Eucharist on this day. Jan Čapek perceived the so-called Mass of St. Peter to be the minimalist form of the mass which included all the basic elements; it was to be composed from the Our Father and the words of consecration upon the eucharistic offerings.[69] Apparently, the Eucharist was celebrated several times daily whenever it was necessary, so that all could receive it. The alternative rite began with confession at the altar, after which the priest was to immediately prepare the eucharistic offering for those present, followed by the washing of hands and the pronouncement of the traditional words of consecration (*Qui pridie* and *Simili modo*) over the bread and chalice of wine, both of which the priest may, but need not, elevate. The conclusion of the service was formed by the Our Father, along with the reception of the Eucharist in both kinds by all baptized. Nevertheless, the alternative rite was not intended for regular use in the celebration of the Eucharist, but rather represented the necessary minimum for exceptional celebrations where people strove to communicate in both kinds.

In 1419, the "pilgrimages to the mountains" helped to strengthen the radical liturgical practices in southern Bohemia. The movement to the hills was part of the reaction to a decree of Wenceslas IV by which all parishes that had been illegally usurped by the reforming party (i.e. Utraquists) were to be returned to their rightful incumbents. This act suddenly decimated the possibilities for

---

68 Zdeněk Nejedlý, *Dějiny husitského zpěvu za válek husitských* (Prague: 1913), 116–22; František Michálek Bartoš, "Z politické literatury doby husitské," *Sborník historický* 5 (1957): 32–4; Josef Dobiáš, "Dva rukopisy z počátku 15. století," *Časopis historický* 1 (1881): 52–60. The latest edition of *The Books*: Jan Čapek, *Knížky o večeři Páně*, ed. Irena Stejskalová: http://vokabular.ujc.cas.cz/moduly/edicni/edice/f5796c7e-5109-4c38-866d215eb95fd277/plny-text/s-aparatem/folio/76r.

69 In this respect, Čapek's exposition is similar to Jakoubek of Stříbro, "De cerimoniis," in Jan Sedlák, "Liturgie u Husa a husitův," *Studie a texty k náboženským dějinám českým* 2 (1915): 149–60. On sources from which both authors drew information on the liturgical developments, see Jana Nechutová, "*Ecclesia primitiva* v husitských naukách," *Sborník prací Filozofické fakulty brněnské univerzity* E 33 (1988): 87–93.

receiving communion *sub utraque* in Prague and eliminated it altogether in many small towns where there was only one church. Faced with the elimination of the chalice and infant communion, reforming (Utraquist) clergy in southern Bohemia led their followers to the hilltops, where they proceeded to preach at length and to celebrate the Eucharist at which all (including children) communicated *sub utraque*, just as they had done in their parishes before Wenceslas's decree.[70]

These assemblies lasted the entire day. First, a canvas tent was erected at the top of a hill, and those present were divided into men and women with children. In the morning hours, three parallel assemblies took place, to which three offices of clergy were connected: the first was based on preaching, in which the priests of this assembly alternated. Elsewhere, priests continually heard confessions (*confessio auricularis*), while the last group of priests celebrated the Eucharist and distributed it in both kinds to men, women, and children. The desire for the renewal of the early Christian sense of community and reciprocity found its expression in the entirely unique practice of the communal banquets which followed the morning assemblies, where all feasted together from the food they had brought and collected. The dinner feast was concluded by a communal thanksgiving to God, a eucharistic procession around the hilltop with spiritual songs, and the orderly return home from the hilltop.[71]

Radical priests, assembled "on the mountains," celebrated the Eucharist without chasubles and communion cloths, required neither a chalice – which could be replaced by any vessel of any material – nor a consecrated altar, which they replaced with a table covered by a white tablecloth, nor even a dedicated space (a church or chapel). Similarly, these priests abandoned the traditional parts of the Roman *ordo missae*: the collects, chants of the mass, and the prayers and gestures of the canon of the mass. The traditional host was not required for the celebration but was usually replaced by common leavened bread. The priests in attendance first kneeled and bowed their heads to the ground (*flexis genibus, capite ad terram prostrates*), then commonly led the Our Father. After this, one of the priests stood up and loudly and comprehensibly (*alta et intelligibili voce vulgariter*) pronounced the words of consecration over the bread and wine.[72] He then distributed the sacrament to the people

---

70   Five contemporary accounts of this popular movement can be found in Kaminsky, *A History*, 278–80.

71   Josef Emler, Jan Gebauer, and Jaroslav Goll (eds.), *Fontes rerum Bohemicarum*, vol. 5 (Prague: 1893), 400–02.

72   It seems that the words of consecration could themselves have taken various forms, from simple wording ("this is my body, this is my blood"), through wording enriched by simple

and priests. Radical priests maintained this simple ceremony not only in the south-Bohemian countryside, but also in Prague, where they avoided churches and chapels. This expressed the fact that they perceived the ceremony as both an authentic representation of the New Testament apostolic practice, and a legitimate and liberating form of celebrating the Eucharist in a time approaching the end of the world.[73]

Vavřinec of Březová attached a list of articles published by the priests of Tábor to his report on the hilltop pilgrimages. According to these priests, only the law of God (*lex Dei*) was obligatory for liturgical practice, while human provisions (*tradiciones humane*) must be abandoned, such as the special blessing (*sanctificacio*) of the chrism, oil, or baptismal water, and the practice of safeguarding (*conservacio*) them for long periods. Similarly, neither chalices, communion cloths, chasubles, nor vestments should be exorcized, blessed, or consecrated. The baptism of children required neither exorcism, godparents, nor special baptismal water. In addition, all liturgical books (missals, graduals, breviaries, etc.) should be spurned, and no one ought to be obliged to participate in auricular confession (*confessiones auriculares*), since internal confession to God sufficed for salvation. Nor should any fasts be obligatory (in the fasting period, quaternary days, etc.), and people should maintain them at their own discretion. Even the daily church prayers were not obligatory, and the only mandatory holiday was Sunday. The Eucharist should be neither elevated nor preserved for the next day (*non est elevandum nec in crastinum conservandum*). People were to avoid holy services performed according to the traditional rite (*missam ritu consueto celebrans*), namely those performed by priests in chasubles, without beards and with tonsures who, in the eyes of the Taborite clergy, represented the church polluted by simony, secular power, and the superiority of human provisions over the truth of the Gospels. The abandonment of traditional liturgical practices was also expressed in the rejection of prayers to the saints and for the dead (in purgatory), as well as to liturgical images.[74]

On 16 October 1424, the university masters, led by Master Jan Příbram, submitted a list of twenty-four articles to be commented on by the Taborites, which included formulations of theological-liturgical foundations that shared

---

narrative context ("that night when…"), to a more complex text that arose from the harmonization of biblical reports on the Last Supper; see Palacký (ed.), *Urkundliche Beiträge*, vol. 2, 522–23.

73 Emler, Gebauer, and Goll (eds.), *Fontes rerum Bohemicarum*, vol. 5, 406–07, cf. 529–30.
74 Ibid., 403–05.

a nearly unanimous consensus among Utraquists.[75] The surprised representatives of the Taborites requested time to prepare their response, for which they summoned a synod of the Taborite clergy in Klatovy on 11 November 1424. It may be said that the position of the Taborites thereafter was largely defined by the Klatovy articles, which expressed a relatively moderate position in liturgical matters, compared to some features of the contemporary radical Taborite practice; the Taborite priests accepted all traditional sacramental rites, though they emphasized the necessity of identifying and maintaining the apostolic form of celebration.

Sundays and Easter held the most important positions within the liturgical year. The celebration of Christ's birth was to be transferred to the nearest Sunday, while the celebrations of the Epiphany and the Purification of the Virgin Mary were to be preserved on their traditional days. The holiday of *Corpus Christi* was to be entirely incorporated into the celebration of Maundy Thursday (*Cena Domini*).

13   Mikuláš Biskupec of Pelhřimov's *Confessio Taboritarum*

The only comprehensive treatment of Taborite liturgical practice and its theological foundations was written during the preparation for the negotiations with the representatives of the Council of Basel by the Taborite bishop, Mikuláš of Pelhřimov, in his *Confessio Taboritarum*.[76] This work had its origins in the disputations held in Prague's Karolinum in April 1431, and was a reaction to the anti-Taborite polemical works of Master Jan Rokycana, especially to his *De septem culpis Taboritarum*. Mikuláš of Pelhřimov recounted the reasons which led the community of Tábor to reject the traditional Roman rite: historically, he argued, many elements had been incorporated into this rite by papal decrees, and thus via their authority. This meant that these additions were human provisions and offered many priests the opportunity for illegitimate enrichment at the expense of the poor, and for the establishment of the spiritual authority of the former over the latter. Traditional elements of *ordinarium* and *proprium*, vestments, gestures (the kiss of peace), and symbols (the cross, candles) ought to be considered *accidentalia*, which could be abandoned by a priest and a congregated community in certain circumstances without fear of sin, as long as the obligatory reverence, devotion, and foundation of the mass were preserved.

---

75   Their text has been reconstituted and published in Kaminsky, *A History*, 500–16.
76   Mikuláš Biskupec of Pelhřimov, *Confessio Taboritarum*, eds. Amedeo Molnár and Romolo Cegna (Rome: 1983).

Based on Mikuláš's text, we can assume that radical Taborite liturgical practice appeared in various forms between two extremes. First among them was the obligatory nucleus, the so-called Mass of Peter, which, as discussed above, contained all necessary elements for the celebration of the Eucharist. This basic form could be expanded by the addition of other elements from the so-called (pseudo-)Dionysian rite, which represented the second variety of Taborite practice. Taborite theologians deemed this rite an authentic ceremony of the apostolic age. According to them, its liturgy of the Word proceeded as follows: it began with the congregated people, along with the priest, singing or reciting the Our Father as the priest approached the altar. This was followed by exclusively scriptural readings in the vernacular (*lecciones de sacris Sripturis in vulgari*), the language also used for singing the psalms, hymns, or God's commandments (*psalmi, ympni vel divina precepta*). The holy service was concluded with a homily (*predicacio verbi Dei*), which could be given by various priests.

Contrary to contemporary practice, the Taborites apparently began the celebration of the Eucharist by selecting participants whose involvement was conditional not only upon baptism and penitence, but also the desire to receive the holy eucharistic gifts. Laymen probably carried with them the bread and wine during the singing of the *Credo* at the beginning of the eucharistic celebration, and the priest followed this with a brief appeal (*exhortacio brevis*), probably recalling Christ's works connected to the act of penitence (*ad recordacionem omnium Cristi beneficiorum et vite*). In utter silence, the priest then approached the altar and loudly pronounced the words of consecration, a feature which sharply distinguished the Taborites from contemporary Utraquist practice, which maintained the traditionally silent recitation of the mass canon as the choir sang the *Sanctus*. After the pronouncement of the words of consecration over the bread and wine, the Taborite priest displayed the eucharistic offerings to the congregated people – to whom he had turned his back until now – and then communicated the offerings along with them. The holy service was closed by a collective thanksgiving (*gracias agere*). In his conclusion, Mikuláš referenced Mt 26:30, in which the Last Supper is finished and followed by the departure to the Mount of Olives, perhaps an allusion to the birth of the Taborite community in the holy services "on the mountains."[77]

In his *Taborite Confession*, Mikuláš Biskupec attempted to briefly summarize and explain the Taborite doctrine on the Eucharist and Christ's presence therein before the commencement of the Basel negotiations. Arguments over the Eucharist permanently polluted the relations between Prague University and the community of Tábor; they were included in most of their disputations,

---

77   Ibid., 298–306.

and were even the cause of cruelty, bloodshed, and executions in the early days of Tábor.[78] Taborite theologians maintained the central role of the Eucharist in the spiritual life of their Christian community, and always promoted its celebration and reception during other ceremonies (baptism, the laying on of hands, marriage, penance, ordination), because the grace given by God in its reception was the foundation of all Christian life, and intensified the effectiveness of the other sacraments. Along with the late work of John Wyclif and the university group of theologians represented by Jakoubek of Stříbro – and contrary to the official position of the church – the Taborites emphasized the persistence of the substance, or the nature (*natura*), of the bread and wine after consecration.[79] Moreover, the Taborite priests also adhered to Wyclif in the concept of Christ's presence in the consecrated eucharistic offerings: the Body (and blood) of Jesus Christ, born of the Virgin Mary and sacrificed on the cross for salvation, is not present in the eucharistic offerings in its nature (*non ydemptice de naturali ydemptitate*), but is present sacramentally, spiritually, really, and truly (*sacramentaliter, spiritualiter, realiter, vere/veraciter*). Yet the university masters insisted upon the designation *substancialiter*, or the substantial (natural) presence of Christ's Body in the bread and his blood in the wine, although generally not supporting the doctrine of transubstantiation.

Recalling their experience with the Pikart heterodox doctrine on the Eucharist and its implications for Christian practice, Taborite theologians, via their bishop, insisted upon the obligatory veneration (*reverencia*) of the consecrated eucharistic gifts, though they rejected all other forms of reverence to the Eucharist (*elevacio, adoracio*) except the worthy reception of the eucharistic gifts by the faithful.[80]

14   Conclusion

It is difficult to pinpoint an exact time when "Utraquist" worship was clearly distinguishable from "Roman Catholic" worship. Certainly, the introduction of frequent communion in the 14th century made Catholic worship in Bohemia unlike Catholic worship anywhere else in Western Europe. By the end of the second decade of the 15th century, the lay chalice and the communion of all

---

78   The so-called Pikart crisis; cf. František Michálek Bartoš, "Kněze Petra Kányše vyznání víry a večeře Páně z r. 1421," *Jihočeský sborník historický* 1 (1928): 2–5; A. Frinta, "Vyznání víry dobré a svaté paměti Petra Kányše. Vyznání o Chlebu živém a věčném (Martina Húsky)," *Jihočeský sborník historický* 1 (1928): 6–12.
79   Jan Sedlák, *Táborské traktáty eucharistické* (Brno: 1918).
80   Mikuláš Biskupec, *Confessio Taboritarum*, 78–9.

the baptized (including infants) were the most visible features that distinguished Roman Catholics from Utraquists. This is not entirely true, however, as there were lay people (usually of high civil status: kings, emperors, etc.) who continued to have the right to communicate *sub utraque* within the Roman Church elsewhere in Europe, and the practice of baptismal communion continued in some dioceses that held firmly to their own ancient practices until the 16th century. These, however, were relatively rare exceptions. After the outbreak of the Hussite revolution in 1419, the lay chalice and infant communion were polemicized and became the particular symbols of Utraquism, so that those clergy and laity in the Czech lands who remained loyal to Roman authority could not observe either practice without compromising their loyalty. Other than those two practices, however, Roman Catholic and Utraquist worship would, at first, have been indistinguishable in parish churches run by the secular clergy, all of whom faithfully used the Prague Use of the Roman Rite.[81]

What would have come to distinguish Roman Catholic worship was its tendency to evolve with the liturgical fashions of the age, while Utraquist practice remained more static and more medieval. In the course of the 16th century, it would have seemed more old-fashioned than Roman Catholic worship. Thus, towards the end of the Reformation era in Bohemia, the contrast between Roman Catholic and Utraquist worship would have been quite stark. Roman Catholic worship had been integrated into the early-baroque liturgical norms which were typical throughout "Catholic Europe"; Utraquist worship remained what, today, would be called "reformed or renewed catholic worship."

The Unity of Brethren and Lutherans accepted the characteristic liturgical reforms of Utraquism such as communion *sub utraque*, the extensive use of the vernacular in the liturgy, and an increased use of vernacular hymnody. The traditional historic ("apostolic") succession remained central for Utraquism, was debated among the Brethren, and eschewed by Lutherans. Utraquism retained traditional ceremonial associated with the Eucharist such as genuflections, processions, and other acts of eucharistic veneration, while these were generally rejected by both the Brethren and Lutherans. Utraquists also preserved virtually the entire *sanctorale* while the Brethren and Lutherans retained a greatly reduced calendar consisting basically of biblical saints. Another fundamental difference – the communion of *all* the baptized – remained

---

81   It must be remembered that in Prague and many other Utraquist towns all parish churches were in Utraquist hands and Roman Catholics could only use the monastic churches to which they still held title and when the members of the religious orders had not fled or been expelled.

a *sine qua non* for Utraquists but was of little interest to Brethren and Lutherans who rejected the practice.[82]

Frequent communion, with which the reformist movement began in 14th-century Bohemia, was an ideal of Luther, Calvin, and Cranmer, but in Lutheranism, Calvinism, and Anglicanism frequent communion did not finally become a part of regular church life until the 19th or, often, 20th centuries. The lay chalice, perhaps *the* symbol of the Bohemian Reformation, was quickly introduced in the churches of the 16th-century Reformation, and the use of the vernacular won its place in these churches more easily than it did in Bohemia. Infant communion, which Utraquism rightly saw as a clear theological consequence of baptism and frequent communion, did not begin to assume a place in the churches of the 16th-century Reformation until the last quarter of the 20th century.

15 Historiographic Survey

The foremost important attempt to reconstruct the liturgical practices of the university and radical Utraquists remains the work of Zdeněk Nejedlý, namely his *Sources of the Synods Between the Praguers and Taborites*, *The Beginnings of Hussite Music*, and *The History of Hussite Music during the Hussite Wars*.[83] With his publications of edited sources and interpretative works, Jan Sedlák transformed the research on the beginnings of Utraquism, the Taborite doctrine on the Eucharist, and the university masters, especially in his works *Taborite Eucharistic Tractates*, *Studies and Texts in Czech Religious History*, and a series of articles called "The Beginnings of the Chalice."[84] These works were drawn on by Augustin Neumann in his 1921 work *On the History of Holy Services in the Hussite Period*.[85] František M. Bartoš expanded the source base of Utraquism's

---

82 On some aspects of Lutheran influence on the existing Utraquist practice, see Pavel Kolář, "The Witness of a New Liturgical Practice. The *Ordines missae* in Three Utraquist Manuscripts," in *The Bohemian Reformation and Religious Practice*, eds. Zdeněk V. David and David R. Holeton, vol. 9 (Prague: 2014), 221–40; idem, "Utraquist Liturgical Practice in the Later Sixteenth Century," 225–36.

83 Zdeněk Nejedlý, *Prameny k synodám strany Pražské a Táborské. Vznik husitské konfesse v létech 1441–1444* (Prague: 1900); idem, *Počátky husitského zpěvu* (Prague: 1907); idem, *Dějiny husitského zpěvu za válek husitských* (Prague: 1913).

84 Sedlák, *Táborské traktáty eucharistické*; idem, *Studie a texty k náboženským dějinám českým*; idem, "Počátkové kalicha," *Časopis katolického duchovenstva* 53 (1911): 97–105, 244–50, 397–401, 496–501, 583–87, 703–08, 786–91; 54 (1913): 226–32, 275–78, 404–10, 465–70, 708–13; 55 (1914): 75–84, 113–20, 315–22.

85 Augustin Neumann, *Z dějin bohoslužeb v době husitské* (Hradec Králové: 1921).

origins in his exceptional heuristic works, and his publication *The Literary Works of Jakoubek of Stříbro*.[86] Foundational interpretative works which incorporate early Utraquist liturgical practice into a broader political, social, religious, and theological context include Howard Kaminsky's *A History of the Hussite Revolution* and Paul De Vooght's monograph on Jakoubek of Stříbro.[87]

The renewal of frequent communion and the issue of communion from the chalice by all baptized Christians have received particular attention in recent research. After the pioneering works of Jan Sedlák and František M. Bartoš, editions and interpretations of important tractates have contributed to this discussion, especially those of Jana Nechutová (the sixth book of Matěj of Janov's *Regulae*),[88] Romolo Cegna, and Helena Krmíčková. Romolo Cegna maintained that the seeds of the restoration of the lay chalice are to be found in the work of Nicholas of Dresden, who lived and worked in Prague along with a group of Germanophones, all of whom, contrary to the inclinations of most of their fellow German speakers, supported their reform-minded Bohemophone colleagues.[89] Helena Krmíčková, on the other hand, has convincingly argued that the defining impulse must be attributed to Jakoubek of Stříbro.[90] A summary of the discussion to date, and the incorporation of the topic into the broader historical context, was most recently attempted by Dušan Coufal in his monograph *Polemics on the Chalice*,[91] while Pavel Kolář has attempted a new

---

86   František Michálek Bartoš, *Literární činnost M. Jakoubka ze Stříbra* (Prague: 1925).

87   Paul De Vooght, *Jacobellus de Stříbro (†1429), premier théologien du hussitisme* (Leuven: 1972).

88   Matěj of Janov, *Regulae Veteris et Novi Testamenti*, vol. 6, eds. Jana Nechutová and Helena Krmíčková (Munich: 1993).

89   The suggestion that Nicholas of Dresden was the first to advocate the restoration of the lay chalice is relatively recent. Romolo Cegna first proposed the idea in his study "Appunti su Valdismo e Ussitismo. La teologia sociale di Nicola della Rosa Nera (Cerruc)," *Bollettino della Società di studi Valdesi* 92, 130 (1971): 10–3, which he then developed more fully in Nicholas of Dresden, *Nicola della Rosa Nera detto da Dresda (1380?–1416?): De reliquiis et de veneratione sanctorum. De purgatorio*, ed. Romolo Cegna (Mediaevalia Philosophica Polonorum) 23 (Wrocław: 1977), 11–16, 46–9.

90   Helena Krmíčková, "The Fifteenth-Century Origins of Lay Communion *sub utraque* in Bohemia," in *The Bohemian Reformation and Religious Practice*, eds. Zdeněk V. David and David R. Holeton, vol. 2 (Prague: 1996), 57–65. Krmíčková's article is the most accessible review of the restoration of the lay chalice. The definitive study is her *Studie a texty k počátkům kalicha v Čechách* (Brno: 1997).

91   Dušan Coufal, *Polemika o kalich mezi teologií a politikou 1414–1431. Předpoklady basilejské disputace o prvním z pražských artikulů* (Prague: 2012).

interpretative approach to Taborite doctrine on the Eucharist based on the polemical works of Petr Chelčický.[92]

Utraquist liturgical practice has become an autonomous topic in the specialized works of David R. Holeton, published mostly in the journal *The Bohemian Reformation and Religious Practice*. Using an interdisciplinary approach, he has focused on specific aspects of this practice, presenting them within the context of medieval liturgical practice in the Western Latin tradition, and suggesting overlaps even up to current ecumenical practices.

Among the modern editions of the sources of Utraquist liturgical practice, *The Litoměřice Gradual of 1517*, the *Jistebnický kancionál* and the *Graduale Bohemorum* are worth mentioning.[93] An urgent task of contemporary research is to make important liturgical sources – and not exclusively those of the Utraquists – accessible in modern editions (*Missale Pragense*, the *Altar Books* of Adam Táborský, the Czech *Agenda*, Tobiaš Závorka Lipenský's *Rules of Services*, among others), the only foundation upon which current comparative and interpretative efforts can reach greater precision and accuracy. The extent of the survival of credible sources on Bohemian liturgical practices, however, remains an open question.

Medieval Czech musical study and hymnology currently face the difficult challenge of unfettering themselves from the influential monographs of Zdeněk Nejedlý,[94] and have for decades been lacking a more ambitious, synthetic study of the issues, despite a series of editorial and analytical achievements.[95] The notion of "Hussite song" is itself the target of critique and seen as an "obsolete concept."[96] For Nejedlý, it generally meant the songs of the Hussites, defined by their doctrinal and social status, and thus its most typical form was "the people's church song," beside which stood "liturgical chant," two

---

92 Pavel Kolář, "'Neb novým angelským obyčejem krmeni budou.' O chiliastickém pozadí sporu o svátostné přijímání v Chelčického Replice proti Mikuláši Biskupci Táborskému," *Husitský Tábor* 17 (2013): 105–52. For a shorter English version of this article see Pavel Kolář, "Petr Chelčický's Defense of Sacramental Communion. Response to Mikuláš Biskupec of Tábor," in *The Bohemian Reformation and Religious Practice*, eds. Zdeněk V. David and David R. Holeton, vol. 6 (Prague: 2007), 133–42.

93 Barry F.H. Graham (ed.), *The Litoměřice gradual of 1517. Lovosice, Státní okresní archiv Litoměřice, IV C 1* (Prague: 1999); Jaroslav Kolár, Anežka Vidmanová, Hana Vlhová-Wörner and David R. Holeton (eds.), *Jistebnický kancionál. MS. Praha, Knihovna Národního muzea, II C 7. Kritická edice. Jistebnice kancionál. MS. Prague, National Museum Library II C 7*, vol. 1: *Graduale* (Brno: 2005); Žůrek (ed.), *Graduale Bohemorum*.

94 Nejedlý, *Počátky husitského zpěvu*; Nejedlý, *Dějiny husitského zpěvu za válek husitských*.

95 The last work of this type is Kouba, "Od husitství do Bílé hory."

96 Horyna, "Česká reformace a hudba," 5–6.

concepts practically in equilibrium, but entirely opposed intellectually.[97] The results of recent source examinations on the Bohemian chant tradition and the hymnological material suggest a range of themes and approaches which complicate, complement, or refute Nejedlý's concept. A relatively representative sample of the Hussite and Utraquist repertoire, comprising the majority of important sources, has been made accessible by modern editions (especially the gradual of the *Jistebnický kancionál* and the numerous mass and office tropes, thanks to David R. Holeton and Hana Vlhová-Wörner; Jiří Žůrek's *proprium de sanctis* in the sources of the 15th and 16th centuries; the selection of the most important parts of the musical repertoire across genres by the research group led by Jaromír Černý; the polyphonic songs of the *Kodex Speciálník* edited by Dagmar Vanišová; the work of Petrus Wilhelmi de Grudencz, edited by Jaromír Černý, among others).[98] Text editions are represented, for instance, by Daňhelka's *Hussite songs* or Novotný's *Hussite songbook*.[99] An edition of the songs of the *Jistebnický kancionál* and a complete edition of the *Kodex Speciálník* are currently in preparation. In addition, a number of other sources are accessible in electronic editions. Certain individual manuscripts have been published monographically (*Kodex Franus, Kolínský kancionál*),[100] as well as a basic synopsis of an entire series of sources from the 15th and 16th centuries written by Barry Graham.[101] After Nejedlý, synthetic works have emerged only within the framework of more broadly focused monographs[102] or journals.[103] In recent periodicals, most attention has been given to topics such as the spread of songs from the *Jistebnický kancionál* and other sources of the 15th and early 16th centuries,[104] and the European context of polyphonous manuscripts with polyphonic music.[105]

---

97 Nejedlý, *Počátky husitského zpěvu*, 2–3.
98 See the many relevant sources by these authors in the bibliography below.
99 Jiří Daňhelka (ed.), *Husitské písně* (Prague: 1952); Václav Novotný (ed.), *Husitský zpěvník. Náboženské písně o Mistru Janovi Husovi a Mistru Jeronýmovi* (Prague: 1930).
100 Dobroslav Orel, *Franusův kancionál z r. 1505* (Prague: 1922); Eliška Baťová, *Kolínský kancionál a bratrský zpěv na počátku 16. století* (Prague: 2011).
101 Barry Graham, *Bohemian and Moravian Graduals 1420–1620* (Turnhout: 2006).
102 E.g. Jaromír Černý, *Hudba v českých dějinách. Od středověku do nové doby*, 2nd ed. (Prague: 1989); the relevant volumes of the *Velké dějiny zemí Koruny české*; and Pavlína Cermanová, Robert Novotný, and Pavel Soukup (eds.), *Husitské století* (Prague: 2014).
103 See, for example, Horyna, "Vícehlasá hudba" and idem, "Česká reformace a hudba."
104 See the relevant articles by Baťová and Žůrek, below.
105 See, for example, Lenka Hlávková, "Die Kompositionen Johannes Tourouts in böhmischen Musikhandschriften. Zur musikalischen Kultur am Hofe Kaiser Friedrichs III. und ihrer Rezeption in den böhmischen Ländern Böhmen und das Deutsche Reich" in *Ideen- und Kulturtransfer im Vergleich (13.-16. Jahrhundert)*, eds. Eva Schlotheuber and Hubertus Seibert (Munich: 2009), 103–11.

Bibliography

Manuscripts

Hradec Králové, Muzeum východních Čech [Museum of East Bohemia], Hr 6.
Hradec Králové, Muzeum východních Čech [Museum of East Bohemia], Hr 7.
Kolín, Regionální muzeum [Regional Museum], př. č. 80/88.
Litoměřice, Státní oblastní archiv [Regional State Archives], sine sign.
Prague, Knihovna Národního muzea [National Museum Library], II C 7.
Prague, Knihovna Národního muzea [National Museum Library], XIV E 7.
Prague, Národní knihovna České republiky [National Library of the Czech Republic], 59 R 5116.
Prague, Národní knihovna České republiky [National Library of the Czech Republic], XVII F 3.

Editions of Sources

Berthold of Regensburg, *Berthold von Regensburg. Vollständige Ausgabe seiner Predigten*, eds. Franz Pfeiffer and Joseph Strobl, 2 vols. (Vienna: 1862–1880).
Bílejovský, Bohuslav, *Bohuslava Bílejovského Kronika česká. Acta Reformationem Bohemicam Illustrantia*, ed. Ota Halama (Prague: 2011).
Boubín, Jaroslav, and Jana Zachová (eds.), *Žaloby katolíků na Mistra Jana z Rokycan* [Grievances of the Catholics against Master Jan Rokycana] (Rokycany: 1997).
Čapek, Jan, *Knížky o večeři Páně* [Books on the Lord's Supper], ed. Irena Stejskalová, http://vokabular.ujc.cas.cz/moduly/edicni/edice/f5796c7e-5109-4c38-866 d215eb95fd277/plny-text/s-aparatem/folio/76r.
Černý, Jaromír (ed.), *Historická antologie hudby v českých zemích (do cca 1530)* [A historical anthology of music in the Czech Lands (to ca. 1530)] (Prague: 2005).
Daňhelka, Jiří (ed.), *Husitské písně* [Hussite songs] (Prague: 1952).
Durandus, William, *Rationale divinorum officiorum* (Venice: 1599).
Emler, Josef, Jan Gebauer, and Jaroslav Goll (eds.), *Fontes rerum Bohemicarum*, vol. 5 (Prague: 1893).
Graham, Barry F.H., (ed.), *The Litoměřice gradual of 1517. Lovosice, Státní okresní archiv Litoměřice, IV C 1* (Prague: 1999).
Jakoubek of Stříbro, "De cerimoniis," in Jan Sedlák, "Liturgie u Husa a husitův,'," *Studie a texty k náboženským dějinám českým* 2 (1915): 149–60.
Kolár, Jaroslav, Anežka Vidmanová, Hana Vlhová-Wörner, and David R. Holeton (eds.), *Jistebnický kancionál. MS. Praha, Knihovna Národního muzea, II C 7. Kritická edice. Jistebnice kancionál. MS. Prague, National Museum Library II C 7. Critical Edition*, vol. 1: *Graduale* (Brno: 2005).

Konáč of Hodíškov, Mikuláš, *Mikuláš Konáč z Hodíškova. Pikartské dialogy* [Pikart Dialogues], ed. Ota Halama (Prague: 2017).

Matěj of Janov, *Regulae Veteris et Novi Testamenti*, vols. 1–4, ed. Vlastimil Kybal (Innsbruck: 1908–1913); vol. 5, eds. Vlastimil Kybal and Otakar Odložilík (Prague: 1913); vol. 6, eds. Jana Nechutová and Helena Krmíčková (Munich: 1993).

Mikuláš Biskupec of Pelhřimov, *Confessio Taboritarum*, eds. Amedeo Molnár and Romolo Cegna (Rome: 1983).

Nejedlý, Zdeněk (ed.), *Prameny k synodám strany Pražské a Táborské. Vznik husitské konfesse v létech 1441–1444* [Sources of the synods of the Prague and Tábor parties. The rise of the Hussite confession in the years 1441–1444] (Prague: 1900).

Nicholas of Dresden, *Nicola della Rosa Nera detto da Dresda (1380?–1416?). De reliquiis et de veneratione sanctorum. De purgatorio*, ed. Romolo Cegna (Mediaevalia Philosophica Polonorum) 23 (Wrocław: 1977).

Novotný, Václav (ed.), *Husitský zpěvník. Náboženské písně o Mistru Janovi Husovi a Mistru Jeronýmovi* [The Hussite songbook. Religious songs about Master Jan Hus and Master Jerome] (Prague: 1930).

Palacký, František (ed.), *Documenta Mag. Joannis Hus vitam, doctrinam, causam in Constantiensi concilio actam et controversias de religione in Bohemia annis 1408–1413 motas illustrantia* (Prague: 1869).

Palacký, František (ed.), *Archiv český čili Staré písemné památky české i moravské* [The Czech archive, or Ancient written documents from Bohemia and Moravia] vol. 6 (Prague: 1872).

Palacký, František (ed.), *Urkundliche Beiträge zur Geschichte des Hussitenkrieges*, 2 vols. (Prague: 1873).

Palacký, František, and Birk, Ernst, (eds.), *Monumenta conciliorum generalium seculi decimi quinti. Concilium Basileense*, Scriptores: vol. 1 (Vienna: 1857).

Petrus Wilhelmi de Grudencz, *Opera Musica*, ed. Jaromír Černý (Cracow: 1993).

Piesničky [Songs] (Prague: 1501).

Vanišová, Dagmar (ed.), *Codex speciálník ca 1500. Písně. Voci e stromenti ad libitum*, (Prague: 1990).

Vlhová-Wörner, Hana (ed.), *Tropi Proprii Missae* (Repertorium troporum Bohemiae medii aevi) 1 (Prague: 2004).

Vlhová-Wörner, Hana (ed.), *Tropi Ordinarii Missae. Kyrie eleison, Gloria in excelsis Deo* (Repertorium troporum Bohemiae medii aevi) 2 (Prague: 2006).

Vlhová-Wörner, Hana (ed.), *Tropi Ordinarii Missae. Sanctus* (Repertorium troporum Bohemiae medii aevi) 3 (Prague: 2010).

Vlhová-Wörner, Hana (ed.), *Tropi Ordinarii Missae. Agnus Dei* (Repertorium troporum Bohemiae medii aevi) 4 (Prague: 2013).

Žůrek, Jiří (ed.), *Graduale Bohemorum. Proprium sanctorum* (Prague: 2011).

Secondary Sources

Bartlová, Milena, "Understanding Hussite Iconoclasm," in *The Bohemian Reformation and Religious Practice*, eds. Zdeněk V. David and David R. Holeton, vol. 7 (Prague: 2009), 115–26.

Bartoš, František Michálek, *Literární činnost M. Jakoubka ze Stříbra* [The literary activity of Master Jakoubek of Stříbro] (Prague: 1925).

Bartoš, František Michálek, "Kněze Petra Kányše vyznání víry a večeře Páně z r. 1421" [The priest Peter Kániš's confession of the faith and the Lord's Supper from 1421], *Jihočeský sborník historický* 1 (1928): 2–5.

Bartoš, František Michálek, "Z politické literatury doby husitské" [From the political literature of the Hussite period], *Sborník historický* 5 (1957): 21–70.

Baťová, Eliška, *Kolínský kancionál a bratrský zpěv na počátku 16. století* [The Kolín cantionale and the Brethren's songbook ant the beginning of the 16th century] (Prague: 2011).

Baťová, Eliška, "'O zpievaní a čtení českém tractat'" [A Treatise on Czech Liturgical Chants and Texts] by Václav Koranda the Younger. A Contribution to the History of Czech Liturgical Language," in *The Bohemian Reformation and Religious Practice*, eds. Zdeněk V. David and David R. Holeton, vol. 8 (2011), 145–61.

Baťová, Eliška, "Denominational Identity as Seen from the Structure and Content of Bohemian Fifteenth- and Sixteenth-Century Hymnals," in *Bohemian Reformation and Religious Practice*, eds. Zdeněk V. David and David R. Holeton, vol. 9 (Prague: 2014), 298–308.

Baťová, Eliška, "Opomíjený pramen husitského zpěvu doby poděbradské a repertoár cantiones hebdomadae sanctae" [A neglected source of Hussite chant in the Poděbrad period and the repertoire of the *cantiones hebdomadae sanctae*], *Hudební věda* 51 (2014): 229–78.

Cegna, Romolo, "Appunti su Valdismo e Ussitismo. La teologia sociale di Nicola della Rosa Nera (Cerruc)," *Bollettino della Società di studi Valdesi* 92, 130 (1971): 10–3.

Cermanová, Pavlína, Robert Novotný, and Pavel Soukup (eds.), *Husitské století* [The Hussite century] (Prague: 2014).

Černý, Jaromír, "Středověký vícehlas v českých zemích" [Medieval polyphony in the Czech Lands], *Hudební věda* 27–28 (1975): 30–56.

Černý, Jaromír (ed.), *Hudba v českých dějinách. Od středověku do nové doby* [Music in Czech history. From the Middle Ages to Modern Times], 2nd ed. (Prague: 1989).

Černý, Jaromír, "Das retrospektive Organum oder Neo-organum?," *Hudební věda* 38 (2001): 3–31.

Čornej, Petr, and Milena Bartlová, *Velké dějiny zemí Koruny české* [A comprehensive history of the lands of the Bohemian Crown], vol. 6 (Prague and Litomyšl: 2007).

Coufal, Dušan, *Polemika o kalich mezi teologií a politikou 1414–1431. Předpoklady basilejské disputace o prvním z pražských artikulů* [Polemic on the chalice between theology and politics, 1414–1431. Preconditions of the Basel disputation on the first Prague article] (Prague: 2012).

De Vooght, Paul, *Jacobellus de Stříbro (†1429), premier théologien du hussitisme* (Leuven: 1972).

Dobiáš, Josef, "Dva rukopisy z počátku 15. století" [Two manuscripts from the early 15th century], *Časopis historický* 1 (1881): 52–60.

Fojtíková, Jana, "Hudební doklady Husova kultu z 15. a 16. století. Příspěvek ke studiu husitské tradice v době předbělohorské" [Musical witnesses of Hus's cult from the fifteenth and sixteenth centuries. A contribution to the study of Hussite tradition before 1620], *Miscellanea musicologica* 29 (1981): 51–142.

Frei, Jan, "Dva pokusy husitologické" [Two essays in Hussite studies], *Hudební věda* 39 (2002): 129–61.

Frei, Jan, "Struktura a funkce písňového oddílu Jistebnického kancionálu" [The structure and function of the song section of the Jistebnický kancionál], in *Litera Nigro scripta manet. In honorem Jaromír Černý*, eds. Jan Baťa, Jiří K. Kroupa, and Lenka Mráčková (Prague: 2009), 33–41.

Frinta, A., "Vyznání víry dobré a svaté paměti Petra Kányše. Vyznání o Chlebu živém a věčném (Martina Húsky)" [The confession of faith of Petr Kániš of good and holy memory. Confession of the living and eternal bread (of Martin Húska)], *Jihočeský sborník historický* 1 (1928): 6–12.

Graham, Barry, *Bohemian and Moravian Graduals 1420–1620* (Turnhout: 2006).

Halama, Ota, "The Martyrs of Kutná Hora," in *The Bohemian Reformation and Religious Practice*, eds. Zdeněk V. David and David R. Holeton, vol. 5, 1 (Prague: 2004), 139–46.

Halama, Ota, "Biblical Pericopes for the Feast of Jan Hus," in *The Bohemian Reformation and Religious Practice*, eds. Zdeněk V. David and David R. Holeton, vol. 9 (Prague: 2014), 173–84.

Hlávková, Lenka, "Die Kompositionen Johannes Tourouts in böhmischen Musikhandschriften. Zur musikalischen Kultur am Hofe Kaiser Friedrichs III. und ihrer Rezeption in den böhmischen Ländern Böhmen und das Deutsche Reich" in *Ideen- und Kulturtransfer im Vergleich (13.-16. Jahrhundert)*, eds. Eva Schlotheuber and Hubertus Seibert (Munich: 2009), 103–11.

Hlávková, Lenka, "*Codex Franus* – a Mirror of the Musical Practice of the Bohemian Utraquist Church around 1500?," *Journal of the Alamire Foundation* 1 (2009): 79–88.

Holeton, David R., "The Communion of Infants and Hussitism," *Communion Viatorum* 27 (1984): 207–25.

Holeton, David R., "The Communion of Infants. The Basel Years," *Communio Viatorum* 29 (1986): 15–40.

Holeton, David R., *La communion des tout-petits enfants. Étude du mouvement eucharistique en Boheme vers la fin du Moyen Âge* (Rome: 1989).

Holeton, David R.,"The Office of Jan Hus. An Unrecorded Antiphonary in the Metropolitical Library of Estergom," in *Time and Community*, ed. J. Neil Alexander (Washington: 1990), 137–52.

Holeton, David R., "Revelation and Revolution in Medieval Bohemia," *Communio Viatorum* 36 (1994): 29–45.

Holeton, David R., "The Bohemian Eucharistic Movement in its European Context," in *The Bohemian Reformation and Religious Practice*, ed. David R. Holeton, vol. 1 (Prague: 1996), 23–48.

Holeton, David R., "'*O felix Bohemia – O felix Constantia.*' The Liturgical Commemoration of Saint Jan Hus," in *Jan Hus. Zwischen Zeiten, Völkern, Konfessionen*, ed. Ferdinand Seibt (Munich: 1997), 385–403.

Holeton, David R., "'All Manner of Wonder Under the Sun.' A Curious Development in the Evolution of Utraquist Eucharistic Liturgy," in *The Bohemian Reformation and Religious Practice*, eds. Zdeněk V. David and David R. Holeton, vol. 3 (Prague: 2000), 161–72.

Holeton, David R., "Fynes Moryson's Itinerary as a Source of Liturgical Information About the Bohemian Reformation," in *Bohemian Reformation and Religious Practice*, eds. Zdeněk V. David and David R. Holeton, vol. 5, 2 (Prague: 2005), 379–411.

Holeton, David R., "The Role of Jakoubek of Stříbro in the Creation of a Czech Liturgy. Some Further Reflections" in *Jakoubek ze Stříbra. Texty a jejich působení*, eds. Ota Halama and Pavel Soukup (Prague: 2006), 49–86.

Holeton, David R., "Bohemia Speaking to God. The Search for a National Liturgical Expression" in *Public Communication in European Reformation. Artistic and other Media in Central Europe 1380–1620*, eds. Milena Bartlová and Michal Šroněk (Prague: 2007), 103–32.

Holeton, David R., "The Evolution of the Celebration of the Daily Office in Utraquism. An Overview," in *The Bohemian Reformation and Religious Practice*, eds. Zdeněk V. David and David R. Holeton, vol. 8 (Prague: 2011), 198–222.

Holeton, David R., "La célébration liturgique de Jean Hus et de ses compagnons en Bohême à l'époque du pluralisme religieux," in *La cour céleste. La commémoration collective des saints, entre accumulation des suffrages et communion ecclésiale (époques médiévale et moderne)*, ed. Olivier Marin (Turnhout: 2015), 51–9.

Holeton, David R., and Hana Vlhová-Wörner, "A Remarkable Witness to the Feast of St. Jan Hus," in *The Bohemian Reformation and Religious Practice*, eds. Zdeněk V. David and David R. Holeton, vol. 7 (Prague: 2009), 156–84.

Horníčková, Kateřina, "A Utraquist Church Treasure and Its Custodians. A Few Observations on the Lay Administration of Utraquist Churches," in *The Bohemian Reformation and Religious Practice*, eds. Zdeněk V. David and David R. Holeton, vol. 6 (Prague: 2007), 189–208.

Horníčková, Kateřina, and Michal Šroněk (eds.), *Umění české reformace (1380–1620)* [The art of the Bohemian Reformation (1380–1620)] (Prague: 2010).

Horyna, Martin, "Vícehlasá hudba v Čechách v 15. a 16. století a její interpreti" [Polyphonic music in Bohemia in the fifteenth and sixteenth centuries and its performers], *Hudební věda* 43 (2006): 117–34.

Horyna, Martin, "Česká reformace a hudba" [The Bohemian Reformation and music], *Hudební věda* 48 (2011): 5–40.

Jakobson, Roman, "Úvahy o básnictví doby husitské" [Reflections on the poetry of the Hussite period], *Slovo a slovesnost* 2 (1936): 1–21.

Just, Jiří, "Bratrské agendy k večeři Páně" [The Brethren's agendas for the Lord's Supper], *Acta reformationem Bohemicam illustrantia*, vol. 6: *Coena Dominica Bohemica*, ed. Ota Halama (Prague: 2006): 39–131.

Kaminsky, Howard, *A History of the Hussite Revolution* (Berkeley and Los Angeles: 1967).

Kejř, Jiří, "Teaching on Repentance and Confession in the Bohemian Reformation," in *The Bohemian Reformation and Religious Practice*, eds. Zdeněk V. David and David R. Holeton, vol. 5, 1 (Prague: 2004) 89–116.

Kolář, Pavel, "Petr Chelčický's Defense of Sacramental Communion. Response to Mikuláš Biskupec of Tábor," in *The Bohemian Reformation and Religious Practice*, eds. Zdeněk V. David and David R. Holeton, vol. 6 (Prague: 2007), 133–42.

Kolář, Pavel, "Utraquist Liturgical Practice in the Later Sixteenth Century," in *The Bohemian Reformation and Religious Practice*, eds. Zdeněk V. David and David R. Holeton, vol. 8 (Prague: 2011), 225–36.

Kolář, Pavel, "'Neb novým angelským obyčejem krmeni budou.' O chiliastickém pozadí sporu o svátostné přijímání v Chelčického Replice proti Mikuláši Biskupci Táborskému ["For they will be fed according to a new angelic custom. On the chiliastic background of the argument concerning the holy communion in Chelčický's Response to Mikuláš Biskupec of Tábor"]," *Husitský Tábor* 17 (2013): 105–52.

Kolář, Pavel, "The Witness of a New Liturgical Practice. The *Ordines missae* in Three Utraquist Manuscripts," in *The Bohemian Reformation and Religious Practice*, eds. Zdeněk V. David and David R. Holeton, vol. 9 (Prague: 2014), 221–40.

Kouba, Jan, "Der älteste Gesangbuchdruck von 1501 aus Böhmen," *Jahrbuch für Liturgik und Hymnologie* 13 (1968): 78–112.

Kouba, Jan, "Od husitství do Bílé hory (1420–1620)" [From Hussitism to the Battle of White Mountain (1420–1620)], in *Hudba v českých dějinách. Od středověku do nové doby*, ed. Jaromír Černý, 2nd ed. (Prague: 1989), 85–146.

Krmíčková, Helena, "The Fifteenth-Century Origins of Lay Communion *sub utraque* in Bohemia," in *The Bohemian Reformation and Religious Practice*, eds. Zdeněk V. David and David R. Holeton, vol. 2 (Prague: 1996), 57–65.

Krmíčková, Helena, *Studie a texty k počátkům kalicha v Čechách* [Studies and texts on the beginnings of the chalice in Bohemia] (Brno: 1997).

Macek, Josef, *Tábor v husitském revolučním hnutí* [Tábor in the Hussite revolutionary movement], 2 vols. (Prague: 1952–1956).

Mengel, David C., "A Monk, a Preacher, and a Jesuit. Making the Life of Milíč," in *The Bohemian Reformation and Religious Practice*, eds. Zdeněk V. David and David R. Holeton, vol. 5, 1 (Prague: 2004), 33–55.

Morée, Peter C.A., *Preaching in Fourteenth-Century Bohemia. The Life and Ideas of Milicius de Chremsir († 1374) and his Significance in the Historiography of Bohemia* (Heršpice: 1999).

Mráčková, Lenka, "Kodex Speciálník – eine kleine Foliohandschrift böhmischer Provenienz," *Hudební věda* 39 (2002): 163–84.

Nechutová, Jana, "*Ecclesia primitiva* v husitských naukách" [The *Ecclesia primitiva* in Hussite doctrines], *Sborník prací Filozofické fakulty brněnské univerzity* E 33 (1988): 87–93.

Nejedlý, Zdeněk, *Počátky husitského zpěvu* [The origins of Hussite chant] (Prague: 1907).

Nejedlý, Zdeněk, *Dějiny husitského zpěvu za válek husitských* [The history of Hussite chant during the Hussite wars] (Prague: 1913).

Nejedlý, Zdeněk, *Dějiny husitského zpěvu* [The history of Hussite chant], 6 vols. (Prague: 1954–1956).

Neumann, Augustin, *Z dějin bohoslužeb v době husitské* [From the history of services in the Hussite period] (Hradec Králové: 1921).

Orel, Dobroslav, *Franusův kancionál z r. 1505* [The *Franus cantionale* from 1505] (Prague: 1922).

Pacnerová, Ludmila, "Die tschechische Variante der kroatischen eckigen Glagolica – Die dritte Periode des Glagolitismus in Böhmen," in *Glagolitica. Zum Ursprung der slavischen Schriftkultur*, eds. Sylvia Richter, Velizar Sadovski, and Heinz Miklas (Vienna: 2000), 192–97.

Pahl, Irmgard (ed.), *Coena Domini. Die Abendsmahlsliturgie der Reformationiskirchen im 16./17. Jahrhundert*, vol. 1 (Freiburg: 1983).

Pátková, Hana, *Bratrstvie ke cti Božie. Poznámky ke kultovní činnosti bratrstev a cechů ve středověkých Čechách* [Brotherhood in honor of God. Remarks on the cult activity of brotherhoods and guilds in medieval Bohemia] (Prague: 2000).

Petr, Stanislav, "A Codicological and Palaeographical Analysis of the Jistebnice Kancionál," in *Jistebnický kancionál. MS. Praha, Knihovna Národního muzea, II C 7. Kritická edice. Jistebnice kancionál. MS. Prague, National Museum Library II C 7*, vol. 1:

Graduale, eds. Jaroslav Kolár, Anežka Vidmanová, and Hana Vlhová-Wörner (Brno: 2005), 55–71.

Poche, Emanuel, and Jan Krofta, *Na Slovanech. Stavební a umělecký vývoj pražského kláštera* [Na Slovanech. The structural and artistic development of a Prague monastery] (Prague: 1956).

Polc, Jaroslav V., and Zdeňka Hledíková, *Pražské synody a koncily předhusitské doby* [Prague synods and councils in the pre-Husite period] (Prague: 2002).

Říčan, Rudolf, *The History of the Unity of Brethren. A Protestant Hussite Church in Bohemia and Moravia*, trans. C. Daniel Crews (Bethlehem, PA.: 1992).

Rubin, Miri, *Corpus Christi. The Eucharist in Late Medieval Culture* (Cambridge: 1991).

Sedlák, Jan, "Počátkové kalicha [The beginnings of the chalice]," *Časopis katolického duchovenstva* 53 (1911): 97–105, 244–50, 397–401, 496–501, 583–87, 703–08, 786–91; 54 (1913): 226–32, 275–78, 404–10, 465–70, 708–13; 55 (1914): 75–84, 113–20, 315–22.

Sedlák, Jan, *Studie a texty k náboženským dějinám českým* [Studies and texts in Czech religious history], vol. 2 (Olomouc: 1915).

Sedlák, Jan, *Táborské traktáty eucharistické* [Taborite eucharistic tracts] (Brno: 1918).

Seltzer, Joel, "Re-envisioning the Saint's Life in Utraquist Historical Writing," in *The Bohemian Reformation and Religious Practice*, eds. Zdeněk V. David and David R. Holeton, vol. 5, 1 (Prague: 2004), 147–63.

Šmahel, František, *La révolution hussite, une anomalie historique* (Paris: 1985).

Šmahel, František, *Die Hussitische Revolution*, trans. Thomas Krzenck (Monumenta Germaniae Historica. Schriften) 43, 3 vols. (Hannover: 2002).

Svejkovský, František, "Dvě varianty husitského traktátu 'De cantu vulgari'" [Two versions of the Hussite tract "De cantu vulgari"], *Miscellanea musicologica* 20 (1967): 49–62.

Tesař, Stanislav, and Kuchař, Martin, *Melodiarium hymnologicum Bohemiae* (Brno: s.a.): www.musicologica.cz/melodiarium.

Vlhová-Wörner, Hana, "The Jistebnice Kancionál – its Contents and Liturgy," in *Jistebnický kancionál. MS. Praha, Knihovna Národního muzea, II C 7. Kritická edice. Jistebnice kancionál. MS. Prague, National Museum Library II C 7*, vol. 1: *Graduale*, eds. Jaroslav Kolár, Anežka Vidmanová, and Hana Vlhová-Wörner (Brno: 2005), 107–33.

Všetečková, Zuzana, "Was the Pyx of Mělnik (with the Image of Christ on the Mount of Olives) Utraquist?" in *The Bohemian Reformation and Religious Practice*, eds. Zdeněk V. David and David R. Holeton, vol. 8 (Prague: 2011), 316–31.

Wagner, Murray L., *Petr Chelčický. A Radical Separatist in Hussite Bohemia* (Scottsdale, PA. and Kitchener, ON.: 1983).

Winter, Zikmund, *Život a učení na partikulárních školách v Čechách v XV. a XVI. století* [Life and education in particular schools in Bohemia in the 15th and 16th centuries] (Prague: 1901).

Zilynská, Blanka, *Husitské synody v Čechách 1418–1440. Příspěvek k úloze univerzitních mistrů v husitské církvi a revoluci* [Hussite synods in Bohemia 1418–1440. A contribution to the role of the university masters in the Hussite Church and revolution] (Prague: 1985).

Žůrek, Jiří, "The Analogies between the Chants of the Jistebnický Kancionál and the Repertory of the Oldest Czech Graduals in the 16th Century," *Hudební věda* 48 (2011): 41–78.

Žůrek, Jiří, *Hymnorum Thesaurus Bohemicus* (Centre for Classical Studies at the Institute of Philosophy of the Czech Academy of Sciences): www.clavmon.cz.

PART 5

Later Developments

The Unity of Brethren (1458–1496)

Ota Halama

The Unity of Brethren is today closely connected with the history of several non-Catholic churches in the Czech Republic, and, on a global scale, with the missionary activity of the international Church of the Moravian Brethren. The most famous figure of the Unity, in the Czech Republic and beyond, is its last bishop, Jan Amos Komenský (Comenius, d. 1670). His work was used to found the new movement of the Lutheran pietist Nikolaus Ludwig Zinzendorf (d. 1760), who helped to found the Moravian Church. Nevertheless, this community of the Brethren was a significant product of Czech Hussitism, including the continuation of the Hussite movement in the post-revolutionary Utraquist Church of the Poděbrad age. The character of the early Unity of Brethren is therefore medieval; the community's ideas, and the lifestyle of its members, are incomprehensible without reference to particular Hussite currents, while its contemporary international character was, to a certain extent, influenced by the idea of the "Hussite-Waldensian International."[1] Nevertheless, the Unity of Brethren is a unique phenomenon due to its alterity and sectarianism, which were conditioned by its social and historical context. The following pages describe the main characteristics of the early Brethren.

1   The Oldest Sources for the Brethren

Generally speaking, the medieval sources for the Unity of Brethren – especially those written by their own authors – have been known for over a century, and constitute a corpus that is mainly edited, and to which no fundamental additions have yet been made.[2] The foremost among these sources is a collection of documents preserved in the first five volumes of the Acts of the Unity of Brethren

---

1   The concept was first introduced by Amedeo Molnár, *Valdenští. Evropský rozměr jejich vzdoru* (Prague: 1973). Cf. Albert de Lange and Kathrin Utz Tremp (eds.), *Friedrich Reiser und die "waldensisch-hussitische Internationale"* (Heidelberg, Ubstadt-Weiher, and Basel: 2006).
2   Among recent discoveries, there is a new manuscript of (previously known) works by Brother Řehoř, found in the 1970s. More recently there was the discovery of a translation into Latin of the Brethren's letters to Rokycana, the interrogation of the Brethren in Kłodzko, and part of the *Sieť viery* [Net of the faith] by Chelčický. See Milada Svobodová, *Katalog českých a slovenských rukopisů sign. XVII získaných Národní (Univerzitní) knihovnou po vydání Truhlářova katalogu z roku 1906* (Prague: 1996), 168–69; Dušan Coufal, "Dva neznámé rukopisy k počátkům

(*Acta Unitatis fratrum*).[3] The collection was assembled by the Brethren after the Litomyšl fire of 1546, in which their existing archive was lost. Also belonging here are the passages of the Brethren's *Necrology*,[4] which describes (in the traditional conciseness of its genre) the lives and deaths of significant figures of the Unity of Brethren, from their beginnings to the 16th century. The records of the Brethren's synods, found in the so-called *Decrees* of the Brethren,[5] are also important, compiled as a collection of the Brethren's "canon law" and simultaneously as the necrological records and *Acta*. The only source which does not have a modern edition is the chronologically ordered collection of records from the Unity's oldest period, called the *Historia fratrum*, originating from the second half of the 16th century.[6]

Our understanding of the life of the first generation of Brethren is supplemented by the texts of the Unity's enemies, particularly the Utraquists (members of the Roman Church began polemicizing against the Unity only after 1500).[7] Foremost within this category are the formularies, letters, and other texts of

---

Jednoty bratrské v benediktinské knihovně v Seitenstetten," *Studie o rukopisech* 39 (2009): 157–88.

3   On their history and content, see Joseph Theodor Müller, "Geschichte und Inhalt der Acta Unitatis Fratrum (sogenannte Lissaer Folianten)," *Zeitschrift für Brüdergeschichte* 7 (1913): 66–113, 216–31; 9 (1915): 26–79; Edita Blažková, "Blahoslavova Akta Jednoty bratrské," *Theologická příloha Křesťanské revue* 31 (1964): 81–8, 97–105; Radek Hobza, "Akta Jednoty bratrské a jejich obsah," in *Československá církev a Jednota bratrská. Sborník prací k 500. výročí staré Jednoty bratrské*, ed. Miloslav Kaňák (Prague: 1967), 152–249.

4   Separate necrologies exist for the Bohemian-Moravian and the younger Polish branch of the Unity; see Joseph Fiedler (ed.), *Todtenbuch der Geistlichkeit der Böhmischen Brüder* (Fontes rerum Austriacarum, 1. Abteilung: Scriptores) 5 (Vienna: 1863), 213–310; Jaroslav Bidlo (ed.), "Nekrologium polské větve Jednoty bratrské," *Věstník Královské české společnosti nauk* (1897): 1–40; Jiří Just (ed.), "Zlomek bratrského Nekrologia z fondů KNM v Praze," in *Acta reformationem Bohemicam illustrantia*, ed. Ota Halama, vol. 5 (Prague: 2004), 59–65.

5   The earliest records of the Brethren's synods were edited as an appendix to Lukáš Pražský, *Odpis proti odtržencom, jenž se malou stránků nazývají* (Mladá Boleslav: 1525). More widely known is their summary rearrangement from the early 1600s: Anton Gindely (ed.), *Dekrety Jednoty bratrské* (Prague: 1865).

6   Cf. *Historie Bratří českých*, vol. 1: Prague, Národní knihovna České republiky, XVII F 51a (vol. 2 deals with the earlier history of the Unity in the 16th century). See Joseph Theodor Müller, *Dějiny Jednoty bratrské*, trans. F.M. Bartoš, vol. 1 (Prague: 1923), 354–55; Pavel Josef Šafařík, "B. Jana Blahoslava Historie Bratří českých u výtahu," *Časopis Musea Království českého* 36 (1862): 99–124, 201–12.

7   Ota Halama, "Tištěná polemika s Jednotou bratrskou v době jagellonské (1500–1526)," in *Knihtisk, zbožnost, konfese v zemích Koruny české doby poděbradské a jagellonské*, eds. Kamil Boldan and Jan Hrdina (Colloquia mediaevalia Pragensia) 19 (Prague: 2018), 139–79.

Jan Rokycana from the 1460s[8] and the work of his successor, the administrator and Master Václav Koranda the Younger, who was bound by his station to resolve the matter of the Unity.[9] Aside from Prague, the administrative center of Bohemian Utraquism, a so-called Kłodzko interrogation of the Brethren was recorded in 1480,[10] which relatively faithfully captures the Unity's contemporary theory and practice. Less reliable is the so-called declaration of Jan Ležka from 1476,[11] which spread many false accusations and fantastical reports about the Unity that held currency until the end of the 16th century. The concluding phase of the Unity's history in the 15th century, up to the secession of the so-called "Minor Party" (*malá stránka*) in 1496, is documented firstly in the contemporary sources contained in *The Acts of the Unity of Brethren*, and again in later printed texts which responded to the revival of the "Minor Party" in the 1520s,[12] reacting especially to the works of the Brethren's bishop, Lukáš of Prague, and the administrator of the Litomyšl congregation, Vavřinec Krasonický. New information regarding the history, thought, and practice of the early Unity of Brethren will probably only be found in the relatively unexplored polemical texts written against the Brethren, as the chance of finding new relevant sources written by the Brethren themselves seems slim.

---

8   František Michálek Bartoš, *Literární činnost M. Jana Rokycany, M. Jana Příbrama, M. Petra Payna* (Prague: 1928), 43–5 (no. 37–39), where the respective editions are listed.

9   Pavel Spunar, "Literární činnost utrakvistů doby poděbradské a jagellonské," in *Acta reformationem Bohemicam illustrantia*, vol. 1: *Příspěvky k dějinám utrakvismu*, ed. Amedeo Molnár (Prague: 1978), 197–98 (nos. 68-3, 68-4, 68-7, 68-8), 199 (nos. 68-19, 68-20), 201 (no. 68-32), 203 (nos. 68-43, 68-44); also listed are Koranda's dubious treatises *Contra picarditas* and *Obrana viery proti pikartom* (209, nos. 82, 83).

10 On the text of the Kłodzko interrogation, see Jaroslav Goll (ed.), "Některé prameny k náboženským dějinám v 15. století. II. Výslech bratří na Kladsku r. 1480," *Věstník Královské české společnosti nauk* (1895): 3–12.

11 Jaroslav Goll (ed.), "Spisek Víta z Krupé proti Bratřím," *Zprávy o zasedání Královské české společnosti nauk v Praze* (1878): 162–70; on the further transmission see Ota Halama, "Tištěná polemika s Jednotou bratrskou v době jagellonské (1500–1526)," in *Knihtisk, zbožnost, konfese v zemích Koruny české doby poděbradské a jagellonské*, eds. Kamil Boldan and Jan Hrdina (Colloquia mediaevalia Pragensia) 19 (Prague: 2018), 139–79, which addresses *Historie Bratří českých (Historia fratrum Bohemicorum)*, vol. 1 (1457–1535), Prague, Národní knihovna České republiky, XVII F 51a; vol. 2 (1536–1603), Prague, Národní knihovna České republiky, XVII F 51b.

12 Jan Kalenec, a literary Prague cutler, contributed to the activities of the "Minor Party" in the 1520s; cf. Wacław Urban, *Der Antitrinitarismus in den Böhmischen Ländern und in der Slowakei im 16. und 17. Jahrhundert* (Baden-Baden: 1986), 23–33; Ota Halama, "Obhajoba biblického kánonu v druhé generaci Jednoty bratrské," in *Amica – sponsa – mater. Bible v čase reformace*, ed. Ota Halama (Prague: 2014), 226–40.

2 Nomenclature

The fundamental authority of the primitive church played an important role in Hussite thought. In a wider sense, the primitive church was understood as the Christian church of the first centuries before its disruption by Constantine, but the apostolic church was foremost for the Bohemian Reformation. From the New Testament Acts of the Apostles and collections of apostolic letters it was possible for the Hussites to reconstruct the intellectual world, conflicting opinions, and everyday life of the oldest Christian community. In the thought of the radical Hussites, then, the example of the primitive church was the premise for the introduction of clerical marriage, liturgical simplicity, and also for the short-lived "communism" of the Taborites. Thus, for the Hussite readers of the New Testament, even the primitive church's naming of their members as brothers and sisters could not be ignored; this was how Christians distinguished themselves from Jews and pagans, while simultaneously conveying to them a new class of interpersonal coexistence under the paternal care of God in the young church. While the New Testament designation "brothers and sisters" was employed in the Middle Ages as a model for religious orders and lay brotherhoods, the Hussites – and especially Hussite radicals – rehabilitated this biblical naming as a title for all the "faithful." After the Hussite revolution, all other non-conforming religious communities in the region in the 15th and 16th centuries were labeled as "brothers." In the Czech lands in the second half of the 15th century, in addition to the members of the Unity of Brethren, non-conformists from Chelčice, Divišov, and the followers of Mikuláš of Vlásenice (called "Mikulášenci" [Nicholists]) were also known as brothers, as were the members of the "Minor Party," mentioned above.

Unlike most sects, it was not characteristic for the members of the Unity of Brethren to be particularly connected to a certain locale or founding figure. Though the Brethren were called the "brothers of Boleslav" in the early 16th century, this was not a self-referential term, but one which originated from the enemies of the Unity who assumed that the seat of the Brethren's bishop in Mladá Boleslav was also their place of origin. From their beginnings, they called themselves "brothers and sisters of Christ's law," and soon called their emerging church the "Unity of Brethren." This first designation expressed the first Brethren's desire to renew the ideal of the apostolic church, and their faith in Christ's law as the absolute authority above individuals and institutions. Simultaneously, however, this name referred to the communal lifestyle of the first Brethren as a sort of lay monastic community. Specifically, it came from the Old Czech vocabulary in which the concept of "law" (*zákon/lex*) overlapped with that of "rule" (*řehole/regula*),[13] and thus the life of the Brethren's lay community, in this sense, was to be conducted according to the rule and law of Christ, much as monks and friars followed the rules of St. Benedict or St. Francis.

The second, better-known, and entirely traditional designation of the first Brethren – the Unity of Brethren – thus emerged from their ecclesiological ideas in which, according to old church belief, they admitted only one church, but one comprised of many units. In other words, the Unity of Brethren considered themselves to be only a part of the holy, universal (Catholic) church. Other members, of course, were the unities of Rome and Bohemia (the Utraquists), which coexisted with the Brethren within the church, and thus kept the Brethren from claiming a superior position above them. Nevertheless, we clearly see from the Brethren's works that the first brothers were especially aware that the "renewal of the holy church" (as formulated in the title of one work by Lukáš of Prague) was primarily realized in their Unity and that, like biblical Israel, they were the "holy nation" (Exodus 19:6).

As soon as they moved beyond the borders of the Bohemian kingdom and the Moravian margravate, the members of the Unity of Brethren became known as the "Bohemian Brethren" at home and abroad. The original connections of this religious community with the Czech language and the Czech lands – reflected in their oldest sources – was soon used only to indicate the origins of the Bohemian heretics, whether during their temporary exile in Moldavia at the end of the 15th century, in the texts of their Catholic enemies from the beginning of the 16th century, or in the lands of today's Poland after 1547. The Brethren were presented as "Bohemians" as early as the beginning of the 1480s in the German-speaking regions of Silesia. Simultaneously, those German Waldensians who established their German-speaking communities within, or according to the model of, the Unity, were also called "Bohemian Brethren" after that period. In Poland and Lithuania they were still called "Bohemian Brethren" at the end of the 16th century, though they had long been communicating predominantly in Polish, and later in German. Finally, those Brethren who were exiled from Bohemia and Moravia after the battle of White Mountain in 1620 were also perceived as "Bohemian Brethren" in all parts of non-Catholic Europe where they settled.

Across Europe, the Unity of Brethren struggled futilely with the fact that they were confused with Waldensians. This identification with the well-known European sect – which also attracted attention in the second half of the 15th

---

13 See *Vokabulář webový*, http://vokabular.ujc.cas.cz, s.v. "zákon."

century due to the inquisitorial procedures against it – was dangerous to the Unity, even though it was factually dubious. To be sure, the Brethren were in contact with the German Waldensians from their beginnings and searched among them for traces of the apostolic church. The groups also shared certain external characteristics of lifestyle, as well as articles of biblically-oriented doctrine. Yet the Brethren clearly distanced themselves from the Waldensians, calling their attitude towards the mainstream church and Christian society hypocritical and thus not worthy of being followed. Nevertheless, the Latin printed polemics against the Unity after 1500 did not distinguish the Bohemian Brethren from the Waldensians. Erasmus of Rotterdam, and Martin Luther shortly afterwards, perceived the Bohemian Brethren as Waldensians.

Another common designation for the members of the Unity of Brethren was the name "Pikarts," a term which may have had limited currency in Europe, but was much more widespread in the Czech lands.[14] While the Brethren rejected their supposed Waldensianism as a well-established error, they saw the label of Pikartism as an unambiguous expression of hatred from their enemies – at first mainly Utraquists, but later members of the Roman Church as well. In the Bohemian context, Pikartism expressed the teaching of certain Hussite radicals whose rejection of the concept of transubstantiation and of giving reverence to the sacrament of the altar were the reasons for their extermination. In the wider European context, the identification of the Unity of Brethren with "Pikarts" was understood as a derogatory reference to lay brotherhoods, beghards and beguines, who stood on the border of heresy. The Bohemian Brethren clearly proclaimed their distance from the Hussite radicals from the beginning, and also emphasized Christ's sacramental presence in the Eucharist to avoid accusations of any radically formulated eucharistic symbolism. In their defense, the Brethren illustrated the foreign origin of the Pikart heresy, from which the Hussite revolution had rid itself, and with which the Unity of Brethren had no connection. Despite all the theory, however, the fact that no brother kneeled before the sacrament of the altar meant that their behavior resembled the practice of the Taborites, thus linking the Brethren to the Taborite radicals.

Today, the label "Unity of Brethren" refers not only to the historical Unity itself, but also to the so-called Renewed Unity of Brethren, which is still active in the twenty-first century. The Renewed Unity was founded on the domains of Earl Nikolaus Ludwig Zinzendorf in Saxon-Lusatian Herrnhut (Ochranov in Czech) in 1727 and known by the Latin name *Unitas fratrum*. This renewed Unity is called the "Moravian Brethren" or the "Moravian Church" in English.

---

14 See ibid., s.v. "pikart."

3   Roots, Influences, Inspirations

The south-Bohemian radical Petr Chelčický is typically referred to as the orienting figure of the first Brethren, namely via his literary works. Master Jan Rokycana, the Týn preacher, originally recommended that the brothers read the works of Chelčický, and it was under his pulpit that the concept of the future Unity of Brethren took form at the beginning of the 1450s. Rokycana did not see Chelčický's writings as erroneous, especially the tractates *O šelmě a obrazu jejím* (On the beast and its image) and *O moci světské* (On secular power), and he understood Chelčický's biblical radicalism – with its emphasis on non-violent spiritual battle – as harmless. Moreover, Rokycana found the conceptual world of the south-Bohemian figure appealing, since Chelčický's literary battle against the Antichrist had clear parallels with his own preaching at the time the Unity was taking shape.[15] Later, the Brethren themselves reminded Rokycana that it was he who led them to the opinion that "the devil encroached into all sacraments and he uses everything for his own benefit"; that "the pope along with all priests who do not follow Christ the Lord in good acts and in virtuous life are that whore sitting on the beast"; that all "priests who enter wickedly into the priesthood are debauched disciples, defeated by sin, and use that office improperly"; that "a faithful Christian should not cause the death of anyone"; that no one should be "subjugated to anything which is against the Lord God," and thus that it is evil "to swear an oath or ride to war with arms in order to strike another," etc.[16]

Rokycana's radical preaching in the 1450s is proven by later collections of accusations against the Prague Archbishop by a member of the Roman Church,[17] as well as by complaints of Catholics against the Prague Utraquist priests and masters, accusing them of breaching the agreement of the *Compactata*. It does not seem that Rokycana – through his personal efforts in the process of limiting the influence of the Hussite radicals, led by the priests of Tábor – fundamentally stepped away from his own vision of enforcing the law of God, nor does it seem that he gave up his efforts to preserve the legacy of his teacher, master Jakoubek of Stříbro. Even Rokycana's reconciliation with Petr Chelčický – which, according to the tradition of the Brethren's second generation, occurred after the fall of the Taborite priests – does not contradict this

---

15   See Jaroslav Goll, *Chelčický a Jednota v XV. století* (Prague: 1916), 68–72, 134–38.
16   Ibid., 69–72.
17   Jaroslav Boubín and Jana Zachová (eds.), *Žaloby katolíků na Mistra Jana z Rokycan* (Rokycany: 1997).

image.[18] According to the Brethren, however, Rokycana remained in the middle of the road, and betrayed his influential position by persecuting the Taborite Pikarts, and later, members of the Brethren themselves.

In the reports of the Brethren, a much more favourable light falls upon the priest Martin Lupáč – who became Rokycana's suffragan by a vote of the Land Diet in 1435 – than on master Rokycana himself.[19] Lupáč's literary works from the 1450s and 1460s were the main source of the Brethren's ecclesiology, and Lupáč also clearly helped implement this theory in 1467, when the Brethren elected their own priests. In contrast to Rokycana, who condemned the election, Lupáč approved it as an entirely legitimate and justified act from the perspective of God. The Brethren's choice for an independent election was most influenced by Lupáč's concept of a universal Christian church,[20] one which cannot be identified exclusively with the one Roman Church lest it contradict the historicity of the other local organizational centers of the primitive church. If, however, the Roman Church, with the pope at its head, is not in accordance with the law of God – especially in the matter of the lay chalice – then it is the church of the Antichrist, according to Lupáč, and thus cannot claim doctrinal and practical authority over the Utraquist Church because it is not, or has ceased to be, the holy universal church.

Thus, the influence of Bohemian Utraquism on the emerging Unity of Brethren in the era after the *Compactata* was strongest regarding ecclesiological matters. Rokycana revealed to the Brethren the church of Antichrist in its practice, its disparagement of the priestly office, its weakening of the significance of the seven sacraments, and especially in the distinction between the "people of the beast" and "faithful Christians."[21] Above all, then, Lupáč provided the Brethren with historical and theological arguments that supported their efforts to materialize their own vision of a "renewed holy church" and to understand the holy church as an eschatological community of worldly "unities" to which the creation of the new Brethren's church was in no way harmful. At the same time, however, the inconsistency of official Utraquist ecclesiology, the adherence of leading Utraquists to the concept of apostolic succession in the consecration of priests, and their simultaneous desire to preserve the community of the Roman Church, led the Unity of Brethren to consult other sources.

---

18   Lukáš Pražský, *Odpis proti odtržencom*, D5a.
19   Goll, *Chelčický a Jednota*, 138–40; František Michálek Bartoš, "M. Lupáč a Jednota bratrská," *Křesťanská revue* 32 (1965): 89–91.
20   Ota Halama, (ed.), "Spis 'De ecclesia' Martina Lupáče z doby poděbradské," *Theologická revue* 75 (2004): 420–35.
21   Goll, *Chelčický a Jednota*, 69–72.

Although the Brethren's election of priests seemed like an act without precedent, and above all an invention coming from Lupáč's theoretical inspiration, it did have a precedent in the events of the autumn of 1420.[22] At this time, Taborite seniors were appointed, equipped with episcopal powers, with Mikuláš of Pelhřimov at their head. Before the election, the Taborite radicals futilely urged the Prague university masters to cut the Gordian knot of the tradition of apostolic succession. Failing in this endeavor, the Taborites took the plunge alone and created an independent bishop's office and church organization, which was thereafter only respected in Hussite Bohemia by the German Waldensians, whose connection to the Roman Church was minimal.

The decision to break with existing church tradition was not the only relation the Unity of Brethren had to Tábor. On the contrary, the Brethren's connections with the Taborites were quite strong, as the communities shared a radical biblicism that was envisioned and formulated by the so-called "Cheb Judge." This emphasized that the example of Christ and the primitive church – along with those church traditions which may be drawn directly from them – are to be the standards of church theory and practice. This shared starting point was expressed especially in the eucharistic and liturgical rejection of transubstantiation, and in the simplification and vernacularization of the ceremony of the mass. Moreover, the Brethren also rejected purgatory, prayers for the dead, the holidays and fasts of the church calendar that were not prefigured in Scripture, and the veneration of saints and their sacred images and relics, on the same biblical grounds as did the Taborites. Finally, the doctrinal similarities of the two churches are expressed by the fact that many former Taborite "warriors of God" later found their way into the Unity of Brethren, and that they prospered in precisely those places that were previously influenced by Hussite radicalism, mainly in southwest Bohemia.

While the south-Bohemian radical Petr Chelčický also had connections to the Taborite Church, his thought and practice were beneficial to the Unity particularly in those areas where he differed from Tábor. This was especially true in his emphasis on non-violent spiritual battle, which was inspired by Jesus' radical interpretation of the biblical command "You shall not kill!" His positon clearly established a border between the true Christian church and the traditional social and ecclesiastical institutions that were externally Christian but were antichristian from the biblical perspective. Yet Chelčický also amended the Taborite teaching on the sacrament of the altar for the first Brethren, accepting Christ's real and sacramental presence therein, and inspired the final

---

22   Vavřinec of Březová, "Kronika husitská," in *Fontes rerum Bohemicarum*, eds. Josef Emler, Jan Gebauer, and Jaroslav Goll, vol. 5 (Prague: 1893), 438.

communal lifestyle of the Unity – their brotherhood – with his own secluded way of life.

Life in seclusion, as was typical for the early Brethren, had a fairly strong following in the Czech lands after the Hussite revolution. In the second half of the 15th and beginning of the 16th centuries in Bohemia, there was an interest in literature connected to the lives of the desert fathers (*Apophthegmata*).[23] This is when the first known historical figures with the surname "Heremita" (Czech "Poustevník") appeared. The fairly wide appeal of an alternative Christian lifestyle among Bohemian Hussites in the post-revolutionary era is also expressed by the fact that, in the Poděbrad and Jagellonian ages, we find nobles – alongside priests and laymen – among the Bohemian hermits. Contemporary hermits, living in secluded communities in central-Bohemian Mount Blaník or south-Bohemian Šumava Mountains, were supplemented by the brothers of Chelčice, along with other rural, spiritually oriented communities in central-Bohemian Divišov, in east-Bohemian Vilémov, and in the region of Kroměříž in Moravia.[24] In all these places, the zealous post-revolutionary Hussites gathered or lived together under the leadership of a priest or layman, and attempted to realize their ideal Christian life. This arrangement was founded, above all, on the radical interpretation of the previous Hussite program, and was connected to their own rejection of the institutional church of the post-*Compactata* era, along with their desire to find salvation in an uncertain age.

Above all, then, we may regard the Unity of Brethren as a church that was born in the crisis of Bohemian Utraquism at the beginning of the 1450s. The Utraquist leadership reacted to the same crisis, as did the laypeople who emancipated themselves gradually in spiritual communities and brotherhoods. Thus, the Unity of Brethren drew from the conceptual world of late Hussitism, which was itself now informed by post-revolutionary developments. It also drew from tendencies of the pre-Hussite era, manifested mainly in the communal experience of the "modern devotion," and particularly stressing the idea of *imitatio Christi*, or, more accurately, the *imitatio ecclesiae primitivae*. The radical biblicism of the Unity was itself influenced mainly by the works of the biblically oriented writer Petr Chelčický, as well as by the theory and practice of the Taborite Church, from which the first Brethren dissented mainly on the matter of the violent enforcement of God's law, though they shared with them many articles of doctrine and church practice.

The separation of the Unity from the Hussite "warriors of God" was expressed by the Brethren with reference to a supposed prophecy of the Parisian

---

23　Emil Smetánka (ed.), *Staročeské životy svatých otců* (Prague: 1909).
24　Goll, *Chelčický a Jednota*, 72–7.

master Matěj of Janov. According to this, the people enforcing God's law with the sword were to fall, while those without the sword were to have a future.[25] Their separation from the Utraquists, with Rokycana at their head, was represented above all by the Unity's election of a priesthood. Yet the Unity of Brethren preserved their separation even from the churches and sects of the European Reformation of the 16th century, and thus their formal connection to the Bohemian Utraquists – influenced by the Reformation – came only after Rudolph II's promulgation of the *Letter of Majesty on Religious Liberties* in 1609, and certainly much later among their European diaspora in the 17th and 18th centuries.

4 Origin and Spread

As already noted, the Unity of Brethren originated at the beginning of the 1450s under the pulpit of master Jan Rokycana, in the Church of the Virgin Mary before Týn in the Old Town of Prague, and under the leadership of Řehoř, Rokycana's supposed nephew.[26] Řehoř was, until that time, clearly connected with the spiritual community at the Utraquist monastery at Slovany in the New Town of Prague (Emmaus), where he acted as the steward (*frater conversus*) and as a lay preacher. Also dwelling there at the time was the English Wycliffite Peter Payne – called "English" in Bohemia – the diplomatic representative of Hussite radicalism. Řehoř was likely the inspiration for the activity of Jan Rokycana, who gained the permission of the Hussite king, George of Poděbrady, to settle his zealous followers and disciples on George's estate in the east-Bohemian village of Kunvald. The actual date of the departure of the first Brethren from Prague to Kunvald is traditionally set in 1457 but may reasonably be moved to the spring of the following year, especially since this region had not yet recovered from the wars with the crusaders.

Unfortunately, it is not possible to estimate the number of the first Brethren who settled in Kunvald and, later, in its surrounding territory. Moreover, it is also impossible to clearly discern the Unity's growing membership in the individual congregations which gradually emerged, due to the organizational competence of Brother Řehoř, in Lenešice near Louny, in Vinařice near Boleslav, in

---

25 Ibid., 140–43.
26 For the life and work of Brother Řehoř, see Goll, *Chelčický a Jednota*, 88–91; Michal Flegl, "K otázce sociálního původu bratra Řehoře a jeho literárních počátků," *Listy filologické* 100 (1977): 88–94; Jiří Just, "Bratr Řehoř, 'patriarcha' Jednoty bratrské," *Nové bratrské listy* 9 (2007): 8–11.

certain locales of Prácheňsko, and in the Moravian feudal towns of Přerov, Prostějov, and Hranice.[27] Thus, to the extent that the sources allow, we may say that, other than the original Praguers, the inhabitants of eastern and southwestern Bohemia, along with those of southern and central Moravia, were most prominently represented among the first Brethren, while inhabitants from other regions were uncommon. In general, then, the members of the early Unity of Brethren recruited mainly from those regions of the former Taborite and Orphan brotherhoods, or from the Žatec-Louny union.

Only two years after their settlement at Kunvald, the Unity of Brethren were exposed to persecution, stimulated by the anxiety of the Prague Utraquist center, and especially that of George of Poděbrady, concerning the re-emergence of Hussite radicalism and the possibility of its militarization. The number of the first Brethren clearly already shocked and confounded their contemporaries.[28] In 1461, several Brethren were discovered in the New Town of Prague and even within Prague University. Some of those captured were jailed, while others were freed after renouncing a mildly worded collection of errors written by Rokycana. Brother Řehoř himself was arrested twice, but – due to either his attributed nobility or his supposed familial relation to the elected archbishop – he was spared interrogation and harsh imprisonment and was protected from the threat of execution.

The first persecutions of the Unity of Brethren were only one illustration of how King George of Poděbrady was fulfilling the duties of his secret coronation oath for the eyes of Christian Europe, and how he was personally engaged in the battle with heretics. However, these actions were more gestures than signs of a consistent policy by the Hussite king, who soon gradually eased his struggle with the Unity in reaction to the pope's cancellation of the agreements of the *Compactata*. Nevertheless, the Brethren immediately interpreted the oppression they experienced as a confirmation of their righteous struggle, and particularly as a tangible expression of the fact that Christ's blessings were being fulfilled within their ranks. Thus, the persecutions were an important impetus for the introduction of the Unity's first "order of Christian life" in 1464, known as the "consent on the Rychnov mountains."[29] Soon, the Brethren also moved to elect a priesthood, an act which took place only three years later.

---

27   The spread of the Unity is followed in detail by Ferdinand Hrejsa, *Sborové Jednoty bratrské* (Prague: 1939).
28   See Goll, *Chelčický a Jednota*, 95–119; Rudolf Urbánek, *Věk poděbradský* (České dějiny) 3 (Prague: 1915–1962), vol. 4, 399–463; Amedeo Molnár, "O příčinách pronásledování Jednoty králem Jiříkem," *Theologická příloha Křesťanské revue* 27 (1960): 35–40.
29   Amedeo Molnár (ed.), *Českobratrská výchova před Komenským* (Prague: 1956), 47–52.

Before this fateful election, the Brethren not only prayed and fasted, but also futilely attempted to find an uncorrupted church, one that was faithful to the ideals of the primitive church, in southeast Europe and among the German Waldensians. In preparation for the election, however, a decisive role was played by the discussions which the first Brethren held with Rokycana's suffragan, Martin Lupáč, and by their thorough knowledge of Lupáč's ecclesiology, mentioned above. The election itself probably occurred in the Autumn of 1467 at the estate of a certain Duchek, located in Lhotka near Rychnov nad Kněžnou.[30] The future of the Unity of Brethren was to be decided by ballot, and thus the process of the draw was set up, above all, to reflect the will of God, so that priests *could* be – but simultaneously *need not* be – elected. The Brethren found inspiration in the practice of the Old Testament priests of the temple of Jerusalem, who sought God's will through the use of oracle stones (I Samuel 28:6). Yet this daring act was mainly directed by Matthew's story on the filling of the ranks of the twelve Apostles after Judas's suicide (Acts 1:26), and thus it could simultaneously be interpreted as a testament to the Brethren's attempts to emulate the practices of the first apostolic church. In the end, the Brethren elected the full number of desired priests – three out of the nine candidates – and the election was immediately accepted by the Unity as legitimate and blessed by God. The first priests were the Silesian Matěj of Kunvald, the miller Eliáš of Chřenovice, and the tailor Tůma Přeloučský, while Brother Matouš was assigned the functions of bishop of the Unity.

Martin Lupáč approved of the Brethren's election, and apparently said to them: "you have attempted great things; even if they are not always pleasant to the people of these times, they are just. May God give you prosperity!"[31] The outcome of the election was also welcomed by Brother Řehoř, to whom – according to a later legend of the Brethren – the result was allegedly already revealed in 1461 during a trance while he underwent a torturous interrogation after his arrest. Soon, however, the Unity's jubilation was replaced by anxiety, as some brothers questioned the legitimacy of the elected priests, given the absence of the traditional connection to apostolic succession. Like the members of the Utraquist Church, even the most radical among the Brethren were unable to abandon this tradition, one which ensured the continuity of the priesthood from apostolic times to the present by the laying on of hands. The Brethren's "Solomonic" problem was finally resolved by the subsequent

---

30   Goll, *Chelčický a Jednota*, 120–34; Amedeo Molnár, "Bratrský synod ve Lhotce u Rychnova," in *Bratrský sborník*, eds. Rudolf Říčan, Amedeo Molnár, and Michal Flegl (Prague: 1967), 15–37.

31   Goll, *Chelčický a Jednota*, 139–40.

ordination of their priests by Waldensians, thus fulfilling the conceptual continuity of their church with the primitive church. Simultaneously, the Brethren adopted the idea, still alive in the contemporary Utraquist Church, that in times of need every priest is a bishop, and thus, insofar as they interpreted their situation as an emergency, the consecration of their elected bishop, Matěj by the Utraquist priest Michael of Žamberk would have to suffice to preserve apostolic succession.

The Brethren likely expected that their election of priests in the Autumn of 1467 – occurring at a time when George of Poděbrady was himself placed under papal ban, and when a new crusade threatened the Czech lands – would not inspire much outrage, and may even get lost in the confusion of these events altogether. Yet they were mistaken: Master Jan Rokycana could now no longer be a passive observer, as the Brethren's establishment of a priesthood ruptured all ties between the Unity of Brethren and the institutional church – represented in Bohemia by the Utraquist Church – for which he was also responsible, as archbishop, on the international scale. The Brethren could now be (and indeed were) punished not only as erroneous and heretical, but also as schismatics; separatists from the holy church and thus pariahs of the entire Christian community. Nevertheless, in letters addressed to Rokycana and King George in 1468, the Unity appeared self-confident and repeatedly reminded Rokycana of his own radical position when the first Brethren were his disciples and audience. Under constant pressure from the Prague center, however, the Unity gradually reflected more and more on the reasons for their actions and, in other texts, imagined the effects. Soon the Brethren endured their first martyrdoms, tormented in dungeons and burned at the stake, or, for those more fortunate, merely tortured and jailed. In later sources, Rokycana was identified as the main enemy of the true faith and of Christ's church of the Taborites and Brethren. This view was echoed in Utraquist sources, which posthumously labeled the Hussite archbishop as the "hammer of the Pikarts."[32] The bloody persecutions of the Unity of Brethren ceased only with the deaths of Jan Rokycana and King George in 1471, and the coronation-amnesty of the newly elected Bohemian king, Vladislav II the Jagellonian. The relative calm and restricted persecution which followed, however, led to a crisis among the Brethren, resulting not only in a schism, but also in a new vision of the future direction of the Unity in both the short and long terms.[33]

---

32   František Šimek and Miloslav Kaňák (ed.), *Staré letopisy české z rukopisu Křižovnického* (Prague: 1959), 281.
33   The schism within the Unity is dealt with in the following surveys: Goll, *Chelčický a Jednota*, 158–247; Müller, *Dějiny Jednoty bratrské*, vol. 1, 150–74; Rudolf Říčan, *Dějiny Jednoty*

In 1474 Brother Řehoř died, and with him the Unity lost not only their founder and earliest organizer, but above all their spiritual leader and capable defender, whose influence exceeded even that of their first priests. The new era of the Brethren's history was symbolically prefigured by the fact that, while Brother Řehoř died in almost eremitic solitude over the town Brandýs nad Orlicí (where he was buried),[34] other administrators of the Brandýs brotherhood found their final resting place inside the town walls. After the persecutions of the Brethren had ceased, cities offered them protection, employment opportunities, and even, in the most favorable conditions, the possibility of financial support for their community. Life in the cities, however, was governed by its own rules, a fact which soon – and frequently – conflicted with the teachings, and especially the way of life, of the Unity of Brethren's first generation.

In 1490 in Brandýs nad Orlicí, the majority of Brethren and their spiritual leaders decided to change the rules governing their relationship with secular authorities, and allowed many among their community to finally legalize their inhabitancy in cities, thus permitting them to receive city offices, participate in the exercise of justice, and swear oaths. Yet some among them immediately resisted, deciding to remain faithful to the legacy of Brother Řehoř. Resistance to the Brandýs decree was strongest in southwest Bohemia – in the regions around the towns of Vodňany and Strakonice – loudly protested by the laity coming from the once Taborite-oriented Moravian region of Kroměříž. Bishop Matěj of Kunvald also soon swayed in this direction and, along with the newly elected spiritual leadership of the Unity, attempted to reverse the decision and opinion of the majority, an act which cost him his future. In 1494 another synod of the Brethren, again in Rychnov – along with a subsequent meeting in Přerov – left Bishop Matěj his holy office but deprived him of authority. In the newly elected leadership of the Unity, this restricted the influence of the inconvenient "unsworn brothers," who rejected the swearing of oaths, and tied their future leaders to adherents of a new direction in the highest administrative organ of the Unity, mainly to the university-educated converts Lukáš of Prague and Vavřinec Krasonický. Another negotiation in Chlumec nad Cidlinou in 1496 officially established the so-called "Minor Party,"[35] a separate group

---

bratrské (Prague: 1957), 68–77; for special accounts, see Erhard Peschke, "Der Gegensatz zwischen der Kleinen und der Großen Partei der Brüderunität," *Wissenschafltiche Zeitschrift der Universität Rostock* 6 (1956–1957): 141–54; Amedeo Molnár, "Die kleine und die große Partei der Brüderunität," *Communio viatorum* 22 (1979): 239–48.

34   New information about Řehoř's burial place was offered by Just, "Bratr Řehoř."
35   On the records from the negotiation in Chlumec, see Josef Dobiáš (ed.), "Psaní jakéhos kněze Jana Appolinářského, učiněné a poslané paní Krescencii Zmrzlíkové na Vorlík," *Časopis historický* 2 (1882): 56–68.

of those who adhered to the old order, led by the laymen Kubík of Štěkeň and Brother Amos. Thanks to the new leadership of the Unity, the works of Petr Chelčický and the writings of Brother Řehoř now made it to the list of prohibited books.[36] Overall, it became clear that those ideas which had inspired the first generation of Brethren would no longer, under the given circumstances, be upheld by the new generation.

Due to the transformation that ensued, the Unity only now gained prominence in the feudal towns of Litomyšl and Mladá Boleslav, centers that would come to be significant for them.[37] Moreover, as Waldensian refugees arrived from Brandenburg and were admitted into the Unity, the first German-speaking communities of Brethren in the east-Bohemian town of Lanškroun and the Moravian town of Fulnek were established.[38] Also for the first time, the Brethren in the Fulnek region became exiles in 1481, expelled into the lands of today's Moldavia under the reign of Matthias Corvinus,[39] and joined there by Brethren from other Bohemian congregations, who together supported the pre-existing Hussite element in eastern Europe. By the end of the 15th century, all traces of the Brethren in Prague and in the royal towns of Bohemia[40] – with the exception of Kutná Hora – had disappeared.[41] After this, we must wait until

36   See Goll, *Chelčický a Jednota*, 209–11.
37   For the history of these towns and the Brethren's communities there, see Zdeněk Nejedlý, *Litomyšl. Tisíc let života českého města*, vol. 1 (Prague: 1954); Amedeo Molnár, *Bratr Lukáš, bohoslovec Jednoty* (Prague: 1948); Hrejsa, *Sborové Jednoty bratrské*.
38   On the Waldensian exiles who settled with the Unity of Brethren in Bohemia and Moravia, see Goll (ed.), "Některé prameny"; Goll, *Chelčický a Jednota*, 151–52, 156–57; Müller, *Dějiny Jednoty bratrské*, vol. 1, 112–14; Jean Gonnet and Amedeo Molnár, *Les Vaudois au Moyen Âge* (Turin: 1974), 262–63; Dietrich Kurze, "Märkische Waldenser und Böhmische Brüder. Zur brandenburgischen Ketzergeschichte und ihrer Nachwirkung im 15. und 16. Jahrhundert," in *Festschrift für Walter Schlesinger*, ed. Helmut Beumann, vol. 2 (Cologne and Vienna: 1974), 456–502; idem (ed.), *Quellen zur Ketzergeschichte Brandenburgs und Pommerns* (Berlin and New York: 1975).
39   Goll, *Chelčický a Jednota*, 152–53, 157; Müller, *Dějiny Jednoty bratrské*, vol. 1, 115–16; Josef Macůrek, "Husitství v rumunských zemích," *Časopis Matice moravské* 51 (1927): 53–98.
40   On the decrease in the Unity's influence in royal towns during the period in question, see Hrejsa, *Sborové Jednoty bratrské*; for the regions of Louny and Žatec, see the edition in Ota Halama, (ed.), "Žatečtí rodáci v pražské bouři 1524. Příloha. Bratrská korespondence v lenešické diaspoře ze 70. let 15. století," in *Poohří 2. Památky a společnost*, eds. Jaroslav Havrlant, Jan Mareš, Jiří Matyáš, and Martin Vostřel (Žatec: 2012), 227–32.
41   The activities of the Unity in Kutná Hora after 1500 are witnessed primarily by the letters of Martin Chlupatý of Třebíč and Jiří Hladík of Kutná Hora from 1501: Prague, Národní knihovna České republiky, XXVI A 8, pp. 1075–98. This information is significantly supplemented by the account of the immolation of the "Pikart" Ondřej Polívka in Kutná Hora in 1511, preserved as part of a text by Vavřinec Krasonický: Prague, Národní knihovna České republiky, XVII F 51a, fols. 152v-167r.

the mid-16th century before we find significant changes in the spread and influence of the Unity of Brethren, during the reign of the Bohemian King Ferdinand I, after the Habsburg victory in the Schmalkaldic War in 1547.

5 Theory and Practice

As has already been noted, the theology of the Unity of Brethren,[42] and its concrete expression in the Christian life of individual members, originated under the strong, lingering influence of revolutionary Hussitism, and was closest to the latter's radical wing. Yet the Brethren's theology simultaneously reflected the conceptual world of Utraquism in the period after the *Compactata*, while also retaining a strong connection to the ascetic ideals of late-medieval Christianity. The Brethren themselves, therefore, did not perceive their establishment of a church as an act that was in any way revolutionary, since their primary motivation was the renewal of the existing church; theirs was a spirit of *restitution*, rather than *institution*. Similarly, the "anxiety over salvation" with which the Brethren rationalized many of their essentially revolutionary acts was expressed neither as Christian individualism, free from the existing church structures, nor as the over-confessional or non-confessional positions of the members of the early Unity, but rather – despite their distrust in institutions – as an entirely traditional and institutional, that is, ecclesiastical, solution. If, despite this, the Brethren's theology was a radical one, it was because they were attempting to resolve the contemporary crisis of the church and Christian society with a return to the roots; a return to an authentic Christianity whose standards and concrete application in human society are plainly found in the Bible. The Brethren's specific standards, therefore, came from the law of Christ (*lex Christi*), the collection of Jesus's expressed commands in the Gospels, and the record of Jesus's life. They found the application of this absolute standard in the life of the first church, the character of which is expressed in the New Testament letters and the Acts of the Apostles. Everything else, in the spirit of the Hussite Cheb Judge of the 1430s, was simply derived from either Christ or the Antichrist.

Formally, the Brethren's theology was one of apologetics, a defense of their theoretical starting points which were introduced into practice in the lives of

---

[42] On the Brethren's theology and ecclesiastical practice, see Müller, *Dějiny Jednoty bratrské*, vol. 1, 125–49; Amedeo Molnár, "O bratrské theologii," in Rudolf Říčan, *Dějiny Jednoty bratrské* (Prague: 1957), 407–42; Craig D. Atwood, *The Theology of the Czech Brethren from Hus to Comenius* (University Park, PA: 2009).

their individual members. Just as Hussite theology was predominantly formed in polemics with members of the Roman Church and in debates between Hussite parties, so too was the first theology of the Unity of Brethren formed in the polemics with the Bohemian Utraquists of the Poděbrad and Jagellonian periods. Nevertheless, the entire range of the Unity's preserved sources from the fifteenth century document the fact that, after the emergence of their own church organization, the Unity could not do without internal documents of a practical nature[43] that did not demand sharp apologetics.

In reference to the binding law of Christ and the practice of the primitive church, and in the spirit of previous intellectual developments, the Unity distinguished foremost between substantial, ministerial, and circumstantial matters (*substantialia, ministerialia, accidentalia*).[44] The Brethren held the first of these as necessary for salvation and unchangeable, as *substantialia* related to the three traditional and fundamental theological qualities – faith, hope, and love – from which "good works and virtuous life" flow. Christians should participate in the second category, the ministerial, as much as possible, but failure to do so in no way threatens their salvation. The third category, along with the second, fulfils only an auxiliary function for the knowledge of substantial matters, and is thus changeable, enactable, and annullable; it includes mainly preaching, the sacraments, and also the church itself, whose main functions were to guide one to faith, hope, and love.

The main instrument of the church to lead people to substantial matters was, according to the first Brethren, the annunciation of the Gospels, which was not limited to preaching. Acceptance of the Gospels by the faithful was supported by the service of the sacraments and the implementation of church discipline. In this framework, as already mentioned, the ministering church is the universal church, standing above its "units" (i.e. local churches), and cannot be identified with any specific church, nor with the Unity of Brethren itself.

Nevertheless, the Brethren themselves understood their own community to be a model of the "renewed holy church."[45] They interpreted their split with the Utraquists as the final consequence of the latter's confusion of substantial and ministerial matters; for Utraquists, the lay chalice was a requirement for salvation, while the Brethren saw it only as a ministerial matter, and thus

---

43 A collection of internal documents survives as *Dekrety Jednoty bratrské*; in the 16th century, the *Akta Jednoty bratrské* were also of largely internal nature.
44 See Molnár, "O bratrské theologii."
45 An example of this perception is Brother Lukáš of Prague's *Spis o obnovení církve* from 1510, which codifies previous opinions of the Brethren.

nonessential. Yet what especially contributed to the self-confidence of the Brethren was their realization that the ideal church could not be found anywhere in the world. This realization was also supported by the experience of repeated persecution, which the Brethren understood to be a sign of the endtimes and also – in the spirit of Matěj of Janov – a distinct mark of the true church.

Life in the Brethren's community, which was defined only as a provisional and, to an extent, temporary one, was understood as life in the one true church, and had an entirely unique character. In the eschatologically oriented early days of the Unity, the lived Christian ideal dominated under the absolute authority of Christ's law. The Christianity of individual brothers and sisters developed foremost in the life of the congregation, which thus became the foundational unit of organization in the Brethren's church. The term "congregation" (*sbor*) itself replaced the traditional terms "church" or "parish."[46] It referred to the service and collective of the church, the assembly of the faithful, which was not bound to a specific building but only to the Brethren's community itself.

In the early Unity, it was especially the lay teachers and leaders, such as Brother Řehoř, who were responsible for the spiritual care of the Brethren's congregations. As the Unity of Brethren was a part of the Utraquist Church until 1467, the search for the "good priest," along with the entrance of some Utraquist priests into the Unity, was a matter which concerned both their early and later existence.[47] The "good priest" did not confuse substantial with ministerial matters; he led believers to the former while practicing what he preached in his own life. Preaching and teaching, therefore, were the main tasks of the priest, while administering the sacraments and employing the "power of the keys" in matters of church discipline were his secondary functions. As a product of the times, however, the Unity of Brethren remained bound to the tradition of clerical celibacy and did not stray from this tradition despite their radicalism in other matters. Moreover, just as in other churches, the Brethren required their spiritual administrators to wear only simple dress and hair. The Unity's essential difference from other churches was foremost represented by the active lives of their priests, who needed to sustain themselves by physical labor according to the example of the Apostles; like St. Peter the fisherman and

---

46 See Josef Macek, "Ze slovníku české reformace: sbor," in *Směřování. Sborník k šedesátinám Amedea Molnára*, ed. Noemi Rejchrtová (Prague: 1983), 117–23.

47 For the definition of a good priest, see, e.g. *Spis o dobrých a zlých kněžiech*, in Jaroslav Bidlo (ed.), *Akty Jednoty bratrské*, 2 vols. (Brno: 1915–1923), vol. 1, 79–180. On the priesthood in the Unity in general, see Müller, *Dějiny Jednoty bratrské*, vol. 1, 65–90, 129–30; Říčan, *Dějiny Jednoty bratrské*, 60–1.

St. Paul the tent-builder before them, the Brethren's priests could not exploit the coffers of the congregation for their own profit and livelihood.

The Brethren's priests divided the administration of their assigned congregations with lay administrators; elders, later called the "Brethren's judges," actively participated in spiritual care, while almsmen were responsible for the congregation's finances.[48] The spiritual administrator himself was subject not only to the oversight of these laymen, but also to the authority of the bishop and the jurisdiction of the so-called "small council," which was gradually introduced as the highest administrative institution of the Unity. It played the role of a kind of consistory for the Brethren, functioning as the deciding mechanism of meetings and synods regarding the clergy and their recruitment, the election of bishops, and the enlistment of new members into its own ranks. Generally, the council was responsible for the life of the Unity in individual congregations and regions, addressing matters first on a provincial scale, and later also on an international one.

In the spirit of medieval mysticism, membership in the Unity of Brethren was distinguished in three degrees: brothers beginning, proceeding, and moving toward perfection.[49] The individual degrees were represented foremost by the extent of an individual brother's participation in substantial matters, and in turn affected his missionary, sacramental, catechetical, and pastoral practice toward each brother within the congregation. The arrival of a new member into the congregation[50] was sometimes preceded by several years of investigation of the candidate's spiritual motives and social position. Once a candidate was accepted, he had to undergo "discipline" and "obedience," which the Brethren's community demanded of its members in both spiritual and temporal matters. He could not, for instance, continue to practice a trade which was contradictory to the ideal Christian life of the Unity. He had to cease participation in worldly power. Above all, he had to be willing to subordinate his life to the authority of his future superiors. If he later erred somehow, he was first cautioned by the leaders of the congregation, then cut off from the Lord's Supper, and only then excommunicated.

---

48 The administration of the Brethren's community, and of the Unity as whole in Jednoty, is described by Müller, *Dějiny Jednoty bratrské*, vol. 1, 146–48; Říčan, *Dějiny Jednoty bratrské*, 60–1; contemporary evidence in Gindely (ed.), *Dekrety Jednoty bratrské*.

49 See Amedeo Molnár, "Počínající, pokračující, dokonalí," in *Jednota bratrská 1457–1957. Sborník k pětistému výročí založení*, eds. František M. Bartoš and Josef L. Hromádka (Prague: 1956), 147–69.

50 Müller, *Dějiny Jednoty bratrské*, vol. 1, 136; Říčan, *Dějiny Jednoty bratrské*, 62–3.

A new member's admittance into the Unity of Brethren was affirmed by his re-baptism,[51] a practice which distinguished the Brethren from all other contemporary churches until the 1530s, when it was terminated in the Unity under the influence of the European Reformation. The Brethren did not recognize the baptism of the Roman or Utraquist Churches as valid, as these confused substantial and ministerial matters, and there were also doubts regarding the moral qualities of individual priests. At the same time, however, the second baptism affirmed the Brethren's doctrine that the dispensation of the sacrament occurred only at the moment that the message of the Gospel was accepted, namely at the age of reason. Thus, the earliest Brethren did not baptize children at all; later only those on the threshold of adolescence were baptized; and only in their second generation did they baptize infants – but still only those who were born to recognized members of the Unity.

Drawing a correlation with the practice of the Brethren in the 16th and 17th centuries, it may be assumed that marriages in the Unity of Brethren from the beginning were subject to the oversight of the church, and thus spouses were often "recommended" to each other.[52] By the end of the fifteenth century, the Unity still did not allow mixed marriages between members and non-members; marriage ceremonies had a certain communal character, to the extent that even the role of the priest was only that of a witness and teacher of the future couple. The character of the married life depended upon whether it took place in a functioning congregation of Brethren or in the diaspora. In the former case, the members of the congregation were subjected to intensive instruction by their spiritual brothers and administrators. In the latter case, small groups of the Brethren met with their administrators only rarely, and often only during common religious services.

For members of the Unity of Brethren, austerity and humility in housing, clothing, and behavior applied without exception.[53] As proponents of physical labor, the Brethren were isolated from worldly pleasures and also from the traditional cycle of the church year, holding fasts only with their church and according to their own deliberation, and, in the beginning, avoiding all holidays except Sundays. The Brethren's distinctiveness from existing ecclesiastic and social norms and traditions was also observable in death; like Brother Řehoř

---

51   On baptism in the first generation of the Unity, see primarily Müller, *Dějiny Jednoty bratrské*, vol. 1: 130–33; the topic is taken up by Říčan, *Dějiny Jednoty bratrské*, 61–2.
52   See Jindřich Halama, *Sociální učení českých bratří 1464–1618* (Brno: 2003), 37–9; Martin Nodl, "Manželství v rané Jednotě bratrské," in *Mezi Baltem a Uhrami. Komenský, Jednota bratrská a svět středoevropského protestantismu. Sborník k poctě Marty Bečkové*, eds. Vladimír Urbánek and Lenka Řezníková (Prague: 2006), 131–47.
53   Halama, *Sociální učení českých bratří*, 35–9.

himself, other brothers of the early Unity had their bodies buried near their own dwelling-places and congregations, attaching no significance to the idea of a sacred ground of final rest, while also understanding death to be a joyous event;[54] only in death did the brothers find the solution to the problem of "necessary salvation" which brought them to the Unity in the first place, and death also strengthened their faith in the Unity of Brethren as the community wherein they found this solution.

6   Later Generations

Even after the secession of the Minor Party, the Unity of Brethren remained a medieval church, and their new spiritual leaders – with Bishop Lukáš of Prague at their head – continued to express their ideas via the scholastic style that they mastered before their conversion, in Prague University and the Utraquist Church.[55] Lukáš himself, like Brother Řehoř before him, resided in the monastic community at Slovany, and acknowledged Chelčický's influence on his decision to enter the Unity. He also experienced the rise and fall of the radical preacher Michal Polák and the revolutionary events in Prague in the first half of the 1480s. However, he did not pass into obscurity like the first Brethren, but gradually joined with the new church, the formation of which he subsequently helped to bring about.

The main task of the second generation of the Unity, and especially of Brother Lukáš, was to build up a functional church institution that was equipped, on the one hand, with arguments to defend its own distinctiveness, and on the other with a means of leading its congregations.[56] The former task was primarily fulfilled by means of disputes with the Brethren's Minor Party, Bohemian Utraquists, the Roman Church, and the European Reformation. The latter task led to the codification of the Brethren's doctrine and practice on specific matters, in the lives of both the whole community and individual brothers.

---

54   Jindřich Marek, "Bratrská nauka o posledních věcech člověka a smrt pana Kunráta Krajíře z Krajku (1487–1542)," *Miscellanea Oddělení rukopisů a starých tisků* 19 (2005–2006): 33–59.

55   Other converts and students of Prague University who gained prominence in the second generation of the Unity, besides Lukáš of Prague, included Prokop of Jindřichův Hradec, Jan Černý, and Vavřinec Krasonický; the majority of them had been ordained in the Utraquist Church.

56   The literary work of Lukáš of Prague is surveyed in Müller, *Dějiny Jednoty bratrské*, vol. 1, 334–50.

Only in the beginning of the 1530s,[57] therefore, do we find a fundamental change in the orientation of the Unity. This was when Lukáš's generation left it and another convert, Jan Augusta, was placed at its head, while significant representatives of the Bohemian nobility also joined the Brethren with their own rebaptism. The Unity thus underwent an internal transformation, instigated mainly by their encounter with Martin Luther and the European Reformation. In 1535 the Brethren's confession was created, following the example of the Augsburg confession, and with the support of domestic noble families. The Brethren's students were becoming acquainted with Reformation teachings and European humanism abroad, and only now did the Unity lose its medieval character. Moving forward, while the brothers of the Unity were still aware of their origins – and continued to name Milíč of Kroměříž, Matěj of Janov, Jan Hus, the priests of Tábor, Petr Chelčický, and Jan Rokycana as their predecessors – they were now foremost a church of the Reformation, with its roots in Hussitism, but its orientation and direction far removed from Hussitism itself and from the Unity's own origins.

7 Historiographic Survey

The beginnings of scholarly research on the Unity of Brethren can be found in the mid-nineteenth century, though even then it was possible to draw from historical works on the topic from the previous two centuries.[58] František Palacký obviously noted the Bohemian Brethren within his monumental *History of the Czech Nation*,[59] but despite his high evaluation of their moral life, he did not establish more than an outline of their history. The first to truly devote himself to the history of the Unity of Brethren was the German historian of Czech descent, Anton Gindely, university professor and Prague archivist, whose work cannot be disregarded even today. His extensive two-volume

---

57 For the further history of the Unity, see primarily Joseph Theodor Müller, *Geschichte der Böhmischen Brüder*, vol. 1: *1400–1528*; vol. 2: *1528–1576*; vol. 3: *Die polnische Unität 1548–1793. Die böhmisch-mährische Unität 1575–1781* (Herrnhut: 1922–1931); Říčan, *Dějiny Jednoty bratrské*; Halama, *Sociální učení českých bratří*.

58 A brief summary of the Brethren's older historiography is found in Müller, *Dějiny Jednoty bratrské*, vol. 1, iii–viii.

59 František Palacký, *Dějiny národu českého v Čechách a v Moravě*, 6 vols. (Prague: 1848–1876), vol. 4, 250–54, 541–44.

synthesis of the Brethren's history,[60] supplemented by several source editions,[61] represented a real turning-point with respect to earlier research. Gindely's work not only encompassed the history of the Unity of Brethren in a complete overview, but for the first time presented the Unity as a European and supranational topic, with roots in Hussitism but simultaneously a phenomenon of the Reformation. Gindely's research on the contacts between the Bohemian Brethren and European reformers (thus a Czech-German topic) was not resumed until long afterwards. Further developments among Czech historians drew inspiration from their esteem for Palacký's conceptualization, and it was foremost the founder of modern historiography at Prague University, Jaroslav Goll, who built upon this. Along with his other works, Goll's German-language, two-volume work of 1878–1882 (expanded and published in Czech in 1916 by his pupil Kamil Krofta) about the Unity in the 16th century – and their relationship with Chelčický and the Waldensians – belongs to a fundamental corpus which still today has not been significantly expanded upon on the level of source heuristics, nor surpassed on the level of interpretation.[62]

A generation of direct and indirect disciples of Jaroslav Goll was inspired by the headway that he, and before him, Palacký had made. Foremost among them was the historian and diplomat Kamil Krofta, particularly his monograph *O bratrském dějepisectví* (On the historiography of the Brethren);[63] the communist politician Zdeněk Nejedlý later added his work on the history of the town of Litomyšl;[64] and Rudolf Urbánek, a professor at Brno University, added his significant chapter in the final volume of his life-work, *Věk poděbradský* (The Poděbrad age).[65] Between 1915 and 1923, the Polonist Jaroslav Bidlo provided editions of the fundamental sources of the Unity from their beginnings – collected in the 16th century with the first and second volumes of the Acts of the Unity of Brethren – and simultaneously dedicated himself to the later

60 Müller, *Geschichte der Böhmischen Brüder*.
61 Gindely (ed.), *Dekrety Jednoty bratrské*; idem, *Quellen zur Geschichte der Böhmischen Brüder*.
62 Jaroslav Goll, *Quellen und Untersuchungen zur Geschichte der Böhmischen Brüder*, vol. 2: *Petr Chelčický und seine Lehre* (Prague: 1882); idem, *Chelčický a Jednota*.
63 Kamil Krofta, *O bratrském dějepisectví* (Prague: 1946).
64 Nejedlý, *Litomyšl. Tisíc let života českého města*.
65 Urbánek, *Věk poděbradský*. On the early history of the Unity, see also Rudolf Urbánek, *Jednota bratrská a vyšší vzdělání až do doby Blahoslavovy. Příspěvek k 400. výročí narozenin Blahoslavových* (Brno: 1923); idem, "Jan Paleček, šašek krále Jiřího a jeho předchůdci v zemích českých," in *Příspěvky k dějinám starší české literatury*, ed. Josef Hrabák (Prague: 1958), 5–89.

history of the Unity in Poland after 1547.[66] A professor of the Hus Evangelical Faculty (today's Protestant Theological Faculty) in Prague, František Michálek Bartoš, also provided a range of studies.[67] Yet the fundamental contribution for research on the Unity was that of Joseph Theodor Müller, a student of Goll, archivist of the Herrnhut Brethren's congregation, and author of the influential and still insurmountable work, *Geschichte der Böhmischen Brüder*. Among the works coming from outside the Goll school, those of the Roman Catholic apologist and Vyšehrad canon Antonín Lenz and the still unsurpassed anthology of the Brethren's confessions by the Petrograd Slavicist Ivan Savvič Pal'mov should be mentioned.[68]

The pre-war interests of Czech, Russian, and especially German historians in the history of the Unity of Brethren and their beginnings was dramatically circumscribed by the communist overthrow in Czechoslovakia in February 1948. Thereafter, researchers devoted time to the history of the Brethren only when it helped to describe the history of certain Bohemian and Moravian regions, when it demonstrated the maturity of local book-printing and music, or when it esteemed the pedagogical genius of the last bishop of the Unity, Jan Amos Komenský. The latter became the main figure of the Brethren's history, which was censured by the totalitarian regime and thus stripped of any ecclesiastic or theological contextualization. The interests of the theologians of the Evangelical Faculty of Prague, however, endured the war and even the fateful year of 1948.[69] Amedeo Molnár published a summary of the theology of the second generation of Brethren titled *Brother Lukáš, Theologian of the Unity*, and in 1956 he was able to publish a fundamental anthology of the Brethren's sources under a title that suited the communist regime: *The Bohemian Brethren's Education before Komenský*.[70] Molnár also wrote a chapter outlining the

---

66 Bidlo (ed.), "Nekrologium polské větve Jednoty bratrské"; idem, *Akty Jednoty bratrské*; idem, *Jednota bratrská v prvním vyhnanství*, 4 vols. (Prague: 1900–1932).
67 See the list of studies in the bibliography below.
68 Antonín Lenz, *Vzájemný poměr učení Petra Chelčického, starší Jednoty českých bratří a táborů k nauce valdenských, Jana Husi a Jana Viklifa* (Prague: 1895); Ivan Pal'mov, *Cheshskie brat'ja v svoih konfessijah do nachala sblizhenija ih s protestantami v konce pervoj chetverti XVI stoletija*, 2 vols. (Prague: 1904).
69 The fundamental work on the Brethren's topography was published before World War II: Hrejsa, *Sborové Jednoty bratrské*.
70 Molnár, *Bratr Lukáš*; idem (ed.), *Českobratrská výchova*; see also idem, *Boleslavští bratří* (Prague: 1952); idem (ed.), *Bekenntnisse der Böhmischen Brüder* (Hildesheim and New York: 1979).

Brethren's theology, which was included in the summarized history of the Unity by the evangelical historian Rudolf Říčan.[71]

After 1948, few contributed to the understanding of the medieval history of the Unity of Brethren apart from Prague evangelical historians and theologians. The main exception was the German Slavicist, evangelical theologian, and professor of church history at the universities of Rostock and Halle, Erhard Peschke. His dissertation of 1935 was dedicated to the eucharistic theology of the Unity of Brethren, and he later clearly described the division of the Unity in the 1490s.[72] Beyond the so-called "iron curtain," the Canadian historian Peter Brock – working in Central Europe and later as professor at the University of Toronto – also dedicated himself to the history of the Unity of Brethren. His interest in the Unity came from his own personal enthusiasm for the history of pacifism and culminated in his Oxford dissertation on the political and social doctrines of the Brethren.[73] Two compilations on the Brethren's history were also recently published by authors affiliated with the American Moravian Church.[74]

Since 1989, the once dominating influence of evangelically oriented historians of the Unity of Brethren in the Czech Republic has been reduced to a single work, that of Jindřich Halama on the social teachings of the Bohemian Brethren.[75] Karolina Justová published a second monograph under new circumstances in 2011, a biography of one of the first priests of the Brethren, Tůma Přeloučský.[76] Otherwise, publications on the early history of the Unity have appeared as journal articles.[77] The lack of contemporary interest in the history of the early Unity of Brethren can be attributed primarily to the determining

---

71 Říčan, *Dějiny Jednoty bratrské*; Molnár, "O bratrské theologii," 407–42. There is a translation into both German and English: Rudolf Říčan, *Die Böhmischen Brüder. Ihr Ursprung und ihre Geschichte*, trans. Bohumír Popelář (Berlin: 1961); Rudolf Říčan, *The History of the Unity of Brethren. A Protestant Hussite Church in Bohemia and Moravia*, trans. C. Daniel Crews (Bethlehem, PA.: 1992).

72 See the list of studies in the bibliography below.

73 Peter Brock, *The Political and Social Doctrines of the Unity of Czech Brethren in the 15th and Early 16th centuries* (The Hague: 1957).

74 C. Daniel Crews, *Faith, Love, Hope. A History of the Unitas Fratrum* (Winston-Salem, NC.: 2008); Atwood, *Theology of the Czech Brethren*.

75 Halama, *Sociální učení českých bratří*.

76 Karolina Justová, *Tůma Přeloučský. Muž znamenitý, kterýž jiné převyšoval* (Prague: 2011).

77 See Coufal, "Dva neznámé rukopisy"; Miloslav Košťál, "Hradeckým, Orebským a Pardidubským. Výzva k pokání a k jednotě všech křesťanů z doby poděbradské," in *Stopami dějin Náchodska. Sborník Státního okresního archivu Náchod* 7 (2001): 135–202; Nodl, "Manželství v rané Jednotě bratrské."

influence of the work of Jaroslav Goll, who was able to gather and interpret all available sources that were significant to the beginnings of the Brethren. The oldest sources of the Brethren have nearly all been available in published editions for some time, and thus are intimately familiar to researchers. In contrast to the history of the early modern Unity, where the number of new sources is always growing, the history of the medieval Unity lacks the external impulse for further research.

Translated by Martin Pjecha

Bibliography

Manuscripts

Prague, Národní knihovna České republiky [National Library of the Czech Republic], XVII F 51a.

Prague, Národní knihovna České republiky [National Library of the Czech Republic], XVII F 51b.

Prague, Národní knihovna České republiky [National Library of the Czech Republic], XXVI A 8.

Editions of Sources

Bidlo, Jaroslav (ed.), "Nekrologium polské větve Jednoty bratrské" [The necrology of the Polish branch of the Unity of Brethren], *Věstník Královské české společnosti nauk* (1897): 1–40.

Bidlo, Jaroslav (ed.), *Akty Jednoty bratrské* [Acts of the Unity of Brethren], 2 vols. (Brno: 1915–1923).

Boubín, Jaroslav, and Jana Zachová (eds.), *Žaloby katolíků na Mistra Jana z Rokycan* [Grievances of the Catholics against Master Jan Rokycana] (Rokycany: 1997).

Dobiáš, Josef (ed.), "Psaní jakéhos kněze Jana Appolinářského, učiněné a poslané paní Krescencii Zmrzlíkové na Vorlík" [A letter of a certain priest Jan Apolinářský, written and sent to Lady Krescencia Zmrzlíková at Orlík], *Časopis historický* 2 (1882): 56–68.

Fiedler, Joseph (ed.), *Todtenbuch der Geistlichkeit der Böhmischen Brüder* (Fontes rerum Austriacarum, 1. Abteilung: Scriptores) 5 (Vienna: 1863), 213–310.

Gindely, Anton (ed.), *Dekrety Jednoty bratrské* [Decrees of the Unity of Brethren] (Prague: 1865).

Gindely, Anton (ed.), *Quellen zur Geschichte der Böhmischen Brüder, vornehmlich ihrem Zusammenhang mit Deutschland betreffend* (Fontes rerum Austriacarum, 2. Abteilung: Diplomataria et acta) 19 (Vienna: 1859).

Goll, Jaroslav (ed.), "Některé prameny k náboženským dějinám v 15. století. II. Výslech bratří na Kladsku r. 1480 [Some sources for the religious history of the 15th century. II. An interrogation of Brethren in Kłodsko in 1480]," *Věstník Královské české společnosti nauk* (1895): 3–12.

Goll, Jaroslav (ed.), "Spisek Víta z Krupé proti Bratřím" [A writing of Vít of Krupá against the Brethren], *Zprávy o zasedání Královské české společnosti nauk v Praze* (1878): 162–70.

Halama, Ota (ed.), "Spis 'De ecclesia' Martina Lupáče z doby poděbradské" [The work "De ecclesia" of Martin Lupáč from the Poděbrad period], *Theologická revue* 75 (2004): 420–35.

Halama, Ota (ed.), "Žatečtí rodáci v pražské bouři 1524. Příloha. Bratrská korespondence v lenešické diaspoře ze 70. let 15. století" [Žatec compatriots in the Prague riots of 1524. Appendix: The Brethren's correspondence in the Lenešice diaspora from the 1470s], in *Poohří 2. Památky a společnost*, eds. Jaroslav Havrlant, Jan Mareš, Jiří Matyáš, and Martin Vostřel (Žatec: 2012), 223–32.

Just, Jiří (ed.), "Zlomek bratrského Nekrologia z fondů KNM v Praze" [A fragment of the Brethren's necrology in the holdings of the National Museum in Prague], in *Acta reformationem Bohemicam illustrantia*, ed. Ota Halama, vol. 5 (Prague: 2004), 59–65.

Kurze, Dietrich (ed.), *Quellen zur Ketzergeschichte Brandenburgs und Pommerns* (Berlin and New York: 1975).

Lukáš Pražský, *Odpis proti odtržencom, jenž se malou stránkú nazývají* [A reply against the apostates who call themselves the lesser party] (Mladá Boleslav: 1525).

Lukáš Pražský, *Zprávy při službách úřadu kněžského v Jednotě bratrské* [Instructions for the services of the priestly office in the Unity of Brethren] (Mladá Boleslav: 1527).

Molnár, Amedeo (ed.), *Bekenntnisse der Böhmischen Brüder* (Hildesheim and New York: 1979).

Molnár, Amedeo (ed.), *Českobratrská výchova před Komenským* [The education among the Czech Brethren before Komenský] (Prague: 1956).

Pal'mov, Ivan (ed.), *Cheshskie brat'ja v svoih konfessijah do nachala sblizhenija ih s protestantami v konce pervoj chetverti XVI stoletija* [The Czech Brethren in their confessions to the beginning of their rapprochement with the Protestants at the end of the first quarter of the 16th century], 2 vols. (Prague: 1904).

Šimek, František, and Miloslav Kaňák (eds.), *Staré letopisy české z rukopisu Křižovnického* [Old Czech annals from the Knights' manuscript] (Prague: 1959).

Smetánka, Emil (ed.), *Staročeské životy svatých otců* [Old Czech lives of the holy fathers] (Prague: 1909).

Vavřinec of Březová, "Kronika husitská" [The Hussite Chronicle], in *Fontes rerum Bohemicarum*, eds. Josef Emler, Jan Gebauer, and Jaroslav Goll, vol. 5 (Prague: 1893), 327–534.

Secondary Sources

Atwood, Craig D., *The Theology of the Czech Brethren from Hus to Comenius* (University Park, PA: 2009).

Bartoš, František Michálek, "Z počátků Jednoty bratrské" [From the beginnings of the Unity of Brethren], *Časopis Musea Království českého* 95 (1921): 30–43, 127–39, 203–18.

Bartoš, František Michálek, "Rokycana za t. zv. druhého pronásledování Jednoty" [Rokycana during the so-called second persecution of the Unity], *Časopis Národního musea* 99 (1925): 71–5.

Bartoš, František Michálek, *Literární činnost M. Jana Rokycany, M. Jana Příbrama, M. Petra Payna* [The literary activity of Master Jan Rokycana, Master Jan Příbram, Master Peter Payne] (Prague: 1928).

Bartoš, František Michálek, "Valdenský biskup Štěpán z Basileje a ustavení Jednoty bratrské" [The Waldensian bishop Stefan of Basel and the establishment of the Unity of Brethren], in idem, *Husitství a cizina* (Prague: 1931), 248–54.

Bartoš, František Michálek, "Neznámý spis proti Chelčickému a prvotní Jednotě bratrské" [An unknown writing against Chelčický and the primitive Unity of Brethren], *Jihočeský sborník historický* 17 (1948): 60–4.

Bartoš, František Michálek, "M. Lupáč a Jednota bratrská" [M. Lupáč and the Unity of Brethren], *Křesťanská revue* 32 (1965): 89–91.

Bidlo, Jaroslav, *Jednota bratrská v prvním vyhnanství* [The Unity of Brethren in the first exile], 4 vols. (Prague: 1900–1932).

Blažková, Edita, "Blahoslavova Akta Jednoty bratrské" [Blahoslav's *Acta* of the Unity of Brethren], *Theologická příloha Křesťanské revue* 31 (1964): 81–8, 97–105.

Brock, Peter, *The Political and Social Doctrines of the Unity of Czech Brethren in the 15th and Early 16th Centuries* (The Hague: 1957).

Coufal, Dušan, "Dva neznámé rukopisy k počátkům Jednoty bratrské v benediktinské knihovně v Seitenstetten" [Two unknown manuscripts on the origins of the Unity of Brethren in the Benedictine library at Seitenstetten], *Studie o rukopisech* 39 (2009): 157–88.

Crews, C. Daniel, *Faith, Love, Hope. A History of the Unitas Fratrum* (Winston-Salem, NC.: 2008).

de Lange, Albert, and Kathrin Utz Tremp (eds.), *Friedrich Reiser und die "waldensisch-hussitische Internationale"* (Heidelberg, Ubstadt-Weiher, and Basel: 2006).

Flegl, Michal, "K otázce sociálního původu bratra Řehoře a jeho literárních počátků" [On the question of the social origin of brother Řehoř and his literary beginnings], *Listy filologické* 100 (1977): 88–94.

Gindely, Anton, *Geschichte der Böhmischen Brüder*, 2 vols. (Prague: 1857–1868).

Goll, Jaroslav, *Quellen und Untersuchungen zur Geschichte der Böhmischen Brüder*, 2 vols. (Prague: 1878–1882).

Goll, Jaroslav, *Chelčický a Jednota v XV. století* [Chelčický and the Unity in the 15th century] (Prague: 1916).

Gonnet, Jean, and Amedeo Molnár, *Les Vaudois au Moyen Âge* (Turin: 1974).

Halama, Jindřich, *Sociální učení českých bratří 1464–1618* [The social teachings of the Czech Brethren 1464–1618] (Brno: 2003).

Halama, Ota, "Obhajoba biblického kánonu v druhé generaci Jednoty bratrské" [The defense of the biblical canon in the second generation of the Unity of Brethren], in *Amica – sponsa – mater. Bible v čase reformace*, ed. Ota Halama (Prague: 2014), 226–40.

Halama, Ota, "Tištěná polemika s Jednotou bratrskou v době jagellonské (1500–1526) [Printed polemics against the Unity of Brethren in the Jagellonian period (1500–1526)]," in *Knihtisk, zbožnost, konfese v zemích Koruny české doby poděbradské a jagellonské*, eds. Kamil Boldan and Jan Hrdina (Colloquia mediaevalia Pragensia) 19 (Prague: 2018), 139–79.

Hobza, Radek, "Akta Jednoty bratrské a jejich obsah" [The *Acta* of the Unity of Brethren and thir contents], in *Československá církev a Jednota bratrská. Sborník prací k 500. výročí staré Jednoty bratrské*, ed. Miloslav Kaňák (Prague: 1967), 152–249.

Hrejsa, Ferdinand, *Sborové Jednoty bratrské* [Congregations of the Unity of Brethren] (Prague: 1939).

Just, Jiří, "Bratr Řehoř, 'patriarcha' Jednoty bratrské" [Brother Řehoř, the "patriarch" of the Unity of Brethren], *Nové bratrské listy* 9 (2007): 8–11.

Justová, Karolina, *Tůma Přeloučský. Muž znamenitý, kterýž jiné převyšoval* [Tůma Přeloučský. "An outstanding man who surpassed the others"] (Prague: 2011).

Košťál, Miloslav, "Hradeckým, Orebským a Pardidubským. Výzva k pokání a k jednotě všech křesťanů z doby poděbradské" [To those of Hradec, Oreb, and Pardubice. An appeal for repentance and the unity of all Christians from the Poděbrady period], in *Stopami dějin Náchodska. Sborník Státního okresního archivu Náchod* 7 (2001): 135–202.

Krofta, Kamil, *O bratrském dějepisectví* [On the Brethren's historiography] (Prague: 1946).

Kurze, Dietrich, "Märkische Waldenser und Böhmische Brüder. Zur brandenburgischen Ketzergeschichte und ihrer Nachwirkung im 15. und 16. Jahrhundert," in *Festschrift für Walter Schlesinger*, ed. Helmut Beumann, vol. 2 (Cologne and Vienna: 1974), 456–502.

Lenz, Antonín, *Vzájemný poměr učení Petra Chelčického, starší Jednoty českých bratří a táborů k nauce valdenských, Jana Husi a Jana Viklifa* [The mutual relationship of the teachings of Petr Chelčický, the older Unity of Czech Brethren, and the Taborites to the teachings of the Waldensians, Jan Hus, and John Wyclif] (Prague: 1895).

Macek, Josef, "Ze slovníku české reformace: sbor" [From the vocabulary of the Bohemian Reformation: "sbor" (congregation)], in *Směřování. Sborník k šedesátinám Amedea Molnára*, ed. Noemi Rejchrtová (Prague: 1983), 117–23.

Macůrek, Josef, "Husitství v rumunských zemích" [Hussitism in the Romanian lands], *Časopis Matice moravské* 51 (1927): 53–98.

Marek, Jindřich, "Bratrská nauka o posledních věcech člověka a smrt pana Kunráta Krajíře z Krajku (1487–1542)" [The Brethren's doctrine of the last things of men and the death of Lord Kunrát Krajíř of Krajk (1487–1542)], *Miscellanea Oddělení rukopisů a starých tisků* 19 (2005–2006): 33–59.

Molnár, Amedeo, *Bratr Lukáš, bohoslovec Jednoty* [Brother Lukáš, the theologian of the Unity] (Prague: 1948).

Molnár, Amedeo, *Boleslavští bratří* [The Boleslav Brehren] (Prague: 1952).

Molnár, Amedeo, "Počínající, pokračující, dokonalí" [The incipients, progressing, and perfect], in *Jednota bratrská 1457–1957. Sborník k pětistému výročí založení*, eds. František M. Bartoš and Josef L. Hromádka (Prague: 1956), 147–69.

Molnár, Amedeo, "O bratrské theologii" [On the Brethren's theology], in Rudolf Říčan, *Dějiny Jednoty bratrské* (Prague: 1957), 407–42.

Molnár, Amedeo, "O příčinách pronásledování Jednoty králem Jiříkem" [On the causes of the persecution of the Unity by King George], *Theologická příloha Křesťanské revue* 27 (1960): 35–40.

Molnár, Amedeo, "Bratrský synod ve Lhotce u Rychnova" [The Brethren's synod in Lhotka near Rychnov], in *Bratrský sborník*, eds. Rudolf Říčan, Amedeo Molnár, and Michal Flegl (Prague: 1967), 15–37.

Molnár, Amedeo, *Valdenští. Evropský rozměr jejich vzdoru* [The Waldensians. The European dimension of their defiance] (Prague: 1973).

Molnár, Amedeo, "Die kleine und die große Partei der Brüderunität," *Communio viatorum* 22 (1979): 239–48.

Müller, Joseph Theodor, "Geschichte und Inhalt der *Acta Unitatis Fratrum* (sogenannte Lissaer Folianten)," *Zeitschrift für Brüdergeschichte* 7 (1913): 66–113, 216–31; 9 (1915): 26–79.

Müller, Joseph Theodor, *Geschichte der Böhmischen Brüder*, vol. 1: *1400–1528*; vol. 2: *1528–1576*; vol. 3: *Die polnische Unität 1548–1793. Die böhmisch-mährische Unität 1575–1781* (Herrnhut: 1922–1931).

Müller, Joseph Theodor, *Dějiny Jednoty bratrské* [A history of the Unity of Brethren], trans. F.M. Bartoš, vol. 1 (Prague: 1923).

Nejedlý, Zdeněk, *Litomyšl. Tisíc let života českého města* [Litomyšl. A thousand years in the life of a Czech town], vol. 1 (Prague: 1954).

Nodl, Martin, "Manželství v rané Jednotě bratrské" [Marriage in the early Unity of Brethren], in *Mezi Baltem a Uhrami. Komenský, Jednota bratrská a svět středoevropského protestantismu. Sborník k poctě Marty Bečkové*, eds. Vladimír Urbánek and Lenka Řezníková (Prague: 2006), 131–47.

Palacký, František, *Dějiny národu českého v Čechách a v Moravě* [A history of the Czech nation in Bohemia and Moravia], 6 vols. (Prague: 1968–1973).

Peschke, Erhard, *Die Theologie der Böhmischen Brüder in ihrer Frühzeit. Das Abendmahl*, 2nd ed. (Stuttgart: 1940).

Peschke, Erhard, "Der Gegensatz zwischen der Kleinen und der Großen Partei der Brüderunität," *Wissenschafltiche Zeitschrift der Universität Rostock* 6 (1956–1957): 141–54.

Peschke, Erhard, *Die Böhmischen Brüder im Urteil ihrer Zeit* (Berlin: 1964).

Peschke, Erhard, *Kirche und Welt in der Theologie der Böhmischen Brüder. Vom Mittelalter zur Reformation* (Berlin: 1981).

Říčan, Rudolf, *Dějiny Jednoty bratrské* [A history of the Unity of Brethren] (Prague: 1957).

Říčan, Rudolf, *Die Böhmischen Brüder. Ihr Ursprung und ihre Geschichte*, trans. Bohumír Popelář (Berlin: 1961).

Říčan, Rudolf, *The History of the Unity of Brethren. A Protestant Hussite Church in Bohemia and Moravia*, trans. C. Daniel Crews (Bethlehem, PA.: 1992).

Šafařík, Pavel Josef, "B. Jana Blahoslava Historie Bratří českých u výtahu" [A digest of Brother Jan Blahoslav's History of the Czech Brethren], *Časopis Musea Království českého* 36 (1862): 99–124, 201–12.

Spunar, Pavel, "Literární činnost utrakvistů doby poděbradské a jagellonské" [The literary activity of the Utraquists of the Poděbrad and Jagellonian periods], in *Acta reformationem Bohemicam illustrantia*, vol. 1: *Příspěvky k dějinám utrakvismu*, ed. Amedeo Molnár (Prague: 1978), 165–269.

Svobodová, Milada, *Katalog českých a slovenských rukopisů sign. XVII získaných Národní (Univerzitní) knihovnou po vydání Truhlářova katalogu z roku 1906* [Catalogue of Czech and Slovak manuscripts under the shelfmark XVII acquired by the National (University) Library after the publication of Truhlář's catalogue from 1906] (Prague: 1996).

Urban, Wacław, *Der Antitrinitarismus in den Böhmischen Ländern und in der Slowakei im 16. und 17. Jahrhundert* (Baden-Baden: 1986).

Urbánek, Rudolf, *Věk poděbradský* [The Poděbrad era], 4 vols. (České dějiny) 3 (Prague: 1915–1962).

Urbánek, Rudolf, *Jednota bratrská a vyšší vzdělání až do doby Blahoslavovy. Příspěvek k 400. výročí narozenin Blahoslavových* [The Unity of Brethren and higher education up to the time of Blahoslav. A contribution to the 400th anniversary of Blahoslav's birth] (Brno: 1923).

Urbánek, Rudolf, "Jan Paleček, šašek krále Jiřího a jeho předchůdci v zemích českých" [Jan Paleček, a jester of King George, and his predecessors in the Czech Lands], in *Příspěvky k dějinám starší české literatury*, ed. Josef Hrabák (Prague: 1958), 5–89.

The Bohemian Reformation and "The" Reformation: Hussites and Protestants in Early Modern Europe

Phillip Haberkern

1   Introduction

Historians have long struggled to delineate the relationship between the movement for religious reform that exploded in the Czech lands during the 1400s and the various reformations that emerged across Europe in the following century. Were the Hussites the embodiments of a "First Reformation" that set political precedents and established theological templates for the "Second Reformation" of Luther, Zwingli, and Calvin?[1] Alternatively, did the Hussites represent a sort of "Premature Reformation" that ultimately foundered on its inability to distance itself from the liturgical framework and institutional hierarchy of Catholicism?[2] Both of these interpretations are loaded with overtones of national self-assertion and undertones of confessional claims about what constituted a true reformation in early modern Europe, and scholars have, in recent decades, happily escaped from these restrictive historiographical tropes. But if we attribute neither primacy nor prematurity to the Bohemian Reformation, then how should it be understood in relation to the 16th-century reform movements that both scholars and the world at large conventionally consider "the" Reformation? To answer this question, it is necessary to understand the Bohemian Reformation's dual status as both an idealized historical construct among 16th-century reformers and a historical process that was still unfolding at that time. By playing off a perception that was founded on both textual representations and actual interactions, Czech "Hussites" were able to

---

1   The great champion of this position was Amedeo Molnár, who identified both the Hussites and Waldensians as the champions of the "First Reformation." See, e.g. his: "Husovo místo v evropské reformaci," *Československý časopis historický* 14 (1966): 1–14 and *Die Waldenser. Geschichte und europäisches Ausmaß einer Ketzerbewegung*, 2nd ed. (Göttingen: 1980), especially 280–99.
2   This terminology was most famously used in Anne Hudson, *The Premature Reformation. Wycliffite Texts and Lollard History* (Oxford: 1988). Cf. the discussion of this terminology in František Šmahel, "Zur Einführung. Häresie und vorzeitige Reformation – causa ad disputandum," in *Häresie und vorzeitige Reformation im Spätmittelalter*, ed. František Šmahel (Munich: 1998), vii–xiv.

achieve a parity with their newly reformed neighbors that was unprecedented within the inter-confessional dynamics of the 16th century.

On the one hand, the Czech churches' status derived from the Hussite movement's prominent place within a history that the anti-Roman movements of the 16th century were creating for themselves. Working backwards from the present to the biblical past, Protestants claimed the Hussites as a key link between themselves and the apostolic, true church that had been driven underground by papal tyranny; the Hussites also served as the most recent example of how a coalition of witnesses to divine truth and pious political elites could resist this diabolical oppression.[3] Catholics, conversely, pointed to the destruction of the Hussite Wars and the century of enmity that had followed in their wake as a warning to the faithful about the inescapable, tragic consequences of tolerating religious dissent.[4] Second-generation Protestants from England to Geneva also looked to the Hussite movement and the martyrs it produced as having inaugurated the heroic renewal of the church in the last age, thus adding an eschatological element to the invocation of the Hussites among 16th-century reformers.[5] No matter which groups claimed the Hussites, though, all of them ultimately constructed an idealized version of the Bohemian Reformation and its protagonists that came to serve as a lynchpin for the historical traditions and apocalyptic expectations that Protestants were formulating.[6]

---

3 A number of specific studies analyse the early Lutheran appropriation of the Hussites, and especially Jan Hus, as forerunners of their movement. On this appropriation, see the recent essays by Gustav Adolf Benrath, "Die sogenannten Vorreformatoren in ihrer Bedeutung für die frühe Reformation," in *Die frühe Reformation in Deutschland als Umbruch*, ed. Bernd Moeller (Gütersloh: 1998), 157–66; and Thomas Kaufmann, "Jan Hus und die frühe Reformation," in *Biblische Theologie und historisches Denken. Wissenschaftsgeschichtliche Studien, aus Anlass der 50. Wiederkehr der Basler Promotion von Rudolf Smend*, eds. Martin Kessler and Martin Wallraff (Basel: 2008), 62–109.

4 On these arguments, see Hubert Jedin, "Die geschichtliche Bedeutung der katholischen Kontroversliteratur im Zeitalter der Glaubensspaltung," *Historisches Jahrbuch* 53 (1933): 70–97; and David Bagchi, *Luther's Earliest Opponents. Catholic Controversialists, 1518–1525* (Minneapolis: 1991).

5 On the proliferation of martyrologies among Protestant authors, see Robert Kolb, *For All the Saints. Changing Perceptions of Martyrdom and Sainthood in the Lutheran Reformation* (Macon, GA: 1987); Brad Gregory, *Salvation at Stake. Christian Martyrdom in Early Modern Europe* (Cambridge: 1999); and Peter Burschel, *Sterben und Unsterblichkeit. Zur Kultur des Martyriums in der frühen Neuzeit* (Munich: 2004).

6 The concept of invented traditions here derives from Eric J. Hobsbawm, "Introduction: Inventing Traditions," in *The Invention of Tradition*, eds. Eric J. Hobsbawm and Terence O. Ranger (Cambridge and New York: 1983), 1–14. On this process of invention in the Protestant reformations, see Euan Cameron, "Medieval Heretics as Protestant Martyrs," in *Martyrs and Martyrologies*, ed. Diana Wood (Cambridge: 1993), 185–207.

On the other hand, the champions of the emergent confessions who wanted the Hussites for themselves also had to contend with the fact that the Bohemian Reformation was not over. Rather, it remained a startlingly diverse religious movement whose various leaders sought to engage with international Protestantism and the Roman curia on their own terms throughout the 1500s, and whose understanding of its own past often conflicted with those that proliferated in the era of the European reformations. Both Utraquists and members of the Unity of Brethren sought a hearing for their distinctive ideas during the 16th century, and each of these parties appealed to the earlier history of the Hussites in articulating their identities and agendas. The presence of these unruly, idiosyncratic dialogue partners who occupied a privileged position in the history of reform therefore demanded efforts to bridge the gap between the Hussite ideal and the actual Hussites that 16th-century reformers encountered. It is only by assessing these efforts that it becomes possible to map out the unique place that the Bohemian Reformation came to occupy among 16th-century reform movements as an equal – a dissident tradition whose history could provide both ideals and admonitions to the nascent religious groups that sought to establish themselves alongside, but as distinct from, the traditional church.

2   We Are All Hussites: From Ignorance to Idealization

In the first decade after the dissemination of Martin Luther's Ninety-Five Theses in 1517, as a wave of popular religious publications rose, crested, and crashed, texts about the Hussites became ubiquitous in central Europe.[7] Luther, his earliest followers, and his most vociferous opponents all sought precedents for contemporary events in the history of the Hussite revolution and its aftermath. Through this search, two main themes came to the fore that colored how writers depicted the Bohemian Reformation throughout the 16th century. The first of these essentially transformed Jan Hus and his followers into proto-Protestants – forerunners who partially espoused the theological positions that the 16th-century reformers developed fully. Best encapsulated in Luther's enthusiastic, if facile, assertion that "without knowing it, we are all Hussites,"

---

[7] On the explosion of popular print and its importance in disseminating Luther's program for reform in the first half of the 1520s, see Mark Edwards Jr., *Printing, Propaganda, and Martin Luther* (Berkeley: 1994), especially 17–25. On Hus's prominence in these texts, see the work of Hans-Gert Roloff, especially "Die Funktion von Hus-Texten in der Reformations-Polemik," in *De captu lectoris. Wirkungen des Buches im 15. und 16. Jahrhundert, dargestellt an ausgewählten Handschriften und Drucken*, eds. Wolfgang Milde and Werner Schuder (Berlin: 1988), 219–56.

this sentiment characterized most Protestant historiography regarding the Hussites until well into the modern era.[8] Linking Luther to Hus was also typical of Catholic polemicists who sought to discredit Luther by associating him with past heresiarchs. This strategy had long been a tried and true method for demonizing religious dissenters, but it did not work in the 1520s. Rather, popular disenchantment with the church at that juncture meant that "the 'heretics' did not drag the Reformers down; the Reformers dragged the heretics up."[9]

The second theme that percolated within the early polemics of the German Reformation was more political and tied the Hussite revolution to the goal of eliminating foreign domination, both political and religious, with the help of secular elites. This *topos* certainly circulated among authors sympathetic to Luther during the early 1520s, but ironically found its most articulate expression in Catholic works decrying Luther's "Bohemianism" and predicting that his reform would result in political unrest as well as heresy.[10] This particular argument tried to undercut Luther's claims to represent the German nation's best interests. After all, how could any real patriot defend the Czech heresiarch whose followers had destroyed their own monarchy and terrorized the Germans during the previous century?[11] Modern scholars have questioned the substance of both these tropes, noting that Luther's self-identification with Hus in particular obscured the two men's substantive disagreement over issues ranging from the papacy's legitimacy to the theology of the Mass.[12] Such arguments, however, miss an equally important point: namely, that Luther's imprimatur (and Catholic authors' opprobrium) for Hus and his followers brought the 15th-century heretics into the center of the public debate that swirled around Luther's criticism of Catholic theology and ecclesiology in the 1520s.

---

8   Martin Luther, "Letter to Georg Spalatin," (Feb. 1520) in idem, *Werke. Kritische Gesamtausgabe, Schriften und Briefwechsel* (Wiemar: 1883–1933), Briefwechsel, vol. 2, 40–2. Luther made this statement after reading *De ecclesia*. On the persistence of the "forerunner" concept into the 20th century, see the introduction to Heiko Oberman, *Forerunners of the Reformation. The Shape of Late Medieval Thought* (New York: 1966).

9   Cameron, "Medieval Heretics as Protestant Martyrs," 187.

10 The ubiquity of this theme in early anti-Lutheran tracts has been clearly demonstrated in Bagchi, *Luther's Earliest Opponents*, 103–10.

11 On the development of this nationalist rhetoric by Catholic authors, see David Bagchi, "'Teutschland uber alle Welt.' Nationalism and Catholicism in Early Reformation Germany," *Archiv für Reformationsgeschichte* 82 (1991): 39–58.

12 For a summary of the arguments minimizing the overlap between Hus and Luther, see Scott Hendrix, "'We Are All Hussites'? Hus and Luther Revisited," *Archiv für Reformationsgeschichte* 65 (1974): 134–61. For an eloquent argument for the contrary position, see Heiko Oberman, "Hus and Luther. Prophets of a Radical Reformation," in *The Contentious Triangle. Church, State, and University*, eds. Calvin A. Pater and Rodney L. Petersen (Kirksville, MO: 1999), 135–66.

It is possible to track the Bohemians' expanding role within this debate by analyzing how knowledge about their Reformation spread at this time. This happened primarily through the publication of Hussite texts, although many of the articles that Hus defended during his trial at Constance also became known at second hand through Luther's writings after the Leipzig Debate in 1519.[13] The first Bohemian texts to be published were two editions of *De ecclesia*, which appeared in print runs of 2,000 copies each in 1520.[14] These editions were, however, anonymous, and their title pages asked readers "to attend not to who speaks, but to what is said."[15] Such reticence about Hus's authorship suggests that the editions' publishers had concerns about his connection to heresy, even though the marginal notes and indices in both revealed a fundamental sympathy for Hus's critique of ecclesiastical authority. Other editors and publishers at this time were less hesitant. In the years 1521–1524, multiple editions of Poggio Bracciolini's account of Jerome of Prague's martyrdom, an edition of the Hussites' Four Articles, and the Czech nobility's defense of Hus's orthodoxy from 1415 were all printed in German or Latin.[16] Collectively, these texts embedded Hus within a larger movement whose critique of ecclesiastical power seemed to presage Luther's, even as they attested to the breadth of actors who made the Hussite revolution possible.

These texts also helped to contextualize the religious debates of the 1520s within a broader history of reform. Poggio Bracciolini's letter, for instance, suggested that the coalition of humanists and preachers that supported Luther's dissent from Rome had a 15th-century precursor. Similarly, both the Four Articles and the 1415 letter highlighted the Czech nobility's role in supporting ecclesiastical reform, a message that resonated with the central message in

---

13   It was at this debate that Johannes Eck accused Luther of being a second Hus. Luther initially denied this charge, but acknowledged that some of Hus's condemned articles were evangelical by the end of this exchange. On the Leipzig Debate and Hus, see Phillip Haberkern, *Patron Saint and Prophet. Jan Hus in the Bohemian and German Reformations* (Oxford: 2016), 149–56.
14   These editions appeared as Jan Hus, *De causa Bohemica* (Hagenau: 1520), and idem, *Liber egregius de unitate Ecclesiae, cuius autor periit in concilio Constantiensi* (Basel: 1520). On the sixth of the editions, see: Martin Luther, "Letter to Georg Spalatin," (19 March 1520) in *Werke. Kritische Gesamtausgabe*, Briefwechsel, vol. 2: 72.
15   Hus, *Liber egregius*, A1r.
16   These texts were published as Poggio Bracciolini, *Eyn sendt brieff wie Hieronimus eyn Junger Joannis Huss im concilio czu Costentz fur ein ketzer vorbrandt* (Erfurt: 1521); Martin Reinhart (ed. and trans.), *Anzaygung wie die gefallene Christenhait widerbracht müg werden in iren ersten standt* (Ausburg: 1524). On these publications, see Siegfried Hoyer, "Jan Hus und der Hussitismus in den Flugschriften des ersten Jahrzehnts der Reformation," in *Flugschriften als Massenmedium der Reformationszeit,* ed. Hans-Joachim Köhler (Stuttgart: 1981), 291–307.

Luther's *Address to the German Nobility*.[17] Martin Reinhardt, who edited the Four Articles in 1524, therefore noted how the Hussites had shown that "the spiritual estate with its disordered life" could be restored to its apostolic purity through such actions, while the editor of the nobility's letter hopefully asserted that "nothing could be a greater consolation to us, than if our leaders became like this."[18]

In terms of linking the Hussites' radical critique and ultimate rejection of the church to current events, though, no text was more explicit than a three-volume edition of sermons and tracts purportedly by Jan Hus that was published in 1524–1525.[19] This collection was shepherded into print by the schoolmaster Otto Brunfels, a minor figure in Strasbourg's reform who nonetheless gained Luther's support for his publishing project. In a letter written to Luther in August 1524, Brunfels stated that Hus's writings "would arouse the whole world" against the danger posed by the papal Antichrist.[20] In his response, Luther concurred, noting that Hus had "emerged in our age to be rightfully canonized."[21] Such overtly hagiographic language was used rarely by 16th-century reformers, but Hus's sanctification served to establish a lineage of counter-saints that could be enlisted as precedents for Luther's dissent.[22] These letters, as well as the apocalyptic sermons, biblical commentaries, and treatises on Antichrist contained in these volumes, also portrayed Hus as an apocalyptic witness, a prophetic individual whose death inaugurated the

---

17 In the *Address*, Luther cited Hus's illicit execution as one of twenty-seven ecclesiastical abuses that had damaged the German nation. See Martin Luther, *An den christlichen Adel deutscher Nation von des christlichen Standes Besserung* (Wittenberg: 1520); idem, *Werke. Kritische Gesamtausgabe*, Schriften, vol. 6: 381–469, here 454.

18 For these quotations, see Reinhart (ed.), *Anzaygung*, A1v; and *Epistola LIIII nobilium Moraviae, pro defensione Iohannis Huss, ad concilium Constantiense* (Basel: 1524), A2r-A3r.

19 These three volumes were published as Otto Brunfels (ed.), *De anatomia Antichristi liber unus* (Strasbourg: 1524); idem (ed.), *Locorum aliquot ex Osee et Ezechiele prophetis cap. v. et viii.*, ed. Otto Brunfels (Strasbourg: 1524); and idem (ed.), *Sermonum Ioannis Huss ad populum tomus tertius* (Strasbourg: 1525). These volumes have been printed in a modern facsimile edition as *Matthias Janov, Opera*, eds. Erich Beyreuther and Werner-Friedrich-Aloys Jakobsmeier (Hildesheim and New York: 1975).

20 Otto Brunfels, "Letter to Martin Luther," (August 1524) in *Werke. Kritische Gesamtausgabe*, Briefwechsel, vol. 3, 332–36, here 333–34.

21 Martin Luther, "Letter to Otto Brunfels" (October 1524), in *Werke. Kritische Gesamtausgabe*, Briefwechsel, vol. 3, 359.

22 On the development of this lineage, see Robert Kolb, "'Saint John Hus' and 'Jerome Savonarola, Confessor of God.' The Lutheran 'Canonization' of Late Medieval Martyrs," *Concordia Journal* 17 (1991): 404–18 and Thomas Fuchs, "Protestantische Heiligen-memoria im 16. Jahrhundert," *Historische Zeitschrift* 267 (1998): 587–614.

last age of the church and whose scathing critique of the institutional church and its diabolical head both foreshadowed and authorized Luther's.[23]

The saintly Hus of this collection was not, however, a figure of veneration and intercession. Rather, he was a martyr whose death revealed the papacy as the seat of Antichrist and whose theological ideals cohered with the German reformers' critique of Rome. In identifying Hus as such a figure, Brunfels played up typological parallels between Hus's trial and those of the biblical and apostolic martyrs, especially Christ. This de-individuation of Hus presented him as the incarnation of a suffering, true church that had finally surfaced with the onset of Luther's movement. The irony of Brunfels's collection of *Hussitica* and its creation of an ahistorical, saintly Hus, though, was that none of the texts it included were actually written by the Prague preacher. All were of Bohemian provenance, but these were the works of Matěj of Janov or later Hussite authors.[24] The enormity of this misattribution did not, however, ultimately matter in 1525. Rather, because the texts published by Brunfels cohered with the image of the Hussite past that Luther and his allies were constructing, they came to constitute a substantial foundation for the Hussites' status as forebears to the German evangelical movement.

Although their decision had unintended consequences, Catholic authors at this time further emphasized the connections between the German reformers and their Bohemian progenitors. Through a host of writings, Catholic polemicists disseminated knowledge of the Hussite movement even as they excoriated it as the most proximate case study of the evils that resulted from political toleration of, or support for, heresy. Catholic authors typically presented Luther and his allies as the descendants of heretics like the Manicheans, Arians, Waldensians, Cathars, Wycliffites, and Hussites. Such an identification linked Luther to movements whose deviance had resulted directly in political unrest and the collapse of Christian North Africa, Byzantium, and the Czech lands.[25] These historical examples were essentially admonitory, then, and Catholic authors predicted the destruction of the German lands if their leaders failed to eradicate heresy from their midst.[26]

---

23 On this idea, see Lawrence P. Buck, "*Anatomia Antichristi*. Form and Content of the Papal Antichrist," *Sixteenth Century Journal* 42 (2011): 349–68.
24 The details of this misattribution are discussed in the introductory essay by Eric Beyreuther to *Matthias Janov. Opera*, 1–27.
25 This rhetoric is analyzed in David Bagchi, "Defining Heresies. Catholic Heresiologies, 1520–50," in *Discipline and Diversity*, eds. Kate Cooper and Jeremy Gregory (Woodbridge: 2007), 241–51.
26 On this argument, see Bagchi, *Luther's Earliest Opponents*, 103–10; and Christoph Volkmar, "Turning Luther's Weapons against him. The Birth of Catholic Propaganda in Saxony in

Exemplary of this rhetoric was the work of Bernhard of Luxembourg, a professor of theology and inquisitor in Cologne whose exhaustive *Catalogue of All Heretics* first appeared in 1522 and went through a half dozen editions during the decade.[27] The *Catalogue* comprised a general description of the nature of heresy, a catalogue of three hundred heretics from the history of the church, and a detailed analysis of Martin Luther's affiliation with them. In describing the Hussites, who occupied a primary place in the *Catalogue*, Bernhard employed an extensive serpentine metaphor. Hus himself became an evil serpent, "a viper begetting vipers," and his brood included Jerome of Prague, Jakoubek of Stříbro, Jan Žižka, Jan Želivský, Jan Rokycana, Mikuláš Biskupec, and Peter Payne, all of whom received separate entries in the catalogue.[28] Bernhard also placed Luther metaphorically among Hus's progeny, because just as Prague ("Praga") was made corrupt ("prava") by Hus, so Luther had transformed Wittenberg into "Viperberg," perverting its university and ruler as Hus had done.[29]

With this imagery, Bernhard emphasized Luther's inheritance from his Bohemian ancestors. Strikingly, such rhetoric also described a narrative arc for the emergence of the German Reformation that was strikingly similar, if inverted, to the one being constructed by Luther and his allies. Catholic polemics reinforced the idea that Luther and his ilk did not represent an isolated outbreak of religious critique, but instead stood at the head of a long line of dissidents who had called for changes to the church. Texts from both sides of the growing confessional divide in the 16th century therefore emphasized how the history of the Hussite movement as a whole could serve as a means of understanding the unfolding religious reforms of the 1520s, even as an individual's or community's interpretation of that history could serve as a cipher for their disposition towards contemporary religious disputes.

3 From Discovery to Dialogue: The Unity and Utraquists among the Reformers

In formulating their interpretations of Hussite history, 16th-century reformers initially proved unaware of, or uninterested in, the Bohemian Reformation's

---

the 1520s," in *The Book Triumphant. Print in Transition in the Sixteenth and Seventeenth Centuries*, eds. Graeme Kemp and Malcolm Walsby (Leiden and Boston: 2011), 115–29.

27 Bernhard of Luxembourg, *Catalogus haereticorum omnium pene, qui a scriptoribus passim literis proditi sunt* (Cologne: 1522). The book was reprinted in Cologne three times (1523, 1525, and 1529), as well as in Paris (1524) and Strasbourg (1527).

28 Bernhard of Luxembourg, *Catalogus*, F4r.

29 Ibid., L3r.

diversity. Early modern writers typically portrayed a unitary Hussite movement exemplified by its martyrs and secular leaders who were under threat from Catholics and from heretical "Pikarts" who initially enjoyed no standing in the nascent Protestant churches' invented traditions.[30] Strikingly, this presentation remained consistent despite the dialogue that developed between 16th-century Protestants, Catholics, Utraquists, and members of the Unity of Brethren. The leadership of both Czech churches quickly initiated contacts with reformers and Catholics in the wake of Luther's emergence, but they found the possibilities for theological dialogue limited by their interlocutors' preconceptions about the Hussite past. Protestant reformers seemed to believe that the Czech churches would seamlessly join with their movements, but this expectation ran counter to the strategies of negotiation and distancing that characterized many of the early interactions between the Czechs and their neighbors.[31]

Certainly both Utraquists and members of the Unity demonstrated substantial interest in Luther's teachings from a very early date. Many of his works were quickly translated into Czech and published in Bohemia and Moravia, and Czech religious leaders applied valedictory rhetoric to Luther as an ally and continuator of the Bohemian Reformation's restoration of God's law.[32] Still, the selectivity of the publication of Luther's works in the Czech lands suggests that the Utraquists and Brethren exercised discretion in their reception of Luther's thought. Some of Luther's earliest devotional tracts – for instance, on the Eucharist, Decalogue, and the Lord's Prayer – were printed in 1520 by Oldřich Velenský, a humanist raised as a Utraquist who later became a member

---

30   On the use of "Pikart" as a term of opprobrium within the Bohemian Reformation, see Howard Kaminsky, *A History of the Hussite Revolution* (Berkeley and Los Angeles: 1967), 353–60. On the persistence of this term into the 16th century, see Martin Wernisch, "Luther and Medieval Reform Movements, Particularly the Hussites," in *The Oxford Handbook of Martin Luther's Theology*, eds. Robert Kolb, Irene Dingel, and Ľubomír L. Batka (Oxford and New York: 2015), 62–70.

31   For influential early articulations of this position, see Ferdinand Hrejsa, *Česká konfesse. Její vznik, podstata a dějiny* (Prague: 1912), 4; and Eduard Winter, *Tausend Jahre Geisteskampf im Sudetenraum. Das religiöse Ringen zweier Völker* (Salzburg: 1938), 146. More recently, see František Kavka, "Bohemia," in *The Reformation in National Context*, ed. Robert W. Scribner (Cambridge and New York: 1994), 131–54.

32   The high view of Luther's success in influencing Czech religious thought, which predominated in much Anglophone Lutheran scholarship of earlier generations, is clearly represented in Jaroslav Pelikan, "Luther's Negotiations with the Hussites," *Concordia Theological Monthly* 20 (1949): 496–517; and S. Harrison Thomson, "Luther and Bohemia," *Archiv für Reformationsgeschichte* 44 (1953): 160–81.

of the Unity.[33] Texts that highlighted Luther's opposition to the pope and emperor were also quickly published in Czech translation, including a version of Luther's self-defense before the Diet of Worms in 1521. This first wave of translations also included Luther's call for communion in both kinds, a topic of obvious relevance to Utraquists and the Unity. The publication of this text demonstrated that Czech translators and publishers sought to enable their audience to understand the full range of Luther's religious teachings, while highlighting his input on the religious issues that continued to shape the Czech lands' native reform.[34]

The publication of Luther's treatises in Bohemia at the same time that Hussite texts were being disseminated throughout the Empire demonstrates that the interest between these reform parties was reciprocal. This impression is confirmed by the travel of Utraquists and members of the Unity to Wittenberg, where their exchanges with Luther and his associates came to serve as the foundations for more substantive intellectual debate. These discussions rarely resulted in full theological agreement, but their lack of resolution did not cut off conversation. Instead, the dialogue between the German and Czech reformers led both to clarify their own beliefs and practices in relatively polite contrast to those of the other. Initially, these exchanges focused on theological issues that had been central to the Bohemian Reformation, especially ordination and the Eucharist. The first of these, which primarily involved Luther and the Utraquists, resulted from a trip taken by the controversial Utraquist leader Havel Cahera to Wittenberg in 1523. According to the contemporary chronicler Bartoš Písař, Cahera wanted to take control of the Utraquist consistory and establish an evangelical church in Prague that would be subordinate to Wittenberg.[35] To this end, Cahera secured a letter from Luther during his stay in Wittenberg that recommended his leadership of such a church. Cahera also

---

33   On the translation of Luther's early writings into Czech, see Rudolf Říčan, "Tschechische Übersetzungen von Luthers Schriften bis zum Schmalkaldischen Krieg," in *Vierhundertfünfzig Jahre lutherische Reformation 1517–1967. Festschrift für Franz Lau zum 60. Geburtstag*, ed. Helmar Junghans (Göttingen: 1967), 282–301. On Velenský, see Antonie J. Lamping, *Ulrichus Velenus (Oldřich Velenský) and his Treatise Against the Papacy* (Leiden: 1976), especially 152.

34   Frederick Heymann, "The Impact of Martin Luther upon Bohemia," *Central European History* 1 (1968): 116. Cf. the more strongly worded, but ultimately similar conclusion in Zdeněk V. David, *Finding the Middle Way. The Utraquists' Liberal Challenge to Rome and Luther* (Washington, Baltimore, and London: 2003), 62–3.

35   Bartoš Písař was a Prague artisan who wrote a chronicle describing the struggles over the leadership of the Utraquist Church and Prague civic government from 1524 to 1537. Although it is difficult to substantiate his narrative independently, Písař did incorporate many primary sources in his account. This text has been published as Bartoš Písař,

prompted Luther to publish a treatise on the topic of clerical ordination entitled *On the Establishment of Ministers in the Church*.[36] And while scholars now question how much support Cahera ever generated for his attempted takeover of the consistory (or even if that was what he desired), it is clear that his journey to Wittenberg did spur an extended debate between Luther and the Utraquists on the nature of leadership in the church.

The Utraquists' maintenance of apostolic succession via ordination by a duly consecrated, Catholic bishop stood in stark contrast to Luther's concept of the priesthood of all believers. Additionally, the Utraquists' historical struggle to gain ordination for their priests meant that Luther's assertion that such a practice amounted to collusion with the Roman Antichrist who had killed Jan Hus and Jerome of Prague was perceived as a direct assault on their tradition.[37] Luther further argued that the Utraquists fundamentally misunderstood the nature of priesthood, which devolved from conduct and function rather than office, and this critique coincided with the German reformers' claims to be the heirs of Hus's reforming vision. As such, this text represented a fundamental challenge to Utraquist legitimacy.

In response to this challenge, the Utraquist leaders in Prague took steps to affirm their independent identity. First, they called a synod in January 1524 that promulgated a list of articles upholding the structures of Utraquist church governance and affirming practices that Luther and his followers rejected, including the communion of infants, the celebration of the Mass as a sacrifice, and the maintenance of the cult of saints (including a feast for Jan Hus).[38] These articles were framed in an intensely biblical rhetoric that was redolent of the emergent Lutheran principle of *sola Scriptura*, but this tonal consonance with the German Reformation's teachings did not obviate the theological differences between Wittenberg and Prague expressed in the articles. This theological retrenchment was complemented by political developments; in the wake of

---

"Kronika," in *Fontes rerum Bohemicarum*, ed. Josef V. Šimák, vol. 6 (Prague: 1907), 1–296. Cahera's story is on pp. 107–33.

36   This text was first printed as Luther, *De instituendis ministris Ecclesiae, ad clarissimum Senatum Pragensem Bohemiae* (Wittenberg: 1523) [see idem, *Werke. Kritische Gesamtausgabe*, Schriften, vol. 12, 160–96]. The text went through a second Latin edition, six German editions, and one Czech edition within the next year.

37   For an overview of the Utraquists' difficulties with obtaining such ordinations, see the fundamental work by Kamil Krofta, "Boj o konsistoř pod obojí v letech 1562–1575 a jeho historický základ," *Český časopis historický* 17 (1911): 28–57, 178–99, 283–03, and 383–420. For this accusation by Luther, see *De Instituendis*, 71.

38   These so-called Candlemas Articles are printed in Písař, *Kronika*, 21–5. For a thoughtful discussion of their content, see Winfried Eberhard, *Konfessionsbildung und Stände in Böhmen, 1478–1530* (Munich and Vienna: 1981), 139–49.

the synod, the Prague city council propagated decrees promoting the practices espoused in the articles, several of Luther's most vocal supporters within the city were exiled, and Cahera allied himself with a new, staunchly Utraquist mayor of Prague.[39]

These political actions effectively closed the first loop in a cycle that would come to characterize relations between the Czech churches, both Utraquist and Unity, and their earliest Protestant neighbors. This cycle was initiated through personal contacts. These interactions prompted the exchange of texts, first letters and subsequently more formal treatises. These writings were then sifted for points of agreement and contention, after which the Czechs would formulate an official position that often disagreed with their interlocutors, but fraternally suggested that more consideration and discussion might clarify the issue. The cycle would then begin again, often taking up new issues rather than rehashing the old. Given the typical inability of sixteenth-century Protestants to sustain this kind of dialogue with each other, the mutual respect that animated these interactions is fairly surprising. Compounding that surprise is the fact that this regard was also extended to the Unity of Brethren.

Indeed, the Brethren's first contacts with the 16th-century reformations largely mirrored those of the Utraquists, despite the fact that Luther and his followers held deep-seated doubts about the Unity's orthodoxy. Their interactions began in 1522, when the Lutheran preacher Paul Speratus sent a list of four Utraquist articles of faith and eleven from the Brethren to Luther for his consideration. Luther's reception of Speratus's report coincided with the presence of two members of the Unity, Jan Roh and Michael Weisse, in Wittenberg, so Luther approached them to discuss the Unity's teachings, particularly with regards to the Eucharist.[40] Afterwards, Luther remained unsure whether or not the Brethren maintained a proper belief in Christ's true presence in the sacrament, which prompted him to enter into correspondence with Brother Lukáš of Prague, the Unity's leading theologian. And in response to Luther's initial inquiry, Lukáš sent him both a general explanation of the Unity's theology and a specific treatise on the Eucharist.[41]

39　On the impact of the articles, see David, *Finding the Middle Way*, 64–69. See also Eberhard, *Konfessionsbildung*, 150–81.

40　Amedeo Molnár, "Luthers Beziehungen zu den Böhmischen Brüdern," in *Leben und Werk Martin Luthers von 1526 bis 1546*, ed. Helmar Junghans, vol. 1 (Göttingen: 1983), 627–39.

41　Lukáš's treatise on the Eucharist was later published in German under the title *Von der siegreichen Wahrheit*; his broader explanation of the Unity's faith, which Luther referred to as the *Apologia*, was never published, but was essential in shaping Luther's opinion of the Unity's orthodoxy. See Joseph Theodor Müller, *Geschichte der Böhmischen Brüder*, (Herrnhut: 1922–1931), vol. 1, 409–17.

Luther struggled with Lukáš's arguments on different modes of sacramental presence in these texts (as did everyone else), but his confusion did not prevent him from writing a preface for the German translation of another text by Lukáš entitled *Christian Instruction in the Faith for Little Children*. This translation of a Unity catechism from 1502 consisted of seventy-six questions and answers on theology, ecclesiology, and religious practice, with questions sixty-one and sixty-two devoted to the Eucharist.[42] Although explicitly didactic, this text still did not satisfy Luther concerning the Unity's eucharistic teachings. He thus offered a response in his 1523 text, *On the Adoration of the Sacrament of the Body of Christ*.[43] This treatise primarily concerned the practice of kneeling before the host as a recognition of Christ's real presence in the elements, but it was framed by a direct address to the Unity. Therein, Luther balanced his respect for the Brethren with his continued belief that they erred in certain of their tenets, including their eucharistic teachings, retention of seven sacraments, defense of clerical celibacy, and belief that faith must be manifested in good works to be truly operative.[44]

Despite these substantial differences, Luther still ended this treatise by asserting that the Brethren were "much nearer to the Gospel than any others that are known to me."[45] This surprising conclusion demonstrated a considerable evolution in Luther's stance towards the Unity, even as the Unity's position towards Luther remained stable. He was a potential ally, to be sure, but his critiques of the Unity's theology up to this point had not spurred any concessions on their part. In this, the Brethren paralleled the Utraquist response to Luther described above, as personal contacts prompted textual exchanges that never quite resulted in theological concessions or institutional unity but allowed both parties to continue the conversation. In the case of both Czech churches, it may therefore be said that while they may have desired to emerge from the isolation imposed on them during the previous century, their histories of sustained religious debate and tenuous coexistence had also trained them to maintain their independence in the face of pressure to surrender

---

42　The Czech original went through twelve editions by 1515, and the German translation went through a dozen editions by 1525. For an overview of the book's publication history, see the modern edition printed as Alexander Kästner (ed.), *Die Kinderfragen. Der erste deutsche Katechismus* (Leipzig: 1902), 1–14.

43　This treatise was published twelve times in German by 1525 and was translated into Czech in 1523. Martin Luther, *Von Anbeten des Sakraments des heiligen Leichnams Christi* (Wittenberg: 1523) [idem, *Werke. Kritische Gesamtausgabe*, Schriften, vol. 11, 417–56].

44　Ibid., 450–55.

45　Ibid., 456.

theological and ecclesiological tenets that did not fit comfortably under any Protestant umbrella.

4 The Imperatives of Confessional Politics

Even as the first contacts between the Utraquists, Unity, and the new Protestant churches were taking shape in the 1520s, the Czech lands themselves were undergoing a dynastic change that would radically affect the political calculus of confessional alliances both internally and externally. With the ascension of the Habsburg Ferdinand I to the Czech throne in 1526, the Brethren and Utraquists came under the direct rule of the dynasty that was tasked with restoring Catholic hegemony in the Holy Roman Empire; and even though Ferdinand was open to finding compromises that respected the confessionally diverse history of the Czech lands, the larger struggle over the political establishment of the German Reformation that took place during the 1530s and 1540s had a dramatic impact on the Utraquists and Unity.[46] On the one hand, that struggle presented the Czech churches (and especially the Unity) with potential allies who could strengthen their position in Bohemia and Moravia. On the other hand, however, the proliferation of Protestant groups within the Czech lands challenged the traditional primacy of the Utraquist Church and forced its leadership to reconsider the strictly bi-confessional status quo that had been established with the Peace of Kutná Hora in 1485.[47] Overall, these opposing pressures forced an evolution in the strategies that the Czech churches employed in their negotiations with the crown and attempts to gain wider recognition of their confessional and political legitimacy.

The Unity, which did not enjoy legal sanction within the Czech lands and had been specifically outlawed in 1503 and 1508, was the most precocious

---

46 On Ferdinand's reign and the confessional politics of the Czech lands, see Kenneth Dillon, *King and Estates in the Bohemian Lands, 1526–1564* (Brussels: 1976), especially Ch. 3; and Winfried Eberhard, *Monarchie und Widerstand. Zur ständische Oppositionsbildung im Herrschaftsystem Ferdinands I. in Böhmen* (Munich: 1985), especially 73–80.

47 On this treaty, see Winfried Eberhard, "Entstehungsbedingungen für öffentliche Toleranz am Beispiel des Kuttenberger Religionsfrieden von 1485," *Communio Viatorum* 29 (1986): 129–53; Anna Skýbová, "Politische Aspekte der Existenz zweier Konfessionen im Königreich Böhmen bis zum Anfang des 17. Jahrhunderts," in *Martin Luther. Leben, Werk und Wirkung*, ed. Günter Vogler (Berlin: 1986), 463–80; and Jaroslav Pánek, "The Question of Tolerance in Bohemia and Moravia in the Age of the Reformation," in *Tolerance and Intolerance in the European Reformation*, eds. Ole Peter Grell and Robert W. Scribner (New York: 1996), 231–48.

religious group in terms of seeking out allies and recognition from abroad.[48] In 1528, Michael Weisse went to Zurich to assess the possibility of unity with Zwingli's reformed church, while the growth of Anabaptist communities in Moravia presented another potential option for the Unity's linking up with the European reformations.[49] These contacts with external groups coincided with a dramatic internal shift in the Unity, as the death of Lukáš of Prague in 1528 allowed a new generation of leaders to reconsider the Unity's insularity. Initially, this re-orientation was political; the Unity began to accept nobles within their ranks around 1530, and these elites provided protection for the Unity within Bohemia and Moravia. They also served as a crucial conduit for negotiations with both King Ferdinand and Protestant nobles in the Holy Roman Empire. The political reach of these nobles was complemented by an increasing number of Brethren who studied in Protestant institutions abroad.[50] By seeking formal higher education in Wittenberg and the Swiss lands, the Unity's members effectively widened the scope of their efforts to secure recognition from the leaders of the nascent Protestant churches.

These efforts were further expanded by the dissemination of the Unity's texts abroad at this time. The most notable of these was a hymnal written in German by Michael Weisse, which made the Unity's theology available through its highly developed hymnody.[51] The hymnal was highly christocentric, with nearly half its songs devoted to commemorating the life and death of Christ; it also contained songs for funerals, communion, and for instructing children. Overall, its contents corresponded closely to those of the *Kinderfragen*, which

---

48 For an overview of the decrees outlawing the Unity and their sporadic enforcement, see Otakar Odložilík, "A Church in a Hostile State. The Unity of Czech Brethren," *Central European History* 6 (1973): 111–27.

49 On the Unity and Zwingli, see František Michálek Bartoš, "L'Unité des Frères Tchèques et les Réformateurs," *Communio Viatorum* 21 (1978): 29–48, 139–55. On contacts between the Unity and Anabaptists, see Jarold K. Zeman, *The Anabaptists and the Czech Brethren in Moravia, 1526–1628. A Study of Origins and Contact* (The Hague: 1969); and the updated bibliography in Martin Rothkegel, "Anabaptism in Moravia and Silesia," in *A Companion to Anabaptism and Spiritualism, 1521–1700*, eds. John Roth and James Stayer (Brill's Companions to the Christian Tradition) 6 (Boston: 2007), 163–214.

50 Craig D. Atwood, *The Theology of the Czech Brethren from Hus to Comenius* (University Park, PA: 2009), 256. It should be noted that the Unity also ceased its practice of re-baptizing adults at this time, which seemed to associate the Unity with Anabaptists.

51 Michael Weisse, *Ein new Geseng Buchlen* (Mladá Boleslav: 1531). At least four editions were published in Ulm by 1540. A modern facsimile edition has been published as Michael Weisse, *Gesangbuch der Böhmischen Brüder 1531 in originalgetreuem Nachdruck*, ed. Konrad Ameln (Kassel: 1957). On this text, see Ute Evers, "Deutsch-tsechischer Melodienaustausch in Gesangbüchern des 16. Jahrhünderts," *Lied und populäre Kultur* 55 (2010): 169–82.

was also republished in a simpler translation at this time. Taken together, these texts represented the Unity's attempts to present their beliefs in ways that were approachable for an audience that had not been previously exposed to its distinctive, often difficult theological idiom.[52]

This popular presentation of the Unity's theology was buttressed by the preparation of two confessions of faith, both of which were eventually published with forewords by Martin Luther. The first of these, entitled the *Account of the Faith, Worship, and Ceremonies of the Brethren*, was written at the behest of Margrave George of Brandenburg-Ansbach in 1532.[53] Its primary author was Jan Roh, and it was translated into German by Michael Weisse. His translation was marked by a Zwinglian, symbolic interpretation of the Eucharist, however, so a second German translation was prepared the following year. This version received a preface from Luther in which he acknowledged the Unity's sacramental orthodoxy. While still asserting that he did not fully understand their eucharistic theology, Luther praised the Unity for their devotion to Scripture, rejection of the papacy, and cultivation of discipline and moral living among themselves.[54]

Two years later, the Unity composed a second confession with the intention of securing King Ferdinand's legal recognition of their church. In an effort to play up the Brethren's legitimacy, this *Confession of the Faith and Religion of the Barons and Nobles of the Kingdom of Bohemia* bore the signatures of twelve Czech barons and thirty-three knights. It also adopted the structure of the Lutheran Augsburg Confession (1530) and reflected some Protestant influence on the Unity's theology.[55] Characteristic of this influence were the *Confession*'s emphasis on salvation by faith alone and declaration that there were only two sacraments. Still, the *Confession* also maintained the necessity of good works and discipline for the Christian community, and it recommended celibacy as

---

52 On the new edition of the *Kinderfragen*, see Müller, *Geschichte der böhmischen Brüder*, vol. 2: 4–6.

53 Martin Luther, *Rechenschaft des Glaubens, der Dienst und Ceremonien der Brüder in Behmen und Mehren* (Zurich: 1532).

54 Martin Luther, *Rechenschaft des Glaubens, der Dienst und Ceremonien der Brüder in Behemen und Mehren, welche von etlichen Pickarten, und von etlichen Waldenser genant werden* (Wittenberg: 1533). Luther's preface has been published in idem, *Werke. Kritische Gesamtausgabe*, Schriften, vol. 38, 78–80.

55 This text originally appeared as *Confessio fidei ac religionis baronum ac nobilium Regni Bohoemiae* (Wittenberg: 1538). It has been published in a modern translation as Jaroslav Pelikan and Valerie Hotchkiss (eds.), "The Bohemian Confession (1535)," in *Creeds and Confessions of Faith in the Christian Tradition*, vol. 1 (New Haven: 2003), 787–833. On this confession, see Jindřich Halama Jr., "The Doctrinal Development of the Unity of Czech Brethren in the Light of their Confessions," *Communio Viatorum* 44 (2002): 128–44.

the ideal state for the clergy. The balance of the Unity's tradition with the influence of 16th-century teachings within this text suggests that it was intended to serve as a summary of the common ground between the Brethren and German Protestants, even as it appealed to the Czech sovereign for his recognition of the Unity's legitimacy.

Externally, at least, this text was a success. After its initial publication in Czech in 1536, the Unity leader Jan Augusta traveled to Wittenberg to discuss its acceptability with Luther and Philip Melanchthon. Their discussion led to some changes regarding clerical celibacy and deathbed absolution, and Luther published the text with his own preface in 1538.[56] This foreword again praised the Unity as "saints and martyrs" who had "set aside the teachings of men" and embraced the Word of God. And while Luther still acknowledged that there were some differences between his teachings and the Unity's, he also enjoined his readers to "remember that all the rites and ceremonies of all the churches never have been nor can be equal and the same."[57] This recognition of historical diversity within Christianity allowed Luther to accept the Unity's overall conformity with his reform program and consequently to argue for their inclusion within the evangelical cause.

Conversely, the decades after Ferdinand I took the throne witnessed a gradual Utraquist retrenchment vis-à-vis international Protestantism, which manifested itself through internal debates about church leadership that marginalized the so-called *Linksutraquismus* of those who promoted Lutheran-influenced theological ideas;[58] the production of new texts affirming a traditional, independent Utraquist identity; and a series of negotiations with King Ferdinand that secured the Utraquists' legal primacy within the Czech religious landscape.[59] The clearest articulations of Utraquist goals and

---

[56] These changes are analyzed in Molnár, "Luthers Beziehungen zu den Böhmischen Brüdern," 636–37. Cf. Milos Strupl, "Confessional Theology of the Unitas Fratrum."

[57] Pelikan and Hotchkiss (eds.), "The Bohemian Confession (1535)," *Church History* 33 (1964): 800–01.

[58] The decline of official Lutheran influence on the Utraquists became evident in 1543, when King Ferdinand helped oust Václav Mitmánek, a Lutheran-leaning member of the Utraquist consistory, after a national synod. Prior to this step, Lutheranism had gained traction among the nobility and in the German-speaking regions of north and west Bohemia. On the growth and then suppression of Lutheranism among the Utraquists, see Winfried Eberhard, "Bohemia, Moravia, and Austria," in *The Early Reformation in Europe*, ed. Andrew Pettegree (New York: 1992), 30–4.

[59] On the Utraquists under Ferdinand more generally, see Eberhard, *Monarchie und Widerstand*, 265–306. On Ferdinand's policies towards the Utraquists, see Paula Fichtner, *Ferdinand I of Austria. The Politics of Dynasticism in the Age of Reformation* (New York: 1982), especially Ch. 3; and Anna Skýbová, "Ferdinand I., der Habsburger, und die Anfänge siener

ideals during this time emerged from meetings of the Czech Estates in 1537 and 1539. At the latter meeting in particular the Utraquist leadership promulgated fifteen articles that largely recapitulated the Candlemas articles of 1524 over and against Protestant sacramental theology and ecclesiology.[60] Beyond such authoritative statements, these years also witnessed the composition of treatises defending distinctive Utraquist practices and affirming the church's independent religious tradition.[61]

This intellectual defense of Utraquist tradition was augmented by political actions undertaken by King Ferdinand, who sought to appease the Utraquist Estates in order to secure their assistance against both the Turks on his southern flank and (potentially) the Lutherans and other Protestant heretics.[62] Practically speaking, Ferdinand supported the Utraquists' efforts to secure recognition of their church's legitimacy based on the Basel *Compactata*, and to these ends he facilitated several meetings between Utraquist leaders and papal representatives throughout the 1520s and 1530s. Ferdinand also introduced legislation that marginalized the Unity and Lutherans in the Czech lands, thereby assuring the Utraquists' and Catholics' privileged positions within the kingdom's government.[63]

King Ferdinand's efforts to secure Utraquist stability in his domains was backed by the efforts of Catholic scholars like the Bishop of Vienna, Johannes Fabri, and the chaplain to Duke George of Saxony, Johannes Cochlaeus, both of whom worked to provide detailed historical and theological justifications for a lasting Utraquist rapprochement with the Roman party. There was certainly a political rationale behind their arguments, as these Catholic leaders realized that the loss of Saxony could be offset by regaining Bohemia.[64] Catholic

---

Regierung im böhmischen Staat," in *Europäische Herrscherr. Ihre Rolle bei der Gestaltung von Politik und Gesellschaft vom 16. bis zum 18. Jahrhundert*, ed. Günter Vogler (Weimar: 1988), 71–84.

60   On these articles, see Eberhard, *Monarchie und Widerstand*, 283. The articles have also been published as "Sjezd stavů strany pod obojí dne 24. srpna 1539," in *Sněmy české od léta 1526 až po naši dobu*, vol. 1 (Prague: 1877), 465–69.

61   On the texts, see David, *Finding the Middle Way*, Ch. 5.

62   Jaroslav Pánek, "Das Ständewesen und die Gesellschaft in den Böhmischen Ländern in der Zeit vor der Schlacht auf dem Weißen Berg (1526–1620)," *Historica* 25 (1985): 73–120.

63   On these meetings, see František Kavka and Anna Skýbová, *Husitský epilog na koncilu tridentském a původní koncepce habsburské rekatolizace Čech. Počátky obnoveného pražského arcibiskupství 1561–1580* (Prague: 1969), Ch. 2. See also Eberhard, *Konfessionsbildung*, 245–54.

64   See e.g. the arguments for recognizing the *Compactata* in Johannes Cochlaeus, "Letter to Johannes Fabri," (28 October 1534) in Walter Friedensburg, "Beiträge zum Briefwechsel der katholischen Gelehrten Deutschlands im Reformationszeitalter," *Zeitschrift für Kirchengeschichte* 18 (1898): 257–63.

leaders also increasingly realized, however, that Utraquism shared many core theological beliefs and liturgical practices with Catholicism. Cochlaeus, for instance, compiled an exhaustive history of the Bohemian Reformation, *The Twelve Books of Hussite History*, which he published along with texts by Jan Rokycana and Jan Příbram that affirmed the fundamental orthodoxy of the Bohemian Reformation.[65] Cochlaeus also published texts that rebuffed Lutheran attempts to claim Hus as their movement's forebear by highlighting Hus's eucharistic orthodoxy and belief in the priesthood's unique status, even as he condemned Hus's obstinacy in refusing to accept the authority of the Council of Constance.[66] It was this juxtaposition of the Hussites' essentially Catholic theology with their rejection of the church's supremacy that defined Catholic efforts to promote the Utraquists' reunion with Rome. If only the Czechs would recognize the church's doctrinal authority, then their shared beliefs and practices could serve as the basis for a lasting unity.

Cochlaeus's contributions towards this argument were largely intellectual, but Fabri undertook his own efforts to convince the Utraquists of their catholicity within a more overtly political context. He served as Ferdinand's representative at Czech diets in 1537 and 1538, and it was in preparation for this role that Fabri composed a lengthy text entitled *A Refutation of the Most Serious Error Held about the Sacrament of the Altar*.[67] In this treatise, Fabri argued that Utraquists must hold to their founding principles and defend the proper understanding of the Eucharist against Luther, Zwingli, the Brethren, and other heretics. In order to spell out the proper understanding, which incorporated a belief in both transubstantiation and concomitance, Fabri referred explicitly to the works of Hus, Příbram, and Rokycana, while also citing the *Compactata*

---

65 Although this book was essentially completed in 1534, it did not appear in print until 1549, as Johannes Cochlaeus, *Historiae Hussitarum libri duodecim* (Mainz: 1549). On the composition and publication of this work, see Ralph Keen, "Johannes Cochlaeus. An Introduction to his Life and Work," in *Luther's Lives. Two Contemporary Accounts of Martin Luther*, eds. and trans. Elizabeth Vandiver, Ralph Keen, and Thomas D. Frazel (Manchester and New York: 2002), especially 50–2.

66 These included a history of Hus's trial published as *Warhafftige Historia von Magister Johan Hussen von anfang seiner newen Sect, biss zum ende seines lebens um Concilio zu Costnitz* (Leipzig: 1537); and a comparative text contrasting Luther's and Hus's theology in ten specific areas: *De immensa Dei misericordia erga Germanos, ex collatione sermonum Ioannis Hus ad unum sermonem Martini Lutheri* (Leipzig: 1538). On Cochlaeus as a historian of the Hussites, see Haberkern, *Patron Saint and Prophet*, especially Chs. 6 and 7.

67 Johannes Fabri, *Confutatio gravissimi erroris asserentis in Sacramento altaris post consecrationem non esse totum et integrum Christum* (Leipzig: 1537). On this work, see Leo Helbling, *Dr. Johann Fabri, Generalvikar von Konstanz und Bischof von Wien (1478–1541)* (Münster: 1941), 112–26.

and decrees from multiple Hussite synods.[68] Such references revealed Fabri's intimate familiarity with Hussite history, while also providing clear evidence for the fundamental differences between the Utraquists, the Unity, and 16th-century Protestants. This text, along with those by Cochlaeus, also sought to use these differences as the foundation for rebuilding ties between Utraquist Bohemia and Catholic Christendom under the umbrella of Habsburg rule.

Despite the learning behind these texts, Catholic attempts to foster unity with the Utraquists failed spectacularly. Copies of Fabri's *Refutation* were destroyed *en masse* in Prague, and Fabri himself went into hiding. Cochlaeus's efforts at rehabilitating the Hussites also proved futile, ultimately landing him on the Index.[69] Even these failures were, however, instructive, as they highlighted the increasingly nuanced interactions of external religious leaders with the Utraquists and Unity (and vice versa). Catholics no longer simply equated the Hussites with heretics of old, while Protestants – especially with respect to the Unity – sought to understand the Czechs' distinctive theologies, rather than eliding the substantive differences they found within them. Significantly, concrete political considerations provoked and sustained these interactions, as Ferdinand sought alliances within his kingdom and the Czech churches continued to seek support from abroad. But even these political imperatives could not entirely erase the incorporation of the Hussites into larger historical and even mythical narratives, which would prove to be the most lasting legacy of the Bohemian Reformation's initial encounters with 16th-century reform, for better or worse.

5   Persecution and the Appropriation of Hussite History

In fact, political developments outside of the Czech lands at this time encouraged the invention (in the sense of both discovery and fabrication) of a Hussite past that was both more elaborate and embedded within a more robust intellectual framework than had heretofore existed. The first of these developments resulted from the papacy's efforts to convene an ecumenical council to address both the need for reform within the church and the threat posed by Protestant heresies in Europe. And while the first push for such a council by Pope Paul III ultimately foundered in 1536–1537, the possibility of its meeting prompted a spike in publications about Jan Hus, Jerome of Prague, and the Council of

---

68   For these references, see Fabri, *Confutatio gravissimi erroris*, K1r-K2v and O4v-P3r.
69   David, *Finding the Middle Way*, 139.

Constance's decision to execute them.[70] These texts included multiple collections of Hus's prison correspondence, translations of Petr of Mladoňovice's passion narratives for Jerome and Hus, and commentaries on Hus's self-defense at Constance and the council's final condemnation of his teachings. In Protestant hands, these specific sources became the foundation for a scathing critique of church councils more generally as kangaroo courts that, under the illicit sway of the popes, served to suppress evangelical truth and promote the absolute supremacy of the papal Antichrist.[71] This broader narrative also portrayed the treatment of the Hussites at both Constance and Basel as a pointed warning about what 16th-century reformers could expect from a comparable assembly.

This attack on the legitimacy of church councils came at a high point for the European reformers, as the ascendancy of the Schmalkaldic League in the Holy Roman Empire, conflict between the Catholic kings of France and Spain, and the withdrawal of England from Roman obedience seemed to create a window of opportunity for international Protestant growth. A decade later, however, that window had slammed shut. In the Holy Roman Empire, the coincidence of Martin Luther's death in 1545, the convocation of the Council of Trent in 1546, and the disastrous Schmalkaldic War in 1547 threatened the existence of the Lutheran church. And while the Augsburg Interim, which allowed certain Protestant practices but largely reinstated Catholic worship throughout the German lands, did not spell immediate doom for the Lutherans, it did result in the exile of many Lutheran preachers and opened up rifts within the Lutheran camp between those who could accept some compromise with the emperor and church, and those who could not.[72] Meanwhile, the accession of the Catholic Queen Mary I to the throne of England in 1553 led to the execution and exile of many British evangelicals, and the continued growth of Calvinist communities had led France to the brink of civil war. Anabaptists and Calvinists in the Low Countries were also experiencing intensified persecution from

---

70   The best analysis of Paul III's efforts to convoke a council at Mantua remains Hubert Jedin, *History of the Council of Trent*, trans. Ernest Graf, vol. 1 (London: 1957), 320. On Protestant responses to these efforts, see Thomas Brockmann, *Die Konzilsfrage in den Flug- und Streitschriften des deutschen Sprachraumes 1518–1563* (Göttingen: 1998), especially 262–87.

71   On these polemics, see Phillip Haberkern, "'After Me There Will Come Braver Men.' Jan Hus and Reformation Polemics in the 1530s," *German History* 27 (2009): 177–95.

72   The Interim's impact on the Lutheran church has been analyzed in Robert Kolb, "Dynamics of Party Conflict in the Saxon Late Reformation. Gnesio-Lutherans vs. Philippists," *Journal of Modern History* 49 (1977): 1289–1305; and Irene Dingel, "The Culture of Conflict in the Controversies Leading to the Formula of Concord (1548–1580)," in *Lutheran Ecclesiastical Culture, 1550–1675*, ed. Robert Kolb (Brill's Companions to the Christian Tradition) 11 (Leiden and Boston: 2008), 15–64.

the Habsburg government, which spurred the formation of churches in exile throughout the cities of the Rhine valley and the Swiss cantons.[73] As a result of all these pressures, then, the middle of the 16th century witnessed the creation of diasporic Protestant communities that shared experiences of dislocation and persecution that led them to identify themselves as the heirs of the captive or wandering Israelites.[74]

The ideologues of these exile communities primarily expressed this shared identity through the composition of martyrologies, which both highlighted the individual authors' confessional and national lineages and created a common pool of martyrs from which all sixteenth-century Protestants could draw. And because many of the martyrologists either worked in the same cities or knew each other personally, their invocations of certain individuals echoed each other's and created an increasingly unified canon of martyrs for the Protestant cause.[75] Unsurprisingly, the Hussites occupied a primary place within this group. Ludwig Rabus, who published the first Lutheran martyrology, made Hus his first medieval martyr and wrote over 100 pages on the Bohemian preacher;[76] the Englishman John Foxe and Frenchman Jean Crespin also began their first, Latin martyrologies with Hus, although subsequent editions of their work

---

[73] On these communities, see Donald Kelley, "Martyrs, Myths, and the Massacre. The Background of St. Bartholomew," *The American Historical Review* 77 (1972): 1323–342; Andrew Pettegree, "Haemstede and Foxe," in *John Foxe and the English Reformation*, ed. David M. Loades (Aldershot and Brookfield, VT: 1997), 278–94; and Nicholas Watson, "Jean Crespin and the First English Martyrology of the Reformation," in *John Foxe and the English Reformation*, ed. David M. Loades (Aldershot and Brookfield, VT: 1997), 192–209.

[74] On the formation of this international Protestant diaspora, see Elizabeth Evenden and Thomas S. Freeman, *Religion and the Book in Early Modern England. The Making of John Foxe's Book of Martyrs* (Cambridge and New York: 2011), especially 56–79. On the leaders of the diaspora and their self-perception as the heirs of Israel, see Philip Gorski, "The Mosaic Moment. An Early Modernist Critique of Modernist Theories of Nationalism," *American Journal of Sociology* 105 (2000): 1428–468.

[75] Strasbourg and Basel, where many of the Protestant exiles settled or published in the 1550s, served as hubs for these networks. Johannes Oporinus's print shop in Basel, for instance, employed John Foxe, John Bale, and Heinrich Pantaleon (all authors of historical polemics), while printing the work of the Lutheran martyrologist Matthias Flacius Illyricus. See Gregory, *Salvation at Stake*, 165. On the intellectual impact of this cross-fertilization, see Euan Cameron, "One Reformation or Many? Protestant Identities in the Later Reformation in Germany," in *Tolerance and Intolerance in the European Reformation*, eds. Ole Peter Grell and Robert W. Scribner (New York: 1996), 108–27.

[76] Rabus's work was first published as Ludwig Rabus, *Der Heyligen ausserwöhlten Gottes Zeugen, Bekennern, und Martyren...Historien* (Strasbourg: 1552). Seven subsequent volumes were published as idem, *Historien der heyligen ausserwöhlten Gottes Zeügen, Bekennern, und Martyren* (Strasbourg: 1554–1558). On Hus's place in this work, see Kolb, *For All the Saints*, 38–9 and 58–60.

incorporated earlier medieval dissenters such as the Waldensians into their genealogies of reform.[77] In composing their collections, these men drew from each other's research and the earlier publication of Hussite texts. Through this process of synthesis, the initial Lutheran adoption of Hus and his followers as forerunners was internationalized and came to reach an audience from the Irish to the Adriatic Sea.

In both the Protestant martyrologies and the texts generated by the debate over church councils, two themes emerged that ensured the continuing relevance of Hussite history for the 16th-century reformers. The first of these concerned Jan Hus specifically, and related to his promotion from a forerunner of Martin Luther to a prophet of the German Reformation. This elevation in status initially derived from a conflation of a letter by Hus with Jerome of Prague's last words at his trial, which Luther himself cited in his response to Emperor Charles v's decision to reinstate the Edict of Worms after the Diet of Augsburg in 1530:

> St. Jan Hus prophesied of me when he wrote from his prison in Bohemia [sic]: "They will roast a goose now (for 'Hus' means 'goose' in Czech), but in a hundred years they will hear a swan sing, and him they will have to endure." And that is the way it will be, if God wills it.[78]

Luther wrote these words in 1531, and this avian association was quickly reproduced in 16th-century medallions, woodcuts, and pamphlets by other authors.[79] On the back of this specific, predictive utterance Hus also came to be seen as the German Reformation's foremost prophet. The collections of his prison letters, for instance, which were published during the second half of the decade, acquired marginal notes that highlighted Hus's prophetic dreams about his successors.[80] Additionally, Johannes Agricola's dramatic retelling of Hus's trial

---

77   On Hus and Foxe, see Thomas A. Fudge, "Jan Hus as the Apocalyptic Witness in John Foxe's History," *Communio Viatorum* 56 (2014): 136–68. See also Gregory, *Salvation at Stake*, 171.
78   This text was originally published as Luther, *Auff das vermeint keiserlich Edict...Glosa* (Wittenberg: 1531) [idem, *Werke. Kritische Gesamtausgabe*, Schriften, vol. 30/3, 321–88], here 387.
79   On the circulation of this prophecy in the German Reformation, see Adolf Hauffen, "Husz eine Gans – Luther ein Schwan," *Prager Deutsche Studien* 9, 2 (1908): 1–27; and Robert Scribner, "The Incombustible Luther. The Image of the Reformer in Early Modern Europe," *Past and Present* 110 (1986): especially 41–2.
80   The most extensive of these collections, published with a foreword by Luther in 1537, included letters detailing Hus's dreams about other individuals furthering the reform he had begun after his death. Marginal notes alongside these letters highlighted their

in *The Tragedy of Jan Hus* (1537) bookended its dramatic action with two soliloquies that explicitly identified Hus as a prophet who had both decried the Antichrist's persecution of Christian truth and foretold its end through the agency of the coming swan.[81] With such references, Agricola's play presented Hus as an apocalyptic figure whose defiance of the Antichrist at Constance and glorious death presaged the culmination of the conflict between the true and false churches.[82]

References to Hus's prophecy abounded in the mid-century martyrologies as well, and the prophecy was also mentioned in the funeral sermons preached and published in the immediate wake of Luther's death.[83] The specific attribution of the prophetic office to Hus, though, represented only one aspect of the predictive value that was ascribed to the Bohemian Reformation by Protestant authors at this time. Indeed, as Protestant authors began to articulate a more substantive historical framework for their respective churches through martyrologies that posited the existence of a "chain of witnesses" that stretched from the biblical past to the present, the Hussite revolution came to serve as a microcosm of that whole history.[84] By understanding the initial struggles that marked the Hussite revolution and subsequent Utraquist attempts to preserve the revolution's gains, then, 16th-century Protestants gained a key for unlocking the dynamics of the entire Christian past.

Emblematic of this more expansive invocation of the Hussite past was the work of the Lutheran historian and polemicist Matthias Flacius Illyricus. Although most famous for coordinating the publication of the *Magdeburg Centuries*, a comprehensive doctrinal history of the true church, Flacius had previously published a prosopography of the leaders of that church entitled *A*

---

prophetic content. See Jan Hus, *Epistolae quaedam piisimae et eruditissimae Iohannis Hus* (Wittenberg: 1537), especially D6v, F6r, and H2r-H3v. Luther's preface appears in idem, *Werke. Kritische Gesamtausgabe*, Schriften, vol. 50, 123–25.

81 This play was a vernacular, rhymed adaptation of Petr of Mladoňovice's account of Hus's trial. Johannes Agricola, *Tragedia Johannis Hus welche auff dem Unchristlichen Concilio zu Costnitz gehalten allen Christen nuetzlich und troestlich zu lesen* (Wittenberg: 1537), Av. and F4v.

82 On this portrayal of Hus in 16th-century polemics more generally, see Rodney Petersen, *Preaching in the Last Days. The Theme of "Two Witnesses" in the Sixteenth and Seventeenth Centuries* (New York: 1993), 149.

83 Haberkern, *Patron Saint and Prophet*, 258–59.

84 On this emergent Protestant historical consciousness, see Irena Backus, *Historical Method and Confessional Identity in the Era of the Reformation (1378–1615)* (Boston: 2003); Matthias Pohlig, *Zwischen Gelehrsamkeit und konfessioneller Identitätsstiftung. Lutherische Kirchen- und Universalgeschichtsschreibung 1546–1617* (Tübingen: 2007); and the essays by Cameron and Grafton in Katherine van Liere, Simon Ditchfield, and Howard Louthan (eds.), *Sacred History. Uses of the Christian Past in the Renaissance World* (Oxford: 2012).

Catalogue of Witnesses to the Truth.[85] This work was a counter to Bernard of Luxembourg's *Catalogue of all Heretics*, and it included 400 individuals who had preached evangelical doctrines despite persecution. In writing this work, Flacius sought to demonstrate that the true church had survived throughout all time, and Flacius made the Bohemian Reformation central to this argument. Altogether, Flacius included eight individuals from the Bohemian Reformation in the *Catalogue*: Milíč of Kroměříž, Matěj of Janov, Jan Hus, Jerome of Prague, Peter of Dresden, Jakoubek of Stříbro, Jan Žižka, and Peter Payne. He also incorporated five German "Hussites" into his account who served as the final span in a bridge that Flacius constructed between Martin Luther and the Waldensians (via the Czech lands), whom he considered to be the most doctrinally pure of all medieval dissidents.[86] Even in granting an intermediary theological role to the Hussites, Flacius bestowed a privileged historical position upon them, since they served as the last link in the unbroken chain that extended from the time of Cain and Abel up to Flacius's day.[87]

While the *Catalogue* placed the Hussites within a larger framework of church history, Flacius also produced the two-volume *History and Monuments of Jan Hus and Jerome of Prague, Confessors of Christ* in 1558.[88] This collection, which included all of the previously published 16th-century materials concerning the two martyrs alongside forty-five new texts, represented the apotheosis of the Hussites in 16th-century Protestant rhetoric. In Flacius's hands, Hus's and Jerome's deaths, along with the consequent rise of the Hussite movement, served as an "infallible argument for the presence of God in the church" by showing "that doctors have repeatedly been awakened who understand and

---

85   Flacius, *Catalogus testium veritatis*. On the methodology and arguments of the *Catalogue*, see Wilhelm Schmidt-Biggemann, "Flacius Illyricus' 'Catalogus testium veritatis' als kontroverstheologische Polemik," in *Reformer als Ketzer. Heterodoxe Bewegungen von Vorreformatoren*, eds. Günter Frank and Friedrich Niewöhner (Stuttgart: 2004), 263–91. On the *Centuries*, see most recently Harald Bollbuck, *Wahrheitszeugnis, Gottes Auftrag und Zeitkritik. Die Kirchengeschichte der Magdeburger Zenturien und ihre Arbeitstechniken* (Wiesbaden: 2014).

86   On these German martyrs, see the introductory essay in Albert de Lange and Kathrin Utz Tremp (eds.), *Friedrich Reiser und die "waldensisch-hussitische Internationale"* (Heidelberg, Ubstadt-Weiher, and Basel: 2006), 7–28.

87   On the chain of witnesses in Flacius's thought, see and Vera van der Osten-Sacken, "Die kleine Herde der 7000 – Die aufrechten Bekenner in M. Flacius Illyricus konzeptionellen Beiträgen zur Neuformulierung der Kirchengeschichtsschreibung aus protestantischer Sicht," in *Matija Vlačić Ilirik [III]. Zbornik radova s Trećeg Međunarodnog Znanstvenog Skupa*, ed. Marina Miladinov (Labin: 2011), 184–213.

88   Jan Hus and Jerome of Prague, *Ioannis Hus et Hieronymi Pragensis confessorum Christi Historia et monumenta*, ed. Matthias Flacius Illyricus, 2 vols. (Nuremberg: 1558; repr. Frankfurt: 1715).

refute errors, preserve the purity of doctrine, and persevere in the footsteps of our Lord."[89] And while this text was the most explicit in elevating the Hussites to this exemplary status, it was not alone in doing so. Rather, the religious conflicts that wracked Europe in the years after 1550 produced a pan-Protestant reaction that sought solace in the past sufferings of faithful Christians and hope from their perseverance in the face of oppression.

6 Conclusion

At the heart of the Czech churches' interactions with the 16th-century reformations was a tension between their conflicting desires to preserve their distinctive theological and ecclesiological traditions, on the one hand, and to be recognized as legitimate reforming churches, on the other. From the outbreak of Luther's movement in 1517 up to the mid-century aftermath of religious war, both the Unity's and the Utraquists' efforts to navigate between these poles led them to engage in extended dialogue with both Protestants and Catholics. These exchanges produced measured theological debate, hagiographic depictions of the Hussite past, and heated polemic in almost equal measure, but never led to any decisive resolution in the form of a more permanent unity. It was only in the second half of the century, as King Ferdinand and his successor Maximilian took steps to build up the Catholic party among the Czech Estates and gain popular support for the church through the appointment of a new archbishop of Prague and the establishment of the Jesuits within the Czech lands, that a new Protestant union could be considered.[90] That union depended first on the abrogation of the Basel *Compactata*, which Czech evangelicals pushed for in 1567, and the preparation of a new Bohemian Confession in 1575 that incorporated the full range of Protestants into a united party.[91] And while this document was not immediately recognized by the crown as the basis for the legal recognition of the various Protestant churches within the Czech

---

89 Ibid., vol. 1, a2r.
90 Habsburg efforts to build up Catholic infrastructure in Bohemia are detailed in Kavka and Skýbová, *Husitský epilog na koncilu tridentském*; and Winfried Eberhard, "Voraussetzungen und strukturelle Grundlagen der Konfessionalisierung in Ostmitteleuropa," in *Konfessionalisierung in Ostmitteleuropa. Wirkungen des religiösen Wandels im 16. und 17. Jahrhundert in Staat, Gesellschaft und Kultur*, eds. Joachim Bahlcke and Arno Strohmeyer (Stuttgart: 1999), 89–103.
91 On the Bohemian Confession, see the foundational work: Hrejsa, *Česká konfesse*; and David Daniel, "Ecumenicity or Orthodoxy. The Dilemma of the Protestants in the Lands of the Austrian Habsburgs," *Church History* 49 (1980): 387–400.

lands, its composition did represent a resolution of the tension that had shaped the first generations of the encounter between the Bohemian Reformation and its European successors.

It would be easy to overlook the significance of the Bohemian Confession as a model for Protestant coexistence, since it was rendered moot by the outbreak of the Thirty Years War in 1618 and the recatholicization of the Czech lands in the ensuing decades.[92] To read backwards from this endpoint, however, and consequently to dismiss the multiple processes of self-assertion, negotiation, and compromise that characterized the Czechs' interaction with Protestants and Catholics in the 16th century, is a mistake. It is a mistake because doing so overlooks the signal achievement of the 16th-century heirs of the Hussites, which was to translate the privileged position they occupied in the invented traditions of early modern reformers into a unique space for conducting debate over issues as central as eucharistic theology and the nature of the priesthood. To put it plainly, past depictions of the Utraquists and Unity primarily as forerunners of the Reformation proper minimizes such debate, rendering it as merely an opportunity for the Czechs to advance past their protean, partial understandings of proper justification, soteriology, and ecclesiology. Such a view neither recognizes the authority that the Hussites maintained within the emergent historical consciousness of the Protestant reformers nor accounts for how the Brethren and Utraquists drew on this Hussite history to treat with figures like Luther and Fabri as equal participants in the effort to shape religious belief and practice in the 16th century. It is only by recognizing the success with which they pressed this claim to equality that it becomes possible to understand the dynamics of the Czechs' interaction with, and partial integration of, the central ideas that animated "the" Reformation in the German lands and beyond.

7 Historiographic Survey

For much of the past century, scholarship on the relationship between the 16th-century European reform movements and the churches that emerged from the Bohemian Reformation has been framed within a series of idioms that interpreted the latter in reference to the former. From the perspective of scholars who work primarily on the 16th century, the Hussites were "forerunners" of the German Reformation, and historians such as Heiko Oberman

---

92 On this process, see Howard Louthan, *Converting Bohemia. Force and Persuasion in the Catholic Reformation* (Cambridge and New York: 2009).

sifted their thought in order to find the germ of ideas that would only find their full expression in the theology of Martin Luther and his ilk.[93] This narrative is certainly teleological, but it had the positive side effect of granting the Hussites a privileged space within the development of early modern reformist ideology.

In the last several decades, this framework has served as the foundation for a number of studies that have looked more substantially at the influence of the Bohemian Reformation on specific aspects of Protestant ideology. Whether focusing on the origins of Luther's eschatology,[94] the identification of the papacy with the Antichrist, or the use of antitheses in the visual propaganda of the early German Reformation,[95] these studies reflect a broad consensus that the Hussites exercised a substantial influence on 16th-century reform. In each of these studies, though, there is still an underlying assumption that the Bohemian templates for these critiques were not fully developed. These studies do, however, open up specific avenues for further research that takes seriously the idea that Protestant reformers were both deeply familiar with the history of the Bohemian Reformation and willing to take up its central concerns as starting points for their own campaigns.

The notion that the 16th-century reformations expanded upon or completed the reform efforts begun by the Hussites has also informed much of the scholarship that has been produced by Czech and foreign scholars who primarily approach this topic via the history of the Bohemian Reformation. Within this larger body of research, several scholars of previous generations marginalized any contributions made by the Utraquist Church after the Council of Basel; it was this institution that domesticated the zeal of the revolutionary Hussites and required an external stimulus to rekindle the Czech lands' spark of legitimate religious fervor.[96] This view is still present – although often implicitly – in scholarship that tends to prize the utopian potential of the Hussite revolution over the institution building of the Utraquists, and it lends itself equally to larger nationalist or Marxist narratives that see the Hussite revolution as a window of radical opportunity that the Utraquists (and later Habsburg monarchs) allowed to be slammed shut. In the last couple of decades, this anti-Utraquist bias has been stridently opposed by Zdeněk David, whose articles and books argue that the Utraquist Church channeled Hussite religious thought into a liberal ecclesiology that offered an alternative to both Rome and

---

93   See Oberman, *Forerunners of the Reformation* and idem, "Hus and Luther."
94   Oberman, "Hus and Luther."
95   Buck, "*Anatomia Antichristi.*"
96   Kavka, "Bohemia," is emblematic of this trend. For a more balanced view, see Tomáš Malý, "The End of the Bohemian Reformation," in *From Hus to Luther. Visual Culture in the Bohemian Reformation (1380–1620)*, eds. Kateřina Horníčková and Michal Šroněk (Turnhout: 2016), 305–23.

Wittenberg.[97] And while David's commitment to Utraquist "liberalism" still places that church in service to a modern ideal, his research has illuminated the substantial theological staying power and intellectual creativity of a church once thought to be isolated and intellectually stagnant.

Beyond studies that place Hussite thought explicitly within trajectories of early modern religious reform, a host of historians have begun to import scholarly concepts from other fields to place the Hussites within larger narratives of Central European history. Some of these concepts – particularly concerning the Bohemian Reformation as an early laboratory for confessionalization or coexistence – are overtly religious.[98] Others, however, that focus on the rise of centralized monarchies and the role of religious rhetoric in opposing their dominance, draw inspiration more from political histories of the 16th century than from confessional historiography. These new frameworks suggest a way forward by positing that the unique circumstances of the Hussite revolution and its aftermath made the Czech lands precocious (rather than premature) in navigating the social and political conflicts that arose from sea changes in religious belief and practice. Such a view still compares the Hussites and their heirs to 16th-century Protestants and Catholics in terms of analysing the respective movements' internal dynamics and relations with external actors. It also, however, emphasizes the Czech churches' unique traditions and identities that were, perhaps surprisingly, resistant to integration within larger and seemingly more dynamic religious bodies.

Bibliography

Editions of Sources

Agricola, Johannes, *Tragedia Johannis Hus welche auff dem Unchristlichen Concilio zu Costnitz gehalten allen Christen nuetzlich und troestlich zu lesen* (Wittenberg: 1537).

Bartoš, Písař, "Kronika" [Chronicle], in *Fontes rerum Bohemicarum*, ed. Josef V. Šimák, vol. 6 (Prague: 1907), 1–296.

Bernhard of Luxembourg, *Catalogus haereticorum omnium pene, qui a scriptoribus passim literis proditi sunt* (Cologne: 1522).

Bracciolini, Poggio, *Eyn sendt brieff wie Hieronimus eyn Junger Joannis Huss im concilio czu Costentz fur ein ketzer vorbrandt* (Erfurt: 1521).

---

97 See especially his *Finding the Middle Way*.
98 Regarding confessionalization, see Winfried Eberhard, "Entstehungsbedingungen für öffentliche Toleranz am Beispiel des Kuttenberger Religionsfrieden von 1485," *Communio Viatorum* 29 (1986): 129–53 and idem, *Konfessionsbildung*. On coexistence, see František Šmahel, "*Pax externa et interna*. Vom heiligen Krieg zur Erzwungenen Toleranz im hussitischen Böhmen," in *Toleranz im Mittelalter*, eds. Alexander Patschovsky and Harald Zimmerman (Sigmaringen: 1998), 211–73.

Brunfels, Otto (ed.), *De anatomia Antichristi liber unus* (Strasbourg: 1524).

Brunfels, Otto (ed.), *Locorum aliquot ex Osee et Ezechiele prophetis cap. v. et viii.*, ed. Otto Brunfels (Strasbourg: 1524).

Brunfels, Otto (ed.), *Sermonum Ioannis Huss ad populum tomus tertius* (Strasbourg: 1525).

Cochlaeus, Johannes, *Historiae Hussitarum libri duodecim* (Mainz: 1549).

Cochlaeus, Johannes, "Letter to Johannes Fabri," (28 October 1534) in Walter Friedensburg, "Beiträge zum Briefwechsel der katholischen Gelehrten Deutschlands im Reformationszeitalter," *Zeitschrift für Kirchengeschichte* 18 (1898): 106–31, 233–97, 420–63, 596–636.

Confessio fidei ac religionis baronum ac nobilium Regni Bohoemiae (Wittenberg: 1538).

De immensa Dei misericordia erga Germanos, ex collatione sermonum Ioannis Hus ad unum sermonem Martini Lutheri (Leipzig: 1538).

Epistola LIIII nobilium Moraviae, pro defensione Iohannis Huss, ad concilium Constantiense (Basel: 1524).

Fabri, Johannes, *Confutatio gravissimi erroris asserentis in Sacramento altaris post consecrationem non esse totum et integrum Christum* (Leipzig: 1537).

Flacius Illyricus, Matthias, *Catalogus testium veritatis, qui ante nostram aetatem reclamarunt Papae* (Basel: 1556).

Hus, Jan, *De causa Bohemica* (Hagenau: 1520).

Hus, Jan, *Epistolae quaedam piisimae et eruditissimae Iohannis Hus* (Wittenberg: 1537).

Hus, Jan, *Liber egregius de unitate Ecclesiae, cuius autor periit in concilio Constantiensi* (Basel: 1520).

Hus, Jan, and Jerome of Prague, *Ioannis Hus et Hieronymi Pragensis confessorum Christi Historia et monumenta*, ed. Matthias Flacius Illyricus, 2 vols. (Nuremberg: 1558; repr. Frankfurt: 1715).

Kästner, Alexander (ed.), *Die Kinderfragen. Der erste deutsche Katechismus* (Leipzig: 1902).

Luther, Martin, *An den christlichen Adel deutscher Nation von des christlichen Standes Besserung* (Wittenberg: 1520).

Luther, Martin, *De instituendis ministris Ecclesiae, ad clarissimum Senatum Pragensem Bohemiae* (Wittenberg: 1523).

Luther, Martin, *Von Anbeten des Sakraments des heiligen Leichnams Christi* (Wittenberg: 1523).

Luther, Martin, *Auff das vermeint keiserlich Edict…Glosa* (Wittenberg: 1531).

Luther, Martin, *Rechenschaft des Glaubens, der Dienst und Ceremonien der Brüder in Behmen und Mehren* (Zurich: 1532).

Luther, Martin, *Rechenschaft des Glaubens, der Dienst und Ceremonien der Brüder in Behemen und Mehren, welche von etlichen Pickarten, und von etlichen Waldenser genant werden* (Wittenberg: 1533).

Luther, Martin, *Werke. Kritische Gesamtausgabe,* Schriften und Briefwechsel (Wiemar: 1883–1933).

Matthias Janov. Opera, eds. Erich Beyreuther and Werner-Friedrich-Aloys Jakobsmeier (Hildesheim and New York: 1975).

Pelikan, Jaroslav and Valerie Hotchkiss (eds.), "The Bohemian Confession (1535)," in *Creeds and Confessions of Faith in the Christian Tradition*, vol. 1 (New Haven: 2003), 787–833.

Rabus, Ludwig, *Der Heyligen ausserwöhlten Gottes Zeugen, Bekennern, und Martyren... Historien* (Strasbourg: 1552).

Rabus, Ludwig, *Historien der heyligen ausserwöhlten Gottes Zeügen, Bekennern, und Martyren* (Strasbourg: 1554–1558).

Reinhart, Martin (ed. and trans.), *Anzaygung wie die gefallene Christenhait widerbracht müg werden in iren ersten standt* (Ausburg: 1524).

Sněmy české od léta 1526 až po naši dobu [Bohemian diets from 1526 to our time], vol. 1 (Prague: 1877).

Warhafftige Historia von Magister Johan Hussen von anfang seiner newen Sect, biss zum ende seines lebens um Concilio zu Costnitz (Leipzig: 1537).

Weisse, Michael, *Ein new Geseng Buchlen* (Mladá Boleslav: 1531).

Weisse, Michael, *Gesangbuch der Böhmischen Brüder 1531 in originalgetreuem Nachdruck*, ed. Konrad Ameln (Kassel: 1957).

Secondary Sources

Atwood, Craig D., *The Theology of the Czech Brethren from Hus to Comenius* (University Park, PA: 2009).

Backus, Irena, *Historical Method and Confessional Identity in the Era of the Reformation (1378–1615)* (Boston: 2003).

Bagchi, David, *Luther's Earliest Opponents. Catholic Controversialists, 1518–1525* (Minneapolis: 1991).

Bagchi, David, "'Teutschland uber alle Welt.' Nationalism and Catholicism in Early Reformation Germany," *Archiv für Reformationsgeschichte* 82 (1991): 39–58.

Bagchi, David, "Defining Heresies. Catholic Heresiologies, 1520–50," in *Discipline and Diversity*, ed. Kate Cooper and Jeremy Gregory (Woodbridge: 2007), 241–51.

Bartoš, František Michálek, "L'Unité des Frères Tchèques et les Réformateurs," *Communio Viatorum* 21 (1978): 29–48, 139–55.

Benrath, Gustav Adolf, "Die sogenannten Vorreformatoren in ihrer Bedeutung für die frühe Reformation," in *Die frühe Reformation in Deutschland als Umbruch*, ed. Bernd Moeller (Gütersloh: 1998), 157–66.

Bollbuck, Harald, *Wahrheitszeugnis, Gottes Auftrag und Zeitkritik. Die Kirchengeschichte der Magdeburger Zenturien und ihre Arbeitstechniken* (Wiesbaden: 2014).

Brockmann, Thomas, *Die Konzilsfrage in den Flug- und Streitschriften des deutschen Sprachraumes 1518–1563* (Göttingen: 1998).

Buck, Lawrence P., "*Anatomia Antichristi*. Form and Content of the Papal Antichrist," *Sixteenth Century Journal* 42 (2011): 349–68.

Burschel, Peter, *Sterben und Unsterblichkeit. Zur Kultur des Martyriums in der frühen Neuzeit* (Munich: 2004).

Cameron, Euan, "Medieval Heretics as Protestant Martyrs," in *Martyrs and Martyrologies*, ed. Diana Wood (Cambridge: 1993), 185–207.

Cameron, Euan, "One Reformation or Many? Protestant Identities in the Later Reformation in Germany," in *Tolerance and Intolerance in the European Reformation*, eds. Ole Peter Grell and Robert W. Scribner (New York: 1996), 108–27.

Daniel, David, "Ecumenicity or Orthodoxy. The Dilemma of the Protestants in the Lands of the Austrian Habsburgs," *Church History* 49 (1980): 387–400.

David, Zdeněk V., *Finding the Middle Way. The Utraquists' Liberal Challenge to Rome and Luther* (Washington, Baltimore, and London: 2003).

de Lange, Albert, and Kathrin Utz Tremp (eds.), *Friedrich Reiser und die "waldensisch-hussitische Internationale"* (Heidelberg, Ubstadt-Weiher, and Basel: 2006).

Dillon, Kenneth, *King and Estates in the Bohemian Lands, 1526–1564* (Brussels: 1976).

Dingel, Irene, "The Culture of Conflict in the Controversies Leading to the Formula of Concord (1548–1580)," in *Lutheran Ecclesiastical Culture, 1550–1675*, ed. Robert Kolb (Brill's companions to the Christian tradition) 11 (Leiden and Boston: 2008), 15–64.

Eberhard, Winfried, *Konfessionsbildung und Stände in Böhmen, 1478–1530* (Munich and Vienna: 1981).

Eberhard, Winfried, *Monarchie und Widerstand. Zur ständische Oppositionsbildung im Herrschaftsystem Ferdinands I. in Böhmen* (Munich: 1985).

Eberhard, Winfried, "Entstehungsbedingungen für öffentliche Toleranz am Beispiel des Kuttenberger Religionsfrieden von 1485," *Communio Viatorum* 29 (1986): 129–53.

Eberhard, Winfried, "Bohemia, Moravia, and Austria," in *The Early Reformation in Europe*, ed. Andrew Pettegree (New York: 1992), 23–48.

Eberhard, Winfried, "Voraussetzungen und strukturelle Grundlagen der Konfessionalisierung in Ostmitteleuropa," in *Konfessionalisierung in Ostmitteleuropa. Wirkungen des religiösen Wandels im 16. und 17. Jahrhundert in Staat, Gesellschaft und Kultur*, ed. Joachim Bahlcke and Arno Strohmeyer (Stuttgart: 1999), 89–103.

Edwards Jr., Mark, *Printing, Propaganda, and Martin Luther* (Berkeley: 1994).

Evenden, Elizabeth, and Thomas S. Freeman, *Religion and the Book in Early Modern England. The Making of John Foxe's Book of Martyrs* (Cambridge and New York: 2011).

Evers, Ute, "Deutsch-tschischer Melodienaustausch in Gesangbüchern des 16. Jahrhunderts," *Lied und populäre Kultur* 55 (2010): 169–82.

Fichtner, Paula, *Ferdinand I of Austria. The Politics of Dynasticism in the Age of Reformation* (New York: 1982).

Fuchs, Thomas, "Protestantische Heiligen-memoria im 16. Jahrhundert," *Historische Zeitschrift* 267 (1998): 587–614.

Fudge, Thomas A., "Jan Hus as the Apocalyptic Witness in John Foxe's History," *Communio Viatorum* 56 (2014): 136–68.

Gorski, Philip, "The Mosaic Moment. An Early Modernist Critique of Modernist Theories of Nationalism," *American Journal of Sociology* 105 (2000): 1428–468.

Gregory, Brad, *Salvation at Stake. Christian Martyrdom in Early Modern Europe* (Cambridge: 1999).

Haberkern, Phillip, "'After Me There Will Come Braver Men.' Jan Hus and Reformation Polemics in the 1530s," *German History* 27 (2009): 177–95.

Haberkern, Phillip, *Patron Saint and Prophet. Jan Hus in the Bohemian and German Reformations* (Oxford: 2016).

Halama, Jr., Jindřich, "The Doctrinal Development of the Unity of Czech Brethren in the Light of their Confessions," *Communio Viatorum* 44 (2002): 128–44.

Hauffen, Adolf, "Husz eine Gans – Luther ein Schwan," *Prager Deutsche Studien* 9, 2 (1908): 1–27.

Helbling, Leo, *Dr. Johann Fabri, Generalvikar von Konstanz und Bischof von Wien (1478–1541)* (Münster: 1941).

Hendrix, Scott, "'We Are All Hussites'? Hus and Luther Revisited," *Archiv für Reformationsgeschichte* 65 (1974): 134–61.

Heymann, Frederick, "The Impact of Martin Luther upon Bohemia," *Central European History* 1 (1968): 107–30.

Hobsbawm, Eric J., "Introduction: Inventing Traditions," in *The Invention of Tradition*, eds. Eric J. Hobsbawm and Terence O. Ranger (Cambridge and New York: 1983), 1–14.

Hoyer, Siegfried, "Jan Hus und der Hussitismus in den Flugschriften des ersten Jahrzehnts der Reformation," in *Flugschriften als Massenmedium der Reformationszeit*, ed. Hans-Joachim Köhler (Stuttgart: 1981), 291–307.

Hrejsa, Ferdinand, *Česká konfesse. Její vznik, podstata a dějiny* [The *Confessio Bohemica*. Its origin, substance, and history] (Prague: 1912).

Hudson, Anne, *The Premature Reformation. Wycliffite Texts and Lollard History* (Oxford: 1988).

Jedin, Hubert, "Die geschichtliche Bedeutung der katholischen Kontroversliteratur im Zeitalter der Glaubensspaltung," *Historisches Jahrbuch* 53 (1933): 70–97.

Jedin, Hubert, *History of the Council of Trent*, trans. Ernest Graf, vol. 1 (London: 1957).

Kaminsky, Howard, *A History of the Hussite Revolution* (Berkeley and Los Angeles: 1967).

Kaufmann, Thomas, "Jan Hus und die frühe Reformation," in *Biblische Theologie und historisches Denken. Wissenschaftsgeschichtliche Studien, aus Anlass der 50. Wiederkehr der Basler Promotion von Rudolf Smend*, eds. Martin Kessler and Martin Wallraff (Basel: 2008), 62–109.

Kavka, František, "Bohemia," in *The Reformation in National Context*, ed. Robert W. Scribner (Cambridge and New York: 1994), 131–54.

Kavka, František, and Anna Skýbová, *Husitský epilog na koncilu tridentském a původní koncepce habsburské rekatolizace Čech. Počátky obnoveného pražského arcibiskupství 1561–1580* [The Hussite epilogue at the Council of Trent and the original concept of the Habsburg recatholicization of Bohemia. The beginnings of the renewed Prague archbishopric 1561–1580] (Prague: 1969).

Keen, Ralph, "Johannes Cochlaeus. An Introduction to his Life and Work," in *Luther's Lives. Two Contemporary Accounts of Martin Luther*, eds. and trans. Elizabeth Vandiver, Ralph Keen, and Thomas D. Frazel (Manchester and New York: 2002), 40–52.

Kelley, Donald, "Martyrs, Myths, and the Massacre. The Background of St. Bartholomew," *The American Historical Review* 77 (1972): 1323–342.

Kolb, Robert, "Dynamics of Party Conflict in the Saxon Late Reformation. Gnesio-Lutherans vs. Philippists," *Journal of Modern History* 49 (1977): 1289–305.

Kolb, Robert, *For All the Saints. Changing Perceptions of Martyrdom and Sainthood in the Lutheran Reformation* (Macon, GA: 1987).

Kolb, Robert, "'Saint John Hus' and 'Jerome Savonarola, Confessor of God': The Lutheran 'Canonization' of Late Medieval Martyrs," *Concordia Journal* 17 (1991): 404–18.

Krofta, Kamil, "Boj o konsistoř pod obojí v letech 1562–1575 a jeho historický základ [The struggle for the Utraquist consistory in the years 1562–1575 and its historical foundation]," *Český časopis historický* 17 (1911): 28–57, 178–99, 283–03, and 383–420.

Lamping, Antonie J., *Ulrichus Velenus (Oldřich Velenský) and his Treatise Against the Papacy* (Leiden: 1976).

van Liere, Katherine, Simon Ditchfield, and Howard Louthan (eds.), *Sacred History. Uses of the Christian Past in the Renaissance World* (Oxford: 2012).

Louthan, Howard, *Converting Bohemia. Force and Persuasion in the Catholic Reformation* (Cambridge and New York: 2009).

Malý, Tomáš, "The End of the Bohemian Reformation," in *From Hus to Luther. Visual Culture in the Bohemian Reformation (1380–1620)*, eds. Kateřina Horníčková and Michal Šroněk (Turnhout: 2016), 305–23.

Molnár, Amedeo, "Husovo místo v evropské reformaci" [Hus's place in the European Reformation], *Československý časopis historický* 14 (1966): 1–14.

Molnár, Amedeo, *Die Waldenser. Geschichte und europäisches Ausmaß einer Ketzerbewegung*, 2nd ed. (Göttingen: 1980).

Molnár, Amedeo, "Luthers Beziehungen zu den Böhmischen Brüdern," in *Leben und Werk Martin Luthers von 1526 bis 1546*, ed. Helmar Junghans, vol. 1 (Göttingen: 1983), 627–39.

Müller, Joseph Theodor, *Geschichte der Böhmischen Brüder*, 4 vols. (Herrnhut: 1922–31).

Oberman, Heiko, *Forerunners of the Reformation. The Shape of Late Medieval Thought* (New York: 1966).

Oberman, Heiko, "Hus and Luther. Prophets of a Radical Reformation," in *The Contentious Triangle. Church, State, and University*, eds. Calvin A. Pater and Rodney L. Petersen (Kirksville, MO: 1999), 135–66.

Odložilík, Otakar, "A Church in a Hostile State. The Unity of Czech Brethren," *Central European History* 6 (1973): 111–27.

Pánek, Jaroslav, "Das Ständewesen und die Gesellschaft in den Böhmischen Ländern in der Zeit vor der Schlacht auf dem Weißen Berg (1526–1620)," *Historica* 25 (1985): 73–120.

Pánek, Jaroslav, "The Question of Tolerance in Bohemia and Moravia in the Age of the Reformation," in *Tolerance and Intolerance in the European Reformation*, eds. Ole Peter Grell and Robert W. Scribner (New York: 1996), 231–48.

Pelikan, Jaroslav, "Luther's Negotiations with the Hussites," *Concordia Theological Monthly* 20 (1949): 496–517.

Petersen, Rodney, *Preaching in the Last Days. The Theme of "Two Witnesses" in the Sixteenth and Seventeenth Centuries* (New York: 1993).

Pettegree, Andrew, "Haemstede and Foxe," in *John Foxe and the English Reformation*, ed. David M. Loades (Aldershot and Brookfield, VT: 1997), 278–94.

Pohlig, Matthias, *Zwischen Gelehrsamkeit und konfessioneller Identitätsstiftung. Lutherische Kirchen- und Universalgeschichtsschreibung 1546–1617* (Tübingen: 2007).

Říčan, Rudolf, "Tschechische Übersetzungen von Luthers Schriften bis zum Schmalkaldischen Krieg," in *Vierhundertfünfzig Jahre lutherische Reformation 1517–1967. Festschrift für Franz Lau zum 60. Geburtstag*, ed. Helmar Junghans (Göttingen: 1967), 282–301.

Roloff, Hans-Gert, "Die Funktion von Hus-Texten in der Reformations-Polemik," in *De captu lectoris. Wirkungen des Buches im 15. und 16. Jahrhundert, dargestellt an ausgewählten Handschriften und Drucken*, eds. Wolfgang Milde and Werner Schuder (Berlin: 1988), 219–56.

Rothkegel, Martin, "Anabaptism in Moravia and Silesia," in *A Companion to Anabaptism and Spiritualism, 1521–1700*, eds. John Roth and James Stayer (Brill's Companions to the Christian Tradition) 6 (Boston: 2007), 163–214.

Schmidt-Biggemann, Wilhelm, "Flacius Illyricus' 'Catalogus testium veritatis' als kontroverstheologische Polemik," in *Reformer als Ketzer. Heterodoxe Bewegungen von Vorreformatoren*, eds. Günter Frank and Friedrich Niewöhner (Stuttgart: 2004), 263–91.

Scribner, Robert, "The Incombustible Luther. The Image of the Reformer in Early Modern Europe," *Past and Present* 110 (1986): 38–68.

Skýbová, Anna, "Politische Aspekte der Existenz zweier Konfessionen im Königreich Böhmen bis zum Anfang des 17. Jahrhunderts," in *Martin Luther. Leben, Werk und Wirkung*, ed. Günter Vogler (Berlin: 1986), 463–80.

Skýbová, Anna, "Ferdinand I., der Habsburger, und die Anfänge siener Regierung im böhmischen Staat," in *Europäische Herrscherr. Ihre Rolle bei der Gestaltung von Politik und Gesellschaft vom 16. bis zum 18. Jahrhundert*, ed. Günter Vogler (Weimar: 1988), 71–84.

Šmahel, František, "Zur Einführung. Häresie und vorzeitige Reformation – causa ad disputandum," in *Häresie und vorzeitige Reformation im Spätmittelalter*, ed. František Šmahel (Munich: 1998), vii–xiv.

Šmahel, František, "*Pax externa et interna*. Vom heiligen Krieg zur Erzwungenen Toleranz im hussitischen Böhmen," in *Toleranz im Mittelalter*, eds. Alexander Patschovsky and Harald Zimmerman (Sigmaringen: 1998), 211–73.

Strupl, Milos, "Confessional Theology of the *Unitas Fratrum*," *Church History* 33 (1964): 279–93.

Thomson, S. Harrison, "Luther and Bohemia," *Archiv für Reformationsgeschichte* 44 (1953): 160–81.

Volkmar, Christoph, "Turning Luther's Weapons against him. The Birth of Catholic Propaganda in Saxony in the 1520s," in *The Book Triumphant. Print in Transition in the Sixteenth and Seventeenth Centuries*, eds. Graeme Kemp and Malcolm Walsby (Leiden and Boston: 2011), 115–29.

von der Osten-Sacken, Vera, "Die kleine Herde der 7000 – Die aufrechten Bekenner in M. Flacius Illyricus konzeptionellen Beiträgen zur Neuformulierung der Kirchengeschichtschreibung aus protestantischer Sicht," in *Matija Vlačić Ilirik* [III]. *Zbornik radova s Trećeg Međunarodnog Znanstvenog Skupa*, ed. Marina Miladinov (Labin: 2011), 184–213.

Watson, Nicholas, "Jean Crespin and the First English Martyrology of the Reformation," in *John Foxe and the English Reformation*, ed. David M. Loades (Aldershot and Brookfield, VT: 1997), 192–209.

Wernisch, Martin, "Luther and Medieval Reform Movements, Particularly the Hussites," in *The Oxford Handbook of Martin Luther's Theology*, eds. Robert Kolb, Irene Dingel, and Ľubomír L. Batka (Oxford and New York: 2015), 62–70.

Winter, Eduard, *Tausend Jahre Geisteskampf im Sudetenraum. Das religiöse Ringen zweier Völker* (Salzburg: 1938).

Zeman, Jarold K., *The Anabaptists and the Czech Brethren in Moravia, 1526–1628. A Study of Origins and Contact* (The Hague: 1969).

Index

Adalbert, St.   36
Adalbertus Ranconis de Ericinio. *See* Vojtěch Raňkův of Ježov
Adamites   207–10, 213
Adso of Montier-en-Der   188, 188n4
Aeneas Silvius Piccolomini. *See* Pius II, Pope
Agricola, Johannes   426n81
Albert the Great   279
Albrecht II of Habsburg   141
Albrecht, King   229
Alexander of Hales   72
Ambrose, St.   86, 268
Amos, Brother   386
Anabaptism   417, 417n49, 423
Andreae, Johannes   36
Anglicanism   356
Anglicus, Peter. *See* Payne, Peter
Anselm of Canterbury, Archbishop   66, 76
Antichrist: and the Apocalypse   82, 148, 166, 190–8, 202, 206, 211, 273
    and Christ   48, 169, 189, 275, 321, 387
    Church of the   79, 116, 160, 170, 172, 189–91, 194, 286, 378–9, 408–9, 413, 430
    and the early Bohemian reform   39, 48, 63, 103, 189, 271
    and heresy   84, 86
    and the interpretation of Scripture   311, 320
    Jakoubek of Stříbro on   68, 116, 190, 194, 197–8, 273–4, 322
    Jan Milíč on   64, 188
    Matěj of Janov on   189, 192, 275
    Mikuláš Biskupec on   165, 175, 197
    Petr Chelčický on   165, 166, 169–70, 211
    Pope as   68, 79, 116, 160, 408–9, 413, 423, 426, 430
    and sacraments   377
    and sin   274–6, 286
    and violence   48, 188–9, 191–2, 194, 197–9, 202, 211, 274
    Wyclif on   188, 190
anticlericalism   31, 45, 72–3, 75–6, 78–9, 88–9, 112–13, 123, 199, 219–20, 262, 267, 281, 284, 299, 308–10, 322–4, 332, 418–19

apocalypticism and chiliasm: biblical prophecies   148, 191, 194, 198–201, 203–4, 311, 321–2, 321n72
    commentaries on   82, 83n57, 126, 310–12, 315, 319
    of early Hussites   187–212
    Final Judgement   148, 187, 197–8, 202, 205, 305, 332, 404, 409
    history   86, 192, 195–8, 202, 204–6
    imagery   187, 188n4, 190, 200, 377–8
    as impetus for reform   187–9, 193–4, 201, 307
    in scholarship   175, 212–13
    of Jakoubek of Stříbro   322
    and martyrs   196
    of Mikuláš Biskupec   175, 190, 194–7, 199n49, 211, 273n56
    and Protestantism   404, 408
    and the primitive church   197, 286, 331–2n2
    Second Coming   202, 205, 208
    of the Taborites   207, 209, 211
    tracts on   157, 191, 211–12
Apostle's Creed   346
Apostolic succession   155, 242–5, 355, 378–9, 383–4, 413
Aquinas, Thomas   76, 81, 88, 165, 279
Aristotle   65, 67, 74, 76, 104
Arnošt of Pardubice, Archbishop   27, 31–5, 52, 63, 219
Art. *See* iconography/imagery
Arundel, Thomas, Archbishop   72
Augusta, Jan, Bishop   393, 419
Augustine of Hippo   66, 73–4, 76, 78–9, 83, 86, 150, 268–9, 277
Augustinians   35, 44–5, 63, 150, 152, 155, 299
Averroes   76
Avicenna   76

Bacon, Roger   76
Bale, John   424n75
Battle of Lipany (1434)   89
Battle of White Mountain (1620)   375
Barak   199

Barbara, Queen   229
Bartoš, Písař   412, 412n35
Basel *Compactata*. *See Compactata*
Bavarian university nation   297
Bechyňka, Jan   338
Bede   196, 197n41
Beghards   207n78, 376
Beguines   45, 66, 73, 277, 317, 376
Benedictines   30, 36, 341, 375
benefices   33, 40, 51, 115, 156, 236–7, 337
Bernhard of Luxembourg   427
Berthold of Regensburg   38, 331n2
Bethlehem Chapel   5, 28, 40–1, 49, 53, 111–13, 121, 156, 224, 297, 315, 338–9n26
Bible. *See* Scripture
Biceps, Mikuláš   47, 106, 106n25
Blackfriars   68, 71
Black Rose (U černé růže)   262
Bohemian Confession (1575)   428–9, 428n91
Bohemian Land Diet (1444)   153
Bohemian university nation   41, 63–4, 116, 297
Boniface IX, Pope   123
Bracciolini, Poggio   407, 407n16
Bradwardine, Thomas, Archbishop   78–9
Bridget of Sweden   37, 52, 322–3n73
Brikcí of Žatec   119–20
Brothers of Boleslav. *See* Unity of Brethren
Brunfels, Otto   408–9, 408n19
Buridan, John   36, 77

Cahera, Havel   412–14
Calixtines   3
Calvin, Jean, and Calvinism   356, 403, 423
Čapek, Jan   304–6, 349, 349n69
Capistrano, John   153
catechism   8, 34, 299, 301–2, 305, 307, 318, 390, 415
Catholic Church: authority and administration of   159, 220n8, 225, 231, 236, 243
   and *Compactata*   141–2, 144–7, 160–2, 172, 241
   on confession   157
   on Czech vernacular   314, 322, 344
   and the early Bohemian reform   28, 43
   on frequent communion   354
   and heresy   266, 270, 344
   and Hus   80, 110, 222–3
   and the laity   235, 237, 336
   on the lay chalice   122, 153–5, 277, 280, 303
   and print   238, 420–2
   Reformation and Counter Reformation   3–4, 7, 403–6, 409–11, 413, 423, 428–9
   and the Taborites   125, 165, 310
   and the Unity of Brethren   168, 324, 375
   and the Utraquists   144–5, 149–50, 163, 166, 171, 229–30, 318, 338, 355–6, 356n81, 377, 416, 420–2
Čeněk of Vartemberk   315
Chalcidius   66
Chalice   2, 4, 171, 193, 277–8, 356
Charles IV, Emperor   38, 40, 63, 340
Charles V, Emperor   219, 299, 425
Charles of Luxembourg   29
Charles University. *See* University of Prague
Charlier, Giles   164
Cheb Judge   159, 161, 163, 165, 269–70, 379, 387
Chelčický, Petr   126
   anticlericalism   323–4
   in historiography   13, 173, 175, 325, 358
   on the Pikarts   210
   and the Unity of Brethren   156, 170, 211, 239, 377, 379–80, 386, 392–4
   on violence   167, 170, 285, 377, 379–80
   works   166–70, 312–13, 315–16
Christ: and the Antichrist   48, 169, 189, 275, 321, 387
   Blood of   120, 279, 303, 354
   Body of   74, 78, 80, 189, 193, 305, 313–14, 415
   as bridegroom of the Church   74, 78
   juxtaposition to the pope   79, 113
   Laws of   84–5, 190, 264–6, 269–70, 274, 278, 282, 323, 375, 387–8
   legislator and ruler   83, 206, 311
   life and Passion   74, 266–8, 275, 319, 417
   real presence   158–9, 164–5, 167–8, 207, 278, 287, 305
   sacraments   126, 156, 278–80
   Trinity   265
Christology   64, 157, 199
Chrysostom, John   270, 277, 300

Church Fathers   35, 40, 42, 47, 84, 103, 143,
    155, 163, 165–7, 191, 192n19, 196–7,
    282n95, 333
Church: of the Antichrist   79, 116, 160, 170,
    189–91, 194, 378, 408–9, 413, 430
    Christ as head   78, 190
    heavenly and eternal   192n19, 193
    militant   47, 78, 269
    organological model   189, 378
Cistercians   27, 34, 35, 45, 105
Clarificator, Petrus   35
Clement VI, Pope   29, 340
Clement VII, Pope   46
clergy; *see also* anticlericalism
    administration   144, 220n8, 231–2, 242–3,
        390
    and civil dominion   88–9, 282
    clerical emigration   225, 238
    and clerical reform   30, 32–4, 38–9
    laity   72, 332–3, 345–6
    offices of the   336, 350, 355
    rivalry with friars   44
    secular clergy and rule   40–1, 49, 116,
        163–4, 236, 241, 282, 355
    sermons addressed to   150, 152–3
    simony   32, 43, 64, 72, 105, 112–13, 123, 171,
        236, 274–5, 285, 351
    and universities   225–6, 347
    usury   43, 149, 151, 285
    Utraquist   227–30, 233–5, 350
    and the vernacular   41, 303–4
Cochlaeus, Johannes   420–22, 420n64,
    421n65, 421n66
Comenius. *See* Komenský, Jan Amos, Bishop
Communion. *See* Eucharist
Communism   130, 325, 374, 394–5
Compactata of Basel   2, 8, 141, 153, 220, 239,
    266, 269, 282–4, 380, 420, 421, 428
    cancellation of   6, 382
    Catholic Church and   6, 142, 147, 241
    confirmation and legislation of   144, 231,
        235
    and Ferdinand I   420, 420n64, 428
    interpretation of   151, 159–61, 172
    negotiations   5, 6, 156, 171, 229, 244
    responses to   145, 151, 223
    Utraquists and   3, 6, 146–7, 150, 222, 225,
        240–1, 387

Constantinople   9, 128, 153, 244
Council of Basel   1, 5, 8–9, 141, 210
    attendees   15, 191, 229, 244
    and the *Compacta* and Four Articles of
        Prague   266, 269, 282–4
    decrees of   230
    Hussite delegation to   86, 125–7, 150–3,
        155, 158, 163, 171, 196, 276, 352–3
    Payne and Wyclif   88–9, 128, 164
    responses to   423, 430
Council of Constance   1–2, 8, 124, 240
    attendees   105, 107–8, 117, 123, 267, 241
    decrees of   4, 121, 123, 305–6
    in historiography   11, 130
    and Hus   81, 87, 110–16, 119, 264, 280,
        302–4
    Hus as martyr   421, 426
    and Jerome of Prague   67
    responses to   122, 321, 338, 407, 423
    on Wyclif   4, 67–8, 71, 78, 107
Council of Pisa   68
Council of Trent   423
Council of Vienne   29
Counter-Reformation   49
Cranmer, Thomas   356
Creation   65, 69, 265
Credo   111, 339, 343, 353
Crespin, Jean   424
Ctibor Tovačovský of Cimburk   146
Cyprian, St.   277, 304
Czechoslovakia   26, 213, 245, 395
Czech university nation. *See* Bohemian
    university nation
Czech vernacular: in historiography   11,
    324–6
    Hus's preaching   5, 297–8, 302, 306–7,
        310, 316, 318, 323
    Jakoubek of Stříbro's preaching   122, 165,
        302–15, 325, 341
    Jan Příbram's preaching   318–23
    and the laity   9, 37, 211, 300–2
    literature   145
    liturgy   42, 275, 299, 301, 304–18, 334–5,
        336, 339–43, 345–6, 353
    and Petr Chelčický's writings   323–4
    sermons at Bethlehem Chapel   5, 111–12,
        297, 302, 315
    Tomáš Štítný's theology   102n7, 168, 332

Czech vernacular: in historiography (cont.)
  translation   27–8, 154, 262
  Unity of Brethren   355–6
  vernacularization   298, 379

Dalimil chronicle   298
Debora   199
Decalogue   74, 109, 111, 115, 411
Denys II, abbot   36
Devotio moderna   34, 35n25, 39, 52, 103n9
Diet of Augsburg (1530)   425
Diet of Bohemia (1435)   152
Diet of Čáslav (1421)   225
Diet of Worms (1521)   412, 421, 425
Dietrichstien Library   173
Dionysius the Areopagite   40
  Ps.-Dionysius   278, 353
Długosz, Jan   242
Dominicans   38, 44, 47, 50–1, 71, 100–1, 106, 299
Donation of Constantine   72–3, 78–9, 145, 169, 323n75
Donatus, Aelius   78
Dresden school   128, 262

Ebendorfer, Thomas   211
ecclesiastical law. *See* law
ecclesiology: Dionysian   40
  of Hus   14, 110, 113
  of Jakoubek of Stříbro   310
  of Jan Milíč   46
  of Matěj of Janov   48, 319
  of the Polish Church   50
  Protestant   406, 415–16, 420, 428–9
  of Šimon of Tišnov   118
  of Stanislav of Znojmo   68, 107, 110
  of Štěpán of Páleč   107–8
  of the Unity of Brethren   375, 378, 383
  Utraquist   7, 145, 151, 210, 378, 431
  of Vojtěch Raňkův   46, 66
  of Wyclif   64, 68, 113, 240n71
Eck, Johannes   407n13
Eliáš of Chřenovice   383
Emmaus monastery   238, 340–1, 381, 392
England: communication with   12, 36, 129, 308
  English masters   36, 87, 127, 147, 164, 227, 244, 382
  English nobility   310
  and Protestantism   423–4

Erasmus of Rotterdam   376
eschatology: and apocalypticism   187, 194, 196–7, 199
  heavenly and eternal Church   192n19, 193
  of Hus   191
  of Jakoubek of Stříbro   116, 158, 192
  Protestant   404, 430
  renewed Church   378
  of the Taborites   172, 202–3, 320
  of the Unity of Brethren   166, 169, 171, 389
Eucharist; *see also* Utraquism4
  Blood of Christ   120, 279, 303, 354
  Body of Christ   74, 78, 80, 189, 193, 305, 313–14, 415
  and the Unity of Brethren   355, 376
  Church councils on   2, 9, 85, 130, 153
  consubstantiation   107
  frequent communion   2, 42n41, 47–8, 50, 54, 103–5, 105n19, 116n56, 119, 171, 192–3, 265, 272, 277, 279, 332–3, 344–6, 354, 356–7
  in historiography   130, 356, 358
  Hus on   112, 119
  Jakoubek of Stříbro on   116, 116n56, 303, 306–7
  Jan Milíč on   331–2, 345
  Jan Příbram on   147–8, 164
  Jerome of Prague on   114
  liturgy of   343, 349, 351, 379
  Mass of St Peter   349, 351, 353
  Matěj of Janov on   27, 48, 119
  Mikuláš Biskupec on   126, 164–5
  Petr Chelčický on   166–8, 312
  and Pikartism   354, 376
  real presence   158–9, 164–5, 167–8, 207, 278, 287, 305
  remanence   64, 68, 104, 107, 117, 156, 167–8, 224, 287, 312
  Stanislav of Znojmo on   105, 107
  sub utraque   2–3, 50, 116–18, 120–1, 123, 151, 153–5, 227, 239, 303, 305, 314, 334, 346, 350, 355
  and the Taborites   312, 318–19, 348, 353–4
  transubstantiation   4, 68, 72, 312, 354, 376, 379, 421
  Wyclif on   64, 68, 79, 105
Eugene IV, Pope   244

INDEX

Fabri, Johannes, Bishop   420–2, 429
Faulfiš, Mikuláš   87
Feasts: calendar   335, 337–8
  Jan Hus   413
  St Wenceslas   225
  the Visitation   54
Ferdinand I, Emperor   387, 416–17, 418–22, 428
Filip of Padeřov   315
Filippo de Villanuova, Bishop   233, 244
Fitzralph, Richard, Archbishop   36, 66, 88–9
Flacius Illyricus, Matthias   424n75, 426–7
Forty-five Articles   68, 71–73, 106, 110
Four Articles of Prague   6, 89, 115, 118, 141, 203, 222, 264, 269, 282, 382, 407–8
Foxe, John   424, 424n75
France   27, 36, 424
Franciscans   42, 155, 375

Gallus. *See* Havlík
Gallicanism   224
George of Brandenburg-Ansbach   418
George of Poděbrady: on clerical poverty   146
  and the conquest of Prague (1448)   143, 152, 156, 230, 232
  and Jan Rokycana   155, 230, 381
  and Jindřich the Elder   242
  as King of Bohemia   6, 142, 144, 235, 381
  and Tábor   144
  and the Unity of Brethren   381–2, 384
George of Saxony   420
Germany: Czech-German antagonism   26, 117, 324–5, 412
  German language   27–8, 38, 207n78, 298, 357, 375–6, 386, 407, 415, 417–8
  German masters   4, 53, 71, 109, 117, 262, 297
  German university nations   64, 68, 128
  German Waldensians   8, 11, 31, 378–9, 383
  preaching benefices   51
  Reformation   406, 408–10, 413, 416, 419, 419n58, 423, 425
Gerson, Jean   8, 15, 50, 70, 122–3, 267–8, 308n29
Glagolitic   340–1
Golden Legend (Jacobus de Voragine)   158
Grace   47–8, 64, 76, 84–5, 243, 278–9, 284, 319

Great Schism   1, 36, 46, 48, 54, 68, 189, 384
Gregory XI, Pope   71
Gregory XII, Pope   68
Gregory the Great, Pope   80, 86, 268
Grosseteste, Robert   36, 76
Grote, Geert   35

Havlík (Gallus)   119, 121–2, 128
Heinrich of Bitterfeld   38, 47, 50, 102, 105, 332
Heinrich Totting of Oyta   26, 66, 104
Henry of Ghent   88
heresy: accusations of   104, 114, 149, 156, 224, 241, 266, 406
  and the Adamites   210
  apocalyptic history of   196
  and books   73–4, 109, 407
  Catalogue of All Heretics   410, 427
  and Church councils   5, 70–1, 242–4, 267
  and the early Bohemian reform   2
  and Hus   73–4, 109
  Hussitism as   4, 211, 262, 270, 285, 409
  Pikartism as   207, 209, 376, 411
  predestination as heretical doctrine   221
  and the Reformation   406, 409–10, 420–2, 427
  suppression of   31
  Taborite movement as   208–9, 211, 314
  and the Unity of Brethren   375–6, 382, 384, 421
  and the vernacular   314, 317, 321, 344
  Waldensianism as   44, 284
  and Wyclif   5, 76, 84, 102, 106–7, 149
Hilarius of Litoměřice (Litoměřický), Archbishop   154, 160–3, 243, 314
Hildessen, Johannes   122
Hoffmann, Johannes IV, Bishop   243
Hübner, Johannes   71, 106
Hugh of Saint-Cher   36, 198n47
Hugh of Saint-Victor   72, 88
Hungary   6, 35
Hus, Jan: apocalypticism of   189
  as authority   127, 149, 167–70, 191, 276, 288
  at Bethlehem Chapel   28, 41, 49, 111–12, 115, 297, 302
  as central figure of reform   1–3, 224, 322
  at Constance   81, 87, 111, 113–14, 122, 280, 303–4
  disputations at Prague   68, 71, 73–4, 77, 283

Hus, Jan: apocalypticism of (cont.)
    and the early Bohemian reform   25, 49, 102
    ecclesiology/ *De ecclesia*   77, 79–80, 110, 113, 222–3, 272
    exile (1412)   82, 113
    in historiography   10, 15, 25, 53, 63n1, 89–90, 101–2
    and Jakoubek of Stříbro   2, 114–15, 155, 165, 307
    and Jan Milíč   103
    and Jerome of Prague   4
    and the laity   112, 344
    on the Law of Christ   103, 264, 270
    letters of   158, 280
    as martyr   143, 274, 315, 321, 338, 338n26, 413, 422–5
    and Matěj of Janov   265
    opposition from Prague masters   107–10, 117–18
    and the Reformation   403–10, 421
    on realist philosophy   3–4
    sermons of   111–12, 302
    students of   116
    on Utraquism   3, 119–21, 279–80
    and the vernacular   5, 297–8, 302, 306–7, 310, 316, 318, 323
    and Wyclif   4, 77, 85, 106–7, 223, 306–7
Húska, Martin   205, 207–9
Hussites: in Europe   7–8
    apocalypticism of   187–212
    authorities   261
    at Basel   8, 88, 125, 153, 158, 229, 240
    Bethlehem Chapel   115
    Cheb Judge   161, 387
    chroniclers of   10, 145
    on clerical poverty   146
    Compactata and the Four Articles of Prague   160, 222, 241, 282, 285
    on confession   157
    conservative Hussite theologians   144, 146, 150–1, 155, 284
    defense of Wyclif   64, 89
    and the early Bohemian reform   105
    and the Eastern Church   153, 280
    in historiography   10–14, 26, 50–1, 129–31, 172–5, 212, 237, 246–7, 256–9, 263, 286–7, 299, 324–6, 429–31

on iconography   347n62
influence on the Unity of Brethren   372, 374, 377, 379–82, 384–8, 393
and Jakoubek of Stříbro   147, 155, 308
on the Law of Christ   104, 172, 269, 286
on the lay chalice   277–8, 283, 355
nomenclature of   1–5, 374
opposition to   118
and the papacy   240
on prosecuting others   156
radicals; *see also* Taborites 125–6, 159, 163, 166, 172, 202–12, 312, 340, 346, 376
and the Reformation   403–18, 421–2
Hussite Revolution   9, 376, 380
on saints   281, 303
and Sigismund   5
on sin   285
and Tábor   126–8, 146, 269
and Utraquism; *see also* Utraquism 2, 50, 119–22, 221
and the vernacular   4–5, 145, 275, 297–9, 305, 312–24
and the Waldensians   262, 379
Hussite wars   220
    and Hussite clergy   228, 232
    and radical ideology   124–5
    Compactata   141–2, 145, 161, 172
    crusading   8
    first war   124
    in historiography   245
    Kutná Hora peace   6, 153
    second war   6
hymnody   238, 334, 342–4, 355, 358–9, 417
Hynce Ptáček of Pirkštejn   144

iconography/ imagery: apocalyptic   187, 188n4, 190, 200, 377–8
    at Basel   128
    of the cross   77
    in historiography   10, 13–14
    and Hus   15
    Hussite art and position on   4, 118, 351
    iconoclasm   10, 103, 347n62
    and Jakoubek of Stříbro   278–9
    in preaching   42
    of the primitive church   194, 204, 211
    sensory perception of   278
    Utraquists on   346

veneration of   48, 84–5, 151, 281, 379
visual propaganda   430
and Wyclif   87
imitatio Christi   9, 43, 88, 148, 192, 195, 201, 266–8, 300–1, 319, 322, 377
Indulgences   8, 37, 39, 48, 54, 107, 110, 113, 145, 151, 224, 285, 297, 302, 309
Innocent III, Pope   85, 168
Innocent IV, Pope   32, 340
Innocent VI, Pope   32
Inquisition   31, 48, 208, 219, 285, 348, 376, 410

Jakoubek of Stříbro: on the Adamites   210
on the Antichrist   68, 116, 190, 194, 197–8, 273–4, 322
apocalypticism of   322
at Bethlehem Chapel   5
in the *Catalogue of All Heretics*   410, 427
as central Hussite figure   115, 147, 149, 158, 170, 277, 377
on communion   2, 115–17, 120–1, 165, 171, 193, 277–80, 302–3, 333, 341
on confession   165, 168
defense of Wyclif   68, 74–5, 115, 119, 266, 281
ecclesiology of   272–5, 282–3, 286
on exegesis   157, 165, 192, 201, 201n60, 268–9, 319–20, 333
and Gerson   267–8
in historiography   90, 114–15, 130, 357
on infant communion   121
influence of Matěj of Janov   50, 116n56, 119, 189–90, 192, 262–3, 266, 276, 281
on the Law of Christ   267, 270, 276–7
and the Taborites   125, 146, 156, 321n72, 354
and the Utraquists   127, 152, 155, 192, 227–8, 302
and the vernacular   122, 165, 302–15, 325, 341
on war   124
Jagellonian period   172, 235, 246, 380, 388
Jan of Chlum   122
Jan IV of Dražice, Bishop   29, 35, 40
Jan Eliášův of Horšovský Týn   110
Jan of Holešov   36
Jan of Hradec   120

Jan of Jenštejn, Archbishop   28–9, 32–3, 35–6, 38, 44–7, 49, 52, 332
Jan of Jesenice   110, 116, 119, 123, 280
Jan of Jičín   74, 76, 205
Jan Milíč of Kroměříž: accusation of heresy   2
on the Antichrist   64, 188
anticlericalism of   272
authority for the Hussite movement   1–3, 66, 103, 300, 393
circulation of texts   50
on devotion   28
on frequent communion   47, 192, 331–2
in historiography   28, 53, 103n9
Jerusalem   44–5, 345
and Pope Urban V   39, 46
as precursor of the Hussites   1–3, 25, 102, 261
in print   320, 427
sermons of   27, 39–40, 42, 79, 103n10, 300
Vita   52
and women   44–5, 47–8, 345–6
Jan Němec of Žatec   167
Jan Očko of Vlašim, Archbishop   32, 39, 45
Jan Papoušek of Soběslav   159
Jan of Pomuk   49
Jan Táborský of Klokotská Hora   341
Jean de Roque   123
Jenek Václavův of Prague   104
Jerome of Prague: in the *Catalogue of All Heretics*   410, 427
disputation   109
in historiography   90–1, 130
and the laity   284, 297–8
as martyr   143, 274, 338, 338n26, 407, 427
at Paris   70
at the University of Prague   114
and the Reformation   413, 422, 423, 425
and Wyclif   4, 67, 75, 114
Jerome, St.   268, 301
Jesuits   52, 428
Jindřichův, Mikuláš   230
Jindřich the Elder of Poděbrady   242
Jiří of Kněhnice   87
Jistebnický kancionál   305, 335, 340–3, 346, 358–9
Johana of Rožmitál   162

Johann of Mühlheim   40
Johannes Andreae   36
Johannes of Dambach   101
Johannes of Marienwerder   104
John of Capistrano   153
John of God   85
John (Quidort) of Paris   193
John Stojković of Ragusa   153, 210
Jošt of Rožmberk, Bishop   162

Kániš, Petr   209
Kardinál, Jan   227–8
Kateřina of Sulevice   45
Komenský, Jan Amos, Bishop   371, 395
Konrad of Ebrach   105
Konrad of Gelnhausen   46
Konrad of Soltau   104
Konrad of Vechta, Archbishop   220, 225–8, 241
Konrad of Waldhausen. *See* Waldhauser, Konrad
Konstantinos Anglikos   128, 244
Koranda the Elder, Václav   200, 205, 348
Koranda the Younger, Václav   161–2, 175, 233, 239, 314, 340, 373
Korybut, Sigismund   225, 227–8
Krajčí, Brother Řehoř   156, 371n2, 381–2, 385–6, 389, 391–2
Krasonický, Vavřinec   373, 385
Křišťan of Prachatice   124, 156, 230, 348
Křižanovský, Václav   154
Kubík of Štěkeň   386
Kuneš of Třebovle   39
Kutná Hora   4, 6, 68, 109, 116, 144, 153, 230, 234, 241, 247, 325, 336, 338, 338n26, 343, 386, 386n41, 416

Ladislas Posthumous   141, 235
laity: and books   300, 334, 344, 346
    in church administration   237, 239
    and the clergy   43, 72, 233–7, 239
    devotion   9, 48, 105n19, 245, 322–4
    and ecclesiastical power   54
    education of   227, 299
    estates   45
    fasting   33
    and frequent communion   2, 47, 103, 193, 272, 332
    and Hus   79, 112
    instruction   36, 38, 112, 162, 299, 308, 314, 318, 322
    in Moravia   385
    and preaching   39–40, 64, 262, 283–4, 348, 381
    and the primitive church   50
    secular defensors of the Estates   233
    and Stanislav of Znojmo   81
    Tomáš Štítný   102n7, 168
    and the Unity of Brethren   374–6, 386
    and the University of Prague   1
    and Utraquism   222, 232, 313, 315, 355, 161, 228, 231–3
    and Wyclif   74, 86
    and vernacular theology   169–70, 211, 285, 299, 301, 304, 315–17, 346
Land Diets   153, 158, 230, 378
Łaskarz, Andrzej, Bishop   123
Lateran IV Council (1415)   2, 28, 40, 79
Law   31–3, 40, 45, 48, 81, 108, 110, 117–18, 151, 224, 233n48, 237, 284, 372, 416
Law of Christ/ God (*Lex divina/ Christi/ evangelica*): and the Antichrist   169, 188, 190–1, 276
    and the clergy   73, 275, 378
    enforcement of   377, 380–1
    Four Articles of Prague   282
    and Gospel law   83–5
    and human law   80, 84, 169, 281, 309
    lex privata   283
    primacy of   104, 113, 150, 162, 168, 274, 286, 374–5, 388–9
    restoration of   411
    as a rule of living   9, 170–2, 200, 203, 264–70, 273, 277–8, 300, 303, 308, 351, 375, 387
    as universal   66
Ležka, Jan   373
literacy   10, 301–2
Lithuania   375
Louis of Bavaria   29
Luciani, Agostino, Bishop   244
Lukáš of Prague, Bishop   338n45, 373, 375, 385, 392–3, 392n55, 395, 414–15, 417
Lupáč, Martin, Bishop   158–61, 174–5, 226, 229, 378–9, 383

INDEX   447

Luther, Martin   14, 174, 221, 376, 393, 405, 418,
    423, 425, 427, 430
  in early print   376, 408–9, 412–13, 425n80,
    425–7
  eschatology of   430
  and frequent communion   356
  in historiography   15, 174
  and Hus   406–7, 410–11, 425
  Ninety-five Theses   405
  Second Reformation   403
  and the Unity of Brethren   393, 411–12
  and the Utraquists   221, 410–11, 414–15,
    418–19, 428
Lutherans   3, 7, 244, 337, 345–6, 355, 371,
    404n3, 411, 419–21, 423–4, 424n75, 428

Malogranatum   27, 34–5, 47, 52
Manichaeism   409
marriage   44, 168, 354, 374, 391
Marsilius of Inghen   48
Martin V, Pope   5, 306
martyrs: and apocalypticism   196
  German   427n86
  Hus and Jerome of Prague   114, 273–4,
    306, 315, 338, 338n26, 407, 409
  of Kutná Hora   338
  martyrologies   404n5, 424–7
  and Protestantism   404, 411, 424n75,
    424–5
  and Unity of Brethren   384, 419
Mary I, Queen   423
Matěj of Janov: on the Antichrist   189, 192,
    275
  ecclesiology of   157, 267, 300, 319
  on the Eucharist   27, 48–9, 103, 119, 192,
    277, 332–3
  in historiography   54, 357
  as Hussite authority   49–50, 75, 116, 152,
    155, 158, 193n22, 261, 263, 266, 273,
    275–6, 278, 281, 283, 307, 316, 381, 389,
    393
  and Inquisition   48–9
  on the Law of Christ   265–6, 269, 271–2
  as precursor of Hus   1, 25, 102–3, 261, 320
  in print   409, 427
  Regulae Veteris et Novi Testamenti   27, 54,
    66, 103, 109, 116, 189, 265, 300
  and Wyclif   79, 286

Matěj of Knín   109, 114
Matěj of Kunvald, Bishop   383, 385
Matouš, Brother   383
Matouš of Zbraslav   105
Matthew of Cracow   27, 37, 47, 50, 52–3, 102,
    104–5, 332
Matthew of Legnica   53
Matthias Corvinus   6, 386
Maximilian II, Emperor   428
Melanchthon, Philip   419
Michael of Žamberk   384
Mikuláš Biskupec of Pelhřimov, Bishop: 263
  on the Adamites   210
  on the Antichrist   165, 175, 197
  on the apocalypse   175, 190, 194–7,
    199n49, 211, 273n56
  and Bernard of Luxembourg   410
  and Jan Rokycana   153
  and Petr Chelčický   167–8, 312, 314
  and Protestantism   404, 408–9, 413,
    426
  as Taborite leader   126, 205, 269, 281,
    379
  works of   126–7, 164–7, 352–4
  and Wyclif   82, 264, 264–5n17, 270
Mikuláš of Vlásenice   374
Moravia   2–3, 28–9, 67, 107, 118, 141–2, 146,
    158, 161, 173, 209, 234, 317, 336, 385, 396,
    411, 416–17
Moravian Brethren   371, 375–6, 380, 382, 386,
    395
music   238, 337, 339–44, 346, 356–9, 395

Neoplatonism   65, 278
Netter, Thomas   71
Nicholas of Cusa, Cardinal   8, 159, 283
Nicholas of Dinkelsbühl   122–3
Nicholas of Dresden: *Apologia*   122
  disputations at Prague   119
  and the Dresden school   128, 262
  in historiography   13
  and Hus   283
  influence on Jakoubek of Stříbro   116, 121,
    263, 269
  and the law of Christ   270, 276
  and Matěj of Janov   49–50
  and Mikuláš Biskupec   127
  Tabulae veteris et novi coloris   194, 275

Nicholas of Dresden: *Apologia* (cont.)
    and Utraquism   120, 277, 283, 303, 357, 357n89
    on violence   124
    and Waldensianism   127
Nicholas of Lyra   83
Nicolaus Magni of Jawór   38
nobility: and the *Compactata*   145
    defense of Hus   407–8
    Hussites   6–7, 224, 302, 308, 310, 380
    and the monarchy   298, 308
    in Moravia   142
    and Petr Chelčický   169
    in Prague   5, 64, 143
    secular defensors of the Estates   233
    Tomáš Štítný   299
    and the Unity of Brethren   382, 393, 417–18
    and the University of Prague   297, 311
    and the Utraquists   224, 315
    Wyclif on the   86, 310

Ockham, William   77
Office of Spiritual Law   228, 230
Ondřej of Brod   28, 110, 117, 119–21, 210, 280, 303, 333
Origen   83
Orthodox Church   9, 153, 244, 280
orthodoxy   28, 44–5, 47, 68, 78, 87, 107, 113, 148–9, 199, 211, 227, 407, 414, 414n41, 418, 421

Páleč, Štěpán   13, 65, 67, 71–3, 79–80, 91, 107, 110, 120, 122, 285, 303
Palomar, Juan   88, 126, 128, 150–1, 164, 210
papacy: and the Antichrist   160, 408–9, 423, 430
    appointments by   33, 155
    in Bohemia   167, 219
    commands and decrees of   81, 352
    and the *Compactata*   8, 161
    and Hus   108, 302
    and Jakoubek of Stříbro   308, 310
    and Jan Milíč   46
    papal monarchy   78
    and Protestantism   404, 406, 418, 422
    and Šimon of Tišnov   118
    and the Utraquists   223, 240, 420
    and Wyclif   64, 68, 71–2, 110

papal bulls   71, 160
papal curia   113, 116, 142, 239, 241, 243, 405
pastoral care   1, 28, 31–2, 36–7, 38–9, 47, 52, 158, 192, 331–2, 390
Pater noster   111
patronage   233, 235, 344
Paul II, Pope   6
Pavel of Janovice   32, 38
Payne, Peter: at Basel   88–9, 128, 164, 284
    in the *Catalogue of All Heretics*   410, 427
    as diplomat   87, 89, 127–8, 163
    disputations at Prague   119, 121, 147–9, 164
    at Emmaus monastery   381
    in historiography   90, 174, 244
    and Jan Rokycana   156
    on oaths   128
    on Utraquism   227
    and Wyclif   82–3, 87, 261, 263
Pecham, John, Archbishop   79
penitence   34, 85, 114, 353
Peter of Pulkau   121
Peter of Zittau   34
Petr of Mladoňovice   423
Petr of Uničov   120
Petr Záhorka of Záhorčí   166
Petr Zmrzlík of Svojšín   202, 315
Petr of Znojmo   110
Philibert de Montjeu, Bishop   229, 241
Pierre d'Ailly   121
Pikarts: on the Eucharist   354
    prosecution of   226
    split from Tábor   3, 207–10, 207n78
    and the Unity of Brethren   376, 378, 384, 411
    and Václav Konranda   162
    and the Waldensians   170–1
pilgrimage   48, 143, 145, 198–200, 272, 338, 347–52
Piotr Wysz of Radolin, Bishop   105
Pius II, Pope   6, 126, 144, 161, 211, 240
Plato   65, 66, 103, 109, 114, 150
Polák, Michal   318, 338, 392
Poland   7, 11–12, 28, 35, 50, 108, 123, 375, 395
Prague: administration of   5, 31, 142–3, 225–9, 234, 237, 414
    as archbishopric   29, 32, 160, 219–20, 242, 314

INDEX

burghers of   5, 143, 144, 297, 302, 337, 344
as center for reform   30, 37–8, 143
as center for Utraquism   6, 142–3, 239, 243–4, 382, 384, 412–13, 412n35
as center of Holy Roman Empire   1, 171
Compactata and the Four Articles of Prague   219–20, 229
conquest of (1448)   144, 156, 232
Hus's exile from (1412)   82, 113, 302
Jan Příbram's exile from (1427–36)   125
New Town   115, 124, 128, 150, 224, 229, 340, 381–2
nobility of   31, 34, 224
Old Town   30, 40–1, 42n41, 44, 115, 146–7, 224, 233–4, 381
parishes of   30, 37, 122, 338, 355, 355n81
riots in (1480s)   227
social conditions in   45
statutes of   27
and Tábor   200, 203
Přeloučský, Tůma   383, 396
Příbram, Jan: at Basel   126, 151
and Petr Chelčický   170
and Peter Payne   125, 147–9, 164
on the Eucharist   125, 164, 171
in historiography   90, 130, 173–4
opposition to the Taborites   82, 147–50, 204, 207, 230, 284–6, 319–23
in print   421
and the Utraquists   125, 143–4, 146, 152, 227, 230, 318, 351
on war   124
and Wyclif   125, 128, 149
Život kněží táborských   126, 148–9, 174, 319
primitive church: and the Antichrist   194–5, 274–5
and apocalypticism   197, 286, 331–2n2
and apostolic succession   258, 270
comparison with the Roman Church   40, 171, 378–9
and the laity   50
and Matěj of Janov   271–7
and Mikuláš Biskupec   82, 127, 164, 194–5
and Nicholas of Dresden   127, 194, 275
and Scripture   269, 274
and the Taborites   206
and the Unity of Brethren   9, 383, 388
and the Utraquists   155, 157, 223, 239
and the Waldensians   384

Prokop of Jindřichův Hradec   392n55
Prokop of Kladruby   76
Prokop of Plzeň: at Basel   150–1
defense of Wyclif   76, 109, 150
De ideis   74, 76
in historiography   174
on the lay chalice   119
sermons of   151
and the Utraquists   143, 152, 227, 230
purgatory   83, 145, 151, 157, 165, 168–9, 379, 203, 351
puritanism   155, 169, 208, 347

Rabus, Ludwig   424
Raymond of Capua   51
Reinhardt, Martin   408
Reinlein, Oswald   210
Roh, Jan   414, 418
Rohan   209
Rokycana, Jan, Archbishop: at Basel   266, 276
biblical commentaries of   154, 157–9
in the *Catalogue of All Heretics*   410
and coup of 1427   143
on the cult of saints   281
on the Eucharist   153–5
in historiography   90, 173–5, 263, 421
at Hradec Králové   143, 230
on the interpretation of Scripture   268
on the Law of Christ   267
opposition to   146
at the University of Prague   127, 144, 243
and the Roman Church   161
at the St Jacob Synod (1434)   339, 342n45
and the Taborites   82–3, 86, 126, 152–3, 164, 168–9, 284, 352
and the Unity of Brethren   371n2, 373, 377–8, 381–4, 393
and the Utraquists   127, 155–6, 158, 172, 226–9, 232–3, 241, 315
vernacular writings of   316–18, 325
Rolle, Richard   36
Roman Church. *See* Catholic Church
Roudnice   35–6, 209, 225, 299, 342
Rvačka, Mařík   123

saints: Hus as saint   338, 408–9
Jakoubek of Stříbro, attitude towards   272–4, 281

saints: Hus as saint (cont.)
  Matěj of Janov, attitude towards 103, 271, 281, 300
  sermons on 150–1, 154, 158–9
  Taborite attitudes toward 83
  Unity of Brethren, attitude towards 379, 419
  University of Prague, debates surrounding 145, 348
  Utraquists, attitude towards 143, 154–5, 157, 165, 337, 351, 355
Scotus, Johns Duns 76
Scripture: biblical prophecies 148, 191, 194, 198–201, 203–4, 311, 321–2, 321n72
  and Church councils 122
  in the Czech vernacular 146, 238–9, 299–301, 304, 308n29, 313, 315, 334, 339, 341, 350–1n72
  in the early Bohemian reform 37, 40, 48, 103–4, 272, 333
  in early print 238
  and Hus 77, 112, 264
  and Matěj of Janov 66, 270, 272, 316
  and Mikuláš Biskupec 82–6, 83n57, 166, 270, 281–83, 166
  and Petr Chelčický 170, 313, 324, 377
  and the Taborites 126, 164–7, 207, 234, 310–11, 321–2
  and the Unity of Brethren 375–6, 379–80, 387, 418
  university commentaries 120
  and the Utraquists 88, 142–3, 148, 151, 154–5, 159–60, 162, 223, 267–70, 277, 311, 316, 318, 319, 355
  and Wyclif 64–5, 72, 83, 270
Seneca 76
Sentences of Peter Lombard 77, 104, 112
Sigismund of Luxembourg, Emperor 5, 13, 141, 143, 171, 200, 229–30
Silesia 40, 50, 53, 123, 297, 375, 383
Simon Fidati of Cascia 36
Šimon of Tišnov 74–5, 109, 118
Speratus, Paul 414
Stanislav of Znojmo 67, 111
  and the condemnation of Hus 72–3, 79–80
  in historiography 91
  synodal sermons of 39, 75
  and Wyclif 65, 68–71, 81, 87, 105–7, 110

Štěkna, Jan 25, 105
Štěpán of Dolany 118
Štěpán of Kolín 39, 53, 105
Štěpán of Roudnice 35, 42
Štítný, Tomáš 26–7, 168, 299, 301, 332
Synods: diocesan 30, 32–3, 38, 47
  Earthquake Synod, Blackfriars (1382) 71
  in historiography 52, 173, 246, 356, 422
  at Klatovy (1424) 352
  at Kutná Hora (1441–1444) 153, 230
  of Prague (1408) 342, (1421) 336, (1524) 413–14
  and the University of Prague 110, 219, 224
  of St Jacob (1434) 234, 339
  of St James's Day (1434) 336
  of St Prokop (1421) 226–7, 234
  of St Wenceslas (1418) 348
  of Tábor (1430) 126, 234
  and the Unity of Brethren 372, 385, 390
  and the Utraquists 222, 228–30, 234–5, 237, 413, 419n58

Taborites: and the Adamites 207–10, 213
  at Basel 127
  Brandýs decree 385
  chiliasm of 195–6, 203–5, 207, 209, 211
  Chronicon Taboritarum 82
  and the *Compacta* and Four Articles of Prague 150, 153, 223, 269, 282, 285–6, 377
  Confessio Taboritarum 82–3, 164, 281, 352–4
  disputations 126–8, 202, 352–4
  eschatology of 172, 202–3, 320
  on the Eucharist 64, 167, 172, 275, 312, 318–19, 348, 353–4
  and Filip of Padeřov 315
  in historiography 130, 167, 173, 213, 246, 356–8
  and Húska 207
  in the Hussite wars 347
  on the interpretation of Scripture 126, 164–7, 199, 205–6, 310–11, 321–2
  and Jakoubek of Stříbro 116, 171, 190, 201, 310–12
  and Jan Příbram 126, 144, 147–50, 174, 318–21
  and Jan Rokycana 82–3, 86, 126, 152–3, 155–6, 164, 168–9, 284, 352, 378, 384

INDEX

and Jan Želivský   200
and Jan Žižka   204, 285
on the Law of Christ   125, 351
liturgy of   347–9, 374
and Martin Lupáč   158
and Mikuláš Biskupec   82, 86, 126–7, 164–5, 168, 190, 269, 273n56, 281, 379
opposition to Prague   3, 72, 82, 125, 144, 201, 223, 234, 239
opposition to the Utraquists   146–7
and Peter Payne   87, 89, 128, 147, 149, 163
and Petr Chelčický   312–13, 379
and Pikartism   171, 207, 210, 354, 378
and Sigismund   200
Synod of Tábor (1430)   126, 234
and the Unity of Brethren   220, 223, 376, 378–9, 382, 384, 393
and the University of Prague   82–6, 125–6, 164–5, 167, 201, 234, 261, 347, 379
and Václav of Dráchov   156
and the vernacular   314, 318
and violence   86, 194–5, 204, 285, 311
and the Waldensians   170
and women   200, 206
and Wyclif   64, 80, 82–6, 146, 149, 166–7, 261, 264, 281, 319, 354
Táborský, Adam   358
Tetragonus Aristotelis   46
Theodoric de Ehrlich   149
Thomas á Kempis   322
Thomas of Ireland (Hibernicus)   34
Thorpe, William   149
Toke, Heinrich   191
Trinity   64, 74, 109, 114, 265, 335

Unity of Brethren: accusations of heresy   375–6, 382, 384, 421
anticlericalism of   418–19
and the Bible   375–6, 379–80, 387
Brother Řehoř   385–6, 389, 392
Brothers of Boleslav   374
Church of the Moravian Brothers/Renewed Unity of Brethren   372, 376
communal lifestyle of   380, 389–90
confusion with Waldensians   375–6
and the early Bohemian reform   26
and the Eastern Church   9
ecclesiology of   383–5, 388, 390
eschatology of   169, 375, 378, 383, 387–8
on the Eucharist   166–8, 312, 355, 376, 414
and Ferdinand I   387
in historiography   371–3, 393–7
influence of Petr Chelčický   170, 221, 239, 377, 379, 386
Kłodzko interrogation   373
and the laity   375
Lukáš of Prague   392–3, 414–15
persecutions of   382
Piesničky (Songs)   342
on Pikartism   376
on re-baptism   391–2
and the Reformation   380–1, 405, 410–12, 414–22, 428–9
relations with the Roman Church   168, 324, 375
and Rokycana   153, 155, 371n2, 373, 377–8, 381–4, 393
and the Taborites   220, 223, 376, 378–9, 382, 384, 393
and Utraquism   3, 156–7, 247, 378, 389
synods   372, 385, 390
University of Cologne   70, 114, 410
University of Heidelberg   38, 70, 114
University of Kraków   38, 50, 104
University of Oxford   46, 66, 87, 114, 127–8, 163
University of Paris   26, 36, 46, 48, 65, 66, 70, 193, 272, 277, 380
University of Prague: and Petr Chelčický   168, 170
and Constance   123
disputations   66, 70–1, 71–3, 75–7, 106–10, 112, 114–15, 117–18, 119, 145, 149, 153, 234, 266, 297, 312, 333, 352–3
Faculty of Arts   67, 109, 111, 114, 117, 142, 144, 150, 160, 237, 297
Faculty of Law   117
Faculty of Protestant Theology   395
Faculty of Theology   71, 101, 104, 107, 109–12, 115, 117, 129, 224–5
first generation theologians   103–5
foundation of   101
and frequent communion   26–7, 47
German nominalists   4
and the Great Schism   36
in historiography   53, 89–91, 129, 173, 356, 395
and Hus   111

University of Prague (cont.)
    and Jerome of Prague   114
    Karolinum college   41, 231, 352
    and the laity   47–8
    liturgy of   348
    privilege of   144
    synods   52, 110, 219, 342, 336, 413–14
    and the Taborites   82–6, 125–6, 164–5, 167, 201, 234, 261, 347, 379
    and the vernacular   162
    and the Utraquists   115, 117–18, 142, 147, 150, 152, 156
    and Wyclif   65–71, 118
University of Vienna   38, 67, 104, 106, 144
Urban v, Pope   39, 46
Urban vi, Pope   46
Use of Roman Rite   337, 344–5, 355
Utraquism   2–3, 50, 114, 116, 119–22, 141–2, 158, 192–4, 208, 212, 222, 303, 333–4, 343, 378
    ban of   122, 305
    at Basel   125, 152, 121–2
    and the clergy   242
    communion of infants/ all baptized   143, 151, 160, 332, 345–6, 350, 354–5
    Compactata   160–1, 171, 220, 231
    Constance   122–3, 125, 128, 130, 150, 153, 267, 303, 305
    disputes over Utraquism   117, 119–21, 123, 225
    and frequent communion   50
    in historiography   356–7, 357n89, 357n90
    and Jakoubek of Stříbro   115–16, 192–4, 116n56, 277–80, 282–3, 278n82, 303–4, 306–7, 333
    and Jan Milíč   331–2, 345
    and Jan Příbram   147–8, 164, 204
    and Jan Rokycana   154–5
    and Matěj of Janov   27, 48, 119
    and Mikuláš Biskupec   126, 164–5, 350
    and the nobility   224
    opposition to   117–18, 120, 122–3, 151, 227, 305, 314
    and Petr Chelčický   166–8, 312
    and the Pikarts   354, 376
    as a practice   2–3, 50, 116, 121, 142, 147, 151, 153–5, 201, 222, 239, 279, 303, 334, 346, 350, 355
    and the Taborites   312, 318–19, 348, 350, 353–4
    and the Unity of Brethren   355, 376
    and the Utraquists   243, 338, 344, 388
    Václav of Dráchov   157
Utraquists: church administration   231–8
    on the clergy   146, 156–7, 220–1, 225–7, 232, 311, 336, 383–4
    and the *Compactata* and Four Articles of Prague   141, 171–2, 283
    on the correction of sin   285
    and the Roman Church   6, 143–5, 155, 160, 163, 166, 223, 235, 240–5, 354–6
    diplomacy of   155, 236, 244
    divisions within   142–3, 324
    and the Eastern Church   9, 128
    establishment of the Utraquist Church   5, 115, 152, 221
    in historiography   7, 172–5, 245–7, 356–9
    and Jakoubek of Stříbro   127, 152, 155, 192, 227–8, 302
    and Jan Rokycana   127, 152–6, 156–8, 172, 226–9, 232–3, 241, 281, 315
    at Kutná Hora   6
    and the laity   161–2, 315
    leadership of   127, 143, 147, 150
    liturgy of   222, 337–47
    preaching of   158–9, 316
    and print   239
    and the Reformation   411–16, 419–22, 426, 428–9, 431
    on religious communities and monasteries   238
    on Scripture   162–3, 201
    structure of the Church   220–2, 223–31
    and the Taborites   144, 146, 205–6, 310, 312, 318–19, 348, 352–4
    transmission of texts   28, 318, 322
    and the Unity of Brethren   371–3, 375–6, 377–8, 380–1, 387–92, 405
    vernacular liturgy of   322, 341

Václav of Dráchov   156–8, 175, 228n34, 315
Václav of Dubá   122
Václav of Křižanov   154, 243
Václav of Krumlov   241
Václav of Litomyšl   239
Václav of Vysoké Mýto   229
Vaněk Valečovský of Kněžmost   146
Vavřinec of Březová   122, 204–5, 208, 210, 351
Velenský, Oldřich   411

INDEX

veneration: of the consecrated host 84, 303, 354–5
  of the cross 151
  of Hus and Jerome of Prague 143, 338n26, 409
  of Mary 159
  of relics and icons 85, 87, 151, 281, 303
  of saints 145, 154, 281, 3
Versor, John 144
Vladislav II the Jagiellonian 6, 338, 384
Vlk, Jakub 229
Vodňanský, Jan 210
Vojtěch Raňkův of Ježov 26, 39, 46–7, 66, 102, 332

Waldensians: German 8, 11, 31, 378–9, 383–4, 386
  Hussite-Waldensian *Internationale* 371
  influence on Bohemia 26, 166, 170, 261–2, 284, 347–8, 403n1
  and the Reformation 409, 425, 427
  transmission of texts 127, 127n92
  and the Unity of Brethren 375, 394
Waldhauser, Konrad: on antimendicantism 44, 272
  and Charles IV 40, 63
  circulation of texts 50
  and German language 26
  in historiography 54
  on Judaism 43
  Postilla studentium 27, 49, 53, 102
  and Prague 66
  preaching of 42, 64
  as precursor to Hus 1, 26, 102, 261
Weisse, Michael 414, 417–18
Wenceslas IV, King 29, 49, 116, 142, 224, 281, 307, 349
Wenceslas, St. 73, 225, 273, 337n20
William of Conches 66
William of Saint-Amour 44, 272
Wodeham, Adam 69
Wyclif, John: on the Antichrist 188, 190
  and anticlericalism 66, 267
  and Augustine 78
  Blackfriars condemnation of (1382) 68
  condemnation of Archbishop Zbyněk Zajíc of Házmburk 73, 307

on the Donation of Constantine 169
and the early Bohemian reform 1–2, 26, 49–50
on the Eucharist 105, 107, 117, 167, 277
as evangelical doctor 4, 166
Forty-five Articles 71–3
in historiography 15, 89–91, 102, 129–30, 261
influence on Hus 73–4, 77, 79–81, 103, 105, 113–14, 118, 264, 269–70, 283
influence on Prague masters 63, 66–71, 81, 104, 106–9, 116–18
and Jakoubek of Stříbro 74–5, 115, 155, 165, 266, 286, 306–10
and Jerome of Prague 297
and Jan of Jičín 76
and Jan Příbram 125, 128, 148–9
and Jan Rokycana 154, 158
on the Law of Christ 264–5
and Peter Payne 87–9, 125, 127–8, 147, 164, 284
on predestination 47, 155, 221
on clerical dominion 284
and Prokop of Plzeň 76, 109, 150
realist philosophy of 3–4, 64–5, 63n4
and the Taborites 82–6, 146, 166–7, 264, 281, 319, 354
and the Utraquists 223, 239, 240n71
and Václav of Dráchov 157–8
works of 64, 64n3
Wycliffites: ecclesiology of 240n71
  as heretics 5, 67–8, 71, 73, 148, 409
  in historiography 13–14, 90
  and Hussites 1–2, 71, 87, 149, 155
  influence on Bohemian reform 4–5, 26
  Opus arduum valde 195, 276
  at Prague 29, 67–8, 107, 224

Zbyněk Zajíc of Házmburk, Archbishop 68–70, 73, 109, 307
Zdislav of Zvířetice 74, 77, 77n39
Želivský, Jan 124–5, 195, 200, 209, 227, 263, 276, 410
Zinzendorf, Nikolaus Ludwig 371, 376
Žižka, Jan 204, 208–10, 285, 325, 410, 427
Zwingli, Huldrych 403, 421
Zwinglians 417–18